Introducing Politics for AS Level

INTRODUCING
POLITICS
for AS level

FULLY COVERS NEW SPECIFICATIONS

PETER HOLMES

polity

Visit the book's accompanying website at www.polity.co.uk/holmes

This feature-packed website includes:

For students

- Chapter summaries
- Multiple choice quizzes for every chapter
- Extra internet links
- Worksheets
- A searchable glossary ideal for revision
- Extra exercises

For teachers

- Sample lesson plans
- Answers to all the activities
- Graphs, tables and diagrams from the book for use in your own slides

First published in 2008 by Polity Press

Polity Press
65 Bridge Street
Cambridge CB2 1UR, UK

Polity Press
350 Main Street
Malden, MA 02148, USA

ISBN-13: 978-07456-2235-4
ISBN-13: 978-07456-2236-1 (pb)

A catalogue record for this book is available from the British Library.

Typeset in 9.5pt on 13pt Utopia
by Servis Filmsetting Ltd, Stockport, Cheshire
Printed and bound in Slovenia by 1010 Printing UK Ltd

The publisher has used its best endeavour to ensure that the URLs for external websites referred to in this book are correct and active at the time of going to press. However, the publisher has no responsibility for the websites and can make no guarantee that a site will remain live or that the content is or will remain appropriate.

For further information on Polity, visit our website: www.polity.co.uk

Contents

Detailed Contents

Part II   The State

Acknowledgements

My thanks are due to the team at Polity with whom I have worked over the years: David Held, Louise Knight, Emma Hutchinson, Rachel Kerr and Neil de Cort. In addition to colleagues and friends on whose help I have relied: Catherine Smith, Katie Cooke, Ross Maggs, Kirsty Bray, Brian Harney, Jon Phelan, Ed Bock, Mark Funnell, Mark Hogarth, Romie Ridley, Cathy Michell, Maureen Murphy, Dave Abbott, Chris Wilkins, Sheelagh Hughes, Richard Till, Kate Latham especially. An enormous debt is also owed to all my students past and present, especially Louisa Loveluck for help with the pictures.

The publishers would like to thank the following people for permission to reproduce copyright material:

16 © Daily Mail/5th June 2003; 65 © Nils Jorgensen/Rex Features; 82 © Rex Features; 94 © Peter Brookes/NI Syndication; 102 © Sipa Press/Rex Features; 110 © Nils Jorgensen/Rex Features; 129 © Patrick Blower, published in the Evening Standard, 1st December 1998, British Cartoon Archive, University of Kent; 142 © Nicholas Bailey/Rex Features; 162 © Tim Rooke/Rex Features; 166 © Ray Tang/Rex Features; 175 © Steve Bell/Rex Features; 185 © Jamie Jones/Rex Features; 188 © Ray Tang/Rex Features; 194 © Rex Features; 196 © Sipa Press/Rex Features; 252 © Rex Features; 255 © Stan McMurtry, published in the Daily Mail, 7th September 1999, British Cartoon Archive, University of Kent; 280 © the Conservative Party Archive; 282 © Steve Bell/Rex Features; 286 © Geoff Moore/Rex Features; 329 © Michael Dunlea/Rex Features; 337 © Rex Features; 338 © UK Parliament and the Parliamentary Recording Unit; 353 © UK Parliament and the Parliamentary Recording Unit; 360 © UK Parliament and the Parliamentary Recording Unit; 361 © UK Parliament and the Parliamentary Recording Unit; 377 © Parliamentary copyright 2007. Photograph by Terry Moore; 385 © Parliamentary copyright 2007; 392 © Parliamentary copyright 2007. Photograph by Deryc Sands; 398 © Parliamentary copyright 2007. Photograph by Deryc Sands; 411 © Rex Features; 413 © UK Parliament and the Parliamentary Recording Unit; 419 © UK Parliament and the Parliamentary Recording Unit; 420 © UK Parliament and the Parliamentary Recording Unit; 422 © Jeff Gilbert/ Rex Features; 428 © Rex Features; 445 © Peter MacDiarmid/Rex Features;

457 © Matt Cartoon/The Daily Telegraph, Matthew Pritchett, published in the Daily Telegraph, 27th February 2002, British Cartoon Archive, University of Kent; 477 © Sipa Press/Rex Features; 481 © Eddie Mulholland/Rex Features; 505 © Balkanpix.com/Rex Features; 520 © Paul Cooper; 535 © Patrick Blower, published in the Evening Standard, 20th May 2003, British Cartoon Archive, University of Kent; 571 © Matt Cartoon/The Daily Telegraph, Matthew Pritchett, published in the Daily Telegraph, 7th May 1999, British Cartoon Archive, University of Kent; 579 © Martin McCullough/ Rex Features; 586 © ITV/Rex Features.

Abbreviations

AMS	Additional Member System
BNP	British National Party
CAP	Common Agricultural Policy
CBI	Confederation of British Industry
CCTV	Closed Circuit Television
CEHR	Commission for Equality and Human Rights
CLEAR	Campaign for Lead-Free Air
CND	Campaign for Nuclear Disarmament
COBRA	Cabinet Office Briefing Room A
COREPER	Committee of Permanent Representatives
CPGB	Communist Party of Great Britain
CRA	Constitutional Reform Act
CRE	Commission for Racial Equality
DCA	Department of Constitutional Affairs
DG	Directorate-General
DRC	Disability Rights Commission
DUP	Democratic Unionist Party
EC	European Community
ECHR	European Convention (or Court) of Human Rights
ECJ	European Court of Justice
EEC	European Economic Community
EOC	Equal Opportunities Commission
EP	European Parliament
ERM	Exchange Rate Mechanism
ESC	Economic and Social Committee
EU	European Union
FPTP	First-Past-the-Post
HRA	Human Rights Act
IGC	Intergovernmental Conference
IMF	International Monetary Fund
MEP	Member of the European Parliament
MP	Member of Parliament
MSP	Member of the Scottish Parliament
MWA	Member of the Welsh Assembly

NAO	National Audit Office
NATO	North Atlantic Treaty Organisation
NEC	National Executive Committee
NFU	National Farmers' Union
NHS	National Health Service
NSMs	New Social Movements
NUM	National Union of Mineworkers
NUS	National Union of Students
NUT	National Union of Teachers
PFI	Private Finance Initiative
PM	Prime Minister
PMQs	Prime Minister's Questions
PPS	Parliamentary Private Secretary
PR	Proportional Representation
QMV	Qualified Majority Voting
RDA	Regional Development Agency
SDLP	Social Democratic Labour Party
SDP	Social Democratic Party
SEA	Single European Act
SF	Sinn Fein
SNP	Scottish National Party
SPUC	Society for the Protection of the Unborn Child
SSP	Scottish Socialist Party
STV	Single Transferable Vote
TEU	Treaty on European Union
TGWU	Transport and General Workers Union
TUC	Trade Union Congress
UK	United Kingdom
UKIP	United Kingdom Independence Party
UN	United Nations
UUP	Ulster Unionist Party
VAT	Value Added Tax

An Introduction to the Study of Politics

Making connections

This chapter is largely introductory and the sort of chapter which is generally skipped by students who want to get down to business as soon as possible. But you will find useful material here, to read initially and then to refer to as you go through your course. A very helpful thing to do in conjunction with reading this chapter is simply to spend half an hour or so leafing through the book, reading the various chapter headings and anything that catches your eye, so that you familiarize yourself with the outline of the subject and the contents of the book as a whole. The final discussion of the war with Iraq is intended to be lively and provocative, but essentially factual nevertheless. If you think it is biased, try to think of what you would say to neutralize it.

An Introduction to the Study of Politics

KEY TOPICS

- Politics: an activity, and a study
- Studying politics
- The new AS specifications and examinations
- Case study: the politics of the war with Iraq

SETTING THE SCENE

This brief but important chapter begins with a stab at defining what we mean by 'politics' and then looks at how to study politics. It should therefore link in with the rest of the book, and should provide some hints as to how you would go about using the book to study the subject. It concludes with what is intended to be a lively case study of a recent controversial political event: the war with Iraq.

I.1 Politics: an activity, and a study

The word 'politics' describes two things: (1) a human activity and (2) the study of that activity. When we talk about politics, we are normally referring most directly to what politicians do: making speeches in Parliament, standing for election, working out how much tax is needed to fund the National Health Service, etc. But the word 'Politics', often spelt with a capital letter, is also used to describe the study of that political activity. The same double usage is true of 'history', 'geography', 'music', 'chemistry', and many other areas.

Politics is a human activity

The word 'politics' derives from the Ancient Greek word 'polis', meaning 'city-state'. The same Greek root gives us many other modern English words: for example, politician, political, policy, polity, politic, metropolitan, cosmopolitan. All these words circle around the idea of political activity or of cities, the cradle of early political activity. Ancient Greece, about two and a half millennia ago, was divided into 'city-states', independent towns sur-rounded by enough land to provide the townspeople with food: Athens, Thebes and Sparta were the best known, but there were many more. These towns were ruled in a variety of different ways, but there was generally intense political activity involved. Since modern Western culture derives from Ancient Greece, the word 'politics' has tended to stick because the first great writers on politics were Ancient Greeks: Plato, Aristotle, Thucydides. Looking at the derivation of words to understand their modern meaning is sometimes a bit misleading, but in the case of politics it works quite well. We can imagine in the great ancient democracy of Athens debates taking place over war and peace, taxation and public spending, leadership and intrigue, which were very similar to controversies in modern politics.

So, politics is the human activity which has to do with running the modern equivalent of a city-state, that is to say, a country or some subdivision of that country. You only have to think for a few moments to come up with a list of areas that will be involved in managing a modern state. There are obviously debates among politicians in Parliament, reports on these in the media, elec-tions to be held and election campaigns to be managed. These areas are those which concern politicians and citizens most obviously and they seem to be what politics is most clearly all about.

A glance at the contents of this book will show you what the politics of the United Kingdom is concerned with. At the base of all politics are the citizens who make up the state, our equivalent to the Greek city. The first part of this book is concerned with citizens. The people of the United Kingdom first and foremost get involved in elections. These take place at a variety of levels and involve choosing representatives for a number of institutions of government, most notably Parliament. The more active citizens will engage in politics by joining a political party or a pressure group, and political activity centres on the work of these important democratic bodies. People are also able to con-tribute directly in politics by voting in referendums. The media and the press keep people informed of political events.

Having looked at the citizens who form the foundations of the political system, it is necessary to look at the system from the top down, from the per-spective of the state, and this is the subject of the second part of this book. The elected representatives work at the top of the system in Parliament, the real heart of British political activity. Parliament is linked in the British system very closely with the executive or government. At the head of the government are the Prime Minister and Cabinet. These elected politicians work with the experts in administration, the civil servants, running the government on behalf of the citizens. Parliament makes laws which the judges, or judiciary, enforce, and their work is also intensely political in the broadest sense of the word. The judges protect the rights of the citizens, another significant aspect of democratic politics. Binding the whole political system together is a complex web of laws and customs known as the constitution. In recent years this constitution has been radically reformed. Among the most recent political reforms and changes that have occurred have been the development of Britain's part in the European Union, and the growth of new institutions of government in the outlying parts of the United Kingdom, notably Scotland, Wales and Northern Ireland.

Politics is the study of political activity

We also use the word 'politics' to mean the academic study of the human activity described above, of what politicians and voters are involved in doing. It is sometimes described as 'political science', the word 'science' here being used in the loose sense of any piece of study involving analysis and research. The study of politics has a long and honourable tradition behind it, starting, as has been said, with the Ancient Greek writers Plato and Aristotle. Politics is an important academic subject at university and is increasingly taught in schools and colleges. The main interest of the political scientist is often to learn about the political system of a particular country, to show how the system works and to evaluate its effectiveness. At university level, academic political scientists tend to specialize in one single aspect of the political system: in Parliament, or in the civil service, or the constitution, for example. Political science draws support from other academic disciplines, especially sociology, history and economics. Sociology and politics overlap at a number of points. The study of political parties and of elections, for example, is helped by an understanding of how society works. The theoretical perspectives used by sociologists are also very useful to political scientists. In return, the study of political power helps sociologists understand their subject better too. History supports the study of politics at so many points that it is difficult at times to see where contemporary history (as the study of really up-to-date events in the past is called) begins and real politics ends. We cannot understand the politics of the present without having a reasonable grasp of the politics of the recent past. For most purposes in British politics, it is generally considered sufficient to begin the historical background in 1945, with the end of the Second World War. But some of the constitutional points in the study of British politics take us right back to the Middle Ages. Economics is important if we are to understand government policy in a wide variety of areas, especially crucial aspects of taxation and public expenditure. These factors in their turn may also help explain how people vote in elections.

The limits of this book are to provide an introduction to the British political system, but political science spreads its net a good deal wider and students at university study a wide range of other topics which also come under the heading of politics. To start with, there is no space in this book to deal at any length with the 'issues' or policies which concern the political institutions of the United Kingdom – education, health, social security, defence, foreign policy, the environment, crime and public order, for example. The study of public administration looks in more detail at how policy decisions are made and how, in general terms, the political issues listed above are dealt with. One very valuable approach to the study of politics is comparative politics, where the institutions and policies of one country are compared with those of one or several others. International relations involves the study of how different states interact, through diplomacy and war. Linked to this are the subjects called Peace Studies and War Studies. Tying the whole study of politics together is an interest in theories which help us understand the political system we study, and it is the work of political theory and political philosophy to try to make this clear. So the study of politics is a very broad one.

I.2 Studying politics

There follow a few hints to help you study politics.

Using a textbook

A textbook like this one is not primarily meant to be read from cover to cover like a thriller or a novel – although please fell free to do so if you like! You will probably be directed in your studies of politics by a teacher who will take you through a course of study step by step. So, when you study, for example, Parliament, you should read the chapters in this book on that subject: there is one on the House of Commons and one on the House of Lords. Although the chapters are grouped around the two great themes (citizen and state), there is really no standard or obvious order in which to take the subjects involved in a course on politics, and it would be quite reasonable to follow them in a different order from how they are presented in this book. The contents page at the beginning of the book will show you where to look, and the index (more detailed and alphabetical) at the end will also help. It is worth bearing in mind also that there is a great deal of overlap in this subject and that it might be very important to cross-refer from one chapter to another. Textbooks are also meant to be used as storehouses of information. Your reading is designed to get you that information. There are a number of types of 'information' communicated in a politics textbook: the definition of concepts and terminology, the analysis and evaluation of evidence and examples, and the use of individual case studies to illustrate this. This information can be understood at the foundational level or extended by students who wish to push their knowledge and understanding up to a higher level.

Analysis and evaluation

Obviously you will be expected in the course of your study of politics to build up a stock of factual information – detailed names, dates and statistics, but also a knowledge of how the systems operate and the specialist vocabulary that surrounds them. In addition, one of the most valuable aspects of the study of politics is the way in which we are called upon to analyse and evaluate the institutions and individuals that make up the world of politics. Analysis involves examining an event or a problem in depth, trying to discover as much as possible about it, looking at its causes and consequences and trying to set it in its context. Analysis may be strengthened by drawing comparisons with other events in the past, or the way in which other countries perform the same functions. Analysis leads naturally to evaluation. Evaluation is judging, saying which aspects of a system are good and which are bad. Evaluation must be based on evidence and/or argument; it cannot simply be a matter of prejudice or 'gut' feeling. In this textbook, you will be given some ideas about the evaluation of key topics. But these are not meant to be exclusive lists of all the points that could be made; nor do they claim to be in themselves right or wrong. It is up to you to add more points and to decide which are the most significant. But, one word of warning, the study of politics is best approached with an open mind. Evaluation must be a two-sided process. If you are evaluating the membership of the House of Lords, for example, it is important to look for things that can be praised as well as things that can be attacked. In the end, you will come up with your conclusion about where the balance lies, but it must be based on evidence and argument.

Concepts and definitions

One way to evaluate a political institution, policy or event is to measure it with the yardstick of a political concept. A 'concept' is an idea or theory, and in the study of politics it is useful to hold in mind a series of such ideas or theories. It is probably easiest to give an example. An absolutely central concept in the study of modern politics is democracy. A definition of the meaning of this concept (democracy) enables the student of politics to examine, say, the British Parliament, or perhaps the European Parliament, and to arrive at an assessment of whether or not these institutions can be properly described as democratic. If there are any questions over the democratic credentials of these institutions, consideration of what constitutes democracy in other countries may help us to understand what aspects of our Parliament or of Europe's Parliament are truly more democratic than others. Democracy is a very broad term. It is helpful as a concept because it can be analysed further into other components, which can themselves be useful in forming an overview of institutions: a standard division is between direct democracy and representative democracy. This provides us with two further concepts, of particular value when judging elections and referendums. In using this textbook, it is useful to consider which concepts have been introduced and which ones are most valuable in order to study a particular section of the subject. Specialist political vocabulary is explained throughout the book, and is then summed up at the end in the glossary.

Defining political vocabulary

Apart from the language of concepts, there are also important pieces of specialist vocabulary which need to be considered when studying politics. All subjects have their jargon; political science is actually quite free from it compared with some subjects. But there will obviously be new words which need to be mastered. As new vocabulary is introduced in this book, it is explained as fully as possible. It is not a bad idea to have a dictionary handy, of course, and there are a number of specialist dictionaries of politics available: the Bloomsbury edition of P. H. Collin's *Dictionary of Politics* can be recommended. A good way of developing this vocabulary is also by reading more widely in the subject.

Extra reading

Your library or local bookshop should have a politics section. If not, you can recommend books to them, which they should then get for you. There are a number of very good textbooks on the market, and authors of specialist works which can be recommended to help deepen and develop your knowledge of the subject. Student journals or magazines also exist, which contain articles on particular topics to give you an up-to-date survey of the academic literature or a new insight into the area: *Politics Review* and *Talking Politics* are the two best student magazines. At the end of each chapter in this book there is a brief list of suggested extra reading.

Current events: newspapers, radio and TV

An important thing for students of politics to do is to try hard to keep up to date with current events. Obviously, it is mainly British political events which will interest the readers of this book. The major 'heavy' daily newspapers provide an important resource for politics students: the *Guardian*, *The Times*, the *Telegraph*, and the *Independent*, as well as their Sunday counterparts, which carry the same names, apart from the *Observer* (which is the Sunday equivalent of the *Guardian*). These newspapers will generally report with a political bias, and their interests are often a little gossipy and humorous, even

Reading one of the major 'broadsheet' newspapers on a regular basis is a good way to keep up to date with current affairs

in the 'heavy' British newspapers. But there are a number of really excellent political journalists writing whose analysis can be very useful. As you read about political events, it is worth trying to see how a consideration of the particular case you are reading about fits into the broader picture you are building up about how British politics works, or is supposed to work. There are good weekly papers too: *The Economist, New Statesman* and *Spectator*. The television news coverage is also quite good in the UK, especially *Channel 4 News* and *Newsnight*. Radio 4 also carries a series of excellent news programmes in the morning, at lunchtime and in the evenings. In addition, both radio and television have 'documentary' programmes on political topics from time to time.

Websites

Current affairs can also be followed on the computer screen: the BBC and *Guardian* websites especially. The major political parties and the key political institutions also have very good websites. There is little in the field that cannot now be researched from your computer. It is obviously worth being a bit sceptical about some sites, but it should be quite clear who has produced the site you are looking at. You would not expect the Conservative Party website to be unbiased, and that is part of its value. If you want to find out what Conservatives believe in, you will be well advised to look at their website. Pressure groups are also a very good source of information about themselves, and some have some very good sites. At the end of each chapter in this book there is a brief list of websites of relevance to the chapter.

Examinations

There are three examination boards which administer AS and A-level exams in Britain, and their websites are given at the end of this chapter. Each follows a slightly different syllabus or specification and you should ensure that you are aware of what the syllabus is before you embark on your studies. This means that you will need to concentrate on slightly different aspects of this present book, which aims to cover all three specifications, when you study the course followed by your particular examination board. Before the examination, you should revise your understanding of the subject matter and also look at past questions which have been set over the years by the examiners. These will be available from the examination boards; also, sample examination questions are included at the end of the relevant sections of this book.

There follows a summary of the specifications of the three examination boards.

I.3 The new AS specifications and examinations

There are three new AS specifications from the exam boards AQA, Edexcel and OCR. This book aims to cover all three of these. Full details of the specifications of each board are to be found on their website; what follows is a brief overview. All three boards divide their subject into two units. The examinations are also described in the grid below. There is no coursework.

Unit 1

AQA: People, Politics and Participation • Participation and voting behaviour • Electoral systems • Political parties • Pressure groups and protest movements	**Examination**: 1 hour 30 mins Candidates answer two questions from a choice of four source-based questions. Each question consists of three parts, worth 5, 10 and 25 marks respectively.
Edexcel: People and Politics • Democracy and political participation • Party politics and ideas • Elections • Pressure groups	**Examination:** 1 hour 20 mins Candidates answer two structured questions from a choice of four. Each question consists of three parts, worth 5, 10 and 25 marks respectively.
OCR: Contemporary Politics of the UK • Political parties • Pressure groups • Electoral systems • UK parliamentary elections • Voting behaviour • Ideology	**Examination:** 1 hour 30 mins Section A: source-based questions on parties and pressure groups. Section B: one essay from a choice of three on electoral systems, elections or voting behaviour.

Unit 2

AQA: Governing Modern Britain • The British Constitution • The judiciary • Parliament • The core executive: Prime Minister and Cabinet • Multi-level governance: devolution • The European Union	**Examination:** 1 hour 30 mins Candidates answer two questions from a choice of six source-based questions. Each question consists of three parts, worth 5, 10 and 25 marks respectively.

Edexcel: Governing the UK	Examination: 1 hour 20 minutes
● The Constitution ● Parliament ● The Prime Minister and Cabinet ● Judges and civil liberties	Candidates answer two structured questions from a choice of four. Each question consists of three parts, worth 5, 10 and 25 marks respectively.

OCR: Contemporary Government of the UK	Examination: 1 hour 30 mins
● The Executive ● The Legislature ● The Constitution ● The European Union ● The Judiciary ● Rights, liberties and redress of grievances	Section A: source-based questions on the executive and legislature. Section B: one essay from a choice of three on the Constitution, the European Union and the judiciary.

Activity

If you are studying AS Government and Politics, ask your teacher which board's examination you will sit at the end of the course. Log on to the board's website (see the list at the end of this chapter) and consult the full specification which you will find there. Look on the website for further information which might be useful: for example, sample examination papers.

I.4 Case study: the politics of the war with Iraq

An important way in which the study of politics can be enriched and enlivened is by undertaking what is called in the social sciences a case study. In making a case study, the student of politics takes a recent event, especially a controversial or complex one, and tries to look at the background to it and to unravel the various strands which come together to form the problem and its solutions. The study will probably not come to any firm conclusion about the case, but will attempt to evaluate it in as impartial way as possible. Topics which might lend themselves to this approach include the abolition of fox-hunting, the reform of the House of Lords, the decline of party membership, devolution to the north-east of England, congestion charging, the resignation of David Blunkett. There are many ways in which a study of this sort could be presented. What follows is a very straightforward narrative account of the war with Iraq; given more space, more analysis and evaluation could have been developed. The purpose of this section is simply to stimulate an interest in how a case study might develop.

In 2003, Britain supported the USA and a number of other countries in an attack on Iraq. It was reported that a third of Britain's army was involved in this military action. Fighting has continued ever since, as the invasion has turned into a form of military occupation, and by March 2008 a total of 175 British soldiers had been killed. Look at the BBC website for the current figure: http://news.bbc.co.uk. This was the biggest foreign and defence policy issue that had faced the country since 1982 and Margaret Thatcher's defence of the Falkland Islands and war with Argentina. The question of whether to go to war in 2003 was much debated in the UK and it divided public opinion quite violently.

The arguments for war were essentially as follows:

- Iraq might have 'weapons of mass destruction' which could threaten Britain. The attack on New York and Washington on 11 September 2001 was the result of terrorist action, and it was generally feared that there would be further terrorist attacks on the USA and her allies, including the UK. Terrorists tend to flourish when they have the support of a 'rogue state', a country which does not choose to keep to the normal rules of international behaviour. Iraq might be, or might become, such a state. It requires the scientific and military support which a state alone can wield to develop biological weapons like anthrax and nuclear weapons. Such weapons might be used by fanatical terrorists. So it was necessary to disarm Iraq as a rogue state or a potential rogue state.
- Britain had a responsibility to get involved in such an attack on Iraq. It would be cowardly to stand aside and let the USA alone take the necessary action against Iraq.
- Britain ought to stand by the USA, her closest ally and a long-standing friend since the USA got involved in both world wars on Britain's side. Britain would probably have been unable to defeat Germany in both these wars without American help. During the Cold War, the Americans had been deeply involved in alliance with Britain in defending the West against Russia. In 1982, the USA had given Britain important support in the war with Argentina. The first war with Iraq (1990–1) had involved Britain and USA jointly, and the two had worked together over Kosovo in 1999. How could Britain not support the USA now?
- Iraq was under the control of a cruel dictator, Saddam Hussein, who ruled by fear and ruthlessly exterminated his enemies – indeed, whole communities. It would be an act of humanity to free the Iraqis from this dictatorship.
- Iraq under Saddam Hussein was in breach of numerous United Nations resolutions, which had been passed following his invasion of Kuwait in 1990 and the subsequent war.
- Iraq had the potential to destabilize the Middle East, which is a very dangerous area, and one where war seems likely to break out almost every year.

A war in the Middle East could seriously upset the peace of the whole world.

- Stability in the Middle East would ensure the supply of oil to the West, which might be threatened by instability caused by Saddam Hussein's continued government of Iraq.
- To remove Saddam Hussein would send a very clear message to the rulers of rogue states, to terrorists and to enemies of the USA and UK that we were willing to make sacrifices to defend ourselves. Osama bin Laden, the perpetrator of the 9/11 outrages, had declared war on 'Western civilization' and believed that the West was too rotten to defend itself. An attack on Iraq, following that on Afghanistan in 2002, would put people right on that score. It would have a deterrent effect.

The case against war seemed to many people just as strong:

- There were no weapons of mass destruction, although this only became clear after the allied troops had occupied Iraq. By the time the war had broken out, the United Nations weapons inspectors had not found

Table I.1 Arguments for and against the war in Iraq	
FOR 👍	AGAINST 👎
Iraq is a rogue state which needs to be disarmed	No proof that Iraq owns weapons of mass destruction
Britain has a responsibility to join forces with the US	The UN Security Council did not support the war
Britain owes a debt of gratitude to the US for American support in previous world wars	Senior British legal advisers questioned the legality of the invasion
Iraq needs to be liberated from dictatorship	No proven connection between Saddam Hussein and international terrorism
Saddam Hussein was in breach of UN resolutions	The human and financial cost of war would be very high
Iraq risks destabilizing the Middle East	The UK risks alienation within the European Union
Iraqi instability would threaten the oil supply to the West	War could cause instability in the Middle East
The removal of Saddam would send a strong message to other rogue states	War could be seen as an imperialist crusade against Islam

any such weapons, and many opponents of the war argued that these inspectors should be allowed more time to continue their search.

- The United Nations Security Council refused to support the war even though its members were being put under great pressure by America to do so. The war was, according to the Secretary General of the United Nations (in a statement made after the war was over), 'illegal'.
- The legality of the war was even questioned by the government's own chief legal adviser, the Attorney General, although he eventually seems to have supported going to war in 2003. When his secret advice to the government was eventually made public, just before the general election of 5 May 2005, it was found to contain many doubts and reservations about whether the war was actually acceptable in terms of international law.
- There was no connection between Saddam Hussein and international terrorism. Since Osama bin Laden was an Islamic fundamentalist and Saddam was a secular leader, there was not likely to be any contact. The only part of Iraq where Islamic terrorists were welcome before the war was an area in the north of the country which was outside Saddam's control and was protected from him by allied air cover.
- The war might turn out to be costly in allied lives and might also kill Iraqi soldiers and civilians. The financial cost would also be high.
- France, Germany and other countries refused to support the USA, and by supporting America, the UK was putting itself outside this group, and disagreeing with its closest neighbours and European allies.
- Far from stabilizing the Middle East, the war would stir up more problems there.
- In addition, the image of the USA and the UK as imperialist powers engaged in a crusade against Islam would be encouraged by a major attack on Iraq.

Political perspectives on the war with Iraq

The war with Iraq is made more interesting if it is studied as a case study in how British politics operate. The main focus of such a study might be an attempt to understand how decisions are made in the UK. A few points might be put forward, not really as absolute facts, but as suggestions for interpretation.

Media and electoral politics

There is a well-known tendency for the press to enjoy reporting wars, especially if they involve the SAS, an organization which the Labour government has expanded. Thatcher was said to have increased the 'feel-good factor' in the run-up to the 1983 election as a result of the successful war against Argentina the year before.

Party image and ideology

Old Labour tended to be seen as being weak on foreign policy. New Labour tried hard in the 1990s to rid itself of this image; in doing so, the party would inevitably make itself more like the Conservatives, and hence might risk losing votes on the left, but would gain them on the right. Labour was generally seen as rather weaker in defence and foreign policy matters than the Conservatives. So part of Labour's modernization strategy involved following a strong line in foreign affairs. Support for NATO over Kosovo in 1999 was a start, and the British support for the USA in Afghanistan in 2002 continued this policy. To intervene in Iraq might help confirm this trend.

Consensus between parties is not uncommon

Given the Labour leadership's desire to fight Iraq, the Conservative opposition had a choice: to do the work of a genuine opposition and point out all the flaws in the government's arguments for war, or – as they chose to do – to support them rather uncritically. Especially in matters of defence, political parties tend to come together and form a united front against the enemy. It is unpatriotic to oppose a government when our soldiers are fighting abroad. But this does mean that genuine concerns about the justice of war and how it was conducted did not surface very clearly in Parliament, except from the Liberal Democrats and some Labour 'rebels'.

Parties disagree among themselves

Another source of opposition to going to war came from within the Labour Party itself. In the crucial votes in 2002 and 2003, the government faced huge rebellions by its backbenchers and only survived these votes with the support of the Conservative opposition. There were a number of resignations from the government, notably that of Robin Cook, the Leader of the House and a former Foreign Secretary, which illustrated the constitutional principle that although MPs can vote against their own party leadership, ministers are expected to give unqualified support to government policy.

The decision about whether to go to war is made by the Prime Minister

Constitutional theory says that decisions on whether to go to war are a matter of 'royal prerogative', which means in practice that the Prime Minister can in effect declare war without a vote in Parliament. But the events of 1956 over Suez showed that a Prime Minister needs to carry the bulk of the political elite along too in making this highly important move. If this is not done, there is a risk that, if things go wrong, he or she will have to resign, as Sir Anthony Eden did over Suez. So Tony Blair needed not only to consult the Cabinet (this, some might argue, was virtually a constitutional requirement), but also to take votes in Parliament, which meant keeping the support of his own political party. Blair, however, had the unswerving support of the Conservative opposition, and as a result he could ride out the opposition of a very large minority of his own MPs.

Governments seek to sway public opinion

A feature of government action which has, according to most commentators, increased in recent years is the use of 'spin doctors', government officials who seek to influence the ideas of the public by feeding the media with the information which presents the government in a good light. The most contentious aspect of the war with Iraq was the use of government information in the months before the war to present the case for war. The Secret Services were asked to prepare reports, which were then used to justify the case for war. A central plank in this case, of course, was the view, held by the Secret Services, that Saddam Hussein might have weapons of mass destruction. The use the government made of this 'dossier' of information was criticized by a BBC journalist, Andrew Gilligan, who claimed that the government (especially Tony Blair's media expert, Alisdair Campbell) had 'sexed' up the dossier, turning the Secret Services' 'might have weapons of mass destruction' into 'has weapons of mass destruction which can be deployed in 45 minutes'.

Daily Mail, Thursday, June 5, 2003

'Dad it's me, Euan. Still no weapons of mass destruction. Only Coke cans and
bent nails . . . when can I come home?'

The first casualty in war is truth: the Hutton Inquiry

The allegations of Gilligan in 2003 led to a huge quarrel between the BBC and the government. Gilligan was sacked by the BBC after pressure from Campbell. A law lord, Hutton, was chosen by the government to investigate the BBC's report and the death, apparently from suicide, of a civil servant, Dr David Kelly, on whose information Gilligan's report had in part been based. The government was completely exonerated from all blame by Hutton when he reported, but the BBC was strongly castigated, so that both the Chairman and the Director General of the BBC resigned. Hutton's report was so one-sided that the press called it a 'whitewash'.

Sofa government: the Butler Inquiry

When things go wrong in government, the opposition calls for an inquiry. The government tries to set up a committee which is framed in such a way as to suit its purposes. The Hutton Inquiry had a narrow remit, and was called following the news of Kelly's death, largely to draw attention away from that event. Another narrow inquiry under a much more effective and impartial chairman, former Cabinet Secretary Lord Butler, was set up at roughly the same time to look into how Secret Service information was used in the preparation for war. On the whole, the Butler Report said little to harm the government, but it did state that government practices were rather too informal under Blair, with many meetings held without agendas or minutes and conducted apparently while sitting on sofas. There was a confusion of government, defence and party political roles at the heart of Blair's administration.

The rise, or revival, of pressure-group politics?

The war with Iraq saw a number of very strongly supported public demonstrations in London and elsewhere. There have been other such demonstrations in recent years, notably from the Countryside Alliance. The Stop the War Coalition spearheaded the Iraqi protests. These have been the first large-scale demonstrations in Britain since the introduction of the 'poll tax' in the late 1980s and are an interesting development in democratic politics in the UK. Large numbers of people from a variety of backgrounds got involved: peace protesters, left-wingers, anti-Americans and also Muslims, who see the War with Iraq as part of a wider anti-Islamic policy followed by the USA. Well-organized, peaceful and strongly supported, these demonstrations bring some comfort to those who fear that people do not participate strongly enough in politics. But on the whole, they made absolutely no difference to what the government decided to do. Even the largest demonstration consists of a small section of the voting population and governments are obviously aware of this. Opinion polls showed that the population was roughly evenly divided on the issue of war with Iraq.

Nothing succeeds like success

The invasion of Iraq was an initial success but the allies did not have a good plan about what to do once they had arrived in Baghdad in 2003. The British forces remained in southern Iraq, with the death toll steadily rising, as insurgents attacked the foreign invaders. The financial cost for the taxpayer was also high, but seldom discussed. By 2004 public opinion had shifted round and tended to be anti-war. The problem would not go away with the BBC–Kelly affair and continued casualties during the occupation. Blair's personal authority in his own party was sapped, partly because so many backbenchers had voted against the war, and also because Blair's party was disappointed in him: he seemed not to have backed a winner. There was a wobbly period in 2004 when his position seemed threatened, but the party decided that Blair was still their best bet, although it was at this point that the already much discussed idea that after the next general election Gordon Brown should take over as PM really began to take shape.

The electoral damage

A general election did not have to be held until 2006 and the electoral damage caused by the war might by then have been quite slight. The people who were most opposed to the war would probably have to vote Labour anyway. On the other hand, there were quite a few Muslims in Labour-held seats, who might vote Liberal Democrat. This was shown in by-elections in Birmingham Hodge Hill and Leicester South in 2004. Blair, however, decided to hold a general election early, in May 2005, and there is no doubt that the war did reduce Labour support. In constituencies with a Muslim population of more than 10 per cent the Labour vote fell on average by 3 per cent more than other constituencies, largely to the benefit of the Liberal Democrats. George Galloway, a former Labour MP who had supported Saddam Hussein, founded a new anti-war party called Respect, and won the strongly Muslim seat of Bethnal Green and Bow from Labour. But all in all the damage done to Labour by the war was limited, in large part because the Conservative opposition could not make any political capital out of the issue because they too had chosen to support it.

Continued impact in Labour's third term

The political damage to Labour from the war continued after the 2005 election. This was largely because the security position in Iraq was going from bad to worse, and the country seemed to be descending into civil war. These concerns were also being expressed in the USA and had a big impact on the American congressional elections of late 2006. The terrorist attacks on London in July 2005 were also harmful politically to the supporters of the war, since they showed that the government's foreign policy had done little to reduce the threat of terror, and may even have increased it. One great asset for the government, however, is the tendency of opposition parties to avoid too much criticism while British troops are abroad and also while Britain faces a terrorist threat. In addition, during 2007 it became clear that the British troops in the area around Basra would be withdrawn as soon as it was reasonable to do so. To some extent this has drawn a line under the affair, as has the replacement in the summer of 2007 of Tony Blair by Gordon Brown, who is less closely connected with the decision to go to war in 2003.

There is a great deal more of interest in the study of a particular problem like the war with Iraq than can be covered here. The object of this exercise is to show that many aspects of the political system can be illustrated by looking at a single issue, especially an important one like this. In terms of exercising power in decision-making, it is still probably true to say that over Iraq Tony Blair made the decisions and then carried them out. But at every turn he was hemmed in by political considerations which made the implementation of his decisions extremely difficult. In the end, though, Blair survived the crisis involved in taking the country into what turned out to be an unpopular war, but he was weakened and probably resigned earlier than he was planning as a result.

 Question: What were the causes and consequences of Britain's decision to support the USA in its invasion of Iraq?

Activity

Having read the account given above of the war with Iraq, consider the following questions:

1 Put yourself in Tony Blair's position in 2002–3: what would you have done?
2 A counterfactual case is one based on denying the facts of the matter. Consider the counterfactual case that Britain did not join the USA in fighting Iraq in 2003. What do you think the consequences of not doing so would have been?
3 Now evaluate the points you have made in answer to question 2 into two categories: good for the UK and bad for the UK.
4 In the last two years there has been much discussion about whether the UK and the USA should go to war with Iran to force the country to stop its nuclear programme. Research this topic using news and other websites (BBC, *Guardian*, for example).
5 Put forward the case for and against intervention in Iran in rather the same way I have dealt with the case study of the war with Iraq.
6 Do you consider that the war with Iraq has made it more or less likely that the USA will attack Iran? Draw up a two-column evaluation of your case.

Part I
The Citizen

The State and the Citizen

Making connections

Probably the most important thing for a student to do at first is to try to get some idea about what the British political system is like in overall terms; this chapter should help with that. Much of the discussion is conceptual and rather dry as a result. Like all introductory material, it sometimes makes more sense when it is reread as a sort of conclusion. The section on the rights of the citizen is rather brief and should be considered in conjunction with the discussion of the subject in chapter 14 on the judiciary.

The State and the Citizen

KEY TOPICS

- The citizen's rights and obligations
- The state, the government, power and authority
- Liberal democracy: uniting the citizen and the state

SETTING THE SCENE

This first chapter introduces you to some initial points about the two building blocks of politics: the state and the citizen. This, then, is yet another introduction, but it is rather different from the last one. The whole of this book centres around these two themes. From below, the political system in Britain is based on the citizens of the country, who uphold the state. Without citizens, there would be no political system at all. Looked at from above, it is the state which, in its turn, rules the citizens. Binding citizen and state together in Britain is our belief in democracy, and this is the subject, one way or another, of the whole book.

1.1 The citizen's rights and obligations

Many efforts have been made to define the essence of politics, all competing for our attention. But the simplest approach is to say that the study of politics is the study of the relationship between the citizen and the state, between the individual and his or her community. This book is organized around these two themes, around the citizen and the state.

Joined together in a democracy, **citizens** together form the state. The adults who live in the United Kingdom (or at least those who are not just visiting the country on holiday, or to work or study here for a limited period) are the citizens of the United Kingdom. The next seven chapters of this book look at how UK citizens are active within the political system: in elections and other democratic forms of participation, by joining political parties and

Citizen: the individual member of a state.

> **Box 1.1 Citizenship, rights, obligations and contract**
>
> Citizenship confers benefits on those who can claim to be citizens of a state. The richer and freer the state a citizen belongs to, the greater these benefits. The first benefit the state confers on its citizens is to defend them from attack from citizens of other, hostile states. Apart from this (it is to be hoped) rather infrequent benefit, the rights listed in this chapter (and expanded on in chapter 14 on the judiciary) are the principal benefits conferred on the citizen by the state. These rights of the citizen are sometimes called civil rights, derived from the Latin word for citizen: 'civis'. But in return, citizenship requires that people should perform certain obligations or duties. According to the great political philosophers of the seventeenth and eighteenth centuries, Thomas Hobbes, John Locke and Jean-Jacques Rousseau, citizenship is based on a contract, an agreement between the citizen and the state, by which the citizen receives benefits, while the state claims duties, or obligations. The obligations of citizenship are both legal (enforceable in the courts) and moral (a matter of conscience). In order to help people understand what the benefits but also the obligations of citizenship involve, the Labour government has, since its election in 1997, made an effort to educate people in citizenship. This involves the developmefnt of a new curriculum area in secondary education, and also efforts to educate immigrants who apply for citizenship. Since 2003, there have been a number of citizenship ceremonies in which new citizens are formally accepted by the British state as its members. Rather controversially, new citizens taking part in these ceremonies swear an oath of loyalty to the Queen, which is more than existing citizens do, many of whom think they have a right not to be monarchists.

getting involved in pressure groups. Citizenship (the quality of being a citizen) is often thought of as involving the exercise of rights and obligations. The citizen is given certain rights by the state which define the relationship between the state and the citizen and also the relationship between each individual citizen. But in return for these rights, the citizen has some duties to perform, some obligations. This reciprocal relationship between rights and obligations is sometimes called by political scientists a 'contract'.

Civil duties: the obligations of a citizen in a democracy

Everyone will come up with a slightly different list of obligations, and disagree with everyone else about which are the most important. It will be noticed that some duties are legal – we have to do them in order to avoid going to prison or being fined; others are moral, we 'ought' to do them, but it is accepted that some people will be happier to get involved than others. The ideal form of citizenship is active citizenship, where the individual goes well beyond his or her legal duties and gets fully involved in the social and political life of the country.

The main duties of a citizen are:

- To defend the state against attack, to serve in the armed forces. This might seem to be a rather brutal point to begin with, but the state will not last long unless its citizens are willing to defend it.
- To pay taxes. In the same way, the state needs our money in order to fund its services.
- To obey the law. This follows from the last point. After all, we as citizens have played a part in making the law, so we ought to obey it.
- To vote in elections. This is not a legal requirement in the United Kingdom, but there is a fairly strong moral obligation on people to participate in politics. Active citizenship involves doing more than simply voting (see chapter 2)
- To act as a witness in court and to serve on juries. The legal system will collapse unless people are willing to do this.
- To engage as fully as possible in the community or in voluntary forms of participation. Again, this cannot be any more than a moral obligation.
- To work for a living, if a job is available. High levels of unemployment sometimes prevent this, but broadly this is a social or political duty, apart from being quite a sensible thing to do anyway if we want to have some money to spend.

In the UK jury service is a civic duty. Around 250,000 jurors are selected at random by computer every year. Once you are 18 you could be called for Jury service and expected to attend the nearest Crown Court for the duration of the trial

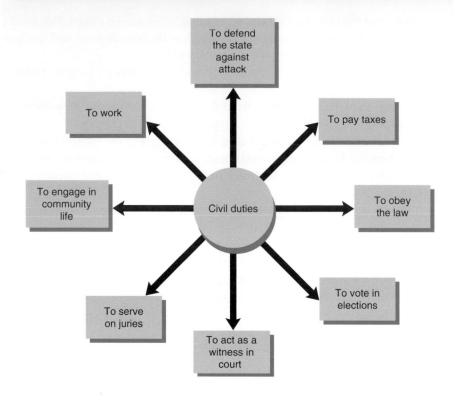

Figure 1.1   Civil duties

Civil rights: the rights of the citizen

In return for fulfilling these obligations, the citizen has certain rights guaranteed by the state. These will vary somewhat from country to country, but here is a brief list of what is generally included:

- Legal rights: the right to a fair trial and to the protection of the law. The right to property and to trade might also be included.
- Political rights: the right to participate in the democratic process – to vote, to stand for election and to join a political party or a pressure group. It will be observed that these are both rights and obligations. The right to free speech and to demonstrate freely are also important political rights, although they have a wider application.
- Religious rights: the right to worship and to believe in whatever religion (or none) the citizen chooses.
- Personal freedoms: for example, the right to follow whatever sexual preferences one chooses, to marry and divorce freely, to dress as one wishes. The right to travel, both at home and abroad, also counts as a personal freedom of a rather different sort.
- Family freedoms: the right to have a family and to bring up children freely.
- Social rights: these vary from state to state, but generally include the right to health care, unemployment pay, old-aged pensions and free education.

> **Civil rights**: special freedoms which citizens of a country enjoy and which are protected by the law.

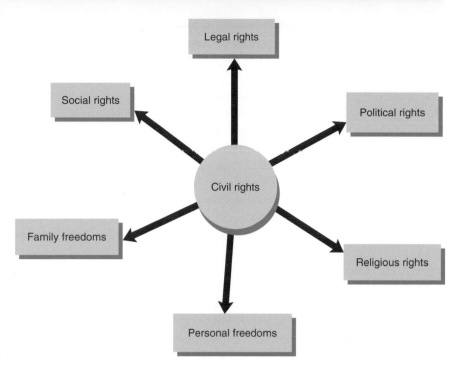

Figure 1.2   Civil rights

 Question: What difference is there between civil and social rights?

Box 1.2 Justice, liberty and equality

Justice means many things, but the most common meaning relates to the rights and duties discussed in this chapter. The contemporary American political philosopher, John Rawls, says that justice is 'fairness'. A just state will be one where a fair balance between rights and duties is protected by the law. All aspects of the state (the politicians, the civil servants and the judges) should be geared towards giving justice to the individual citizen. A just state will also be one where individual freedom, or liberty, is guaranteed. According to what might be called a right-wing view of justice, it is *liberty* which is the real basis for justice. If people are free, justice is preserved. But those on the left of politics tend to stress the need for equality as well. *Equality* means treating every citizen in the same way,

and having no privileged groups at the top or under-privileged groups at the bottom of society. This is not just saying that people should all have the same legal rights and responsibilities, because the rich will be far more likely to be able to enjoy these rights than the poor. So, on the left of politics there is often a demand for what is called 'distributive justice'. *Distributive justice* involves sharing the wealth of society more equally among all citizens. This might limit the freedom of the rich to spend their money because they would be taxed more heavily. But it would also allow the poorer, and more numerous, members of society to acquire the education, leisure and security which are necessary to enjoy rights and freedoms.

1.2 The state, the government, power and authority

The citizen's rights are given to her or him by the state, and the obligations or duties which the citizen must in return perform are imposed by the state. In terms of its institutions, the state is the subject of the second half of this book, which looks, amongst other things, at Parliament, the government (or executive) and the judiciary. These later chapters also deal with the relationship between our state (the United Kingdom) and the European Union, and with local, regional and national government, especially in Scotland, Wales and Northern Ireland. Here, we will give a brief introduction to the state, and try to show how it differs from the government. We shall also deal with key concepts concerned with the state and government, and which have a bearing on the citizen: power and authority.

The official name for our country is the United Kingdom of Great Britain and Northern Ireland. This is, understandably, abbreviated as either the United Kingdom (UK) or Great Britain (GB), or just Britain. The word 'country' describes a geographical place, somewhere we can point to on the map. When we think of a country politically, we can call it a 'state'. So Britain is a state.

The state

The **state** is the most important unit of politics; most students of politics study a particular state, or a number of states in relation to one another. We also use the word 'state' to describe the permanent political authority within an independent country. So, it is possible to talk about the whole political system as the state, or even to refine the meaning to cover a particular aspect of the political system, as when we talk about 'the welfare state' (meaning the welfare system run by the state) or 'the secret state' (meaning the spies employed by the state).

We could elaborate on the concept of the state in the twenty-first century as follows:

A state covers a particular territory

It can be located on a map, and is usually consolidated in one single piece of land or group of islands. The rivers that run through the country, and their water, are also the property of the state. The air space above the country belongs to state, and the sea that flows around it, up to a certain distance form the shore, belongs to the state. Minerals underground are also claimed by the state.

> **State**: a country which is independent of all others; the permanent political authority within an independent country.

A state has sovereignty

Within its geographical limits, the state contains complete authority or sovereignty. It has, in the famous words of the German sociologist Max Weber, writing in 1919 (and himself citing Tolstoy, the Russian novelist), 'the monopoly of legitimate physical violence within a certain territory'. The state is responsible for defending its borders and for maintaining law and order within its frontiers. This right to use force is the ultimate political power.

The state is an association of citizens

It is impossible to conceive of a state with no one living in it, and the main point about any political system is that it involves a collection of people working together. The state's main responsibility is to its citizens, those who live within its borders. In the same way, it is virtually impossible to be a citizen without being the citizen of a particular state.

The state comes in a variety of forms

Precisely what political system the state adopts varies from place to place. These forms of the state can be classified in many different ways. The main modern varieties are liberal democratic (as in Britain), communist (as in China) and authoritarian (as in Saudi Arabia).

The state may be centralized or decentralized

Another way of classifying states is to consider whether the power within the state is strongly focused at the centre, in the capital, or whether power is dispersed to the various parts of the country. An example of a strongly decentralized country would be the United States of America. Small countries like Israel or Ireland are often quite centralized. Federalism is connected to this point and will be discussed in the chapters 9 and 16 (on constitutions and devolution respectively).

Box 1.3 The state of Texas

The terminology used in the social sciences – for example in politics – is formed from the words used in everyday language, and this can lead to confusion, since everyday language can be employed differently in different places. In the USA, the word 'state' is used to describe one of the 50 subsidiary units of the United States, such as Texas, California, etc. The USA itself tends to be called 'the nation' by Americans. This, of course, turns the political science definition almost completely on its head. The only way in which the American usage can be brought together with political science terminology is to point out that under the US federal constitution, Texas does share its state sovereignty with the central, national authority of the USA, so even the political scientist would agree that Texas has some of the marks of statehood.

State and government

A crucial conceptual distinction used in political science is that between state and government. The state, as has been said, is the permanent political authority in a country. As long as the country remains independent, the state survives. The Head of State is often a symbolic figure, who represents the country on ceremonial occasions: in the UK this role is taken by the reigning monarch, currently Queen Elizabeth II. The functions of the monarch are dealt with in chapter 9 on the constitution. The citizens of a state owe their loyalty to the state, and when they fight in a war they do so in defence of the state. In fact, in a democracy the state is really no more than the community of all the citizens: we pay our taxes to the state; civil servants and other public employees work for the state.

The government (also known as the executive), on the other hand, is the temporary, removable group of people who are appointed by the citizens in a democracy to run the state on their behalf. Chapter 12 deals with this subject in greater detail. The head of the government in the UK is not the monarch, but the Prime Minister. In a dictatorship, like Hitler's Germany, the distinction between state and government is not clear because the dictator will not allow himself to be removed, and becomes permanent. But in a liberal democracy, the people can change the government, and whatever the government does – in terms of raising taxes, going to war or making peace – it does in the name of the people and with their approval.

The state and the government bring us to the heart of politics, to questions of power and authority, and we will now briefly explore these concepts. Power seems to be at the heart of a political system.

Political power

Ultimately, **political power** may involve forcing someone to do something they may not wish voluntarily to do. The government possesses this power. Take, for example, the case of an old age pensioner in 2005 who decided to withhold paying all of his council tax, a tax which we pay to our local council in return for local services like street lights and refuse collection. The pensioner refused to pay all his tax because he said that it had been going up in recent years much more quickly than his pension. There was a general protest movement in the country at that time which shared the same views, and a number of pensioners were prosecuted for non-payment of council tax. In the end, the pensioner was taken to court and sentenced to a short term in prison as punishment for not paying his tax. The state ultimately had the power to force this old man to pay his tax or to put him in prison if he refused. The state, looking at it from one angle, could use violence to deprive him of his property: a real display of power. But looked at from another angle,

> **Political power**: the ability to get things done, to change something in the country or to decide to keep it the same.

the state in this case had every right to do what it did. The citizen agrees to pay taxes by being a member of the political community in which he or she lives and also agrees to obey the law. If citizens dislike this, they should campaign legally to change the law, so that the level of taxation fits in better with how they feel about things. The state therefore exercises power in this case, but it is lawful power; the state has the authority to do so.

Authority

> **Authority**: the quality possessed by a political leader or a government which has legitimacy or a right to rule.

Max Weber, the German sociologist of the early twentieth century already referred to here, in a famous analysis, said there were three types of **authority**. The first was traditional authority, which derived from heredity or religious sources; it was the authority claimed by medieval kings or by religious leaders like the Pope. The second form of authority according to Weber was charismatic authority, the claim to rule which outstanding individuals with magnetic personalities or with great powers of oratory had. Weber borrowed the word charisma from the Old Testament of the Bible, where it was the God-given power of leadership granted to the prophets. Third, in the modern world, Weber argued that authority was legal-rational: it derived from a legitimate constitution and the right to rule conferred by democratic elections. Clearly, the authority of the government of the United Kingdom is of this third sort. But we cannot completely reject the other planks of Weber's analysis: our Head of State (the monarch) is of the traditional variety, and in a sense the ancient grandeur of our institutions (like Parliament) is also traditional. The power of charisma is also a significant factor, especially in the modified form which the advent of television and the mass media requires. The popularity of leaders like Tony Blair and Margaret Thatcher derives still to some extent from their public-speaking abilities and their ability to put a message across with conviction to large audiences.

Box 1.4 Political culture

Within a particular state there is generally a dominant outlook about political matters held by most people, which unites the country: a shared political culture. In Britain, this political culture could be described as liberal democratic. Most of the citizens of Britain and most of their politicians happily accept that this is the best way in which to run the country. If we did not share this outlook, the country would be very difficult to run. Questions remain, however, over this idea of a single, shared political culture.

1 The major political parties compete for our support on the basis of competing ideologies and principles. Those on the left of politics stress equality as one of their main ideas, while those on the right are more keen on liberty. Those on the left support a strong state sector in the economy and a generous welfare state. Those on the right are in favour of a vibrant capitalist economy and a lot of private welfare provision. The answer that can be made to this is that, nevertheless, both Labour and Conservative supporters agree that the

Box 1.4 (*continued*)

way in which these issues should be settled is by using elections and debates in Parliament. It might also be said that these old divisions between left and right are to some extent no longer relevant in this age of a new consensus.

2 Another objection to the idea of single political culture is to say that we now live in a multicultural society in which people from a variety of religious and ethnic backgrounds live together. This makes it difficult to see us all as sharing a single political culture: a Muslim fundamentalist will have very different views on society from an atheist. The answer to this is that these differences are to do with lifestyle and religion, and do not impinge on politics: everyone benefits from the tolerance of liberal democracy as a result of which different racial and faith groups can live together in harmony.

3 A final objection is that there is in fact no shared culture since the majority of people are essentially ignorant and apathetic about the responsibilities of citizenship. People think of themselves as individuals, each with separate interests, and not as part of a big happy family called the United Kingdom. What is more, the political culture they are expected to share is essentially one which benefits the ruling class, and therefore it is not surprising if many people feel excluded from it. The answer to this is that such an outlook of alienation and rejection only applies to a minority and, in effect, as Abraham Lincoln said, 'you can't please all of the people all of the time'.

Question: What are the main differences between power and authority?

1.3 Liberal democracy: uniting the citizen and the state

What is it that links the state to the citizen, that ties together the two themes which are explored in this book? What is it, as Max Weber would put it, that translates the power of the state (and government) into authority, which provides it with legitimacy? The answer is that in modern Britain the magic formula which binds together the individual citizen and the great powerful state is democracy – which is the subject of chapter 2. It is democracy in the modern world which provides the state and its governments with the legal-rational (as Weber would put it) legitimacy to rule. The state and the government could not claim the authority to put an old age pensioner in prison for not paying his taxes unless the law allowing this to be done had been voted for by a majority of the people of the country. The United Kingdom is usually described as a liberal democracy, and we will now briefly explore what this means.

The different types of state around the world can be classified according to where the political power is located within the political system. The Ancient

Box 1.5 Max Weber (1864–1920)

Max Weber was a German philosopher who contributed most to the study of sociology. He is described as a classical sociologist, one of the founding fathers of the subject. He added to the theories of Karl Marx, by stressing that in addition to material factors, ideas were also significant in shaping society. This is seen in his attempt to show that capitalism developed in Europe at the end of the Middle Ages as the result of the spread of Protestantism. He developed this idea by looking at his native Germany, where Catholic Bavaria was largely agricultural and Protestant Northern Germany had more industry. Although now almost entirely discredited, this theory certainly inspired a great deal of discussion. His analysis of authority is most often quoted in politics textbooks, although he only rather briefly sketched it, and his main authority was, as he said, the Russian novelist Leon Tolstoy. Nevertheless, it seems to express an important truth: namely, that authority is a complex concept.

Greek philosopher, Aristotle (384–322 BC), said that there were in the end only three ways to classify states: according to whether they were ruled by one person, by a few people or by many people. He felt that we should evaluate these systems, and he believed there were good and bad versions of each (see table 1.1).

Table 1.1 Aristotle's classification of political systems

Number of people who rule	Good form	Bad form
Government by one	Monarchy	Tyranny
Government by few	Oligarchy	Aristocracy
Government by many	'Polity'[a]	Democracy

[a] This is a word not used in this sense by us

Source: Aristotle, *Politics*, book III, ch. VII

Democracy: the system of government where the people rule themselves.

Although Aristotle felt that **democracy** was a bad form of government, he preferred government by the many to the alternatives. His 'polity' would have been government by the many, but in the interests of all. In Greek, democracy means people-power ('demos' is the people). The most famous definition of democracy in the modern world comes from the President of the USA, Abraham Lincoln (1809–65), who called it 'government of the people, by the people, for the people'. Lincoln meant that it was a system where the people ruled themselves, and did so in their own interests. The mature, modern form of democracy which we claim to operate in the United Kingdom is sometimes described as '**liberal democracy**', and it brings the focus back to the rights of the individual citizen.

It is important for democracy to operate against a solid legal and constitutional framework which protects individuals and minorities from the dangers of over-ambitious or unscrupulous politicians. It is also important that the majority should not use their democratic power to tyrannize the minority. There must be some limits set to the power that the elected representatives are given. An effective liberal democracy will be what is described as pluralist. There will be a number (plurality) of institutions which influence those people with political power: a free press and media, pressure groups, free churches and religious groups, and political parties.

The liberal democratic political system in the United Kingdom can be summed up in a number of stages, illustrated in figure 1.3. This at least is the theory. By the time you have finished reading this book you should be able to question how truly democratic the country actually is. What follows is a brief evaluation of British democracy.

> **Liberal democracy**: a state where the people rule themselves but in addition the rights of the citizen are protected by law.

Positive points

In theory, the United Kingdom is a liberal democracy, as can be seen from stages illustrated in figure 1.3. In comparative terms, also, we are a true democracy. Anyone who has lived under the cruel dictatorship of certain countries (Hitler and Stalin come to mind, but there are still regimes rather like that around today) will tell you that we are certainly a democratic country. People seeking asylum in the country, fleeing the cruelty of dictators, can also give a very clear account of the positive value of living under a political system like ours. Arguably, Britain would also seem to have become rather more democratic in recent years than in the past as the result of devolution, the Human Rights Act, reform of the House of Lords, and the growing use of referendums, for example.

Criticisms of democracy in the UK

There are doubts about how far the system of elections used in the UK is truly representative and hence democratic. Question-marks hang over the real democratic credentials of both pressure groups and political parties. The fact that we do not have a written constitution in the UK and that we have unelected and hereditary elements in the monarchy and in the House of Lords also adds to our doubts over how democratic Britain really is. The rise in the power of the unelected judiciary and of the European Union with its 'democratic deficit' may also lead us to question in two different ways whether we live in a true democracy. All these points will be dealt with at greater length in the rest of this book.

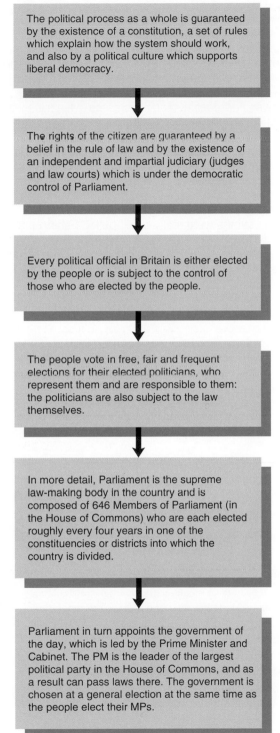

The political process as a whole is guaranteed by the existence of a constitution, a set of rules which explain how the system should work, and also by a political culture which supports liberal democracy.

The rights of the citizen are guaranteed by a belief in the rule of law and by the existence of an independent and impartial judiciary (judges and law courts) which is under the democratic control of Parliament.

Every political official in Britain is either elected by the people or is subject to the control of those who are elected by the people.

The people vote in free, fair and frequent elections for their elected politicians, who represent them and are responsible to them: the politicians are also subject to the law themselves.

In more detail, Parliament is the supreme law-making body in the country and is composed of 646 Members of Parliament (in the House of Commons) who are each elected roughly every four years in one of the constituencies or districts into which the country is divided.

Parliament in turn appoints the government of the day, which is led by the Prime Minister and Cabinet. The PM is the leader of the largest political party in the House of Commons, and as a result can pass laws there. The government is chosen at a general election at the same time as the people elect their MPs.

Figure 1.3   Stages of the UK political system

Box 1.6 Karl Marx's critique of liberal democracy

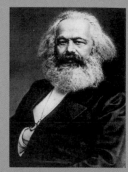

The great political philosopher Karl Marx (1818–83) believed that all human relationships were determined by material forces, by economics. Men and women were essentially workers and struggled with the material world to create the means of survival. In order to produce, they formed social relationships – families, towns, factories and social classes. Man's life was formed by these economic and social forces. What people call politics was, according to Marx, just a result of these social relationships. If people were ruled by a king it was simply because the politics of royal government fitted in with the facts of agricultural production and land ownership at that stage in human history. Marx said that the politics of liberal democracies was just a mask behind which the power of big business hid itself. Although people were given the illusion of having some impact on their own lives through the political process, in practice they could change nothing because the strings were really being pulled behind the scenes by the people with economic power. Even these people were essentially powerless, according to Marxist analysis, because they themselves were subject to the invisible forces of the world market and economic conditions, which could remove their fortunes in a bad day at the stock market. So, for the Marxist, the realities of human life and the changes it underwent were to be found not in politics but in people's relationship with the forces of production, with materialism. Obviously, such a dismissive view of politics and of liberal democracy needs to be challenged by students of politics. First of all, even Marx seems to accept that there is such a thing as politics, there is a world of political activity in Parliament and in the 'corridors of power'. What Marx rejects is the idea that it is of fundamental importance, that it is causative in shaping human existence. The answer that can be made to this is that it is palpably untrue: people with political power can use the police force and the army, and can have a very considerable impact on everybody's life. Moreover, it is simply not true that politicians in a liberal democracy invariably act as the agents of the bourgeoisie, of the middle-class factory owners and stockbrokers. The history of Britain is full of examples of social and economic reform (passed by all three major political parties) which have benefited all the people and not just the rich middle classes.

Activity

This is an activity for you to do at the very end of your course, by way of revision.

1 Draw up your own democratic audit of the United Kingdom.
2 Draw a line down the middle of a sheet of A4, label one column 'Successfully democratic' and the other column 'Undemocratic or of dubious democratic credentials'.
3 Go through each of the chapters of this book and make points drawn from each one to fill in your two columns with evidence.
4 At the end, draw up a list of reforms you would like to see introduced to improve Britain as a democracy.

Question: How democratic is government in the UK?

SUMMING UP

The individual in the United Kingdom enjoys certain rights as a citizen, but in return is expected to perform duties to the state. The state exists to protect the citizen, and acquires authority over the citizen in a democracy by having the support of the bulk of the population. The state transfers its power to the government of the day. The form of government used in each state varies around the world; in the United Kingdom it can be described as a liberal democracy.

The citizens of the UK are largely united by the idea that this is the best, and most legitimate, form of government. There are many criticisms that can be levelled at democracy in the UK, but in the end most people agree that we make a reasonable attempt at achieving a workable system which represents most of the people well, protecting their rights and receiving in return their loyalty and support.

Further reading

A. Heywood, *Politics* (Macmillan, 1997): a valuable, straightforward introduction to the main concepts covered in this chapter.

Websites

www.citizenship.org.uk (Centre for Citizenship Studies in Education)
www.hansard-society.org.uk (Hansard Society)
www.politicsassociation.co.uk (Politics Association)

CHAPTER

2

Democracy and Participation

Making connections

This chapter is, in a way, an introduction to the three chapters that follow it, which deal with elections and with voting behaviour. So, your understanding of the subjects discussed in this chapter will be deeper after you have studied the next three chapters as well. Liberal democracy has already been discussed in chapter 1.

CHAPTER

2

Democracy and Participation

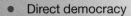

SETTING THE SCENE

The subject of this chapter follows from the last one, where the idea of democracy was introduced. It is probably the most important topic in modern politics, since we consider democracy to be the central and most valuable aspect of how Britain is run. This is where the people themselves get involved in the political process, through elections at various levels and then through referendums. But how successfully do we run the democratic process in this country?

2.1 Direct democracy

Democracy can be analysed within two main types: direct and representative. In both types, what is often most important is the participation of the people in the process, and this leads us to a consideration of what is called 'participatory democracy'. We will examine these three strands in turn, beginning with a consideration of direct democracy.

Direct democracy is the ideal form of democracy, with the people genuinely ruling themselves and making decisions on political matters on a day-to-day basis. In practical terms in the modern world, it is only through the use of referendums that direct democracy can be put into use. There

Direct democracy: government of the people by the people, immediately and with no intervention from elected politicians.

have been suggestions that with the development of new technology a modern form of direct democracy might develop, nicknamed predictably 'e-democracy', or '**digital democracy**'. Here, people would express their political views over the internet. It doesn't take much thought, though, to realize that if this was to be genuinely democratic, everyone would need a computer and everyone would need to be computer-literate. We are a long way off achieving that. Even if it were achieved, it is doubtful whether people would actually want to participate anyway. Nevertheless, in 2007, 1.8 million computer addicts signed an electronic petition on the Downing Street website against road-charging, so perhaps this form of direct democracy may have a future.

> **Digital democracy** or e-democracy: a form of direct democracy where the people make political decisions, or are consulted by the government, using the internet.

Box 2.1 Athenian and modern direct democracy

The great model for direct democracy takes us back more than two thousand years to Ancient Greece, where in Athens the citizens could all meet together in the market place and decide political matters by debating and voting among themselves. When the Athenian democrats had to choose representatives, they did so by lottery and for limited periods – a sign that they distrusted representative democracy, which will be discussed in the next section of this chapter. Historians tell us that in fact this was not really a matter of democracy, since women and slaves played no part in the process. So the decisions were only taken by about a third of the total adult population: the male freemen. In addition, we might add that the Athenians were very often led by great statesmen like Pericles, which rather calls into question the claim that they really practised direct democracy. Still, the Athenian model stands as the great ideal of how a direct democracy might work. It is worth emphasizing that the population of Athens in ancient times was relatively small. Obviously it would be difficult to replicate the circumstances of direct democracy in the modern world. However, developments in electronic technology might in the future enable people to make decisions at home, like voting on the TV show, *Big Brother*. More realistically, the use of referendums, where the people are directly consulted on a specific issue, is a modern form of direct democracy. Referendums are dealt with later on in this chapter (sections 3 and 4).

 Question: Close your book and answer the following question from memory: 'What are the main advantages and disadvantages of direct democracy?'

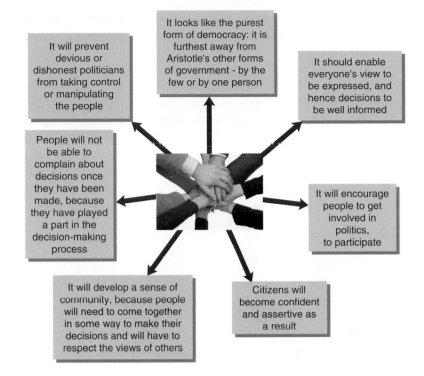

Figure 2.1   The advantages
of direct democracy

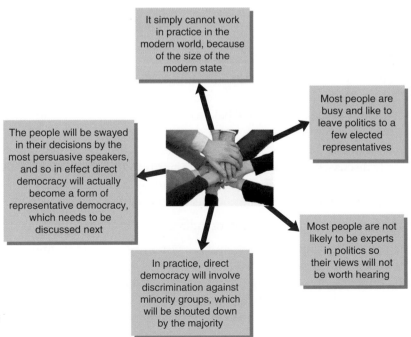

Figure 2.2   The disadvantages
of direct democracy

2.2 Representative or indirect democracy

In a large modern state the only practical way in which democracy can be made to work is if the people elect representatives to rule them. In Britain the most important of these elected representatives meet in Parliament, so we can also call this system parliamentary democracy. It is important that these elections are quite frequent in order to make sure that the system is really democratic. With frequent elections, the representatives can be held to account, be held responsible for what they have done in the past and replaced by other politicians if they are judged to have failed.

The advantages of **representative or indirect democracy** are as follows:

- It is the only practicable system for the modern world.
- It enables a few people to specialize in government and politics and hence the state will be run efficiently.
- It is still democratic, but with some modifications; it is 'government of the people by some of the people for the people'.
- The representatives can protect minorities and prevent the people from coming to rash or hasty decisions; it will prevent the 'tyranny of the majority'.
- If it works properly, a variety of views will be expressed (probably when the politicians organize themselves in political parties).
- Different groups in 'civil society' (farmers, business people, members of particular religious groups, those living in remote areas, for example) will form pressure groups and even political parties in order to achieve representation and protect their interests. This representation of many different groups is known as pluralism, a topic discussed more fully in chapter 6, which deals with pressure groups.
- The process of democratic accountability keeps government running smoothly and makes elections into an important part of the political system. A system of 'checks and balances' allows representatives to check the work of government.
- Representative democracy is often associated with liberal democracy (briefly discussed in chapter 1), where minority and individual rights are further protected, and where freedom of expression and freedom to associate are key aspects of creating an effective pluralist system.

The disadvantages of representative or indirect democracy are as follows:

- The politicians simply take over and the system becomes government by one person or by a few.
- Even if the politicians do not become dictators, they can manipulate the voters at the elections and so maintain themselves in power.
- The politicians will pander to the majority, so the views of minorities will not be heard.

> **Representative or indirect democracy**: the system in which the people elect politicians to govern on their behalf.

- The people will not participate in politics, leaving it to the representatives, so in the end the system will cease to be democratic.
- The politicians will quarrel among themselves and spend their time chasing votes when they should be running the country. The impact on democracy of political parties is not always positive: see chapter 7 on political parties.
- Pluralism will actually ensure that the rich and powerful make themselves heard and the poor and weak (sometimes in a majority) are ignored. The dangers to democracy of pressure groups are discussed in chapter 6.

Representative democracy is the best system we can manage. Winston Churchill said that democracy was the worst form of government until you came to consider the alternatives – at that point it begins to look like the best. The same could be said to be true of representative democracy. Above all, it can be made to work in the modern world, whereas direct democracy cannot. Modern representative democracy can be made to work even better than it sometimes does, given some conditions: by establishing true liberal democracy and by encouraging participatory democracy, which is the subject of the final section of this chapter.

 Question: Evaluate representative democracy.

Box 2.2 Sir Winston Churchill (1874–1965)

Winston Churchill was Britain's war-leader during the Second World War, as the Conservative Prime Minster at the head of the last Coalition government to rule Britain (1940–5). He was Prime Minster again from 1951 to 1955. Churchill came from an aristocratic background: his father had been a controversial Tory politician before him, and his mother was American. His early career was as a reforming Liberal MP and associate of Lloyd George in the New Liberal government of 1906–16. But he then became a Conservative and his views were typical, in domestic policy, of the paternalist, Disraelian, progressive Toryism of that era (although, in a speech in 2006, David Cameron depicted him as a right-wing Conservative in his attitudes to poverty, which was very far from the truth). After a disastrous contribution to the First World War (the unsuccessful Gallipoli campaign was his responsibility), he was nevertheless chosen in 1940 by the Conservatives to lead the nation during the Second World War. He made fewer mistakes this time round, and was best known for his stirring radio broadcasts (some of which were made by an actor who could imitate his voice), exhorting the people to stand firm against Germany, and for his photographs in the newspapers shaking his two fingers at Germany as a sign of victory. He inspired both love and hatred among British voters and, to the surprise of his fans, he lost the 1945 general election comprehensively. He recovered power, however, in 1951, largely because his Labour opponent, Clement Attlee, made a disastrous decision to call an election unnecessarily, which he then lost.

2.3 Referendums

We now move on to look at the most significant aspect of direct democracy currently used in Britain: the **referendum**. Referendums are comparatively new political developments: the first one to be used in this country was in 1973, and since the election of Tony Blair's government in 1997 their use has increased (see table 2.1). Does the increased use of referendums enhance democracy?

A referendum is an exercise in direct democracy, and sometimes called a plebiscite. Generally in a referendum there is one simple question (though in the case of the Scottish referendum of 1997 – see below – there were two linked questions). The voters are simply asked to vote 'yes' or 'no' to the question given. These devices are used widely abroad for a variety of purposes. In Switzerland, for example, there have been 500 referendums in the past 150 years. In some states of USA they have also become very popular, especially in recent years. In the November 2004 elections in USA, there were more than 200 referendums of one sort or another in 40 states. In the UK they are used much more rarely. Technically, in the UK, they can be divided into **pre-legislative** (or advisory) and **post-legislative** (or mandatory) referendums.

In practice, there is little difference between the two types of referendum, because Parliament would find it very difficult politically to ignore the result of a pre-legislative referendum, and, on the other hand, could technically repeal the legislation which preceded the post-legislative referendum (although again this would have great political costs).

National referendums

There have been seven important referendums covering the whole country or one of the 'national' components of the United Kingdom, as well as a number of local ones. In addition, there have been proposals for a number of national referendums in the future. The detail given here may be rather difficult for you until you have studied the questions of Europe and devolution, which are dealt with in chapters 15 and 16.

Local government referendums

As in London, a number of other towns have been balloted in local referendums on whether to establish a directly elected mayor. There were 34 such referendums between 2001, when the process began, and 2006 (almost all in 2001–2), and they resulted in a 'yes' vote in only 12 of these towns. They were largely conducted by all-postal ballot, in a desperate effort to boost turnout.

> **Referendum**: a vote on a specific issue (or specific issues) by the electorate as a whole.

> **Pre-legislative referendum**: one held before legislation has passed Parliament on the issue in question. In pure constitutional terms, Parliament could ignore the result; it is only a piece of advice given to Parliament by the people.
> **Post-legislative referendum**: one that gives the electorate the say on whether to adopt a piece of legislation or not – legislation which has already passed Parliament; so if the people agree, the government is mandated, or commanded by them, to act.

Table 2.1 UK referendums since 1973

1973 referendum on Northern Ireland	The referendum asked the people of Northern Ireland whether they wanted to remain part of the UK. It was boycotted by the minority, Catholic population (who wanted to leave the UK and become part of the Republic of Ireland); that is to say, the Catholics organized a protest campaign and did not turn out to vote, because they knew in advance that they would lose. *Result: Yes, 98.9%; No, 1.1%; Turnout, 58.1%*
1975 referendum on whether to stay in the EEC (forerunner of the EU)	This is the only referendum to be held in the UK which has covered the whole country and not just one part of it. Britain had joined the EEC in 1973 without a referendum; when Labour came to power in 1974 they said they would renegotiate the arrangements (largely financial) made with EEC by the previous Conservative government and then give the people of the whole country the chance to say 'yes' or 'no' to staying in the EEC. *Result: Yes, 67.2%; No, 32.8%; Turnout, 63.2%*
1979 referendum on devolution to Scotland	The Scottish people were asked whether they wanted the Act for the devolution of power to Scotland, which had already been passed by Parliament, to be implemented. It was decided that on such an important issue at least 40% of those entitled to vote (the electorate) would have to agree. The supporters would have to cross a higher threshold (or achieve a larger target) than normal. All other UK referendums (apart from the 1979 Wales referendum, which was the same as this one) had a simple first-past-the-post (FPTP) rule: if over 50% of the voters supported a measure, it would be taken as a 'yes' vote. By saying that over 40% of the electorate, whether or not they bothered to turn out and vote, had to support devolution, it had been made rather more difficult to achieve a 'yes' vote. Although the 'yes' vote passed the 50% of the voters threshold, it failed to reach the 40% of the electorate threshold, so the result was held to be 'no'. *Result: Yes, 51.6% (32.5% of electorate); No, 48.4% (30.7% of electorate); Turnout, 63.8%*
1979 referendum on devolution to Wales	Essentially the same as the Scottish referendum. The result was decisively 'no' here with not even 50% of the voters supporting the idea. *Result: Yes, 20.3% (11.8% of electorate); No, 79.7% (46.5% of electorate); Turnout, 58.3%*
1997 referendum on devolution to Scotland	Unlike the 1979 effort, this was pre-legislative. Unusually, it asked two questions: one on devolution, and the second on whether the voter supported giving the new Scottish Parliament tax-varying powers (that is, powers to increase or decrease income tax by 3p in the £). No artificial barriers were set to the voters as they had been in 1979. The result was a convincing 'yes' on both counts. *Results: devolution: Yes, 74.3%; No, 25.7%. Tax-varying powers: Yes, 63.5%; No, 36.5%; Turnout, 60.1%*
1997 referendum on devolution to Wales	This did the same thing in Wales as the previous referendum did in Scotland, with the difference being that there was only one question: the proposed Welsh Assembly was not going to have tax-varying powers, and the Welsh were not to be asked whether they wanted it to have them. *Results: Yes, 50.3%; No, 49.7%; Turnout, 50.1%*
1998 referendum in Northern Ireland on the 'Good Friday Agreement'	This asked people in the province whether they would accept the power-sharing system of government and the cross-border arrangements with the Republic of Ireland which had been painfully negotiated over the years since the first IRA ceasefire in 1993. The people were not also asked if they preferred a united Ireland or some form of return to Unionist domination. There were some question-marks over the result, since the 'yes' result seems to have included a rather low number of supporters from the majority Unionist community. *Results: Yes, 71.1%; No, 28.9; Turnout, 81%*
1999 referendum on proposed changes to London's local government	The proposals were to create a directly elected mayor and a Greater London Assembly. *Result: Yes, 72%; No, 28%; Turnout, 34%*

Very infrequently

On the whole, referendums are rather unpopular among politicians (see below) and we can conclude that they are only held in fairly exceptional circumstances, at least at the national level. There has only ever been one referendum covering the whole country (in 1975 on the European question).

Local matters

As has been seen, referendums are held surprisingly often on local matters. This goes back as far as the 1850s, when the decision on whether to open public libraries was made one on which local referendums could be called. Their use has increased in recent years, mainly to decide on the use of local amenities which have tax implications.

Matters of nationality

Six of the seven major referendums that have been held to date have concerned the status of the nations which make up the United Kingdom, or the national status of the UK itself. These are major topics of nationality and statehood itself, and since they concern the individuals who make up the state so closely, it is reasonable to consult them directly on such matters. This has been a common role for referendums in other countries too. In a sense, the English referendums on mayors and assemblies just follow from the devolution referendums to Scotland and Wales, and so, loosely speaking, could be seen as part of the same thing.

Constitutional issues

Matters of nationality are constitutional issues, although many other aspects of the constitution have been changed by Parliament without reference to the electorate, as have other national matters.

Not for controversial social or moral questions

In some countries difficult moral or social questions (for example, abortion, euthanasia, gay marriage) are dealt with by referendum, but not in the UK. Such matters are often decided in the UK by a vote in Parliament. This is generally taken outside the party struggle and decided by a 'free' vote among MPs. In other words, the MPs vote on their own conscientious beliefs on these matters and are not forced to adopt a party line on them. There has been little appetite for using referendums in this way in Britain, at least no appetite among MPs. The death penalty was abolished, and such issues as hunting, drugs, pornography, abortion, divorce and prostitution have all been dealt with by MPs without reference to the public, even at general elections, since these are free-vote matters. In 2000, a Scottish businessman,

Brian Souter, arranged for all Scottish voters to be sent an unofficial ballot on Clause 2a, which was known as Section 28 in England. This was a clause in the 1988 Local Government Act which Margaret Thatcher had passed and which banned the promotion of homosexuality in schools. The Labour government planned to repeal this clause, and Mr Souter felt that this was wrong. Having failed to stimulate the government into holding a referendum on the subject, he decided to hold his own postal ballot. Perhaps surprisingly, a third of the electorate returned the forms. Whatever one may feel about the rights and wrongs of the subject which interested him, Mr Souter was at least highlighting the difficulties faced by pressure groups in Britain in persuading a government to hold a referendum. In many states in the USA, this process is frequently resorted to and is called an initiative: if enough citizens support a petition, it can lead to a referendum on the subject. The same is true of the lowly parish polls in the UK, which can be triggered by as few as ten signatures. The Liberal Democrats have proposed to introduce a system of national initiatives.

To get politicians out of a difficult situation

If a controversial issue threatens to divide a political party, or to cause a rift between people and politicians, it is perhaps not unreasonable to hold a referendum. But there is generally some political in-fighting associated with the decision to call a referendum. The 1975 referendum on Europe was designed by Harold Wilson to put an end to squabbling within the Labour Party on the subject. All sorts of political tensions also lay behind James Callaghan's Labour government's decision to hold the 1979 referendums on devolution for Scotland and Wales: the Labour backbencher's amendment demanding that the 'yes' vote get more than the 40 per cent of the support of all those qualified to vote (whether they actually voted or not – see table 2.1) was essentially a wrecking manoeuvre. The post-1997 referendums look more straightforward, although the tax-varying clause was imposed on the Scottish Labour Party by a nervous Tony Blair who did not want to be portrayed as an advocate of tax increases in the run-up to the 1997 general election. The referendum on the euro has also been useful to Labour because they have been able to avoid discussion of an unpopular issue by saying that in the end it is up to the people to decide. The announcement in 2004 by Tony Blair that there would be a referendum on the European Constitution was designed to take this issue off the agenda for the coming general election.

 Question: Under what circumstances have referendums been held in the UK? Give three examples.

2.4 The case for and against referendums

The case for referendums

There is a good deal of overlap between the case for direct democracy and against representative democracy (dealt with already in the chapter) and the case for referendums.

Direct democracy is the purest form of democracy

If Britain is a democracy, why should the people not decide, especially on such significant issues? Elected representatives are often out of touch with the views of the people, and they can make decisions that are unpopular and hence bring the whole system of representative democracy into disrepute. This argument was made about the way in which the Prime Minister took the country to war against Iraq in 2003 despite considerable opposition to this policy in the country. It is difficult to see how a referendum could be held over this, however. A better example is the question of whether to join the euro zone: this is too important a decision to leave to the politicians.

Referendums encourage political participation

People can become detached and cynical about the political process, but referendums are a way of involving them more directly and hence removing apathy and alienation. In the 2004 presidential election in USA it is reckoned that turnout increased because in a number of states controversial matters (like gay marriage) were included on the ballot papers as referendums.

Referendums remove the threat of 'elective dictatorship'

Politicians can become arrogant and unresponsive between general elections, after they have been elected. This was described as 'elective dictatorship' in 1976 by Lord Hailsham. Two hundred years earlier, the French philosopher Voltaire had said that the British were only free for one day every few years: election day. Frequent referendums will prevent this development.

If politicians cannot agree, the people should decide

As has been said before, politicians tend to use referendums when they cannot, for a variety of reasons, decide on an issue themselves. For example, parties are divided over whether to adopt the euro, as they were in 1975 over whether to stay in the Europe Economic Community (which later became the European Union): so, it is better to preserve party unity by passing the decision to the people.

Single issues cannot be decided in general elections

It is therefore better to hold a referendum on single issues. In a general election voters choose between parties on a whole range of issues, not just one.

Only the people can directly decide on matters of national identity

To date, this has been the main focus of UK referendums: the people are the nation.

Constitutional changes require the support of the people

This is especially true in the UK, where there is no formal provision, as there is in most countries, for constitutional amendment.

General elections are an unfair way of deciding the status of a region/nation within the UK

Only the people of Scotland, Wales or Northern Ireland are qualified to decide the future of their particular region, so this should not be decided in a general election, which involves everyone in the whole country voting. Between 1979 and 1997, Scottish supporters of devolution were thwarted by the repeated election south of the border of Conservative governments determined not to give Scotland its own Parliament.

Table 2.2 The case for and against referendums	
FOR 👍	**AGAINST** 👎
Direct democracy is the purest form of democracy	Referendums are a device of dictators and demagogues
Referendums encourage political participation	Representative democracy is preferable to direct democracy
Referendums remove the threat of 'elective dictatorship'	The people lack the knowledge to decide
Only the people can directly decide on matters of national identity	Referendums can be manipulated by politicians
Constitutional changes require popular support	Politicians decide when to hold a referendum
General elections are an unfair way of deciding the status of a region/nation within the UK	The legitimacy of the result can be questioned

The case against referendums

Again, this tends to overlap with the case against direct democracy and in favour of representative democracy given above.

'A device of dictators and demagogues'

Clement Attlee, Labour Prime Minister (1945–51), used this phrase. The first referendums were used, or misused, by dictators and rabble-rousing demagogues like the French Emperors, Napoleon I and Napoleon III, and then, in the twentieth century, by Hitler and Mussolini. They were frequently accompanied by the use of force, fraud and propaganda. This is clearly not a good precedent.

Representative democracy is preferable to direct democracy

The views of the people need to be filtered through the mechanisms of parliamentary democracy and discussion at party level.

The people lack the knowledge to decide

Left to themselves, the people cannot be trusted, and do not have the knowledge required to make difficult decisions. For example, whether to join the euro zone is a highly complex economic question which divides academic economists. The people can hardly be expected to have a well-informed view on this.

The people make short-term decisions

In a referendum, people vote on a spur-of-the-moment basis, considering the immediate circumstances of a question, rather than reflecting on how their decision will look in the future. But a referendum does usually decide the question for some time to come. It is through responsible, representative government that such decisions should be made.

The people are swayed by other factors

Evidence from abroad suggests that some people tend to vote in referendums as if they were voting in elections. They will punish a government during a period of recession or while the government is generally unpopular by voting in a referendum against the preferred option of the government. It has been suggested that this explains why the French voted against the European Constitution in 2005. This may also account for the 'no' vote in the devolution referendums in Scotland and Wales of 1979, since they were taken after the 'winter of discontent', when the government was unpopular.

The referendum can be manipulated by politicians

The wording of the question used in the referendum itself is all-important; the timing of the referendum may be significant; the amount of money spent promoting the 'yes' or 'no' vote; the support or otherwise of prominent figures: all these points are true, but manipulation that is too blatant will generally be uncovered and revealed by the media. In addition, the Electoral Commission set up in 2000 has been given powers to limit expenditure on referendums and to ensure that the campaigns are properly conducted.

Who decides whether to have a referendum?

It is entirely up to the politicians in Parliament to decided on what subjects a referendum should be held and when. So they are not genuinely an example of direct democracy. On the other hand, a powerful campaign in favour of holding a referendum can work, as was shown in 1997 by the pressure for a referendum on the euro from the Referendum Party.

The legitimacy of a result can be questioned

The setting of an artificially high threshold in 1979 has been questioned and led to criticisms of the legitimacy of the result of the Scottish referendum, which otherwise would have been in favour of devolution. But this does highlight an important issue. If turnout is low and the result is close, the whole purpose of a referendum is called into question. The point seems to be for the people to make up the national mind when the politicians cannot do so themselves. But what if the people cannot decide either? The Welsh result in 1997 is open to criticism on these grounds, since it was so close on a low turnout. In 1992 Denmark held a referendum on the Treaty of European Union and the result was an indecisive 'no'. The politicians renegotiated the Treaty (a little) and another referendum was held in which the people gave a slightly more decisive 'yes'. Which result should we trust when the votes are so close? This example also shows how politicians can manipulate referendums to suit their own views. Similarly, in Ireland in 2001 and 2002 there were two referendums on the same question, about the Treaty of Nice (the European Treaty which led to the enlargement of the EU). In the first referendum a small majority of the Irish said 'no', but the politicians were not happy and asked the electorate again the following year, this time receiving a 'yes' vote, which is now considered final.

> **?** *Question:* Outline two differences between referendums and general elections.

Activity

Together with a classmate, draw up a list of topics which you feel ought to be put to a referendum. Try to draft a neutral question to be put to the electorate on that issue – one which will not be accused of being weighted to one side or the other. Imagine a campaign on each of these topics and devise points which would be made on each side of the campaign. Test the views of your whole class, by putting these referendums to a secret ballot in the classroom, after the case has been argued on either side. Do the results of these referendums show that the class is largely nationalist or internationalist? authoritarian or liberal? left-leaning or right-leaning? Are males or females more on one side of the line than the other?

2.5 Political participation

Representative democracy can take on some of the virtues of direct democracy. One way in which this can be done is to use referendums (a form of direct democracy – see above) more widely in conjunction with the normal methods of representative democracy. Referendums, for example, are important to validate any changes to the rules by which liberal democracy operates. In addition, representative democracy works best (in a way, it becomes more direct) if more people are involved in the political process, by joining political parties or pressure groups, becoming local councillors and, above all, simply by voting in elections conscientiously.

Active participation at a number of levels in politics is described as active citizenship. There are a number of ways in which people participate in politics in a democracy:

- *Voting*. The most fundamental democratic right is the right to vote and although rather a simple form of participation, this is the most important form of all. The term used to describe the level of voting in a country is turnout. Turnout is important at all types of election: national, regional and local. Participation may also involve turning out to vote in referendums.
- *Political activism in party politics.* A more active form of participation is to join a political party, to attend the local meetings of the party, and offer to help canvass for votes and deliver leaflets. Parties encourage their members to get involved in policy forums and the regular conferences held by the party. Local parties need volunteer officers and committee members to support and maintain their work.
- *Recruitment into the world of politics itself.* The most active participants in party politics will become involved in local politics and may then graduate from this to national politics, as John Major did. Others, like Tony Blair, will be directly recruited as parliamentary candidates, without having had any experience in local politics.
- *Political activism in pressure politics.* Political participation can also involve playing a role in a pressure group. This may come out of a local issue, like the building of a new by-pass or objections to the siting of a mobile phone mast. It may also result from deeply held convictions about a cause, or support for a particular interest group. A citizen can join a pressure group or go further and attend meetings, stand for office in the group and help run it.
- *Demonstrations and direct action.* The most active pressure politics involves demonstrations, protest marches and even more extreme forms of protest, picketing and blockading.

Political participation: the way in which citizens get involved in the political process. A participatory democracy is one in which citizens are encouraged to take an active part in political life.

2.6 Is political participation in decline?

The really big question surrounding political participation is whether it is in decline and, if it is, what the reasons are for this declining participation. The answer to the first question seems to be 'yes', although there is a debate over how far this decline has gone and whether it matters. We will look at each of these points in turn, starting with the evidence for a decline in participation, concentrating mainly on turnout in elections, but also looking at the other forms of participation: membership of political parties, political recruitment, membership of pressure groups and, finally, involvement in direct action.

Table 2.3 Turnout in post-war general elections	
General election	Turnout (%)
1945	73
1950	84
1951	83
1955	77
1959	79
1964	77
1966	76
1970	72
1974 (Feb)	78
1974 (Oct)	73
1979	76
1983	73
1987	75
1992	78
1997	72
2001	59
2005	61

Source: http://news.bbc.co.uk

Turnout: the measure of how many people vote (or 'turn out' to vote) in elections. In the UK it is usually expressed as the ratio of voters (those who actually do vote) to electors (those entitled to vote because they are on the electoral register), expressed as a percentage.

Turnout

Table 2.3 shows that the general elections of 1997 and 2001 did see a decline in **turnout**. In 1997 the turnout was the lowest, up to that point, in the post-war period, although it was close to the figures of 1970 and 1945. The 2001 turnout was quite shocking, the worst since 1918 (57 per cent), which was an exceptional year partly because of the sudden increase in the electorate and because the First World War had just ended, making it difficult to record the votes of the armed forces. It is possible to argue that there has been a steady decline in turnout since 1945. Obviously the 1945 figure itself is a problem in that argument, but, again, at the end of the Second World War the disruption meant that the figure is not a reliable guide to participation. It does look as if there is a slight erosion of participation if we compare the 1950s with the 1980s, but then the figure for 1992 crops up to cast some doubt on that argument. Still, we can probably argue for some slight long-term decline in turnout, and then a dramatic fall in 2001. The 2005 figure (61 per cent) is very little better than that of 2001, especially in the light of the strenuous efforts that were made to make voting easier in 2005, by the expansion of postal voting.

Geographical and social factors in turnout

There are a number of long-term or sociological factors which may affect turnout, including geographical factors and those connected to gender, social class and age.

Table 2.4 Regional turnout, general election 2005 (2001 in brackets)

Region	Turnout (%)
England	
South-East	64 (62)
South-West	67 (65)
London	58 (55)
Eastern	64 (62)
East Midlands	63 (61)
West Midlands	61 (59)
Yorkshire and Humberside	59 (57)
North-East	57 (56)
North-West	57 (56)
Wales	62 (61)
Scotland	61 (58)
Northern Ireland	63 (68)

Source: Electoral Commission website, www.electoralcommission.org.uk

First, there is a slight geographical aspect to turnout, as table 2.4 shows. The geographical differences shown here are too small to justify much comment. The low northern turnout is likely to be a function of Labour strength in many constituencies there, which makes voting for anti-Labour candidates rather unnecessary. The more rural a constituency, the higher on the whole the turnout will be, and the figures for London tend to confirm this. The lowest turnout in 2001 was in the safe Labour constituency of Liverpool Riverside, where it was 34.1 per cent. In 2005 this constituency was still the lowest in the country, but turnout had risen to 41.49 per cent. The highest turnout in 2005 was leafy Hampshire East, where it was a staggering 90.5 per cent. There was a tough battle there between the Liberal Democrats and the Conservatives. In 2001, the turnout in Hampshire East had only been 63.82 per cent. The figures for 2005 do not show a very much higher turnout in Northern Ireland than in the rest of the country (largely because the moderate SDLP and UUP failed to inspire their supporters), but in 2001 Northern Ireland turnout was 9 per cent above the national average: this has been used to support the view that it is conflict which makes people vote and contentment which prevents them from doing so.

There is a slight gender gap in turnout, a rather pronounced difference in turnout according to age, and some social differences too (see table 2.5). The pronounced differences in turnout between different age groups and

Table 2.5 Social factors in turnout, general election 2005 (2001 in brackets)	
Social Group	Turnout (%)
Men	62 (61)
Women	61 (58)
Social group AB (professional and managerial)	70 (68)
Social group C1 (clerical)	62 (60)
Social group C2 (skilled manual)	57 (56)
Social groups DE (semi-skilled and unskilled)	54 (53)
Age group: 18–24	37 (39)
Age group: 25–34	49 (46)
Age group: 35–44	61 (59)
Age group: 45–54	65 (65)
Age group: 55–64	71 (69)
Age group: over 65	75 (70)

Source: http://www.mori.com

between different social groups are on the whole not surprising. They may suggest that voting is a sign of social inclusion, of a belief that you belong to society and can alter how it works by exercising your democratic right. Hence the people at the bottom of the social system do not vote as much as the people at the top, and the young do not vote as consistently as the old. On the other hand, the very old often seem marginalized in modern society and yet they vote more regularly than anyone else. An explanation offered for this is that the old have been socialized into voting, coming from an age when turnout levels were higher. In addition, the old rely quite a lot on the state and therefore have a big stake in the outcome of elections. They also have more time to get to the polling stations than those who are younger and at work. In terms of whether turnout will improve or not in the future, we could argue in both directions from these figures. On the one hand, if the population is getting older, as is often said to be the case, as the young get older, more responsible and more conscious of their responsibilities, perhaps they will turn into voters. The contrary argument says that the young who have lost the habit of voting will gradually replace the conscientious elderly voters who acquired the habit in more politically active days, and as a result participation will decline even further.

Participation through membership of political parties

There is no question that membership of the major political parties has declined since the Second World War. Membership is now almost a tenth of what it was in the 1940s. It is true that Labour membership grew in the 1990s, but that increase has since tailed off and the increase did not reach very high levels. It is also true that the growth of the Liberals/Liberal Democrats has seen a revival in their membership base, which started in 1981 with the foundation of the Social Democratic Party. The nationalist parties in Wales, Scotland and also England (UKIP) have also developed a new membership. New parties spring up from time to time and must have some sort of membership: the Green Party, United Kingdom Independence Party and, more recently, Respect and Veritas. But this does not seriously alter the fact that there has been a dramatic change in the nature of the major political parties. The Labour Party was once seen as a 'Movement', as 'the People's Party', a mass mobilization of the working class, which struggled in conjunction with the trade union movement to defend the interests of the people. Such a description was always an exaggeration, but now it is just laughable as a description of what is a tightly controlled mechanism for winning national support for the leadership's views. Nowadays, neither of the two major political parties seems to want a mass membership. They distance themselves from their youth movements, they control their annual conferences to a ridiculous extent and they seek funding from the rich and famous, not from ordinary people. Political parties and participation are discussed again in chapter 7.

Participation: the evidence of recruitment

There seems to be no great shortage of politicians and, according to political scientist (himself a member of the House of Lords) Lord Norton, MPs are now of a high calibre. People are always willing to serve as members of the House of Lords. Politicians are increasingly people who look on politics as a career, rather than people who try to combine politics with another career or see politics as an act of public service which interrupts or concludes some other employment, as was the case in the past.

Questions have been raised about the **political recruitment** of women and racial minorities, and the Labour Party especially has tried to do something to improve the recruitment of women. Figures for the recruitment of different social groups into Parliament are given in chapter 10. The new devolved assemblies in Wales and Scotland have seen the recruitment of more women into politics.

Political recruitment: the way in which people are drawn into politics itself at an active level, generally by becoming politicians.

Tony Blair with some of the 101 newly elected female Labour MPs after the general election in May 1997

The modern politician is seldom drawn from the ranks of 'ordinary' people or the working classes; the decline in links between the Labour Party and trade unions has ensured this. There may be problems in recruiting able people for local government, and this is perhaps connected to the lack of a mass membership of political parties. Local councillors do tend to be, frankly, elderly. The need for a rejuvenation of local government is quite widely recognized.

Participation through pressure politics

It is sometimes argued that as party politics has declined, so pressure politics has taken its place. Membership of 'cause' pressure groups has grown in the last 40 years, and this growth does appear to coincide with the fall in party membership. On the other hand, interest groups have been in decline since the 1980s. The membership of trade unions has fallen considerably in recent years (although there has been a slight revival since 1997), and their role has also become less political, as they have marketed themselves as providers of insurance rather than defenders of collective rights. In 1992, 35.8 per cent of employees were in trade unions; by 2005 the figure was 29 per cent. This still equates to 6.39 million people, though. Pressure politics and direct action, and the question of whether pressure groups are in decline or rising in importance, are dealt with more fully in chapter 6.

Participation through protest and demonstrations

In 2003 there were major demonstrations against the invasion of Iraq, led by the pressure group Stop the War Coalition. In the years after 1997 the Countryside Alliance has also organized well-attended rallies in London. In 2000, fuel protesters paralysed the country for a few days by blockading the petrol distribution depots. There have also been spectacular individual demonstrations, such as that of Fathers4Justice, which involved the Prime Minister being pelted with condoms filled with dyed flour in the House of Commons in 2004. These events show that direct political action still has a value, especially when media focus is attracted by photogenic displays. This is clearly a form of rather desperate participation. It seems to support one of the arguments which people use to explain a decline in regular participation in politics (for example, by turning out to vote), since it calls for the alienation of people from the normal channels of representation. Furthermore, direct action is a volatile thing, dependent on swings in fashion and mood. When in September 2005 petrol and diesel prices rose dramatically and there were calls for another mass fuel protest, as in 2000, there was very little response and no great direct action protests resulted.

New forms of participation

'New' Labour has tried to claim that citizens are increasingly getting involved in political activity in new ways, and that this should encourage those depressed by the thought of declining turnout in elections. In February 2007, 60 people, selected as a cross-section of the population by a professional polling organization, were invited to Downing Street to debate policy. In the last 15 years, such policy forums have played an increasingly prominent role in the structures of political parties, and indeed in the world of market research and advertising. The 2005 Labour election manifesto spoke of 'a flowering of innovative forms of public engagement' and cited as evidence the Citizens' Councils used by the National Institute for Clinical Excellence to advise on ethical dilemmas. In reply, it might be argued that these innovations are actually another symptom of declining participation: top-down initiatives to compensate for the wilting of the grassroots. But in February 2007, 1.8 million people signed the on-line petition organized by the Downing Street website against road-charging; so maybe we should avoid cynicism about new forms of participation. In September 2007, Gordon Brown announced that one aspect of the 'new politics' he wished to pursue involved wider consultation of the electorate through the use of citizens' juries – a new version of policy forums, or groups of people selected at random who would be consulted by the government on policy developments in specific areas like health care, education, etc.

 Question: What is 'political apathy'?

2.7 Reasons for the decline in electoral turnout

It is worth emphasizing initially that the evidence for whether there is a real long-term decline or whether we should be explaining a 'blip' in 2001 and 2005 is unclear. But most authorities tend towards the former view, and in any case both issues need explaining.

One reason for thinking there is a long-term decline in participation in elections in Britain is that there has been a decline in other similar democracies in Europe and around the world. This has been most remarked upon in the USA, although the 2004 presidential election there saw an increase in turnout. But before that there had been a pronounced decline in participation rates to levels generally lower than in Britain, and the turnout in the 2006 US midterm elections saw no continuation of the increase observed two years earlier. Hence the explanations used in other countries for a fall in turnout may also explain the British decline. Some of these are discussed below.

Voting is not a legal obligation

Where voting is enforced by law, turnout tends to rise sharply, with a fine as the penalty. Countries like Belgium and Australia achieve high rates of turnout as a result, but Britain has not been in favour of adopting this policy. However, the UK is not completely opposed to enforcing civic duties by making it a criminal offence not to do them. For example, you are fined if you deliberately omit to fill in a Census form, and in a few years time we will probably have compulsory ID cards.

Voting is a difficult process

Many people claim to be too busy to vote, and the process of voting is not always easy. Elections are normally limited to one day, which in Britain is, by tradition, a Thursday, a part of the working week. In some European countries, voting is on a Sunday, which might improve turnout, since people are largely not at work then. Puritan opposition to Sabbath-breaking seems to have been the reason for using Thursdays in Britain. In July 2007, Gordon Brown announced that the government was going to consider changing voting day from Thursday to Saturday or Sunday, in an effort to increase participation. To vote, the British go to a polling station, which is opened up in a school, public library, church hall or similar place. It is often the case that this polling station may be difficult to find and too far to walk to. One service performed in the past by party workers in rural areas was to give voters a lift to the polling station. It was sometimes alleged that this boosted the Conservative vote in these areas, since the Conservative volunteers had better cars. If you are on holiday or too ill to vote, you can obtain a postal vote or get someone to vote officially on your behalf (a proxy vote). The Labour government elected in 1997 has been keen to improve turnout and has been a little embarrassed by its continued decline while they have been in power. It has therefore tried to develop ways in which voting might be made easier.

In 2000, by the Representation of the People Act, the government allowed new experiments in voting methods to be used in an attempt to improve turnout in local elections. The first experiments began in 2001 in some areas in local elections, and have continued ever since: polling stations have been set up in places where people were more likely to find them (e.g. supermarket car parks); in some cases voting has been spread over a number of days; and even voting by phone and by electronic means have been used. The most popular new method seems to have been the extension of postal voting. In the 2001 general election, anyone wanting a postal vote could apply for one without needing any medical or similar reason (as had been the case in the past). There have also been local experiments with all-postal ballots, where everyone in an area votes by returning a form through the post. The experiments made in 2003 in local elections and in other votes were judged a success. The turnout nationally in local elections in 2003 was 36 per cent, but in areas where universal postal voting was introduced it rose to 50 per cent (and in Hertfordshire it rose as high as 61 per cent). E-voting made little difference, however, and in Basingstoke where it was trialled as an alternative alongside traditional methods, turnout actually fell. So the all-postal experiment was extended to the June 2004 European Parliament elections in four UK regions. It did seem to be the simplest way in which turnout could be increased. The results were not brilliant in June 2004, with accusations of corruption and problems with delivering the ballot papers. The thing about the old method of voting was that it was at least reasonably secure and safe from corrupt practices.

As a result of these accusations of fraud, an enquiry by the Electoral Commission was set up, and the government called off two of the three regional referendums it had planned to hold in November 2004 to decide on the question of whether to create regional assemblies.

The Electoral Commission reported on new voting systems in August 2004 and concluded that all-postal ballots had in 2004 increased turnout by 5 per cent (previous experiments had increased it by 15 per cent), but that the problems associated with this method outweighed the advantages. It recommended that after November there should be no further all-postal ballots, but that a system based on choice should be developed, by which voters could choose from a variety of methods, including easy access to the postal vote if they wanted it, but not the use of a compulsory postal vote. In the 2005 general election, more than 6.5 million postal votes were applied for – a huge increase on 2001. There were concerns raised over the use of postal votes again in 2005, and the police investigated a number of allegations of fraud. After the election, the Electoral Commission called for legislation to tighten up on the use of postal votes and the government announced that it was considering this suggestion. It may be that 2005 represents the high-watermark of attempts to increase turnout by making it easier to vote.

On the whole, the idea that people are too busy to vote does not provide anything like a complete explanation. But it does seem that there will be greater choice in voting methods allowed in the future to voters, most of whom will probably continue to choose to vote in the old-fashioned way, using a polling station.

Political apathy

This point is one that could be made about decline in all forms of participation. People do not take part in politics because they do not care about politics. They are ignorant and bored by the subject and hence do not wish to participate. It may be that politics is no longer of as much relevance to people's lives as it was in the past, when the state owned more of the economy

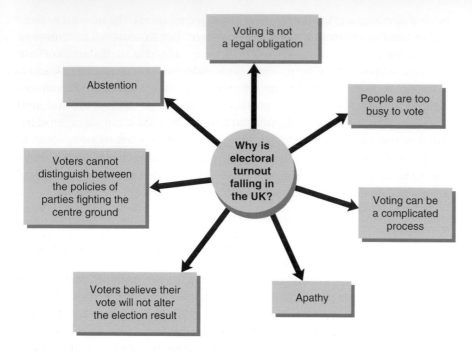

Figure 2.4   Why is electoral turnout falling in the UK?

and employed more of the population. The government has been trying to counter this problem by introducing the teaching of citizenship into the curriculum in state schools. This will certainly help combat ignorance about the political process and may help to off-set the very low turnout levels among young voters when school-age children grow up to be of voting age. The introduction of citizenship lessons for newly arrived immigrants has also been suggested as a similar reform to improve turnout. Another suggestion that has been made, and is currently being seriously considered by Brown's government, is that young people should get the vote at 16 so they may acquire the voting habit young.

Alienation or contentment?

If people are apathetic and do not vote, is it because they are happy and contented and do not see the point of political involvement? There may seem to be some point in this positive, and rather unusual, interpretation of apathy. Political activity and interest historically does seem to rise at times of crisis and times of disagreement among citizens. The people of Northern Ireland have in the past been keen participants at election times, but largely because they are discontented. On the other hand, the suggestion is often made that not voting is actually a positive rejection of the whole democratic political system, an expression of alienation. In support of this view, we could say that the lower down the social scale you are, the less likely it is that you will vote.

In addition, people are put off politics by the reputation some politicians in the 1990s gained for 'sleaze'. In 2005 there was a good deal of comment along the lines that 'all politicians are liars', and this might also be a continuing symptom of a popular disengagement from the political process. If it is not a sort of anarchist alienation, not voting may be a symptom of the declining 'civic culture' that some people, notably the American sociologist Robert Putnam, have seen as an aspect of the modern world. People have retreated into their own private sphere and are reluctant to play any voluntary part in communal activities. They will not participate socially, let alone politically. Putnam's potent symbol of this disengagement from society was the image of Americans going ten-pin bowling alone, rather than as part of a team, as used to be the case in the 1950s.

People will not vote if the result is a foregone conclusion

This simple, short-term argument probably explains a great deal about declining turnout, especially in 2001, and probably also in 2005. Everyone knew the result of the election of 2001 before it was even held. Even the Conservatives had more or less given up hope of winning before the contest started. In such circumstances, the citizen makes the rational choice not to bother to vote. This is shown by the fact that turnout in 2001 was lower in safe seats than in marginals (there was an average 3 per cent difference). Although the result in 2005 was closer, it was still largely expected to be a Labour victory and this helps explain the low turnout then. Looking back at previous elections, it does seem to be the case that a close election result enhances turnout: 1992, 1974 (February), 1950 and 1951 being good examples. People will vote if their vote is likely to make a difference.

Parties fighting on the centre ground

People will vote if their vote will make a difference in another sense. In 1997, 2001 and 2005, the two major political parties were both offering very similar policies, even on issues like Europe and immigration, where they seemed to present very different images. This closeness of the two major parties is likely to depress turnout. It will also make the campaigns rather boring and hence reduces media coverage, both of which have been put forward as reasons for the low turnout in 2001 and 2005.

Abstention: deliberately not voting, as a positive act, having carefully considered the alternatives (as opposed to not voting through apathy). A genuine act of abstention is a piece of political participation.

A deliberate act of abstention

Far from being the action of feckless ignoramuses, not voting may be a rational political action: an act of **abstention**. In countries like Australia, where voting is compulsory, there is a space on the ballot paper for people to

attract protest votes for smaller parties. It is not surprising, therefore, that voters do not turn out and vote in them.

Too many elections?

It is clear that voters do not like being asked to vote too often, and that this can depress turnout. In both 1910 and 1974, there were two elections in one year, and in both cases turnout fell in the second one. This reluctance on the part of voters to vote too often may also explain the low turnout in 'second-order' elections. It may affect the turnout in the new elections and referendums introduced since 1997. In fact, however, by international standards, British voters are not faced with a huge number of elections.

Does a decline in turnout matter?

There is controversy over whether a decline in voter participation actually matters. Here are some arguments that could be put on either side of the question.

Yes, turnout is important

It does matter, because democracy depends on participation. In fact, voting is a fairly low level of political participation. If people do not vote, they are not really represented by the elected politicians, and so their voice is not heard. They may therefore feel shut out of the political process and this can, in the long term, have harmful effects on democracy. Democracy

---

Box 2.3 Under-registration

British turnout figures are arrived at by dividing the number of people who vote (voters) by the number of people who are registered to vote (electors). Registration in Britain is a publicly administered and very thorough process. But it does depend on people responding to postal invitations to register, and some people are reluctant to be included on the register because they are suspicious of authority and resistant to bureaucracy. There are indications that quite a large proportion of the adult population is not registered to vote. This may simply be because they slip through the net, or because they tend to move about a lot. It may also be that some people deliberately do not wish to be recorded on a public document. A report by the Electoral Commission in September 2005 suggested that 3.7 million people were left off the electoral roll – that is, one in twelve of the adult population (8.5 per cent). In London, this figure might be as high as 18 per cent according to the Electoral Commission. If this is true, it means that we should actually subtract this 8.5 per cent from the turnout figures, because if you are not on the electoral register you cannot vote. Turnout levels may therefore be a lot worse than the figures normally given suggest.

is only about a century old in the modern world. In the 1920s and 1930s it was challenged by ideologies of the Right and Left which argued that it was a sham, and that people were not really involved in a democracy, but were just given the illusion that they were. If people do not vote in elections, this in a sense gives support to such a view and undermines the whole democratic process. On a low turnout, extremists are more likely to be elected. So, low levels of participation do matter. Representative democracy is only a sort of second best to direct democracy, where the people genuinely rule themselves, and one way of bridging the gap between direct and representative democracy is to encourage participatory democracy. Voting is so important that in some countries it is not just a civic duty, but also a legal requirement. Even if it is not considered right to make voting compulsory, it should certainly be considered an obligation of citizenship, the very least that a responsible citizen should perform. The sharp decline in turnout in the UK since 1992 has led some commentators to write about a 'legitimacy crisis'. In a democracy, the political system acquires legitimacy (a moral authority to govern) through elections, but if fewer people are voting than those who do not vote, it looks as though the system is losing this claim to legitimacy. The question of authority and legitimacy is discussed in chapter 1.

No, concerns about falling participation are exaggerated

On the other hand, it could be argued that there is a problem only if we can demonstrate that there really is a long-term decline in turnout. If people are not voting because they are making rational political decisions not to vote on certain occasions or in certain elections, then it is difficult not to see the decision not to vote as a sort of act of democracy in itself, as a reasonable political act. The situation in the last few years has been rather exceptional in British politics, since the two major parties have been so similar in policies but so different in terms of electoral support. In addition, the introduction of new elections and referendums since 1997 has hardly helped increase electoral turnout. Perhaps the new voting methods being tested at the moment will help people to vote in more convenient ways. But it would be wrong to sacrifice the purity and trustworthiness of the result for the sake of pushing up voting statistics. It would also be paradoxical in the extreme to make voting compulsory: in the words of the eighteenth-century French political philosopher, Jean-Jacques Rousseau, 'to force men to be free'.

Question: Is voting predominantly a middle-class activity?

SUMMING UP

There are two versions of democracy: representative and direct. Direct democracy is the purer form, but in the modern world the only practical type is representative. But we can inject a little direct democracy into our politics by using referendums, which have been used intermittently in this country since 1973, especially under Labour governments. Democracy can only survive if people participate in politics, but in recent years concerns have grown over declining rates of involvement. Most serious of all, fewer people are turning out to vote in elections. There are a number of reasons for this, which have been proposed in this chapter. It may only be a temporary phenomenon, and a really hard-fought and close election might see turnout rates recover to a more healthy level.

Further reading

A. Arblaster, *Democracy* (Open University Press, 1988): high-level analysis of the various theories of democracy.

D. Butler and D. Kavanagh, *The British General Election of 2001* (Palgrave, 2002): this and the next book give a detailed breakdown of the election results, their causes and consequences.

D. Butler and D. Kavanagh, *The British General Election of 2005* (Palgrave, 2006).

G. Evans, 'Political culture and voting participation', in P. Dunleavy, A. Gamble, R. Heffernan and G. Peele, *Developments in British Politics 7* (Macmillan, 2003): valuable detailed study of recent trends in turnout.

D. Held, *Models of Democracy* (Polity, 1996): study of how the concept of democracy has developed since it first appeared in Ancient Greece.

Websites

www.edemocracy.gov.uk (government site to encourage participation)

http://news.bbc.co.uk (BBC site, for election results)

http://www.mori.com (MORI, the opinion pollsters)

http://www.powerinquiry.org (2006 think-tank report on the state of democracy in the UK)

http://www.electoralcommission.org (Electoral Commission: body established to supervise elections in UK)

Elections and Electoral Reform

Making connections

The real difficulty with this topic seems at first to involve getting a clear idea in your mind about how each electoral system works. In fact, some of the systems are actually quite mathematically challenging, but the level of technical detail which it is necessary for a student of politics to know is rather limited. Through the course of this chapter there are summaries of the chief components of each of the major electoral systems. Although you ought to be able to explain how, broadly speaking, each system works, it is more important to understand the reasons behind using the systems, and the arguments in favour of each one. The analysis of electoral reform will probably become clearer if you have a knowledge of devolution, a topic dealt with later on in chapter 16. Before thinking about electoral systems in detail, you should be quite sure that you grasp the purpose of a British general election, and how the British parliamentary system of government works.

3

Elections and Electoral Reform

KEY TOPICS

- The British first-past-the-post electoral system
- An evaluation of the first-past-the-post system
- Proportional representation, majoritarian and hybrid systems
- An evaluation of proportional representation
- Electoral reform in Britain since 1997

SETTING THE SCENE

In the previous chapter we discussed representative democracy and participation, and these themes are now explored in greater depth. The most significant way in which people participate in politics is through voting for their representatives in elections. Over the years, the way in which we vote in Britain has been subject to scrutiny and debate and there have been calls for a major reform of the electoral system. The system used in the UK until recently for all elections was the first-past-the-post (FPTP) system, but in other countries a variety of other systems have been used, based on proportional representation (PR). As a result of the criticisms of FPTP, there have been changes made to methods of voting in recent years, especially when new opportunities to hold elections have arisen, in Scotland, Wales, Northern Ireland and London, and also in connection with the elections for the European Parliament.

First-past-the-post (FPTP): an electoral system that involves two or more candidates standing for election, the electors being given one vote each, and the candidate who wins most votes being declared the winner. In recent years it has also been called the single-member plurality system (SMPS) and is sometimes confusingly called a majoritarian system, or majoritarian representation (this is explained later on in this chapter).

3.1 The British first-past-the-post electoral system

Almost all elections carried out in Britain before 1997 followed the **first-past-the-post** (FPTP) system. It is still the way we conduct elections for Parliament (what are also called general elections or Westminster elections, since Parliament meets in Westminster), and also how local government elections in England are run. The most important aspects of the system are, first, that voters only have one vote and cannot rank the candidates in order of preference as they can under some other systems: it is not a 'preferential system'. Second, the constituencies are on the whole single-member constituencies – i.e., each constituency is represented by one Member of Parliament (MP). This is certainly true in parliamentary elections, but in local elections, some 'wards' (or local government constituencies) have three members, which is why the 'single member plurality' description is actually not a very good one. Third, the winner does not have to achieve an absolute majority of the votes (more than 50 per cent, or more than all the other candidates put together), which is the case under some alternative systems. All that is required is a

---

Box 3.1 The mechanics of general elections: who can stand and who can vote?

Voters

You have to be on the electoral register to vote. This is drawn up annually by the local Electoral Registration Officers, who write to every household and have the power to prosecute people who refuse to give information needed to draw up the register, or who give false information. There still does seem to be some under-registration (discussed in chapter 2). In order to register and vote in a general election, you must be 18 and a citizen of the UK or of the Republic of Ireland (other EU nationals resident in the UK can vote in local elections and European Parliament elections). Members of the House of Lords, those detained under the Mental Health Act and convicted prisoners are all refused the right to vote. There has been some discussion recently about prisoners' rights, and in many countries they are given the vote. There has also been discussion about extending the vote to 16–18-year-olds.

Candidates

Any UK national over the age of 21 can be a candidate, either as an Independent, or as the official candidate of a party. There is an anomaly in the fact that someone can vote at the age of 18 but not stand for election until the age of 21. Since 2007, people have been able to stand as a candidate in local elections from the age of 18. Since 2000, parties have had to be registered nationally, and must submit a list of their official candidates in each constituency (this is to prevent people from claiming to be, for example, a Conservative candidate when they do not have the official backing of the party). Each candidate, or their party, has to put down a deposit of £500 to stand in the election, to prevent frivolous candidates; this sum is returnable if a candidate gets over 5 per cent of the vote. This law was made by the 1985 Representation of the People Act, which reduced the threshold from 12.5 per cent set in 1918, following a spate of frivolous candidacies. Legislation has been drafted recently to reduce this threshold to 2 per cent, in order to save the money of small parties. In 2005, 1,386 candidates (39 per cent of the total) lost their deposits. The selection of candidates by a political party is a very contentious matter, involving the central party organization and that in each constituency – this is discussed in chapter 7 on political parties.

'plurality' (sometimes confusingly called a simple majority) – that is, one more vote than the runner-up. It is not infrequent for an MP to be elected on less than 40 per cent of the vote, and occasionally on less than 30 per cent.

Constituencies

For general elections in the UK, the country was divided in 2005 into 646 constituencies with, in theory, roughly equal numbers of electors in each one. Generally, there are between 60,000 and 70,000 electors in each constituency. There is quite a lot of variety in terms of numbers of electors per constituency, but this is largely because there is a desire not to allow constituencies to become too large in terms of area, and also to respect traditional boundaries. The size of constituencies is regulated by independent bodies, the Boundary Commissions, which change the electoral map of the country from time to time in light of movements of population revealed by the Census every ten years. There is a great deal of negotiation between the Commission and the political parties before a final decision is made. The Parliament elected in 2005 has 13 fewer constituencies than that elected in 2001, because, as a result of setting up the Scottish Parliament in Edinburgh, the number of Scottish constituencies in Westminster has been reduced (previously, Scotland had been over-represented in Westminster). The latest major change in boundaries came into effect after 2007, when the results of the Census of 2001 were factored into the equation. This redrawing of boundaries is expected to hit Labour hardest since Labour constituencies are often found in places of declining population like inner city areas.

What is the purpose of general elections?

It is crucial to be absolutely clear about what a general election is aiming to do before we can evaluate the different systems that are used or might be used. General elections have at least five functions, which are listed below; the first two are the most important.

1 To elect a constituency's MP, its representative in Britain's legislative assembly. This person is there to speak on behalf of the local community and also to act as a link between individuals in the constituency and the world of politics at the centre, in Westminster.
2 Probably more important is to choose the government of the country. In the UK, the Parliament or legislative body is elected at the same time and by the same process as the executive or government. This is known as a parliamentary system of government. When the result of the election in all the constituencies in the country is known, the government of the country is formed by the political party which has more MPs in the House

of Commons than any other party. Since 1945 this has always been a single party, although it is quite possible for the winning party to form a coalition government with one or several other parties. This would be likely to happen if the winning party did not have a working majority (that is, more than all the other parties put together) of the MPs behind it. Not achieving an absolute majority has only happened once since 1945, when the Labour government of James Callaghan was in a minority in the Commons from 1977 to 1979. Callaghan did not form a coalition, but ruled with a 'minority government'. But apart from that exception, all governments since 1945 have ruled with an absolute majority in the Commons.

3 Elections are an opportunity for the electorate to remove an unpopular government. They hold the previous government to account and make a judgement on how well it has performed, voting against it if they disapprove. Of course, they could also endorse a government which they think has ruled well, and give it a mandate (or command/permission) to rule for a further term.

4 Elections in a representative democracy are also a great political occasion, well covered in the media, and the subject of much public interest and

Tony Blair being greeted by jubilant Labour Party supporters as he arrives at Downing Street after his election victory in 1997. New Labour won a total of 419 seats which represented 63.6 per cent of total seats and 43.2 per cent of the popular vote

debate. They are the most significant chance for people to participate in politics.

5 Elections allow small parties to put their views across. They may never get an MP and it would be absurd to imagine that they could form a government. But an election allows these small parties to put pressure on the larger parties and also to get some attention from the media and hence influence the public. The Green Party, the UK Independence Party, the Referendum Party and Respect (an anti-war party) are recent examples of minor parties which have used elections to apply democratic pressure.

Box 3.2 By-elections

Under our FPTP system it is relatively easy to hold a by-election, to elect a new MP (or local councillor) when one dies or resigns. A by-election can be held at any time in between general elections. It is a little difficult under some PR systems to replace representatives as efficiently or democratically. Since FPTP is supposed to give a strong constituency link between people and representative, it is a significant aspect of the system that by-elections can easily be held. But voters tend to behave rather differently at by-elections than at general elections. First, there is a very marked tendency for voters not to turn out so readily at by-elections (this is discussed in chapter 2), which suggests that they do not care much about a constituency link. Second, voters sometimes use the by-election to vote in a negative way, attacking the party in government for any national misfortunes that may have befallen it. The recipients of these protest votes have often been the Liberal Democrats or occasionally the nationalist parties in Scotland and Wales. Often, though, these parties lose the seat they have won in a by-election when the next general election comes round. Thus, in 2003, the Liberal Democrats won Brent East (with a large Muslim population) from Labour in a by-election and even held it at the next general election, and in 2004 they also took Leicester South, a similar sort of constituency in a by-election, but then lost it at the next election. By-elections

become far more important to political parties than to the constituents. A great deal of effort is made by the party in power to avoid humiliation in a by-election, and by the opposition parties to ensure that some punishment is handed out to the government. The focus on the by-election by the national media can become quite intense, and parties get very nervous when they select their candidates, leading occasionally to struggles between the central party organization and the constituency leadership. Some by-elections are credited with having a significant impact on the national fortunes of a political party, acting as a tipping-point, a time when public opinion changed. But in reality they are symptoms rather than causes of changing opinion. Since 2005, the only really exciting by-election has been in Dunfermline and West Fife, where the Liberal Democrats snatched away a Labour seat in an area supposedly very loyal to Gordon Brown. The 2007 by-elections that followed very shortly after Brown's promotion to Prime Minister were hailed as a sign that the Conservatives had failed because of a 'Brown bounce', but what they mainly showed was a failure by the Liberal Democrats to perform their historic role of winning by-elections mid-term, as a result of Brown's honeymoon period. In other respects they were typical, in terms of a fall in turnout and a fall in support for the previous winning party (see table 3.1).

Table 3.1 Recent by-elections

Constituency	Date	Reason by-election	Result	Turnout	Share of vote of winner	Previous general election result	Turnout at previous general election	Share of vote of same party at previous election
Cheadle	14/7/05	Death	LibDem	55.2%	52.2%	LibDem	69.6%	48.9%
Livingston	29/9/05	Death	Lab	38.6%	51.1%	Lab	58.1%	51.1%
Dunfermline & West Fife	9/2/06	Death	LibDem	48.7%	35.8%	Lab	59.9%	20.4%
Blaenau Gwent	29/6/06	Death	Ind	51.7%	46.2%	Ind	66.1%	58.2%
Bromley & Chislehurst	29/6/06	Death	Con	40.5%	51.1%	Con	64.8%	51.1%
Sedgefield	19/7/07	Resignation of Blair	Lab	41.6%	44.8%	Lab	61.8%	58.9%
Ealing, Southall	19/7/07	Death	Lab	42.9%	41.5%	Lab	42.9%	56.4%

Source: http://www.parliament.uk

Question: Describe the first-past-the-post electoral system.

3.2 An evaluation of the first-past-the-post system

Arguments in favour of FPTP

FPTP is simple and effective

The ballot paper is not intimidatingly long, and there is only one choice to be made. Giving people two or more votes (as under other systems) complicates the matter. When choosing between candidates, the idea of being able to have preference votes seems essentially a bogus one. The important preference, it could be argued, is simply to be able to vote once in favour of the person you want. Elections are like a competition between the candidates. The losers know when they put themselves up for election that they might lose, and it is stupid to try to arrange elections in such a way as to allow the losers to act as representatives on the same basis as the winners (as some alternatives to FPTP seem to do). The same is true of voters. If their candidate loses, they know they have an opportunity next time to win him or her more support, but for the moment they have to accept the democratic decision and accommodate themselves to the fact that the candidate they did not vote for has won. It is further argued that because FPTP is simple, people will be happy to use it, and that the adoption of a new system would reduce turnout. The result under FPTP is usually known within a few hours of the polling booths closing. It is easy to count the votes, and this tends to develop public confidence in the whole system. Under PR systems, it can take days for the result to be declared.

Strong links between the MP and the constituency

FPTP results in effective representation by establishing strong links between the MP and the constituency. One of the key concepts which helps us to evaluate electoral systems is representation. The problem is that representation means many different things to different people. But according to one valuable view of representation, people need to have close links with their representatives. The representative needs to understand what the people want, and needs to be able to put their views across. Interests vary from one part of the country to another; people have different jobs and different outlooks. So, the single-member constituency is a good representative mechanism. The local MP understands his or her constituency and can look after the interests of the people locally. In turn, the local people feel that the MP is someone that they can look to if they are in difficulties. Over the last 30 years or so, MPs have developed a role as advisers and consultants to their constituents on a whole range of issues, often rather outside what in purely constitutional terms would be seen as their true area of concern. They hold 'surgeries' and write letters on behalf of constituents who have a problem with some aspect of the system of government. This role demonstrates that MPs are fulfilling an important representative function. It is argued that only small constituencies can effectively deliver this sort of representation, and these are not possible except under the FPTP system.

Manifesto, mandate and legitimacy

The FPTP system also represents the opinions of people effectively, it is argued, because it makes government representative. When a general election is called, the political parties publish their manifestos, in which they set out their policies and the reasons why we should vote for them. Although most people do not have the time to read all the manifestos, what is contained in them filters down to the voters during the course of the election campaign, which will be widely covered in the media. The voters then vote for the party they prefer, and, once elected, the victorious party is mandated (or commanded/permitted) to do what it does by the electors. The government is given legitimacy by the FPTP electoral system: a democratic endorsement of its right to rule the country until the next election. This is the doctrine (or theory) of the **electoral mandate**. Alternative electoral systems, it is argued, do not produce this direct representation of the views of the electors, because voters under these systems do not know what the impact of their vote will be. Under proportional systems (to be discussed below) we could end up with a coalition government, where the views of the parties are mixed together, and no one can really argue that they have a mandate to do anything.

> **Electoral mandate**: the authority to implement a programme or policy given to a government as a result of winning an election.

Governments can be held to account and dismissed easily

There are doubts about the doctrine of the mandate in terms of whether the government actually does do what it is mandated to do, whether it keeps to its manifesto promises. But the mandate argument can accommodate this, because it says that voters then have the power to vote out a government which breaks its promises. More broadly, a general election under FPTP can be a national judgement on the record of a government, a way of holding that government to account, or holding it responsible for what it has done. This is more difficult to achieve under proportional systems. The FPTP system is very good at reflecting changes in national opinion and translating them into changes of government – for example, the decisive rejection of the Conservatives in 1997 and election of a Labour government. FPTP leads to responsible government, in the sense that the government can easily be held responsible at an election to the people for its work.

Strong, stable, majority government

The most important function of our general elections is to produce a government for the country. The FPTP system has the effect of producing single-party governments which have good majorities in Parliament and which can therefore get the work of government done. They can legislate, putting into law their manifesto, and they can deal effectively with crises at home and abroad. In alternative systems, there would be less government stability, frequent changes of government and also weak government more generally because coalitions would be elected, which, it is argued, are inherently weak. If there were not coalition governments, there might be 'minority governments' elected more frequently under alternative voting systems, ones which cannot command a clear majority in the House of Commons and which have to rely on the neutrality of opposition parties. Again, there is justice in this argument. Since 1979, our governments have all been elected with a good majority (although John Major's majority was not very large after 1992), and we have had single-party government since 1945. Whether strong government is always a good thing could be debated, especially in the light of Margaret Thatcher's record and also, some would say, that of Tony Blair. There are also legitimate doubts to be raised over whether the strength of British governments is due entirely to the FPTP system or whether it is mainly due to the parliamentary system of government, which guarantees a majority in

Parliament. It shouldn't be forgotten that, even under FPTP, there were two brief periods of minority government in Britain (1974, 1977–9).

Arguments against FPTP

MPs are often elected without an absolute majority of votes

FPTP leaves many people essentially unrepresented and it is therefore unfair. It results in 'wasted votes', because the votes of those who voted for losers do not count. The main reason for this is the rise of 'minor' parties in the British system. FPTP would not produce this result if we still had a two-party system in the UK, but this is no longer the situation. The problem can be illustrated by the result in the Scottish constituency of Argyle and Bute in 2001, the worst case of this effect in recent years (see figure 3.1). The result shows that in Argyle and Bute in 2001, more than 70 per cent of the voters voted against the victorious candidate; these voters, according to critics of FPTP, were therefore unrepresented.

Parliament is not proportionally representative of the views of the population as a whole

This argument takes the last one a step further. It looks beyond each individual constituency and focuses on the composition of the assembly that is elected – that is, on Parliament. Parliament simply does not reflect the opinion of the people accurately. Under the FPTP system, many votes are wasted, and votes do not carry equal value. Looking at the result in 2005, if you are a Labour voter your vote seems to be worth more than a Conservative vote, and far more than a Liberal Democrat vote (see table 3.2). So, the Conservatives were deprived of nearly 2 per cent of the share of the seats they

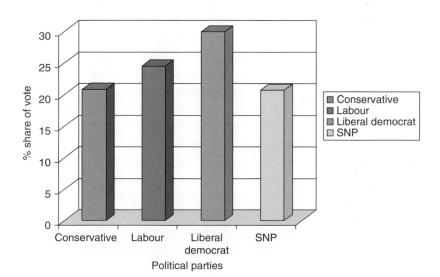

Figure 3.1   General election, 2001: Argyle and Bute constituency result expressed as % share of the vote

Table 3.2 General election, 2005: votes cast and seats won as percentages of total

Party	% of votes in country as a whole	Seats in Parliament[a]	Seats as % of total in Parliament
Labour	35.2	356	55.1
Conservative	32.3	197	30.5
Lib Dem	22.0	62	9.5

[a] 645 of the 646 seats were contested on election day

Source: Based on results given on the Electoral Commission website: www.electoralcommission.org.uk

deserved, Liberal Democrats of over 11 per cent, while the Labour Party got nearly 20 per cent more than its share. The Liberal Democrats always suffer badly under FPTP. It is arguably even worse for minor parties like the Green Party. In 2005, the Greens won 1 per cent of the vote, which should have won them six or seven seats under a proportional system, but under FPTP they got no MPs. In the same election, the UK Independence party gained more than 600,000 votes – 2.3 per cent of the vote – worth about 15 MPs under proportional representation, but under FPTP they got nothing.

A government can be formed by the party which does not win a plurality of the national vote

It is a feature of our electoral system that it can produce the strange result that the party with most votes in the country does not receive the most seats in Parliament (see table 3.3). This is obviously unfair when we consider the composition of the legislative assembly, but it is catastrophic for FPTP when we consider the fact that the nature of a government (whether Labour or Conservative) depends not on the number of votes cast, but on the number of seats won. This is a feature of FPTP, combined with the way in which in the UK the government is indirectly elected as a result of a general election.

The reason this evidence is so damaging to FPTP is that this system is often justified on simple, common-sense grounds that it is a way of giving a mandate to rule to the most popular political party in the country; but in 1951 and 1974 the complete reverse of this happened. We might also mention here that in the 2005 general election, in England alone (i.e., not counting Scotland, Wales or Northern Ireland), Labour gained 63,000 fewer votes than the Conservatives, even though – in England alone – it won 93 more seats in Parliament (largely because its voters were more concentrated in certain regions and hence constituencies).

Table 3.3 Governments elected as the smaller of the two main parties since 1945

Date	Votes of party forming government	% of votes of party forming government	Seats won by party forming government	Votes of 'losing' party	% of votes of 'losing' party	Seats won by 'losing' party
1951	13,717,538 (Con)	48 (Con)	321 (Con)	13,948,605 (Lab)	48.8 (Lab)	295 (Lab)
Feb 1974	11,646,391 (Lab)	37.1 (Lab)	301 (Lab)	11,872,180 (Con)	37.8 (Con)	297 (Con)

Source: http://www.electoral-reform.org.uk

Box 3.3 The exaggerated Labour majority in 2005

In 2005, Labour won a comfortable rather than an overwhelming majority of 66, but this still grossly exaggerated Labour's victory, since the party was only 3 per cent ahead of its great rivals, the Conservatives, who had to put up with winning 159 fewer seats. Labour won this majority on a mere 35.2 per cent of the popular vote. Political scientist Professor John Curtice comments: 'Never before in British electoral history has so much power been secured with so few votes.'

Governments are elected which are unrepresentative of the range of opinion in the country

FPTP tends to result in single-party government, and not coalition government. These single-party governments represent only a narrow range of opinion. Typically since 1974, a government is formed by a party which has about 42 per cent of the popular vote, but in 2005 it was only 35 per cent (see box 3.3). No government since before 1945 has been elected on an absolute majority (more than half of the total) of the popular vote. Under a different electoral system, coalition government would be more likely to result, which would mean that a wider range of views would be represented in government.

The performance of the winning party is exaggerated, leading to large majorities in Parliament

Between 1997 and 2005, Britain was ruled by a Labour government with two huge majorities, won in two general elections. In 1997, their majority (the amount by which the number of their MPs exceeded the total of all the other MPs) was 171, and in 2001 it was 165. These huge majorities did not reflect some great shift in opinion in favour of Labour (although arguably there had been quite a shift in opinion against the Conservatives) but were a result of the FPTP system. This feature of FPTP has been called the 'cube rule': 'If votes are in the ratio a:b then the electoral system will convert this ratio into the ratio $a^3:b^3$ in terms of seats', as political scientist David Denver puts it. While this tendency to exaggerate majorities has seldom been as great as the cube rule suggests, in 1997 and 2001, with Labour's large lead over the Conservatives, the effect was close to what the cube rule said it should be. Large majorities can, therefore, be a feature of FPTP. Large majorities are open to criticism in our system. They demoralize oppositions, they make MPs seem redundant, they prevent governments from acting responsively and they bring the whole political process into disrepute if ministers seem arrogant and if Parliament seems irrelevant.

The danger of extreme and confrontational governments being elected

The earliest opponents of FPTP argued that it was necessary to have an electoral system which blunted the tendency towards electing extreme governments. John Stuart Mill, writing in 1861 in his book *Representative Government*, supported proportional representation because he feared the 'tyranny of the majority', the election of an extreme government supported by the majority, which then brought in laws harmful to the interests of minorities. Modern opponents of the FPTP system tend to argue in the same way. They show that it is the centre party (the Liberal Democrats) which is most disadvantaged by the FPTP system, and that if the Liberal Democrats had more input in government (by joining coalitions, for example) this would tend to have an impact in dulling the extremism of governments dominated either by the Left (Labour) or Right (Conservatives). Would governments elected under PR have brought in the economic 'reforms' of the Thatcher era? Would a PR coalition have backed the war with Iraq?

Box 3.4 Confusing terminology: majoritarian

There are two uses of the word 'majority' in politics. First, simple majority, which means the same as plurality – in other words, first-past-the-post. A simple majority is when a candidate wins at least one more vote than the number of votes won by the runner-up. In other words, FPTP or SMP systems can also be called majoritarian, or forms of majoritarian representation. I have avoided doing so in this book, since it is a bit confusing. But the examination boards are not so squeamish. The second use of the word 'majority' is better qualified as absolute majority. An absolute majority is one more than 50 per cent – in other words, the number of votes won by a candidate is greater than the number of votes received by all the other candidates put together. So, in most descriptions, a majoritarian system is one which tries to give the winner an absolute majority of the votes, by giving the voter two or more votes. These majoritarian systems are described next in this chapter.

Question: Advance a case for maintaining the present electoral system.

3.3 Proportional representation, majoritarian and hybrid systems

As can be seen from what has been said above, there have been many critics of the FPTP system. But what are the alternatives? In this section we look at three different types of system which are alternatives to FPTP. Before looking at proportional representation (PR), the most popular alternative, it is necessary to look briefly at **majoritarian electoral systems**, which you could think of as a halfway house between FPTP and PR.

There are a number of different systems which can be called majoritarian, the most famous of which are the supplementary vote, the alternative vote and the second ballot systems. See box 3.5 on how they work in more depth.

> **Majoritarian electoral system**: one which ensures that the winning candidate is elected with an absolute majority (more than 50 per cent) of the vote.

Box 3.5 How majoritarian systems work

Constituencies: These systems are made for single-member constituencies or where one person is to be elected.

Voting: The essence of a majoritarian system is to give the voter a chance to express a first preference, and then a second and maybe a third (and so on) preference. So, you choose your first choice from among the candidates and then go on to choose your second, third, etc., depending on how precisely the system is run.

Counting: The first preference votes are counted and if the result does not give an absolute majority to one of the candidates, then a second round of counting begins, with the candidates at the bottom of the poll being eliminated, and the second preference votes of those who voted for them being redistributed. There may be a number of rounds held, until a candidate emerges with a clear majority of the votes.

Supplementary vote: Under this system, voters are only given two votes. There are only two rounds of counting, and all but the two front-running candidates are eliminated after the first round of counting. This is the system adopted after 1999 for the election of directly elected mayors in the UK (e.g. the mayor of London). In 1993 a Labour commission under Lord Plant advised that this system should be used for UK parliamentary elections.

Alternative vote: A more complicated version, with the voter allowed to express a number of preferences, and a number of counting rounds taking place. It is used to elect the Australian House of Representatives.

Second ballot system: The French Presidential elections are essentially run on the supplementary vote system, but the first round of voting and counting is separated from the second by a week. In the first round there are as many candidates as are nominated. By the second round (or run-offs) these have been whittled down to two. A variant of this system was used to elect the Conservative Party leader in 2005.

There is debate over whether we should classify majoritarian systems as being proportional or not. They do have some limited proportional effects, but this is largely accidental. (What proportionality means is discussed in the next section.) The reason that they produce a more proportional result is that if voters are given two votes, their second vote often strengthens the centre parties (like the Liberal Democrats), and since it is a weakness of FPTP that it unfairly discriminates against the centre, the introduction of majoritarian systems would help produce proportionality. But their main intention is to strengthen the claims of elected representatives to legitimacy by producing a rather artificial majority for them. They are therefore good systems to adopt where one candidate is being elected – for example, to the French presidency, to the leadership of a political party or to the London mayoralty. They could be adopted by our British parliamentary system quite easily, which is why Plant liked them. Voters would just be given two or more votes in each constituency instead of one. This would preserve the famous 'constituency link', the link between the MP and his or her constituency. It would not, however, produce anything very close to a true proportional result in Parliament, and hence probably would not have much impact on the complexion of governments either. Whether you approve of majoritarian systems or not depends on whether you think it is reasonable to count people's second preferences at the same time as you count other people's first preferences. Should voting be a matter of expressing preferences between candidates (this makes politics into a rather negative business) or voting positively for what you want?

Proportional representation

Proportional representation (PR) is not a 'system' in itself; there are many different electoral arrangements which are based on this principle. The most famous are the single transferable vote (STV) and the party list systems. Most European countries use some form of PR in their electoral systems. For over a century, the UK Electoral Reform Society has campaigned for STV in particular, and for PR in general. The Liberal Democrats and their ancestors the Liberal Party have also campaigned for an STV system. Labour has toyed with the idea over the years, and the electoral reform which followed the 1997 election was based to some extent on ideas of PR. These reforms are discussed below.

If the election of 2005 had been conducted strictly according to PR principles, the result would have been a coalition between Labour and the Liberal Democrats (see table 3.4 and contrast it with table 3.2). The Labour Party would not have been able to rule with 227 seats since this is not a majority in a House of 646 seats, but with the help of the 142 seats of the Liberal Democrats it could have formed a coalition government. It is also argued by those in favour of PR that the introduction of some PR systems would encourage

> **Proportional representation**: under an electoral system run according to the principle of PR, the number of votes cast for each party is matched more or less exactly by the proportion of seats in the assembly allocated to each party.

Table 3.4 PR principles applied to the 2005 general election			
Party	Actual seats under FPTP	Proportion of votes (%)	What they would have got under a perfectly proportional system
Labour	356	35.2	227
Conservative	197	32.3	209
Lib Dem	62	22.0	142

Source: Calculated by the author from the election results (http://news.bbc.co.uk)

people to vote for smaller parties. At the moment people do not do this, because it looks as if they are wasting votes in doing so. So, if this is true, the result of an election under PR would certainly produce coalitions, and perhaps even 'rainbow coalitions', drawn from several parties, as happens in some other countries under a PR system. Such a broad coalition would cover a spectrum of opinion, and hence allow a much wider range of views to be represented in government.

Box 3.6 How do proportional systems work?

Single transferable vote

Used in Northern Ireland for local, European and Assembly elections in Northern Ireland, from 2007 for local government elections in Scotland and Wales, and also in the Republic of Ireland and for elections to the Australian Senate.

Constituencies: Multi-member, large constituencies (typically, five MPs would be returned).

Voting: You have a single vote, but you can 'transfer' it, ranking the candidates in order of preference. So, unlike a List System, it allows voters to rank candidates from different parties in order of preference.

Counting: There are several rounds of counting. The magic number, or quota, that a candidate requires to be elected is determined in advance, according to a formula; the best known is the Droop formula. According to this method, the quota (Q) = (number of votes/number of seats +1) +1. In the first round, those candidates who achieve this number will be elected, and the candidate at the bottom of the poll will be eliminated. A second round of counting will redistribute the second preference votes of those candidates who have been eliminated, and the second preference of the winning candidate's surplus voters (those in excess of the quota that the candidate received). This continues until five members have been elected.

List systems

Used in mainland Britain for European Parliament elections.

Constituencies: These need to be very big or actually to disappear. The purest list system is used in Israel, where a national list is drawn up, so in effect there are no constituencies. In larger countries, regional lists will be used; the larger the region, the more proportional the result.

Box 3.6 (*continued*)

Voting: You vote once for the party list you prefer. In *open list* systems, you can change the order of candidates in the list (the nearer the top the candidates the more likely they are to get elected), or even add a name of your own. In *closed list* systems, the list is fixed by the party.

Counting: The number of seats allocated to each party is determined by the number of votes they receive, and how many times this fulfils a quota. The candidates nearer the top of the list are more likely to be elected. There are a number of different mathematical methods used to determine the quotas needed to achieve this result; the best known is the d'Hondt system used quite widely in Europe. The aim of the quota is simply to achieve a result where the seats allocated to each party are directly proportional to the votes they receive.

Hybrid systems

Under a **hybrid electoral system**, the voter would choose a constituency MP (elected by FPTP or on a majoritarian system) and then the voter would elect 'top-up' representatives, usually from a regional party list. This obviously is aimed at achieving the benefits of both systems: constituency links, possibly a majoritarian outcome in the constituency and a degree of proportionality between votes cast and seats allocated. It has the disadvantage of electing two different types of representative, and is not strongly proportional. Perhaps the best known is the system of voting used in Germany, called the additional member system (AMS).

The elections introduced since 1997 for the Scottish Parliament, the Welsh Assembly and the Greater London Assembly are also conducted by AMS.

Hybrid electoral system, also known as a mixed system: one which combines features of FPTP and PR, or even combines features of majoritarian and PR systems.

These work on a sort of hybrid system and will be discussed below, as will the recommendations of the Jenkins Commission, called the alternative vote plus system (see, in particular, box 3.7).

Question: Define proportional representation.

3.4 An evaluation of proportional representation

The case for and against PR to some degree mirrors the case for and against FPTP which has been discussed above, but here are a few additional points, not covered already.

Arguments in favour of PR

The system is fairer for the voters

There are no wasted votes, since every vote will go towards the proportion of seats in Parliament received by the party voted for. Each vote is of equal value. The election seems a much more efficient affair, therefore. This is the essential point in favour of PR, and is best illustrated by table 3.4 above on the impact the introduction would have had in 2005.

Parliament and government are more representative of the range of national opinion

Representation in Parliament reflects (represents) the make-up of the country in terms of its political views. In turn, government may become more representative of the country, since a broader range of parties might be included in coalition governments. This effect can be exaggerated, however: a coalition will only need to be broad enough to command a majority in Parliament.

Coalitions are good

A range of opinions will be aired in a coalition government. One party can keep an eye on the other in government. A bit of healthy debate within the government will be tolerated, since two or more parties will be involved. Governments may be more inclined to pursue the national interest rather than a narrow party interest. During the two world wars, Britain adopted coalition governments, and there was a reason for this; it helped produce national unity and a sense of common purpose. Why could this not be useful in peacetime as well as during war? It is also argued that coalition governments will be less able to dominate Parliament, and that backbenchers will become more independent and hence better able to represent their constituents and control the activities of an executive which under the British system can sometimes become too powerful.

Small parties are given a chance

Minor parties get a chance of a place in the coalition, perhaps, but certainly will win a seat or two in Parliament. This helps defuse tension by allowing extremists to express their views. It may produce a useful injection of new ideas (for example, from Greens) into the political system. Anyway, it is fairer if such views are represented and expressed.

The power of party is reduced

The Big Two – Labour and Conservatives – have dominated the political system for nearly a century, but a democracy should allow new parties to be formed and to grow. This is much more likely to happen under PR than under FPTP, because it can give small parties a first foothold on the ladder to power. This would possibly make all political parties less strong in our political system, and allow MPs greater freedom to represent the views of their constituents rather than just toe the party line. Whether PR actually has this effect can be debated (see below).

The selection of candidates can be more representative of women and minority groups

One way to think of representation is to consider that a representative body (like Parliament) should be a cross-section or sample of society as a whole. Hence about half the MPs should be women, and ethnic minorities should be represented in roughly the same proportions in Parliament as in society as a whole. Party list systems – and also to a lesser extent STV – would seem to be an easy way to produce a Parliament which in this sense is more representative of society than one elected under FPTP. The political parties could simply ensure that their lists were more representative. This argument can be countered by saying that there is actually no intrinsic reason why FPTP favours white males, and that a more proactive approach to what is called 'political recruitment' on the part of the major parties would do the job without resort to PR.

Arguments against PR

Representation of constituency views may be weakened

STV involves usually five-member constituencies, and it is argued that this would destroy the link between what, under our present FPTP system, is a relatively small constituency and its representative. Party list systems would have even bigger constituencies than STV, or none at all if a national party list system were used. Local views would not be represented so well, since it

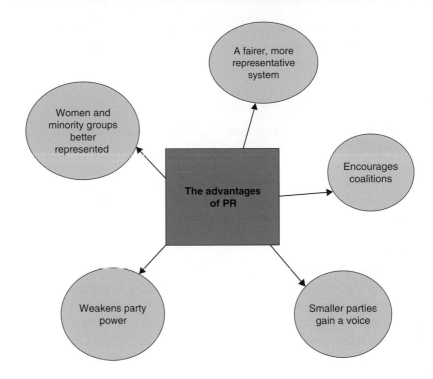

Figure 3.2   The advantages
of PR

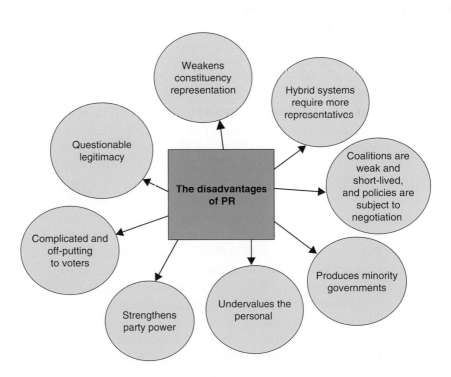

Figure 3.3   The
disavantages of PR

would be regional views that were being looked after by the MPs – that is, the interests of a wider area than the small local constituency. In addition, there may be problems if a number of people from different parties are claiming to act as the constituency representative.

Hybrid systems have two types of representative

One solution to the objection raised against PR that it removes the link between representative and constituency is to have a hybrid system. But this can create a further problem in that it involves having two types of representative: those with a constituency link and those who are 'top-up' representatives. This has the potential to create difficulties in the representative assembly, with tension developing between the two types of MP.

Coalitions are bad

They are weak, quarrelsome and short-lived. The experience of coalition government and PR in Italy, for example, demonstrates its drawbacks. In the 50 years after 1945, there was a new government in Italy almost once every year. As a result, in 1994 the Italians decided to move away from PR. In addition, under our constitution in this country, it is likely that the monarch will be drawn into politics in naming the leader of a coalition if there is any prolonged dispute between the parties. It is likely that a coalition in the UK would always contain the Liberal Democrats. This is the experience in Germany where a small party in the centre, rather like our own Liberal Democrats, has almost always been in government, whether the government is led by a left- or a right-wing party. This exaggerates the importance of this party, and seems to be essentially contradictory of the principles of PR. It is possible for very small, extremist parties to have an exaggerated importance when coalitions are formed. This has been the experience of Israel at certain times, when fundamentalist parties can hold the balance of power and therefore impose their policies on the larger parties as a price for allowing them to form a coalition government.

'Smoke-filled rooms'

The make-up of the coalition is dependent on negotiations which follow the election, taking place in the proverbial 'smoke-filled rooms' – in other words, in secret. Coalitions can take weeks to be formed and in the period that this is going on the country is effectively without a government. In 2007, it was more than two months after the Welsh Assembly elections (held under AMS) that the coalition executive for Wales was finally settled. As the coalition is formed, so its manifesto is developed, as a combination of the manifestos of two or more parties. In other words, the manifesto is written after the election. So voters cannot really make a choice between parties on grounds of policy. This seems to be contrary to democratic principles.

Minority governments

If a coalition cannot be formed, it might be necessary to set up a minority government – that is, one which cannot command a majority in the legislature, but which is composed of the party with most votes there. This is likely to lead to unstable or weak government. The election in 2007 to the Scottish Parliament under AMS led to a minority government being set up under the Scottish National Party.

The personal element in politics is undervalued and the significance of ideology exaggerated

This is true of the constituency link, but also in other ways. The theory behind PR is that people are essentially divided according to ideological type: there are so many people on the left, so many on the right, and so many in the middle. These ideological types then correspond to political parties, and the point of an election is to see that these ideological groups (these parties) are fairly represented in the assembly. But is this true? First, it could be said that people want a constituency MP who is an individual and not just a symbol. Second, in strong two-party systems (generated by FPTP) there is still a range of ideological opinion because the two major parties tend to be ideological coalitions themselves. But PR systems often involve just voting for a party list, or for candidates in large constituencies under STV who are unlikely to be very well known to the voter.

The grip of parties on the political system is strengthened

This follows from the last point. Under PR systems there will probably be more parties, but they will be firmly grouped according to a particular ideological view-point, and they will be run on dictatorial lines, especially if a party list system is used. The party list, and to a lesser extent STV, involves the political parties in exercising considerable, probably centralized, power over their candidates in drawing up the list. It assumes that the voter will not wish to vote for an individual, but for a party.

Good-bye to the doctrine of the mandate

Under FPTP, the argument runs, what you vote for is what you get, provided a sufficient number of your fellow citizens agree with you. The party issues a manifesto, and, if elected, is given authority, or a mandate, to rule. The successful political party introduces the policies set out in its manifesto, and at the next election it is held to account by the electorate, who will vote against it if it has not fulfilled its pledges at the last election. Under PR, this does not happen. You might vote for the centre party, in the hope that it will form a coalition with the left-wing party, for example. But you might find to your horror that what you get is a centre-right coalition.

Is preference voting really legitimate?

Some PR systems involve voting more than once or having the vote transferred (which is the same). This means that the voter is persuaded to express a preference where in fact he or she may not actually have one. I might feel that I simply want to vote for my favourite candidate or party. This seems in some ways the best way to resolve political differences: after all, we generally do not ask MPs to express a range of preferences when they vote on a bill in Parliament. Voting once simplifies political choice and makes people think about it seriously. It develops stronger feelings and perhaps a stronger sense of involvement. When the counting of votes begins under PR, the voter has no control over whether his or her first, second, third, etc. preference vote is counted. When these preference votes are counted, my third preference vote may count in the same way as your first preference vote. This seems to resurrect the problem of 'wasted votes', or attempt unsuccessfully to hide it. I could fairly claim that my vote had been wasted if, in the end, it was my third preference vote that was counted. You could claim that it was unreasonable for your first preference vote to count for the same as my third preference vote. So in the end, votes under a preference system do not seem to be of equal value. In attempting to solve certain problems associated with FPTP, some PR systems seem to run straight into the same difficulties themselves.

Voting is difficult and depresses turnout

People do not fully understand complicated PR systems and hence are put off voting altogether. This was shown in 2007 in the Scottish Parliament and local elections (although it was less remarked upon in Wales). A large number of votes for the Parliament in Scotland were disallowed because voters used the STV system rather than the AMS system: they were confused by the fact that, in its wisdom, the government had decided to run two elections (for Parliament and for local councils) at the same time, using different systems where voting was conducted in different ways. Under STV, voters write numbers against names; under AMS they put two crosses in boxes. The result was frustration among voters. The *Guardian* reported: 'A 36-year-old man walked into an Edinburgh polling station and began smashing ballot boxes with a golf club.'

 Question: 'Different electoral systems result in different ways of governing.' Discuss.

3.5 Electoral reform in Britain since 1997

Since 1997, electoral reform has been introduced to the United Kingdom in a number of areas. We will describe the reforms introduced, and discuss briefly what their impact has been. First, a brief overview of where reform has been introduced or proposed:

- elections for the European Parliament in mainland Britain (i.e., excluding Northern Ireland, where the system introduced there in 1979 has been retained);
- elections for the Scottish Parliament;
- elections for the Welsh Assembly;
- elections for the Mayor of London and other directly elected mayors;
- elections for the Greater London Assembly and other regional assemblies;
- elections for the Northern Ireland Assembly;
- creation of the Electoral Commission;
- the Jenkins Report;
- elections for Scottish and Welsh local government;
- elections for the reformed House of Lords.

Elections for the European Parliament in mainland Britain

Before the reform

Initially, members of the European Parliament (EP) were appointed by the governments of each country. In 1979, this was replaced by direct elections: each member state of the European Economic Community (EEC: the predecessor of the European Union) could decide how to conduct these elections for themselves. Almost every country apart from UK adopted a form of PR, but mainland UK stayed with FPTP. By 1994, there were 84 large constituencies, which elected their EP member (MEP) in the same way as for general elections. There was a difference, in that these elections were fixed-term elections, once every five years. In Northern Ireland, a different system had been adopted in 1979 for elections to the EP, which was the single transferable vote (STV), with the whole of the province of Northern Ireland forming one single constituency, returning three MEPs. The use of STV was to reduce the tendency of elections in Northern Ireland to follow narrowly sectarian or religious lines, and to allow the minority faith (Catholics) a chance to be represented in Europe. It was hoped that STV would strengthen moderate parties in Northern Ireland. It was a system used for Northern Irish local elections and also in elections in the Republic of Ireland.

European Parliament members voting on a resolution at the start of negotiations for Turkey's possible membership of the European Union

The reformed system

Following legislation in 1998, the 1999 EP elections in mainland Britain were conducted using the party list system. The country is divided into 11 regions (Northern Ireland forms a twelfth) and MEPs are elected in groups for these regions. Each party publishes a list of its candidates and the voter chooses which party to vote for. The number of seats in each region is distributed according to the proportion of votes given to each party. This produces a reasonably proportional result, but not one which is completely proportional, because the number of MEPs to be elected is rather small in relation to the number of regions into which the country is divided, and, in addition, these regions are not of equal size. One criticism of the new system as it passed through Parliament was that it involved a closed party list. In open party list systems the voter can determine in what order she or he wishes to rank those on the party list and can even, in some countries, write new names onto the list if there are people she or he wants to vote for whose names are not there. The closed party list system gives power to the party bosses to decide where to put candidates on the list, and those near the bottom of the list are highly unlikely to be elected. It is nevertheless possible for individuals to stand as independents under this system.

The impact of the reform

There have now been two elections to the European Parliament under the party list system: in 1999 and 2004. The details of these elections are given in table 3.5.

Table 3.5 European Parliament elections, 1999 and 2004

Party	1999		2004	
	Percentage share of the vote	Number of MEPs elected (of 87)	Percentage share of the vote	Number of MEPs elected (of 78)
Conservative	35.8	36	26.7	27
Labour	28.0	29	22.6	19
UKIP	7.0	3	16.2	12
Lib Dem	12.7	10	14.9	12
Green	6.2	2	6.3	2
Others	10.3	7	14.2	6

Turnout: 1999: 23%; 2004: 38%

Source: www.europarl.org.uk

Turnout

In European Parliament elections, turnout under the old system (FPTP) was low: 36 per cent in 1989 and 1994, and 32 per cent in the previous two elections. Under the new system it remained very low: in 1999 it was 23 per cent; in 2004, it was boosted to 38 per cent, partly by the campaigning of the UK Independence Party, which attracted media attention, and partly by the introduction of postal voting in some regions. One could argue both ways about turnout from the 1999 and 2004 evidence, but it is reasonable to conclude that the introduction of PR probably did not affect it much. Some people have argued that PR will depress turnout because voters do not understand it, but the party list system is arguably easier to understand than FPTP. Most voters simply do not see European elections as important: they are 'second-order' elections. Lessons about turnout are therefore difficult to draw, and, indeed, any lessons at all are difficult to draw about how PR affects voting behaviour in other respects, because turnout in these elections is low.

All parties strengthened

Parties, big and small, had complete control over drawing up their candidate lists.

Small parties did benefit

The election saw the return of two members of the Green Party in 1999 and 2004, and of three members of the UK Independence Party in 1999 and a staggering twelve members in 2004. Back in 1979 the Green Party had won (in a very surprising result) nearly 15 per cent of the vote in the EP elections, but got no seats in return because the election was fought on FPTP lines. After the reform, in 1999 and 2004, on about 6 per cent of the vote, it won two seats. It is true that low turnout also helps small parties, as do elections which are considered by many to be pointless: the small party can turn out its own core supporters, while the major parties do not bother, and people vote for parties like the Greens as a protest. The UK Independence Party campaigns against Europe, so perhaps its supporters were the people most interested in the elections. The small nationalist parties also gained seats: the Scottish National Party (SNP) got two in both elections and Plaid Cymru won one in 1998 and two in 2004. On the other hand, in 2004 neither Respect (the anti-war with Iraq party of George Galloway) nor the British National Party gained representation although they each had 5 per cent of the vote. There is therefore a sort of unofficial threshold which small parties must cross, due to the slight disproportional effect of using regional rather than national lists.

The centre party did benefit

In 1994, the Liberal Democrats won two seats when the elections were conducted under FPTP. In 1999, under the party list system, the Liberal Democrats won ten seats, and twelve in 2004. This was to be expected.

The result was more proportional than under FPTP, but not completely so

The two major parties were still somewhat over-represented, but not by as much as they would have been under FPTP. Smaller parties, like the Green Party, benefited slightly. This general lack of true proportionality is what one might expect, because the regions are not large enough to produce a purely proportional result. But other considerations called for regional lists rather than a national list: the EU likes to work with regions, and there was still a lingering desire to keep a sort of constituency link. In any case the results were much closer to proportionality than under FPTP.

Elections for the Scottish Parliament and the Welsh Assembly

The 1999 reforms

A hybrid system, known as the additional member system (AMS), was adopted for the four-yearly fixed-term elections to both these bodies. There are two parts to the AMS election in Scotland and Wales. First, in the Westminster parliamentary constituencies, a FPTP election is held to choose a single Member of the Scottish Parliament (MSP) or Member of the Welsh Assembly (MWA). Second, additional members are elected at the same time

---

Box 3.7 How does AMS work?

Constituencies: A proportion of the seats in the elected assembly are reserved for constituency members; the rest are reserved for additional members, elected in regions (larger groupings of constituencies).
Voting: Everybody has two votes. The first vote is for the constituency representative, the second for a regional party list.
Counting: The constituency members are elected by FPTP. The list representatives are allocated in such a way as to make the overall representation of the parties in the assembly proportional to the votes they receive. In other words, if a small party gets, say, 15 per cent of the vote, but no constituency members, it will be compensated by getting a fair share of the list representatives. Conversely if a large party with, say, 40 per cent of the vote on the constituency vote, is fairly represented already in the assembly, or over-represented, it will not get any additional members from the list. This balancing effect is achieved by using the d'Hondt formula to calculate how many representatives should be allocated from the Party Lists.

and on the same ballot paper, with voters choosing between closed party lists. The additional members are representatives for regions (the regions employed are those used until 1999 in European Parliament elections), or groups of constituencies. There are 5 regions in Wales and 40 constituencies; in Scotland there are 7 regions and 73 constituencies. This hybrid system was adopted because the constituency link was considered important for bodies which, after all, were being set up precisely to provide more local representation. But it was also thought to be desirable to work towards a greater degree of proportionality. This was crucial in Scotland and Wales where there was, effectively, in some constituencies a four-party system (see table 3.6 below).

Impact

There have been three elections in both Wales and Scotland (in 1999, 2003 and 2007). The impact of AMS has been considerable, and suggests that the introduction of PR in the country as a whole would radically change the face of British politics. The details of these elections are summarized in tables 3.6 and 3.7.

Turnout

This was low: in 1999, it was 59 per cent in Scotland and 47 per cent in Wales; in 2003, it was 49 per cent in Scotland and 38 per cent in Wales; in 2007, it revived to 52 per cent in Scotland and 44 per cent in Wales. It is obvious from this that the Welsh were less overjoyed by devolution than the Scots, but the Scottish turnout in 1999 is close to the 2001 general election turnout, so it might be possible to conclude from this that the introduction of AMS had little impact, either by depressing or encouraging turnout. Disillusionment with devolution was thought at the time to be the best explanation for the low turnout in 2003; the revival in 2007 might be due to disillusionment with Blair (i.e., people were using these elections to register a protest).

Smaller parties benefited

AMS is not a completely proportional system, but it certainly benefited smaller parties. Greens gained seven seats in Scotland in 2003, all from the regional list element of the AMS system. Another small party in Scotland and Wales was the Conservative Party. In the 1997 Westminster general election, the Conservatives had won no seats at all in Scotland or Wales, but in these devolved elections they were able, under PR, to have a minor revival, in Wales winning nine seats in 1999 and eleven in 2003, and in Scotland eighteen in both elections. The Scottish Socialist Party, another small party, grew from one seat in 1999 to six in 2003. This was also a new party, and more proportional systems are expected to allow new parties to be formed. But in 2007, this effect was greatly reduced, as voters concentrated on the Big Four in these nations. In Wales, a fragmented vote for minor parties (over 16 per cent

Table 3.6 Elections to the Scottish Parliament, 1999, 2003 and 2007 (Results for 1999 in brackets, for 2003 in bold, for 2007 in italics)

Party	Constituency percentage share of vote	Constituency seats	Regional list percentage share of vote	Regional list seats	Total
Labour	(39) **35** *32*	(53) **46** *37*	(33) **29** *29*	(3) **4** *9*	(56) **50** *46*
SNP	(29) **24** *33*	(7) **10** *21*	(28) **21** *31*	(20) **17** *26*	(35) **27** *47*
Conservative	(16) **17** *17*	(0) **3** *4*	(16) **16** *14*	(18) **15** *13*	(18) **18** *17*
Lib Dem	(14) **15** *16*	(12) **13** *11*	(16) **12** *11*	(5) **4** *5*	(17) **17** *16*
Green	(0) **0** *0*	(0) **0** *0*	(4) **7** *4*	(1) **7** *2*	(1) **7** *2*
Scottish	(1) **6** *0*	(0) **0** *0*	(2) **7** *1*	(1) **6** *0*	(1) **6** *0*
Socialist Party					
Others	(2) **3** *1*	(1) **2** *0*	(6) **9** *9*	(0) **2** *1*	(1) **4** *1*

Turnout: 1999: 59%; 2003: 49%; 2007: 52%

Source: Electoral Commission website

on the regional list vote) did not result in more than one seat for such a party. The same was true to a lesser extent in Scotland. Very small parties will struggle to be represented on any PR system.

The dominant party suffered

Labour did rather poorly in the 1999, 2003 and especially the 2007 Scottish and Welsh elections. Again, this was a predictable feature of a move even towards a hybrid system. The 'cube rule' effect in FPTP elections was gone. Nevertheless, Labour still did well in these elections, emerging as the front-runner, with the single exception of 2007 in Scotland where it was very narrowly beaten by the SNP. A more proportional system allowed the left wing of the Labour Party to break away in Scotland and gain representation as the Scottish Socialist Party, but a series of scandals burst the SSP bubble in 2007.

'Split ticket' voting

AMS allows voters to vote twice: once for their constituency MSP and once for the party list. They can, therefore, vote, if they choose, for two different parties at once, or to 'split the ticket', as the practice is called in the USA. This seems a bit against the spirit of PR (which some people argue should be introduced so that people stop tactical voting), but it does show that the electorate is sophisticated enough not only to cope with PR (sometimes people have argued that it is too complicated) but also to use it to express more than one preference. The second vote seems to have been used by voters to benefit minor parties: an intelligent move for voters to make, since minor parties cannot generally win in the constituency contest. The electorate did this more in 2003 and 2007 than in 1999, and this suggests that new voting systems will change the party system as they become established.

Minority government and coalition government in Wales

In 1999, Labour tried at first in Wales to form an executive as a minority, expecting that in practice it would get support from the minor parties. This might have worked had the Labour Party not been subject to internal divisions in the Welsh Assembly, largely because the Welsh Labour Party was interfered with by the Labour Party in London, especially over the vexed question of who was to lead it and hence become the first head of the Welsh executive. This in-fighting within the Labour Party was a consequence of devolution rather than of electoral reform, but it led to the fall of the minority government and the creation of a coalition government with the Liberal Democrats. The coalition ended with the election of 2003, which gave Labour exactly half the seats in the Welsh Assembly, which it used to form a single-party executive. But in 2007, Labour lost seats and, to most people's surprise, was able to form a coalition with Plaid Cymru.

Minority government and coalition government in Scotland

Somewhat to its surprise, the Labour Party could not form a majority government in Scotland after 1999, and as a result it had to ask the Liberal Democrats to form a coalition with it. This coalition survived the 2003 election, but

Table 3.7 Elections for the Welsh Assembly, 1999, 2003 and 2007 (Results for 1999 in brackets, for 2003 in bold, for 2007 in italics)

Party	Constituency percentage share of vote	Constituency seats	Regional list percentage share of vote	Regional list seats	Total
Labour	(38) **40** *32*	(27) **30** *24*	(35) **37** *30*	(1) **0** *2*	(28) **30** *26*
Plaid Cymru	(28) **14** *22*	(9) **5** *7*	(31) **20** *21*	(8) **7** *8*	(17) **12** *15*
Conservative	(16) **20** *22*	(1) **1** *5*	(16) **19** *21*	(8) **10** *7*	(9) **11** *12*
Lib Dem	(13) **14** *15*	(3) **3** *3*	(12) **13** *12*	(3) **3** *3*	(6) **6** *6*
Others	(5) **5** *8*	(0) **1** *1*	(6) **12** *16*	(0) **0** *0*	(0) **1** *1*

Turnout: 1999: 47%; 2003: 38%; 2007: 44%

Source: Electoral Commission website

fell in 2007 after the SNP 'victory' in the election. In 2007, the SNP formed a minority government after emerging as the leading party, but without a majority of the seats in the Scottish Parliament.

'New politics'?

There was a good deal of talk about 'new politics' in Scotland (in Wales there was less enthusiasm for devolution generally). The creation of a coalition government in Scotland had the curious effect of drawing a Scottish 'New' Labour Party back to the left, probably much to its secret satisfaction. The Liberal Democrats supported more favourable treatment of students (over loans and grants), public employees (especially teachers) and the sick and elderly. In terms of its public policy decisions, Scotland stood out therefore against the drift to the right of the Labour Party in the UK as a whole, because ironically it was in coalition with a party which was supposed to be in the centre. This was directly attributable to the new electoral system adopted there.

Increased female representation

One aspect of 'new politics' which followed the new electoral systems was the increase in the representation of women. After 2003, half the members of the Welsh Assembly were women; in 2007, the number had been cut to 28 out of 60. After 2007 in Scotland, exactly one-third of the MSPs were women. This relatively high level of female representation is a predictable consequence of using party lists, since parties (especially the Labour Party) were able to select more female candidates using the list system. Selection of candidates under the old constituency system (used in FPTP elections) tends to be less favourable towards women because the local constituency members tend to favour choosing male candidates, who are considered to be a safer electoral bet.

Elections for the Mayor of London and other directly elected mayors

The reforms

In 2000 a mayor was elected for the first time in London under the majoritarian supplementary vote system, and a second election followed in 2004. No proportional system, of course, can be used in the election of a single person. The voters of London were given a first choice vote and then a supplementary vote. If the front-runner in the election received more than 50 per cent of the first preference votes, he or she would be declared elected. If not, then a second round of counting begins, with the two top candidates having their first-preference votes supplemented with the second preference votes of the eliminated candidates. The same system has been used to elect the rather

30-foot high balloons of four of the candidates for London Mayor in May 2000

limited number of other directly elected mayors who have been appointed around the country, following referendums.

Impact

The details of the results of these two elections are given in tables 3.8 and 3.9, respectively. One of the most interesting facts about the 2000 election was that Ken Livingstone was elected mayor as an Independent candidate. This strange fact owed nothing to the electoral system and everything to the fact that Labour had handled the process of selecting candidates so poorly that, as a result of not being selected, Livingstone had resigned as candidate for the Labour Party and decided to put himself forward as an Independent. In 2000, he would still have won if the election had been been conducted under an old-fashioned first-past-the-post system. He gained 39 per cent of the first preference votes, compared to Steve Norris's (Conservative) 27 per cent. When the second round of counting had redistributed the second preference votes of the other unsuccessful candidates, Norris had 42 per cent and Livingstone had 58 per cent: they had increased their vote almost exactly in the same proportions! By 2004, Labour had seen the error of its ways and Livingstone had been readopted as Labour candidate, and duly won the election. Turnout in 2000 was only 34 per cent, and 37 per cent in 2004, but this low figure probably has nothing to do with the electoral systems, although they were very complex in London, with two different methods being used, one for the mayor and one for the assembly. Many voters simply did not see these elections as important.

Table 3.8 London mayoral election, 2000

Candidate[a]	First preference votes	Percentage share of first preference votes	Final votes (including second preference votes)	Percentage share of final votes
Ken Livingstone (Ind)	667,877	38.96	776,427	57.92
Steven Norris (Con)	464,434	27.09	564,137	42.08
Frank Dobson (Lab)	223,884	13.06	Eliminated	Eliminated
Susan Kramer (Lib Dem)	203,452	11.87	Eliminated	Eliminated

[a] Only the top 4 (out of 11) candidates are listed here
Turnout: 34.43%

Source: http://www.londonelects.org.uk/results/mayor/index.html

Table 3.9 London mayoral election, 2004

Candidate	First preference votes	Percentage share of first preference votes	Final votes (including second preference votes)	Percentage share of final votes
Ken Livingstone (Lab)	685,541	35.70	828,380	55.39
Steven Norris (Con)	542,423	28.24	667,178	44.61
Simon Hughes (Lib Dem)	284,645	14.82	Eliminated	Eliminated

Turnout: 36.95%

Source: www.londonelects.org.uk

Elections for the Greater London Assembly and other regional assemblies

The reforms

At the same time Livingstone was elected mayor, in 2000 and 2004, a separate electoral system was used to elect an Assembly for London. This was conducted under the same sort of system as the Scottish and Welsh elections, the AMS system. Fourteen candidates were elected by FPTP in London constituencies, and a further eleven were elected on the list system, to top up the numbers and make them more proportional. A similar system will be used if any of the English regions decide by referendum to opt for an elected regional assembly, which seems unlikely.

The impact

The details of these election results are given in tables 3.10 and 3.11, respectively. Again, the smaller parties benefited, with three Green candidates returned in 2000, on 11 per cent of the vote, and two in 2004 on a reduced vote. The United Kingdom Independence Party (UKIP) gained two London Assembly seats in 2004 (the London elections were held at the same time as the European Parliament elections). A more consensual form of politics also ensued in London, but this was largely inevitable since the Assembly had to

Table 3.10 Greater London Assembly results, 2000

Party	Constituency seats	Percentage share of vote	Additional members
Conservative	8	28.99	1
Labour	6	30.30	3
Liberal Democrat	0	14.80	4
Green	0	11.08	3

Turnout: 34.34%

Source: www.londonelects.org.uk

Table 3.11 Greater London Assembly results, 2004

Party	Constituency seats	Percentage share of vote	Additional members
Conservative	9	31.20	0
Labour	5	24.70	2
Liberal Democrat	0	18.50	5
Green	0	7.70	2
UK Independence	0	8.18	2

Turnout: 36.97%

Source: www.londonelects.org.uk

cooperate with the Independent mayor. It is also worth emphasizing that local politics is often less strongly confrontational than politics in Westminster, even though every council (apart from the Greater London Assembly) is elected by FPTP.

Elections for the Northern Ireland Assembly

The reforms

By the time of the Good Friday Agreement of 1998, a settlement of Northern Ireland had been arrived at, with extremely complex constitutional arrangements put in place, designed to create a political system which was not dominated by the majority Unionist section of the population. One of the safeguards put in place was to have the Northern Ireland Assembly elected by single transferable vote (STV). This would have the effect of ensuring that the two hostile communities in Northern Ireland would be represented as fairly as possible. There are four major parties in Northern Ireland and a number of smaller parties too. STV, being one of the most proportional of the electoral systems, would allow for the greatest degree of fairness in the representation of these rather numerous parties. It was also hoped that under STV people would transfer their vote from one moderate party to another, even if it meant crossing the religious divide, hence reducing support for the extreme parties in each community. There was also a tradition of using STV in Northern Ireland: elections to the European Parliament in Northern Ireland and also local elections there were held under this system. It is also a system used in the Republic of Ireland.

Impact

Elections were held in 1998, then, after a delay, in 2003, and most recently in 2007: details are given in table 3.12. The second election was delayed because of the continuing strife in the province. The political situation in Northern Ireland was so fragile and so complex, and the Good Friday Agreement itself was such a complicated document, that it is hardly possible to comment on the impact of the STV system here in isolation. It did seem to produce a very proportional result, and the strong representation of small groups in the Northern Ireland Assembly has probably been a factor for stability there, with parties like the Alliance, the Women's Coalition and the minor Unionist parties acting as something of a buffer between the four major parties which, under FPTP, had dominated politics in the region. But the elections of 2003, when they were eventually held, actually resulted in an increase in the support for the two more extreme parties, the Democratic Unionist Party and Sinn Fein. This trend was confirmed in 2007. So STV had had no impact in reducing the strength of the more hard-line political parties, but it would be wrong to single out the electoral system for blame here.

Table 3.12 Northern Ireland Assembly election results. 1998, 2003 and 2007 (Results for 1998 in brackets, for 2003 in bold, for 2007 in italics)

Party	Percentage share of vote	Seats
Democratic Unionist	(18.1) **25.7** *30.1*	(20) **30** *36*
Sinn Fein	(17.6) **23.5** *26.2*	(18) **24** *28*
Ulster Unionist	(21.3) **22.7** *14.9*	(28) **27** *18*
SDLP	(22.2) **17.0** *15.2*	(24) **18** *16*
Alliance	(5.6) **3.7** *5.2*	(6) **6** *7*
Independent	(0) **2.8** *3.2*	(0) **1** *1*
Progressive Unionist	(1.9) **1.2** *0.6*	(2) **1** *1*
Others	(9.3) **3.5** *4.5*	(10) **1** *1*

Source: www.electoralcommission.org

Creation of the Electoral Commission

One further reform brought in by Labour since 1997 has been the creation of a body to oversee the conduct of elections: the Electoral Commission. Since there are now so many different types of election, it is important to have a watchdog to ensure that the rules are observed. The Commission was set up under the 2000 Political Parties, Elections and Referendums Act. The body also looks at the funding of party election campaigns, and tries to ensure that parties spend and raise money in the ways legally allowed. In addition, the Commission has been given a role in the conduct of referendums. In 2000, Parliament also passed the Representation of the People Act, which allowed the introduction of novel methods of voting like all-postal ballots; this is discussed in chapter 2.

The Jenkins Report

In its 1997 election manifesto, Labour announced that it would look into the question of whether to introduce PR to British general elections. This had been discussed in Labour circles for many years, but especially since their third electoral defeat in 1987. At that stage a Labour Party commission had been established under Lord Plant to look into the matter, and it had recommended that the majoritarian system known as the supplementary vote system should be introduced for general elections, that AMS ought to be used for any future devolved assemblies, and that regional lists should be used for European Parliament elections and also for a reformed House of Lords. But although Plant was clearly influential in some areas, his recommendations were not adopted for general elections. However, in its manifesto of 1997, Labour did promise that a further commission should look into the question of electoral reform for parliamentary elections and that the matter should then be put to the people in a referendum. In 1997 Lord Jenkins, a former Labour politician and at the time a Liberal Democrat peer, was given the job of looking at the matter again. When published in 1998, the Jenkins Report recommended that a PR system more ambitious than that suggested by Plant should be introduced for British general elections. The Report's proposals were in favour of a hybrid system, which has been called an alternative vote plus system. The main features of his proposals were:

- It would be a sort of watered down AMS system.
- Voters would have two votes.
- 80 per cent or 85 per cent of MPs should be elected by the majoritarian alternative vote system in what were very like parliamentary constituencies (voters rank all their candidates in order of preference and these votes are then used as the basis for arriving at a majority for the winner by eliminating the least popular candidates successively until a majority is achieved).
- The remaining MPs would be elected by an open party list system in regions, which grouped together a number of constituencies. The purpose of this would be to achieve greater proportionality. The voter could still vote for individuals on the party list by name if he or she preferred this to accepting the full published party list.

Jenkins's suggestions were not very extreme, and not particularly proportional either. He was probably trying to put forward a plan which would be acceptable to the Labour government. It must be remembered, though, that in 1997 Labour had won the general election with a huge majority on the FPTP system, and it was to do the same again in 2001 and with a comfortable majority in 2005. So there was no real incentive for Labour to adopt a PR system by the time Jenkins had reported. It seems that the Jenkins Report has been quietly forgotten, and it is unlikely that any firm proposals for electoral reform in British general elections will be made by Labour in the foreseeable future. The 2005 Labour manifesto merely repeated what had been said in the last two manifestos – that electoral reform was best decided by a referendum – but did not make any promises about holding one. Still, if Labour slips in the opinion polls (as it did in Blair's last two years as Prime Minister) and as the next general election approaches, perhaps we should expect them to resurrect the idea of this final piece of electoral reform.

Elections for Scottish and Welsh local government

A footnote on electoral reform in Britain in recent years is that, since 2007, local council elections in Scotland and Wales have been held under the STV system. As has been said, this caused confusion among voters, especially in Scotland. This recent development suggests that the final word on this subject has not yet been written.

Elections for the reformed House of Lords

In 2007, proposals for further reform of the House of Lords suggested that if there were to be an elected element of the reformed chamber, it should be done by partially open party lists in the European Parliament elections, and at the same time as them. Politics students will be overjoyed to see that yet another new system is being proposed here.

The parties and the future of electoral reform

The attitude of Labour to future electoral reform has been discussed when looking at the Jenkins Report. The Liberal Democrats remain the main enthusiasts for electoral reform in Westminster elections. They still prefer STV. The great hope for the Liberal Democrats is that a future FPTP election would produce an outcome with no very clear winner among the two main parties (a 'hung Parliament') and hence the right conditions for the creation of a coalition government in which they could play a part. In return for supporting one or other of the main parties, they would demand a change in the electoral system for Westminster elections. This was the demand made in February 1974 by the Liberals as the price for joining a coalition with the Conservatives, whose leader, Ted Heath, refused. It was too great a price to pay by a political party which generally did quite well under FPTP. If the Conservative Party could manage a sustained revival and if Labour's support were to undergo a serious decline, this might become a possible scenario again. And the Conservatives, under David Cameron, are open to new ideas in the field of constitutional and hence possibly electoral reform. Would Cameron act differently from Heath if faced by the chance of power in a future general election? Only time will tell.

> **Activity**
>
> At the beginning of chapter 5 is a table giving the results of all the British General Elections since 1945 (see pages 156–7). Look carefully at the table – it takes a bit of puzzling out. Then use the data given there to illustrate a case for and against electoral reform for UK general elections.

Question: What have been the effects of the use of proportional representation in elections in the UK?

SUMMING UP

Until 1997, the system used almost without exception for elections in the UK was FPTP, a method of voting which had grown up organically since medieval times. In the middle of the nineteenth century, criticisms had been voiced against this system, most notably from John Stuart Mill, who felt that it encouraged what he called 'the tyranny of the majority'. But the system also had its supporters, especially among those who benefited most from it – the two major political parties. But in the 1990s, after a long, depressing period in opposition, the Labour Party was converted (or more correctly reconverted) to the idea of some sort of electoral reform. The result has been that, since its election in 1997, Labour has opened the door to the introduction of no fewer than four different electoral systems, especially in connection with other constitutional reforms like devolution. The result is a bit of a mess. The poor London voter is called upon to use no fewer than four of these electoral systems: AMS for the London Assembly, SV for the Mayor of London, party list for the European Parliament and FPTP for general and borough elections. This is probably unique, a state of affairs not found anywhere else in the world. What Labour has consistently refused to do is to take forward its commitment to hold a referendum on electoral reform for parliamentary elections. The reason for this is obvious: Labour has, to date, won three elections running under FPTP. It is conceivable that the situation may change, however, if the electoral fortunes of the two major parties draw closer together, and if the dreaded prospect of a 'hung Parliament' with the Liberal Democrats holding the balance of power, becomes once again more of a possibility.

Further reading

D. Butler and D. Kavanagh, *The British General Election of 2005* (Palgrave, 2005): detailed analysis of the 2005 general election.

D. Farrell, *Comparing Electoral Systems* (Prentice Hall, 1997): careful dissection and comparison of the main electoral systems used around the world.

Websites

www.electoralcommission.gov.uk (Electoral Commission, the official body which regulates elections)

www.electoral-reform.org.uk (Electoral Reform Society, a group which campaigns for electoral reform)

Voting Behaviour

Making connections

This is not a topic for those who like certainty and hard facts. Almost everything about the study of voting behaviour is speculative. There are many theories competing for attention, and the data which need interpreting are constantly changing and build up in volume with each election. It is a very useful topic, however, in terms of providing a background to the study of elections and political parties.

CHAPTER

4

Voting Behaviour

KEY TOPICS

- An introduction to the study of voting behaviour
- Long-term or sociological factors in voting behaviour
- Other long-term factors in voting behaviour: geography, gender, age and race
- Short-term or political factors in voting behaviour

SETTING THE SCENE

The previous chapter looked at the way in which elections are organized; this chapter looks at how people vote in them. Why do some people always vote for the same party? What makes people shift suddenly in large numbers from supporting the government to voting for the opposition party in a general election? There are links here to be drawn with the earlier discussion in chapter 2, which looked at why people vote at all, why they participate in politics. The same sort of analysis that was used in the treatment of political participation in that chapter will be used here.

4.1 An introduction to the study of voting behaviour

One of the most interesting aspects of political science is the study of voting behaviour. 'Voting behaviour' is the social psychologists' way of saying 'how people decide to vote in elections'. People who study the details of voting are sometimes called psephologists, a word which derives from the Greek word 'psephos', which was the pebble the Ancient Greeks put into large jars (the equivalent of their ballot boxes) when they voted. The study of voting behaviour attempts to answer a number of questions, which can be put into two groups. First, there are sociological questions about what might be called the long-term factors involved in determining how people vote. Second, there

121

are the political, or short-term, questions which try to discover why people vote the way they do in any particular election.

Long-term or sociological questions

- Do certain types of people tend to vote for a particular political party or candidate?
- Do people in one part of the country vote one way and those in another part of the country vote another?
- Do rich people or people in well-paid jobs tend to vote for one political party?
- Does how people vote vary according to what social class or job they are in?
- Are women more likely to vote one way than men?
- Does age enter into the account?
- Are religion and race factors in deciding how people tend to vote?

These questions are sometimes called long-term factors in voting behaviour, because presumably they are not likely to change much between elections: people in certain sociological groups will tend to vote the same way from one election to another, and any changes in their voting behaviour will be gradual. I have called them sociological factors here because they seem to me to deal with the sort of questions a student of society (or sociologist) is interested in, by classifying people into different groups – old, young, rich, poor, etc. If we can establish some sort of pattern to voting behaviour along the lines set out above, the next thing may be to answer the question 'Why?' Why do people in Scotland vote more strongly one way than another? Why do the young or old vote in a particular way?

Short-term or political questions

Further questions also need to be answered:

- Do people vote for a party because they find the party leader in some ways sympathetic?
- Do people vote for a party because they like its ideology or political philosophy?
- Do people vote by looking at political issues, and in essence by ranking the opposing parties in an election according to how much they like their policies?
- Is it correct to say that people in effect vote with their wallets – i.e., vote for a party which will keep inflation or unemployment down or which will impose fewer taxes?
- Are people inclined to vote by looking back at a government's record or by looking forward to a party's promises?

- Do election campaigns matter?
- Are newspapers significant in swaying the opinion of voters?
- Do public opinion polls make a difference?

These further questions are sometimes called short-term questions, because they affect how voters behave in a particular election. They are also obviously the political questions which directly affect people's conscious decisions about how they are going to vote at each election.

How can we answer these questions?

A quick glance at the lists of questions above immediately tells us that there is unlikely to be a very clear answer to any of them, and that the answers are liable to be rather inconclusive and conditional. The simple fact is that although we are never going to be able to answer these questions fully or very clearly, there are various types of evidence we can use in helping us to do so.

Election results

We have a great deal of very hard statistical data in the election results. This can be analysed and used to produce evidence. The best evidence it can give us is geographical: we know exactly how the people in, say, Aberdeen or Plymouth voted and we can compare the results. It is also very good historical evidence since we know how people voted in specific elections on specific dates. It is still rather difficult to use, however, because we only know in broad terms how people voted; we do not know how each individual voted because there is a secret ballot.

Census and similar statistical information

Election results can go beyond geographical questions when they are compared with other fairly hard data. From the ten-yearly census and other similar official statistical information, we can work out the age profile and get a view on the occupational nature, even the class structure, of a constituency. That might help us to answer the sociological questions above.

Public opinion polls

In addition, there is the evidence which political scientists draw from surveying public opinion. This is the evidence which is used to answer what have been called the political questions above. There are all manner of opinion polls, some designed for an academic audience, some to be used by the political parties and some for publication in the media. Opinion polling is nowadays a very exact social and mathematical science. But the problem is that they can never be completely reliable or objective sources of information. People sometimes conceal the truth, even from themselves, and people often do not really know what they think on very complicated and difficult political issues. We know for a fact, for example, that the opinion polls in 1992 were predicting a Labour victory in the general election, but in fact the Conservatives won reasonably comfortably. This has been put down to a tendency for people who voted Conservative to deny that they were going to do so. All polls rely on sampling: the pollsters cannot ask everyone in the country, but need to choose, say, 1,000 people chosen as a cross-section. It does not take much thought to see that there are likely to be problems in selecting that sample.

Other political data

In order to make sense of the answers people give to opinion pollsters, we need to set them in their contemporary background: we need other political data. Some of this data is quite hard and reliable: the economic statistics are likely to be quite good, although seldom entirely acceptable to all economists. They will help us look for a correlation between voting behaviour and the rise in prices or the fall in employment. But some of the political background is difficult to fill in. Obviously, some sort of measurement can be made here, but it is likely to be rather unscientific, and we may simply be thrown back on correlating findings from various different opinion polls. For example, how could we objectively establish whether a party had fought a good election campaign? Or whether a party leader was really a good leader? In the end all the opinion poll evidence may be telling us is that more people voted for a particular party in an election because it was more popular than its opponents. This may not be thought really worthy of note. We could try to analyse this answer further, asking people what they thought about the party leader, or its policies, or its values and beliefs. But it is important to realize that as soon as we analyse in this way, we are imposing the subjective views of the pollsters onto the people who are being polled. Again, we will probably, as a result, end up with some rather unsurprising results.

No agreed framework

Finally, political scientists disagree quite strongly on how to use any data they are brave enough to come up with as a result of conducting their research. There is no agreement, for example, on social class and how to define it. This is a real problem, since how particular social groups vote is an important question in the study of voting behaviour. There is a fundamental problem also in looking at the two types of question used in the study of voting behaviour. The long-term questions tend to assume that people are programmed like robots to vote in a certain way. On the other hand, the short-term questions treat people as rational agents, as making a considered choice. Obviously, people cannot be both, and it is also a little unlikely that the population can be divided into two groups: robots and rational choosers. Still, these problems on the whole make the study of voting behaviour more not less valuable. But it is worth emphasizing that the answers we give to the questions outlined above are bound to be a little uncertain.

 Question: Discuss three major factors which have influenced recent voting behaviour.

4.2 Long-term or sociological factors in voting behaviour

The 'social structures' model of voting behaviour

We will begin in this section to look at what is considered the really significant factor in long-term explanations of voting behaviour: social class. Put crudely, the working class has tended to vote Labour and the middle class to vote Conservative. The Labour Party was, after all, formed to represent the 'labouring' or working class.

Behind this view of voting behaviour lie theories of 'socialization', the psychologist's way of describing how we form our ideas of the world by absorbing the views of those around us in our families, our neighbourhoods and places of work. Butler and Stokes, writing in 1963 when the social structures model of voting was very popular, conducted research which discovered a close correlation between the political views of teenagers and those of their parents (who obviously shared the same class): teenagers had been socialized into their political views by these 'primary' influences. But while the link between class and party support may be strong, there have always been middle-class supporters of Labour, typically the 'intellectuals', especially those in state employment as teachers or civil servants. There have also always been 'deferential' working-class supporters of the Conservatives, often in rural areas – people who looked up to their social superiors and were happy to vote for them. In addition, many people who were classified as working class and who voted Conservative were actually lower-middle-class small businessmen. But by and large, the straightforward division of British party politics along class lines has been true. To quote political scientist Peter Pulzer: 'Class is the basis of British party politics; all else is embellishment and detail.' This is called 'class-based voting': voting along class lines. The standard view of political scientists is that while this may have been true in 1967, when Pulzer wrote it, now it is no longer true. They point to what is called **class dealignment**.

Class dealignment: the tendency since about 1970 for the decline of the simple link between the working class and voting Labour and the middle class and voting Conservative.

Box 4.1 What is meant by social class?

There is a huge part of sociology which deals with this question, which is technically called 'stratification'. Until quite recently, political scientists were happy to deal with the old-fashioned division of British people into three classes: working, middle and upper. The working class consisted of people who worked in manual jobs, working literally with their hands, in factories, farms, mines, transport and service industries. The middle class was made up of the better-paid office workers, professional people like lawyers, clergymen and doctors, and business people. The upper class comprised the big landowners and people rich enough not to need to work at all. Broadly speaking, the assumption was that the working class was inclined to vote Labour and the middle and upper classes had a tendency to vote Conservative. There were always problems with this division into three classes: (1) the upper class was too small to be of much interest to political scientists; (2) the working class is best divided into an unskilled and a skilled part; (3) the middle class also divides into an upper-middle class of rich professional and business people and a lower-middle class of teachers, civil servants and senior clerical staff. Sociologists and political scientists argue endlessly about these classifications, since they are important for understanding voting behaviour. At present, the generally accepted classification, which follows a pattern invented by the advertising industry, is more complex, and divides people into the following six groups:

A = professional
B = managerial
C1 = clerical
C2 = skilled manual
D = semi-skilled
E = unskilled

According to MORI (the professional pollsters) in 2005, these groups constituted the following as a percentage of the total electorate:

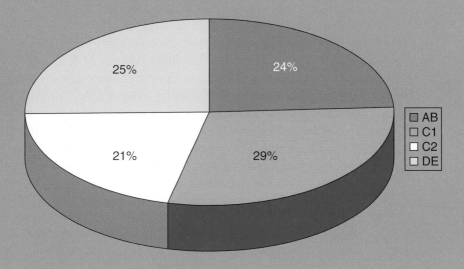

Table 4.1 Changes in class voting: Conservative % lead over Labour in different social groups in selected elections, 1974–2005

Social group[a]	Oct 1974	1983	1992	1997	2001	2005
ABC1	+37	+39	+32	+5	+4	+7
C2	−23	+8	−1	−23	−20	−7
DE	−35	−8	−18	−38	−31	−23

[a] See box 4.1

Source: MORI final aggregate analysis

Class dealignment is connected to the rise since the 1960s of a third party, now known as the Liberal Democrats, which obviously makes the simple link described above difficult to sustain. It is also linked to changes in social class itself: people are now less easily identifiable in class terms. It is often said that the industrial working class has declined, but it is worth pointing out that the suburban middle class has also changed, as job security has been eroded in the private sector and as the 'new public management' has replaced professionalism in the state sector. But two points need to be made before we accept the class dealignment theory completely. First, the Conservatives under Margaret Thatcher made great efforts to appeal to working class voters, by privatizing council houses for example. Thatcher was credited with winning the heart of 'Essex man', a cartoon character typifying the southern working class. In the same way Tony Blair bent over backwards to win the support of the middle class, of 'Mondeo man', an upwardly mobile suburbanite caricature. This seems to confirm the idea of class dealignment. But looked at from another perspective, Thatcher was simply trying to expand the 'deferential' Conservative vote, which is as old as Disraeli, while Blair was building on the 'intellectual' middle-class Labourite, again an aim as old as the Fabian Society. The second warning about swallowing the class dealignment theory completely is to look at the statistics from recent elections: they still show quite a strong link between voting behaviour and social class – see table 4.2.

It is true that the correlation between class and voting is less firm than it was, but a few moments studying table 4.2 shows that it still is there. The lower down the social scale you are, the more likely it is that you will vote Labour. The richer you are, the more likely it is that you are a Conservative voter. The Liberal Democrats are a bit like the Conservatives in this respect, but their appeal is somewhat broader.

Table 4.2 Social class and voting: the 1997, 2001 and 2005 general elections (% share of the vote: 1997 in brackets; 2001 in bold; 2005 in italics).

Social group[a]	Conservative	Labour	Liberal Democrat
AB	(41) **39** *37*	(31) **30** *28*	(23) **25** *29*
C1	(37) **36** *37*	(39) **38** *32*	(18) **20** *23*
C2	(27) **29** *33*	(50) **49** *40*	(16) **15** *19*
DE	(21) **24** *25*	(59) **55** *48*	(13) **13** *18*

[a] See box 4.1

Source: MORI final aggregate analysis

Box 4. 2 Embourgeoisement

The French word *bourgeois* means middle class. So, embourgeoisement means 'becoming more middle class'. It describes the way in which individuals as they become more prosperous become socially mobile and can move from the working class to the middle class. As the country as a whole also becomes richer, so the number of people who can be described as working class declines. In the post-war period, especially since the 1960s, industry has declined in Britain and the service sector of the economy has grown, providing people with more middle-class jobs in shops and offices. The impact of this on British politics has been, according to some commentators, very significant. This is most clearly seen in the voting behaviour analysis which connected the rise of the new middle class with the decline of the old Labour Party and the success of Margaret Thatcher's Conservative Party in the polls. This can then be linked to the development in the 1990s of 'New' Labour, a party which has appealed to the middle class as much as to the working class. The situation, however, is probably more complex than it seems. Opinion polls show that people are often reluctant to call themselves middle class even after they should have become bourgeois. People cling to their roots and typically working-class habits like die-hard football fans. From a political perspective, the Conservative Party has remained very much middle class in its appeal since 1997, but until 2006 saw no significant growth in its support.

The 'party identification' model of voting behaviour

But how important are these long-term or sociological explanations for how people vote? According to political scientists like David Denver, they are less important than they were before about 1970. One reason for this is because what is called **party identification** has declined.

Party identification is clearly linked with some of the long-term factors connected with voting behaviour which have been discussed above. Class alignment, which is also discussed briefly above, is obviously linked to partisan

Party identification (or partisan alignment): the way in which particular people consistently support the same political party, adopting its ideology and voting for it on a regular basis.

Margaret Thatcher's period in office saw the rise of an aspiring new middle class which changed the social landscape of modern Britain

alignment: people in a particular social class will be aligned to the political party which they identify as being the one which has the interests of their class at heart.

There is good evidence for the decline of party identification, and most commentators take the year 1970 as very roughly the date when things changed. Between 1945 and 1970 there were high levels of party identification, but in the years 1970 up to the present this has less clearly been the case. Evidence for a decline in party identification includes the following:

1 The decline of the two-party system with the emergence of the Liberals (currently the Liberal Democrats). The effect this had on voting in general elections can be seen from table 4.3. Before 1974 the Labour and Conservative Parties between them generally won something in the region of 90 per cent of the votes. After 1970 (with the exception of 1979), the two main parties sometimes struggled to get more than 70 per cent of the votes, and failed altogether in 2005. Clearly there has been a change in party identification and a decline in identification with the major parties.
2 Opinion poll evidence shows that people do identify less than they did in the past with political parties. There are simply fewer people around today who say they 'strongly support' a political party. This looks like a symptom of the disengagement with politics which is demonstrated most clearly by declining turnout at elections.

Table 4.3 Support for Labour and Conservatives as a % of total vote, 1945–2005

Election	% of voters supporting the two major parties
1945	88
1950	90
1951	97
1955	96
1959	93
1964	88
1966	90
1970	89
Feb 1974	75
Oct 1974	75
1979	81
1983	70
1987	73
1992	76
1997	74
2001	72
2005	68

Source: Compiled from Butler and Kavanagh, *The General Election of 2001*, and MORI final aggregate analysis

3 Membership of political parties has declined. Membership of the Conservative Party in the 1950s was two million, and there were one million full Labour Party members. In 2002 it was 330,000 and 280,000 respectively. By 2005 Labour Party membership had fallen again to about 198,026, although the Conservatives had risen slightly to 290,000. There were also 72,000 Liberal Democrats. Obviously this loss of party membership suggests a general decline in party identification.

4 Parties change. The Labour Party radically altered its ideology in the 1990s and it is with party ideology that people tend to identify. After all, what else would they identify with? Labour has openly said that it wishes to attract middle-class voters. The same could be said of the Conservative rejection of the ideology of one-nation Toryism (on which, see chapter 8) under Thatcher, and its revival under Cameron.

It still remains the case that many people do regularly vote for the same party. The lowest point in the fortunes of the Labour Party was the 1983 general election, when it was reduced to its absolute core support. This still amounted to 27.6 per cent of the voters. If 1997 was the lowest point of Conservative support, it means that their core is slightly bigger, at 31 per cent. In 2001, MORI found that 70 per cent of those polled said they felt strongly or fairly strongly attached to a party. This was a decline by 5 per cent on 1997, but it showed quite a large amount of continued party identification. What is more, the period 1945–70 did see some remarkable swings in support, especially the landslide Labour victory of 1945 and then the Conservative recovery in the 1950s. But the general view among political scientists is that there has been an increase since the 1970s in the number of **floating voters** and in **voter volatility**. Clearly floating voters are not strong party identifiers.

> **Floating voters** (or swing voters): voters who are not naturally or reliably attached to a particular party and who vote for different parties at different times.

> **Voter volatility**: the changeable nature of modern voters, who are willing to switch their votes from one party to another. The opposite is voter stability.

Question: Discuss the major changes in voting behaviour since 1979.

4.3 Other long-term factors in voting behaviour: geography, gender, age and race

Having considered the influence of social class on voting habits, we need to look at the correlation between other significant factors in people's lives and how they vote: where they live, their sex, their age and what ethnic group they belong to.

Geographical factors

If we know where someone lives, we can predict their voting behaviour with greater certainty than anything else about them, apart (in some cases) from their race. Labour is supported very strongly in Wales and Scotland. This effect has grown in the last three decades. In 1945, the Conservatives won as many seats in Scotland as Labour. The rise of Scottish nationalism may account for the Conservative decline (if one adds together the Conservative share of the vote with that of the Scottish National Party in Scotland and of Plaid Cymru in Wales, one arrives at roughly the Conservative share of the vote in England). Labour's devolution policy is clearly a success in shoring up their vote in Scotland and Wales. The large number of Scottish ministers in the Labour Cabinet presumably makes a difference too. Since its foundation, Labour has been successful in the industrial north of England – and this is still the case. In order to win a general election, however, Labour needs to appeal to the populous south of England, and in 1997, 2001 and 2005 it did

Table 4.4 Geographical support for parties in the 2005 election: % share of the vote

Region	Conservatives	Labour	Liberal Democrat	Nationalists
London	32	39	22	
South-east England	45	24	25	
South-west England	39	33	23	
Eastern England	43	30	22	
England: East Midlands	37	37	18	
England: West Midlands	35	39	19	
England: Yorkshire & Humberside	29	44	21	
North-west England	29	45	21	
North-east England	23	53	20	
Wales	21	43	18	13 (Plaid Cymru)
Scotland	16	40	23	18 (SNP)

Source: MORI final aggregate analysis

very well there, although it was still behind the Conservatives, except in London itself. The Conservatives have held onto their rural and suburban vote in England quite firmly, having done well in these areas for centuries. In 2005, they won more votes in England as a whole than did Labour, but because of the FPTP system, they won fewer seats there. The Liberal Democrats have support which is more evenly spread across the country than that of other parties, although in 1997 and 2001 they made an effort to build on a power-base in the West of England; by 2005, however, they were beaten into third place by Labour even there. The full figures are given in table 4.4.

Gender

It used to be the case that women had a greater tendency than men to vote Conservative rather than Labour. This is described as the 'gender gap': the difference between men and women in terms of their voting behaviour. This was not a very pronounced effect, but was definitely there. It may have been connected to the age factor, since women live longer than men, and the old tend to vote Conservative. It was also explained by saying that Conservative values tended to appeal to women, who were said to like an ordered, hierarchical society, and who wanted to improve their social position more than men. The fact is, however, that in 1997 and 2001 there was virtually no difference between how men and women voted (except in turnout, which is discussed in chapter 2), although women still tended towards the Conservatives and the Liberal Democrats very marginally more than men. This was despite the fact (or possibly because of the fact) that New Labour was trying hard to win women's votes, by selecting women candidates more than the other two parties, for example. By 2005, however, Labour was certainly appealing to women more than the Conservatives were – see table 4.5.

Age

The old tend to vote Conservative and the young tend to vote Labour or Liberal Democrat. This is generally attributed to psychological factors: the rebelliousness of the young, and the 'small-c' conservatism of the

Table 4.5 Women and men voters in the 1997, 2001 and 2005 general elections: % share of the vote (figures for 1997 in brackets, figures for 2001 in bold, figures for 2001 in italics)

Gender	Conservative	Labour	Liberal Democrat
Men	(30) **32** *34*	(45) **42** *34*	(17) **18** *22*
Women	(32) **33** *32*	(44) **42** *38*	(17) **19** *23*

Source: MORI final aggregate analysis

Table 4.6 Different age groups and voting behaviour in the 1997, 2001 and 2005 general elections: % share of the vote (figures for 1997 in brackets, figures for 2001 in bold, figures for 2001 in italics)

Age group	Conservative	Labour	Liberal Democrat
18–24	(27) **27** *28*	(49) **41** *38*	(16) **24** *26*
25–34	(28) **24** *25*	(49) **51** *38*	(16) **19** *27*
35–44	(28) **28** *27*	(48) **45** *41*	(17) **19** *23*
45–54	(31) **32** *31*	(41) **41** *35*	(20) **20** *25*
55–64	(36) **39** *39*	(39) **37** *31*	(17) **17** *22*
65+	(36) **40** *41*	(41) **39** *35*	(17) **17** *18*

Source: MORI final aggregate analysis

old. As can be seen from table 4.6, however, Labour in 2005 was able – as it had been in the two previous elections – to maintain or build on support among the older age groups, without losing the support of the young. Conversely, the Conservatives were unable to extend their support among the young. The Liberal Democrats had a more even range of support among both young and old. This seems to support the psychological explanation if one accepts that the Liberal Democrats are a party of the centre.

Race

All the evidence suggests that immigrant groups since the 1940s have felt far happier voting Labour than voting Conservative or even Liberal Democrat. In 2001, it is reckoned that 76 per cent of black voters and 69 per cent of Asian voters voted Labour compared with a paltry 9 per cent of black voters who supported the Conservatives and 11 per cent of Asian voters who did. Only 4 per cent of each group is said to have voted Liberal Democrat. Labour's policies tend to be more favourable towards ethnic minorities, and they field more candidates from ethnic minority groups. It may simply also be that immigrants and people from the ethnic minorities tend to be lower down the social scale, and such people tend to vote Labour anyway. They also tend to live in inner-city areas, where Labour constituencies are often to be found. Afro-Caribbean Britons tend to vote Labour a little more than Asians, some of whom are likely (as businessmen) to be natural Conservatives anyway. Since the Iraq War of 2003–4, Labour has lost support among the Islamic community and this support has generally gone to the Liberal Democrats. Labour's poor showing in the by-elections in July 2004 in Birmingham and Leicester demonstrates this, but it may just be a typical by-election protest. The figures for the 2005 general election are worth comparing with those for 2001 given above: the non-white population voted 19 per cent Conservative, 56 per cent Labour and 22 per cent Liberal Democrat. The slump in the Labour black vote owed much to changes in how Muslims voted. In seats with a more than 10 per cent Muslim electorate, the Labour vote fell on average by 3 per cent more than in other seats. The loss of the safe Labour seat in Bethnal Green and Bow to George Galloway, the anti-war candidate for the Respect Party, at the general election of 2005 also shows this: this was a seat with a large Islamic population of Asian origin.

Question: 'Voting behaviour is influenced more by political issues than by social factors such as class, age or gender.' Discuss.

Activity

Draw up a questionnaire to test the political views of your class and other willing participants you can find. The questions could include the following:

1 What party would you vote for? (force them to answer this!)
2 What party did your mother/father/grandparents/elder siblings vote for? (Try to build up a picture of the family's views)
3 What social class is your family?
4 What ethnic group?
5 Where do you live (which region in UK)?
6 Where do you live (which neighbourhood in your locality)?

Try to devise some more, relevant questions. When you have got a reasonably large response, analyse your findings. Do your findings support any of the theories given above, especially those linked to the social structures model?

4.4 Short-term or political factors in voting behaviour

There have always been voters who are non-aligned and who are willing to vote differently at different elections. There seem to be more such voters in recent years (since about 1970). These voters respond to the direct appeal of the political parties, to short-term campaigning and to real political factors. These are what political scientist Denis Kavanagh called matters of 'recency', by which he drew attention to the fact that people take into account recent experiences when voting, and do not rely on the long-term socialization associated with the sociological theories given in the previous section. This approach to understanding voting behaviour is called 'consumer-model voting', or 'issues voting'. Behind it lies a broader theory of human behaviour, made popular in America in the 1950s, which is called 'rational choice theory'. Hence, we have yet another term which can be used to describe this view of voting – the rational choice model of voting behaviour. It sees the voter as a shopper, who studies the political scene like someone going around the supermarket, and who decides how to vote on the basis of making a rational decision about what he or she thinks is the best thing for the country and/or for themselves.

There would seem to be a number of factors that this supermarket voter takes into account – see figure 4.1 for a list of these. It is quite a list, and it raises a problem straightaway with this analysis of voting behaviour: namely, what if the voter has different opinions on each of the headings given in figure 4.1?

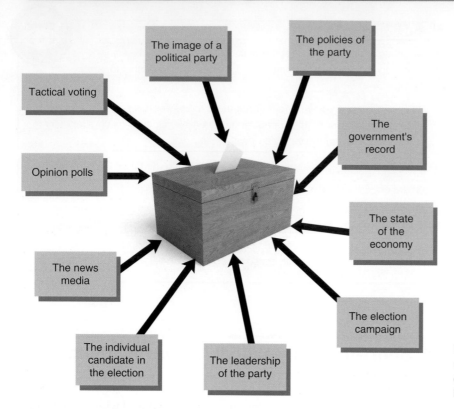

Figure 4.1 Consumer model voting: what the voter considers when deciding how to vote

What if he or she prefers the Liberal Democrat image, likes the Conservative leader and loves Labour policies? Obviously, this is likely to happen to some extent. In 2005, many more voters in opinion polls said they respected Charles Kennedy than were prepared to vote for his party. The Holy Grail of political scientists is to find a model of voting behaviour which helps place these various factors in order of importance. Like the Holy Grail, it is probably true to say that a formula of this sort is never likely to be found. We shall now briefly examine each of these factors in turn.

Party image

If we pursue the analogy with shopping further, marketing experts say that when buying a product (say, a motor car) consumers tend to consider the 'brand image' – an intangible, vague sense of what the product will say about them when they buy it. Branding a political party therefore becomes important in winning a general election. A brand may in some ways be very close to old-fashioned ideology, repackaged for the modern world. The image will consist of a sense of what the party stands for, or which principles lie behind what it aims to achieve in power. A modern party brand image is less specific than ideology: it is a matter of broad values rather than political philosophy.

But it is still important. The danger in modern politics is that the political parties tend to get closer and closer together as they distance themselves from their old ideologies. So 'values' or 'image' are still important in giving the party an identity. A party must somehow differentiate itself from its rivals. In 1995 Labour adopted a new statement of ideology, a new Clause IV. Many commentators pointed out that it was such a broad and vague wish list that it was very difficult to disagree with it or to complain that some area was neglected. It looks rather like the statements of principle which the other two major British parties have from time to time put forward. But Labour was successful under Tony Blair in putting across a clear image. It became 'New' Labour, modern and young, thus rejecting 'Old' Labour and trade-union extremism. It was sober and sensible in economic terms, but also caring and compassionate on the social front. In the elections of 1997 and 2001, the Conservatives could not shake off a negative image: old-fashioned, faintly bigoted, sleazy and obsessive. In 2005, they were probably beginning to do so, partly perhaps because by then Labour was developing some of those traits itself.

Policy

Salient issue: one which the voters consider to be important.

It seems altogether right that voters should look at the policy proposals of the major parties on the current political issues when making their decision to vote. Political scientists rank issues according to their saliency. Obviously, it ought to be the **salient issues** which decide the outcome of the election.

Table 4.7 The salient issues in 2005: % of people who rated these issues as the most important in helping them decide how to vote	
Health	21
The economy generally	15
Law and order	15
Education	14
Taxation and public services	13
Asylum and immigration	8
Iraq	3
The fight against terrorism	3
Europe	2
Source: MORI final aggregate analysis	

Once the consumer-model voter has decided which the salient issues are, he or she then has to decide which political party has the best policies on them. Saliency is obviously very important. On some issues in 2005, the voters preferred the Conservative approach to that of Labour. This was true of policy on asylum and immigration. But, as can be seen from table 4.7, asylum was not considered a very salient issue. So, the Conservatives were wasting their time concentrating on this topic, because voters did not see it as a really significant political problem. The important issues to the voters in 2005 were the economy and health, and on these Labour was thought to have the best policies. In theory, the election will be won by the party which has most popular support for the most salient issues. But it is worth striking a note of caution here, by considering the evidence given in figure 4.2

Obviously, the data in figure 4.2 supports the idea of consumer-model voting perfectly when we look at the elections of 1997 and 2001. Clearly in these two instances Labour had better policies, according to the sample of people polled, and as a result they won. In fact, it is a bit surprising that they did not do even better in these elections, judging from the evidence in figure 4.2. But the problem lies with 1992 and 2005. In 1992 Labour had the better policies, not by a wide margin, but the better policies nevertheless. Yet that year, the Conservatives actually won the election quite comfortably.

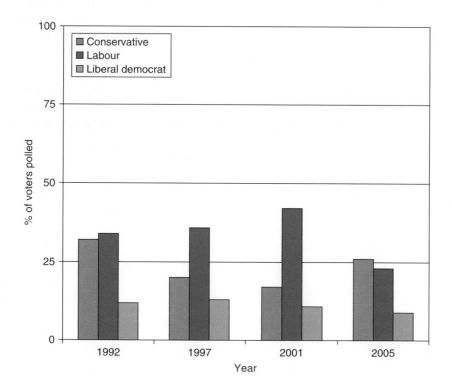

Figure 4.2   Which party had the best policies, 1992–2001?

However, there were doubts about the accuracy of the opinion polls, largely because they all seemed to exaggerate Labour support, so perhaps the problem is no more deep-rooted than that and may be very slight. But the phenomenon re-emerges in 2005, with voters seeing the Conservatives that year as having a lead on the major issues.

The government record

Do voters vote retrospectively or prospectively? Do they look back and judge the past when they vote, or do they look forward, having evaluated the policies of each of the parties in turn? The conventional wisdom is that there is a tendency for governments to lose rather than for oppositions to win elections. Obviously, however, the answer is to some extent a bit of a mixture. The points that follow include some of the retrospective and forward-looking factors which the discerning issues-voting citizen will consider.

The state of the economy and the 'feel-good' factor

One variant of the rational choice model of voting behaviour stresses the importance not just of policy and party image, but of the political circumstances in which the election is fought, and how these interact with the competing policies of the parties. This is the 'voting context' model of voting behaviour. The most important in these factors influencing voting are economic ones, and also a wider question of a national 'feel-good' factor.

According to the evidence of table 4.7, in 2005 economic issues were considered less salient by the voters than the state of the health service. This may have been because the economy was strong in 2005. However, there is a good case for arguing that the economy is the chief concern of voters. David Sanders has shown that there is a complex relationship between the economy and voting behaviour. When we talk about the economy, we mean a large number of things which affect people's lives very closely and which the voters know the politicians can do something to change: unemployment, inflation, interest rates and taxation, for example. Sanders's studies have covered a large number of elections, and his theory has been refined and improved over the years as the evidence has built up. The picture is not a very simple one, but there is clearly a link between the economy and voting behaviour. It is still possible for voters to vote for a government which seems to have given them a slump – they did this in 1983 and (possibly) 1992. They do so because they do not think the opposition has got a better plan for dealing with the slump than the government has.

It is also safe to conclude that voters will vote for a government which has given them economic prosperity, a 'feel-good' factor, and tend to punish a government which has not. John Major's government after 1992 presided over one major economic catastrophe (Black Wednesday, when the currency lost initially 15 per cent of its value) and a mini slump, so it is not surprising that the voters punished it in 1997. In fact, the economy was improving by 1997, but the voters did not 'feel' any better, because the Chancellor of the Exchequer, Ken Clarke, had followed a prudent course and not wasted money on tax cuts. In the same way, by 2001, the economy was in very good shape and the voters were grateful to Tony Blair and Gordon Brown, although they ought also to have been grateful to John Major and Ken Clarke (but obviously could not vote for them!). The 'feel-good' factor can also result from other causes: many people say that the victory won by Margaret Thatcher in the Falklands in 1982 contributed to her success in 1983. Harold Wilson even attributed his victory in 1966 to England winning the World Cup. In 2005, the economy was perceived to be strong and Gordon Brown had succeeded in persuading people that this was due to his work. A Guardian/ICM poll found that 46 per cent of voters thought that Labour had the best economic policies, compared with 21 per cent who thought the Conservatives did.

The election campaign

If voters are consumers, then a marketing campaign can make a difference. Modern election campaigners have clearly used modern marketing techniques. It is common to say we have learnt these techniques from the USA, but advertising tends to be a global business these days. What follows are some of the main points about modern election campaigns.

Expense

Campaigns cost more and more. Much is spent on buying advertising space in newspapers. On the face of it, if campaigns matter, the Conservatives should always have won elections, since they could, until recently, always raise more money to spend than Labour. In 2000, however, national party expenditure in general elections was capped by law: for the 2005 election the figure was fixed at £19.23 million per party. Whether expenditure makes much difference is open to question. The Liberal Democrats always spend far less than the Big Two parties, but generally increase their share of the vote during the campaign. The reason may be that they often enjoy almost as much as the Big Two of that best of all marketing commodities – free publicity, on the TV and in the media.

Professional approach

Each party has its expert campaign advisers. Labour relied in recent years on figures such as Philip Gould, Peter Mandelson and Alastair Campbell; Thatcher notoriously employed the up-market advertising agents, Saatchi and Saatchi;

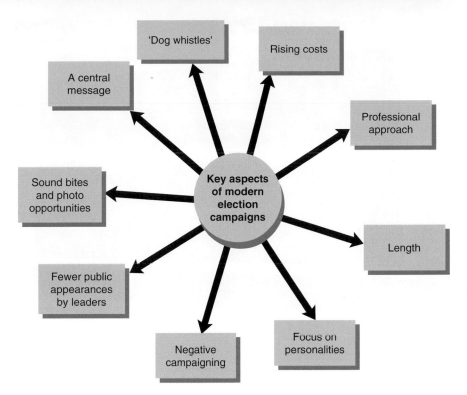

Figure 4.3 Key aspects of modern election campaigns

and in 2001 Labour used a firm called TWBA, the creative director of which, Trevor Beattie, was well known in the trade for his Wonderbra campaign. The well-fought Conservative campaign of 2005 was masterminded by a veteran of a number of Australian elections, Lynton Crosby.

The long campaign

One problem with assessing the impact of a modern election campaign is that it is not clear that a party is ever not electioneering. Spin-doctors will be advising the party all the time on the value of and methods for winning publicity and support, and not just at election time.

Concentration on personalities

Campaigning tends to focus on the personalities of the leaders of the main parties. However, although election broadcasts do this, so far there has not been in Britain a face-to-face televised debate between the party leaders, although it has become one of the rituals of the campaign for the possibility of such a debate to be discussed. This is one aspect of US elections which has not been copied in the UK. In 2005, we came quite close to it, however, with the three leaders answering questions on TV before the same audience one after the other.

This anti-Labour Party advertisement was used by the Conservative Party during the 1997 general election campaign. The rise in negative campaigning over the past ten years has been heavily criticized by political commentators who believe it leads to a greater degree of apathy and disenchantment among voters

Negative campaigning

Often also said to be an import from America, the use of the campaign to make negative points about the other parties is now a normal part of an election. Another aspect of negative campaigning much used by the Liberal Democrats is to make private polling claims about the position of the parties in three-way marginals in order to persuade voters to give their tactical votes to the Liberal Democrats.

The absence of genuinely public appearances by leaders

Public speeches and debates were commonplace until the 1980s. They now rarely happen. Leaders are afraid of being covered in eggs and flour by the people they wish to represent. What happens instead is that they appear before carefully selected audiences of supporters, giving the impression of being out and about, but without risking any dents to their pride. Labour seemed to be moving away from this trend in 2005, with a number of highly reported appearances of Tony Blair in public, but these were actually stage-managed, with Labour Party employees and trusted supporters forming the audience of 'real people'. On the other hand, Charles Kennedy did hold genuinely public meetings in marginal constituencies, like Cambridge, where his courage in speaking before a large audience was very favourably received: his party went on to win Cambridge for the first time in living memory.

Sound bites and photo opportunities

One reason for not wishing to be attacked by voters in public is that it would result in a photograph which would be used very widely on television. It is important that the photographs that are used give a positive image. Television likes people to be concise, and hence the need for handy slogans and smart comments which can be broadcast without troubling the patience of the viewers for too long.

A central message

In a world of sound bites it is important for politicians to stay focused on the main message they wish to convey to the electorate. Leaders will constantly repeat what they think are the vote-winning slogans, and other candidates will be carefully drilled by the party organizer on the need to stick to these simple messages.

'Dog whistles'

Lynton Crosby was credited with introducing this technique in 2005: politicians maintain the support of their core voters by making oblique references to topics of interest to them: e.g. 'It's not racist to talk about immigration.'

But although all this looks very slick and professional, the fact is (as every person in marketing knows) that if the product is no good, you cannot sell it, no matter how wonderful your campaign is. It is well known that the Labour campaign in 1987 was generally very well run, but Labour still lost hands down. Similarly, there are claims that the 2001 and 2005 Conservative campaigns were quite good technically in terms of presentation, and they seem to have succeeded in shifting some votes back to the party during the month before each election, but Labour still won convincingly.

Local campaigns are also important. Each party will target specific 'battleground' constituencies – seats where they are particularly keen to win. This enhanced attention on the locality will tend to boost the party's results to a small degree, and it may be enough to secure victory if the seat is very marginal. The place will be frequently visited by the prominent figures in the party, and the local media will therefore cover the election in more depth. This local campaigning effort may be cancelled out, of course, if the opposing parties also think that this is a 'key' marginal.

The party leader

One thing which will influence people when they come to vote is the personality of the person who is standing for election. There are two aspects to this. First, the 'personality' of the party leader may count as one of the policy issues on which the consumer-voter bases his or her vote at a general election. Voters presumably want their country to be run by someone who is honest, reliable, clever, eloquent, strong and good at talking to foreign politicians. The election campaign tends to focus public attention on the party leaders, whose face is generally put on the front of the party manifesto, which the party leader is responsible for drawing up. Party election broadcasts and other television programmes often feature the leader and tell a story (give a 'narrative', to use the modern jargon) about the life of the leader. Tony Blair was keen to stress his family life, the fact that he did not have early ambitions to become a politician, and generally to portray himself as a young, ordinary sort of person. It is always helpful when giving a narrative of this sort to have come from a humble background. Blair could not do this, but at least he could stress the ordinary nature of his hobbies and interests. The rise of presidentialism in British politics is often connected to this growth of voters' interest in the party leader. We might say that in the British parliamentary democracy, according to constitutional theory, the general election is held to elect a collective leadership and also a constituency representative for the legislature, and hence it is not right for the voters to concentrate their attention too much on the character of the party leaders. But, on the other hand, there is a widespread belief that, in practice, the general election is, among other things, a sort of prime-ministerial election.

How significant a factor is the leader in an election? It presumably counts as one factor among many. The important thing is not the absolute value

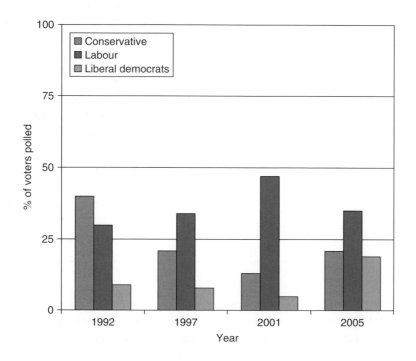

Figure 4.4 Which party was seen as having the best leader, 1992–2005? (% of those polled who said that the party had the best leader)

placed by voters on the leader's attributes, but the relative value, in comparison to those of the leaders of the opposition parties. Leadership qualities also seem to be variable: a leader can appear to the voters to have a lot of them at one time but fewer at other times: in 1992 Major was perceived to be better than Kinnock and won, while in 1997 Major was perceived as worse than Blair and lost. There is a case for saying that this factor in voting behaviour has grown in recent years with the increased media focus on party leaders, and the growth of 'presidentialism'. The appointment of David Cameron as Conservative leader in 2005 and then of Gordon Brown as Labour leader in 2007 both had a considerable impact on the opinion polls, increasing support for their parties by between 5 and 10 per cent as a more popular person took over.

The individual constituency candidate

How important is the individual candidate who is put up for election in each constituency by the parties? Parties expend a great deal of effort in choosing the right candidate and we are told that the role of the constituency MP has in the last generation become more significant. Is this reflected in a candidate-based approach to voting behaviour? Only to a very small extent, it seems. There is what is called an incumbency effect, the benefit received by the incumbent MP, or the MP who already has the seat. The incumbent has the advantage that he or she will have been well exposed in the local press and will also have helped a number of constituents in the MP's role as adviser and supporter of those in dispute with some public body. It is generally thought that this incumbency factor is worth something like 4–5 per cent extra votes. This effect is rather more strongly felt by Liberal Democrat incumbents and those from other small parties like the nationalists, and seems to be less significant in the case of the Conservatives. In 2005, it was recent incumbents who gained the biggest boost; that is, MPs who were elected in the previous election.

The news media

The news media covers television, radio, newspapers and, more recently, electronic communications. The impact of the media on voting behaviour and on politics in general is a huge and hotly disputed topic. Most of what the voter knows about politics comes to him or her through the media, rather than directly from the candidates and parties. On the whole, coverage by television and by radio is governed by stringent regulations which ensure impartiality. The political parties also strictly monitor television and radio to ensure that they keep to these rules on impartiality. Each party is allocated some broadcasting time in proportion to its voting strength in the last election and the number of constituencies it is contesting. This broadcasting time can then be used (without charge) for party election broadcasts. The neutrality of television is important, since most people get their political information this way.

The really contentious area concerns the newspapers, privately owned and subject to no rules concerning impartiality. The political parties can place advertisements (at considerable cost) in the newspapers. But mostly they have to rely on the news coverage of a biased editorial team. Until 1992, most newspapers in Britain were Conservative in their bias, and many commentators linked this to the fact that the Conservative Party was the most successful party in British politics. After 1992, this began to change and a number of high-circulation newspapers began to criticize the Conservatives and support Labour instead. The loss of support for the Conservatives was very significant in that John Major was undermined as Prime Minister in the very papers that his most loyal supporters actually read. This change in attitude was particularly true of the papers owned by the Australian-American Rupert Murdoch, who controls the largest circulation tabloid (or 'red-top', popular, down-market newspaper), the *Sun*, and the most famous broadsheet (or up-market, intellectual newspaper, formerly printed in large format), *The Times*, in which William Rees-Mogg, a true-blue Conservative journalist, was very outspoken in his attacks on Major.

The switch from Conservative to Labour in the *Sun* was also most dramatic. In 1992, on election day, the *Sun* devoted a large part of its paper to a savage attack on the Labour leader Neil Kinnock. After Kinnock had been defeated in the election, the paper claimed in an illiterate (but charming) headline: 'It's the *Sun* wot won it.'

But by 1997 and 2001, Murdoch had decided to back Tony Blair's New Labour; Labour duly won the elections. There were some doubts in 2005 over whether Murdoch would still support Blair, since the Conservatives were improving their poll ratings under the Euro-sceptic Michael Howard – Murdoch is also concerned about Europe, since it has quite a strict regulatory regime which might affect his media empire. But in the end Blair was simply too much of a winner to lose the support of News International, Murdoch's firm.

It is certainly helpful to Labour to have newspaper support, but it would be wrong to take the view that this is decisive. Labour was able to win elections before 1997 despite the opposition of a majority of the newspapers. Academic psychologists have studied the impact of the media on people and confirm that most people do not 'believe everything they read in the papers'. We tend to filter out opinions with which we disagree, and only accept as true what conforms to our own personal world-view. This certainly seems to be borne out by the evidence of table 4.8, which shows how in 2005 newspapers with quite solid Conservative support among their readers were still supporting

Newspaper	Broadsheet or tabloid	Party supported in 2005	Readership in 000s	% of readers supporting Con	% of readers supporting Lab	% of readers supporting Lib Dem
Mirror	T	L	4,657	15	60	18
Express	T	L	2,132	41	29	19
Sun	T	L	8,825	31	41	13
Mail	T	C	5,740	53	21	17
Star	T	L	1,965	17	53	16
Telegraph	B	C	2,181	61	15	17
Guardian	B	L	1,068	5	44	37
Times	B	L	1,655	40	26	29
Independent	B	LibDem ?	643	12	36	39
Financial Times	B	L	453	45	23	24

Table 4.8 National daily newspapers and the 2005 general election

Source: MORI, NRS

Labour in their coverage in the election. On the other hand, when Rupert Murdoch switched sides in the 1990s, it was after it had become quite clear that Labour would win the forthcoming election anyway. Who was leading whom: Murdoch or Blair? It remains to be seen whether Murdoch's support for Labour will be a permanent feature of British politics if the Conservatives develop a sustained opinion poll lead.

Dominant-ideology model of voting behaviour

Karl Marx argued that the main beliefs of a community were shaped by the 'ruling class', by which he meant the rich and powerful. In the days of Conservative dominance in British politics (the 1980s), political scientists P. Dunleavy and C. Husbands applied this important insight to the question of voting behaviour. They argued that the dominant ideology communicated to the voting population by the powerful institutions of government, business and the mass media was likely to influence how people voted. This helped to explain why the Conservatives tended to win elections more frequently (at that time) than Labour. It might also help explain why Labour was forced in the late 1980s and early 1990s to change its ideology and adopt a more centrist approach in order to be in a position to win elections. While this model is a useful corrective to ideas that people vote rationally as consumers, it might be said that it gives us very little guidance as to why in detail different people vote differently from one another at different times and in different

people 'swap' votes tactically. So, a Liberal Democrat who wanted to vote tactically for a Labour candidate in his or her constituency could link up with a Labour voter in a different constituency who was intent on doing the opposite. There was no way, of course, of ensuring that either person kept to the agreement. In 2005, the Liberal Democrats also benefited from negative voting, in this case as a result of disillusioned Labour supporters voting for them. It is unlikely, though, that such voters would also vote for the Conservative Party if it was the party more likely to unseat a Labour MP.

? *Question:* Assess the impact of campaigns on voting behaviour in general elections.

Activity

Review the contents of this chapter, and use the evidence given to evaluate (by giving points for and against) the current value of the following models of voting behaviour:

- social structures model
- party identification model
- rational choice model
- dominant ideology model
- voting context model

Which of these five models do you think fits the facts best?

SUMMING UP

The best approach to the study of voting behaviour is an interested scepticism. There does not seem to be any magic formula to explain why people vote as they do. The background is a dynamic one, with social change affecting how people vote, and with the parties themselves changing too. It would be wrong to deny that sociological factors are not still a highly significant indicator of how people vote. But people do not explain their voting behaviour by saying, 'I voted Conservative because I live in Surrey'. They give short-term political explanations instead: 'I am voting Conservative because I believe they have a tougher approach to defence policy, which for me is the most important issue.' It would seem

to be true that long-term or sociological factors are of declining importance, and that increasing numbers of voters make up their minds according to political or short-term factors. Political parties will be successful if they make sure their core supporters (in sociological terms) are secure. Then the party has to reach out to attract the floating voters and with luck some of the core supporters of the opposition. Just because Margaret Thatcher won working-class votes in large numbers and Tony Blair won middle-class votes in large numbers does not mean that class is not a significant factor in voting behaviour. Thatcher and Blair still relied on their core class support as well as winning over new voters.

Further reading

D. Butler and D. Kavanagh, *The British General Election of 1997* (Palgrave, 1997): this and the next two books are the great academic studies of the elections, brim full of statistics and insights.

D. Butler and D. Kavanagh, *The British General Election of 2001* (Palgrave, 2001).

D. Butler and D. Kavanagh, *The British General Election of 2005* (Palgrave, 2005).

D. Denver, *Elections and Voting in Britain* (Palgrave, 2002): a very clear analysis of changes over time in voting behaviour.

Ron Johnston and Charles Pattie, *Putting Voters in Their Place: Geography and Elections in Great Britain* (OUP, 2006): academic and up-to-date.

D. Kavanagh, *Election Campaigning* (Blackwell, 1995): a careful and engaging dissection of how election campaigning has changed in recent years.

Websites

www.electoralcommission.gov.uk (Electoral Commission)

http://www.essex.ac.uk (British election study, academic study from University of Essex)

http://www.mori.com (MORI, the pollsters)

http://www.nrs.co.uk (National Readership Survey, newspaper circulation figures)

www.YouGov.com (YouGov, the pollsters)

www.icmresearch.co.uk (ICM polls)

Case Studies of
Recent General
Elections

Making connections

This chapter fills in background which will help you understand the chapter on electoral behaviour and also help with the discussions of parties and their ideologies and policies which follow in chapters 7 and 8. There is great scope for making recent elections the subject of a case study, or looking in depth at the work of a particular government (e.g. the Labour government 1997–2001) on which there is much information.

5 Case Studies of Recent General Elections

KEY TOPICS

- Elections as turning-points and landslides
- The 1997 general election
- Why Labour won in 1997
- The 2001 general election
- Why Labour won again in 2001
- The 2005 general election
- Why Labour won again in 2005

SETTING THE SCENE

The last three chapters have focused largely on voting and elections, participation and referendums, the electoral processes themselves and why people vote the way they do. This chapter looks at how these work out in practice, by investigating the results of three general elections:1997, 2001 and 2005. We start by outlining the outcome of these three elections, all of which resulted in a Labour victory, and then move on to trying to give explanations for these results. The explanations are largely of the political, or short-term, sort, to use the classification given in the previous chapter.

5.1 Elections as turning-points and landslides

> **Landslide election**: an election which gives the winner a large majority and which is also a turning point, bringing in a new party to government.

The history of the past half-century or so of British politics is broken up by political scientists into three periods, each one starting with a great election victory. The first of these significant turning points was 1945. As can be seen from table 5.1, this produced a huge majority for the Labour Party under Clement Attlee; it was a **landslide election**. This result was to some degree unexpected and was highly significant because it gave Labour what seemed at the time like a huge majority. As a result, Attlee brought in a great series

Table 5.1 Results of British general elections, 1945–2005*

Year	Total no. of MPs	Conservative votes Share of vote (%) No. of MPs	Labour votes Share of vote (%) No. of MPs	Liberal votes Share of vote (%) No. of MPs	Party forming government
1945	640	9,577,667 39.8% 213	11,632,191 48.3% 393	2,197,191 9.1% 12	Lab
1950	625	12,502,567 43.5% 299	13,266,592 46.1% 315	2,621,548 9.1% 9	Lab
1951	625	13,717,538 48% 321	13,948,605 48.8% 295	730,556 2.5% 6	Con
1955	630	13,311,936 49.7% 345	12,404,970 46.4% 277	722,405 2.7% 6	Con
1959	630	13,749,830 49.4% 365	12,215,538 43.8% 258	1,638,571 5.9% 6	Con
1964	630	12,001,396 43.4% 304	12,205,814 44.1% 317	3,092,878 11.2% 9	Lab
1966	630	11,418,433 41.9% 253	13,064,951 47.9% 363	2,327,533 8.5% 12	Lab
1970	630	13,145,123 46.4% 330	12,178,295 43% 288	2,117,033 7.5% 6	Con
Feb. 1974	635	11,872,180 37.8% 297	11,646,391 37.1% 301	6,058,744 19.3% 14	Lab
Oct. 1974	635	10,464,817 35.8% 277	11,457,079 39.2% 319	5,346,754 18.3% 13	Lab
1979	635	13,697,923 43.9% 339	11,532,218 37% 269	4,313,804 13.8% 11	Con
1983	650	13,012,315 42.4% 397	8,456,934 27.6% 209	7,780,949 25.4% 23	Con

Table 5.1 *(continued)*

Year	Total no. of MPs	Conservative votes Share of vote (%) No. of MPs	Labour votes Share of vote (%) No. of MPs	Liberal votes Share of vote (%) No. of MPs	Party forming government
1987	650	13,763,066 42.3% 376	10,029,778 30.8% 229	7,341,290 22.6% 22	Con
1992	651	14,092,891 41.9% 336	11,559,735 34.4% 271	5,999,384 17.8% 20	Con
1997	659	9,602,857 30.7% 165	13,516,632 43.2% 418	5,242,894 16.8% 46	Lab
2001	659	8,357,622 31.7% 166	10,724,895 40.7% 412	4,812,833 18.3% 52	Lab
2005	646**	8,772,473 32.4% 197 (198**)	9,547,944 35.2% 356	5,981,874 22.0% 62	Lab

* Three major parties only

** The election in the safe Conservative seat of Staffordshire South was delayed because of the death of one of the candidates, but the results are included here

Source: http://www.electoral-reform.org.uk

of reforms: nationalizing large parts of British industry and setting up the welfare state. This election also ushered in a period which later historians have called the 'post-war consensus' (discussed in chapters 7 and 8) and which ended with another important election in 1979. Although not technically a landslide, in that it did not give the new government a huge majority, the 1979 election was nevertheless very significant because it was the start of the Thatcherite period: 18 years of uninterrupted one-party government under the Conservatives, which lasted until 1997. Then, in 1997, the 'New' Labour Party under Tony Blair won an important election victory, ushering in the long period of Labour government. A landslide accompanies a great change in public opinion, and the fact that they occur at all challenges some of the assumptions made in the previous chapter about how people vote.

5.2 The 1997 general election

As long as it is held within five years of the previous general election, a Prime Minister can decide when to hold the next one. Since his government had become more and more unpopular as time went by, it was not at all surprising that the Conservative Prime Minister, John Major, decided to hang on until he had enjoyed the fullest period possible as Prime Minister. When the election was finally held it produced a landmark result, which changed the shape of British politics. The 1997 election was one of the great turning-points in British politics, on a par with 1945 – the election of Clement Attlee's Labour government – and 1979 – the election of the first Thatcher Conservative government. The result can be summarized as follows.

1 Labour won 418 seats in the House of Commons, giving them a majority of 179. This was an outstanding result: Labour's biggest majority in its history and the biggest parliamentary majority for any party since 1832. It was a landslide, a major change, not least because Labour had been out of power for 18 years.

2 The Labour victory was won on 43.2 per cent of the popular vote. This represented an important improvement on Labour's recent previous achievements – in 1992 they had won only 34.4 per cent of the vote. But it was hardly an outstanding share of the vote (less than nine post-war governments).

3 The Conservatives went from having 336 MPs in 1992 to having only 165 in 1997. This was a desperate result for the Conservatives – their worst since 1832. Their share of the vote was reduced to 30.7 per cent. Although a poor result, this was better than Labour had managed in 1983, when they were at the bottom of their electoral cycle and only received 27.6 per cent. Some commentators argue that the Conservatives have a slightly stronger core vote than Labour.

4 Turnout in the election was very low. The proportion of those eligible to vote who voted was 71.5 per cent. This was lower than for any previous general election since 1935. The main reason for this low turnout is probably that the result was widely predicted in advance, and so people did not bother to vote because they thought they could not affect the outcome. In addition, the two major political parties were rather similar in terms of their policies.

5 The Liberal Democrats did very well in terms of how many seats they won: 46, which for them was a post-war record. This was despite the fact that they won a slightly lower share of the vote than they had done in 1992 (when they got 20 MPs). The Liberal Democrats benefited from the overall swing against the Conservatives, in which they were associated by the

voters with Labour. They also successfully targeted seats in the south-west of England, building on a regional base there.

A new party called the Referendum Party also did surprisingly well in the 1997 general election, gaining 811,827 votes, the largest number to have been won by a fourth party in any election. The Referendum Party campaigned in favour of holding a referendum on the subject of the European single currency. Essentially, however, it was an anti-European party: most of those who wanted a referendum on Europe basically wanted the opportunity to vote 'no'. If elected to government, the party said it would hold a referendum and would then resign from government and call another general election in which it would not stand. Despite the fact that, under pressure from their campaign, all the other three major political parties also agreed to hold a referendum on the single currency (although they did not say when they would do it), the Referendum Party still contested the election and gained from this interesting protest vote – but won no MPs. No referendum has been held on this issue to date and the UK has not joined the euro zone, probably in large measure because of the Referendum Party. It might be said, though, that after Labour, the Referendum Party was, in a sense, the most successful party in 1997.

5.3 Why Labour won in 1997

A simple, but straightforward, way to explain an election result in a two-party system is to do so in terms of why one party was unpopular (in this case the Conservative governing party of John Major) and also in terms of why the alternative party (the Labour Party of Tony Blair) was popular.

Conservative unpopularity

'Black Wednesday'

Almost as soon as he had won the general election of 1992, John Major slipped on a major banana skin. On Black Wednesday – 16 September 1992 – there was a currency crisis, as a result of which the pound initially lost 15 per cent of its value on the currency markets. The causes of this crash were little to do with the government – the Exchange Rate Mechanism of the European Union was not functioning well, and speculators in New York found that they could make money by buying sterling cheap and then selling it back to the British government at a higher price (this was due to a policy of intervention to keep up the price of the pound which any reasonable government would have followed). Arguably, the collapse of sterling was not such a bad thing, since it meant that exports could be sold more cheaply abroad and this would boost the economy. The total cost of intervention on the markets in support of the pound was revealed in 2005 to have been £3.3 billion – a large, but not colossal, sum (it was estimated in the press to have been more at the time). But the government got the blame for it. Conservative governments had always claimed to be better at running the economy than Labour, and the only occasions in the past when similar crashes had taken place had been under Labour governments. Major had won the election of 1992 by claiming that the economy would be safer in Conservative hands than in those of Labour. It was not surprising, therefore, that public confidence in the the party slumped after Black Wednesday and, according to the evidence of opinion polls, it never really recovered.

Sleaze

Most Conservative MPs and ministers were (and are) admirable, public-spirited people of high moral character. But there were a number of cases in the 1990s which hit the headlines and which showed up some Conservative politicians in a much worse light. There were sex scandals involving ministers, and some allegations of corruption. The Scott Report revealed a less than completely straightforward approach by some ministers over the 'arms to Iraq' scandal. As a result of this, Major appointed a Commission to look into standards in public life under a senior judge, Lord Nolan, which reported in 1995. When the Nolan Report was published, Major began to implement some of its recommendations. But nevertheless, by 1997, the Conservative Party had acquired a reputation for sleaze, while Labour appeared to be fresh and pure.

No feel-good factor

John Major had won the 1992 election when the economy was in rather a poor state. The housing market had slumped and a lot of people were suffering from high interest rates on their mortgages, and in some cases from 'negative equity' – the unpleasant experience of owing more on their house than it was worth. By 1997, the economy was actually recovering quite strongly, and was in the capable hands of Kenneth Clarke, the Chancellor of the Exchequer. Interest rates by 1997 were low, as was inflation and there was expansion in the economy. But the general perception was that the economy was not particularly strong. Taxes remained quite high and public spending was relatively low, since the Chancellor was busily paying off the national debt. The result was that there was not a very strong feeling either that people were prosperous or that public services were being well funded.

Time for a change

The Conservatives were stale, and it was time for a change. In 1990, the party had successfully given the impression that it could change and renew itself by dumping Margaret Thatcher as leader. In 1992 it projected a new image under John Major, who, in contrast to Thatcher, had quite a youthful appeal. But by 1997 it was clear that it was still the same old party. Major added little that was very novel to Thatcherism and he himself was looking distinctly grey and unimaginative. It was time for a change. People were fed up with the Conservatives and wanted to give the alternative a chance.

Tactical voting

The unpopularity of the Conservative Party is shown by the prevalence of tactical voting in 1997. Tactical voting involves the voter in deciding to vote for anyone who has a chance of defeating the candidate of a particular party, in this case the Conservatives. So, voters who wished to vote tactically against Major's unpopular government would either vote for the Liberal Democrat candidate in their constituency or for the Labour candidate, depending on which one they thought was likely to win more votes. The widespread use of tactical voting helps also to account for the success of the Liberal Democrats in the 1997 election.

Reasons for Labour popularity

Tony Blair

It is very difficult to know how much voters are influenced in their voting intentions by the leader of the political party they are voting for. It would not be surprising if they were, because the result of the election will decide who is to be Prime Minister and the media pay huge attention to the holder of that office. Blair was certainly personally very important by 1997. He appeared young, intelligent and lively in contrast to Major. He had none of the apparent extremism or volatility of previous Labour leaders like Kinnock and Foot.

New Labour

But the Labour Party itself had changed considerably since the 1980s and it would have won the election in 1997 whoever was leading it. It was Blair who adopted the title 'New' in 1995, and this symbolized the change in Labour which had occurred over the previous few years. Labour was now less closely associated with trade unions, and even tried to appear to be linked to business. Labour won the support of powerful newspapers, especially those owned by Rupert Murdoch: the *Sun*, *The Times*, the *News of the World* and the *Sunday Times*. By 1997, most newspapers supported Labour, which was very unusual, since in the past the press had tended to be pro-Conservative. The biggest symbolic step for Labour was steered through by Blair in 1995, when the party ditched the old Clause IV of the party's constitution, which had promised the nationalization of the economy, and introduced a much more moderate and middle-of-the-road statement of ideals in the new Clause IV.

Tony Blair, John Prescott and Robin Cook launch the new Labour Party manifesto in April 1997

New policies?

The Labour Party in the post-war era had been a left-of-centre social democratic party which believed in relatively high levels of state welfare, a mixed economy, a foreign policy founded on international cooperation and a nuclear deterrent, and a criminal justice policy which involved removing the causes of crime by social reform. In the early 1980s these policies had shifted a few degrees to the left and had incorporated the desire to withdraw from the European Union. After 1983 there had been a gradual movement of Labour away from the left and back to the centre, a point which Tony Blair made a very good job of advertising. In fact, he claimed it was all very 'new'. The return to the centre meant the party was left with policies in 1997 which were hardly new, however, in comparison with those of the Conservative Party. Blair was keen to win Conservative waverers over to his side, and he therefore promised that there would be no change from Conservative policies in taxation and spending for two years after the election. Since economic and social policy are determined almost entirely by taxation and spending and, in addition, since these are for most voters the main election issues, the Labour Party was offering itself to the voters as a brighter version of Major's government. Labour placed emphasis in 1997 on small specific areas of policy where it said it could make a difference: the size of reception classes in primary schools, waiting lists for hospital appointments, the timetabling of court appearances for young criminals. In comparison with the Labour shopping-list in 1945, which had caused the last landslide in British politics, this was a laughable policy programme. Even on Europe, the difference between

Labour and the Conservatives was a matter of emphasis: both parties were pro-European, but Labour seemed more genuinely in favour of the euro and of the EU than its rivals. The major difference between the two parties was, according to political scientists, a huge one: Labour was promising a good deal of constitutional reform, including devolution to Scotland and Wales, electoral reform, changes to the House of lords, a Human Rights Act, freedom of information and reforms to local and regional government. The Conservatives opposed all of this. Although political scientists get excited by these matters, the majority of voters – even in Scotland and Wales – do not, and these were not therefore decisive issues in the election.

The electoral system

It is quite clear that the main factors in Labour's victory in 1997 were the Conservative unpopularity and voters' desire for a change. The image of the Labour Party in 1997 was very good, and that owed a lot to Tony Blair and his 'New' Labour colleagues. But what is less easy to explain is the sheer size of Labour's victory, especially given the fact that the real difference between what Labour and the Conservatives were offering was so slight. The reason for the landslide is certainly that the British electoral system tends to favour the victor in elections disproportionately. Once a party begins to cross a magic threshold in terms of the 'swing' from the rival party, it starts to benefit very strongly in the number of seats it wins.

 Question: Why did Labour achieve the landslide victory of 1997?

5.4 The 2001 general election

Since the early 1990s, the Labour Party had floated the idea that there should be a fixed term for Parliament of four years. In 1992 Neil Kinnock suggested that this should be made a legal, constitutional requirement. When new representative assemblies were set up in Scotland, Wales, Greater London and Northern Ireland, they were given four-year terms. But since 1997, Labour has not moved (perhaps predictably) to legislate on this matter. Nevertheless, after four years Tony Blair did decide to call another general election. To a very large extent, this turned out to be a re-run of the 1997 election. The main points to emerge from the election results were as follows:

1 Labour won. The party got almost exactly the same number of seats (412) as in 1997 (418), but with far fewer votes. In 1997 it had received 13,516,632 votes; in 2001 it won 10,724,895 – nearly 3 million fewer. The turnout was

much less for all parties. As a result of this, Labour was able to get virtually the same number of seats on a 2.5 per cent reduction in proportion of the vote. In 1997, it received 43.2 per cent of the popular vote; in 2001, it was only 40.7 per cent – the British electoral system produces curious results! This was still an impressive victory, with a Labour majority of 167: i.e., another landslide. Labour was confirmed as the new dominant party in British politics.

2   The Liberal Democrats also continued to do well, increasing their vote to 18.3 per cent and gaining 6 more seats (to 52). This was their best result since 1987 in terms of percentage of the vote (although well below their 1983 peak), and the best since the 1920s in number of seats. The disproportional British electoral system is responsible for producing such an odd state of affairs. It is still difficult to talk about a three-party system in the UK in the light of this result, but a two-and-a-half party system is a reasonable description.

3   The Conservatives, to be honest, did poorly again. They gained one more seat (to 166), and an extra 1 per cent of the vote, but this was still an appalling result for the formerly dominant party. They at least secured a single seat in Scotland after their disastrous whitewash there in 1997.

4   Turnout was 59.4 per cent, the lowest since the war, and much worse than 1997 (when it had been 71.5 per cent). In reality, since some people also seem to have stopped registering to vote, experts put the true turnout at 53 per cent. The fact that the result was a foregone conclusion was probably the chief factor in turnout.

5   Minor parties did not flourish much. The Scottish National Party lost a seat, and Plaid Cymru stayed the same. This suggested, according to some commentators, that devolution had had the effect of reducing nationalism in Scotland and Wales, at least at that stage. The Northern Ireland result was worrying, in that it saw an increase in support for the more extreme parties (Sinn Fein and DUP), thus putting a strain on the Good Friday Agreement. The other minor parties did not feature at all in terms of seats, but did get some votes (United Kingdom Independence Party (UKIP): 1.5 per cent; Green Party: 0.6 per cent). There was no surprise minor party result as in 1997 when the Referendum Party got more than 750,000 votes. The British electoral system is bad for minor parties, a fact which also depresses turnout.

5.5 Why Labour won again in 2001

The result in 2001 was so similar to that of 1997 that we can claim that many of the same sort of factors applied in both cases.

Labour popularity

Two principal factors accounted for Labour's continuing popularity in 2001:

1 Blair's leadership. Tony Blair remained popular with voters in 2001. His youthful vigour, good looks and charm remained. Added to that, voters had begun to appreciate his robust leadership style. He could seem arrogant and a bit of a know-all, but people rather respected this in a leader. Blair lost no opportunity to present himself as tough and able to take unpopular decisions. Shortly before the election, his wife had another child, Leo, and this added to his appeal as a family man. In objective terms he was clearly a 'winner' and people liked that. Hague offered nothing at all that could compete with this.

2 'It's the economy, stupid!' In 1992, Bill Clinton had coined this phrase so he and his team would remember that the election he was fighting in the USA then would be won or lost on the economy. People would vote for a government which was delivering prosperity and punish one which was not. The economy in the UK in 2001 was very strong, and people respected Labour for its economic achievements. In contrast, people still remembered the economic problems of the 1990s and blamed these on the Conservatives, who had nothing fresh to offer in terms of economic policy in 2001. The economic success of the Labour first term reassured former Conservative voters and gave them the courage to vote Labour in 2001.

Conservative unpopularity

The Conservative Party remained almost as unpopular as ever in 2001. It had not shaken off the poor reputation it had won in the 1990s, and in a sense voters were still angry with it for the perceived failures of the Major government.

Leadership

As soon as the results of the 1997 election were announced, John Major resigned and was replaced by William Hague after a leadership election among the party membership. Hague was elected leader because he was quite young, and it was thought that he would give the party a new image, which would win votes in the same way that the youthful Blair had won votes for Labour. Although young in years, Hague came across as faintly elderly to the voters, partly because he was bald. He was actually highly intelligent and a brilliant House of Commons debater, but he was not telegenic and was soon the butt of cruel cartoons.

Following the Conservative Party's disastrous showing in the 2001 general election, leader William Hague decided to stand down. Speculation was rife regarding his possible successors. After three months of in-party campaigning, Iain Duncan Smith was elected leader with 61 per cent of votes

Party disunity

The Conservative Party had been disunited and prone to quarrelling in the years of Major's government and this made it unpopular with the electorate. These quarrels continued after 1997. The main area of dispute was over Europe, with an increasingly large number of Conservative MPs tending towards Euro-scepticism, or distrust of the European Union. The party also quarrelled over whether it should remain Thatcherite or return to its Disraelian, One-Nation roots. There were also bitter disputes over the leadership, with Hague being undermined by an ambitious Michael Portillo, who wanted to be leader himself.

No new ideas

Portillo argued that the Conservative Party should move back to the centre of British politics and fight the Labour Party on its own territory. This would involve accepting multiculturalism and sexual diversity and it might also involve a wholehearted acceptance of the welfare state and of Europe. Broadly speaking, Hague and most of the party did not accept this new agenda, which made them seem old-fashioned and faintly xenophobic as a result. The party did not learn the lesson that Labour had learnt in the 1990s – namely, that it needed to present itself as new and different, not from its rival, but from its former unpopular self. It is fair to say, though, that it had taken Labour over a decade to realize the importance of this. The Conservatives had only had four years to do so.

An obsession with Europe

Although a sizeable part of the party disagreed with this view, Hague decided to make Europe the main issue of the 2001 election campaign. The Conservatives tried to paint Labour as pro-European and themselves as suspicious of the European Union. Although opinion polls suggested that this was a popular line to take, the problem was that Europe was not really what is called a salient issue, or one which is very important to the voters. Most people wanted to forget about Europe, and were more interested in their own living standards and the state of the public services. On these issues, the Conservatives had nothing to offer.

Labour's first term (1997–2001)

The Labour Party's victory in 2001 is best seen as a judgement by the electors on its previous four years of government: Labour's first term had largely been a successful and popular one. The main achievements and setbacks are now outlined.

The economy

As has been said, the economy flourished under Labour. Inflation remained low and unemployment began to fall. The economy grew at a good rate, at a time when other countries were having economic difficulties. Gordon Brown never ceased to tell people that this was a result of his 'prudent' approach as the 'Iron Chancellor' of the Exchequer. In fact, it is at least arguable that it was also the result of the Thatcherite policies of the previous 20 years, which had prepared the way for growth. It was certainly true that, after taking office in 1997, the New Labour government followed for two years precisely the same economic policy as its predecessor, and thereafter that Brown's prudence was based on exactly the same principles as had been followed under the Conservatives by their last Chancellor, Kenneth Clarke.

Public ownership

There was no return either to public ownership or to the redistribution of wealth. The New Labour government could not privatize much more, because most of it had already been sold off by the Conservatives, but they refused to take even the railways back into public ownership, as many people wanted.

Taxation and the minimum wage

For the rich, taxation levels remained comfortably low, with a maximum income tax rate of 40 per cent. The gap between the rich and the poor in Britain remained very great and in fact continued to grow a little. But Labour, after initial delays, did help the very poor by introducing a minimum wage

there had not been much 'delivery' on the public services, and no great improvements in education, health or transport, but it claimed that a further electoral mandate would enable it to complete the work of modernization which it had already begun. A programme of extra spending on the police, education and the health services had already begun before 2001, and the feeling was that if the Conservatives were elected they would stop this development. Old Labour supporters were impatient at the apparent lack of achievement, but were assured that a second term would be more effective and that the rewards of careful economic management could now gradually be shared out in the social field.

 Question: Why did Labour achieve a second election victory in 2001?

5.6 The 2005 general election

More or less four years after the election of 2001, on 5 May 2005, the Prime Minister again called a general election. The main features of the result were:

1 Labour won again. This was the first time Labour had won three elections in a row and it gave the party a good, working majority of 66.
2 But the Labour bubble seemed to have burst. This was not the landslide of 1997 or 2001. Labour won on a paltry 35.2 per cent of the vote: no post-war government had won on such a small percentage. Labour lost well over one million votes compared to 2001 and had nearly four million fewer than in 1997.
3 The Conservatives showed signs of climbing out of the abyss. Although their share of the vote only increased slightly (to 32.4 per cent), they gained an additional 31 MPs and more than 400,000 more votes.
4 The Liberal Democrats had their best election since 1987 in terms of votes, winning 22 per cent of the vote, and they increased their number of MPs to 62, the best result in these terms since the days of David Lloyd George in the 1920s.
5 There was an interesting increase in support for minor parties and for independents, but the first-past-the-post electoral system made it difficult to translate this into seats in Parliament. Respect (the anti-war with Iraq party) won a seat; Dr Richard Taylor, the independent campaigner for Kidderminster Hospital, retained the seat he had won in 2001; and an Independent Welsh Labour activist, Peter Law, took the safe Labour seat of Blaenau Gwent in Wales in protest against the Labour Party's use of all-women short-lists in the selection of the candidate for the seat. The Greens gained their highest ever general election result: 1 per cent of the

popular vote, but no MPs. The United Kingdom Independence Party was in fourth place for the parties, with more than 600,000 votes (2.3 per cent of the vote).

6   Turnout increased a little in comparison with 2001, but was still very poor (61.3 per cent); this was despite a real drive by all parties to turn out their vote, and despite a big national effort to encourage greater turnout by increasing the issue of postal votes. Turnout in the UK 2005 general election was very close to that in the US presidential election of the previous year, and for decades the British had smugly condemned the low level of American participation.

5.7 Why Labour won again in 2005

Labour had performed reasonably well since 2001 in terms of its economic and social policy. The economy was remarkably strong after about a decade of almost continuous growth. This provided the all-important 'feel-good factor', which is so significant if a government is to win an election. Despite all the scare stories, most people were actually quite happy with the health and education services. As a result, there seemed no good reason to punish Labour too hard. In addition, Labour continued to appeal to both the old working classes and a reasonably large portion of the middle classes. Blair, although less popular than in the past, still had something of his old magic touch with the British people. As far as most voters were concerned, it was not really time for a change. Also, Labour retained the powerful support of Rupert Murdoch's press. So in this sense, the election victory of 2005 was a repeat of 1997 and 2001, but on a smaller scale.

Labour ran another slick campaign in 2005. Once more, Blair proved himself a good campaigner, especially on the *Question Time* programme which showcased all three party leaders. Also, Gordon Brown was paraded as the likely successor to Blair, in an effort to firm up the Labour core vote. He could appeal to left-wing voters, and Blair to right-wing voters.

Finally, the Conservative and Liberal Democrat challenge was not sufficiently strong to dislodge Labour. The Conservatives still seemed out of touch and obsessed with right-wing issues like immigration. Everyone knew that a vote for the Liberal Democrats was just a protest vote and that there was no realistic prospect of them forming a government or even replacing the Conservatives as the official opposition.

Labour's second term (2001–5)

As in 2001, the 2005 election result is probably best seen as the voters' judgement on what the Labour government had achieved in its previous term.

for both men in exaggerating their differences: Blair could win Conservative votes and Brown could attract Labour voters, who hoped that in the future he would take over. The real political problems for Labour's second term did not rest on an alleged quarrel between Blair and Brown, but on an increasing tendency for Labour backbenchers to vote against the government. There were some staggering rebellions in 2002–4: over Iraq, top-up fees and foundation hospitals. But since Labour had such a huge majority, large-scale rebellions were perhaps to be expected.

One-party dominance

Labour's political problems were really not very serious when one considers the strength of their continued lead, throughout the second term, over the main opposition party. It might have been expected that the election in 2003 of Michael Howard as Conservative leader, in succession to the truly poor Iain Duncan Smith, would help revive Conservative fortunes. Howard was a clever man, quite capable of humiliating Blair publicly at Prime Minister's Questions, but after a slight bounce in the opinion polls after he had been chosen (unopposed) as the new leader, the Conservatives remained well behind Labour. It has to be admitted that the damage done as a result of the war in Iraq to Blair and Labour had been limited partly because their policy was so staunchly supported by the Conservatives. The Liberal Democrat opposition to the war helped that party with some by-election successes, and Charles Kennedy talked about replacing the Conservatives as the main opposition to Labour. This was very unlikely to happen, since the Conservatives' 'natural' base of support is nearly twice that of the Liberal Democrats, and is, moreover, nicely concentrated in the suburbs and countryside of England. In 2004, the United Kingdom Independence Party squeezed the Conservatives from the other end of the political spectrum, as was shown by their strong electoral performance in the European elections.

Why the Labour vote was reduced

Although Labour won the 2005 election, the party's majority was substantially cut. The reasons for this have to some degree been sketched in above, but it is worth emphasizing why it was that there was a general feeling among Labour voters that the government had failed them in some respects. This dissatisfaction was reflected in the increase in protest votes to the Liberal Democrats, independents and minor parties like Respect and the Green Party. It was also reflected in the abstention of Labour voters, and the low turnout. It was reckoned that the Labour turnout was 58 per cent while the Conservative turnout was 65 per cent. The factors that contributed to this dissatisfaction are discussed in what follows.

Anti-war protesters mark the anniversary of the start of the war in Iraq in Trafalgar Square on 20 March 2004

The impact of the war with Iraq

In Muslim seats especially, voters were angered by the government's part in the American attack on Iraq in 2003. More broadly, the attack on Iraq was symbolic of a wider dissatisfaction among Labour's core vote with the rightward drift of policy under Blair, and on the less than straightforward approach of the government to explaining the reasons for the war. In order to go to war, many people believed that at its worst the government had misled Parliament and at its best the government had seriously mishandled the diplomacy and politics involved. On the other hand, the Liberal Democrats had always opposed the war, and benefited at the polls in 2005 as a result.

Student university fees

Despite having said that it would not do so in its 2001 manifesto, the government had legislated to introduce a system by which students would pay their university fees themselves (rather than have the state pay them). When the bill to introduce this reform was passing through Parliament, it provoked large Labour backbench rebellions and seemed again to be symptomatic to those on the left that government was drifting further to the right. So in 2005, Labour found that it did poorly in constituencies with large student populations, losing Withington (Manchester) and Cambridge, for example, to the Liberal Democrats, both with large anti-Labour swings. Of course, this cannot have been decisive, but again is an interesting symbol of wider Labour dissatisfaction with its own government. Labour ought to win the support of young people, but in 2005 it tended to lose it.

Tony Blair

By 2005, Blair was becoming personally less popular, especially with Labour core voters. He seemed arrogant and duplicitous, by turns pompous and flippant. It is true, however, that he still had some of his former charisma and on balance was more of a vote-winner than any of his rivals. The opposition tried to link Blair's unpopularity with the issue of trust: could voters still support Labour if they did not trust its leader, after what he had done over Iraq and over university fees?

The Conservatives

Although the party fell far short of winning in 2005, the Conservatives under Michael Howard enjoyed something of a modest revival, especially in the heartlands of southern Britain. They conducted a slick campaign, using the skills of Australian spin-doctor, Lynton Crosby. The party played on fears about immigration, crime, hospital cleanliness and school indiscipline. These were relatively minor points on which to fight a campaign, and the Conservatives could not really harm Labour over Iraq, the economy or social policy. In addition, they were keen to steer clear of Europe as an issue in case they helped their great rivals UKIP by highlighting the question. What Howard did succeed in doing, however, was to attack Blair quite successfully personally (calling him directly a 'liar'), and this may have lost Labour votes.

The Liberal Democrats

Led by the most human of the party leaders, Charles Kennedy, the Liberal Democrats mopped up a large number of anti-Labour protest votes (over Iraq and university finance). They targeted some seats quite effectively, and built on their previous successes in local government and by-elections. It is generally reckoned that they did not entirely succeed in being all things to all men, and in the end lost votes on the right to the Conservatives, but they gained them on the left from the disaffected ranks of Labour. In the end, the electoral system was, as usual, hard to them, but they did succeed in denting Labour's lead.

 Question: Why was Labour's majority reduced in the general election of 2005?

Activity

Work out who will win the next election!!

1 After some research on the internet and using your own recollection of current events, with the help of a classmate, draw up a balance sheet of achievements and failures of the three main political parties since 2005, in rather the same way that we have done in this chapter for the last three elections.

2 Look at the following: the state of the economy, the popularity of the leaders, the policies of the parties, recent events at home and abroad which reflect on public perceptions of the parties, the unity of parties, the public image of the parties and their promise for the future. Try to weight these factors according to which you think most important and what impact they may have on the outcome.

3 Get your class to vote on the outcome of the next election, and then ask for the reasons behind these votes.

4 To get some objective decision as to who came closest in their estimate, try to find the odds given by Ladbrokes for each party; or check out the opinion poll websites for their view of how the parties currently stand.

SUMMING UP

However much they may be criticized, New Labour has been the most successful election-winning machine for a century. Not since the period 1951–64 has a party won three elections in the row, and when the Conservatives did that half a century ago, they did not achieve the huge majorities of Blair and his colleagues. These victories have been a classic case of winning from the middle ground of politics. While Labour appealed to the essential moderation of the British voter, their Tory opponents were lost in a right-wing wilderness. In 1997, the country was sick of the Conservatives after 18 years, but in 2001 and 2005, as has so often happened in British politics, it was as much the opposition which lost the election as the government which won it.

Labour will certainly not have such an easy time of it when they come to face the next election. By then, the party will have been in power for more than a dozen years; it will have lost Blair (at least at first their great vote winner) as its leader; the economy may be weaker; and it will probably still face a moderate Conservative party under a youthful leader, David Cameron, who, when he was first appointed, raised the Conservative poll ratings very successfully.

On the other hand, Gordon Brown may just pull it off – again! He portrays himself as different from Blair, and may be able to do what Major did in 1992: win a fourth successive election in a row for his party by appearing fresh and new. Brown may be able to relaunch New Labour and avoid the 'time for a change' threat, which always haunts parties after a long time in power. But political scientists have discovered through their research that the best way to find out who will win the next election is to consult a bookmaker, so perhaps we should leave the speculation to the experts.

Further reading

D. Butler and D. Kavanagh, *The British General Election of 1997* (Palgrave, 1997): since 1945, the veteran political scientist David Butler, now working with another great expert in the field, Dennis Kavanagh, has published a volume of analysis on the most recent election. It is here and in the next two books mentioned that you will find the best guide to the subject.

D. Butler and D. Kavanagh, *The British General Election of 2001* (Palgrave, 2001).

D. Butler and D. Kavanagh, *The British General Election of 2005* (Palgrave, 2005).

Websites

www.electoralcommission.gov.uk (Electoral Commission)

http://www.essex.ac.uk (British election study, academic study from University of Essex)

http://www.mori.com (MORI, the pollsters)

http://www.nrs.co.uk (National Readership Survey, newspaper circulation figures)

www.YouGov.com (YouGov, the pollsters)

www.icmresearch.co.uk (ICM Polls)

6 Pressure Groups

Making connections

This topic lends itself particularly to a research-based approach. It is very easy to find examples of pressure groups and they are generally very keen to provide information about themselves. Look on websites (there is a brief list at the end of the chapter); get in touch with a group that interests you: for a small fee you may be able to join, and then you will be deluged with information. So, in a short time you can undertake case studies on individual examples of the different types of group.

6

Pressure Groups

SETTING THE SCENE

This chapter will deal with the world of pressure groups and pressure politics. Is this where the real power is to be found in British politics – behind the scenes, in the organizations which work to influence the government and also the citizens, by persuading them that policy needs to be changed or new political approaches adopted?

6.1 What are pressure groups?

Pressure group: an association of people who try to influence those who have political power.

Perhaps the best way to illustrate what a **pressure group** is to give a list of some of the well-known ones. Examples include the following:

- British Medical Association
- Automobile Association
- Friends of the Earth
- National Union of Students
- Refugee Council
- Amnesty International
- Royal Society for the Protection of Birds
- Confederation of British Industry
- Adam Smith Institute

- Oxfam
- Farmers for Action
- The Society for the Protection of the Unborn Child

As can be seen from the list, many different bodies can be described as a pressure group. In fact, the term is used so broadly that political scientists have had to distinguish between different types of pressure group, as will be shown later in the chapter. However, a general definition, which should cover all the examples above, would say that a pressure group consists of a group of people whose aim it is to influence those in political power.

This definition involves a crucial distinction between *power* and *influence*. The people with power are the ministers, MPs, civil servants, judges and, ultimately in a democracy, the people themselves. They have power because they can change things. Pressure groups seek to influence the people with power so that the changes in policy are changes in the direction the pressure groups want. To illustrate this, we could take the campaign launched in 1982 to promote lead-free petrol. Until then, all types of petrol had contained a lead additive, which helped lubricate the engine. But the burning of petrol in cars resulted in high levels of emissions of lead into the atmosphere. Lead is poisonous, and once it begins to build up in a person's internal organs, it cannot be removed. Studies showed that children who went to school near major roads had lower IQ levels than children whose schools were well away from roads, and experts said that this was a result of breathing in lead in the exhaust fumes of the cars. Veteran campaigner Des Wilson and a number of others set up a pressure group to campaign to reduce lead emissions, which was called the Campaign for Lead Free Air (CLEAR). CLEAR mustered the support of some 25 other pressure groups in the fields of environmentalism and health. Within a very short time (by 1983), this group had persuaded the government, using its political power, to pass laws increasing taxes on petrol containing lead. Pressure in the UK, further lobbying in Europe, and contacts with other campaigners in the USA and around the world then persuaded motor manufacturers only to sell cars which run on lead-free petrol. So, the pressure group persuaded the people with power to change public policy in this area. Successful pressure is able to influence those with political power (and economic power –like the manufacturers) into taking action.

Difficulties with our definition of pressure group

One problem is that many groups are pressure groups according to our definition, but *they are other things as well*. Take, for example, the Automobile Association (AA) and its rival organization, the Royal Automobile Club (RAC). These groups will feature in most lists of pressure groups, and they do campaign on behalf of motorists, trying to influence government policy on road safety, speed limits and the building of new roads, for example. But the fact is that the members of the AA and RAC, which number millions of people, join these organizations mainly to use them as a sort of breakdown insurance, and to be frank most of them could not care less about their pressure-group activities. Does this matter for our definition? It probably does if we consider that almost any body of people can try to influence the policy-makers, the people with political power. For example, the Football Association will work with the Minister of Sport to promote football in this country, but is not normally thought of as a pressure group, since its main job is to organize, with other groups, how football is run in the UK. It will, however, lobby on behalf of football and try to ensure that the government gives the sport its encouragement and support. Another example would be a huge pharmaceutical company, GlaxoSmithKline. Its main business is to manufacture and sell its products, but it will also have a department which will be very keen to promote these products by lobbying, when necessary, the government and indeed the European Union, especially in areas like health-care policy, industrial regulation, labour relations law, etc. But this hardly means that GlaxoSmithKline is a pressure group.

The fact is that there is pressure and influence everywhere in our political system, and the problem with a narrow definition is that it does not really recognize this. It might be better to talk in more general terms about 'pressure politics', as the political scientist John Kingdom does. This implies that pressure is felt at all points in the political system from all sorts of groups, whether they are technically pressure groups or not. In fact, if you really want to get your way in the political system, it may sometimes be best to conceal the fact that you are from a pressure group.

One useful distinction which helps with this problem is between **primary pressure groups** and **secondary pressure groups**. Primary groups are the chief pressure groups, the ones that come easily to mind: often, perhaps (according to the definition given in the next section) 'cause' pressure groups. Secondary groups are the businesses, the fundraising charities or the groups which bring people together for a variety of purposes in different ways, but which also make contact with parts of the political system from time to time. One problem with this category is that it is quite large, and brings us back to the point that in the end almost every group or association of people can from time to time use political pressure.

Primary pressure groups: those which have political pressure as their main concern.

Secondary pressure groups: those which have other primary concerns, and which use political pressure occasionally and incidentally to their chief interests, which may be commercial, charitable or social in nature.

Box 6.1 What is the difference between a political party and a pressure group?

This is a question which makes us reflect seriously on how to define both parties and pressure groups, because there tends to be some overlap, especially between the smaller parties and pressure groups. Political parties are dealt with in chapters 7 and 8, and this topic may make more sense when you have studied that too.

Pressure groups on the whole do not seek to achieve political office – but some do, in the sense that they contest elections. For example, the Pro-Life Alliance (an anti-abortion pressure group) has put up candidates for election in Scotland. Respect, a group opposed to the war with Iraq, also contested elections in 2004 and 2005. The reason pressure groups do this is probably largely to put pressure on the 'real' political parties, in order to make them change their policies. So this is a form of pressure-group activity, but it still involves typical party behaviour. The small political parties also tend to behave in this way too, as the Referendum Party showed in 1997.

Pressure groups should, according to the usual definition, concentrate on a single issue (this can be called 'single-issue politics'). This is especially true of cause pressure groups. But some pressure groups behave like political parties in taking an interest in a whole range of policy areas. Some large trade unions have taken a view on nuclear weapons and on foreign policy matters as well as the more predictable economic and social issues we would expect them to be concerned with. This looks like political party behaviour. Environmental pressure groups like Friends of the Earth also have a range of policy interests, looking at them from a specifically 'green' angle. Indeed, it is hard to see how such pressure groups differ from the Green Party itself, which generally counts as a political party, not a pressure group. Small parties like the Greens and Respect are often themselves engaged in single-issue politics in a rather similar way to pressure groups.

If we take ideology as our measure, pressure groups should generally be expected to leave ideological concerns to political parties. But in fact, in recent years parties have shied away from ideology. In contrast, trade unions have very strong ideological commitments to left-wing theories, and environmental pressure groups adopt a clear ideology – environmentalism! It might be argued that in present circumstances, if you want ideology, you should look to pressure groups, not parties.

In other respects, there are also similarities between pressure groups and parties. Both seek to enrol a large membership, both raise funds for political purposes, both have leaders and 'constitutions' and both tend to compete for media attention. According to some commentators, the fact that parties have had a declining membership in recent years, while cause pressure groups have a growing support, can be linked. This suggests that in terms of participation, parties and pressure groups are to some extent interchangeable.

  Question: What is a pressure group?

6.2 Cause pressure groups and sectional pressure groups

Pressure groups, as the list at the beginning of the chapter shows, are often very different from one another; to help us understand them, they are divided into two types: cause pressure groups and sectional pressure groups.

Cause pressure groups: associations which have as their main aim the achievement of influence over a particular area of policy. In other words, they focus above all on a single aim, or a cause. Because they try to promote their cause, these pressure groups are also called promotional groups.

A **cause pressure group** can have a very narrow focus or it can have a broad focus. The example of CLEAR given above is an obvious case of such a pressure group. Environmental pressure groups, like Friends of the Earth or Greenpeace, campaign across a very broad range of green issues, but still ought strictly to be called cause pressure groups. On the other hand, a pressure group can be extremely local and narrow in its focus: for example, a group set up to stop the building of a new airport terminal or runway. An instance of such a group is Stop Stansted Expansion, which has campaigned since 2000 to prevent the growth of Stansted Airport, and which receives wide support in the area around the airport. On the face of it, these cause groups seem to be the 'purest' and the best form of pressure group: they seem to be campaigning freely for what they believe in. If you believe in the same things as they do, you can join them, and help to achieve their cause.

Sectional pressure groups: associations which have as their main aim the defence of the interests of a particular section of the community. For this reason they are sometimes called interest groups.

Sectional pressure groups will try to influence those with power in such a way as to ensure that public policy is geared to what their members, who will be drawn from a particular section of the community, want. The two most famous examples of such pressure groups are trade unions, which represent workers, and the groups which act as representatives of employers.

To take an example of a trade union, the National Union of Teachers (NUT) tries to defend the interests of the teaching profession. Above all, it wishes to improve the pay of teachers and to reduce their workload, but also campaigns on other issues relating to education. The NUT, and all the teaching unions, opposed the introduction of SATs, and as a result the Conservative government of John Major made some modification to the number of the tests, and the Welsh Assembly has abolished them in Wales. The NUT has also

With around one million members, UNISON is one of Britain's largest trade unions. It represents workers in public services including the NHS, local government, education and transport

Box 6.2 Peak pressure groups

The world of pressure politics is complex. Some work together to achieve their ends. This is especially true of sectional groups. They sometimes organize themselves so that they appoint a super-pressure group, or peak group, to represent their interests. The best example is the Trades Union Congress (TUC), a body set up in 1868 to bring together all the other trade unions in the country. It holds an annual conference and has an important General Secretary (at the time of writing, Brendan Barber), who is the person to whom government and the media often turn if they want to know the opinions of the trade unions. In the same way, the Confederation of British Industry (CBI) is a peak group, set up in 1965 on the basis of earlier groups, and represents all the separate associations which protect the interests of British business. Again, this body has a Director General (Martin Broughton at the time of writing) who is an important spokesperson for industry. For example, in August 2004, Broughton's predecessor, Digby Jones, was interviewed at the time of the publication of the GCSE results, saying that business was finding that many of the people it employed straight from school had poor literacy and numeracy skills. Presumably this was designed to put pressure on the government to improve basic skills teaching in schools.

In Brussels, pressure groups from all over the European Union organize themselves into peak groups, representing the different industries and also bringing all trade unions together too. This is not just a feature of sectional pressure groups: it can also happen with cause pressure groups. The Countryside Alliance, for example, as its name implies, is a peak group which brings together a number of different pressure groups with allied interests.

campaigned to reduce bureaucracy and red tape in education, and all political parties claim that they are in support of such campaigns. To look at the employers' organizations, the Road Haulage Association has worked hard to defend the interests of a whole industry: heavy-goods road transport. It has campaigned to allow larger lorries on the roads of the UK, and has been successful in that; it has also supported improvements in the building of new roads and has campaigned to reduce the excise duty on diesel fuel and the road tax paid by trucks.

Problems with the distinction between cause and sectional pressure groups

On the face of it, it is a good, solid distinction, which expresses a real and important difference (rather better than that between insider and outsider groups discussed later on). But like all distinctions, it can be dissolved, if we can find examples which can easily be put into both categories. Take the National Union of Railwaymen. This is obviously a sectional pressure group, representing the interests of the people who work on the railways. But it is also a cause pressure group since it will focus its campaign on better railways, more rail safety, government investment in the industry, etc. Or take a gay rights pressure group, like Stonewall. Obviously, this has campaigned for changes in the law on homosexuality (same-sex marriages, equalizing the age of consent, an end to discrimination against gays, etc.); at the same time, most of its members and supporters are presumably drawn from the gay and lesbian community.

The problem with the cause/sectional distinction is that it combines two rather different criteria or yardsticks in order to make the distinction. If we talk about cause and non-cause groups, we are looking at the aim of the group. If we talk about sectional or non-sectional groups, we are looking at the membership. Perhaps the crucial point to focus on when considering whether a group is cause or sectional is to ask which comes first, the cause or causes it is promoting, or its members' interests? This won't always be an easy question to answer.

 Question: Explain what is meant by 'single-issue politics'.

6.3 Insider and outsider pressure groups

Insider pressure group: one which has strong links with those people who have political power and is therefore in a good position to influence policy.

The great example of an **insider pressure group** was, and continues to be, the National Farmers' Union (NFU). This body represents British farmers, and it enjoyed a very close relationship with governments in the post-war era. Farming was not nationalized after 1945, unlike many other industries, but remained in private hands, with a government department, which has been given various names, but which started life as the Ministry of Agriculture, to channel government money into agriculture via the farmers. It was government policy at the time to subsidize agriculture because the Second World War had shown how desperately Britain needed to produce food if it were to survive a blockade preventing it from importing food from abroad. But the ministry needed to remain in close touch with the hundreds of thousands of farmers up and down the country in order to keep them up to date with the latest agricultural methods and so that it could direct them to produce certain crops which the civil servants and politicians thought needed to be developed. Hence, it was very important that the ministry and NFU worked closely together, so that the NFU could communicate with farmers on behalf of the government and so that farmers' concerns could be expressed to the politicians.

Outsider pressure group: one which is not blessed with the degree of contact enjoyed by an insider group, and which cannot therefore have such influence.

A good example of an **outsider pressure group** nowadays would be the Countryside Alliance. This body was set up in the 1990s to fight for the preservation of the rural way of life. It has generally quite friendly relations with the Conservative Party, but since 1997 has taken a rather hostile attitude towards the Labour government. It has campaigned against a number of policies which it considers harmful to the countryside: the 'right to roam' for walkers, for example, and the banning of fox-hunting. The Countryside Alliance has

In September 2002, around 400,000 people descended on London for the Countryside Alliance's 'Liberty and Livelihood' march, bringing the streets of Westminster to a halt

organized a number of demonstrations against government policies, an indication of its outsider status.

How good is the distinction between insider and outsider pressure groups? It certainly is valuable, and the examples above show how it can be used. The main difficulty with it is that it oversimplifies what is a complex relationship between the people in power and the people applying pressure. Rather than having two distinct categories (insider and outsider), it is probably better to think of a spectrum, with some groups very closely linked to the government and others very much marginalized and out in the cold, but with very many gradations in between. Taking the two examples given above, it is clear that the NFU is likely to have a friendlier relationship with Conservative governments in power than with a Labour government, because farmers have traditionally been Conservative voters. In addition, the recent problems in the farming industry (BSE and foot-and-mouth, for example) have to some extent been blamed on the close relationship between the government department responsible for agriculture and the pressure group. The closeness of this relationship, it has been argued, has prevented civil servants and ministers from taking a firm enough line with farmers, and from enforcing strict regulations on them, with the result that problems concerning the health of farm animals have developed. Such concerns have led to a loosening of the ties between the NFU and the government, although it is still consulted on all-important agricultural matters. In the same way, the present Labour government has been unwilling to ignore everything said by the Countryside Alliance, and it was certainly rather slow in the years between 1997 and 2004 in its pursuit of a ban on fox-hunting, sensitive as it was to the impact on the media of demonstrations by annoyed countryside campaigners. Potentially, even the most uncooperative pressure groups can become an insider group if they appear to be of sufficient value to the government for it to make friends with them. Another defect with the insider/outsider distinction is that it ignores the fact that pressure groups apply pressure at a variety of points. So a group which is an outsider in relation to the UK government may get a much warmer reception from the opposition parties, or at the European Commission. Pressure groups also tend to vary their approach according to what produces the best result: at some times it may suit them to be on the inside, but at other times it may not be to their advantage.

Question: Briefly explain, with an example, what is meant by 'an insider group'.

Box 6.3 Protest movements

A pressure group is a single, organized body, but the world of pressure politics sometimes involves attempts to apply pressure on a broader front. This would be especially true in the field of cause or promotional pressure. A good way to describe this broader, less tightly organized approach would be to use the term 'protest movement'. Recent examples would include opposition to the war with Iraq and attempts to stop the ban on hunting. In both these cases there was something to protest about: a piece of public policy. In both cases also, there was an umbrella organization involved (which could be called a pressure group): the Stop the War Coalition and the Countryside Alliance. But the protest movements both had wider support, and many of the people involved were not connected to the specific group mentioned.

Protest movements tend to operate through more active forms of action: marches, demonstrations, even 'direct action'. The fuel protests of 2000 could be described as a protest movement, in this case against the high price of petrol and diesel, and they resorted to quite extreme methods. They were not responding to government policy so much as trying to mould it to the way they wanted – by getting the government to reduce taxation on fuel. Some protest movements are more positive: they do not want to stop something or change policy,

their aim is to respond and protest about something on which there is a lack of legislation. An example would be the Snowdrop Campaign in 1997, following the Dunblane massacre (the murder of 16 children and an adult in a Scottish primary school in 1996), which campaigned for gun control. Another example is the G8 protest of 2005, headed by a group called Make Poverty History, which persuaded nearly a quarter of a million people to join a protest march in Edinburgh at the time of the G8 summit near there, and which was trying to get world leaders to reduce third world debt.

Protest movements do not have to be national: they could involve a local protest against a hospital closure or a piece of planning, involving road-building for example, or airport expansion, as in the case of Stop Stansted Expansion. While we can usefully distinguish between pressure groups and protest movements, it is worth emphasizing that it is difficult to conceive of a protest which did not lead to the setting up of a group of some sort. The important example of a piece of protest action, the Camp for Climate Action, set up near Heathrow Airport in August 2007 to express opposition to the development of a third runway, was extremely well-organized by a consortium of groups including the wonderfully named Plane Stupid.

6.4 How do pressure groups operate? Who do they try to influence?

It is important at this point to return to the key concepts concerned with pressure groups: power and influence. Pressure groups will clearly need to influence those people who have power in modern British society, or influence at one remove those forces which themselves have influence over those in power. In a modern pluralist society, there are many **access points** for pressure groups to employ, as a way of bringing their influence to bear on those with power.

> **Access point**: a point of contact between the people with power politically and those protest movements or pressure groups which seek to influence them: e.g. Parliament, government departments, law courts, local and devolved government, the EU.

The government in power

Most obviously, a pressure group will attempt to persuade the government in power to change or keep its policy. This will be through influencing the Prime Minister, the Prime Ministers' advisers and the government minister(s) responsible for a particular area of policy. The ability of pressure groups to make any real, direct headway here should not be exaggerated, however. While certain groups may have privileged access (e.g. the trade unions under a Labour government, the Institute of Directors under a Conservative government), mostly a pressure group will have to attempt to influence those who influence the people in power. In other words, they will need to be patient.

Civil servants

Insider pressure groups will have much more access to the civil servants in the departments which relate to their particular areas of interest. Members of important, high-profile pressure groups will often be included on government advisory committees and will be quite frequently contacted by the civil servants responsible for their particular area. Oxfam will play a part with other famine-relief agencies, like Save the Children, in the work of the Department for International Development. Civil servants will need to consult most widely when a piece of legislation is being planned in their department; the publication of a green or white paper is intended to be a way in which pressure groups can contribute their views on a proposed change in the law.

Members of Parliament

Members of the government are most sensitive to what is said in Parliament, especially by MPs from their own party. Pressure groups will therefore attempt to lobby MPs in a variety of ways. Local pressure groups, for example, involved in a major planning decision (over a motorway, an airport development, etc.) will clearly try to work through local constituency MPs. The people of Kidderminster, for example, who were campaigning to stop the closure of the accident and emergency department in their town's hospital, were so keen to have a voice in Parliament that they elected a local doctor, Richard Taylor, who was a key figure in their campaign, as their MP in 2001. Pressure on MPs may be most intense when a piece of legislation is being debated, or when a committee in Parliament is enquiring into a specific matter of interest to a pressure group.

House of Lords

Because members of the House of Lords are more independent than MPs, they may be more susceptible to pressure, and more able to bring causes which are not supported by the governing party onto the agenda. On the other hand, since their powers are limited, there is less point in the end in pressure groups focusing much attention on the Lords. The support there for the opponents of the ban on fox-hunting proved ineffective in the end, when, in 2005, the House of Commons overruled the Lords, and it enabled anti-hunt protesters to portray the fox-hunting lobby as upper class and out-of-touch.

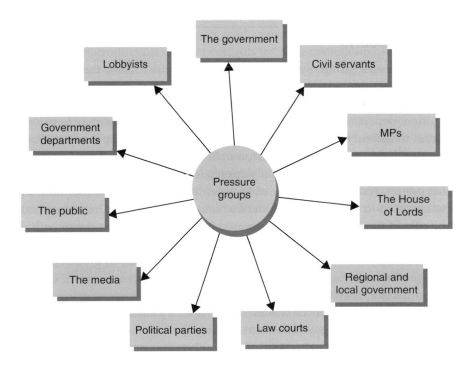

Figure 6.1 Which bodies do pressure groups seek to influence to achieve their aims?

Fathers 4 Justice protestor Jason Hatch attracted considerable media attention when he scaled Buckingham Palace dressed as Batman to protest for improved rights for fathers to see their children

and in its negotiations with government the size of its membership will be an influential factor.

Changing values

Perhaps the real struggle, for a cause group especially, is to change social values. If the background in public opinion is favourable to the cause, then it is much easier for the group to have success on particular issues. The environmentalist movement (represented in a number of pressure groups) has over the last generation shifted opinion on green issues to quite a considerable extent. This then makes it easier for the pressure groups to influence those with power to adopt recycling or sustainable energy policies. The same may be said for the influence over the last few decades of anti-racist groups like the Anti-Nazi League.

Knowledge is power

Pressure groups are often most successful if they have good information at their disposal. The passing in 2000 of a Freedom of Information Act, which allows access to some government sources of information, helps pressure groups. The broad campaign against the war with Iraq in 2002–3 made as much use as possible of the information it could glean from the government about the reasons for the war. Well-informed pressure groups often find they can achieve greater access to government if they can themselves supply information and research to particular departments. The Confederation of British Industry publishes influential reports on a regular basis on the state of British industry, which help it to lobby on behalf of its members. Some pressure groups (known as think-tanks) deal only in information and research; their sole purpose is to develop policy on a broad range of topics.

Direct action

Pressure groups need publicity, and it has long been recognized that 'propaganda by action' is often a more valuable way of commanding attention than 'propaganda by word'. Greenpeace has been very good at raising the profile of green issues by giving television companies exciting pictures, usually involving a high-speed boat and activists chaining themselves to a source of pollution. Their campaign against the sinking of the Brent Spar oilrig in the Atlantic, mentioned already, involved such an operation, and was combined with demonstrations by supporters of the movement outside the petrol stations owned by the oil company concerned. Nothing is ever straightforward, and within a few months the oil company had commissioned a report which suggested that the environmental cost of dismantling the rig in a Scandinavian fjord (Greenpeace's solution to what to do with it) was greater than that of sinking it in the North Atlantic.

In 2000, direct action was also seen in an anti-environmentalist direction when a combination of farmers, hauliers and motorists blockaded petrol-distribution yards and, as a result, cut off supplies of petrol to petrol stations. The result was that many people ran out of petrol and were unable to get to work, and students (much to their regret) were unable to get to school or college. This highlighted the high taxes on British petrol. The government was extremely sensitive to this sort of criticism, especially since they planned a general election within a few months. In order to placate the demonstrators, the government reduced taxes on petrol, although not by very much. The government also applied pressure to the managers of the oil-distribution centres to ensure that such blockades would not work in the future. There was more than a suspicion that the direct action had been successful because the oil companies wished to cut taxes on petrol in order to boost demand – and hence profits – and as a result had not done much to ensure that supplies got through. In 2005, the price of fuel had risen well beyond the levels of 2000, but threats of direct action did not lead to any real protests. Perhaps this shows that such forms of pressure have a short-lived impact.

communism in 1989, this argument continues, was the major factor in the decline of defence spending all over the world, and the successful negotiation of arms reduction between West and East in recent years. If it is a little difficult to say when a cause pressure group succeeds, it is even more difficult to say when a sectional pressure group succeeds or fails, since the interests of a group or a section of society need long-term protection. Hence, although a sectional pressure group may run individual campaigns on particular issues, which can be judged in terms of success or failure, its overall protection of interests over a long period is a little difficult to gauge.

Insider groups are successful, while outsider groups are unsuccessful. This looks like a good answer to the question of what makes a successful pressure group. It is probably the case, especially with sectional groups, that they wish to become or remain insider groups, with close connections to government. But some groups do not really want to become insider groups, and it may be possible to change policy without becoming an insider. Insider groups have to compromise, they may lose credibility and hence members, and so, becoming an insider may be very far from what they consider a success. Or, if they do wish to have influence, it is on their own terms, and they will therefore be an arms-length insider, always keen to avoid being seduced into moderation or respectability by the support they receive from government. Greens in Britain and abroad have debated for a long time whether it is better to be realists or fundamentalists. Realists will attempt to have inside influence, but realize that they may have to compromise to do so; fundamentalists stay true to their principles on environmental matters, but risk being marginalized as a result. Some recent outsiders have had considerable success. Fuel duty has not been increased by as much as probably would have been the case if it had not been for the 2000 direct action of the fuel protesters, who were very much outsiders. The Countryside Alliance probably had the effect of delaying the anti-hunting legislation Labour had promised in 1997 as a result of their large demonstrations. Fathers 4 Justice in 2004–5 forced some consideration of the issues they highlighted (largely concerning the rights of access for separated or divorced fathers to their children) with a series of illegal stunts. These mainly involved men dressed up in fancy dress climbing up prominent London landmarks, including Buckingham Palace and the tower of Big Ben. On the other hand, the Stop the War Coalition, after mass rallies in 2003, did not manage to stop the war.

Launched in 1958, the Campaign for Nuclear Disarmament reached its peak in the mid-1980s with more than 100,000 members. It has since been in steady decline. Can you think of the reasons for this drop in membership?

Factors in the success of a pressure group

There are a number of factors which will clearly make for pressure-group success.

Size of membership

With a large membership, a pressure group cannot be ignored by a political party, since votes may be involved. However, members of pressure groups will obviously vote in an election on a range of issues, not just in support of their group. Thus, trade unions have a large membership, but in recent years they have become politically more diverse than in the past. Surveys show that 21 per cent of trade unionists voted Conservative in 2001, while 19 per cent voted Liberal Democrat and 50 per cent voted Labour. The trade union movement, even in 2005, provided a large part of the Labour Party's campaign finance for the election, despite the fact that only half of all trade unionists would vote Labour. Hence, a pressure group cannot necessarily deliver the votes of its membership. The voting intentions of trade unionists may not really depend on whether a political party supports the trade union movement or not.

Solid finances

A large membership will generally mean strong finances, although a rich individual backer may be just as useful. Publicity campaigns obviously cost money. Some pressure groups have been described as 'cheque-book groups' because the contribution that many of their members make is solely to pay their membership fee or to respond to a financial appeal. Greenpeace and Friends of the Earth may fall into this category.

An active membership

An active membership will turn out for demonstrations and volunteer to put leaflets in envelopes.

A charismatic leadership

This will help to raise the profile of a pressure group. Bob Geldof added a great deal to the campaigns run by Live-Aid in the 1980s and 1990s, and then again in 2005 in the Live-8 campaign to put pressure on world leaders to write off third world debt. In 2002, high-profile figures in the field of entertainment, including Geldof, were used on adverts in the campaign against adopting the euro.

Salient campaign issues

A salient issue is one that is in the public eye, with lots of media focus; hence politicians will wish to support it if it seems to be popular. The Snowdrop Campaign, which has already been discussed, is a good example.

Media interest

A pressure group with favourable television and newspaper coverage is far more likely to succeed than one which is ignored by the media. This was certainly true of the Snowdrop Campaign, which led to a successful change in the

6.6 Are pressure groups in decline or are they growing in importance?

Political scientists are interested in comparisons geographically, looking at the USA, for example, and asking what a comparison between its politics and ours can tell us. But they are also interested in comparisons between the politics of today and the politics of the recent past. This leads to a mini-obsession with decline, and a small industry devoted to discovering it within the political system. Candidates for decline include political parties, Parliament, local government, political participation and pressure groups. Of course, if we can establish decline of some sort in all these areas, we might establish some general theory about democratic decline all round. For the moment, we shall stick to pressure groups. On the other hand, some commentators have been more optimistic about recent developments in the world of pressure politics and have been able to detect very interesting signs of a revival.

Evidence for decline

The golden age of interest groups has passed

There is a reasonable case for saying that interest groups have declined from a sort of golden age in the 1960s and 1970s. The membership of trade unions has certainly been substantially reduced in recent years (although numbers have increased slightly since 1998). This is a phenomenon which is observed in all other advanced economies too. The reasons are to be found in the decline of industrial employment, especially full-time, skilled work for men, which provided the bulk of the membership of the trade unions. In the 1970s there were more than half a million coalminers in the UK, all without exception members of the National Union of Mineworkers. Now there is scarcely a tenth of that number, there are other unions apart from the NUM and many miners do not even join a union. As clerical work has increased, and employment of women, especially in part-time or casual jobs, has grown, so the great industrial unions of the past have gone into decline. Strikes by trade unionists were a significant feature of the politics of the period 1945–85, when trade unions were still powerful, but they have fallen in number steadily from a high point under Thatcher, and are now relatively uncommon. The employers' organizations have also declined in number, size and importance. Part of the reason for this is that such organizations were set up to combat the unions, so as the unions have declined, so have these employers' associations. Another reason is that new industries have developed in the past 20 years or so, and they have been less ready to join bodies of this sort. Individual firms will lobby on their own behalf, rather than rely on an outside body, which charges high membership fees. At the same time, and not surprisingly, the interest group peak organizations (the TUC and CBI) have also become less prominent. In the 1960s and 1970s, the TUC Conference was widely reported in the press and on television, not always favourably; nowadays, it gets almost no coverage.

The end of tripartism or corporatism

Political scientists refer to the years from 1945 to 1979 as the years of corporatism (sometimes called neo-corporatism, or new corporatism). Corporatism involved government and the interest groups representing business and those representing workers cooperating together, or at least trying to, in order to encourage economic growth. There were three sides to this relationship – government, workers and employers – and hence it was also called tripartism. The best example of how this worked was under Labour Prime Minister Harold Wilson (1964–70, 1974–6). Wilson was most concerned to keep inflation down and spent a great deal of time negotiating with trade union leaders to stop them having strikes for more pay. This was the era of 'beer and sandwiches at Number 10', when the Prime Minister would meet representatives of striking unionists in an effort to bring an end to an industrial dispute. At the same time, he applied pressure on the manufacturers and retailers to try to stop them from increasing their prices. This was called a prices and incomes policy, and much of the time it relied on frequent interaction between the three partners in the corporatist relationship. This policy was not followed just by Labour: Conservative governments had their own (slightly tougher) variant. When Mrs Thatcher came to power, she was determined to bring an end to this system, which the New Right political philosophers whom she followed felt was harmful to the economy. It was better, they said, to allow the economy to develop freely without government intervention, and so tripartism came to an end.

Thatcherism

Thatcher was ruthless in her attack on trade unions, and under her government and that of John Major an act of Parliament was passed on average every two years which limited the powers of trade unions to picket, strike and engage in support for one another. But Thatcher was careful to reduce the power of the CBI too. New Right ideology held that if a government supported business, it would probably support the old-fashioned industries which should be replaced with new businesses by a simple process of competition and 'market forces'. So it was actually harmful to the economy to allow the representatives of industry and business to have too much influence on government.

Governments have learnt to live with cause pressure groups

Since Thatcher's time, governments have become generally more robust in their relationship with all forms of pressure. There is a great desire under New Labour to get legislation through Parliament quickly and there is often less time for consultation than there was in the past. This tends to squeeze out some pressure groups. The development of insider pressure groups might also be seen as a symptom of pressure group decline. Some groups have in essence been 'captured' by the government and, in return for gaining the valuable access to civil servants and ministers that they seek, may have compromised their independence and ability to fight effectively for their cause.

Evidence for growth

Growth of cause pressure groups

There is a general feeling that there has been a rise in the number of cause groups in the post-war era, filling in the gap left by the decline of interest groups. In the 1960s and 1970s, the rise of New Social Movements (NSMs) led to the growth iin the number of cause pressure groups dedicated to the new political issues of that period: nuclear disarmament, environmentalism, gender and racial politics, for example. These NSMs encouraged cause pressure groups to put the case for their particular area of concern. In addition, as these new groups developed, so too did groups opposed to these movements, justifying the pluralist view of how pressure groups can operate successfully in a democracy. Feminists defending the 'woman's right to choose' were opposed by anti-abortionist groups like the Society for the Protection of the Unborn Child. There seems little doubt that such cause bodies have increased in importance. Cause group activity in the UK remains strong. The *Directory of British Associations* lists more than 7,000 organizations, of which half date from after 1960. It is estimated that in 2004, 29 per cent of the British population belonged to a group of some sort; 16 per cent belonged to two and 5 per cent to three. These groups included many secondary pressure groups (for example, motoring organizations like the AA), but nevertheless they show that more of the British belong to some sort of a group than do not. The National Trust has 2.7 million members; the Countryside Alliance has 100,000 ordinary members and 250,000 associate members.

Direct action and protest movements

Supporters of the view that pressure groups have to some degree revived as cause groups point to the recent growth (since 1997) of Direct Action and the activities of Protest Movements: fuel protests, Countryside Alliance rallies, Stop the War Coalition demonstrations, the stunts by Fathers 4 Justice, and the Camp for Climate Action in 2007 outside Heathrow. There does seem to have been a rise in prominence of protest movements in the last decade.

Think-tanks

In their quiet way, the growing strength of think-tanks also provides evidence for the continued strength of pressure politics. In addition, even the trade union movement has, according to some, been strengthened by the recent years of struggle and decline, and is emerging leaner and fitter. As has been said, New Labour has also encouraged links with business.

Lobbying

The rise of lobbying in the 1980s and 1990s suggests that business has needed somehow to gain access to government and that individual businesses have resorted to employing professional experts to do this rather than working through large trade associations. This would support the case for saying that pressure-group politics is not in decline. However, in the 1990s allegations of sleazy relationships between business and MPs, and question-marks over party funding led to investigative journalism and an inquiry under the Nolan Committee (1994–5), which has restricted the activities of lobbyists and made the process of sponsoring MPs and funding parties more transparent. Lobbying remains significant, however.

New points of access

Lobbyists are now found not just in Westminster and Whitehall, but also in Belfast, Cardiff, Edinburgh and, of course, Brussels. Multi-level governance has given the pressure world new points of access to exploit.

The development of new technology adds an extra dimension to pressure politics: an e-petitioner at work (see 'Cyber-activism' on page 206)

Cyber-activism

Pressure groups exploit new forms of communication. People find out about protest movements and demonstrations online. Of members who used the internet, 31 per cent said that the Countryside Alliances website was what inspired them to turn up to a large London demonstration in 2002. At the time of G8 in 2005, a massive 360,000 Make Poverty History protesters emailed Tony Blair to support reduction in third world debt.

New Labour, business and the unions

In the 1980s and 1990s, Labour began to distance itself from the trade union movement, and since achieving power Labour has done little to undo the anti-trade union legislation brought in by Thatcher and Major. As a result, some trade unions have disaffiliated themselves from Labour, breaking links with the party which go back often as much as a century. There has been no real revival of corporatism since 1997. But business has much more influence on New Labour than on Old. Gordon Brown has spoken to the CBI conference, and a former Director General, Lord Adair Turner (significantly ennobled), was commissioned by the government to prepare a report on state pensions, which was published in 2005. In addition, Labour still takes funds from the trade unions and they play a part in the party's structure. Before the election of 2005, senior Labour officials met with trade union leaders and agreed the 'Warwick Accord' which led to Labour dropping some of its plans to make a raid on public sector pension funds; in return, Labour received £12 million towards its election fighting fund. Labour in power has been more receptive to interest groups than had been the case under Thatcher. It is worth noting, perhaps, that since the end of the 1990s, the steady decline of trade unions in Britain has been stopped and there has even been a modest revival.

The best conclusion is probably that interest pressure groups in the UK, especially those which represent economic interests, have declined, but from a position of great strength. There are still, however, signs of vitality in the field, especially from the newer cause groups. Much depends on the framework of consultation and response, from government, Parliament and the political parties, in which groups operate. The political climate since 1979 has been hostile to pressure groups generally, and this has tended to depress this area of political participation. But pressure groups have a wider range of options now open to them with the development of 'multi-level governance'. In Europe and in the devolved assemblies, there is often a more positive response than in Whitehall and Westminster. Pressure groups have shown their strength in responding to the challenge of gaining a voice in these new areas.

 Question: To what extent have pressure groups become more important in recent years?

Box 6.5 Think-tanks

These have developed strongly since the 1970s. They are pressure groups without members, which do not campaign. Instead, they think! Small groups of like-minded researchers and academics join together and essentially write pamphlets and articles urging the government to develop the sort of policies they like. The first great examples were the Adam Smith Institute (1978), the Institute of Economic Affairs (1955) and the Centre for Policy Studies (1974). They developed right-wing ideas, which chimed in well with the thinking of Margaret Thatcher and the New Right of the Conservative Party. In the 1990s, left-of-centre think-tanks began to emerge, developing the ideas of New Labour: Demos (1993), the Institute of Public Policy Research (1988), for example. Predictably, Labour in office after 1997 has also been seen to take some advice from the Adam Smith Institute. These bodies are cheap to run: academics will work for them on a part-time basis, and do not expect huge salaries. But their influence can be immense. They have tended to take over the work of developing policy alternatives from political parties and the civil service. They show the strength, but also the dangers, of pressure groups. Who elected the Adam Smith Institute (or a similar body)? To whom is it responsible for its ideas? What genuine academic status can it claim for studies which will not be subject to peer review and which will probably not be properly understood by politicians, who tend to get stars in their eyes when confronted by academics who agree with them? For a list of think-tanks and links to their own sites, go to: http://politics.guardian.co.uk/thinktanks.

Activity

1 Research think-tanks by going to the website mentioned in box 6.5 and using the links there.
2 Try to sort these think-tanks into right-wing and left-wing ones (there is an explanation of 'left-wing' and 'right-wing' at the beginning of chapter 8).
3 Try to work out whether these think-tanks are insider or outsider groups.
4 Consider when they were set up: make a time line to illustrate this. Do you find any chronological trends? Which decades saw the largest number of think-tanks being set up?

6.7 Do pressure groups benefit or hinder democracy?

A controversy surrounds the status of pressure groups in a liberal democracy. At first sight, they clearly seem to be democratic bodies which contribute well to the political life of the country, but they also have critics who call into doubt their democratic status. There follows a discussion of some of the arguments which might be used on either side of the debate.

Arguments that pressure groups benefit democracy

Pressure groups have rights

Liberal democracies involve a belief in rights, and the European Convention on Human Rights is now incorporated into British law. Pressure groups exercise the right of association (the right to form and run groups) and the right of free expression. These are core political rights and to condemn pressure groups would be to attack them merely for exercising their democratic rights.

Pluralism

A pluralist society is a democratic one in which individuals relate to a number (plurality) of focuses of power and influence. It is sometimes contrasted with a totalitarian society in which a fascist or communist government tries to monopolize power. A plurality of different pressure groups helps balance the tendency of all governments, even democratic ones, to try to monopolize power. Even if some pressure groups are too powerful and may themselves start to look a bit undemocratic in the way they try to bully the rest of the people (see below on this), the pluralist theory says that for every pressure group there will generally emerge a rival group arguing in the opposite direction. Thus, the League Against Cruel Sports faces the Countryside Alliance and other groups in favour of hunting and shooting.

Participatory democracy

It is important for people to be active citizens and to involve themselves in politics. There has been a decline in the support given to political parties since the mid-1970s, but to balance this, membership of pressure groups (especially cause groups) has grown. This is a significant way in which people can play a part in politics, and it helps counteract the apathy and lack of interest in politics increasingly shown towards the more mainstream parts of the political system.

Development of policy

Policy initiatives cannot be reserved for political parties and civil servants. Everyone ought to be able to play a part in developing new thinking on politics. Pressure groups play an important role in bringing issues to the attention of government and putting matters on the political agenda. This is especially true of cause pressure groups, and the specialized pressure groups called think-tanks.

Representation

Democracy is all about ensuring that the views of the people are known by the government of the country: that the people are, as far as possible, represented

Functional representation: the representation of different interests (professions, or social or economic groups, for example) through the existence of associations (generally sectional pressure groups) dedicated to representing their views, and keeping government informed of their needs and grievances.

by the government. The existence of sectional pressure groups, especially, enables this to happen. This is known as **functional representation**. How would government know about the particular concerns of small businessmen if the pressure groups that represent them did not exist? In addition, representative democracy only allows people to express their views on government policy at infrequent intervals when elections are held. Pressure groups allow citizens to make their opinions known in between elections. Elections only allow opinions to be expressed on the whole range of policy options, put forward in their manifestos by the competing political parties, whereas pressure groups allow people to express themselves on specific individual topics.

Political communication

Pressure groups not only allow the people to communicate with the government and help in policy-making, they also act as a channel of communication between the government and the people. This is especially the case with trade unions and employers' organizations, which are an important way in which a government department can spread information. One way for the Department of Health to communicate with doctors, for example, is via the British Medical Association – the doctors' trade union.

Scrutiny

Pressure groups are an important way in which government actions can be kept under scrutiny. Trade unions through the TUC press for changes in government policy on employment law, while employers' groups like the CBI watch the way in which taxation may affect business. Civil rights groups like Liberty and Justice carefully examine legislation – for example, the various anti-terror laws introduced since 2000. Pressure-group scrutiny can then help develop media interest in such issues.

Compensation for the deficiencies in political parties

Modern political parties tend to be catch-all parties, which seek to represent all interests and all sections of the community. It is therefore difficult for particular groups to make their points heard through the mechanisms of the political party. Pressure groups supply this need.

Important and beneficial changes have been achieved

One notable contributor to recent changes has been Charter 88, a pressure group set up in 1988 to press for the introduction of reforms of the constitution. It is difficult not to see this pressure group as a significant factor in developing the great raft of constitutional reforms brought in by Labour after 1997. The pressure against the introduction of GM crops from a variety of environmental pressure groups after 1997 certainly seems to have led to their introduction being slowed down, despite quite strong support for it at the heart of government. There are many more examples which could be given of what seems to be effective pressure-group activity. It is difficult to claim, of course, that without pressure-groups none of these changes would have been brought about. It is also a matter of personal political judgement as to whether these examples are in themselves good and therefore whether they support our argument here.

Box 6.6 Terrorism

On 7 July 2005, four bombs exploded on the London transport system, killing 52 people and injuring many more. They had been exploded by four suicide bombers. As far as can be gauged, the bombers wished to protest against British foreign policy, which they viewed as anti-Islamic, especially as a result of the war in Iraq. Two weeks later, a very similar attack failed because the bombs did not explode. Nearly exactly two years later (29–30 June 2007), there were two failed car-bomb attacks at Glasgow Airport and in central London, arranged apparently by a group of doctors of Middle Eastern origin who worked for the NHS. These terrorist outrages were similar to the infamous attacks of 11 September 2001 in the USA. In the UK, terrorist attacks connected to the politics of Northern Ireland were quite common in the last 30 years of the twentieth century, but have now declined as a result of the Good Friday Agreement there in 1998.

Terrorism can be defined as the use of illegal violence to apply pressure to people or governments. So terrorist organizations are rather similar to pressure groups in what they seek to achieve (in general terms), but it is important to emphasize that they are not the same. They use different methods – illegal methods.

Is such terrorism ever justified? The usual answer is 'no', but it may be worth adding, 'not in a liberal democracy'. In a dictatorship, it is generally part of the liberal tradition, as set out clearly by the founder of liberalism John Locke (1632–1704), that people have a 'right to resist' tyrannical government, and this would seem to cover terrorism. But in a functioning liberal democracy, there is no right to resist because people have the normal methods of political protest and influence to use in order to change policy or to express political grievances. Above all, they can set up a pressure group.

Does direct action amount to terrorism? This is a difficult question. On the whole there seems to be a difference in that direct action may involve breaking the law, but does not threaten wholesale death and destruction. On the other hand, any breaking of the law is wrong, however minor, and it seems unreasonable to give legitimacy to direct action while denying it to terrorism. Taken to extremes, direct action can be extremely intimidating, which is presumably the point of terrorism. Case studies of the most extreme forms of direct action might include the animal rights protesters recently involved in the campaign against Huntingdon Life Sciences and other organizations involved in experiments on animals. These have involved damage to property, assaults and the desecration of a family grave. Some people have called this terrorism: it clearly goes beyond holding protest rallies and demonstrations. If terrorism is clearly distinguished from pressure-group activity, then it could be said that it is unfair to invoke terrorism as part of an attack that argues that pressure groups are undemocratic. According to this argument, terrorism in a liberal democracy makes the case in favour of pressure groups look good: if people with a grievance concentrated their energies on forming and working for pressure groups and avoided terrorism, they ought to achieve more. Generally, terrorists put people off the cause they champion rather than winning their support.

Table 6.1 Are pressure groups good or bad for democracy?	
GOOD 👍	BAD 👎
They promote the right of free association and expression	They can be structurally undemocratic
They encourage pluralism	They may not be inclusive
They promote public involvement in politics	They may enable a minority to exercise too much power
They influence policy-making	They undermine democratic structures
They represent public interests	They may encourage corporatism
They act as a channel of communication between government and the people	They may encourage elitism
They keep the government under scrutiny	They may be 'captured' by government
They compensate for the deficiencies of political parties and can achieve significant change	They are open to corruption

Arguments that pressure groups harm democracy

Pressure groups are often not democratic in structure

In the 1970s and 1980s, the New Right in British politics, whose views strongly influenced Margaret Thatcher, expressed very strong criticisms of pressure groups, especially trade unions. They pointed out that these bodies were often unrepresentative of their membership and were led by people who were beyond democratic control. For example, Arthur Scargill, the leader of the National Union of Mineworkers, had had himself made president of that body for life. The reforms of the trade unions made by Thatcher and John Major in the 1980s and 1990s meant that these pressure groups now have very strong democratic structures in place, with elected officials and frequent consultation of members. Ironically, this has strengthened trade unions, which was not really the intention of the New Right. It remains true, though, that pressure groups are often dominated by a few enthusiasts, who do not fairly represent the views of their members.

allow this ban, since other countries would not follow suit and the sponsorship money would therefore be transferred abroad. Ecclestone had also made large donations to the Labour Party. His views prevailed.

Conclusion

Are pressure groups good for democracy or are they bad? On balance, most people would accept that they are not only good, but essential. But they need to be looked at with a critical eye. Some pressure groups are 'better' than others, more democratic, genuinely representative, sincere and open about their role and funding. Unfortunately, the pressure that really succeeds is often not from such well-motivated or straightforward bodies.

Box 6.7 Policy networks and policy communities

Over the years, political scientists have tried to develop a formula which explains the nature of pressure politics and the relationship between government and pressure. Karl Marx (1818–83), the founder of communism, argued that in a capitalist state (a state run on free market lines, like Britain at the moment), there was really no difference between power in society and power in the state. In other words, the government did what the bosses told it to do: the bosses were the 'ruling class'. It is difficult not to see some truth in this, when we consider the Formula One incident, mentioned above. A much more optimistic view can be summed up as pluralism: according to this view, we need a variety of inputs and democratic points-of-contact between people and government, and pressure groups supply this basic need. Professor Wyn Grant developed the idea of insider and outsider groups as a way of analysing how, in the real world, pluralism actually operates. Pluralism flourishes in a world where outsider and insider groups compete for attention and influence. More recently, political scientists have explored the idea of *policy networks*, or, according to a subtle variant, *policy communities*. These apply to insider groups and their relationship to government. Take the case of health. The policy community here would consist of the government ministers in power (with the appropriate select committee of the House of Commons) and the specialist civil servants in the government department. They would need to have links to the various trade unions involved in health care: the National Union of Public Employees (NUPE), the British Medical Association (BMA) and the various nursing unions. The private sector agencies involved – like BUPA (a health care insurance company) – would also have an input into the community, as would the representatives of the primary care and hospital trusts which run the National Health Service. In addition, any interested think-tanks, academics in the field of health care economics and social policy, and specialist journalists would also form part of this complex web. Finally, the policy network (or community) would also contain the various voluntary associations and cause pressure groups involved: Mind, Mencap, Britsh Heart Foundation, etc. There would then be the representatives of the pharmaceutical industry. No policy community would be complete these days without some input from the European Union. So, the world of pressure politics is a complex one, and any simplistic generalizations about how it works or whether it works successfully are likely to fall foul of the facts the deeper you dig.

Question: 'Pressure groups make already powerful interests even more powerful.' Discuss.

Activity

1 Choose a pressure group to research. There is a list at the beginning of this chapter, but there are thousands more to choose from. Find out as much as you can about the group. Examine their website; 'google' them and find out what you can from some other sources; look them up on the BBC or Guardian websites for more information; find out if there is a book written about them – see Amazon; you could even join them and receive a mail-shot or endless emails (but it might cost money – or you might not be eligible to join!).

2 Write a brief research paper about the pressure group you have chosen. Classify it according to the types described earlier in this chapter. Does it challenge any of the distinctions made in these classifications? Try to find out about the history of the group: its membership; its funding; its links with political parties; its main campaigns; its successes and failures; its links with other groups; its opposing groups (if any); its international links; its leading figures and supporters. Add in anything else you can find out which seems interesting or useful.

SUMMING UP

The political system in a modern liberal democracy like the UK is complex, and beneath the surface there is more political activity than might at first be apparent. Pressure groups play a vibrant role in the modern world. People need the support of interest groups, of trade unions and professional associations, and businesses need to apply pressure on the government through similar organizations. As issues arise, cause groups will be formed to try to change policy in those particular areas. Controversy surrounds the topic. There are those commentators who suggest that the great days of pressure-group activity are at an end, and that the small-scale activity of a myriad of cause groups is not the same as the power exercised in the 1960s and 1970s by traditional interest groups like the trade unions and the industrial organizations representing employers. Other political scientists see recent developments in the last decade or so as showing that there has been a significant growth of a new pressure politics, as shown by the anti-war and pro-hunting demonstrations. It is particularly interesting to see such obviously different groups using the same methods of protest. Another controversy associated with pressure groups surrounds the question of whether their activity can be justified in a properly functioning democracy. In the end, it is difficult to disagree with the view that says that the existence of strong pressure groups is a sign that democracy is flourishing rather than otherwise. But we can still afford to be concerned about the influence of big business on politics, and concerned also that a small group using bullying tactics can sometimes change policy, against the interests of the silent majority.

Further reading

P. Byrne, *Social Movements in Britain* (Routledge, 1997): sets the topic in a wider context.

Bill Coxall, *Pressure Groups in British Politics* (Pearson Longman, 2001): solid summary of the current state of research.

Rob Baggott, *Pressure Groups Today* (Manchester University Press, 1995): a good overview of the topic.

Wyn Grant, *Pressure Groups and British Politics* (Macmillan, 2000): significant contribution to the debate about how to define the various types of group.

S. Mazey and J. J. Richardson (eds), *Lobbying in the European Community* (Oxford University Press, 1993): explores the all-important EU connections.

Websites

A sample of websites produced by prominent pressure groups:

www.adamsmith.org (Adam Smith Institute)

www.amnesty.org (Amnesty International)

www.cbi.org.uk (The Confederation of British Industry)

www.countryside-alliance.org (The Countryside Alliance)

www.fathers-4-justice.org (Fathers for Justice)

www.foe.co.uk (Friends of the Earth)

www.greenpeace.org (Greenpeace)

www.liberty-human-rights.org.uk (Liberty)

www.spuc.org.uk (Society for the Protection of the Unborn Child)

www.stopwar.org.uk (Stop the War Coalition)

www.tuc.org.uk (The Trade Union Congress)

Political Parties

CHAPTER

7

Making connections

This chapter and the next one go together. In the next chapter, we look at the Labour, Conservative and Liberal Democrat Parties in depth. So it may help if you understand the rather theoretical discussion of parties in this chapter when you get down to some detail in the next one. All political parties have websites and it is worth making a case study of one of the major parties, or one of the more mainstream minor parties. A good time to examine one aspect of the life of parties is in the month of September, when all three major parties hold their annual conference. These are always widely reported in the press and on TV and radio and give a good flavour of what the parties are really like at grass-roots level.

Political Parties

SETTING THE SCENE

We move on from pressure groups to the other main organizations which involve people in politics: political parties. According to some commentators, this is where real political power is to be found, since almost all the politicians with power in Britain will be members of a political party. This is the first of two chapters on this important topic. The next chapter looks at the ideas and recent history of the three major political parties in Britain.

7.1 What is a political party?

A political party is a group of like-minded people who join together to achieve political office. The achievement of political office is crucial, but it does not imply that all political parties wish to form a government (many political parties cannot ever hope to do so), merely that political parties are generally formed to fight elections and to achieve representation. Other features that most (but not all) political parties tend to share are discussed in the following paragraphs.

Key features

A political party usually has an identifiable political outlook or ideology. An ideology is a set of political beliefs. Members of a political party join because they share these views. The problem with saying that a political party is a group of people who share an ideology is that ideology tends to be something which also, in some cases, divides political parties. We often speak of the left wing or right wing of a single political party and this suggests that the party does not have a common ideology. A further problem is that modern political parties, as they have developed in Britain and in other democratic countries in the last 20 years or so, have tended to move away from ideological commitments and have become what is described as 'catch-all' parties, appealing to as many people as possible – people with a wide range of different beliefs.

A political party has a programme, a range of policy commitments which differentiate it from other parties. Most major political parties are like this, but there are two problems with including this in our definition. First, some minor parties are effectively 'single-issue' parties, or at least tend to concentrate on one issue at the expense of others. The Referendum Party, which won more than 750,000 votes in 1997, campaigned largely on the issue of holding a referendum about the European single currency. In 2003 a party called Respect was set up whose main interest was opposition to Labour's policy on Iraq. Obviously, such a party is likely only to have a brief life. The nationalist parties in Scotland and Wales do have a range of policy concerns, but they tend to stress their nationalism above all else. Second, there is a tendency towards 'consensus politics' in modern democracies, a tendency in effect for political parties (especially the major ones) to agree with one another on a number of policy areas. So in some ways, even with the major parties the idea that developing separate policies defines a political party seems not to be fundamental.

A political party generally has a 'constitution' or system of rules which define its structure, and also has a leader with a clear role. This could certainly fit most political parties, but it is conceivable that a party would not wish to adopt this format. The Green Party, for example, has tended to have a very loose structure and to avoid too great an emphasis on leadership. In the 1980s, the Liberal-SDP Alliance had two leaders, although this did not prove to be a very successful arrangement. In addition, many other organizations, from social clubs to commercial companies, have rules and leaders, so this is not really by itself a defining characteristic of a political party.

Question: Outline two features of a political party.

7.2 What functions do political parties perform?

Democratic function

Parties (in the plural) play an essential role in a modern liberal democratic political system. Political parties exist in almost every country all over the world, and have done so for at least a century. About the only countries where they have not existed, or do not exist, are those dominated by an ancient tribal or feudal system. In what we might call modernized societies, there generally are political parties. But parties have also existed not only in liberal democracies like Britain but also in countries ruled by dictatorships of the right or the left. The Communist Party in Russia and the Nazi Party in Germany were, by their own standards, among the most successful parties in recent times, and the Communist Party in China continues in power. The significant difference, of course, between a democracy and a dictatorship is that under a dictatorship there is only one party, while in a democracy the function of a party is to operate within what is called a plural-party system, alongside one or more other parties. Indeed, it is virtually a defining characteristic of liberal democracies that they have more than one political party, and, conversely, dictatorships are defined by the existence of only one political party. A totalitarian country under a dictator is generally a one-party state. A liberal democracy operates with a plural party system, where two or more parties compete for power.

Representative function

Parties in a liberal democracy are the mechanism by which citizens exercise their essential democratic right to be represented. Representation in Britain takes place at a number of levels: at the supranational level in the European Parliament, in the UK Parliament at Westminster, in national assemblies like the Scottish Parliament and Welsh Assembly, at regional level in London and, finally, at the local level in county, city, borough, district or parish councils. Almost always, the representatives to be found at all these levels are members of particular political parties. Occasionally, independent candidates are elected; that is to say, people who do not stand as a candidate of a particular party, but as independents. This is especially true at the local level, and there are some MPs elected on this basis too – for example, the MP elected in 2001 (and again in 2005) for Wyre Forest, Kidderminster was a candidate, Dr Richard Taylor, who was protesting against the closure of the accident and emergency department in a local hospital. Another independent was elected in 2005, Peter Law, MP for Blaenau Gwent, and on his death in 2006 was replaced by another, Dai Davies. They were elected as local activists who were resentful that the Labour Party was trying to impose a candidate on the constituency with no real local links.

Aggregation and reconciliation of interests

Why should individuals not stand as representatives by themselves, as independents? Why should pressure groups not stand for election in order to bring about the changes in the law which they advocate? Of course, in some cases this does happen, but on the whole it does not. But if this were the general rule, it would produce confusion, both at the time of elections and then in the representative assembly. Hundreds of individuals and hundreds of pressure groups would be clamouring for support and attention, and little would be achieved. In fact, fairly soon these individuals and small groups would form alliances between themselves, so that they could cooperate in getting things done. In effect, political parties would emerge. This shows the value of parties. They link together (or aggregate) different interest groups and different individual politicians, who cooperate in order to achieve political office. At the same time, it is argued, party aggregation of

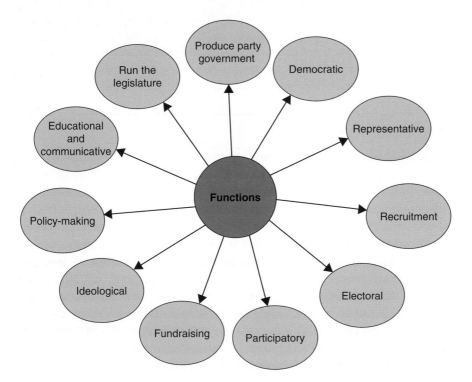

Figure 7.1   The primary functions of a political party

interests results in a softening of conflict between interests and hence leads to a reconciling of opposing positions.

Recruitment function

Parties are the first stage in this process of representation. The parties choose the candidates for election before the electorate gets a chance to vote on them. This is known as a 'recruitment' function. If the party selects someone for an election, the party is said to 'endorse' that candidate, to give him or her the official party stamp of approval. Conversely, if the candidate then misbehaves, the party reserves the right to 'deselect' the candidate, and refuses to support him or her in a subsequent election. In performing this function, parties may also show their democratic credentials by trying to recruit a diverse range of candidates, representative of society as a whole, including women and people from black and ethnic minorities.

Electoral function

This obviously follows from the last points. In order to gain representation, parties need to contest elections, and this is perhaps the most useful and most visible party activity in a democracy. Parties organize themselves so that they contest elections with the utmost vigour. They publish statements of their beliefs and of their intended policies (called manifestos). They advertise their political wares in the media, and they aggressively combat the ideas of their opponents. Electioneering in a democracy without parties is almost inconceivable. Parties give voters a choice at elections between competing views of how the country should be run. First, parties develop and advertise broad visions of how things should be done, or ideologies. These principles or beliefs are then refined and developed into specific policies on the range of issues which the political system has to deal with. Voters can choose between the ideologies and policies of the various parties. In a democracy, the majority view on this choice prevails, and the direction for legislation and government over the next few years is set by it.

Participation function

To fulfil their recruitment, representation and electoral functions parties need to encourage political participation. They try to get people to join their party as members, they raise funds from supporters, they get members to stand as their candidates in elections and, above all, they try to get voters to turn out and vote. This last point can be quite literally the case, since one of the historic functions of political parties in Britain has been organizing local volunteers to give people a lift to the polling station on election day, or ensuring in other ways that they turn out and vote.

Fundraising function

In countries like the UK, where state funding for political parties is limited, political parties also have to raise money from the public in order to fund their democratic functions. This can lead to controversy and scandal, but it is difficult to see how political parties could work without funds.

Ideological and policy function

Parties need ideologies, or at least some people argue that they do. If modern parties seem reluctant to talk about 'ideology', they are nevertheless keen to stress their belief in 'vision', 'values' or 'principles', which comes to the same thing. The ideologies of political parties also change and develop as time passes. Parties therefore have a function in developing political ideas, and in communicating them to the people. These ideologies then narrow down into specific policy proposals and these programmes and policies are also developed by parties. It is on the basis of their ideological commitment, programmes, and the policy suggestions published in the manifestos that parties stand for election.

Educational and communicative function

In order to develop participation and to mobilize party supporters at election time, parties need to educate the population (or perhaps we should say indoctrinate the population) with their viewpoints. They need to communicate their views to the electorate and to their membership. In this, of course, they work with the news media, with TV, radio and the newspapers.

Parties run the legislature

Essentially, Parliament, and the various other representative assemblies that parties get involved in, are run by the political parties. It is true that Parliament has its own permanent administrators and its neutral Speaker, but apart from that, the political parties control what happens there. Following a general election, the winning party forms the governing party in Parliament, and it then works through the whips and the Leader of the House, in conjunction with the Cabinet, to dominate almost every aspect of the running of Parliament. The timetabling of business, the legislative calendar and the composition and work of committees are decided directly or indirectly by the dominant party. In running Parliament, the governing party will need to cooperate to some degree with the opposition party in Parliament. The whips of the two parties work 'through the normal channels' (the phrase used to describe this cooperation) and there will also be some minimal input from the minor parties. When votes on legislation are taken, it is on party lines that MPs vote in Parliament. When debates take place, they speak in the main according to a party script.

Party government

The elected component of the government (the Prime Minister, Cabinet and junior ministers) is drawn from the majority party in Parliament. This is the basis of what is called the parliamentary system of government in Britain.

Box 7.1 Ideology and policy

Parties are held together by their beliefs: by their ideology and policy. The word 'ideology' is used in a number of different ways in the social sciences, but in the discussion of political parties it means a political philosophy, a set of political beliefs which present in broad terms a coherent world-view. Conservatism could be described as an ideology, as could socialism, liberalism and social democracy, etc. An ideology starts with a view of what people are like and what they need from a political system; it also has a vision of what would be best for people; and then it presents a broad picture of how the political system can be moulded to achieve this.

For example, the socialist starts with a view that people are essentially good and wish to do their best, and that they are more or less equal in their intellectual capacities; it sees a world of sharing and community as the ideal; and it sees redistribution of resources and welfare polices as the way to achieve this goal. The conservative is more suspicious of people's motives and thinks that they vary greatly in ability. The ideal for the conservative is a world of freedom, where everyone is left alone to achieve their personal ambitions. The way to achieve this is by reducing the role of government in people's lives and cutting taxation.

Policy explores the third part of the ideology equation in greater detail: it gives a more precise and more focused view of how to achieve the ideological aims of a political party. It is usual to assign the word policy to a particular area of government activity: we talk about education policy, foreign policy, defence policy, etc. It is then usual to break down overall education policy into a series of points which are more detailed still: a policy to improve literacy levels at Key Stage 2; a policy to charge more for school dinners; a policy to expand higher education teaching of drama, etc. The education policy will develop from those aspects of ideology which relate to education: for the socialist, education policy may derive from a belief in equality and hence in comprehensive schools; for the conservative, the policy might be deducible from a belief in intellectual differences between people and hence lead to a policy of selection. It is difficult to imagine a political party which did not have some policies; obviously, they are the selling point for the party when the election comes around.

Politicians like to see themselves as pragmatic or practical in their approach, interested in real problems and real solutions, interested, in short, in policy rather than ideology. But politicians still talk about values and principles, which may be just another way of saying ideology. Some political scientists argue that ideology is in decline and all that really matters now is policy. But in the last 30 years we have seen the birth of Thatcherism and then in the 1990s of 'New' Labour's Third Way. So perhaps it is a little early to claim that the only ideology is pragmatism. Voters seem to like ideology; it gives them something to identify with and is easier to absorb than hundreds of fiddly little policies on all manner of different things.

The Prime Minister is not directly elected by the people as happens under a presidential system like in the USA. The Prime Minister and Cabinet are acutely aware that this means that, ultimately, they are answerable to their party. In 1990, Conservative MPs removed the Prime Minister, Margaret Thatcher, and replaced her with John Major. On the whole, parties and their governments exist on a basis of symbiosis (mutually beneficial dependence), but in the end it is the party which controls the government and not vice versa. It is arguable that it is not Cabinet government or prime ministerial government that we have in Britain, but what Richard Rose called 'party government'. The ultimate power over the system of government is in the hands of the party which wins the general election.

 Question: How do political parties achieve their aims?

7.3 Are parties good or bad for democracy?

There is an important debate among political scientists about whether political parties are a positive force in a democracy, or whether they can be criticized for weakening democracy. Some of the points which can be made on both sides of the debate are given here.

Good: political parties are essential to a liberal democracy

What has been said about the functions of parties in the last section will be seen to be slanted to a large extent in favour of parties. There is no need to recap the main positive points made above, but there is a final point to make.

Freedom of association

Parties are, for all their faults, largely unavoidable. In a liberal democracy, one of the most important rights we have is the 'freedom of association', the right to join together with other people, to form a club, church, trade union, etc. Political parties are just rather exaggerated versions of these associations, and although they need to be regulated by the law (like all clubs), they have a perfect right to exist, and it is probably good in general terms that they do exist, because people cannot easily cope with life all by themselves. This does not mean, of course, that individuals and other forms of association cannot play a part in politics alongside political parties. The real point which ought to be debated, then, is not so much whether parties are good or bad for democracy but whether in Britain political parties are too powerful.

Bad: political parties are essentially undemocratic

This extreme argument contains more than a grain of truth, and we will spend a little longer on it because the discussion of functions given in the last section gave a very positive view of parties. What follows are the main points that could be made in criticism of parties.

Marxist critique

The follower of the ideas of Karl Marx, the founder of communism, would argue that in a liberal democracy all political parties are essentially very similar to one another. So the idea that parties really do compete and offer voters choice is bogus. In a liberal democracy, according to this view, you can vote for any party you like as long as it is liberal democratic. Obviously, an answer to this is that Communist Party candidates are sometimes elected to Parliament in Britain: the last time was in 1945, when two members of the Communist Party of Great Britain were elected for Scottish constituencies. But the Marxist would come back against that argument by pointing out that this very seldom happens, and that the media and every other institution in the country ensure that people are not given access to the information that would allow them to judge whether or not to vote communist, and in fact are all strongly biased against communism.

Manifestos and choice

Swing voters (or 'floating' voters): those who can swing in either political direction, and are willing to vote for any party that convinces them it is right for them to do so.

Essentially, parties generally compete at a very trivial level and agree on the big issues. This is due to the tendency towards consensus in liberal democracies. Elections are often decided in marginal seats by a small number of uncommitted or '**swing' voters**. Parties therefore need to appeal to the voters who are probably most inclined to be centrists, and may not be very interested in either policy or ideology. So, the parties will try to be similar to each other on the important political issues of the day because they do not want to alienate the swing voters. If post-war politics is analysed, it does not show that there was often a very big difference between the political parties. It is only if parties compete in terms of having very different policies that they can be said to satisfy the democratic case that the essential role for parties is to provide the voters with a clear choice.

In a classic study in 1974, Richard Rose analysed party manifestos, the statements of policy and ideology which parties publish in an election campaign and on which they fight the election. Voters are supposed to choose between parties on the basis of what they promise to do in these manifestos. Rose felt that he could show, first, that much of what a government did once elected was not actually promised in the manifesto at all; and, second (this point has been disputed), that parties tended to have a poor record in terms of carrying out their manifesto promises. To take a modern example, in 1997 the Labour Party made five specific 'pledges' about social and economic policy (waiting lists in hospitals, class sizes in schools, reducing unemployment, taxation levels, law and order issues) that they promised to fulfil if elected. By 2001, when the next general election came round, they had only fulfilled two of these promises. In fact, most people had forgotten about the five pledges by then. Labour argued that they had only promised to fulfil them in a full five years of a parliamentary term, conveniently ignoring the fact that they themselves had called the election of 2001, a year early. Questions were raised also over Labour's apparent manifesto commitments in 1997 to make the House of Lords democratic (repeated in 2001), to abolish fox-hunting, to have referendums on the euro and on electoral reform; and in 2001 about not charging 'top-up' fees to university students. There have also been many policies adopted by Labour since 1997 which were not advertised in their manifestos. For example, within a week of winning the election in 1997, Gordon Brown had given the Bank of England the power to determine Britain's interest rates, one of the most significant economic changes made in the post-war era and one not even hinted at in the manifesto.

'The iron law of oligarchy'

One problem with political parties is that they seem to be rather undemocratic, and slightly shabby organizations themselves. Robert Michels coined the phrase 'iron law of oligarchy' in a work published in 1906 to describe the tendency of parties to be run by a few people at the top. 'Oligarchy' is government by the few. In some respects, parties seem more democratic now than they did in Michels' day: party leaders and other party officials are now routinely elected in a way that involves the members of the party. Party finances may also have been cleaned up to some degree by recent reforms, and there should be more transparency in terms of donations. This openness has, however, confirmed that parties receive large donations from individuals and rich organizations. The scandal over 'cash for peerages', which the police began to investigate in 2006, also suggests that there may still be problems in this area. The decline in the influence of the Labour Party Conference in the 1980s has tended to reduce the democratic element in policy-making in that party. The Conservative Conference had never really been very influential. Similarly, the growth of the 'control-freak tendency' in Labour Party head-quarters has tended to centralize power in the Labour Party rather like the Conservative Party. The election of Michael Howard in November 2003 in succession to Iain Duncan Smith, without the membership of the Conservative Party being involved (since Howard's nomination by MPs was unop-posed), also suggests a continued centralization of control in that party. So Michels' description still has some relevance.

Centrist critique: excessive partisanship

One argument against parties made in Britain comes from the centre of the political spectrum, and is often used by Liberal Democrat politicians. According to this view, political parties spend a great deal of time in pointless arguments, when they often basically agree. It would be better, according to this view, if politics could be conducted in a more cooperative way and if a genuine desire to improve matters for the population could inspire politi-cians. This is probably an argument not so much against parties, but against the two-party system, from which the Liberal Democrats are of course excluded. But the depiction of parties as essentially factious, quarrelsome and determined only on winning power from the other 'team' is as old as the Ancient Greek philosopher Plato, and obviously has much to recommend it.

Party decline

Political scientists in recent years have argued that political parties in Western democracies are in decline, and this argument may perhaps be used to support the view that there is something wrong with parties, and that, as a result, they have declined. The arguments for party decline often overlap with the discussion about declining turnout in elections (see chapter 2). If a function of parties is to encourage participation and if participation is in decline, this seems to suggest that parties are failing. Parties are said to be failing in terms of developing policies. They now rely increasingly on inde-pendent think-tanks for this, and indeed for ideological developments too. In fact, they are retreating from ideology in any case. Parties leave communica-tion and education to the media. Parties in some senses are retreating from elections too, perhaps. Why bother to turn out the voters if a majority of elec-tors cannot be relied upon to vote for you? It is better if your enemies stay at home and do not vote. This may describe the attitude of the major British parties in recent years to European and local elections. But the best evidence for party decline comes simply from the records of falling membership, which is discussed briefly at the end of this chapter. There is also good evidence from opinion polls to suggest that levels of partisan alignment are decreasing. This is dealt with in more detail in chapter 4. Partisan alignment (or attachment) is the tendency of people to vote throughout their lives for the same party, and to feel strongly attached to that party, even if they do not join it. Since the 1970s this tendency has been in decline, and partisan dealignment (as the opposite tendency is called) has taken place. There are important social reasons for this, but it would seem that partisan dealignment is the result, to some degree, of the failure of parties to be consistent in ideological terms. People are reluctant to continue to support a political party, like the modern Labour Party, which has moved too far away from what they think the party ought to stand for.

 Question: How effective are political parties at promoting democracy in the UK?

7.4 Party systems

There are really two separate points involved in the study of Britain's party system, although they are linked. First, does Britain have a two-party or a multi-party system? Second, do British parties operate within a party system which tends, at certain periods, to produce one-party dominance? These will be dealt with in turn. But before doing so, we can briefly evaluate the different systems on offer.

Which is better: a one-, two-, multi- or dominant party system?

One-party system

This can be dismissed as inconsistent with liberal democracy and as a feature of Fascist or totalitarian systems, as in Hitler's Germany, where only one party, the Nazi Party, was allowed.

Two-party system

This may lead to strong and stable government; it gives the voters a clear choice; it will lead to broad and diverse political parties; and it was once said to be consistent with the realities of capitalist society, the different sections of which (the working class and the middle class) could be represented by a party on the left and a party on the right. It might well lead to strong and stable one-party government, but it also leads to adversary politics (discussed in chapter 7), deprives small parties of the chance to express their views in Parliament or government, depresses turnout and participation as a result and can drive out new and useful ideas. It will be noticed that the arguments which can be used here mirror those used in favour of and against the first-past-the-post electoral systems which are outlined in chapter 3. This is because the two-party system is encouraged by a non-proportional electoral system.

Multi-party system

The advantages of this are that it gives voters more choice, and hence may boost turnout and membership of parties; it represents a wider range of views in Parliament (e.g. those of small parties like the Green Party), and possibly in coalition governments; and it enables new parties to be set up and new ideas to be heard. But critics argue that such systems lead to unstable and weak coalition governments, as was the case, for example, in Italy in the recent past. Multi-party systems only *seem* to give the voters a choice; actually, they enable politicians to decide the composition of the government after the election. Such systems may exaggerate the influence of harmful extremist parties of the left or right, or conversely they may allow small, unrepresentative centre parties to find a place in government whatever the outcome, more broadly, of an election, as has been the case in Germany. Once again, the arguments here need to be used in conjunction with those in favour of and against proportional representation, discussed in chapter 3.

Dominant party system

The state of affairs where one party can dominate the political scene in a liberal democracy for a number of terms of office (e.g. Labour since 1997 and the Conservatives from 1979 to 1997) has its supporters and its critics. Supporters argue that one term in office is insufficient for a party to change the country radically and to consolidate its reforms. It would lead to weak and unstable government if at every election there were a change of government. Critics, however, argue that a government can become arrogant, secretive, even vindictive towards its enemies, if one party stays in power for too long. A dominant party system, argue critics, denies the very principles of competition and democracy on which the two- or multi-party systems rely. On the other hand, supporters reply, if that is what the people vote for, it is surely what they want.

7.5 Does Britain have a two-, three- or multi-party system?

Modern liberal democracies generally have either a two-party or a multi-party system. The USA is an example of a country with a very pronounced two-party system; most European countries have a multi-party system. According to some, Britain seems to be somewhere between these two extremes, with, arguably, a three-party system. Evidence for these different views of the British **party system** (two-party, three-party, multi-party) is now discussed.

> **Party system**: the way in which parties operate together within the wider political system, specifically, the number of parties in the country, and the relative strengths of the parties.

A two-party system?

Two-party domination of central government

Since 1922, every Prime Minister has been from either the Labour or the Conservative Party; no other party has won a general election since then. It is true that the coalition governments that ruled continuously from 1931 to 1945 all had some Liberal input, but this was largely because of a token gesture. Britain has been dominated by two parties ever since the late seventeenth century, although before the 1920s, when the Labour Party first began to emerge, the two dominant parties were the Conservative Party and the Liberal Party.

Two-party domination of Parliament

It goes without saying that if two parties have dominated government since 1922, in Britain these same two parties have dominated Parliament. This is less clearly true than the first point, since it is possible for minor parties to be represented in Parliament without this affecting the composition of the government. In addition, the way in which Labour and the Conservatives jointly dominate Parliament has been in decline since 1970. But the fact remains that only for a few years in the 1970s, when the two major parties were very closely balanced, have minor parties had any chance of making any real difference in Parliament.

One of the same two parties always wins the general election

Again, this is pretty obviously true in the light of the two statements made above. Between 1945 and 2001, the two major parties have always won more than 70 per cent of the vote between them, although in 1983 – and then again in 2001 – they came close to falling below this figure. In 2005, for the first time since 1924, the proportion of voters supporting Labour and Conservative candidates slipped below this magic figure, to 67 per cent.

The structure of Parliament and of the wider system of government

Ever since the modern British political system came into existence about 300 years ago, there have been two main parties, and this has left its mark on our wider political system, with the result that the two-party system is somehow institutionalized in Britain. The House of Commons is conveniently divided into two halves, one half for the government MPs and the other for the opposition MPs. This emphasizes the two-party system and, incidentally,

Box 7.2 Party systems and electoral systems: Duverger's law

The French political scientist Maurice Duverger noticed the close correspondence between particular types of electoral system and particular types of party system. Generally speaking, countries with first-past-the-post electoral systems tend to have two-party systems. This is because small parties find it difficult to establish themselves since there is quite a high initial threshold to cross in single-member constituencies before a party can get itself elected (generally about 40 per cent of the vote). In multi-member constituencies, a small party can gain some representation with a far smaller proportion of the vote. Conversely, countries with electoral systems based on proportional representation tend to reduce the importance of the two major parties, and hence smaller parties get more power in the representative assembly and in government.

makes it difficult for the Liberal Democrats and other minor parties literally to make themselves heard, assuming they can even find somewhere to sit. We have a government – and also Her Majesty's Loyal Opposition. We talk about the Cabinet – and also the Shadow Cabinet. It is true that since 1970 and the rise of the Liberal Democrats (as the Liberal Party is now known), some efforts have been made to allow minor parties to get a look in, but the essential two-party structure in Parliament remains. This tendency of the main parties to dominate the system and to rig things (such as access to state funding) so that minor parties are weakened has been described as the activity of cartel parties: a 'cartel' is an arrangement in business by which large firms conspire together to squeeze out small competitors.

A three-party system?

The rise of the Liberal/Liberal Democrat Party: general election results

Two-party dominance of the British political system was particularly marked in the years 1945–70, but in the 1970s, a revival occurred in the Liberal Party (now known as the Liberal Democrat Party). Since 1974, the Liberal Democrats have generally gained a little under one-fifth of the popular vote, and in 1983 they won 25.4 per cent of the vote which placed them 2.2 per cent behind Labour. In 2005, they won 22 per cent of the vote. In addition to growing general election success, the Liberal Democrats have also been particularly successful from time to time in by-elections. The Brent East by-election victory of 2003 and the Leicester South by-election victory in 2004 are good examples.

Liberal Democrat parliamentary representation

There has been a steady growth in the Liberal Democrat presence in Parliament. In 1951 they had only 6 MPs; by 2004 they had 54 (nearly a third of the number of Conservative MPs). In the 2005 general election, they gained their largest number of MPs for 75 years: 62. Of course, because of the unproportional first-past-the-post electoral system, this does not fully reflect the growing strength of the party in the country, but it clearly shows some improvement.

Liberal Democrat strength in local government

The Liberal Democrats have also enjoyed some successes in the unglamorous world of local politics, and at various times have claimed to be the second party of local government. They have also made a good showing recently in European elections, and to some extent in the elections for the two devolved assemblies in Scotland and Wales. It is worth emphasizing that European, Scottish, Welsh and Greater London elections have been held since 1997 under proportional electoral systems.

Liberal Democrat involvement in government

In 1977, the Liberal Party had formed a 'pact' with Labour, which meant that the Liberals refused to vote Labour out of office – Labour was at that point in a minority in the Commons. This 'Lib–Lab Pact' was criticized by some Liberals at the time because it did not in return win any concessions for themselves from the Labour government, but it did at least emphasize how important a third party could be when the other two parties were evenly matched in the Commons. Later, between 1997 and 2001, the leader of the Liberal Democrats, Paddy Ashdown, was a member of a Cabinet committee on constitutional reform. This was little more than a gesture made by Tony Blair, but one which emphasized how close the Labour Party and the Liberal Democrats were in policy terms on constitutional reform. In both Scotland and Wales, Liberal Democrats between 1999 and 2003 helped form coalition administrations alongside Labour. The Scottish coalition continued after the 2003 election, and led to some changes in policy in Scotland, which again demonstrates that the Liberal Democrats now wield greater political power than in the past.

The evidence given above may support the view that there is a multi-party system developing in Britain (to be discussed next), but it does not really support the idea that we have at the moment a three-party system. Liberal Democrat gains have been too modest. In fact, for much of the period, the Liberal Democrats have wished not to establish themselves as a successful third party, but to oust one of the major parties and to become themselves once again one of the Big Two. This was the over-ambitious claim made by the Liberal Democrats after their success in October 2003 in the Brent East by-election. Indeed, it is difficult to imagine what a three-party system would actually look like. Does it mean that each of the three parties would take it in turns to form a government? Would we have to build a triangular House of Commons? Some people have unkindly suggested that we now have a two-and-a-half-party system, but it can be argued that even that exaggerates the role of the Liberal Democrats.

A multi-party system?

The rise of the Liberal Democrat Party

While the evidence given above about the Liberal Democrats does not support the idea that we have a three-party system, it does undermine the idea that we merely have a two-party system. It shows that we have moved away from a two-party system, but that our first-past-the-post electoral system in parliamentary elections is preventing us moving very far away. Taken in conjunction with the evidence given below, it might support the case for saying that we have a multi-party system. Or, to express it rather differently, we have different party systems in different parts of Britain. At Westminster it is a modified two-party system, but in Scotland, Wales, Northern Ireland and even Greater London, there is a multi-party system at work.

Nationalist parties

Apart from the Liberal Democrats, the other minor parties to have made a significant mark on British politics have been the Scottish National Party (SNP) and the equivalent party in Wales, Plaid Cymru (the Party of Wales). The SNP was founded in 1928 and Plaid Cymru in 1925, but at first both made little impact. The story of the rise of these two nationalist parties is rather similar to the story of the revival of the Liberal Party. In the case of all three of these parties, dissatisfaction with the 'old politics' as represented by Labour and the Conservatives began to grow in the 1960s, and became most apparent in October 1974 when the two nationalist parties in Scotland and Wales between them gained 14 MPs and 3.5 per cent of the vote. This was their greatest Westminster success, but in 2005 they still achieved 9 MPs and 2.1 per cent of the vote between them. In the late 1970s they had some parliamentary impact as a result of the closeness of the gap between Labour and the Conservatives and were able to contribute to the toppling of Callaghan's Labour government on a vote of no confidence in 1979. The greatest achievement of the two parties was to bring devolution onto the political agenda and, in 1998, to secure devolved assemblies in Scotland and Wales. These in turn have further boosted the impact of these parties, as has been seen by the results of the 2007 elections in Scotland and Wales, which resulted in a minority SNP government in Edinburgh and a Labour/Plaid Cymru coalition in Cardiff.

No similarly successful nationalist party has developed in England, although there are some signs of a nationalist tendency. We can probably

funded party election broadcasts, a minor party also has to cross a threshold in terms of the number of constituencies it contests (one-sixth of the seats in England, Scotland or Wales). The media generally is biased in favour of the two major parties; national newspapers tend to support either the Labour or Conservative Party. Television is anxious to balance coverage on the three leading parties at election time, and the only coverage of minor parties is a cursory race through the names of the whole range of candidates (lasting a few seconds) when there is any focus on a particular constituency. There is fairly strong overall political bias in Britain against minor parties; it is not just a matter of the electoral system. Nevertheless, in 2005 there were more than 45 independent candidates, and more than 165 parties contested the election, the great majority with absolutely no prospect of success.

7.6   Does Britain have a dominant party system?

Relative party strength and party systems

When political scientists talk about 'party systems', they are not only interested in whether there is a two-party or a multi-party system operating in a particular country, but also in whether one of the parties is dominant. We may have a modified two-party system in the UK, but is one of the two parties dominant? It is important to look at this in a historical perspective: clearly, dominance can only be defined in terms of control of the political system for a number of years. There seem to be two possible theoretical models:

1 A single dominant party over a long period. In Sweden and Japan, for example, one party dominated the political landscape for four decades in the years after the Second World War, although in both cases that dominance has recently come to an end. Obviously, this model seems to present some challenges to democracy, since parties in a democracy are meant to keep one another in a state of balance, to ensure scrutiny and full representation of views.
2 A regular interchange of two parties, swapping power, turn and turn about. This seesaw model seems more democratic than the last, since it allows different views to be represented, and ensures there is a strong opposition party, waiting in the wings to take over after the next election.

British party dominance

Which of these two models gives the better view of the British position? Over the years, each of these models has seemed appropriate.

One-party dominance

The idea that the Conservative Party was the dominant British political party had strong support in 1992, when John Major had just won a fourth successive election victory for the party. To win four election victories in a row was unprecedented in modern British history. The Conservatives were certainly the most successful party in the twentieth-century: Labour only had a Prime Minister for about a fifth of the century; the Conservatives were in power, one way or another (in coalition or alone) for about two-thirds of the century. Moreover, Labour governments – apart from that elected in 1945 – generally had small or non-existent majorities. Looking back even further, the Conservative Party enjoyed great success in the nineteenth century, and could trace itself back to the Tories of the seventeenth century. Various theories have been advanced to explain this Conservative dominance, but they mainly emphasise that the British people were, in the words of the Victorian political scientist Walter Bagehot, a 'deferential people', respectful of their social superiors, who liked being ruled by people claiming to come from the upper classes. The Conservative Party was especially strong in England, and there are far more English people than there are Scots or Welsh. Arguably, the English are more deferential than their Celtic cousins. This theory of Conservative dominance received some nasty shocks in 1997, 2001 and even 2005. There is still something in it, though, bearing in mind that Labour had to turn itself into a party which looked very like the Conservative Party before it could gain power. This is sometimes explained in terms of a dominant ideology: what matters, according to this view, is not which party is in control, but which ideology it follows.

Democratic seesaw: a 50–50 party system

This model seemed to fit the picture of British politics in the post-war era, especially in the 1970s. Between 1945 and 1979 the Labour and Conservative Parties were each in power for almost exactly half the time. It is true that there were solid periods of Conservative dominance when they were in power for 13 years (1951–64) and then, less clearly, Labour dominance under Wilson and Callaghan (1964–79, with Heath for the Conservatives intervening in 1970–4), so it was a rather erratic seesaw. But the democratic process of checks and balances did seem to operate quite well, especially in the 1970s, to such an extent that commentators thought that a dangerous level of instability was developing, with 'a crisis of ungovernability', and they longed for the 'smack of firm government'.

Alternating longish periods of one-party dominance

The beginning of the new century gives us a fresh perspective on this question. The Conservative Party had 18 years of uninterrupted government after

1979, and seemed to dominate the political world. Then they lost three general elections in a row, in one of which (1997) they were reduced to their smallest number of MPs since 1832. Labour, in contrast, after slumping in 1983 to a mere 27 per cent of the popular vote, enjoyed unobstructed power for three parliamentary terms after 1997. There are signs of a revival for the Conservative Party after Labour's setbacks in 2003–4, and the party made some gains in 2005, but it did lose that election too. We therefore seem to have moved into an era when periods of one-party dominance alternate between

Box 7.3 Incumbency effect

Incumbency is the position enjoyed by the holder of a political office, as an individual MP, or by a whole party when it is in government. The incumbency effect is the advantage which incumbency can give an MP or a government at an election. In other words, the incumbent candidate is more likely to be re-elected. This is a very strongly marked effect in American politics, so much so that it has led to a movement towards 'term limits' – laws preventing candidates from standing repeatedly.

Incumbent MPs
British incumbent MPs have a small advantage (about 5 per cent) over challengers, which can be demonstrated statistically. As an MP works at righting the wrongs of his constituents and as his or her photograph appears more and more frequently in the local free newspapers, a sort of fan club develops. This must collectively give a marginal advantage to an incumbent party as a whole.

Incumbent parties
The party in power attracts more donations from businessmen, keen (for example) not to see a ban on advertisements for cigarettes. The news media tend to support a party in power, especially if their proprietor wishes to prevent legislation limiting media monopolies. Above all, the party in power can set the media agenda, by making announcements of policy initiatives, etc. Patronage in the hands of the government also helps. Margaret Thatcher put a surprising number of newspaper editors up for knighthoods. A party in power can also use its patronage to keep its own supporters happy, and thus prevent splits and disunity. Government information and party spin-doctoring will be difficult to separate. An incumbent party can use foreign policy to its advantage, and the leader can become a sort of *Hello* magazine 'personality', photographed shaking hands with Nelson Mandela, or directing a (hopefully successful) war in a distant land of which we know little. The incumbent party can manufacture an economic boom, conveniently timed to coincide with a general election. The Chancellor of the Exchequer can cut taxes, increase public spending and generally use the economy to create a 'feel-good' effect. Above all, in Britain the Prime Minister can choose when to call an election, as long as he or she does so within five years of the last election.

The dangers of incumbency
Incumbency needs careful handling. Events can arise which no government can turn to its advantage: for example, economic downturns or unsuccessful wars. The government tends to get the blame, even if it is not responsible. Parties become disunited as they remain in power: ministers get sacked and become critics of the government; mavericks on the backbenches appear, as it becomes clear to them that the Prime Minister will never promote them. Worst of all, Prime Ministers can mis-time the general election, as Callaghan did in 1978–9.

the two major parties. This would seem to provide both democratic checks and balances, thus removing the danger of corruption and elective dictatorship, while at the same time producing strong effective leadership – at least in theory. One reason for this state of affairs may be the incumbency effect.

 Question: 'Britain now has a multi-party system.' Discuss.

7.7 Adversary and consensus politics

How do political parties behave in relation to one another? How do they operate within the wider political framework? There are two models which describe the ways in which this happens, both rather extreme views of how, in practice, the political system actually works. These are adversary politics and consensus politics.

Adversary politics: the way in which political parties conduct themselves in constant disagreement and debate.

The phrase **adversary politics** can be used to describe what seems to be the obvious disagreement that exists on a regular, day-to-day basis between the political parties. Clearly, the adversarial conflict will be strongest at the time of general elections. Each party will seek to undermine the other, to condemn the activities of their opponents in the past, particularly the record of the government, and also to discredit the policy proposals of their rivals. This is important if voters are to make a sensible choice when they cast their votes. They need to have a clear idea of where parties stand, and how they differ from one another. It is also important that there should be adversarial conflict if the government's actions are to be properly scrutinized and if legislation is to be debated in parliament effectively. There may be a way in which adversarial politics links to democratic representation too. The antagonism between different social classes or different interest groups is played out in the political debate between the parties, thus perhaps defusing the conflict and helping prevent a resort to violence. It acts as a sort of safety valve when tempers are running high. The adversarial system in British politics tends to emphasise a two-party system, however. Where does the third party place itself? This has always been a dilemma for the Liberal Democrats, who can either attack both the other parties, in which case they appear negative, or side with one party against another, in which case they appear redundant. Adversary politics can be criticized. It seems rather artificial and childish to be quarrelling all the time. If government is a business which is important, surely politicians should cooperate a little more? It was to tap into this feeling that, when he set up his government in June 2007, Gordon Brown tried to be inclusive, to set up a 'government of all the talents', by inviting Paddy Ashdown, an ex-Liberal Democrat leader, to join his Cabinet; Ashdown refused. On the other hand, when it works well, the adversarial system helps stimulate effective scrutiny of the executive in Parliament from a strong opposition.

Consensus politics occurs at two levels. First, there is a tendency in times of crisis for political parties to stop quarrelling and to unite to fight a common enemy. This leads to what is called a bipartisan approach on some issues, or agreement between the two major parties. Cooperation at certain times can even lead to the setting up of coalition governments. A coalition government is one that consists of members from a number of different political parties.

Second, and more interestingly, consensus – or 'moving consensus' as Dennis Kavanagh calls it (because it is best understood as a process moving through time) – is used to describe the tendency in post-war politics for the major political parties to agree broadly on many issues for long periods, without ceasing at the same time to quarrel over details and to present to the voters an image of being engaged in strong adversarial disputes.

> **Consensus politics**: agreement, so when parties agree this can be seen as consensus politics.

Bipartisanship and coalition

On a day-to-day basis, parties clearly agree quite frequently in some areas of public policy: especially on matters of defence, foreign policy and national security. This is sometimes described, in a two-party system, as a bipartisan (or two-party) approach. Thus, after the Northern Ireland troubles re-emerged in 1969 there was generally not much to choose between the policies of the two major mainland parties on this matter. The invasion of Iraq in 2003 also commanded the support of the leadership of both Labour and Conservative Parties in the end, although the Liberal Democrats opposed it. It is perhaps natural that when the country is faced with external threats, there should be a suspension of adversary politics. During the two world wars of the last century, coalition governments were set up, which is the ultimate stage of consensus. Other areas sometimes also command agreement. Environmental issues, for example, seem to be ones on which the major parties generally seem reluctant to disagree. Back in 1931, very severe economic problems and the onset of the Great Depression led to the creation of a 'national' or coalition government, which contained Labour, Conservative and Liberal MPs, and lasted until the formation of the war-time coalition government under Winston Churchill. Even outside these exceptional areas of bipartisan agreement and periods of coalition government, on a day-to-day basis it is important for an opposition party to be seen to be acting responsibly and it is sensible for it to give support to a government when it is seen to be popular with the media and the electorate to do so. The government itself may also see some political advantage to be gained from appearing consensual. Brown's attempt to be inclusive when he formed his government in June 2007 were probably largely undertaken in an attempt to destabilize the other parties, and amounted to little, but giving a peerage to a non-member of the Labour Party, Digby Jones, and then including him as spokesman on industry in the government was at least an interesting consensus innovation. Brown also appointed a number of non-Labour politicians as 'government advisers'.

Consensus and adversary politics during the post-war period

Some political scientists use the term consensus politics to refer to a broader tendency in British politics that is, the tendency, at least for most of the time, for parties to follow what are broadly very similar policies despite, on the face of it, disagreeing quite violently about the detail of these policies. On a day-to-day basis, adversary rather than consensus politics generally seems to be more the norm, but if we step back and look at issues over 10 or 20 years, agreement or consensus look more prominent. There have been two main periods of consensus in recent years: the first from 1945 to 1979 and the second from about 1990 to the present. But in between there were also periods of quite prolonged conflict, or adversarial combat, periods of what is sometimes called polarization, when Labour and the Conservatives appeared to be unable to agree about anything much. It looks, then, according to this theory (which has received some criticism, it is fair to say), as if, in the post-war period, there have been two periods of consensus and one major period of polarization.

The post-war consensus (1945–79)

This period of consensus is said to have started with what is called the Attlee Settlement, the period of reform under the Attlee Labour government of 1945–51. Clement Attlee established new lines of policy by setting up the welfare state on the basis of the Beveridge Report. He also worked for full employment, following the economic theories of John Maynard Keynes. His government established a nuclear defence policy based on a close Atlantic alliance with the USA, and began to dismantle the British Empire. At first, many of these reforms were opposed in good adversarial fashion by the Conservatives. But when, in turn, Winston Churchill, Anthony Eden, Harold Macmillan and (to a lesser extent) Edward Heath became Prime Minister, none of them overturned much of what Attlee had done. Indeed, they mostly continued it, thus establishing a consensus. So the post-war consensus was essentially left-of-centre in political terms, established by Labour but then accepted by moderate Conservative administrations. In addition, the Labour leaders who were elected after Attlee tended to stick with what he had achieved and were reluctant to move any further to the left. Thus they also kept to the consensus.

The period of adversary or polarized politics (roughly 1979–90)

The post-war consensus is said to have broken down in the 1970s in the face of economic and social problems (although the foreign and defence aspects of it were rarely questioned). Margaret Thatcher condemned consensus, calling believers in it 'Quislings' (a reference to a Norwegian traitor of the Second World War who had collaborated with the Nazis). Thatcher was ready to abandon full employment, Keynesian economics and even some parts of the welfare state. At the same time, the left of the Labour Party seized control of their party and tried to steer it away from consensus in the opposite direction. Basically, Thatcher won the struggle, and was able to establish her new settlement and then consensus, while the Labour Party split down the middle, with its right wing going off to form a separate party, the Social Democratic Party.

The new Thatcherite consensus (1990–present)

Thatcher left an indelible mark on British politics, as much as Attlee, and we are still living in her shadow. She shifted economic and social policy substantially to the right. There was little she could do about the imperial and foreign policy she inherited from Attlee, although her resolute defence of the Falkland Islands suggested a return to imperial days. John Major continued as Thatcher had begun, and there was no retreat from her domestic policy, except over the poll tax. As the Labour Party itself moved back into the centre of British politics, it largely adopted Thatcher's approach, only adding one new element – namely, its distinctive constitutional policy, of which Thatcher and Major strongly disapproved. By the time Blair was elected Prime Minister in 1997 it was possible to talk about a new consensus, based on the Thatcher settlement. It seems unlikely that history will judge that Brown has moved far from this Blairite Thatcherism

Consensus and party competition

Faced with a popular and successful line of policy such as that pursued by Thatcher or Attlee, an opposition party can either fight it (and risk, as Labour did in the 1980s, being seen as extremist) or it can accommodate itself to the successful policies and accept the consensus that is established. So party dominance is linked in a complex way with consensus and adversary politics. Parties have to compete, but since they are competing for our votes, they have to adapt themselves to what is popular. This can put a strain on their ideology and can risk disunity. It is probably not possible to develop a coherent theory to explain the relationship between all these themes (consensus, ideology, party dominance and party unity), but there is clearly a subtle and interesting inter-relationship between them.

Question: Distinguish between consensus and adversary politics.

7.8 The internal structures and politics of parties

Political parties have their own internal structures, which provide political scientists with a fruitful area to study. A survey will be given here of the chief points, concentrating on the Conservative, Labour and Liberal Democrat Parties. In recent years there has been convergence, or a tendency towards similarity, between all three major parties in terms of their internal structures, but some differences will be highlighted.

Quasi-federal structures

In recent years, all three major parties have developed structures which are in part federal (quasi-federal), devolving some power from London to their national organizations in Scotland and Wales. The Liberal Democrats inherited from the Liberal Party a basic structure which was already federal, with Scottish, Welsh and English organizations. The other two parties have developed more in the same direction in recent years as a result of the need to work in the environment created by devolution, the policy which Labour has followed since 1997 of giving greater independence to Scotland and Wales. It is important as a result of devolution to have a devolved national framework for selection of Scottish and Welsh leaders and candidates, and the development of distinctive policies for each devolved nation. Further down the line, the parties are essentially structured according to the parliamentary constituency boundaries; each constituency has a committee of some sort, with a chairman. The major parties are also able to employ in each constituency (or a group of constituencies) a paid party agent who runs the elections and keeps the administration of the constituency party ticking over between elections. The two major parties have a more or less costly administrative machine in London, although Labour recently opened some offices in Newcastle upon Tyne. The Conservative Party chairman has for many years been an MP who generally has a seat in the Cabinet or Shadow Cabinet. Recent Conservative reforms have seen the appointment of two party chairmen, who work in partnership together. In contrast Labour's organization was run by a less prominent figure who was not an MP: the General Secretary. But in 2001 Labour followed the Conservatives in this, appointing a chairman with a seat in the Cabinet. The Labour Party has a National Executive Committee, which was originally an important body, representing the party membership

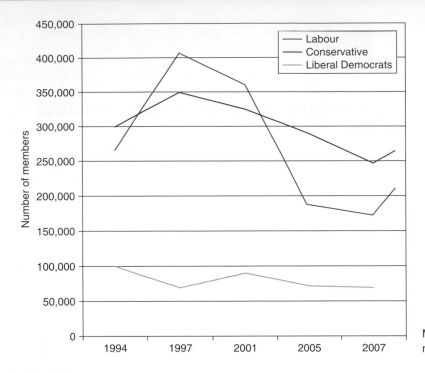

Membership of the three main parties, 1994–2007

and deciding policy and matters of party governance. In the 1970s this body occasionally came into conflict with the parliamentary leadership of the party, but by the 1990s it became far less active than it had been, and is now almost entirely subservient.

Membership

Political parties try to develop a mass membership, although it is an uphill struggle at the moment. A large membership helps raise funds, is useful for canvassing, leafleting, etc. in the election campaign, is important in maintaining a presence in local government and simply raises the core support of a party. But membership has declined from the middle of last century, when there were two million Conservative members, and one million ordinary Labour members. By 2005, there were 198,000 Labour members and 290,000 Conservative members. In the same way the Liberal Democrat membership has shrunk from 100,000 in 1994 to fewer than 72,000 in 2005. The Labour Party made a great drive to increase its membership in the 1990s, which was successful, but this growth has not been sustained, and there has been a significant loss of members since 2001, due in part, it is said, to opposition to Labour policy over Iraq among the membership. By May 2007, Labour Party membership had slumped to 177,000 (well under a half of its 407,000 peak in the heady days of 1997), but the fall of Blair led to an increase of 130,000 during three weeks in the summer of 2007. In the same way, the appointment of David Cameron as leader of the Conservative Party encouraged a significant growth in Conservative membership. The Labour Party is different from the other parties in that, in addition to its ordinary membership, it has a large number of what are called 'affiliated' members, mainly those who belong to trade unions which have links to the Labour Party and who contribute through their union dues to party funds. It may be that membership is actually not as important to parties as it was in the past. Funds can be raised from large donors more easily than from a mass membership. The election campaign is conducted increasingly centrally rather than locally, using electronic communication methods and the mass media, so it does not depend on a large number of volunteers.

Selection of leaders

All three major parties now have a formal system for the selection of their leaders by the membership. This has replaced a system by which party leaders were once chosen only by their MPs. The Liberal Democrat Party ballots all its members after its MPs have nominated candidates. The Conservative Party has a two-stage process, which involves initial ballots among MPs and then the membership voting in a run-off, when the MPs have reduced the field to two. As the events of 2003 showed, the Conservative membership only becomes involved when the MPs disagree over who should be leader. The election of Michael Howard in that year was uncontested by his fellow MPs, so he was elected, in a so-called 'coronation', without any input from the membership. There were moves afoot in 2004–5 to propose a reform of the Conservative leadership election rules, which would return the power of choosing a leader entirely to the MPs, which was how the process had operated before the fall of Thatcher in 1990 led to a change in the system. It was felt that the membership could make mistakes in electing leaders, as was the case with Iain Duncan Smith (chosen in 2001). When, following the general election of 2005, he announced his decision to retire as leader, Michael Howard said that he would reintroduce the former system for electing the leader before he stood down. But in a vote among the leading figures in the party held in September 2005, Howard's proposals for reform were turned down, and the election of his successor, David Cameron, was conducted under the two-tier system, involving both MPs and the membership. It seems that in the case of Cameron's election, it is arguable that the membership were more sure-footed than Conservative MPs would have been, since, if left to themselves, they would probably have selected David Davis, who had less mass appeal to the electorate as a whole than Cameron.

The Labour Party system now involves a so-called Electoral College, which is divided into three equally weighted groups of electors: MPs and MEPs, trade union affiliated members and the 'ordinary' members of the party. Each

Table 7.2 Female party candidates in the 2001 and 2005 general elections

Party	2001			2005		
	Female	Total	%	Female	Total	%
Labour	148	640	23.1	166	627	26.5
Conservative	92	643	14.3	123	630	19.5
Lib Dem	140	639	21.9	145	626	23.2
Green	38	145	26.2	37	183	20.8
Plaid Cymru	7	40	17.5	5	40	12.5
Respect	n/a	n/a	n/a	9	26	34.6
SNP	16	72	22.2	13	59	22.0
UKIP	58	424	13.7	64	496	12.9

Source: Adapted from Lisa Harrison, 'Electoral Strategies and Female Candidacy: Comparing Trends in the 2005 and 2001 General Elections', 2005

the introduction of party lists in European and national devolved elections after 1997, the input of the party leadership increased. The desire on the part of the central organizers in all major parties to involve more women and more minority ethnic groups in the process has also led to disputes with their local constituency parties, who may not sympathize with positive discrimination, or with central interference. Labour efforts to impose a female candidate in 2005 in the constituency of Blaenau Gwent led to a split in the constituency party and in the end to a disgruntled local Labour activist, Peter Law, standing as an independent and winning the seat. The 2000 Political Parties, Elections and Referendums Act strengthens the central control by parties of the selection of their candidates, since every candidate now needs central endorsement before his or her name can be included on the ballot paper in an election.

Greater diversity of candidates

As has been said, the process of trying to get more women and (to a lesser extent) black and minority ethnic MPs has been one which all the mainstream parties have shared. Labour began the process by adopting all-women shortlists for half its winnable seats in preparation for the 1997 election. This did lead to a growth in female representation, but was strongly resisted in some sections of the party, and in 2001 had to be dropped because of a judgement in an industrial tribunal, which ruled that the practice was discriminatory (against men). As a result, Labour passed the Sex Discrimination (Election Candidates) Act in 2002, which allowed such discrimination. This was then applied to the selection of candidates for 2005, and allowed Cameron to develop his A-list strategy. The use of party lists in AMS elections has also hastened this process of achieving greater female representation. The position for black and minority ethnic candidates has, however, been less satisfactory.

Party conferences

All parties hold meetings of members, the most important of which are the annual party conferences, held in the autumn, usually in a holiday town. In the 1980s, these used to be rather different affairs from what they are nowadays. The Conservative Conference was always a well-managed process with long speeches from the leading figures of the party applauded politely by the party faithful. Apparently, the behind-the-scenes lobbying under Thatcher at conference time could actually be quite effective and she always took the conference seriously. But essentially these were calm events, where the Conservative Party put on a brave face for the news media.

The Labour Party Conference, in contrast, claimed to be a genuine process of consultation, with real policy decisions arrived at after real debate. In practice, in the 1970s and 1980s Labour conferences became riotous assemblies where the long-suffering Labour leaders were harangued about the brotherhood of man by activist delegates from the trade unions or constituency parties. Since those days, Labour has cleaned up its act to such an extent that the Conference now looks as though it has been scripted by Downing Street spin-doctors. At the 2005 Labour Conference, Walter Wolfgang, an 82-year-old member of the party, was forcibly ejected from the Conference chamber for shouting out 'Rubbish' in the middle of a speech by the Foreign Secretary. This attempt to prevent dissent turned out to be a mistake when the TV pictures of the event received almost universal condemnation from those who saw them.

Again, on the subject of conferences, the main theme is convergence: the two major parties becoming more like one another. Only the Liberal Democrat Conference seems at present to contain the occasional genuine debate. The Labour Party Conference retains one significant point of difference from the others, since the trade unions still retain half the voting power there. This is a remnant of the old days when Labour was extremely closely linked to the trade union movement. On the whole, modern trade unions have been quite supportive of the new party leadership, although in 2005, the unions used their votes to pass resolutions in favour of a return to more trade union legal powers, which embarrassed the New Labour spin-doctors.

Tony Blair arriving at the annual Labour Party Conference in Manchester, 2006

Policy forums

In the 1990s, all three political parties developed mechanisms by which they could consult their core supporters away from the glare of publicity – away, in fact, from the conferences. These bodies tend to be strictly managed by the party organizers and amount to glorified focus groups, or groups of people brought together by experts in marketing (and increasingly by political campaign strategists) to test public opinion at depth on a range of issues. The Labour Party has a complex policy-forming process which involves a National Policy Forum and a Joint Policy Committee: these bodies then pass their ideas to the National Executive Committee and to the conference for approval. No one can doubt, though, that at each stage the behind-the-scenes intervention of the party leadership can be decisive. In any case, policy is increasingly made now in think-tanks, some of them funded by the parties, but essentially detached from them.

Top-down or bottom-up?

Are British political parties democratic? Robert Michels' 'iron law of oligarchy', which has been referred to already in this chapter, still applies. Parties in Britain are still run by their leaders and the small group of people who associate themselves with the leadership. Parties (even the Liberal Democrats) are essentially top-down organizations; that is to say, the people at the top have the power. The Labour Party had to change most of all to achieve this dubious goal, but it succeeded, to such an extent that after 1997 there were complaints that Labour was run on a basis of 'control-freakery' from the top. This led to real problems when it came to the selection in 1999 of a London mayoral candidate, and also to the selection in 1998 of a Welsh Assembly party leader. In both cases, the party at the centre tried to impose its will on the local party members, with disastrous consequences for the party in both cases. It is hardly surprising, given this top-down approach, that party membership figures are in decline. According to recent political science analysis, we have moved from mass-membership parties characteristic of the first half of the twentieth century to cadre parties, run by a small elite oligarchy (or 'cadre'), sometimes also described according to the coinage of P. Webb as electoral professional parties – parties designed to win power by professionally marketing themselves.

7.9 Party funding

State funding

Parties play a valuable part in the democratic process, and in some countries they are funded largely by the taxpayer. There has been much discussion in Britain about whether this should be done here, and the general view among the parties is that it would be wrong to develop a system of state funding. But it needs to be emphasized that the state already does fund political parties to some extent in Britain. Opposition parties receive 'Short Money' (named after the politician who first introduced the policy in 1975), which is given to help them maintain their structures and organization. In 1996, Cranborne Money (again named for a politician who set up the scheme) was introduced to help fund the opposition party in the Lords. These grants recognize that, one way or another, the party in government can use state money to strengthen itself, for example by putting political advisers on the civil service pay-roll, or by making the party chairman a cabinet minister, and hence that the opposition needs some compensation. It is reckoned that about £25 million goes each year direct from the taxpayer to the parties.

Party political and party election broadcasts are controlled by legislation and are broadcast free of charge to the parties. This represents a significant saving in election costs for political parties – in the USA, parties spend most of their money on television broadcasts. It is estimated that free party election broadcasts are worth about £68 million. In addition, free postage is provided to all parliamentary candidates so they can send out leaflets: a saving of about £20 million. But, despite these elements of public funding, there are

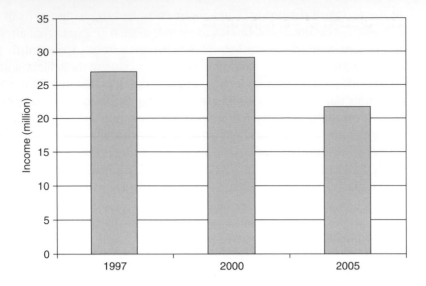

Labour Party income, 1997–2005: three-quarters of funding received by the Labour Party now comes from trade unions

still large sums of money which need to be found by the political parties themselves.

Party fundraising

Funds are raised from membership subscriptions and from constituency fundraising efforts – for example, social events. Individual contributions from wealthy donors are a topic which has excited controversy over the years, especially if (as was the case until regulations prevented this) the donor was a foreigner. Business provides some funding for political parties, in the past especially in the case of the Conservative Party, but increasingly also for the Labour Party. Trade unions have always helped to fund both individual Labour MPs and the party as a whole. In 2005, the unions gave Labour £12 million. This funding is to some degree in decline, and voices on the left of the trade union movement are sometimes raised against it, but the practice still continues. These corporate and union donations have been called into question as being potentially corrupt.

Party spending

The central organizational structures and the running of local constituency parties require money. Parties need research and media departments, which will be expensive to run. But the real drain on resources comes at election time, and there are now more elections to finance as a result of European integration and devolution. Huge sums are spent, above all, on mounting newspaper advertising campaigns and employing staff at the party's headquarters.

Regulation of party funding

The amount that each individual candidate in a general election can spend has been strictly regulated since 1883 in an effort to prevent the bribing of voters. The funding and expenditure of political parties at the national level has long been an area of interest and sometimes of concern. In the 1990s a number of scandals came to light, especially, but not exclusively, affecting the Conservative Party, some of which had to do with party funding. The result was that Labour, when it was elected in 1997, asked the Neill Committee on Standards in Public Life to report on the law governing party funding. The Neill Report was published in 1998 and resulted in legislation in 2000, when the Political Parties, Elections and Referendums Act was passed. The main provisions of the Act are:

- An independent electoral commission has been set up to supervise party spending on elections (among other things). The limit set on national spending on a Westminster general election was, in 2005, set at £19.23 million over a period of one year before the election for each party which contests all constituencies in Great Britain.
- Large donations (of more than £5,000 nationally) must be publicly disclosed.
- Foreign donations to parties are forbidden.
- Parties must publish details of donations quarterly, and weekly during the election campaign.
- Companies which make contributions to parties must ballot their shareholders every four years on this.
- Blind trusts (financial devices to pay money to parties without the origin of the money being made clear) are forbidden.
- Nominations for honours to major party donors are to be scrutinized.

"... So I says to my mate, Shamus back at the mission, what am I goin' to do with me lottery win? Why not make a donation to the Labour Party he says ..." *Cartoonist of the Year*

Cash for peerages

Following the 2005 election, scandalous allegations were made about the fundraising activities of all three political parties. The first problem concerned the way in which donations to parties were being disguised as loans. Loans are not subject to disclosure and auditing by the Electoral Commission, so a supporter can lend money to a political party without the public knowing about it. This seems to be against the spirit of the 2000 Act, and if the loan is made on non-commercial terms, and worse still if it is not expected to be repaid, it is downright illegal. Part of the problem for Labour was that these loans seem to have been made direct to Downing Street, without the Treasurer of the Labour Party knowing about them. In addition, it became clear that there appeared to be a link between loans and the recommendation of people for peerages: these allegations mainly surrounded Tony Blair and his Downing Street advisers, especially his chief fundraiser Lord Levy. The other two parties were also investigated, however, although clearly Labour was in a stronger position to sell peerages than the opposition parties.

The sale of peerages, although widely understood to have been a feature of British political life for several centuries, is against the law, following the scandals surrounding David Lloyd George, the last Liberal Prime Minister, who resigned in 1922. A long police inquiry dogged the last years of Blair's premiership, reaching its climax in 2007, the year of his resignation. In response to these difficulties, in 2006 the government set up a commission under a former civil servant, Sir Hayden Phillips, which has sought to achieve agreement among the three main parties on how to develop an acceptable system of party funding. In the end, the police inquiry led nowhere and no

Box 7.4 Sir Hayden Phillips's Report

In March 2007, Sir Hayden delivered his report and recommended the following:

- Individual donations from organizations and individuals to political parties should be capped at £50,000. This immediately caused a great deal of fuss in the Labour movement, since it seemed to threaten trade union links with the Labour Party.
- State funding of parties would be raised to £23 million per year.
- Online donations of £5 per person to political parties would be matched by state funds.
- Parties would receive state funding of 50p a year for each vote they got in a parliamentary election and 25p a year for each vote in other elections.
- Spending between elections by parties would be cut; with a limit set of £20 million by each of the main parties per year over the term of a Parliament.

It is generally felt that this report will not be implemented by Parliament in full, since the political parties are unlikely to reach agreement on it. It will probably, however, be a catalyst for some sort of change.

charges were brought against Blair or any of his associates in connection with the 'cash for peerages' affair.

The difficulties of party funding were again exposed when the Labour Party General Treasurer, Peter Watt, resigned in November 2007 after it became clear that the party had accepted donations totalling £663,975 from a businessman, David Abrahams. The problem was that he had given his money through other people, without declaring his name. It then emerged that Abrahams had also given money secretly to a number of candidates for the position of Deputy Leader of the Labour Party, to fund their campaigns. This prompted further investigations and as a result, in January 2008, the Cabinet minister, Peter Hain, resigned after it became clear that he was being investigated by the police.

Activity

There has been much debate recently about party funding. In the UK, relatively little party funding is provided by the taxpayer, but in some countries a great deal more is. In conjunction with a classmate, debate the advantages and disadvantages of state funding for parties. In addition think about the following:

1 Would all parties be eligible for state funding?
2 How would you allocate the amount to be paid to each party?
3 How would you raise the money through taxation? What would you tax?
4 In the USA taxpayers make a voluntary contribution to party funding through the tax system. Is that a good idea? Would it work?
5 Would you fund everything that parties do?
6 Would you allow parties to raise some money of their own?
7 How would you limit what they can raise?
8 How would you limit party expenditure?
9 When you have come up with your plan for party funding, debate it with the others in your class who have done the same.

? *Question:* Discuss the advantages and disadvantages of the current methods of funding British political parties.

> **Factionalism**: the way in which political parties often divide into sub-groups, divided over policy, ideology or strategy; if they become very serious, these divisions can even lead to a party splitting up.

7.10 Party unity and division

The whole point about a political party is that it should present a united front and fight in a determined way to achieve power. It is therefore important that the party should be united. But parties often become disunited, and are prone to **factionalism**, and can even split up.

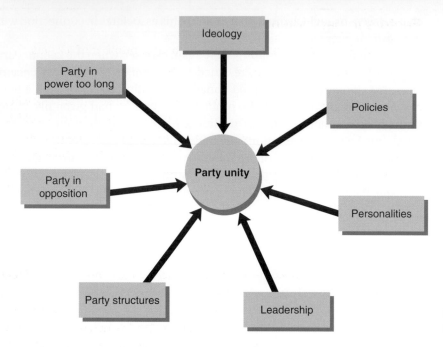

Figure 7.4   Factors affecting party unity

Factions and tendencies

Richard Rose introduced this helpful distinction into the study of political parties in 1974. Factions are groups that have the potential, for one reason or another, to cause real problems within a political party because the members of the faction feel almost more committed to their factional cause than they do to the party itself. The Euro-sceptics in the Conservative Party after 1991, who opposed the signing of the Treaty of Maastricht, qualify as a faction on this basis. They were committed to opposing the ratification of that treaty and although Major's majority in the Commons was thin, they repeatedly voted against a three-line whip. Major became so exasperated by this that in 1994 he effectively expelled nine of them from the party (technically they had 'the whip removed'), but they were then readmitted to the party the following year when it became clear that the government needed their votes on other matters. Tendencies are less troublesome groups which seek to steer the party in the direction they prefer, perhaps over a wide range of issues. The left wing of the Labour Party, sometimes known as the Tribune Group (from the newspaper of that name which distributes their ideas to a Labour Party readership), probably still qualifies as a tendency, although it has been much less active than it was. Right-wing MPs in the Conservative Party have formed a new group, called Cornerstone.

Factors in party disunity

Parties can disagree among themselves for a large number of reasons.

Ideology

There are often disagreements over basic political philosophy at work when a party seems disunited. They can still be best understood in terms of the old division between left and right. In the post-1997 period, the Conservative Party was essentially divided between left-wing, sometimes called 'modernizers' – such as Kenneth Clarke and David Cameron – and, on the other hand, right-wing 'traditionalists', who stayed loyal to the views of Margaret Thatcher – such as Liam Fox and David Davis. These disagreements seemed to come to an end in 2006 with the election as leader of David Cameron.

Policy

Disagreement over ideology leads to disagreement over policy, fuelled perhaps by the constituency interests or the conscientious scruples of individual MPs. The war with Iraq caused considerable division in 2003 within the Labour Party, with a majority of Labour backbenchers opposing the Cabinet on the issue, and two Cabinet ministers (Robin Cook and Clare Short) disagreeing with their colleagues and resigning.

Personality

Politicians tend to have large egos and to be ambitious people. This can lead to personality clashes, and rivalries. Gordon Brown and Tony Blair are said to be great rivals and the creative tension which results from their rivalry is often a positive force, but could potentially divide their party. Michael Portillo in the Conservative Party was at one time a rather troublesome presence because of his great ambition and his evident political ability, which always tends to excite jealousy.

Leadership

Disagreements about who should be leader often stem from these personality disputes. If a leader is perceived to be weak or unpopular in the country, a movement may develop in the party to depose him or her. Question-marks about the Conservative leadership have surfaced from time to time in the case of every leader since Thatcher – including Cameron. Within a year of his appointment as leader in 2003, Michael Howard's position was being called into question in the press. The problems involved with arranging a transfer of power between Brown and Blair was a source of disunity within the Labour Party, especially in Blair's third term. The Liberal Democrats quarrelled in 2005–6 over Charles Kennedy's leadership difficulties; but no sooner had they replaced him with Sir Menzies Campbell, than they began debating whether the new leader was up to the job. In October 2007, they decided that he wasn't, and in December Campbell was replaced by Nick Clegg.

Party structures

These can be a cause of disagreement, and also a vehicle for the expression of opposing views. The great struggles in the Labour Party in the 1970s and 1980s between the left and the right were accompanied by debates over the role of the party conference, the methods of electing the leader and of selecting candidates.

Opposition

Parties in opposition tend to quarrel more fiercely than parties in power. The Labour Party after 1979 and the Conservative Party after 1997 are good examples. However, if matters get too desperate, then a party in opposition can pull itself together in order to recover power: this was true of Labour between 1987 and 1997 and may be true of the Conservative Party after the election of David Cameron as leader. The Liberal Democrats are always in opposition, but have tended not to quarrel very much among themselves, at least not until 2005–7, when leadership issues began to plague them.

Too long in government

There is some evidence that if a party is in power for too long it will lead to disunity and internal feuds. The backbenches fill up with disgruntled ex-ministers who have been sacked by the Prime Minister, and the 'mavericks' (politicians who have no desire for promotion and who have made a name for themselves for having independent views) become more active. This describes the Conservative Party under Thatcher in the late 1980s and may be an accurate description of the Labour Party in its third term, after a reasonably long stretch in power.

Party splits

The ultimate stage of party disunity is a party split. If an individual MP leaves one party to join another, this is unfortunate, but can generally be shrugged off. It is more serious if a faction (or tendency) consisting of a number of people does this. In the post-war period this has only happened once, in 1981, when four prominent Labour Party right-wingers left to set up a new party, the Social Democratic Party. This split helped keep Labour out of power for the next 16 years.

SUMMING UP

Political parties, like pressure groups, have had their critics, but they play a vital role in a liberal democracy. Above all, they are the means by which we are represented in government and Parliament as a result of voting in elections. But they tend to quarrel fruitlessly between themselves and at times look like vehicles by which ambitious people gain power rather than institutions essential to the proper functioning of a democracy. The United Kingdom has two principal parties and a strong third party, the Liberal Democrats, which is about half as strong as Labour and the Conservatives. This is a little strange given our disproportional electoral system, which ought to produce a strong two-party system. In addition, the 2005 election involved a large number of minor party and independent candidates, but not many winners. Although often accused of simply fighting for the sake of it, politicians in political parties have, since 1945, more often been in broad agreement (consensus politics) with one another than in conflict (adversary politics). Political scientists also study the internal organization and structures of political parties. Although they work in a democracy, British political parties are still run largely as oligarchies, in fact increasingly so over the last 20 or so years. The main theme in party organization in recent years has been a tendency towards 'convergence', with the three main parties looking, in terms of their structures, increasingly similar. Perhaps the biggest challenge facing political parties at the moment is over funding and spending, with Tony Blair having been the only Prime Minister in Britain's history to have been questioned by the police – over the 'cash for peerages' scandal.

Further reading

S. Ingle, *The British Party System* (Pinter, 2000): straightforward academic account of the nature of the party system in the UK.

S. Jenkins, *Thatcher and Sons* (Penguin, 2006): looks at the new consensus.

R. McKenzie, *British political parties*, 2nd edn (Heinemann, 1967): the classic text on post-war political parties, giving invaluable historical background.

R. Rose, *The Problem of Party Government* (Pelican, 1976): another classic text, fizzing with ideas, and based on careful research.

D. Simpson, *Political Parties* (Hodder and Stoughton, 1998): very good for the beginner.

P. Webb, *The Modern British Party System* (Sage, 2000): inventive and stimulating academic study.

Websites

www.greenparty.org.uk (Green Party)
www.conservative-party.org.uk (Conservative Party)
www.labour.org.uk (Labour Party)
www.libdems.org.uk (Liberal Democrats)
www.snp.org.uk (Scottish National Party)
www.plaidcymru.org (Plaid Cymru)

The Three Main Political Parties in the UK

Making connections

The overlap with the last chapter may require some cross-referring. This always happens in a subject like politics. There are also links to be made to the chapters on elections. The main exam focus in this chapter is on the ideologies and current policy differences of the main UK political parties, but it is very difficult to talk intelligently about these areas without knowing something about their history. Why not join a political party to find out about what it believes in and what it does? This would provide useful material for a case study. (You could even join two – there's nothing to stop you!)

CHAPTER

8

The Three Main Political Parties in the UK

KEY TOPICS

- Left, right and centre
- A brief history of the Labour Party
- Labour Party ideology
- Policy: Labour's manifesto proposals, 2005
- A brief history of the Conservative Party
- Conservative Party ideology
- Policy: Conservative manifesto proposals, 2005
- A brief history of the Liberal Democrat Party
- Liberal Democrat Party ideology
- Policy: Liberal Democrat manifesto proposals, 2005

SETTING THE SCENE

The last chapter looked at political parties in general and how they operate within the wider political system. It was said there that Britain has, arguably, a two-party system with a strong third party. This chapter now examines the three principal political parties in the UK in more depth: Labour, Conservative and Liberal Democrat. The main focus will be on their ideologies, or core beliefs and values (which were discussed briefly in the previous chapter). There will also be a brief analysis here of the key policy proposals made by each party in the run-up to the 2005 general election.

8.1 Left, right and centre

This chapter is mainly concerned with ideology or political beliefs. Ideologies are often described as being either left or right wing, or being in the centre. Before looking in detail at the three main political parties, it is important first to be clear about what we mean by these words: left, right and centre.

Essentially, a right-winger is a conservative, someone who does not wish to change things very much. A left-winger is someone who sees him- or herself as progressive and reforming. Someone in the centre tries to combine the best of these approaches, believing in only moderate change. This well-known and useful way of classifying political beliefs goes back to the French National Assembly after the French Revolution of 1789, when members of the Assembly sat on the right or left of the chamber according to their political opinions.

The left/right division seemed very clear during the past century in British politics, and mainly concerned how the economy should be run: should it be controlled by the state, in public or national ownership, which was what the left wanted, or should it be in private hands, as the right preferred? This is the classic ideological split between socialism (state ownership) and capitalism (private ownership), and it defined very clearly the views of the Labour Party on the one hand and Conservative Party on the other. Linked to it was the division between those on the left who believed that social problems could be cured by taxation and public spending, and those on the right who felt dubious about this. Even in the years of the classic divide between left and right, there were problems with this analysis, largely because there were 'cross-cutting issues', like law and order, defence, Europe and Northern Ireland, which could not be easily fitted into the left–right spectrum. A further problem was that both major political parties were themselves divided into left and right wings, which inevitably meant that some right-wing Labour members were actually to the right of some left-wing Conservatives. Since the advent of Thatcher's radical reforming brand of conservatism, and then New Labour's rejection of state ownership, the old divisions between left and right seem even less relevant. Having said this, the descriptions 'left', 'right' and 'centre' are so useful as a starting point for discussion that they are very unlikely ever to be completely abandoned by political scientists.

8.2 A brief history of the Labour Party

The Labour Party is the youngest party among the three principal British political parties. It was set up at the beginning of the twentieth century to fight for the rights of working people. In the 1990s it transformed itself into 'New' Labour, a party which seeks to appeal to all classes with radical left-of-centre policies.

1900: the founding of the Labour Party

The Labour Party was founded, as its name suggests, to represent labour, or the working class. A significant factor in the founding of the party was the input from the trade unions, organizations set up to improve the working conditions and wages of ordinary people. It was felt in 1900 by many trade unionists and working men that the other two parties that existed at the time (the Liberal Party and the Conservative Party) represented different sections of the middle class, leaving ordinary people unrepresented. As a result of a series of reforms in the previous century, working men now had the vote; until 1900 the industrial workers had tended to vote for the Liberal Party because of its radical traditions.

1924, 1929–31: Ramsay MacDonald

The party grew steadily after 1900, and by 1924 it was in a position to form a government under its leader, James Ramsay MacDonald. Neither the government of 1924 nor that formed in 1929, also by Ramsay MacDonald, was very strong, having to work without a majority in the Commons, and against a background of economic crisis, but obviously Labour had now made an important breakthrough. Above all, these governments symbolize the fact that in the 1920s the Labour Party replaced the Liberal Party as the chief alternative to the Conservatives, as, in effect, the party on the left of British politics.

1945–51: Clement Attlee

At the end of the Second World War, Labour won a landslide election victory and with its huge majority brought in a series of reforms which defined the party's position as a democratic socialist party capable of massive social and economic reform. Clement Attlee nationalized many key industries, taking them into state control, and compensating their former owners. He set up the welfare state, based on a generous social security system, a new National Health Service and large-scale public housing projects. He adopted an economic policy based on the ideas of John Maynard Keynes, and was committed to government intervention to achieve full employment (Keynesianism). Attlee, however, was no revolutionary. He built on previous Liberal reforms, and in defence and foreign policy he stayed closely linked to the USA and strongly opposed to Stalin's USSR. The achievements of this government created the post-war consensus (see chapter 7), establishing a basis on which future Conservative and Labour governments were to build until the arrival of Margaret Thatcher in 1979.

1951–79: the post-war consensus

Labour and the Conservatives both had their share of power in the years after Attlee: there were 11 years of Labour government and 17 years of Conservative

Box 8.1 Clement Attlee (1883–1967)

Clement Attlee was the greatest Labour Prime Minister before Tony Blair. Like Blair (and many leading figures in the 'people's party'), he came from an upper-middle-class background, attending public school at Winchester, university at Oxford, and serving as an officer in the First World War. He was Deputy Prime Minister to Winston Churchill during the Second World War, and won the 1945 general election for Labour with a landslide majority. He campaigned by being driven round the country by his wife in the family Rover and making speeches every evening in large public halls. In an age which, to judge from some political scientists, was marked by Cabinet government, Attlee was famously frosty with his colleagues and ran a very tight ship. He took the decision to develop a British nuclear weapon without consulting the Cabinet, and certainly without consulting Parliament. He nationalized many major industries: steel, road haulage, railways, air transport, gas, electricity, water, coal and telephones. He established the welfare state and began the process by which the British Empire was disbanded when in 1947 India was given its independence. In the 1950 general election, the voters swung strongly away from Labour, and Attlee only managed to cling onto power with a tiny majority. He made the mistake of trying to recover a larger majority by calling an election the following year. The Conservatives won and were in power for the next 13 years.

government, so Labour was generally less successful that the Conservatives. But Attlee had set the agenda for the post-war consensus, giving this period its distinctive flavour. Harold Wilson and James Callaghan, the two Labour Prime Ministers at this time, were both cautious and essentially rather moderate figures. As a result, the left wing of the party became dissatisfied with its leaders, and the party generally became less united. A struggle developed between the right and left wings of the party to see who should control it.

1979–83: triumph of the left, breakaway of the right

Labour lost the 1979 election to Margaret Thatcher, and the left wing gained the upper hand within the party, with Michael Foot being elected leader. This was the culmination of quarrels between the left and right which had been present from the very beginning, and which had developed strongly in the 1960s and 1970s. As the result of the triumph of the left, four prominent Labour right-wing politicians (David Owen, Roy Jenkins, Shirley Williams and Bill Rodgers) left the party and in 1981 set up the Social Democratic Party (SDP), which then formed an electoral 'alliance' with the Liberal Party. The left were now in control of the Labour Party, and they developed a programme which would have shifted the country decisively towards socialism. They advocated withdrawal from the European Economic Community, unilateral nuclear disarmament, further nationalization, higher taxation and more welfare spending. This programme was put to the people in the 1983 election, which Labour decisively lost, gaining a mere 27 per cent of the vote, which was only 2 per cent ahead of the SDP–Liberal Alliance. Peter Shore, a Labour right-winger, aptly described the 1983 manifesto as 'the longest suicide note in history' (it had been both an extreme and a very long document).

1983–97: the birth of 'New Labour'

Labour remained in opposition for 18 years after 1979, and struggled, following the colossal defeat of 1983, to make itself electable. The obvious lesson to draw from 1983 was that the party had to move not to the left but to the right if it was to gain popular support. This lesson was gradually learnt under three successive Labour leaders, each more right wing than the last: Neil Kinnock, John Smith and Tony Blair. It was Blair who completed this process after 1994. The modernization of the party involved, above all, abandoning left-wing ideology and developing instead more centrist policies. In addition, there was an overhaul of the internal structures of the party and a concerted attempt to make it more electable and to develop support in the news media. Blair added to this strategy a very media-friendly personality and a greater willingness than his predecessors to move to the right.

The great symbolic gesture made by Blair in 1995 was when he persuaded the party to abandon the old Clause IV of the Labour Party's constitution and adopted a new version of it (this will be discussed further below). The name 'New' Labour began to be used by Blair and his supporters at this time. The party did not in fact change its name – it is still the Labour Party. But the adoption of the word 'New', an approach to marketing a product well known to be successful in the advertising industry, was a stroke of genius, since it emphasized to the cautious British voters that Blair was leading a party which had rejected the extremism and squabbles of its past.

1997–present: 'New Labour' in power

In 1997, the Labour Party led by Tony Blair won a stunning victory: they gained 418 MPs, more even than Attlee had done in 1945. The Labour majority was the largest any political party had held in Parliament since 1832. The Conservatives were reduced to a mere 30.7 per cent of the popular vote. This Labour victory was then repeated in 2001, when the party gained only six fewer seats. In 2005, Labour's majority was reduced to 66, but they still won nevertheless. By the time he stepped down in 2007, Tony Blair had become the Labour Party's longest-serving Prime Minister.

Since 1997, Labour has presided over a period of great economic prosperity (largely beyond their control) and has introduced the most comprehensive programme of constitutional reform ever seen in recent British history. Under Blair the party became a formidable political machine and, at the

Table 8.1 Labour Party leaders since 1945	
Clement Attlee	1935–55
Hugh Gaitskell	1955–63
Harold Wilson	1963–76
James Callaghan	1976–80
Michael Foot	1980–3
Neil Kinnock	1983–92
John Smith	1992–4
Tony Blair	1994–2007
Gordon Brown	2007–

same time, changed out of all recognition from 'Old' Labour. But problems began to beset the party in its third term in government, and before Blair gave way to Gordon Brown as leader the electoral prospects for the new Prime Minister seemed much bleaker than they had done at any time since 1992. However, Brown produced a rather unexpected revival in Labour's popularity. Perhaps the New Labour experiment has run its course, or perhaps not! The next election will tell.

Question: 'Old Labour was concerned with implementing socialism; New Labour is concerned with winning power.' Discuss.

8.3 Labour Party ideology

Labour, like the Conservatives, has always been a divided party in terms of ideology, with the left wing essentially socialist in outlook and the right wing essentially social democratic. A third distinctive element is provided in the 'Third Way' associated with New Labour and Tony Blair. It would seem that Brown, a close associate of Blair's from the very beginning, is also part of this movement. The history of the party is the history of how these ideologies have developed and how their supporters have competed for power.

Socialism

The word '**socialism**' dates from the early nineteenth century and there were a number of British writers and activists associated with a wide variety of forms of this belief: Robert Owen, William Morris, Charles Kingsley, for

Socialism: the view, founded on a strong belief in human equality, that private property should be replaced by 'social ownership'.

example. These writers stressed a number of key principles. First, cooperation: the belief that people should work together rather than in opposition to one another. Second, equality: the belief that people deserved equal, or fair, treatment from the state and from one another. Socialism grew up as a protest against the appalling working and living conditions in the nineteenth century, which were based on exploitation and inequalities which derived from a strongly defined class system. Socialists rejected private property and the capitalist system and wanted, in a variety of ways, to take the economy into state or public control, to 'nationalize' large sections of it.

The person who developed a most influential strand of socialism (often known as communism) was the German writer Karl Marx (1818–83), and his ideas, directly or indirectly, had an important impact on the Labour Party. But Marx's ideas were essentially a more extreme form of socialism than that adopted by the party. What was distinctive about the Labour Party, and a number of similar parties in Western Europe, was that they supported a parliamentary route to socialism, rather than a belief in revolution as the way to achieve it. This approach differentiated the Labour Party very clearly from the Communist Party in Russia (and, while it existed, the Communist Party of Great Britain). A belief in reform not revolution is sometimes called democratic socialism, since it involved using the democratic processes as the way to achieve socialism. There was a difficulty, however, in such an approach, since it implied that a Labour Party could achieve social ownership but that a subsequent election could overturn this achievement. Another aspect of Labour Party socialism which marked it out as different from communism was its acceptance that the achievement of socialism might be a slow, laborious process. This gradualist approach is sometimes described as Fabianism – from the Fabian Society, a club of Labour intellectuals who named themselves after the Roman general (Quintus Fabius Maximus), who defeated Hannibal by slowly wearing him down. The left wing of the Labour Party was essentially democratic socialist. But the right wing adopted a different approach: social democracy

Social democracy

Social democracy: the ideology which seeks to gain gradual and moderate social improvements for the people through democratic processes, and which is based on a belief in the value of social cooperation, but not necessarily state ownership.

Social democracy is essentially a watered-down version of socialism, and comes close to some approaches adopted by reforming Liberals and Conservatives. The difference between the social democrat and the democratic socialist is that the former has abandoned the ultimate goal of social ownership and accepts the value of various forms of property ownership. What the social democrat wants are practical steps to improve working conditions and living standards for ordinary people. The social democrat wishes to improve welfare: housing, health, social security and provision for children and the elderly. But he or she accepts that these improvements may depend on economic growth and that economic growth may come best through a mixed economy, where private and public ownership are combined. The social democrat may see socialism as a wonderful ideal, since he or she also feels that people should cooperate on a basis of equality, but realizes that socialism is no more than an ideal, and in practical terms it is not realizable. The social democrat may also be a more genuine democrat than the democratic socialist since the social democrat accepts that socialism may never really command majority support, and that in electoral terms only a more moderate programme is actually achievable. Social democracy is a convenient way of describing the pragmatic (or practical, level-headed) approach taken by most of Labour's leading politicians in the past 50 years, who tended to be drawn from the right wing of the party. When the left of the party briefly seized control after 1979, the four right-wing politicians who left in 1981 formed what they called the Social Democratic Party. But as the supporters of the right who stuck with Labour recovered their strength after 1983, a new version of Labour Party ideology developed.

The Third Way

The Third Way is a term that grew up after the election of Tony Blair as Labour Party leader in 1994. The phrase New Labour was adopted by the party in imitation of what Bill Clinton had done in USA (he and his associates used the term 'New Democrats' to describe their reformed party). The significant feature of Blair's approach was to draw up in 1995 a new Clause IV for the Labour Party and this is a statement of the Third Way. The Third Way is described by its critics as a sham, lacking in intellectual rigour. But this is unfair, and well-known academics like Anthony Giddens have given the ideology respectability. Another criticism is that Labour has tended to be closer to Thatcherism than to socialism, and there is some truth in this. But a better criticism is to say that the Third Way is not really very different from old-fashioned social democracy.

The key ideological aspects of the Third Way are said to be three. First, communitarianism, a set of beliefs deriving from the USA and involving a stress on community, with people accepting that they have responsibilities as well as rights and that these responsibilities involve attempting to live together in a caring and supportive environment. Second, Tony Blair himself and other supporters of the Third Way have been influenced by Christian socialism, or ethical socialism, a belief which can be traced a good way back in Labour Party history and which tries to root its political views in religious beliefs in the brotherhood of man and the need for good neighbourliness. Third, the Third Way is based on stake-holding, an outlook developed by the journalist Will Hutton, which stresses the importance of 'social inclusion', giving all elements of society a 'stake' in the nation, and which sees equality of opportunity (through 'education, education, education', which Tony Blair said summa-

The Third Way: New Labour's ideology, which is an attempt to steer a centre path between old-fashioned socialism and Thatcherite conservatism, but one based on Labour principles of community and social justice.

rized his ideology well) as essential to achieving this. In short, the Third Way seeks to reconcile community with individualism, and stresses equality of opportunity as a way for every individual to achieve his or her full potential. It accepts, however, that social justice has to be based on the creation of national wealth, and that a mixed economy with a strong private sector is a better way to achieve this than state ownership of the means of production, distribution and exchange, as the left of Old Labour had believed.

Brownism?

People talk of Blairism, as a shorthand term for the Third Way of New Labour. In another decade's time, will we also be writing about Brownism? Gordon Brown stands in the Third Way tradition, largely because of his 'prudent' and 'cautious' economic instincts, but his social policy may possibly nudge him back towards a rather Old Labour social democracy. As soon as he was chosen Labour Party leader in 2007, Brown announced a change of style, but maybe not of substance. His appointment of an ex-leader of the CBI, Digby Jones, as government minister in the Lords suggests that the New Labour project is still on track: in the days of Old Labour, such an appointment would have been the equivalent of the college of cardinals choosing a Methodist as Pope.

Box 8.2 Clause IV

Clause IV (technically Clause IV, part 4) used to be part of the Labour Party Constitution of 1918 and was a statement of socialist intent: 'To secure for workers by hand and by brain the full fruits of their industry and the most equitable distribution thereof that may be possible upon the basis of common ownership of the means of production, distribution and exchange, and the best obtainable system of popular administration and control of each industry and service.' The precise meaning of this sentence has been much debated, but on the face of it, it is in favour of nationalization, or taking businesses out of private hands and putting them under state control.

Attempts to reform Clause IV
Throughout the history of the Labour Party, Clause IV has been a cause of debate between the left of the party (who supported it) and the right (who criticized it). In 1959 Hugh Gaitskell, the right-wing leader of the party, tried to get Clause IV removed from the party's constitution, but the move was defeated at the conference. When the left of the party took control after 1979, they had the clause printed on party membership cards. As the party moved back towards the centre, the view taken by Kinnock and Smith, the leaders at the time, was that it was better just to ignore Clause IV and not stir up a hornets' nest by trying to do what Gaitskell had tried. Tony Blair, however, decided to take the bull by the horns, and after a lengthy period of consultation he persuaded the party members in a referendum to support a new version of Clause IV.

The New Clause IV (1995)
'The Labour Party is a democratic socialist party. It believes that by the strength of our common endeavour, we achieve more than we achieve alone so as to create for each of us the

Box 8.2 (continued)

means to realize our true potential and for all of us a community in which power, wealth and opportunity are in the hands of the many not the few, where the rights we enjoy reflect the duties we owe, and where we live together freely, in a spirit of solidarity, tolerance and respect.' In order to achieve this, the clause continued, the Labour Party works for (1) a dynamic mixed economy, based on enterprise and competition as well as some public ownership; (2) a just society, which protects the weak and the poor while it promotes equality of opportunity; (3) an open democracy, focusing on local decision-making and human rights; (4) a healthy environment. The Labour Party also committed itself to a defence policy and foreign policy based on cooperation with Europe, the UN and the Commonwealth, and designed to secure peace, freedom, democracy, economic security and environmental protection for all. Finally, the party reaffirmed its links with trade unions and cooperative societies, but also with voluntary organizations, consumer groups and other representative bodies. Clearly, this new statement of Labour values is far more comprehensive than the old one; it rejects wholesale nationalization and tries to find a 'third way' between the free market and socialist beliefs in equality.

Box 8.3 Labour manifesto proposals, 2005

Economy: Continued economic growth and stability, combined with higher levels of public spending than promised by the Conservatives.

Education: A promise to make 'every secondary school an independent specialist school'. There should be at least 200 academies ('independent non-selective schools') by 2010 – building on the 17 currently in existence. Discipline in schools to be a priority. Everyone should be 'learning' until the age of 19.

Crime: The promise of a new system of neighbourhood policing teams, and legislation on buying replica guns. The age limit to buy knives to be raised to 18 and head teachers given the power to search students for weaponry. ID cards with biometric data to be introduced, and new terror legislation (including a crime of glorifying or condoning acts of terror). Tough policy on asylum and immigration promised, although the value of immigration is also emphasized: a points system for immigrants to be introduced.

Health: Continued investment in the NHS and, by the end of 2008, no patient should have to wait more than 18 weeks between a GP's referral and an operation. The 'independent' sector to continue to be used to expand NHS capacity.

Pensions: Pensions to be reformed, hopefully by consensus. Families to be helped and child poverty addressed. By 2010, all parents of 3- and 4-year-olds to have access to 15 hours of nursery provision. Rights to paid maternity leave to be increased to nine months in 2007.

Foreign Policy: Support for the EU constitution and campaign for a 'Yes' vote in a referendum on it. An interest in securing international agreements on the arms trade, fair trade and climate change to be balanced by a commitment to defence and to a continued presence in Iraq, helping the 'fledgling democracy' there.

The Constitution: A 'vibrant civil society' to be fostered and political participation encouraged. The Welsh Assembly to be strengthened with 'enhanced legislative powers'. The powers of London Assembly and Mayor to be reviewed and regional government generally given more responsibility. A free vote on the composition of the House of Lords to be allowed, and also some changes to its powers and functions. 'A referendum remains the right way to agree any change for Westminster' elections'; a review of the new electoral systems so far introduced to take place.

8.4 Policy: Labour's manifesto proposals, 2005

There is not enough space to say very much about the development of Labour Party policy, but it is important to give a brief survey and the best way may be to look at the Labour election manifesto published in 2005. Under the banner 'Forward not back', Labour promised much, while also dwelling on past achievements in a very long manifesto (see box 8.3).

Question: Explain what is meant by New Labour.

 Conservatives

8.5 A brief history of the Conservative Party

Late seventeenth century: Whigs and Tories

The first political parties in British history (Tories and Whigs) date from the period when Parliament was beginning to establish its independence from the control of the monarchy. Although there have been many twists and turns since then, the Conservative Party can claim a continuous existence since those days. The ancestors of the Conservatives were the Tories, while the Whigs changed in the nineteenth century to become the Liberal Party. The Tories were given their name by their enemies – it was a term used by the Irish and Scots to describe robbers and outlaws. The Tories of the seventeenth century were the royalist, or cavalier, party which wished to preserve as much as possible of the power of the King.

1832: the Tory Party adopts a new name

At the time of the Great Reform Bill, the label 'Conservative Party' began to be used, to replace the Tory label (although Tory is still used as a nickname). The Conservatives wished to conserve or maintain as much of the old constitution as possible in the face of the reforms proposed by their Whig rivals. But Conservative leaders like Robert Peel and Benjamin Disraeli refused to oppose all change, understanding that some was inevitable and might even be good.

Twentieth century: the dominant party

With the decline of the Liberal Party and the only very gradual growth of the Labour Party, the twentieth century was the century of the Conservatives.

Between 1900 and 2000 there was a Conservative government or a Conservative-dominated coalition government in power for two-thirds of the time.

1945–79: the post-war consensus

Conservative Prime Ministers of the post-war period were essentially moderate and prepared to accept many of the Labour reforms established by Attlee in the years immediately after 1945. This proved to be a popular approach and for 17 of these 34 years there were Conservative governments, under Winston Churchill, Anthony Eden, Harold Macmillan, Alec Douglas Home and Edward Heath. But many on the right of the party were dissatisfied by their approach because they seemed to be too willing to accept the policies of Attlee.

1979: Margaret Thatcher

The 1979 election ushered in 18 years of Conservative government, and seemed to create a permanent dominance for the party over British politics. Thatcher won large majorities in three successive elections, and in 1992 John Major (who replaced her in 1990) surprised everyone by winning a fourth term for the party. Thatcher moved her party back to the right and is credited with creating a new consensus, just as Attlee had created the first post-war consensus. Thatcher stood for low taxation, low public spending, privatization, a tough approach to law and order and an assertive foreign policy. Her greatest personal achievement (to become the first woman prime minister in Britain) went almost unnoticed.

1997–2005: in the wilderness

The Conservative Party showed symptoms of disunity and division in the late 1980s. Thatcher was a difficult person to work with, and was surrounded by ambitious colleagues who were keen to replace her. Her brand of right-wing conservatism had always been opposed by some in the party, and her decision to impose an unpopular poll tax (or community charge, a local tax which tried to tax the rich at the same rate as the poor) on the country seemed to her ideological opponents to illustrate her extremism only too well. In 1990, Thatcher was voted out of office by her own MPs and replaced by the more approachable and likeable John Major. He held things together for a further seven years. The great source of division within the party became Europe, with a growing body of opinion voicing criticism of the powers of the European Union. After crashing to a humiliating defeat in 1997 and then again in 2001, the Conservatives had two leaders (William Hague and Iain Duncan Smith), who struggled to unite the party and win back votes. They remained hampered by the fact that most of their best policies had been adopted as part of Labour's Third Way. The few policies which they were left with were rather unpopular. The election – unopposed – of Michael Howard, a pragmatic right-winger, in November 2003, led to a modest revival of Conservative fortunes. But even with an experienced and intelligent leader, the Conservatives did not succeed in making very great headway against an able Labour leadership and a revived Liberal Democrat challenge in the 2005 election.

2005–present: Conservative revival

There is a clear indication that, after the general election of 2005, the Conservatives began to climb back up the greasy pole of politics, helped by the growing unpopularity of the Labour government and a decline in Liberal Democrat fortunes. The election of the media-friendly David Cameron as their leader late in 2005 set them on the right path. Cameron moved his party quickly and sharply back onto the centre ground of politics. Throughout 2006, it looked as if he was the Conservative version of Tony Blair, in the sense that his charm and flair won public sympathy. But since the replacement of Blair by Brown in 2007, Cameron has faced a new challenge, and it may be that the 'Tory Blair', as he has been called, is open to the same accusations of superficiality as the real Blair, especially when faced by (what Blair himself called) the 'clunking fist' of a solid no-nonsense Brown.

Question: How successful have the Conservative Party leaders been in changing the party since 1997?

8.6 Conservative Party ideology

There is an element of continuity in the long history of the Conservative Party, provided by the beliefs or ideologies which over the years have been the foundation for the political message they have tried to deliver. As with the Labour Party, the principles on which conservatism is based have changed and developed over the years. There are three main ideological strands in the history of the party: traditional conservatism, Disraelian or one-nation Toryism, and Thatcherism.

Traditional conservatism

Traditional conservatism is well expressed in the writings of an eighteenth-century political philosopher who was actually a Whig, but who later joined the Tories, Edmund Burke (1729–97). Burke revered the monarchy and the aristocracy. He believed that the most successful constitutions were those that grew naturally rather than those which were written by reformers and intellectuals. He condemned the French Revolution of 1789 as the inevitable and bloody result of the failure of people to accept their position in society. Traditional conservatism involves support for a structured hierarchical society, where people are satisfied with their social position, but where the upper classes realize that they have responsibilities to help look after the lower classes. Burke had little respect for the lower classes, whom he described as 'the swinish multitude'. Obviously, such ideas are largely out of date now, but support for the family, for law and order, for a society based on a recognition of the right to wealth, and a belief that love of country can be combined with support for the monarchy still appeal to many supporters of conservatism. The problems of the twentieth century, with its extreme ideologies of fascism and communism, seem also to suggest that a desire for stability has a place in the modern world.

> **Traditional conservatism**: values are based on a love of the past, a respect for tradition and a desire for stability.

One-nation Toryism

The dominant approach of Conservative politicians in the twentieth century is best described by the **one-nation Toryism** which derives from the writings and speeches of the Conservative novelist and Prime Minister, Benjamin Disraeli (1804–81). Disraeli, building on the work of Sir Robert Peel (1788–1850), an earlier leader with rather similar views, believed that the country was being divided into two nations by the development of the Industrial Revolution. The two nations were the rich and the poor. Disraeli felt that the job of the Conservative Party was to reunite the country, and that the way to do this was by bringing in social reforms, to improve the living and working conditions of the people. At the same time, he aimed to win the votes of the newly enfranchised working class and thus become a truly national party, rather than one that relied just on the votes of the aristocracy and their tenant farmers. Disraeli also emphasized patriotism and support for the monarchy, and while he was Prime Minister he developed an expansionist foreign and imperial policy. This nationalism was to be a feature of conservatism in the years that followed. The acceptance of the post-war consensus by Conservative politicians after 1945 is understandable in the light of this Disraelian willingness to grasp the need for reform, and a feeling that there was a responsibility on the rich to help the poor. The Conservative leaders in this period – Churchill, Eden, Macmillan,

> **One-nation Toryism**: the idea, derived from Disraeli, that the Conservative Party should aim to reunite the country by working to reduce the gap between rich and poor and by developing a strong sense of patriotism.

Home and even Heath – consciously adopted this reforming Disraelian approach and sought to win votes in the centre ground of British politics. Even in the Thatcherite and post-Thatcherite era, Conservative politicians, largely but not exclusively on the left wing of the party, still refer to the need to unite the country behind a progressive 'one-nation' approach. David Cameron's ideology must surely be seen as lying within this broad Conservative tradition.

Thatcherism

The right of the Conservative Party never fully accepted the post-war consensus or Disraelian one-nation Toryism, and in Thatcher they found a champion. Thatcher developed her outlook from the writings of the New Right, a term used to describe the theorists in USA and Britain who revived conservatism in the 1960s and 1970s with their new brand of right-wing views. Prominent among the theorists of the New Right were the American economist, Milton Friedman, and the Austrian-British political philosopher, Friedrich von Hayek. Thatcherism was based on a belief in the power of what is called 'economic liberalism' (a slightly confusing term). Thatcher believed that free enterprise, the market, was the best way in which to run an economy. Free enterprise is based on the freedom of individuals to trade and prosper with the minimum of government interference. Here, Thatcher was keying into long-standing Tory beliefs in the individual's freedom. The main elements in this Thatcherite economic policy were the reduction in government taxation, spending and borrowing. The aim was to stop inflation and allow private enterprise to develop free from state interference. This would, in the short term, lead to a rise in unemployment and hence conflict with the trade unions, best shown by the very bitter and violent miners' strike of 1984–5. But the long-term benefits would be that the impetus provided on the 'supply side' of the economic equation would lead to a growth in national prosperity and hence eventually to more jobs and more opportunities for people to run their own businesses.

The policy of privatization was the most dramatic aspect of what Thatcher did. After a hesitant start, large parts of the state-run economy were sold off to small investors and the big financial institutions. Electricity generation and supply, gas, water and telephones became privately owned. The coal and steel industries, or what remained of them, were also sold off. Buses and, eventually under John Major, railways were also privatized. The mixed economy established by Attlee was becoming increasingly a mixture, where private ownership predominated. Thatcher's aim was to 'roll back the frontiers of the state', but at the same time to make sure that what remained of the state should be strong and effective. The idea of 'market forces', of using the

Created by the Saatchi brothers, this poster is cited as instrumental in the downfall of James Callaghan's Labour government in the 1979 election

techniques of private business in running the public services and the civil service, became the principal ideology of the 1980s and 1990s. The huge army of people employed by the state to govern the country and to provide social policy was divided up and put under a sort of ill-defined 'mixed economy', not entirely privatized, but less clearly under state control than in the past. It was hoped that in this way the work of government would be more efficient and cheaper. The application of these new principles to the public services is sometimes called 'marketization'.

The logic of Thatcherism was that the welfare state would be dismantled. Why shouldn't people pay for their welfare benefits, for education and hospital care in the same way that they paid for other services: either directly out of their pockets, or, if they couldn't afford that, by means of insurance schemes? Why should the government get itself involved in delivering services which could quite easily be provided by business? This was the logic of Thatcherism – to replace a social solution to problems with an individual one. But Thatcher had enough political sense to realize that she could not sell these extreme policies to the British people, who remained attached to ideas of welfarism and social responsibility. The result was that the post-war consensus remained to some degree intact when it came to the welfare state. The biggest area for change was in public housing. Almost by accident, Thatcher developed one of her most popular policies, which was selling off council houses to their tenants. By the end of the Conservative period in government, the majority of council houses had been transferred into private ownership.

In other respects, though, the welfare state was not very seriously threatened by Thatcher. In education, the comprehensive revolution of the 1960s and 1970s remained, although there were efforts to give some state schools greater independence, to encourage competition between schools and also to use parental choice as a device for developing improvements in the quality of teaching. The National Health Service was also restructured and efforts were made to make it conform more to the business practices of the private sector. But it would have been electoral suicide for the Conservatives to try to replace state-funded health care with a private insurance system – and they were very well aware of it. In terms of social security and pensions, the Conservatives found they had to fund the welfare state with large amounts of money because their economic policies in the 1980s led to high levels of unemployment. There were cheese-paring attempts to cut costs here, but, again, no major dismantling of the system. What Thatcher did do was to start a debate about welfare in the United Kingdom and, for the first time since Attlee had set up the welfare state, people were prepared to question the principles on which it was based. But apart from housing, in practice not much actually changed.

The Conservative Party after Thatcher

John Major, who took over leadership of the party in 1990, moved away from Thatcherism to some degree, but it was more a matter of style than substance, and William Hague and then Iain Duncan Smith both defeated leadership contenders on the left of their party to get elected. So the party continued by and large to follow the Thatcherite path. It was difficult for the party to return to one-nation conservatism when their main political opponents, New Labour, were stressing their own commitment to a sort of diluted Thatcherism. The election of Michael Howard as party leader in November 2003 seemed to point in two directions. On the one hand, like Hague and Smith before him, Howard came from the Thatcherite right of the party. On the other, he was a pragmatist with a desire to win, and in his earliest pronouncements after announcing his candidature for election he went out of his way to describe himself as a one-nation Conservative in the tradition of Disraeli. The 2005 Conservative election campaign, with its stress on issues like asylum, immigration, travellers, Europe and the dangers of the Human Rights Act, showed that Howard was still essentially on the right of the party. After defeat at the polls in that election, Howard announced his retirement and another leadership contest began. Essentially, it was between three candidates on the left of the party (David Cameron, Kenneth Clarke and Malcolm Rifkind) and two on the right (Liam Fox and David Davis). The candidates on the right were to a large degree still Thatcherites, who felt that the party could eventually win by sticking to its guns. The three candidates on the left took another view, and felt that the party needed to modernize and seize the

David Cameron was elected leader of the Conservative Party in December 2005. He has since sought to cultivate a progressive image championing green causes, illustrated by his much-publicized decision to cycle to work, although he apparently needed a car to follow him to carry his papers

'centre ground' of politics; in other words they wished to return to the one-nation approach which Thatcher had abandoned. The election of David Cameron in December 2005 suggests that the Conservatives were beginning to return to their Disraelian roots.

Cameronism

David Cameron has brought an end to the Thatcher era in the history of Conservative ideology. Although respectful to the memory of Thatcher, he and his colleagues have been careful to distance themselves from aspects of her ideology. His approach in this resembles that of New Labour under Blair in the period of opposition. Cameron can clearly be bracketed with the progressive or one-nation Conservatives of the pre-Thatcher era, but Cameron adds his own twenty-first-century ingredients. On the environment, he has enthusiastically adopted a more green outlook, speaking on the subjects of global warming and renewable energy. He visited the Arctic to see the evidence of climate change at first hand, and also to be photographed on a dog-sledge. And he cycles to work.

Cameron has distanced himself from the rampant capitalism of Thatcherite economics, speaking of the need to finance public services before tax cutting could begin. This moves his ideology decisively back into the consensual centre ground. He has given his support to the welfare state, saying that his policy can be summarized in three letters ('NHS'), in imitation of Blair's earlier mantra ('education, education, education'). He has spoken warmly of the way in which the NHS has supported his disabled son. Cameron has also abandoned the social authoritarianism of Thatcher, emphasizing the need to prevent crime through an active social policy. He hit the headlines by saying that we should 'hug a hoody'. He has also avoided appearing fanatical or right wing on the touchy questions of Europe and immigration. His approach to refugees, race relations, homosexuality and drugs has been studiously liberal. He has even admitted to having smoked cannabis at school, which one cannot imagine Thatcher doing. It remains to be seen whether this movement to the left on so many issues will continue to gain electoral support, and also whether Cameron will be able to carry all his party with him. When he (an Etonian) announced that his party disliked grammar schools and preferred Labour's city academies, a low rumble of Tory complaints was heard from the more middle-class grassroots of his membership. The real test may come if he faces the tough challenges of an election campaign against a reinvigorated Labour Party headed by Gordon Brown. But it is undeniable that Conservative ideology under Cameron is very different from that followed by the party leadership in the 30 years before he took control.

8.7 Policy: Conservative manifesto proposals, 2005

There follows a concise analysis of the contents of the Conservative election manifesto of 2005, in order to a give a flavour of Conservative thinking, at that (pre-Cameron) stage, on policy. The Conservative manifesto spoke proudly of the 'British Dream', stressing 'freedom, security and opportunity'. The main points were summed up by the Conservatives themselves under seven headings (see box 8.4).

Box 8.4 Conservative manifesto proposals, 2005

More police: 5,000 new police officers to be recruited every year — as part of a general proposal to toughen up in the treatment of criminals, and restore 'respect, discipline and decent values'.

Cleaner hospitals: A stress on the need to prevent outbreaks of MRSA (a serious infection prevalent in many British hospitals) in hospitals by reintroducing the senior rank of nurses, the matron, and by encouraging hospital cleaning. Generally plans for the NHS to involve greater 'choice', especially giving half the NHS cost of an operation to people without private health insurance who have operations privately. Professionals (doctors and nurses) should be allowed to work with fewer bureaucrats controlling them.

Lower taxes: A suggestion that £12 billion could be saved from the budget by reducing 'bureaucracy' and waste. This would involve removing '235,000 bureaucratic posts'. As a result, spending at Labour's rate on health, education, transport and international development would be maintained, and increased on the police, defence and pensions, while at the same time £4 billion worth of tax cuts would be made in the first budget. Government spending to be increased over the next seven years by 4 per cent instead of Labour's proposed 5 per cent. This would then help produce 'a lower tax economy'.

School discipline: A stress on the need for respect. The most specific proposal to involve setting up special 'Turnaround Schools' for difficult and disruptive pupils. Schools to be given more freedom, and parents more choice. University fees to be abolished.

Controlled immigration: Much tougher policies proposed. A British Border Control Police to be set up, to 'take proper control of our borders'. A points system for work permits to be established, as in Australia. An annual quota for immigrants, including those granted asylum, to be set. Britain to withdraw from the 1951 Geneva Convention on asylum and also from EU rules in order to have national control of immigration.

Accountability: Under Labour, politicians had not been held effectively accountable for their decisions: Conservatives, in contrast, make specific promises. For example, an immediate date to be set for a referendum on the European Constitution, in which the Conservative government would campaign on the No side. Parliament — specifically the select committees — to be strengthened to make it more accountable, and the number of MPs to be reduced by a fifth. A commitment to make devolution work, but English laws to be passed in Parliament on the votes of English MPs alone and plans for regional assemblies to be abandoned in England.

Defence: Promises for increases in defence spending. Labour attacked for its Iraq policy; commitment expressed to rebuilding Iraq. On Europe, reform, a reduction in regulation, reform of the the Common Agriculture Policy and an opt-out of the Common Fisheries Policy all to be addressed.

Question: To what extent has the Conservative Party's ideology changed since Margaret Thatcher's resignation in 1990?

8.8 A brief history of the Liberal Democrat Party

Late seventeenth century: the Whigs

The party which developed in the seventeenth century alongside the Tories was the Whigs, a name they were given by their enemies and which derives

LIBERAL DEMOCRATS

from a group of Scottish rebels. This was the party that was willing to reform the political system and give more power to Parliament and to the people, and to reduce the power of the King. It derived from the old Roundheads, or Parliamentarians, of the Civil War period and was, at first, remarkably successful. Throughout most of the eighteenth century, the Whigs were supported both by the people and by monarchs who were willing to compromise.

1832–54: the birth of the Liberal Party

As the Tories developed into the Conservative Party, so the Whigs developed into the Liberal Party. They stood for change and progress, and opposed the old-fashioned world of the past. They drew their support from the new urban middle classes but also from the working class produced by the Industrial Revolution. Their great achievement was to reform the political system, by giving more men the vote in the 1832 Reform Act.

1854–94: Liberal hey-day

William Gladstone, Disraeli's great Liberal rival, dominated late Victorian politics. He stood for further political reform and modernization. Under the Liberals, or as a result of pressure they applied, almost all men were given the vote and the civil service, army, schools and universities, judiciary and the Church of England were to some degree modernized. Gladstone also attempted, but failed, to give Ireland the devolution it had been pressing for.

1906–14: new liberalism

This great reforming trend continued after the Liberals won a massive landslide victory in 1906. They began the reform of the House of Lords and took further steps to free Ireland. But they also adopted a policy of social reform, in order to win the working class away from the newly formed, and growing, Labour Party. David Lloyd George epitomized this new approach, and he helped bring in old-age pensions, the beginnings of social security and heavier taxes on the rich.

After 1914: Liberal decline

For reasons over which there has been much controversy, the Liberal Party then went into a very rapid decline. The main factor is certainly the rise of Labour, but also the continued success of the Conservatives. The last Liberal Prime Minister was David Lloyd George, who during and after the First World

War led a coalition government largely composed of Conservatives. By the 1950s the Liberals seemed to be in terminal decline and in 1955 only succeeded in getting six MPs.

1970 onwards: Liberal revival

The Liberal Party revived in the 1960s, largely because of voter dissatisfaction with the performance of the other two main parties. By October 1974 the Liberals had won 18.3 per cent of the vote, although this only translated into 13 MPs. They also won a number of important by-elections and gained an increased number of seats on local councils. This revival was significantly helped by the formation of the Social Democratic Party (SDP) in 1981. Shirley Williams, David Owen, Roy Jenkins and Bill Rodgers, the 'Gang of Four', leading figures on the right of the Labour Party, resigned from that party because of the rise to power of the left wing, and launched the SDP. In the next two elections, they formed an electoral alliance with the Liberals, under which the two parties agreed not to run candidates against each other in certain designated constituencies. In 1983, the SDP–Liberal Alliance gained 25.4 per cent of the vote, but only 23 seats between them in Parliament, which was insufficient to make the breakthrough they wanted. In the election of 1987, the alliance vote slipped back a few points to 22.6 per cent, and again they only won a disappointing 22 MPs – largely due to the disproportional electoral system.

After the SDP/Liberal merger that formed the Liberal Democrats, Paddy Ashdown was elected as the new party's leader in 1988

1988: formation of the Liberal Democrat Party

The SDP–Liberal Alliance had been a cumbersome organization, and in 1988 it was decided to join the two parties. In many ways this looks, with the benefit of hindsight, like a Liberal takeover of the SDP. The Liberal Democrats, led by, in turn, Paddy Ashdown (1988–9), Charles Kennedy (1999–2006), Menzies Campbell (2006–7) and Nick Clegg (2007–), have continued to play a respectable, if undramatic, part in British political life. The party has regularly scored about 18 per cent of the vote in general elections, and somewhat surprisingly in 1997 and 2001 this translated into a slightly higher number of MPs than had been the case in previous elections (46 and 52 respectively). This increase in representation was the result of a policy of targeting certain seats, tactical voting and also the collapse of the Conservative vote. It only represents a small part of the number of seats they would win under a genuinely proportional system. The same problem was clear in 2005, when they increased their share of the vote to 22 per cent but still only got 62 seats as a result.

Menzies Campbell gives way to Nick Clegg

Having, in 2005, won their greatest election victory for more than 80 years, the Liberal Democrats promptly sacked their leader, Charles Kennedy, after he had admitted to having a drink problem. This had been largely unknown to the voters, but a cause for concern for some time to Kennedy's colleagues. In 2006, the party elected as its leader one of its elder statesmen and a great expert on foreign affairs, Menzies Campbell. Whereas Kennedy had been amusing and youthful, Campbell was sober, respectable and over 60 years old. After his election as leader, the party's poll ratings fell. Campbell made little impact in the House of Commons. He seems to have decided to respond to the challenge of Cameron by steering his party a little to the right on the political spectrum. This seems to be a curious response to a Conservative who is becoming increasingly popular by moving to the left. But, Campbell was in a difficult position, and the decline in his party's fortunes after 2005 probably had little to do with his own leadership, and everything with the rise of Cameron. In October 2007, after months of bad headlines, Campbell decided to resign, and a protracted leadership contest began. The main front-runners were Nick Clegg and Chris Huhne. Nick Clegg, the favourite – sometimes dubbed a 'David Cameron clone' – emerged as the eventual winner.

8.9 Liberal Democrat Party ideology

Liberalism in the Victorian age was a very clear set of ideas and principles, and it influenced to a greater or lesser extent all three of the modern British political parties. Partly as a result of this, although the modern Liberal Democrats are clearly positioned as an alternative to Labour and the Conservatives, it is a little difficult to define Liberalism now in ideological terms.

Box 8.5 What is liberalism?

Liberalism is one of the most widely used words in political science, and one which can cause most confusion.

Derivation
The Latin word *liber* meant 'free', so liberalism means a belief in freedom.

History
Liberalism emerged as a result of the American and French Revolutions of the late eighteenth century, but could trace its origins to English writers of the seventeenth century, and above all to John Locke (1632–1704). His writings were used to justify the Whig party and the Glorious Revolution of 1688–9, which established the power of Parliament over the King. Locke defended a political system in which the members of the community freely agreed to be governed. The people, Locke said, could remove this consent, and rebel against the rulers if they abused their power. This was the theory of the social contract, the belief that men left the original freedom which they enjoyed in 'the state of nature' and became citizens of a state only because they freely agreed to do so. Liberalism developed in the nineteenth century on the foundations laid by Locke into an ideology which supported government by the people and the establishment of free political institutions. Liberals were essentially distrustful of the government of kings and the existence of hereditary elites. But nineteenth-century liberalism had its limits. Its commitment to complete democracy was qualified and it was strongly in favour of private property. It appealed therefore to the middle classes, and the support it received from the majority of the people was limited, especially when socialism developed as

an alternative. Once democracy and free political institutions had been achieved (everyone over 21 in Britain had the vote by 1928), political liberalism was, arguably, redundant.

What Americans mean by 'liberalism'
The word liberalism is still widely used in USA to describe people on the left, especially members of the (American) Democratic Party. It implies a support for the rights of racial and sexual minority groups, a commitment to welfare programmes, a lenient approach to crime, a peaceful foreign policy and generally a rather civilized approach. This usage has never been very popular in UK, although Liberal Democrats might welcome it, and it is certainly rooted in Locke.

Economic liberalism (also called neo-liberalism)
Supporters of capitalism, the free market and laissez-faire economics can quite reasonably be called economic liberals. Their views enjoyed a revival at the hands of the New Right in the 1970s, and such views were sometimes called neo-liberalism. This economic liberalism is consistent with the writings of Locke and the beliefs of most Victorian members of the Liberal Party. The modern Liberal Democrats are rather suspicious of unrestrained capitalism, drawing their inspiration from the new liberalism of Lloyd George (which is discussed below). According to this usage, Thatcher was an economic liberal. But her economic liberalism was combined with a social and political conservatism, which set her apart from what in America and Britain is generally called liberalism.

Traditional liberalism and new (or progressive) liberalism

The nineteenth-century Liberal Party stood for liberalism (see box 8.5). In practice, it supported constitutional reform, religious freedom, the modernization of British society, devolution to Ireland and free trade. These themes can still to some degree be found in the modern Liberal Democrat Party, but they have also been widely adopted by the other two main parties, so it is difficult to see them clearly as a distinctive ideology today. Early in the twentieth century, Lloyd George and Asquith added a sort of social democratic element in their new (or progressive) liberalism, which involved a belief in social reform and the redistribution of wealth from the rich to the poor. Again, this looks like Disraelianism or Labour social democracy, so it is difficult to see it as distinctive. The Liberal Party in its heyday stood for a civilized and peaceful approach to international and defence matters, and this again is a clear strand in modern Liberal Democratic values. It is, for example, the only party which can claim to have been consistently pro-European in recent years, and in 2003 it was the only party to come out clearly in opposition to British involvement in the war on Iraq.

Liberal democracy: an ideology of the radical centre

But can the Liberal Democrats of the last two decades be clearly differentiated in terms of their outlook from the other two parties? Do they have a distinctive ideology? This is a little difficult to say. On the whole, their political philosophy is what one would expect of a party generally positioned in the centre: it is one of moderation and reconciliation, a desire to avoid conflict on grounds of class or on grounds of political philosophy. According to this ideology, consensus and indeed coalition is a sensible way in which to solve the economic and social problems of the modern world, while confrontation and adversarial politics are not helpful. So, Liberal Democrat ideology confronts the two other parties with a challenge, a challenge to cooperate and to progress as a result. The Liberal Democrat belief in constitutional reform is seen as a way to achieve this cooperation. Above all, Liberals have argued for a long time that electoral reform and the adoption of proportional representation would force all parties to work together in the national interest rather than compete with one another in order to achieve selfish partisan advantage. The beliefs of those in the centre of politics are bound to be a mixture of ideas from the two other parties, but what Liberal Democratic ideology offers is a way of actually putting these ideas into action through consensus and cooperation. If people vote for the Liberal Democrats to protest about Labour and the Conservatives, it is in order to persuade the other two parties actually to get something done. But the Liberal Democrats are also radical; a radical claims to examine politics in depth and to get to the root of problems. Over the years, they have been willing to debate questions like cannabis, the monarchy, gay rights, abortion, etc. – areas that the other parties have often been too timid to look at. There may be a tension between their centrism, which places them equidistant between Labour and the Conservatives, and their radicalism, which, especially in recent years, has tended to put them increasingly to the left of New Labour, which has famously repositioned itself more in the centre.

8.10 Policy: Liberal Democrat manifesto proposals, 2005

The Liberal Democrat manifesto of 2005 gives an outline of the party's current policy interests. The Liberal Democrats claimed to be the 'Real Alternative' party, and to be 'open and straightforward'. The main detailed points are given in box 8.6.

Box 8.6 Liberal Democrat manifesto proposals, 2005

Health: As in Scotland, a return to the situation where personal care for the elderly and disabled is provided free. Dental and eye checks also to be made free of charge, and long-term prescription charges made free too.

Education: All university tuition fees to be abolished and more grants to be made available to poorer students. Also, a substantial reduction in class sizes, funded by abolishing Labour's Child Trust Fund. The number of SATs to be reduced.

Crime: 10,000 more police promised, and an end to plans to introduce ID cards. The Liberal Democrat stress here is tougher than it had been in the past on law and order. In a brief reference to immigration and asylum, asylum-seekers to be allowed to work rather than subsist on benefits.

Economic policy: A promise to introduce a top rate of income tax of 50 per cent on earnings around £100,000 per annum, which would be used to fund education and health spending. Money to be saved in a number of ways, for example by abolishing a whole government department, the Department of Trade and Industry.

Pensions and benefits: Council tax to be abolished and replaced with local income tax, thus helping pensioners. The Child Support Agency also to be scrapped, its work being done by the Inland Revenue.

Foreign affairs: war in Iraq should not have happened: British troops to be withdrawn by the end of the year. EU Constitution supported, but also some reform of EU institutions and the Common Agriculture Policy.

Transport and environment: Plans to improve the railways and reduce pollution by introducing in the long run a national 'congestion-charging' system to replace car tax and fuel duty.

Stop the abuse of power: Constitutional change a priority. The royal prerogative powers currently exercised by the Prime Minister should be subject to Parliament, especially on decisions about war and peace. The vote to be extended to 16-year-olds, and STV to be used for all British elections. The Welsh Assembly to be given primary legislative powers.

Question: Is liberalism a coherent ideology?

Activity

Go on the websites of the three main political parties (see below) and research their key beliefs and policies. Try to come up with a coherent statement of their current views by examining their websites, and attempt to classify the beliefs found there.

- Does the Conservative website suggest that the current party is Thatcherite or one-nation in its emphasis?
- Is there evidence on the Labour website for 'Old' Labour socialism, or a greater emphasis on the 'Third Way'?
- Is the Liberal Democrat website authentically 'liberal'?
- If you find this exercise rather tricky, what does it tell you about 'ideology'?
- Do parties still have ideologies?
- Is policy taking over?
- Or is it just a matter of 'image' and 'vision'?

SUMMING UP

There are three main parties in the British political system: Conservative, Labour and Liberal Democrat. Each has a distinctive set of ideologies and policies and a proud history. Over time, the ideologies of the three parties have changed, but the parties still retain something of their past. The Conservative ideology is, as its name suggests, one that highlights tradition and stability. But one-nation conservatism, the party's dominant ideology over the past century and a half, also stressed the need for social reform and a progressive approach generally. Thatcherism emerged in the 1970s as a challenge to this progressivism, but was itself a new, radical ideology, based on a belief in private enterprise and social authoritarianism. Recently, David Cameron has pulled the party back to its Disraelian roots, and has moved to the left of the Thatcherites.

Labour has moved in the opposite direction. Founded in 1900 as a left-wing party, it was until the 1990s a coalition of democratic socialists on the left and social democrats on the right. In the early 1980s, the socialist left briefly took control of the party, only to be thoroughly defeated in 1994 with the election as leader of Tony Blair. Blair was an advocate of the Third Way, a more right-wing Labour ideology, reminiscent in some ways of the views of the social democrats but with some elements of the Thatcherite consensus added. It remains to be seen whether under Gordon Brown there will be any real move on the part of Labour back to the left of British politics. It seems rather unlikely.

Liberalism as an ideology has a great history behind it, but the Liberal Democrats (and their predecessors) have suffered from the way in which both the Conservative and Labour parties have sought to incorporate the best bits of their beliefs within their own system of beliefs. The modern Liberal Democrat party is at the centre of British politics, but with a distinctively radical outlook, especially on matters of foreign policy and constitutional reform.

Further reading

R. Blake, *The Conservative Party from Peel to Thatcher* (Fontana, 1998): the classic study of the history of the Tory party.

D. Coates, *Prolonged Labour: The Slow Birth of New Labour Britain* (Palgrave, 2005): links Labour ideology and policy well.

D. Coates and P. Lawler, *New Labour in Power* (Manchester University Press, 2000): an attempt to interpret the phenomenon of New Labour.

S. Driver and L. Martell, *New Labour: Politics after Thatcherism* (Polity, 1998): early attempt to sum up the nature of New Labour aims and intentions.

A. Gamble, *The Free Market and the Strong State: The Politics of Thatcherism* (Macmillan, 1994): classic summary of Thatcherism.

A. Giddens, *The Third Way and its Critics* (Polity, 2006): brilliant academic analysis of that fragile ideology, the Third Way, by the man who more or less invented it.

A. Heywood, *Political Ideologies* (Macmillan, 1998): remarkably clear and sensible analysis of all the major ideologies of modern politics.

Greg Hurst, *Charles Kennedy: A Tragic Flaw* (Politico's, 2006): biography of a recent Liberal Democrat leader.

S. Ludlum and M. Smith (eds), *New Labour in Government* (Palgrave, 2001): detailed analysis of the politics of the early Blair government.

S. Ludlum and M. Smith, *Governing as New Labour* (Palgrave, 2004): academic essays bringing the previous book up to date.

Kieron O'Hara, *After Blair: David Cameron and the Conservative Tradition* (Icon, 2007): sets the new leader in the context of the ideological traditions of the party.

H. Pelling and A. J. Reid, *A Short History of the Labour Party* (Macmillan, 1997): classic study of Labour history.

A. Seldon and D. Kavanagh (eds), *The Blair Effect 2001–5* (Cambridge University Press, 2005): fascinating series of essays by the leading experts in the field on various aspects of Blair's second government.

Websites

www.labour.org.uk (Labour Party)
www.conservative-party.org.uk (Conservative Party)
www.libdems.org.uk (Liberal Democrats)

Part II

The State

The British Constitution

Making connections

It is difficult to get into the right way of thinking to study the Constitution. It is clearly a very significant aspect of the political system, and in every other country apart from Britain a book of this sort would begin with a discussion of the Constitution. But in the UK the unwritten nature of the Constitution gives the whole thing a rather surreal feeling. It is important to bear in mind that there are constitutional points that can be made about how the British Constitution works in theory, but there are also political facts about how it actually works in practice. The section in this chapter on constitutional reform links to many other parts of the book, and hence is rather brief. The monarchy had to be fitted somewhere into this book: it shows up in this chapter. The monarchy is an extremely important political and sociological topic for a student of the British way of life, but unfortunately it looms rather small in most politics syllabuses.

The British Constitution

SETTING THE SCENE

The previous chapters have dealt with the way in which the people can participate in politics through elections, pressure groups and political parties. We now move on to look at politics from the top, where power is really exercised. Before doing so, it is necessary to look at the curious British Constitution. It is through the Constitution that the people are linked to the governing institutions which form the subject matter for the rest of the book. But how powerful can the British Constitution really be if it is, as will be shown, 'unwritten'?

> **Constitution**: a set of rules, or constitutional laws, setting out how a political system in a particular state should operate, how the citizen is related to the state and what rights the citizen can claim.

9.1 What is a constitution?

In the light of the definition given here, we can say that in a perfect world a **constitution** would have the following functions:

- to give the members of our legislature, executive and judiciary a clear statement of what their functions are;
- to settle any disputes there might be between the members of the legislature, executive and judiciary about their powers;
- to inform citizens about what the powers of these three branches are;
- to inform citizens, judges, politicians and civil servants what the rights of the citizens are; and
- to prove a legal framework on these points, enforceable like all laws.

Does the UK Constitution perform these functions well? On the whole, we have to say that there are more doubts about whether it does than in any other liberal democracy in the rest of the world. Whether this really matters to British citizens is another matter. The reasons for these difficulties with the British Constitution are largely because it is 'unwritten'.

Historical background

The first modern constitution was adopted in 1787 by the United States of America when they successfully achieved their independence from Britain. The US Constitution is contained in a document – often now printed as a small booklet – consisting of a few thousand words, which sets out in simple terms what the powers and functions of the President, Congress and Judiciary should be. It then contains a number of changes or Amendments to the original Constitution which have been made in the past 200 years or so. Since then, constitutions have been extremely popular. Most countries have had several, and generally they have followed the pattern of the US Constitution: they have been short, concise statements of how the political system within the state should operate, and what rights the people should have in relation to the state. They have generally been issued after a revolution or when a country has made itself independent from an imperial power, as happened to the USA.

9.2 The uncodified or unwritten British Constitution

The great exception to the picture painted above is the United Kingdom, which does not have a codified constitution. The British Constitution is called unwritten or uncodified. One or two other countries also are in this position, notably Israel and New Zealand; in Israel there are moves afoot to adopt a codified constitution. The reason the United Kingdom has this rather unique form of unwritten constitution is that there has not been a successful revolution in Britain in recent times, and Britain has not been liberated from any imperial invasion. In other words, the conditions which led to the drawing up of written constitutions in other countries have not operated here. The British Constitution has developed or grown over many centuries and this *organic* development is reflected in the rather odd unwritten form in which it now exists.

Uncodified, not unwritten

The old way of describing the British Constitution was to call it 'unwritten', but this gives a rather bizarre impression that the Constitution is somehow virtual, or a fantasy, existing perhaps only in the memory of some courtiers in Buckingham Palace. The fact is, of course, that the Constitution is to be found in a bewildering series of sources, which are almost all written down in some form or another and which will be discussed below. It is in fact not unwritten, but uncodified. That is to say, it does not exist in the manageable format of an official code: there is no brief, concise summary of the Constitution.

Box 9.1 Two uses of the word 'constitution'

Before there were codified constitutions, the word constitution was already being used, simply to mean 'the political system'. This use of the word still persists in Britain, where there is no codified constitution. In the technical jargon of philosophy, this is an *analytical* use of the word: it simply analyses what actually is the case. Political philosophers distinguish between *analytical* and *normative* statements. When we talk about the US Constitution or the French Constitution, for example, we are using the word 'constitution' in the *normative* sense, to describe what are the norms or rules which describe how the American/French system ought to work. Many of the difficulties that sometimes arise in discussions about the British Constitution stem from the confusion between these two uses of the word. When we are talking about the British Constitution, do we mean simply what actually happens, or do we mean what we think, according to the rules, ought to happen? The two greatest writers on the constitution in the UK were Walter Bagehot, who wrote *The English Constitution* in 1865, and A. V. Dicey, who wrote *The Law and Custom of the Constitution* in 1885. It is clear from both these writers that they thought of the word 'constitution' as meaning 'the political system', in an analytical sense. In 1893, Dicey wrote a pamphlet about whether to hold a referendum on devolution for Ireland or not, and he answered the accusation that to do so would be unconstitutional by saying 'this word holds no terrors for me; it means no more than unusual'. So, according to this use of the word, in conditions where there is no written or codified constitution as in the UK we are driven to the odd conclusion that, to quote John Griffiths, writing in 1985: 'the constitution is what happens'.

 Question: Distinguish between a written and unwritten constitution.

voted on by the Houses of Parliament and some are just customs. For example, the work of whips, the Speaker and the leaders of the two houses are matters of parliamentary custom.

European treaties

Recent textbooks say that European treaties constitute a source of the British Constitution. Since we joined what is now the European Union (EU) in 1973 and signed up to the Treaty of Rome, EU law has become our law, and this has certainly affected key aspects of the British Constitution. A purist might say, though, that it has only done so through the Act of Parliament by which we joined the EU, and so it could be argued this is not a new source. The scope of the EU has been enlarged by subsequent treaties which have altered the British Constitution to some degree: the Single European Act of 1985, the Treaties on European Union signed at Maastricht in 1991 and at Amsterdam in 1997, and the Lisbon Treaty of 2007 are the most important. These treaties are also confirmed by Acts of Parliament.

Works of authority

Because there is such complexity involved in deriving a constitution from the sources described above, various textbooks have acquired an important status as guides to what the British Constitution is. The works of authority generally cited are:

- Thomas Erskine May, *Parliamentary Practice* (first published in 1844)
- Walter Bagehot, *The English Constitution* (1865)
- A. V. Dicey, *The Law and Custom of the Constitution* (1885)

To this list we could probably add *Questions of Procedure and Code of Conduct for Ministers*, mentioned above. This document summarizes what ministers should and should not do, and hence covers the doctrine of ministerial individual responsibility. It is reissued and re-edited by the Prime Minister at each change of government, but remains much the same.

In the end, the most important sources of the British Constitution are really just two: Acts of Parliament and convention. This was the approach taken by Dicey in his famous work of authority. If we want to find information about these two sources, we look at the authorities (for example, at Dicey himself), although in a way they are now rather old-fashioned, and we might be better off looking at a modern textbook of constitutional law. The other sources listed above are not to be neglected, but are perhaps of secondary importance.

 Question: What are the main sources of the UK constitution?

9.4 The chief features of the British Constitution

The most significant, and distinctive, features of the UK's constitution may be said to be as follows:

- Constitutions may be codified or uncodified: this has already been discussed, and the British Constitution has been defined as uncodified.
- The British Constitution is said to be based on the 'rule of law' and a defence of the rights and liberties of its citizens. We will deal more fully with this in chapter 14 on the judiciary, although there is a brief discussion of the 'rule of law' in box 9.2 below.
- Constitutions may be flexible or rigid: Britain is said to have a flexible Constitution.
- Constitutions are unitary or federal: the British Constitution is still best described as unitary.
- There must be a location for sovereignty defined in a constitution: in the UK, sovereignty is said to be located in Parliament.
- The British Constitution is not based on a strong belief in what is called the separation of powers; indeed, in some respects it is founded on the opposite: on a fusion of powers.
- Britain is sometimes described as being a constitutional monarchy, as opposed to a having a republican constitution, where the Head of State is not hereditary.

The last five points here will now be discussed in turn.

9.5 The British Constitution is flexible

A constitution is said to be flexible if it can be amended or changed easily. In contrast, a rigid constitution is difficult to amend, and its provisions are said to be entrenched (protected). Rigidity is also ensured by having a constitutional court to enforce the provisions of a constitution.

Amending the British Constitution

The British Constitution can be amended in two ways: first, and most obviously, an Act of Parliament can be passed and this will change the Constitution. For this to happen, a simple majority in the Commons and the Lords is required. By the Parliament Act of 1911, the House of Lords can veto a constitutional amendment, which would mean that more than five years could pass between general elections. But it is very doubtful whether in practice the Lords could actually do this. In practice, during the First and Second World Wars the main politicians decided among themselves not to hold a general election, using something called a Speaker's Conference to do this. Setting this exception aside, Parliament can amend the Constitution and in reality could do so remarkably quickly. Hence in 1999, an Act of Parliament changed the way in which the House of Lords was composed, excluding most hereditary peers, who had sat in the House of Lords for more than 600 years. In the UK there is no difference between constitutional statutes and any other acts passed by Parliament: they are all required to be passed by the two Houses on a simple majority. This is even true of the Human Rights Act of 1998: in the UK the rights of the citizen are not 'entrenched' as they are in other countries. They can be modified or even removed by a simple majority in both Houses of Parliament. This flexibility depends on the idea of parliamentary sovereignty, which will be discussed later on.

The other way in which the British Constitution can be changed is simply by using the vagueness of the customary parts of the Constitution as a sort of smoke screen behind which to bring in constitutional innovations. Harold Wilson allowed his Cabinet to disagree over trade union law in 1969 and over Europe in 1975; he was said to have 'suspended' the constitutional convention of Cabinet collective responsibility. This looks a bit like amending the Constitution, although there was an earlier precedent for what Wilson did. The whole point about a custom or convention is that it has grown up organically and hence that it can change a little over time as it grows further. The rules governing what to do in the event of a Prime Minister asking the monarch for a dissolution of Parliament, and hence for the chance to hold a general election, were clarified only in 1950 in a letter written anonymously by a senior adviser of the King, printed in the correspondence columns of *The Times*. So, custom continues to be made to meet new possibilities as they arise. The British Constitution is sometimes described as organic, because it has a tendency to grow and develop to fit in with new circumstances.

Amending written constitutions

In comparison, most countries with written constitutions have more obstacles in the path of constitutional amendment. Constitutional laws in these countries are described as entrenched (or specially protected) because they cannot easily be changed. In the USA, for example, a constitutional amendment requires a two-thirds majority in both houses of Congress and then agreement by three-quarters of the individual states of the Union. This is such a difficult process that one amendment took two centuries to pass, and there have in total only been 27 amendments to the US constitution since 1787. Still, written constitutions can in fact be quite flexible: the US constitution is so brief, so codified in fact, that it does not cover the political system in much detail, and as a result the system has developed considerably without needing these difficult constitutional amendments to be passed.

Enforcing the British Constitution

In the UK, there is no constitutional court to ensure that the Constitution is observed. It would be impossible to have such a court, because to do so would breach the constitutional principle that Parliament is sovereign. There is a process called judicial review which allows decisions made by government agencies to be judged, to see whether the agencies have followed their rules correctly, but this is very different from true constitutional review. The courts can also enforce the rules of electoral law, for example, and those who break them (perhaps by voting twice) can be prosecuted in the same ways as ordinary criminals. The courts can also enforce the new Human Rights Act, but not by overturning Acts of Parliament which go against the Act. All in all, it is true that in the last 20 or so years the judiciary has played a greater role in politics in the UK and indeed, broadly speaking, has shown a greater willingness to make decisions in the field of constitutional law. But the fact remains that there is no body that can enforce our unwritten constitution. This must mean that the UK Constitution is more flexible than others, since there is no court to ensure that the Constitution is exactly followed.

Enforcing written constitutions

In these cases, there generally is a Supreme Court, or a constitutional court of some sort, which can enforce the Constitution and ensure that it is not so flexible as to undermine at least its most important guiding principles. The US Supreme Court is so powerful that in 2000, for example, it effectively decided the outcome of the general election, and it can rule on whether an Act of Congress, any action of the President or any measure taken by an individual state (e.g., Texas, California, etc.) is constitutional or not.

9.6 The British Constitution is unitary, not federal

Unitary constitutions

The United Kingdom is a **unitary state**, and one of its most important principles, which will be discussed below, is that of parliamentary sovereignty, a principle which is essentially dependent on the unitary status of the UK. This means that although there are local councils and regional assemblies (and a Parliament now in Scotland), in the United Kingdom their power is completely dependent on that of the centre. Parliament can change their boundaries, change their powers and even abolish them altogether. It is difficult to imagine having an unwritten, flexible constitution which was not unitary, because it is only through the mechanism of a written constitution, enforced by a constitutional court, that the rights of local or regional government can be preserved from the encroachments of the centre.

> **Unitary state**: one in which sovereignty is located in one place, concentrated at the 'centre' of the state.

Federal constitutions

In a **federal state**, the rights and powers of local or regional government are preserved by constitutional law, and cannot be encroached upon by the centre. In the USA, for example, there are areas of policy that are reserved under the US Constitution for the federal authorities in the centre (in the capital: Washington, DC), and others that belong exclusively to the individual states of the Union. This is overseen and enforced by the Supreme Court. Sovereignty is said to be shared under these circumstances between the federal and the state authorities. In some senses, the US Constitution itself can be seen as sovereign. The rights of the individual states in the US are said to be entrenched, protected by the Constitution; they cannot be overturned by action taken at the centre of the federal system.

> **Federal state**: one in which the constitution lays down that sovereignty is shared between the central authority and local and regional authorities.

Is the UK constitution still unitary?

There have always been some doubts about whether the UK is really a unitary state. It is, after all, the United Kingdom of Great Britain and Northern Ireland, which consists of four different nations: England, Northern Ireland, Scotland and Wales. Since these four units have joined together, their individual rights and differences have always been to some degree protected. This has been especially true of Scotland, which has preserved its own legal system since the Act of Union of 1707, when it joined England. As a result, the political scientists Stein Rokkan and Galen Irwin coined the term 'union state' to describe the UK, since it has been formed by Acts of Union between England and Wales (1536–43), Scotland (1707) and Ireland (1801, amended in 1920). In other words, the need to recognize the ancient traditions of the different parts of the UK has always been an important political reality. But the Westminster Parliament has over the years modified the Union, especially with regard to Ireland, which it could legally do because of the unitary nature of our state, and because of the British principle of parliamentary sovereignty.

Since 1997, changes have been made to the relations between the UK and Scotland, Wales and Northern Ireland, which political commentators have said have moved us towards a quasi-federal state – a semi-federal state, a 'sort of' federal state. Scotland now has a Parliament with primary legislative and tax-varying powers; and the Welsh and Northern Ireland Assemblies have lesser, but still important powers. The question is: are these measures permanent, or can they be revoked by Westminster? If they can be revoked, the UK cannot really be called federal. As far as Northern Ireland goes, its devolved system is certainly dependent on the continuance of peace in that area, so it may not be permanent. In fact devolution for Northern Ireland, as re-established in 1998, has been suspended by the UK government in London four times since then. In Wales and Scotland, it is true in strict legal terms that devolution could be overturned by the UK's Westminster parliament, but in political terms it is almost unthinkable that it could be repealed in the immediate future, especially in Scotland. We might therefore think of there being political federalism, if not legal federalism, in the UK now, to adapt phrases used in relation to sovereignty, which is discussed below.

The development of the European Union suggests that the UK may be moving away from being a unitary state and towards being a federal state in another way. According to some commentators on the EU, it seems possible that in the future the nations of Europe will be regarded as states within a federal United States of Europe. Others take a less extreme view and see the EU as being a loose **confederation** of states. It is therefore much less demanding on its members than a federation. It is reasonable to say that, at the moment, the EU is a sort of confederation, but that some enthusiasts of the European project are working towards a future when it will become a federal state, a genuine 'union'.

> **Confederation**: an association of states which retain their independence but which join together for their mutual economic or diplomatic benefit.

9.7 Parliamentary sovereignty

When discussing the British constitution, it is usual to distinguish between national sovereignty and parliamentary sovereignty.

National sovereignty

> **Sovereignty**: supremacy or ultimate political power.

A state (or nation) is said to be **sovereign** when it fulfils two conditions. First, when it has external sovereignty, and no foreign power has control over it.

Second, when it has internal sovereignty, in that it has complete control over all territories and individuals within its frontiers.

Parliamentary sovereignty

National sovereignty is said to have a location, a place where it is to be found within the state. Where is sovereignty located in the UK? The answer until about 400 years ago was that sovereignty belonged to the monarch: to the king or queen. As a formal mark of respect, we still use the title 'Sovereign' when referring to our monarch. But during the course of the seventeenth century, Parliament won power from the monarch, and hence Parliament itself became sovereign. However, Parliament never claimed to be anything more than the mouthpiece of the people, and with the growth of mass democracy in the past 200 years, we can say that Parliament exercises sovereignty on behalf of the people. Ultimately, at the time of the general election it is the people who are supreme, it is the people who are sovereign.

There are two main aspects to **parliamentary sovereignty**. First, Parliament can make any law, and this law then takes precedence over all previous laws. Parliament can also repeal any laws. Parliamentary law is superior to all other forms of law in the country: the common law and the law made by judges in their courts (so-called case law) can be overturned by Parliament. From the point of view of the present discussion, constitutional laws can be made and repealed by Parliament. It can be seen how crucial to the British Constitution the idea of parliamentary sovereignty is. Since there is no written constitution, and no special formula for making constitutional amendments, there is nothing to prevent Parliament from legislating on the Constitution as easily as it can pass laws in other areas. If there were a written constitution to limit Parliament, then Parliament could not be sovereign. Similarly, if there were a constitutional court to judge on the constitutionality of laws, Parliament would not be sovereign either. Finally, if the various regional and 'national' (Scotland, Wales and Northern Ireland) representative bodies had entrenched powers, as they might under a federal structure, then Parliament in Westminster could not be sovereign, but would share its sovereignty with the devolved bodies.

The second aspect to parliamentary sovereignty is that Parliament cannot bind its successor: no Parliament can pass an Act which cannot later on be repealed. If a Parliament did this it would, of course, present us with a logical paradox. Were a Parliament to try to tie the hands of a future Parliament, it would also deny the sovereignty of the people, which in a democracy is the

> **Parliamentary sovereignty**: the ultimate political power in the United Kingdom, exercised on behalf of the people by their elected representative body.

Box 9.2 A. V. Dicey's two features of the British Constitution

Writing in his great 'work of authority' on the Constitution, *The Law and Custom of the Constitution* (1885), Dicey said: 'two features have at all times . . . characterized the political institutions of England': these were the sovereignty of Parliament and the rule of law. This was Dicey's way of contrasting the British Constitution with written constitutions in other countries. Rather than having a written constitution, we have relied on Parliament to define the Constitution; rather than having a Declaration of Rights, we have relied on the rule of law to define the rights of the citizen. On the last point, Dicey was probably following J. S. Mill, who, in his *On Liberty* (1859), put forward the idea that freedom (or liberty) was best defended by drawing up laws on the basis of principles which allowed considerable freedom but also protected people from harm (negative liberty), rather than by working on the basis of a declaration of rights (positive liberty). Dicey defined the rule of law as having three main elements. First, no one should be punished except after a fair trial for breach of a law. Second, no one – no government minister or official – should be considered above the law, and no one should be able to argue, as the Nazis argued at Nuremberg in 1945, that they were 'only obeying orders'. Third, Dicey said that previous legal judgements had built up a series of precedents which guaranteed free speech and freedom to hold public meetings, and which showed there was therefore no need for a statement of rights in Britain. After more than a century, Dicey can be said still to have a strong point here, in that the rise of 'judicial review' shows how the courts can enforce the rule of law on government agencies. On the other hand, the passing of the Human Rights Act in 1998 seems to move the agenda on from where Dicey left it, moving our Constitution potentially away from ideas of parliamentary sovereignty, and our idea of rights away from his rather flimsy legal protection under the umbrella of the rule of law.

justification for parliamentary sovereignty. If Parliament were to pass an Act and insist that it should not in the future be repealed, and then there was a general election and a new Parliament was elected which did want to repeal this Act, it should surely have the right to do this in a democracy. Each individual elected Parliament between elections is sovereign; not the institution in itself.

9.8 Is Parliament really sovereign?

Parliamentary sovereignty is a crucial constitutional principle in the United Kingdom. But in practice, in the world of political reality, is Parliament really sovereign? Especially in recent years there have been many who have argued that it is not.

Table 9.1 Is Parliament really sovereign?

NO: recent changes have meant that the sovereignty of parliament has been eroded	YES: Parliament is still sovereign
The European Union	*The arguments that parliamentary sovereignty has been eroded can all be answered*
The development of the EU is the biggest threat to national sovereignty and hence to the sovereignty of Parliament. By signing the Treaty of Rome and its subsequent modifications, the UK accepted that European law would take 'immediate effect' in the UK. That is to say, European law does not have to be turned into British law by being passed by Parliament: it already is British law as soon as it is formally enacted by the institutions of the EU. This means that in certain circumstances parliamentary statutes can be overturned if they conflict with European law. The agreement to adopt a constitution for the EU – which was made in 2004 but has not yet been ratified by the member states of the Union, and as a result may never be formally adopted – seemed to threaten British national sovereignty and hence the sovereignty of Parliament.	As has been seen so far, all the arguments that parliamentary sovereignty has been eroded can be answered to a greater or lesser extent. The 'official' line on the subject adopted by the government and Parliament itself is certainly that Parliament in a sense reserves its sovereign right to resume the powers it has granted to the judiciary, and to Europe, Scotland, Wales and Northern Ireland.
Factortame Case	*Sovereignty is not lost if it is 'pooled'*
This famous case, which reached the House of Lords (as the UK's highest court of appeal) in 1991 demonstrated the last point with great clarity. A Spanish fishing company, Factortame, sued the British government for restricting their fishing in the seas near the UK. The British government claimed that under the 1988 Merchant Shipping Act, they were not qualified to fish there. But Factortame replied that under EU law they were. The House of Lords heard the appeal and consulted the European Court of Justice before reaching the decision that Factortame was in the right, and the Merchant Shipping Act, an Act of Parliament, was 'struck down', or overruled, by the Lords. This seems to indicate that EU law takes precedence over laws passed by Parliament, which can therefore hardly be described as sovereign. It could be argued in answer to this that the fact that EU law takes immediate effect in the UK itself stems from An act of Parliament – the 1972	By granting some national sovereignty away to Europe, we have not actually reduced the stock of sovereignty, but in a sense have benefited from mixing it together with the sovereignty of other nations in the EU. Britain, in short, has become stronger by being a member of the EU.

Table 9.1 (continued)

NO: recent changes have meant that the sovereignty of parliament has been eroded	YES: Parliament is still sovereign
European Communities Act – by which we joined the EU. According to this argument, the judgement made in the Factortame case was in accordance with Parliament's views, and hence with parliamentary sovereignty. But the problem with this is that one key aspect of parliamentary sovereignty is that 'no Parliament can bind its successor', so the Factortame case still seems to destroy the principle on these grounds, since it involved overturning an Act of 1988 by virtue of an Act of 1972.	
Devolution	*Parliamentary sovereignty still survives because it is based on the sovereignty of the people*
The granting of devolved powers to Scotland, Wales and Northern Ireland also suggests that parliamentary sovereignty is under threat, because these are alternative locations of power, which in Scotland include the power to levy taxes and to pass primary legislation. More significantly, it is very unlikely that in the short term these devolved powers will actually be revoked to the UK Parliament. So Parliament seems to have tied its hands for the future by passing laws which look as if they are entrenched. As has been said, the development of a diluted form of federalism in the UK is likely to erode the sovereignty of Parliament. The answer made to this is that Parliament still retains the power to repeal the Scotland Act of 1998 and the other devolution acts, just as in 1972 the Act of 1920 granting devolution to Northern Ireland was overturned.	The positive case in favour of the view that Parliament remains sovereign is much briefer than the arguments that can be used to support the idea that it has been undermined, but it is still powerful. The most important point to make is that, since Parliament has made these grants of power to the EU and the devolved nations, it can as easily revoke them. If it did so in answer to the demands of the British people, it would be performing a legitimate function in a democracy. A belief in democracy is part of the reason for the doctrine of parliamentary sovereignty. The supremacy of Parliament derives from the will of the people who elect Parliament.
The 1998 Human Rights Act	*Steps have been taken in recent legislation to ensure that the principle of parliamentary sovereignty is upheld*
It is sometimes said in recent years that the judiciary has become more powerful, especially through its growing use of judicial review. This is just about consistent with parliamentary sovereignty, since Parliament can, in constitutional theory, remove the power of judicial review. In any case, judges can only ensure when they hear this sort of case that the legislation passed by Parliament has been correctly observed. But the Human Rights Act	The 1998 Human Rights Act rules that legislation coming out of Parliament is checked before being passed, to ensure that it is consistent with the Act. This is a sensible, pragmatic way of making sure that parliamentary sovereignty is not dented. Also, as has been said, judges cannot use this Act to strike down others. All they can do is to write to

Table 9.1 (continued)

NO: recent changes have meant that the sovereignty of parliament has been eroded	YES: Parliament is still sovereign
seems to interfere to a greater extent with Parliament's supremacy, especially since cases can go on appeal to the European Court of Human Rights at Strasbourg. This last point also looks like an attack on national sovereignty, since these appeals are heard outside the borders of the UK. However, the Human Rights Act was carefully drawn up to preserve, at least in theory, the sovereignty of Parliament, and judges cannot 'strike down' acts of Parliament on the strength of this Act.	Parliament asking for some amendment to the law to be made if a case which has come before them shows that some part of the law seems to be inconsistent with the Act. Similarly, the devolution acts passed in 1998 granting powers to the Scottish Parliament and Welsh and Northern Ireland Assemblies have clauses in them laying down a precise definition of the devolved and reserved powers and a series of complicated mechanisms, designed to avoid any clash between the sovereign Parliament in Westminster and the new assemblies in the regions.
Decline of national sovereignty: international organizations	*Unwritten constitution*
National sovereignty and parliamentary sovereignty are separate issues, but they are connected. If national sovereignty is eroded, so is the sovereignty of Parliament. One way in which national sovereignty can be undermined is as a result of the UK joining alliances and entering into international treaties which bind us to future action. In the modern 'globalized' era, when countries are increasingly linked together, it is difficult to think of any country which is completely independent of others. Examples of such restrictions on our independence include our membership of NATO, the United Nations, the Commonwealth and also our signature of international treaties like the 1999 Kyoto Treaty, which limits environmental pollution.	Since we still have an unwritten constitution, there is nothing to put in the place of the principle of parliamentary sovereignty and nothing therefore to say that parliamentary sovereignty has been given up.
Decline of Parliament	*It is impossible to deny parliamentary sovereignty*
This is also a rather separate issue, but can be linked to the constitutional question of the decline of parliamentary sovereignty. There have been more cases in recent years when Parliament has been by-passed by the use of referendums. Parliamentary sovereignty can be preserved here by saying that these referendums are only advisory and that Parliament in the end will still actually make the	Logically there is no way of denying that Parliament still retains the power to overturn the various pieces of legislation – such as the 1972 European Communities Act or the 1998 Human Rights Act – which it has passed and which suggest that parliamentary sovereignty has been overturned, because they look like permanent fixtures. In addition, there is certainly no constitutional source

Table 9.1 (*continued*)

NO: recent changes have meant that the sovereignty of parliament has been eroded	**YES**: Parliament is still sovereign
final decisions, or by saying that these referendums were called as a result of an Act of Parliament. The other way in which Parliament is said to be undermined is by the steady growth in the power of the executive, so much so that in practice, it is argued, the sovereignty of Parliament has become the sovereignty of the executive.	which tells us that Parliament cannot overturn them.

Box 9.3 Legal and political sovereignty

One way to get round the problems posed by parliamentary sovereignty and the question of whether it has been breached or not is to make a distinction between legal and political sovereignty. According to this view, legal sovereignty still exists because legally speaking (in terms of constitutional law) Parliament still has a constitutional right to overturn the various threats to parliamentary sovereignty which have grown up in recent years (joining EU, the Human Rights Act, devolution, etc.). But in terms of sheer political realities, it would be very difficult and unpopular to do so, and so parliamentary sovereignty has been surrendered. To withdraw from the EU after being a member for more than 30 years would harm trade and business, and would make enemies of our closest neighbours abroad. To go back on devolution for Scotland and Wales would disappoint many people in those nations, and certainly lead to a great protest movement which would play straight into the hands of the Scottish and Welsh nationalists. To repeal the Human Rights Act would also provoke very great criticism; although the Conservative Party did suggest in 2004 that it might do so if elected, its reasons were not connected with the issue of parliamentary sovereignty. There certainly is an important point to be made here about the difference between constitutional theory (where sovereignty remains) and political reality (where it does not), but whether it is right to see it as a contrast between 'legal' and 'political' factors is dubious. In fact, it is in legal matters that parliamentary sovereignty seems to be most under attack: over Factortame and over the claims of the judiciary as a result of the Human Rights Act (see table 9.1). Conversely, it is the politicians who seem most keen to speak in rhetorical terms about how parliamentary sovereignty is still preserved.

Question: Discuss the view that Parliament is no longer sovereign.

9.9 The fusion and separation of powers

The separation of powers is a constitutional principle strongly emphasized in the USA, based on the writings of the eighteenth-century French philosopher, Montesquieu. According to this view, the three 'powers' of the system of government (executive, legislature and judiciary) should be kept separate and should balance one another. No single power should dominate the others, otherwise it was thought that tyranny might develop. Montesquieu believed that in his day Britain had a Constitution which guaranteed this sort of balance. By 1865, when Bagehot wrote his authoritative study of the Constitution, it was clear that the executive and legislative branches were no longer separate, but were more or less 'fused' or joined together. Bagehot said it was the Cabinet which achieved this fusion, because Cabinet ministers were members of both the executive and the legislature and, in effect, it was they who ruled the country. Hence, according to modern commentators, there is in practice a fusion of the executive and legislative powers at the heart of the British Constitution. This is sometimes described as 'parliamentary government' and is discussed at more length in chapter 10. It is a constitutional principle which produces strong government, but may fail to deliver the checks and balances which Montesquieu and his American followers felt were essential to the maintenance of liberty.

The British Constitution may not, however, be quite so dangerously unbalanced as it might appear at first sight. Although it is clearly the case that in the UK the legislature and executive are not in practice separate, it is probably going too far to say they are exactly 'fused', since they do maintain some distance from one another. This distance enables proper parliamentary scrutiny to develop, which is the best defence against executive tyranny. Most important of all, even in the UK there is no fusion between the judiciary and the other branches of government. A significant principle of the British constitution is the idea of the 'rule of law' and the independence of the judiciary. This is discussed at greater length in chapter 14.

9.10 Do we need a written constitution?

Since the British constitution is virtually unique among liberal democracies, because of its unwritten or uncodified nature, and also because it has had its critics for this and for other reasons, there has been a long-standing debate over whether or not Britain should adopt a written constitution. In what follows, the arguments on each side are briefly summarized.

Yes: the UK should have a written or codified constitution

A lack of constitutionalism

Because the Constitution is unwritten and uncodified, people in the UK do not think in constitutional terms: there is a lack of constitutionalism, of a belief in the value of constitutional government. This leads to a feeling of contempt for and cynicism about the political process. In countries where the constitution is codified, people are aware of the nature and scope of the constitution because it is easily available in a small printed form.

A useful educational aid

School students could be taught the Constitution more easily in their citizenship classes if it were a written constitution. A better awareness of politics and of the Constitution among the young might lead to an increase in participation in the future.

Legitimation of the political process

Without a written constitution there is danger that the political process may seem to be a game played by politicians, rather than a process governed by rules and subject to control.

A written constitution would be entrenched

The Constitution would be protected from easy amendment if it were written and if, as in most other countries, its written clauses could only be changed with a large degree of popular support. It would be entrenched. Entrenchment does not necessarily mean inflexibility. There could still be a chance to change the Constitution if it were written, but it would require a considered and careful process to do so, possibly subject in every case to a referendum.

Subject to the judgement of a constitutional court

In countries where there is a written constitution, there is generally a court staffed by legal experts who can be called upon to judge whether or not an action of the executive or legislature is consistent with the Constitution. This strengthens the Constitution and encourages respect for it.

Better protection of human rights

The 1998 Human Rights Act has extended the protection of rights that UK citizens enjoy, but it is not entrenched and can be overruled by a future Act

of crisis an executive is able to adopt quite large powers. Parliament can reform the Constitution very quickly and sensibly. The numerous constitutional reforms of the past few years under New Labour would not have been possible without parliamentary sovereignty. They would have been less likely to have happened if we had had a codified constitution. The British Constitution has evolved gradually over centuries in a way sometimes described as 'organic' or natural; this is a virtue and needs to be preserved.

Who wants a weak executive?

Strong government is a good rather than a bad thing, and if the uncodified constitution strengthens the executive, that is to be praised not condemned.

Who wants an over-powerful judiciary?

Judges are unelected and unaccountable, so it is not a good idea to give them additional powers by entrenching the Constitution and creating a constitutional court. It is better that an elected Parliament should be sovereign than that unelected judges should adopt that role. We already have some recent cases where politicians (e.g. David Blunkett, the Labour Home Secretary in 2001–4) have come into conflict with the judges, and we do not wish to see more.

Human Rights are protected

Some people argue that there were very few problems over civil rights in the UK even before the passage of the Human Rights Act. Now that we have passed the Human Rights Act, British citizens are just as well provided for as they would be if there were a codified constitution. It is only a technical difference to have human rights entrenched, and it would make no practical difference.

There has been little demand for constitutional codification

Support from the Conservatives has been unclear, Labour was officially opposed and in recent years even the Liberal Democrats have tended to steer away from constitutional matters, concentrating instead on political issues of more direct relevance to ordinary voters. All this may change, of course, under a Brown premiership.

Who wants to be like Europe?

There is really no case for trying to become like every other European country simply for the sake of it. It is in fact quite pleasant to have some cultural and traditional differences in our own country which help define us as a nation, especially since globalization tends to produce uniformity anyway.

How would a codification be performed?

Could Parliament do this? This is problematic, because Parliament would in a way be binding its successors, which is contrary to the principle of parliamentary sovereignty. If the government of the day whipped the reform through Parliament in the face of strong opposition, the legitimacy of the resulting constitution might be called into question. There would have to be extensive debate and consultation about what to include in a new codified constitution, and this would involve years of preparation.

What would become of parliamentary sovereignty?

At the heart of the British Constitution is the idea of parliamentary sovereignty, which is essentially a democratic one that helps strengthen government at the same time as securing the representation of the people. The writing of our constitution would remove parliamentary sovereignty, already under threat, once and for all, because the Constitution, enforced by the unelected judiciary, would become sovereign. It would be impossible logically to write a constitution which contained a clause defining Parliament as sovereign. The consequence of writing a Constitution would be that future generations would be ruled by their ancestors – ruled by an inflexible constitution inherited from the past.

There can be no right or wrong answer to the question of whether or not we should have a codified constitution. Strangely, the large volume of constitutional reform since 1997 seems to be the best argument not in favour of a codified constitution, but against one. Labour would have had much more trouble bringing in these reforms if the UK had had a codified constitution with a long and laborious process of constitutional amendment laid down in it. Instead, because of our uncodified Constitution, and because of the principle of parliamentary sovereignty, it has been able to bring about a great string of radical reforms without very much difficulty at all.

 Question: Why has the UK's uncodified constitution been criticized?

9.11 Labour's constitutional reforms since 1997

In 1997 Labour was elected to power for the first time for 18 years, promising to bring in a great deal of constitutional reform. Labour did not attempt a complete reform of the Constitution or the drawing up of a written constitution, but it did introduce piecemeal reform of how the British political system works in a whole range of areas. This section will examine why Labour decided to bring in this constitutional reform. It will then briefly survey the main areas of constitutional reform that Labour has brought in (briefly, because they are dealt with more fully in other sections of the book). It will then look at the attitude of the other political parties to constitutional reform.

Why did Labour bring in constitutional reform?

The case for reform was seen to be strong in the 1990s

There are arguments in favour of each item of constitutional reform that Labour introduced. According to political scientist Neil McNaughton, there are four underlying themes in the reforms. First, Labour wished to modernize the political institutions of the country; second, the aim was to make the political process more democratic; third, there was a desire to decentralize power away from Westminster and Whitehall; and, finally, the aim was to improve and safeguard minority rights.

There was an internal logic behind many of the reforms

By the 1980s, both Labour and Conservative leaders were beginning to see that only a new constitutional arrangement in Northern Ireland could solve problems there. This new consensus began to replace the attempt to achieve a 'military solution' there. The growing integration of the European Union was also a driver for constitutional change in this and other areas. Perhaps most important in the 1990s for the Labour Party, a party increasingly led by Scots, was the continued strength of the Scottish National Party (SNP) and the need to support devolution there in order to outflank demands for independence. Devolution for Scotland suggested the need for devolution in Wales, as well as those parts of England which might like it, and also the development of electoral reform in order to prevent the SNP from gaining control of a devolved assembly in Scotland.

Labour had a tradition of constitutional reform

The party had inherited this strand of its outlook from the Liberal Party. Much of what Labour has achieved since 1997 has been unfinished business. In 1949 Attlee reduced the power of the House of Lords, and in 1969 Wilson attempted a major reform of the Lords, but was prevented by opposition from within his own party, led by left-winger Tony Benn (himself a former member of the aristocracy), who felt that a reformed House of Lords would weaken the power of the House of Commons. In 1949 and again in 1969 Labour had reformed the electoral process, removing plural voting and giving the vote to 18-year-olds. Labour used referendums on three occasions in the 1970s, and the referendums of 1979 attempted to devolve power to Wales and Scotland. Much of what Labour has been doing since 1997 has been following on in this tradition.

New Labour gave constitutional reform a higher priority than Old Labour

Despite what has just been said, the post-war Labour Party (Old Labour) had been mainly interested in social and economic reform, not in the Constitution. The change in the 1990s in the Labour Party meant an abandonment of these old socialist priorities. New Labour needed something to fill its policy vacuum, and part of the answer was constitutional reform. This was announced in the new Clause IV of 1995, which committed Labour to 'an open democracy, in which government is held to account by the people: decisions are taken as far as practicable by the communities they affect; and where fundamental human rights are guaranteed'.

Left-leaning pressure groups favoured constitutional reform

There were a number of pressure groups associated with the left in politics which were pressing for constitutional reform. Charter 88 had been set up in 1988 to mark the anniversary of the Glorious Revolution of 1688, which had established parliamentary government in Britain. Charter 88 campaigned for constitutional reform of the sort that Labour eventually introduced when it achieved power. There were also active single-issue constitutional reform pressure groups: the Campaign for Freedom of Information, Liberty (in favour of a Human Rights Act), the Electoral Reform Society and Justice (supporting reform of the judicial system).

Opposition to Thatcher strengthened the demand for constitutional reform

Margaret Thatcher's Conservative government and, to a lesser extent, that of John Major had been seen by the left in British politics as presenting a strong case for constitutional reform. After 18 years of 'elective dictatorship' there was seen to be a need for some reform of Parliament, and devolution to the regions. Scottish and Welsh devolution were strongly supported on the left as a way of stopping Conservative dominance in those areas, which relied on votes from England. By 1997, the Conservatives were so unpopular in Scotland and Wales that they won no parliamentary seats in those countries. Thatcher was accused of having removed rights in the UK as a result of a number of cases, especially, the Ponting Case in 1985 and the attempted prosecution under the Official Secrets Act of Peter Wright, the former spy, for publishing his memoirs, *Spycatcher*. The removal by the 1992 Criminal Justice Act under Major of the 'right to silence' in a piece of populist law-and-order legislation confirmed that the attack on human rights in the UK was, if not a reality, at least a possibility. All this must be set against a background of clashes between trade unionists and police in the 1980s and the imposition of the poll tax (or community charge) in Scotland in 1988, and then in England and Wales the following year, which sparked great controversy and a few riots.

Support from the Liberal Democrats

Tony Blair's great political idea in the early 1990s (which proved to be wrong in the end) was sometimes called the 'Project'. He believed that the only way for Labour to achieve power was in coalition with the Liberal Democrats. Such an alliance would heal the split of 1981 when the right wing of the Labour Party had broken away from Labour, and even annul the events of 1900 when the Labour Party had been created by people who had formerly been Liberals. A new alliance of the left-of-centre parties would create an anti-Conservative group and overturn the Conservative dominance in British politics which had persisted for so long. The price of such an arrangement, it was well known, would be concessions by Labour on electoral reform. In order to make such a concession palatable, Blair believed that it could be presented to people as being part of a wider package of constitutional reform, which his new Liberal Democrat friends also supported. In the end, the landslide election of 1997 made the 'Project' unnecessary, but its basis in constitutional reform remained – apart, of course, from any change to the first-past-the-post system in Westminster elections.

Labour's constitutional reforms since 1997

The following is a list of the constitutional reforms made by Labour since 1997:

1 Devolution for Scotland, Wales and Northern Ireland.
2 The introduction of various new electoral systems (Wales, Scotland, Northern Ireland, European Parliament, London Assembly and directly elected mayors); the creation of an electoral commission and the passing of laws controlling party spending at elections and referendums; the encouragement of voting by allowing pilot schemes involving postal voting, e-voting, etc.
3 The greater use of referendums (Scotland, Wales, Northern Ireland, London, directly elected mayors, devolution for the north-east of England).
4 Reform of the House of Lords.
5 The Human Rights Act.
6 The Freedom of Information Act.
7 The introduction of a directly elected mayor for London (and other towns), the creation of a Greater London Assembly and proposals for the reform of regional government elsewhere in England.
8 The modernization of the House of Commons: attempts to strengthen select committees; the removal of some archaic ceremonial, and changes to working hours; the reform by which the Prime Minister is exposed to

six-monthly questions in front of the Liaison Committee consisting of the chairpersons of the Commons select committees.

9   Judicial reforms: these include the setting up of a Supreme Court, new rules for the appointment of judges and reform of the office of Lord Chancellor.

10   Changes in the European Union since 1997 could also be linked to constitutional reform in the UK.

11   Independence from government to the Bank of England in the setting of interest rates. This is an important step, but may not technically be seen as a constitutional reform. It is true, however, that in some countries the position of the central bank is referred to in their written constitutions.

It is reasonable to conclude by saying that in the future Blair's governments will be remembered for this great array of constitutional reform, which is almost unprecedented in its scope and breadth. But there are critics who have said that these constitutional reforms have not gone far enough, and who argue that Blair and some of his leading colleagues were too timid and lukewarm in their commitment to reform: devolution has not been as generous in Wales as it has in Scotland, and would never satisfy the committed nationalists; reform of the House of Lords is as yet incomplete and has not touched the powers of that body; the Human Rights Act and the Freedom of Information Act do not go as far as similar measures in other liberal democracies do; reform of the House of Commons has been tinkering; there has been no reform of the electoral system for general elections; the use of referendums has been fitful and limited; no regional government has been extended to England, largely because the English do not want it. Unsurprisingly, there has been no attempt to tackle the power of the executive – or, indeed, the over-concentration of power in 10 Downing Street itself.

The 2005 Labour election manifesto promised further reform: a review of the new electoral systems and even a mention of a referendum on electoral reform for parliamentary elections, but no firm commitment to hold one. It was promised that the powers of the Welsh Assembly would be extended, and there was a commitment to complete the reform of membership for the House of Lords. The Welsh reform was carried through in 2006, and the following year the first steps towards reform of the Lords were taken. This suggested that constitutional reform would continue, but that it was a lower priority for Labour than it had been back in the heady days of the party's first term.

Further constitutional reform after 2007

One of the first actions taken by Gordon Brown after being appointed Prime Minister was a speech in Parliament on 3 July 2007 in which he announced his intention to consider a range of new constitutional reforms. At the same time a Green Paper, *The Governance of Britain*, was published. This was probably partly done to undermine David Cameron, who had been making many of these suggestions himself since becoming Conservative leader. But Brown's commitment to reform comes across as both enthusiastic and genuine. What he suggested we should expect under his government in this field is as follows:

1   A new Bill of Rights, setting out responsibilities as well as rights.
2   A revival of the right to demonstrate near Parliament.
3   A reduction of the voting age to 16.
4   Elections on a Saturday or Sunday, to boost participation.
5   Improvements in mechanisms for petitioning Parliament.
6   A limit put on the government's power to use the royal prerogative: to declare war, make treaties, appoint bishops and other key officials, to dissolve and recall Parliament, give honours and grant pardons. These prerogative powers would in future all require parliamentary involvement and oversight rather than be exercised by the executive. The Green Paper announced that 'the government will seek to surrender or limit powers which it considers should not, in a modern democracy, be exercised exclusively by the executive'.
7   There would therefore be an increase in the power of parliamentary oversight, as in the USA, with parliamentary committees interviewing judges and other public appointees (e.g. the Chief Inspector of Prisons) before their appointments.
8   There would finally be a Civil Service Bill, putting the powers and role of the civil service on a statutory footing.
9   The power of the Attorney General (the government's chief legal adviser and a Cabinet member) to stop individual criminal prosecutions should be removed, and the Attorney General's advice to the Cabinet should be made public. These reforms would answer criticisms made of Blair's Attorney General, Lord Goldsmith, who was embroiled in controversy over his advice on the war with Iraq and on the 'cash for peerages' scandal.
10 A National Security Council to be created to coordinate anti-terrorism policy.
11 There were hints that this would be accompanied by the drawing up of a written constitution.

At the same time, the new Brown government announced plans to scrap unelected regional assemblies, which presumably also puts a final nail in the coffin of the idea of English elected regional assemblies, as an answer to the 'West Lothian Question', an important (and dismally ineffective) plank of Labour constitutional policy since 1997. It seems likely also that the setting up of an SNP executive in Edinburgh following the May 2007 elections there will bring the question of the powers of the Scottish Parliament back on the

agenda, and hence also bring the West Lothian Question back into prominence. As Cameron pointed out in response to Brown's announcements of
further constitutional change, this was the one thing that Brown had omitted.

We will now look at the attitude of the other main political parties to constitutional reform.

The Conservative Party

Opposition to reform

The Conservative Party has in the past been rather divided over constitutional reform, but largely opposed to it. The party supports tradition and
wishes to 'conserve' the ancient institutions. It is therefore likely to be
opposed to reform of the Constitution. Since Victorian times, the Conservative Party has been associated with Unionism, the desire to preserve the
Union of Scotland, Wales, England and Ireland. Until the resumption of
Direct Rule over Ulster in 1972, the Ulster Unionist MPs in Westminster took
the Conservative whip and the party was technically called 'The Conservative
and Unionist Party'. It seemed logical then that they should be opposed to
devolution. Defence of 'the Union' formed a significant part of John Major's
successful election campaign in 1992. The Conservatives had an in-built
majority in the House of Lords, and hence would not welcome reform there.
In the past, the party had often done well out of the first-past-the-post electoral system and was therefore not well disposed towards proportional representation. In the 1990s Conservatives became increasingly Euro-sceptic
and hence did not welcome developments there. The fact is that during 18
years of the most recent Conservative governments (1979–97) there was no
great progress made in terms of constitutional reform, and any change that
did occur in this area was incidental, almost accidental, and undertaken for
other reasons.

The party of pragmatism

But while the Thatcherite party was, on the face of it, strongly opposed to
constitutional reform, there was a strand in Conservative tradition which was
willing to support, on common-sense practical grounds, some reforms. The
first major referendum to be used in the UK was introduced in 1972 by Ted
Heath, the Conservative Prime Minister, to try to solve the problem of Northern Ireland. Heath had also supported devolution for Scotland in the late
1960s and nearly fought the 1970 general election with that policy in his manifesto. He would have done so in exactly the same spirit as Labour did a little
later – to remove support for the Scottish National Party. It was Heath who,
as Prime Minister, took Britain into Europe, an important constitutional
development. And it was a Conservative government which, in 1958,

introduced life peerages. In fits of depression during periods of Labour electoral success, some Tories supported proportional representation, and the normally optimistic Lord Hailsham (former Conservative Lord Chancellor) in 1976 proposed that Britain should have a written constitution to protect citizens from the threat of socialist 'elective dictatorship'. So there is sufficient evidence to show that the post-war Conservative Party, in the tradition of Peel and Disraeli, was willing to support any constitutional reform which might benefit it.

Opposition to Labour's reforms after 1997

The Conservative Party that faced Labour from the opposition benches after 1997 was a Thatcherite party, by and large, and opposed, as best it could, the majority of Labour's constitutional reforms. At first sight this opposition seems to have been ineffectual and to have failed to stop the programme of reform from being implemented. But it is worth suggesting some areas where a certain pragmatic cunning has at least delayed reform. The first stage (and at present the only stage) of House of Lords reform envisaged the removal of all hereditary peers from the second chamber. But in order to secure the difficult passage of this legislation through the Lords itself, Labour was forced to accept the 'Weatherill amendment', named after the Tory, Lord Weatherill, former Speaker of the House of Commons. By this amendment, 92 hereditary peers are still in the Lords. Labour has also been forced to moderate its enthusiasm for the European Union because of Conservative populist opposition, especially to the euro. Conservative opposition in 2004 to the adoption of regional devolution in the north-east of England may also have contributed to Labour's failure here. The caution of Blair and the right-wingers in the Labour Party on a number of issues (electoral reform, human rights, freedom of information, for example) has probably been strengthened by Conservative opposition to radicalism in these areas.

Conservative acceptance of the new constitutional consensus

Conservatives are still pragmatic. It is very unlikely that, despite their opposition to the reforms as they passed, the Conservatives, if elected to government even in the near future, would attempt to overturn many of them. On Europe, the Conservatives have recently floated the idea that they would modify in some respects Britain's relations with the European Union. In 2004, David Davis, Shadow Home Secretary, suggested that the Conservatives would repeal the Human Rights Act if they won power again, in order to remove the 'compensation culture' which he said was associated with it. The 2005 manifesto committed them to a review of the Act. In other respects they have decided to keep most of what Labour has achieved, although they would abolish proposals for regional government in England. They may also be prompted into further Conservative reforms by what Labour has done:

most notably some attempts to solve the West Lothian Question by giving England equality with Scotland and Wales in terms of devolved powers. The 2005 manifesto also proposed to reduce the size of the House of Commons by 20 per cent, to strengthen parliamentary committees in order to make government more accountable, and to reform the composition of the Lords. Some Conservatives have even suggested that there is at last a need for a written constitution to preserve the independence of Britain in the face of growing European integration.

A new constitutional agenda under Cameron?

The instinctively pragmatic David Cameron, who became Tory leader late in 2005, has broadly accepted much of the New Labour constitutional reform and it seems very unlikely that he will attempt to overturn much of what Labour has achieved if he becomes Prime Minister. He would, however, almost certainly attempt to address the West Lothian Question, even if some of his party's proposals made before he became leader are not followed through. Cameron has also expressed his desire for a 'modern British bill of rights', intended to remove some of the problems associated with the Human Rights Act of 1998. Cameron has said that he is interested in constitutional matters. In a speech in the summer of 2006, he identified the need to modernize and strengthen Parliament, to ensure the integrity of the civil service, and to address alienation from the political process as areas which concerned him. Most interesting of all, he suggested that the royal prerogative powers held by the Prime Minister should be made subject to parliamentary scrutiny. Above all, Cameron suggested, decisions on war and peace should be subject to democratic approval in the House of Commons, as should the prime-ministerial power to make appointments, and to reorganize government departments. Unfortunately for him, however, Gordon Brown stole almost all these policy suggestions in one fell swoop when he became Prime Minister in summer 2007. This was an interesting reversal of roles: a Labour Prime Minister adopting the constitutional reform proposals of a Conservative leader of the opposition.

Liberal Democrats

The Liberal Democrats had worked quite closely with Labour in the 1990s as the Labour programme for reform over devolution, rights and electoral reform developed. As has been said, the Liberal Democrats were more strongly identified with this reform programme than Old Labour had been. Although in other respects rivals, Labour and the Liberal Democrats had cooperated on some areas of constitutional policy, especially devolution for Scotland, where they were united by a fear of the SNP. In 1997 Paddy Ashdown was included on the Cabinet committee on constitutional reform; it was an unprecedented step to have a member of an opposition party on a Cabinet committee. In both Scotland and Wales, the two parties worked in devolved coalition administrations. Lord Jenkins, a Liberal Democrat peer, and, in his past, both a Labour right-winger and a founding father of the Social Democratic Party, was appointed by Blair to lead a commission to look into electoral reform. This was done to fulfil a Labour manifesto pledge made in 1997, but after the landslide – under FPTP – it was unlikely anything would be done. The Liberal Democrats have pressed, with little success, for more radical constitutional reform than Labour has carried out. They have supported more powerful human rights legislation, a more effective freedom of information measure, full regional devolution in England, the adoption of the euro and a European constitution, a substantially elected House of Lords, the vote at 16 and a written constitution. But Labour's constitutional reforms are also in broad terms a victory for the Liberal Democrats, who, while pressing for more radical steps to be taken, have been supportive of Labour's general thrust. In a way, this has removed a large area of the Liberal Democrat purpose, and more recently the party has tended to turn its attention to social, economic and foreign policy concerns. Liberal Democrat leaders have in recent years been reluctant to appear to be leading a party with a single obsessive desire to secure electoral and constitutional reform, preferring to campaign across the whole political spectrum. Nonetheless, the commitment to further constitutional and especially electoral reform is to be found in the Liberal Democrat 2005 manifesto, and the party continued to press the case for proportional representation in answer to Brown's 2007 announcements on constitutional reform.

Question: Discuss the view that there have been only limited changes to the British constitution since 1997.

9.12 The constitutional monarchy

A final feature of the British Constitution that needs briefly to be discussed here is that it makes provision for an hereditary monarch. It is by no means unique in the modern world for a state to have a hereditary leader, perhaps especially in Western Europe, where there are monarchs in Belgium, the Netherlands, Denmark, Sweden, Norway, Luxemburg and Spain. A hereditary monarch of this sort in a liberal democracy is usually described as a 'constitutional monarch'. So, Britain can be said to be a constitutional monarchy. This is reflected in the official name of our country; it is the United Kingdom. But, although there are other countries with a constitutional monarch, the equivalent role is generally taken in most countries by an elected figure, generally known as a president. Since 1952, when Queen Elizabeth II succeeded

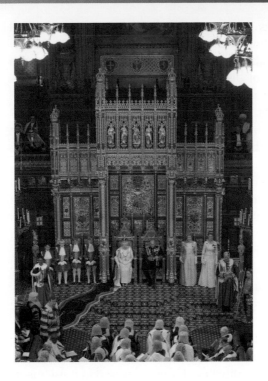

Queen Elizabeth II and Prince Philip at the State Opening of Parliament

her father, King George VI, the position of the British monarch has declined in importance, and since the 1990s has become less popular. Once accepted as the single most popular institution in British politics, the position of the monarchy has come increasingly under scrutiny. Most elected politicians, however, accept that the British monarchy is here to stay; in part because they cannot think of anything else to put in its place.

The political role of the monarch in Britain is largely that of a head of state. The head of state is to be distinguished from the head of government, who is the Prime Minister. The head of state is the symbolic representative of the nation as a whole, while the head of government is a temporary figure who rules the nation as a political leader. Since the state is permanent and in a sense non-political, there is something to be said for having a non-elected, non-political life holder of the office of head of state such as an hereditary king or queen. Very briefly, the constitutional role of the British monarch can be summarized as follows:

- The monarch is head of state and represents the country abroad by visiting foreign countries and by receiving diplomats and other heads of state when they visit the UK.
- The head of state represents the nation on ceremonial occasions like Remembrance Sunday and plays a role in times of national mourning and celebration.

- The monarch has a limited political role to play in giving formal approval to the decision of a Prime Minister to call a general election and officially appointing the government after the election. In the past, monarchs have exercised a certain amount of discretion in these areas, but nowadays almost all decisions are made according to rules established by precedent. There may be some need for a personal royal decision if the two major parties win exactly the same number of MPs in an election (resulting in a 'hung Parliament'), but even then a complicated set of rules exists, and the monarch will not be lacking in those keen to give their expert advice.

- The Prime Minister and Cabinet and the government as a whole rule, in theory, on behalf of the monarch; that is to say, they exercise the power of the state, of which the monarch is head. So the ancient prerogative powers of the Crown are transferred to the government of the day (although if the proposals for constitutional reform made by Gordon Brown in July 2007 are implemented, these powers will be more under parliamentary scrutiny in the future). The Prime Minister meets the monarch on a weekly basis to talk about current policy; according to Bagehot, this gives the monarch the 'right to warn' the Prime Minister of the dangers of some controversial piece of policy. But the decision to go ahead after such a warning belongs, ultimately, to the elected politicians. Such discussions are private: the monarch is 'above politics', so views expressed in these meetings are not made public.

- The Crown has a role to play in Parliament: the monarch formally opens sessions of Parliament by reading a speech, which is written for her by the Prime Minister and government. Technically, all legislation requires the Royal Assent to pass, but this assent has not been withheld in modern times.

- All honours and medals are given in the name of the Crown, but almost all decisions are actually made by the government.

- The monarch is head of the British Commonwealth, the influential club of former members of the British Empire. Again, this is a symbolic role, and all decisions which involve the Commonwealth are made by the government.

- The monarch has a role to play as a leader of that intangible thing, British society. The charitable work of the Royal Family sets a good example to the rest of the population. In addition, the monarch is Governor of the Church of England, and plays a part in the religious life of the country, although all religious decisions are taken by the Church itself.

The case for having a constitutional monarch is strong. Queen Elizabeth II has performed the function with great success for more than half a century, and has built up a huge experience of British politics and foreign diplomacy. The monarchy remains popular. The non-political role of the British head of state is a significant advantage, and may be best performed by a hereditary figure. But the case against the constitutional monarchy is also strong. In a democracy, the hereditary element is open to question. The wealth of the royal family seems to exaggerate officially the divisions within British society. It might limit the power of the Prime Minister (often said to be too great) if there were an elected head of state, who was drawn from a political background and was able to play a rather stronger role than the monarch can. But this last point probably makes the best case for saying that in the near future it is very unlikely that this aspect of the British Constitution will be reformed. Those with political power in Britain will not create a potential rival by creating an elected presidency.

Activity

1 Look for information about the US Constitution, and consider it in the light of this chapter on the UK Constitution. Make brief notes after skim-reading the US Constitution on the main differences and similarities between the UK and US Constitutions.

2 The US Constitution begins with three Articles setting out the powers of the three main branches of their system of government: the legislature, the executive and the judiciary. Bullet-point the main powers that you would give to each branch in the UK, first if you were drawing up a real description of what actually happens at the moment and then if you were describing what you think ought to be our ideal constitution in a perfect world.

SUMMING UP

The British Constitution seems almost ludicrous, because it is 'unwritten'. It is better to describe it as 'uncodified', since it is based on about half a dozen different types of written documents. There is a customary or conventional part of the Constitution, but even for this there are written guides. But there is no brief summary of the Constitution as there is in almost all other countries around the world. This makes the British Constitution flexible and easy to amend, but also, from another perspective, pliable and subject to manipulation, especially by the over-powerful executive. In recent years, controversy has developed around other descriptions often made of the British Constitution: is it really still unitary, or quasi-federal? Is Parliament still sovereign? There has been a long-running debate among political theorists, and to a lesser extent among politicians, over whether there should be a written constitution to define these points more clearly. In the ten years of Blair's term in office, there was a great deal of constitutional reform, and this will stand as New Labour's lasting legacy. It seems set to continue under Gordon Brown, who has given a new impetus to such policies. As partial reform has been piled on top of partial reform, the case for a thoroughgoing constitutional settlement of some sort is made stronger. As Britain moves into a new era, under Gordon Brown and David Cameron, it may be that this will result finally in the creation of some sort of definitive written code. Or perhaps we will continue with more piecemeal reform, correcting the problems created by the earlier reforms, largely because the difficulties of drawing up a written constitution are so great.

Further reading

W. Bagehot, *The English Constitution* (Fontana, 1963): surprisingly readable, one of the great 'sources' of our Constitution.

R. Brazier, *Constitutional Reform* (Clarendon, 1997): intelligent discussion by a constitutional lawyer of how the Constitution works in practice.

A.V. Dicey, *An Introduction to the Study of the Law of the Constitution* (Macmillan, 1959): the other great work of authority, also very readable.

R. Hazell, *Constitutional Futures* (Oxford, 1999): inspiring attempt to suggest reform of the Constitution.

P. Hennessy, *The Hidden Wiring* (Indigo, 1996): fascinating and highly readable analysis of how the system works.

A. King, *Does the UK Still Have a Constitution?* (Sweet and Maxwell, 2001): brief essay on the Constitution by one of the country's foremost academic political commentators.

Websites

http://www.unlockdemocracy.org.uk (The new incarnation of the constitutional pressure group Charter 88)

www.ucl.ac.uk/constitution-unit (The Constitution Unit, an independent research body)

www.official-documents.gov.uk (For CM 7170, 'The Governance of Britain' Green Paper, 2007; and other official government documents – free online)

CHAPTER

10

Parliament: The House of Commons

Making connections

The House of Lords is also a part of Parliament and is dealt with separately in chapter 11. Much of what is said in this chapter contains a discussion not just of the House of Commons but also of the whole Parliament. It is very difficult to think of Parliament in the British system without considering the government or executive too, which is also the subject of chapter 12. The most important thing to get sorted out is the relationship between the executive and Parliament, which is discussed here in section 10.2: the so-called 'Westminster model of parliamentary government'. The initial difficulty people often face is differentiating between 'government' and 'Parliament' and also between 'MPs' and 'ministers'. It is important not to confuse these terms when discussing the British political system.

Parliament: The House of Commons

- What is Parliament and how is it composed?
- Parliamentary sovereignty and the 'Westminster model'
- The functions of Parliament
- Representation
- Legislation
- Taxation and finance
- Scrutiny of the executive
- Parliamentary debate or deliberation
- Legitimation
- Recruitment and training of members of the government
- Recent reforms of the House of Commons
- Does Parliament matter?

SETTING THE SCENE

At the centre of the British political system is Parliament, or, as we should now emphasize, the Westminster Parliament. This is where the citizens of the United Kingdom are represented by their Members of Parliament or MPs. Is this where the real power in the country is found? Or is Parliament in decline and in fact so dominated by the government and Prime Minister that it is little more than a rubber stamp for decisions made elsewhere?

10.1 What is Parliament and how is it composed?

First, Parliament is our legislature, or law-making body. Second, political scientists also call bodies like Parliament 'representative assemblies', to emphasize this further important function. As we shall see, these two descriptions do not exhaust the list of roles or functions performed by Parliament, but they do make a good simple analysis. Since 1999, we have had to be careful in using the word 'Parliament', because in that year the Scottish Parliament was revived (having abolished itself in 1707), so there are now two Parliaments in Britain. The phrase '**Westminster Parliament**' has come into greater use since 1999 to deal with this problem: it refers to the UK Parliament which meets in Westminster, a part of London. There are also other law-making and representative assemblies: local councils at various levels, and the Welsh and Northern Ireland Assemblies. The Westminster Parliament is the leading assembly of this sort, but not the only one.

> **Westminster Parliament**: the United Kingdom's supreme legislative and representative assembly.

The composition of Parliament

Parliament in Britain is an extremely ancient institution, which dates back to the thirteenth century, when the English people began to develop a body which would assist the king in the government of the country. Even before that there had been assemblies of some sort. This antiquity perhaps explains the curiosities surrounding the composition of Parliament. Parliament is technically composed of three elements: the House of Commons, the House of Lords and the Crown. Let us now look at these in reverse order of importance.

The Crown

This refers the ruling monarch of the day – currently Queen Elizabeth II – but the role of the monarch is now almost entirely ceremonial, especially as a part of Parliament. The monarch is not allowed to enter the House of Commons at all, a symbolic reminder that in the 1640s Parliament fought the King and executed him. Once a year, generally in the autumn, the Queen attends the State Opening of Parliament, a ceremonial occasion, at which she delivers the Queen's Speech. This is a brief statement, drawn up by the Prime Minister and government, setting out their legislative programme for the coming parliamentary session, which lasts until the following summer unless a general election is called before then. The monarch's other parliamentary role is to give Royal Assent to all pieces of legislation. That is to say, the Queen puts her signature on the final version of all bills that pass through Parliament. This sounds like an important job, but although in theory she can refuse to assent to a piece of legislation, in practice Royal Assent has not been withheld since the days of Queen Anne 300 years ago. The last time a monarch seriously threatened to refuse Royal Assent was in 1800, when George III prevented a bill on the subject of Catholic emancipation from being introduced, thus holding up this important matter for 29 years. On both occasions, it was over matters which the monarch of the day thought were closely connected with the Crown, so it is just about possible that a

The Palace of Westminster, also known as the Houses of Parliament, sits on the banks of the Thames. It consists of two main chambers – the House of Commons and the House of Lords

monarch might refuse to sign a bill dealing with the monarchy, or abolishing it, if one were ever introduced, but this refusal would presumably not have any effect if things had already gone so far. It is, of course, absolutely correct that the monarch's role in Parliament is ceremonial, since we live in a democracy; there is also no indication that any member of the House of Windsor has had any problem with this at all. What the Queen adds to Parliament, her supporters would say, is a touch of glamour, without which Parliament is a little drab, and an additional element of legitimation (see below).

The House of Lords

The House of Lords is a much more active part of Parliament than the Crown, but still far less significant than the House of Commons. In the Middle Ages it was superior to the Commons, and in the eighteenth century probably of equal importance to it, but by the twenty-first century the House of Lords has limited powers, which will be discussed in the next chapter, as will a detailed analysis of its membership.

The House of Commons

The real centre of Parliament is here. In 2005, the nation elected 646 Members of Parliament – or MPs, as members of the House of Commons, perhaps

Michael Martin, the current Speaker of the House of Commons (2000–)

significantly, are always called; the number varies a little as constituency boundaries and electoral law change. Members of the House of Lords are not called MPs, even though they are clearly members of Parliament. MPs are elected in single-member constituencies on the first-past-the-post system. We can divide MPs into two groups: backbenchers and frontbenchers. Front-benchers are the MPs who are also government ministers or opposition shadow ministers. They are so called because they sit on the benches at the front of the chamber. Backbenchers are the rank-and-file MPs who have not been given a government or shadow role to play and who sit behind their leaders. They are a more numerous group, constituting about three-quarters of the MPs.

The House of Commons has the support of a rather limited number of civil servants, called House of Commons clerks. There are also domestic officials headed by the Serjeant at Arms, the 'men in tights' as the press calls them because of their comical fancy dress. But the real work of running the politics of the Commons is done by MPs themselves, especially those from the major-ity party in the House. It is from the governing or majority party that the main officers of the House of Commons responsible for running the place are drawn: the Speaker, the Leader of the House and the government whips.

The Speaker of the House of Commons (currently Michael Martin), who is supported by a number of Deputy Speakers, chairs debates – and is an MP. The chairing of debates involves keeping order, which is sometimes difficult, and calling on people to speak, which is also difficult, since MPs in large

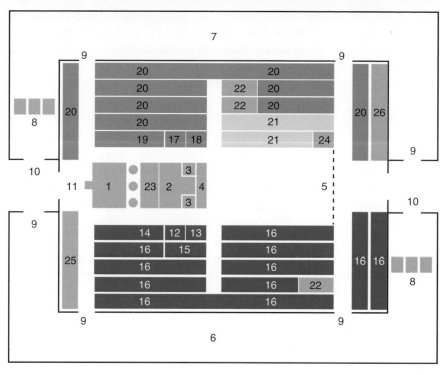

Figure 10.1 Floor plan of the House of Commons

The Commons Chamber

1	Speaker's Chair	14	Other ministers
2	Table of the House	15	Parliamentary private secretaries
3	Despatch boxes	16	Government backbenches
4	The Mace	17	Leader of opposition
5	The Bar of the House	18	Opposition Whips
6	Aye division lobby	19	Shadow ministers
7	No division lobby	20	Opposition backbenches
8	Division clerks' desks	21	Liberal Democrats
9	Entrances to lobbies	22	Other smaller parties
10	Exits from lobbies	23	Clerks at the table
11	Petition bag	24	Serjeant at Arms
12	Prime Minister	25	Civil servants
13	Government Whips	26	Strangers

numbers are often trying to speak, but need to 'catch the Speaker's eye' before they can do so. The Speaker will have been elected to Parliament as a member of a political party like any other MP, but on being chosen Speaker, he or she will need to become impartial and cannot participate in debates. In the event of a tied vote, the Speaker has a casting vote, which has to be used according to strict rules, so this is a situation that is avoided as much as possible. The Speaker will not vote in favour of a measure which might otherwise be defeated, because it is possible that a future vote by MPs could produce a decisive outcome, whereas if it were passed it might be difficult to repeal. But the Speaker would oppose a vote of no confidence in the government (leading to the resignation of the government if it passed) in the event of a tie, so that there could be a chance in the future for the majority of MPs to come to a conclusion themselves on the matter, which would have been impossible if the government had already fallen as a result of the Speaker's vote.

The Leader of the House of Commons is the government minister, currently Harriet Harman, responsible for running the House of Commons, as what is called the 'business manager' for his or her political party. This mainly involves deciding on the timetable for debates and the passing of bills, and keeping closely in touch with the Prime Minister and Cabinet (of which he or she is a member) on this. The Leader is also responsible for bringing in any reforms that are thought to be necessary in the management and procedure of the Commons.

The whips are the party officials who also play a large part in running the House of Commons, their main concern being that MPs support the party line on whatever is being debated at the time. They publish a daily list of debates with instructions to members of the party on how important each vote is considered (this document is also known as a 'whip'): the highest level of importance is attached to a vote which is underlined three times in this document – known as a 'three-line whip'. MPs are expected to turn up and vote for their party on a three-line whip. Whips enforce party loyalty by a mixture of threats and promises. The ultimate threat is to 'withdraw the whip' from an MP, which means ejecting an MP from the party. Party discipline in the House of Commons is generally very strong. The whips also listen to the concerns of MPs and are expected to pass on these concerns to ministers. All the main parties represented in the Commons have whips: there is generally a Chief Whip (the government Chief Whip is currently Geoff Hoon) with a team of about a dozen assistants in the two main parties.

 Question: Describe the main features of the membership of the House of Commons.

10.2 Parliamentary sovereignty and the 'Westminster model'

Parliamentary sovereignty

This is a key constitutional principle in Britain and is discussed at more length in chapter 9. Essentially, this principle claims that Parliament is sovereign or supreme in its law-making capacity. This means that it can overrule any other political bodies (like the newly created devolved assemblies) which play a part in the life of the country. Laws made by Parliament are superior to any law made by judges, and when an Act of Parliament is passed the judges must immediately enforce it. Parliament can also repeal any law passed by an earlier Parliament. According to this constitutional theory, Parliament can make and break the Constitution itself. This gives to Parliament immense theoretical power, far more than most other legislatures around the world would claim. This idea of sovereignty links with the other rather exalted claims that are made for Parliament. Parliament's great antiquity is often stressed, its position as the 'Mother of Parliaments', the ancestor in the modern world of all other democratic assemblies, especially those in former British colonies. Parliament has an iconic status: the buildings which house it, especially the Tower which contains Big Ben, are instantly recognizable, and in graphic form they mean British politics to us when we see them.

The parliamentary system of government: the Westminster model

The 'Westminster model' is a way of describing how Parliament fits into the broader political system in Britain, and also in those countries which use the same sort of political methods. So when we talk about the Westminster model, we mean 'the system of government used in the UK'. Another way of describing the Westminster model is to call it a 'parliamentary system of government', a phrase that is sometimes abbreviated into 'parliamentary government'. Around the world, in liberal democracies, there are essentially two models of how to run a system of government: the parliamentary system and the presidential system. The presidential system is often said to follow the model of the USA. The main differences between the two systems are presented in table 10.1. The key point about parliamentary government is that it involves a fusion of the legislative and executive branches of government. On the whole, the real effect of this in Britain is not to strengthen Parliament but to reduce its power, because in practice the executive is able to dominate Parliament. So there are question-marks over the reality of Parliament's power and sovereignty. These doubts will be discussed later in the chapter.

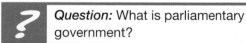

? *Question:* What is parliamentary government?

Table 10.1 Parliamentary and presidential government

Parliamentary government	Presidential government
The members of the executive (often confusingly called 'the government') are also members of Parliament	The President and the other members of the executive are not members of the legislature
The members of the executive are elected as Members of Parliament, and then the executive is formed by the largest party in Parliament	The President is directly elected by the people
There is no real 'separation of powers'; in fact there is a 'fusion' of the executive and legislative powers	There is a 'separation of powers' between the executive and legislature: they are kept apart
The executive is responsible to Parliament, and accountable to Parliament	The President and his ministers are directly responsible to the people
Parliament can in theory dismiss the executive, using a 'vote of no confidence', which will then result in a general election. There are therefore no fixed-term elections	The timing of elections is inflexible, and it is at the election that the President can be dismissed by the people, or re-elected
Since the Prime Minister is part of both the executive and legislature, it would make the position too powerful if he or she were head of state as well as head of government (or executive), so a separate head of state is required	It may be possible to combine the roles of head of state and head of government (or executive), as in the USA

10.3 The functions of Parliament

Figure 10.2 illustrates the main functions of Parliament. The remainder of this chapter will analyse these roles and evaluate how far they are effectively fulfilled by Parliament.

 Question: Outline the main function of the House of Commons.

10.4 Representation

Representation is a rather complicated concept, and hence it is difficult to be very definite about how far Parliament is an effective representative assembly. According to political theorist Hanna Pitkin, there are four ways in which the word representation can be used:

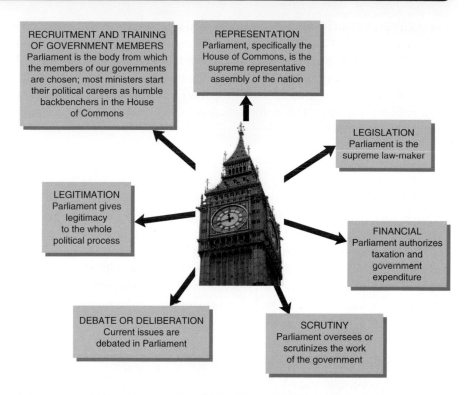

Figure 10.2 The main functions of Parliament

A representative is freely and fairly chosen by those whom he or she represents

This is probably the most important point and provides a simple and clear definition of a representative. Only the House of Commons is elected, in contrast to the House of Lords; so only the Commons can be called representative. To evaluate whether, according to this definition, the House of Commons is truly representative brings us back to the old debate about first-past-the-post elections as opposed to proportional or majoritarian electoral systems, which is dealt with in chapter 3.

A representative acts on behalf of those whom he or she represents

How well do MPs act on behalf of those they represent? There are two difficulties here. First, should the representative be allowed discretion in doing this, and if so how much? Second, who actually is the MP representing?

Representative or delegate?

A delegate does what his or her voters want, and refers back to them if he or she doesn't know what it is they want. A representative (according to this specialist use of the word) uses his or her own intelligence to decide what is best for the voters. The standard view of the role of an MP says that on the whole the MP should act as a representative not a delegate. After all, the MP cannot consult widely enough on all issues to become an effective delegate. However, it is fair to say that MPs will probably try to have some view on what their constituents want. This point is dealt with more fully in box 10.1 on the ideas of Edmund Burke.

Who is the representative acting for?

This links to the last point. To simplify, the main dilemma here is whether MPs act on behalf of their constituency, or whether they act on behalf of their political party. On the face of it, the best answer seems to be the constituency. After all, the great strength of the first-past-the-post system is often said to be the constituency link, and surely MPs should be aware of local issues and go to Westminster to set them before Parliament. But, on the other hand, an MP is elected on a party ticket. The great majority of voters really do not care whether their MP is Mrs X or Mr Y, but vote for the candidate because he or

Box 10.1 Edmund Burke's view of representation

A famous discussion of representation is to be found in political philosopher Edmund Burke's letter to his Bristol constituents of 1774. Burke said, first, that he would feel himself bound, now he was elected, to represent *all* his constituents in Bristol, not just those Whigs who had voted for him. He therefore seemed to be saying that he thought that he should be a constituency representative before being a party representative. This would not be a popular view of things nowadays, at least among the whips, the people responsible for party discipline in Parliament. On the other hand, in their constituency role (answering the enquiries of constituents and trying to help them if they have problems), MPs nowadays do agree with Burke, and make every effort not to discriminate in favour of those constituents who voted for them and against those who did not. Of course, it is actually impossible nowadays, since voting is secret, to know how votes have been cast. Second, Burke said that he would make his own mind up, once elected, on matters of policy and legislation. He would use his conscience to

decide what the right course of action was, and use his intelligence and knowledge to decide what was most in the interests of his constituents. He would not be consulting his constituents on what they felt. This is generally taken to define the difference between a delegate (bound to act on the commands of those who elect the MP) and a representative (free to do what is best when elected). This view of things also looks very outdated now, for two reasons. First, MPs are allowed by their whips to vote freely according to their consciences only on a small range of moral matters, like the death penalty, for example. Second, MPs now believe that they are bound to act according to the party manifesto and they feel that it is this manifesto that links them to their constituents. The reason is that constituents have elected the MP on the basis that he or she would follow the manifesto. So Burke's views seem largely outdated, mainly because our modern democracy has strengthened the power of parties to a great extent since his day.

she 'represents' at election time the political party whose manifesto they prefer. If at the end of four or five years the MP stands again for election, the voters will be judging his or her party's record when they come to vote, not the MP's individual performance (unless it has been spectacularly bad, as in the case of Neil Hamilton, the disgraced MP for Tatton, in 1997). At least, this seems to many political scientists to be how our democratic system works. If it is, we actually want our MPs to be party delegates (to go back to the last point) and not constituency representatives. Perhaps the really effective MP is the one who succeeds in balancing these two representative functions most effectively.

A representative body is a cross-section of the whole community

This is another use of the word 'representation' which is quite common – for example, when we talk about a 'representative sample'. As is well known, however, the House of Commons (let alone the House of Lords) fails quite badly in this respect. In terms of gender, the Commons seriously under-represents women, although things have improved a little in recent years. There has been very little change, however, in the way in which the Commons represents ethnic minority groups, which are still seriously under-represented in Parliament. In addition, the House of Commons is largely dominated by middle-aged, if not elderly, men. On the whole, MPs are over-educated in comparison with the rest of the population, and a large number of them have been to private schools and to university. There are more Old Etonians (17) than there are members of the ethnic minorities, although one of the Etonians is of Ghanaian parentage and another is Anglo-Chinese. Finally, in terms of social class, MPs are overwhelmingly middle class, with lawyers grossly over-represented. The House of Commons, in short, is not a good representative cross-section of the country.

The remedy for this lies in the hands of the political parties; it is a problem with what political scientists call 'recruitment'. Political parties need to recruit or select more candidates for election than they do at present from minority racial groups, more females and people from a wider range of trades and professions. All political parties are to a greater or lesser extent aware of this, although probably the Labour Party has moved fastest to remedy the situation. The first-past-the-post electoral system used in Westminster elections is also a factor in delaying change here. Proportional systems like AMS and the party list system enable political parties at the centre to recruit more women and minority candidates. The fact that the Welsh Assembly after 2002 was 50 per cent female, elected on the AMS system, shows this.

A representative is an ambassador of the people

Hanna Pitkin's final point is that a representative is seen as a role model, a figurehead, someone who represents his or her locality as a leading figure in the community, and also someone who, as a politician, has a sort of ambassadorial role to play for the nation as a whole. Whether all voters really see their MPs in this way is probably open to question, but there is clearly some truth in it. In recent years the prestige of MPs has suffered from accusations of corruption ('sleaze') and from scandals of one sort and another affecting a small number of individual politicians. This creates cynicism about democratic politics and may, some argue, have an impact on participation rates. It can affect Parliament's role in terms of legitimation too. The appointment of a Parliamentary Commissioner for Standards following the Nolan Inquiry (1995) into allegations of sleaze among MPs, and the introduction of legislation in 2000 on party funding, may result in some improvements here.

All in all, representation is such a tricky concept that it is difficult to make any snap judgements on how effective Parliament is as a representative body. Broadly speaking, we could conclude that it can be criticized especially on issues of recruitment, and possibly in terms of the other categories dealt with above (although that is less clear). The really important issue is connected with the great debate over electoral systems, and the arguments on each side of that debate are probably quite evenly balanced.

 Question: Why has Parliament been criticized for being insufficiently representative?

10.5 Legislation

Legislation: law-making; laws, especially those passed by Parliament.

Passing laws, or **legislating**, is the primary role of Parliament. There is no point in electing MPs, however representative they are, according to whatever definitions, if they do nothing once they are elected.

In Britain, Parliament is the supreme law-maker. But law is also made by judges: this is called 'case law' and is said to be set by 'precedent'. Judges are sometimes put in the position where a case they are trying involves a completely novel problem and the judge then has to make a ruling in this new area. This ruling then becomes a precedent for other judges to follow. In this way judges can make new law, or legislate. But Parliament can then change this judge-made law, if it sees fit, and set out what it wants to be done in such cases in the future. The national assemblies in Wales and Northern Ireland, and the new Scottish Parliament, can also make law, each body in a slightly different way. Again, this legislation in the devolved assemblies is subject to the overriding sovereignty of Parliament. The Europe Union also passes legislation which is binding in Britain. According to constitutional theory, this European law is also subject to parliamentary supremacy. At a lower level, local councils (of the borough, city, district and even parish) can make by-laws, on minor matters, which can be overruled by Parliament if necessary.

How effective is Parliament as a legislator?

This is a difficult question to answer because it is hard to say what constitutes success in a legislator. But the following points seem valid:

Positive points

- In 1997–8, Parliament passed 52 bills; in 2000–1, it was 21; in 2005–6, it rose to 42. These low numbers suggest that the process is a slow, careful one. Most legislation is professionally drafted, and seems to keep pace with

Box 10.3 How does the process of parliamentary legislation work?

1 The government will probably proposes a piece of legislation in its manifesto (this is not an essential starting point).

2 The government may decide to consult about the matter. If it does, there may be a 'Green Paper' issued, a longish document, which is a preliminary statement of policy intentions, or increasingly in the last few years, more informal discussion papers will be published. These are meant to stimulate debate and allow the government to take advice from interested parties. Alternatively, or in addition, a 'White Paper' may be published. This is a more detailed and more focused statement of government intentions, and may be very close to the final published bill. Again the idea is to get opinions and comments from interest groups and people who may be affected by the proposed legislation. There is no compulsion on a government to use this stage of the process.

3 The first formal part of the process of legislation is when a bill is published. The government 'draftsmen', the lawyers skilled in the arts of drawing up (drafting) legislation, produce the bill, which is what the government will ask Parliament to enact. It is often a very long and complicated document, divided into hundreds of clauses.

4 The first reading is when the bill is formally presented to the Commons. In the past it was actually a time to read out the bill, but now it is merely made available for MPs to read. The real debate will be held on the second reading, when a full-scale discussion involving government ministers and the shadow ministers, and as many on the backbenches as are interested, takes place.

5 Committee and report stage: The bill is now generally given to a so-called standing committee, a small group of MPs from both government and opposition parties, but with a government majority. The purpose of this stage is to analyse the bill in detail, searching for problems of drafting and discussing possible amendments, or changes to the bill which might be thought useful. The committee then reports back to the Commons, who vote on the bill and any amendments which have come out of the committee or are proposed on the floor of the House. Finally, there is a third reading, which is a final set-piece debate on the bill.

6 The House of Lords now debates the bill (occasionally a bill starts off here, but normally not). The House of Lords cannot completely overturn it, but it can propose amendments and it can delay the bill by a year and a month by voting against it. In each case if this happens, the bill has to be voted on again in the Commons.

7 Royal Assent: the formality of royal signature complete, the bill is now called an Act of Parliament, or a Statute, and has become the law of the land.

changes in society which require changes in the law. Obviously, Conservative and Labour supporters will prefer the bills passed by the government they voted for, so evaluation is particularly difficult here.

- In legislative terms, Parliament has considerable scope – far more than legislatures abroad. This is because Parliament can pass constitutional amendments on a simple majority. In fact, in Britain there is no difference between constitutional law and other forms of legislation.
- Parliament can be very quick in passing legislation in times of crisis. For example, in March 2005, anti-terrorist legislation was rushed through the Commons in two days, although the speed with which this was done was not without controversy.
- What is called, rather confusingly, 'legislative scrutiny' – the process by which proposed legislation is examined for problems with drafting – seems to work quite well because of the adversarial nature of British party politics. The thoroughness of the process can be seen in box 10.3.
- Almost all government bills become laws. If their content was included in the manifesto, these bills can be said to have been approved, at least in broad outline, by the electorate. If this has not happened, the electorate can pass its judgement on them when it holds the government to account at the end of its term. This leads, it is alleged, to strong, responsible government, but it also means that the process is democratic.

Negative points

- The central point here is the standard criticism of the Westminster model of parliamentary government. This is the simple point that Parliament does very little more than 'rubber-stamp' government proposals. Hence, what is called executive dominance, combined with the strength of party adversarial conflict, means that Parliament is a weak body.
- Bills can be passed through too quickly. The usual example given of this is the Dangerous Dogs Act (1991), a measure which followed a newspaper scare about pit bull terriers, Japanese tosas and even the dogo Argentino, three breeds that were condemned to death after a bill had been rushed through Parliament. In the following years, cuddly looking mutts on death row were featured widely in the same newspapers that had called for action in the first place. The fact is that the legislation was a knee-jerk reaction to a press scare, and should not have been passed through Parliament so quickly and with so little thought for the consequences.
- It is wrong to launch into constitutional reform on the basis of simple parliamentary majorities. Matters of this importance should require a fuller procedure, as is generally the case in countries with entrenched, written

constitutions. The use of referendums to validate important constitutional changes to some degree answers this point. But there is nothing to force a government to have a referendum on a constitutional reform if it does not want one.

- Legislative scrutiny may not be very effective, given the strong party adversarial conflict in Parliament. Is there any point in effective scrutiny by the opposition if it means that the credit for good legislation goes to the government? This is the downside of the Westminster model of account-able government. In other words, strong government is not always good government, even in a liberal democracy. Specifically, the standing com-mittees might be criticized for not doing a very good job. In 1979 a reform of the committee structure in the Commons made it possible for special standing committees to be used to scrutinize a particular bill. These would

Box 10.4 Private Members' Bills

Most pieces of legislation passed by Parliament are government bills. They are initiated by the government, which whips them through Parliament. But about one in eight of all bills passed are initiated by MPs in their own right – these are called Private Members' Bills. Peers can also propose Private Members' Bills in the House of Lords. Technically, there are three ways in which this can be done in the Commons:

1 Under the Private Members' Ballot, the most common way, where MPs put their names into a ballot and those who win are given time to introduce a bill.
2 Under the Ten-Minute Rule.
3 Under Standing Order 58.

On the one hand, it seems to be a good thing that MPs can do this. Some major changes in the law, largely of a moral sort, have been brought about by Private Members' Bills; e.g., the abolition of censorship on plays, the legalisation of homosexuality. The system allows backbench MPs to take up a worthy cause, sometimes one that is suggested by a pressure group, and to play a genuine role as legislators outside the party struggle. But the weakness of the process needs emphasizing. It is very difficult to get controversial measures through the Commons without the support of the government whips, and many Private Members' Bills fail to pass. The organization of the Commons is such that a fair hearing is not necessarily given to a Private Member's Bill, and there is no compulsion on legislators even to turn up and vote for or against a measure that is not whipped by the government or the opposition. A second criticism is that the government sometimes uses Private Members' Bills as a way in which to get things passed in the Commons without seeming to be associated directly with them. 'Handout bills', which are bills the government wants passed through the private members' system, are given to MPs who win in the ballot. Conversely, a government sometimes opposes a Private Members' Bill in an underhand way, using a sort of secret whip to get a measure it opposes dropped. Governments are also known to hijack Private Members' Bills which they think will get them some glory, and pass them as government measures. All in all, how the system operates in practice tends to emphasize the weakness of Parliament and the strength of government.

have acted much more like such committees in the United States, calling witnesses and drawing in contributions from a number of sources. But in the end this reform was not made much use of, and only a handful of such Committees have ever been set up.

- There is very little opportunity for backbench and opposition MPs to propose subjects for legislation. The main way in which legislation is initiated (to use the technical term) is by the government. There are some opportunities for what are called Private Members' Bills, but they are few and far between.

 Question: How effectively does Parliament fulfil its role as a legislator?

10.6 Taxation and finance

Since the Middle Ages, Parliament – and especially the House of Commons – has developed a role as the supreme financial institution in the system of government, as the sovereign taxer. Technically, taxation and expenditure are authorized through parliamentary legislation, so in a sense this is really only a matter of legislation again. Similarly, the 'power of the purse' is also expressed by Parliament's close scrutiny of government spending, so this too overlaps with another of Parliament's functions, to be discussed in the next section. But there are some separate points that need to be emphasized.

Parliament is the sovereign body

The European Union receives much tax revenue, although only by Parliament's approval. Similarly, the Scottish Parliament (alone of the national assemblies) can vary tax by three pence in the pound over or below the rate set in Westminster, but only as a result of a prior Act of the Westminster Parliament. Local councils can increase or decrease council tax (local taxes), but are closely supervised in this by the central government and Parliament.

No interference from the House of Lords

The House of Commons allows absolutely no interference in this power of taxation from the House of Lords. Essentially, this is based on a tradition that taxation does not concern the Lords which stretches back to the Middle Ages, and was confirmed in 1911 in the Parliament Act, which allows the Lords the right to delay all Commons legislation apart from financial measures.

The budget

The budget is announced in the House of Commons in the spring, and is the annual statement of the government's plans for taxation and expenditure. It gives rise to one of Parliament's grand occasions, with the Chancellor of the Exchequer making a speech that is answered by the leader of the opposition. There follow several days of debate. There is intense media interest in this occasion.

Party unity

No area of policy is more subject to the pressure of party discipline and the adversarial nature of British politics. It is on taxation and expenditure that elections are often largely fought, and absolute party unity on these matters is expected, and generally achieved.

Scrutiny

Among the great strengths of Parliament is scrutiny of financial matters, partly because it takes place a little outside the party battle. The oldest and most successful committee is the Parliamentary Accounts Committee (PAC), which dates back to 1861 and is always chaired by a member of the opposition, currently Edward Leigh. It is responsible for a large department called the National Audit Office (NAO), which was set up, on the basis of an earlier body, by a Private Member's Bill in 1983. There are 800 staff employed by the NAO, headed by the Comptroller and Auditor General, who is an officer of Parliament, not the government. The PAC is a very effective body, which combs through the government's accounts and looks hard for ways of using taxpayers' money more effectively. It also carries out inquiries into various government departments and agencies to see if they are working as economically as they should. In 2005, for example, it gained publicity when it inquired into the finances of the Prince of Wales.

10.7 Scrutiny of the executive

An important function of any representative assembly in a liberal democracy is to **scrutinize** the executive. There are several main ways in which the House of Commons does this.

Legislative scrutiny

This has been dealt with already. It takes place during the long, complicated process of debate and committee work through which all legislation passes.

> **Scrutiny**: the act of overseeing or examining the work of one of the branches of government by another. It generally applies to the oversight of the executive by the representative assembly. The purpose of scrutiny is to expose the errors of government, thus ensuring accountability and good government.

Since the government is the main source of legislation, legislative scrutiny can be said also to be scrutiny of the government.

The Public Accounts Committee and National Audit Office

These have also been discussed above as examples of how Parliament undertakes important financial scrutiny of the work of the executive.

Prime Minister's Questions

PMQs are a very significant aspect of scrutiny. Because of the fusion of legislative and executive powers under our parliamentary system of government, the head of our executive (the Prime Minister) is a member of the legislature. This means he or she is available for what is called 'interpellation', or direct questioning by MPs. This now occurs once a week and is currently timetabled at 12 noon on Wednesdays, lasting half an hour. A complicated ritual surrounds this process, but in the end it does mean that the Prime Minister answers questions on most aspects of policy and is cross-examined to some extent by the leader of the opposition. PMQs draws a good deal of media interest and parts of it are often televised on prime-time news programmes. Some people complain that the process is rather trivialized, which does not really lead to much scrutiny. Instead, it simply emphasizes the

Tony Blair is applauded by MPs from all parties after his last Prime Minister's Questions on 27 June 2007

rhetoric of conflict between the two parties, and tests the performance skills of the Prime Minister and leader of the opposition. Favourable questions are sometimes planted by pro-government backbenchers, to enable the government to look good. Sometimes PMQs is made to look like a cross-examination of the leader of the opposition and this is criticized, but it could be said that parliamentary scrutiny should also involve scrutiny of the opposition.

Questions to ministers for oral answers

In the same way, other ministers in the government also answer questions orally, on a rota which allows for two sessions a week devoted to each government department in turn. Obviously, this comes closer to real scrutiny than PMQs, since it involves more specialized, detailed questions. Ministers are aware of the questions in advance, and consult their advisers and civil servants on what to say by way of answer.

Questions for written answer

MPs can give any number of questions to ministers for a written answer. The answer is prepared by a departmental civil servant who is expert in the field. These questions will enable an opposition party to keep up with detailed matters of government, and also enable MPs to pursue matters of concern to their constituents. The answers given to these questions may also help an MP who is campaigning on a particular issue of public concern. A surprising number of such questions are made each session: in some years up to 50,000. The answers are printed in *Hansard*, the official record of parliamentary business.

Departmental select committees

In 1979, the select committees of the House of Commons were reformed by Norman St John Stevas, Conservative Leader of the House in the biggest reform of the Commons arguably in the whole century. This reform established a committee to shadow and scrutinize the work of each major government department. There are now 18 such departmental select committees, composed generally of 11 MPs, drawn from the parties in rough proportion to the number of seats they hold. These committees are therefore dominated by the governing party and the chairman is generally (but not always) drawn from this party too. Obviously, these fundamental points about membership blunt their scrutinizing edge. The committees make inquiries and issue reports on matters of public interest connected to 'their' department. They are televised and witnesses can be called, in the form of civil servants, ministers and anyone they like. The Prime Minister so far has refused to attend these committee meetings, however. Margaret Thatcher sent her Cabinet Secretary (a senior civil servant) to appear on her behalf when she was asked to attend herself.

Select committees do provide good scrutiny. For example, the 1999 Report of the Select Committee on the newly formed Department for the Environment, Transport and the Regions was a devastating attack on how John Prescott had run his ministry. But on the other hand, the dominance of these committees by the governing party means that criticism is often muted. There have been persistent rumours that the party whips have been involved (under both Labour and Conservative governments) in selecting members and chairmen of these committees, and there are suspicions of collusion between the committees and the departments they are supposed to be scrutinizing. In 2003, the chairman of the Foreign Affairs Select Committee admitted to the Hutton Inquiry that he had allowed Geoff Hoon, Minister of Defence, to dictate to the committee what questions were to be put to Dr Kelly, a senior civil servant who was attending the inquiry. That select committee produced a report which essentially backed up the government's position on the reasons for going to war with Iraq. It is very difficult to see it as having applied independent scrutiny to the inquiry. However, this is perhaps to be expected on such a high-profile matter. By and large, these committees do very useful work. A list of departmental select committees is given in figure 10.3.

Prime Minister's Questions before the Liaison Committee

In 2002, Tony Blair offered to submit himself to questioning on all topical matters by the Liaison Committee, which is composed of all the chairmen of select committees. These public, televised meetings take place twice a year, and clearly add a further element of scrutiny. It is fair to add that the chairmen whom the Prime Minister meets are mostly from his own political party, which means that he or she is likely to be treated quite gently.

Debates

Parliament works through debates, set-piece arguments with opposing sides of a question being put by MPs. Debating is so important that it is sometimes described in itself as a function of Parliament. The main debates which focus on scrutiny are as follows.

The Annual Debate on the Address

This is the five days of debate which follow the Queen's Speech and the 'address' or reply of the Commons to it. So it can cover the whole range of government proposals for the coming parliamentary year which have been

Figure 10.3   House of Commons departmental select committees

announced at the State Opening of Parliament. In 2007, Gordon Brown announced that the government would unveil its legislative programme in advance of the Queen's Speech (he did so in 2007 – about four months earlier), which should enable a greater degree of scrutiny to take place.

Debate on a motion of no confidence

This is the most famous debate in Parliament because if the government loses the vote at the end, it has to resign and there will be a general election. However, there is very little point in the opposition proposing a motion of this sort (that is, calling for such a debate) because, by definition, it will lose the vote. At times of crisis for the government, the opposition can call for such a debate, but simply in order to focus public attention on the issue, even if they know they will lose the vote. Only once since 1945 has a government lost such a debate, and this was in 1979, when James Callaghan's government was already in a minority and when a general election would have had to be called in a few months in any case, since it was nearly five years since the previous one.

Opposition days

Twenty days a year are set aside for the opposition parties to propose subjects for debate, which clearly gives a chance for scrutiny to take place.

Estimates days

On three days a year, there are debates on what are called 'estimates', or the estimated expenditure of individual government departments – these generally tie in with select committee reports which have raised questions.

Private members' debates and adjournment debates

These provide a chance for individual backbenchers to propose topics for debate. The adjournment debate takes place in the half an hour before the Commons closes for the day and is frequently used by MPs to raise constituency matters or to highlight matters of particular concern to them.

Early day motions

The House of Commons is full of quaint antiquated procedures which tend to baffle outsiders. Early day motions are a good example of this. MPs can suggest a subject for debate 'at an early day' – i.e., as soon as possible. In fact, these motions are almost never debated, but the process does provide a certain amount of scrutiny and can (on rare occasions) prompt a change in government policy. This is because the printed list of these motions is made available to other MPs who have an opportunity to sign the motion themselves, a bit like a petition. If a large number sign it, the government is obviously made aware that there is some sort of problem. Labour backbench opposition to top-up fees in 2003 was announced to the government in no fewer than four critical early day motions.

The Ombudsman, or Parliamentary Commissioner for Administration

This official's role was created in 1967 in imitation of a similar one in Sweden. If an MP receives a complaint from a constituent about maladministration (mismanagement) by a government department, he or she can try to sort it out by applying to the Ombudsman. In some ways, the work of the Ombudsman is more about a sort of judicial redress of individual grievances and the representative function of MPs, but the process will also act as a form of scrutiny. The decisions of the Ombudsman are not binding, and the office has not really enjoyed the success that was hoped for it when it was created. There are now other ways in which a citizen can obtain redress, under the Human Rights Act, for example, and through a large number of tribunals. In the past

20 years or so, a number of other officials called 'Ombudsmen', with a specific area to deal with (like the health service or local government ombudsmen), have also been set up. These officials have little or nothing to do with Parliament. As a result, the parliamentary Ombudsman has quite a small workload.

How effective is parliamentary scrutiny?

Positive points

- There is no escape for government ministers under a parliamentary system of government. They are part of the legislature and hence can be questioned directly and frequently by the opposition and by their own backbenchers. They have to lead debates on the legislation they propose and have to defend their policies and proposals. This goes right to the top, and the Prime Minister likewise has to appear regularly in Parliament to answer questions. This would be impossible under a system based on the separation of powers, a presidential system of government.
- The motion of no confidence is a highly significant reminder that the theoretical position is that Parliament is in control of the executive. This is supported by the constitutional principle of collective Cabinet responsibility, by which the whole government (not just the Prime Minister) have to resign in the event of defeat on a vote of no confidence.
- The British constitutional doctrine of individual ministerial responsibility (discussed in chapter 12) supports the idea of parliamentary scrutiny: ministers are responsible to the people by way of Parliament. If they have lied to Parliament they must apologize, and can be held responsible. In the end they can be forced to resign if they are found in breach of the rather hazy rules of ministerial conduct.
- The lines of accountability are made very clear in Britain. Ministers and the government as a whole are accountable to Parliament, and through Parliament to the country. The voters can make a very clear link between the success or failure of a government and how they will vote in a general election. This is more difficult to do in a country run under a system of the separation of powers. In the USA, it is not always clear who is to blame for a failure: President or Congress.
- There is a great range of methods of scrutiny available to Parliament as the list above shows.
- Parliament has added to its armoury in recent years. The introduction of the reformed select committees in 1979 was a significant step forward.

Recently, the appearance of the Prime Minister before the Liaison Committee is also significant. Proposals made in 2007 for the prerogative powers of the executive (e.g. declaration of war) to be routinely subject to Parliament's consent may also strengthen its scrutiny powers.

Negative points

- In practice, the executive dominates Parliament to such a degree that effective scrutiny tends to be difficult. It is difficult for Parliament to hold ministers to account, because the government can dominate Parliament. The presence of ministers in the legislature (seen as a strength in the positive list of points) actually means that the executive is running things in Parliament. The parliamentary timetable is decided by the government, and day-to-day management is the responsibility of government whips and the Leader of the House, who is a Cabinet minister. A government with a majority has nothing to fear from a vote of no confidence, and John Major used the threat of calling such a vote as a way of making sure that the party supported his government in the Commons. This seems to turn the whole idea of accountability on its head. The composition of select committees favours the governing party, which also appoints the Chairmen of most of these committees.
- Strong party discipline combines with the power of the executive to produce a Parliament where genuine criticism of the government is confined just to a minority, to the opposition, whose powers are limited. The strength of party loyalty and the power of the party whips is such that the governing party is seldom troubled by scrutiny.
- The strength of party adversarial politics is such that the governing party is unlikely to question the government itself too closely. The opposition may also be careful not to work in a true spirit of scrutiny, pointing out mistakes the government makes, from of a desire to make British government work more smoothly, because British party politics depends on the opposition exploiting the mistakes of government rather than rectifying them.
- True scrutiny depends on a weak governing party in the Commons. If the government has a large majority in the Commons and if the governing party is united behind the leadership, it is unlikely that they will be very thoroughly scrutinized or genuinely be held to account by the opposition. It is the presence of a substantial body of government 'rebels' within the governing party that makes Parliament really work as a body that successfully holds the government to account. If the government has a small majority in the Commons, effective scrutiny is also more likely.

Box 10.5 The opposition

The greatest institution of both legislative and executive scrutiny is 'Her Majesty's loyal opposition', defined as the Conservative Party when Labour is in government, and vice versa. When there was a simple two-party system in operation, the adversarial nature of Parliament highlighted the role of the opposition, led by its Shadow Cabinet. The whole parliamentary system continues to revolve around the opposition and government, which together manage the timetabling of business. It is the leader of the opposition who replies to the Chancellor's budget speech and who leads the criticisms of the government programme as set out in the Queen's speech. The leader of the opposition heads the attack in Prime Minister's Questions, and the Shadow

David Cameron, Leader of the Opposition

ministers confront their opposite numbers in ministerial questions and other debates. But the opposition's role is always very difficult. There is clearly no very strong interest in sorting out the government's poor drafting of legislation or offering constructive solutions to any problems it may face. In addition, if the opposition is too adversarial, it risks being accused of opportunism and being obsessed with nit-picking for its own sake. The opposition needs to appear statesmanlike and a genuine government in waiting. On foreign and defence policy, it has little alternative but to support the government if it wishes to avoid being accused of a lack of patriotism. Opposition is particularly difficult if the government has a large majority. After 1997, the tiny Conservative opposition group was demoralized and many of its front bench spokesmen seemed to be busy quarrelling among themselves or carving out part-time careers in business. In addition, the rise of the Liberal Democrats and other minor parties can undermine the whole concept of the opposition and the adversarial system on which Parliament is based. After 1997, the Liberal Democrats appeared to be more inclined to support Labour and criticize the Conservatives, although they were sitting in their places on the opposition benches. When the government is weak, as Major's was after 1992, the opposition will concentrate its energy on opposing the government through the media, and will tend to ignore Parliament if it feels it won't have much impact, because even a weak government has (normally) a built-in majority. Sometimes the work of the opposition is undermined because the strongest criticisms of a government come from its own rebellious backbenchers, as was the case over the war with Iraq in 2003–4.

Question: Through what mechanisms does Parliament hold the executive accountable?

10.8 Parliamentary debate or deliberation

It is often said that debating is one of the separate functions of Parliament (the deliberative function), but this is probably not acceptable as a theory. Debating is a highly significant parliamentary tool, a method used to achieve its true functions. The ways in which parliamentary debates help the smooth passage of legislation and the achievement of good scrutiny have already been discussed. But these are the means to an end: they are not an end in

Debate in the House of Commons

themselves. The case for there being a separate deliberative function depends on the view that some debates fall outside the normal scope of legislation or scrutiny. Some debates, it is argued, are merely ways in which the representatives of the nation clarify their collective views on a topic. This may then feed, in the long term, into policy formation. Since the executive is the really important part of the political system, it is important for Parliament to influence how the executive behaves by supplying some of the ideas which help shape policy. Debates may contribute to this. In the end, though, even this aspect of the deliberative function is probably better seen as just a rather generalized form of scrutiny of the executive. The representatives of the nation are, through certain debates, not scrutinizing individual pieces of policy, but trying to influence the general tendency and direction of government policy, even of ideology. To this extent, perhaps, there is a separate deliberative function, but it is rather nebulous.

10.9 Legitimation

Legitimation: the conferring of legitimacy, the process by which political 'power' is transformed into 'authority', by which force is made legitimate or morally acceptable.

The concepts 'power' and 'authority' are discussed in chapter 1. Parliament, the representative assembly in the UK, plays an important part in the process of **legitimation**, of transforming power into authority. As R. A. Packenham argued in the 1970s, there are two types of legitimation: manifest and latent.

Manifest legitimation is clear and open. The best examples of this are in the fields of taxation and legislation. Taxes are justified in a democracy by being the result of a vote in the representative assembly – in Parliament. If we ask why it is that we should be morally (and legally) bound to pay taxes, the answer is that it is because we have assented to this taxation through our representatives. The same is true of all laws. Why should I be imprisoned if I break a law? Because I have agreed to this being the case through the fact that Parliament is elected by me and everyone else, with the legitimate authority to pass laws. The doctrine of the mandate fits into these theories of legitimation. The governing party has stood for election on the basis of its manifesto. Once elected it can claim to have a mandate, or permission, from the electorate to fulfil its manifesto commitments.

Latent legitimation is hidden, or behind-the-scenes. This means that the whole political process is made legitimate by having at its heart an elected, representative body. In the end, Parliament links the people to the government. People can appeal to their MP if they are concerned by what has happened to them as individuals or collectively as members of a group. Parliament is the symbol of our national unity and of our democracy; it gives legitimacy to the whole state. This underlying legitimation role surfaces from time to time, perhaps most notably when Parliament is recalled in times of national emergency – for example, at the time of the Falklands crisis (1982), the Gulf War (1990–1), the Omagh bomb (1998) and the 11 September 2001 attack on New York and Washington. Parliament is recalled so that the government can be reassured that the representative assembly of the people has been consulted and gives its support to whatever steps the government feels should be taken in response to this sort of crisis.

How successful is Parliament in the field of legitimation?

Legitimation is such a nebulous concept that it is a little difficult to see how we would measure how successful Parliament is in this area. If Parliament is fulfilling its other functions, presumably it will command greater respect and hence will be an important source of legitimation. If MPs are held in respect, then people will trust Parliament. Curiously, while the reputation of 'politicians' has suffered in recent years as a result of accusations of sleaze and scandal, people continue to write to their local constituency MPs, who are welcomed at local functions and on visits with a great deal of respect, even affection. Still, the declining levels of participation in politics are worrying for the view that Parliament is a legitimizer of the political process. So also is the way in which the growth of European and devolved institutions threatens Parliament's power. It is also arguable that what legitimizes our legislation and our political system is not just Parliament but the whole political system: parties, executive, judiciary, the various levels of governance and even the media and pressure groups. So, the whole idea of parliamentary legitimation may be open to question.

10.10 Recruitment and training of members of the government

This function of Parliament is a consequence of the British parliamentary system of government and fusion of powers. The people elect the House of Commons, and from the House of Commons the government is chosen. The majority party in the Commons provides the personnel of government. Almost all members of the government will be drawn from the House of Commons, and a few from the House of Lords. In addition, the process by which a party selects those destined for high office is based on an assessment of their performance as MPs. Successful MPs will show debating skills, a willingness to work on committees and the key parliamentary virtue: party loyalty. These skills will develop during an MP's career, so in a sense he or she will be trained as well as recruited through Parliament. The first step on the road to a ministerial career will probably be appointment as a Parliamentary Private Secretary (PPS), attached to a minister. Sometimes called 'bag carriers', PPSs will be able to observe what a ministerial job involves, while providing support to their minister. The next stage is to become a junior minister and then, if the MP shows exceptional promise, to join the Cabinet. Much of this will be the result of what the MP does in Parliament. This emphasizes the importance of parliamentary performance in the achievement of ministerial office for an MP.

10.11 Recent reforms of the House of Commons

In 1997, Labour came to power committed to a wide range of reforms, including the 'modernization of Parliament'. Apart from the changes to the Lords, which will be discussed separately, the reforms of the Commons were, in the Blair years, rather limited in scope, and amounted to little more than tinkering. The first step was to set up a select committee on the modernization of the House of Commons. In 2001, Robin Cook was appointed Leader of the House and he announced further proposals for reform, but he achieved little in practice and his resignation from the Cabinet in 2003 meant the end of these plans.

The main changes that actually took place while Tony Blair was Prime Minister were:

● In 1997, Prime Minister's Questions was reshaped. Before, there had been two 15-minute sessions on separate afternoons. Since 1997, there has been one half-hour session before lunch on Wednesdays. MPs have been known to become rowdy after lunch. This change, it was argued, would lead to a more thorough examination of government policy. But from another perspective, it meant that the Prime Minister would only have to come to the Commons once a week instead of twice.

- In 2002, the Prime Minister announced he would submit himself to a six-monthly interrogation by the Liaison Committee, a committee consisting of the chairs of the various departmental select committees.

- Select committees are allowed to see bills while they are in draft stage and hence to give some 'pre-legislative scrutiny' of government proposals.

- The chairmen of select committees have been awarded an additional annual payment. In the past, they were paid exactly the same as back-bench MPs, while government ministers received more money. The hope is that this will give MPs a parliamentary career path, so that the best or most ambitious are not siphoned off onto the front benches. Since 2002, select committee chairmen have served a limited term of office, in that they can only serve as chairman for eight years, or two parliamentary terms, whichever is the longer.

- Select committees are given more staff time and additional resources.

- There has been a general attempt to modernize the House of Commons by improving the office accommodation for MPs. A large new office block was opened in Portcullis House across the road from the old Palace of Westminster.

- Efforts have been made to remove some of the more unusual ceremonies which give the Palace of Westminster the appearance of what the MP Dennis Skinner calls 'the Palace of Varieties', or pantomime. For example, by putting on a top hat (called an 'opera hat'), an MP could stop debate on a private member's bill. This practice has been brought to an end, although it remains the case that an individual MP can still veto a decent piece of private member's legislation out of spite or in support of some special interest which dislikes it.

- There has been a change in the working hours of MPs, reducing the evening and all-night sessions, and introducing morning sessions. This is expected to be particularly valuable for women MPs and for those with young families. However, in January 2005 the Commons decided to return to longer hours on Wednesdays. This looked like a move on the part of MPs away from the modernization agenda, and was followed by the announcement by a female MP that she had decided not to stand at the following election, in part because of Parliament's continued use of these old-fashioned work practices.

- Timetabling bills: to prevent log-jams from developing at the end of a parliamentary session, when there is a great rush to pass all the bills before Parliament goes into recess, bills now have a rigorous timetable imposed on them so that they will pass through by the deadline. Critics say this is a way of strengthening the executive and preventing thorough parliamentary scrutiny.

- Attempts have been made to allow bills to be carried over from one parliamentary session (roughly a year long) to another, but the problem with achieving this important reform is that the Lords have to be allowed to debate all bills and have to have a chance to hold them up for a session. So in practice it is unlikely that this reform will be possible as long as the powers of the House of Lords remain the same.
- Additional, parallel sessions of the Commons are now held in a committee room off Westminster Hall, allowing extra debating time without interfering with the passage of legislation. In the past, it has been argued that governments steamroll legislation through Parliament without allowing all MPs to contribute to the discussion. The institution of this additional talking-shop may justify the view that one of Parliament's functions is simply to debate.

Supporters of these reforms suggest that it is only possible to change Parliament gradually and that these modest measures represent a first step in altering the culture of an ancient institution. Critics say that little has been achieved, essentially because the government does not wish to see Parliament's powers extended, and that any meaningful reform would be likely to have this effect. In addition, cynics argue that some of Labour's reforms of the Commons have actually strengthened the executive in its relations with Parliament. Government business can now be more rapidly dealt with as a result of these measures; the loyalty of most select committee chairmen has been bought by a pay increase; the Prime Minister now has an easier time at PMQs and is televised twice a year hitting the slowly bowled balls of the Liaison Committee, which consists largely of the party faithful who have recently been awarded a pay rise.

Gordon Brown's proposals for further parliamentary reform

In a dramatic move on 3 July 2007, shortly after becoming Prime Minister, Gordon Brown announced that he intended to strengthen the power of Parliament over the executive. If enacted, this would make the Labour parliamentary reforms started in 1997 seem much more significant than the comments given above suggest. Brown's proposals are as follows:

- Parliament should be involved in decisions on war and peace.
- Parliament should scrutinize the patronage powers of the Prime Minister, in terms of appointments of bishops (who sit in the House of Lords) and government officials. In the same way, Parliament should also vet senior judicial appointments.
- The power of the executive to dissolve Parliament and to call it into special session should be limited.

- The government's legislative programme will be announced well in advance of the Queen's speech, to allow for full discussion.
- There shall be a debate every year in the Commons on each government department's annual objectives.
- Nine regional Commons select committees will be set up, to scrutinize the work of the nine English regional ministers whom Brown has appointed.
- The ability of citizens to petition Parliament should be improved.

These are major steps to take, although, were they enacted, the cynic might argue that with tight party discipline in the House of Commons, the power of the Prime Minister would not, in practice, really be reduced, nor the power of Parliament much increased.

 Question: Why have the parliamentary reforms brought in by Tony Blair's government been considered inadequate?

10.12 Does Parliament matter?

In conclusion, what follows are two contrasting perspectives on the British Parliament.

The decline of legislatures

For many years Parliament has been subject to strong criticism. These criticisms generally revolve around the part played by Parliament in the wider political system, especially in relation to the executive. According to this view, Parliament had a glorious past, defeating over-mighty kings in the seventeenth century and then exercising a decisive role in forming and destroying governments even as late as the mid-nineteenth century. But then the rot began to set in, ironically just at the time when Parliament was becoming more democratic. When Walter Bagehot wrote *The English Constitution* in 1865, he was keen to undermine the idea that Parliament was at the heart of the political system, and argued instead that we had a system of Cabinet government. Writing in 1921, Lord Bryce spoke of the 'decline of legislatures' and said that Parliament was suffering from a number of 'chronic ailments'. This decline is a common feature, to be found not just in Britain but around the world; in the USA the decline of Congress has also been complained about by some political scientists. Philip Norton, a modern authority on Parliament, points to the rise of pressure groups and political parties as another factor in the decline in legislatures. Concerns about the impotence of Parliament are to be found in the writings of recent commentators of both the left and right, from Tony Benn to Lord Hailsham.

They stress the rise of executive dominance as involving a corresponding decline in the power of Parliament. It is easy to see how it is that these writers could come to such a view. The parliamentary system of government in Britain, as has been emphasized earlier in this chapter, depends on executive control of Parliament.

We could point to further ways in which the power of Parliament might be said to have diminished in recent years. The development of European integration and devolution for Scotland, Wales and Northern Ireland clearly involve some dilution of parliamentary authority, and even threaten the precious constitutional theory of parliamentary sovereignty. The increased use of referendums undermines the representative function of Parliament and may even strengthen the executive. The rise to prominence in recent years of the judiciary presents Parliament with a new rival. Labour's half-hearted reform of the House of Lords has focused attention on that decaying and unattractive part of Parliament. But Blair's Labour governments did not replace the House of Lords with anything that can command respect or act as an equal partner in what is supposed to be a bicameral legislature. The instances of sleaze – largely, but not entirely, under the Major governments of 1990–7 – have done little to raise public confidence in MPs. The large majorities under Labour since 1997 and previously in the 1980s under the Conservatives served to emphasize executive dominance. The apparent subservience of Labour MPs after 1997, at least until the 'rebellions' over Iraq and other domestic issues in 2003–4, and talk of a 'control freak tendency' in the Labour Party have helped brand MPs as 'lobby-fodder', people whose only purpose is to march like soldiers into the voting lobbies and record their support for the party line. The decline of participation might also be linked to this declining respect for politicians, and hence of Parliament.

A more positive assessment

What has been written above is clearly exaggerated. A useful antidote to such exaggeration is provided by David Judge in his 1992 book, *The Parliamentary State*. The central argument of the book, as its title suggests, is that the British political system revolves around Parliament, not only constitutionally (because of the constitutional principle of parliamentary sovereignty), but also in terms of political realities. Judge shows that in all aspects of political life, Parliament is involved, because of the fusion of powers. Rather than seeing this as executive dominance, he interprets it as parliamentary involvement. What is more, the great advantage of this parliamentary state over systems based on separation is that it delivers strong government, and avoids the sort of gridlock which can develop – as in USA, for example.

Norton, writing in 1993, gives a balanced answer to the question posed by the title of his own book, *Does Parliament Matter?* (republished in 2005 as

Parliament in British Politics). Norton compares the British Parliament with other legislatures around the world. He has three categories into which he places legislatures:

1 *Legislatures with little impact on policy.* These weak bodies are really just acting as rubber-stamps to the decisions of the government. They debate and give advice, but their only real function is to give laws what legitimacy they can by publishing them formally. The real power lies with the government. Norton gives as an example of this the present-day legislature in China.

2 *Legislatures which make policy.* Here, the legislature is very much in charge. Above all, its members initiate much of the legislation for themselves and can make law. The executive is then bound to work according to this law and enforce it. This type of power is to be found in the US Congress, and was perhaps how the British Parliament worked in the so-called 'golden age' of Parliament (1832–67).

3 *Legislatures which influence policy.* In this case, midway between the two extremes described above, the executive formulates policy, but the legislature can amend it, and has the job of applying scrutiny to how the government creates and implements its policy. This description applies, according to Norton, to most Western European and Commonwealth legislatures and to the British Parliament too.

Norton's assessment of Parliament is not uncritical: he has advocated a number of reforms which would improve Parliament's work. But he points to some aspects of the work of Parliament which he feels have improved in the past few decades, and which have served to strengthen Parliament. Among these could be counted the growth of backbench independence and the improvement generally in the calibre and professionalism of MPs.

Backbench independence

On most votes in the Commons, MPs are expected to support their party. There is an elaborate system of control run by the party whips to ensure that this happens. Frontbench MPs are ministers and are bound by the principle of ministerial collective responsibility, and hence they must toe the party line or resign. Backbench MPs are also expected to support their party, and the ultimate sanction is that they will have the whip 'withdrawn' – that is to say, they will be thrown out of their party. This happens very rarely: under John Major it occurred in 1995 when nine opponents of government policy on Europe were excluded, only to be readmitted a few months later. This was unprecedented in post-war politics. Party loyalty also extends to general conduct in Parliament, in asking questions at PMQs and when other ministers face questions. The exceptions – the times when an MP is allowed freedom to vote and speak according to his or her conscience – are rather few.

On Private Members' Bills, since the government is not sponsoring the bill, MPs have the freedom to vote as they like, at least in theory. There are also matters over which a 'free vote' is taken, either because the government is genuinely unclear about what approach to take, or because these are matters of conscience – moral matters where it would be unreasonable to force MPs to vote against their beliefs. The votes on the death penalty are of this latter sort. The vote in 2003 on the future shape of the House of Lords was presented to MPs as a series of alternatives, because the government said it did not have a very clear view on which was the best one to adopt. The same process is likely to be adopted in 2007 when the Commons tries again to decide on the future composition of the Lords. But generally, the government takes a view on things, and the opposition parties also decide their approach. In such circumstances MPs generally accept what the whips instruct them to do. The result is that a government with a working majority has only once since 1945 been defeated in the Commons on a vote on the second reading of a bill. This was in 1986 on the Shop Hours Act, which aroused opposition from Christian groups opposed to Sunday opening of shops. Many Conservative backbenchers thought this was really a matter of conscience, although the government tried to apply a three-line whip (the strongest form of command to the party to support a vote). The danger with all such loyalty is that it can seriously undermine the functions of Parliament, especially scrutiny. The advantage is that it does make lines of accountability very clear: voters vote for a party whose policies and ideology are known to them, and then MPs are bound to act on this electoral mandate.

Research by Philip Norton and by Philip Cowley indicates that MPs have in recent years been less willing to support this level of party loyalty, and more willing to 'rebel' than in the past. The change seems to have come in the early 1970s, and figures show that a tendency to oppose the party line, although fluctuating over the years since then, has generally increased. Clearly, this would seem to strengthen Parliament as an institution, and broadly speaking to remove some of the criticisms that Parliament is prevented by executive dominance and party loyalty from fulfilling its scrutiny functions. The difficulties that John Major faced in 1993 – especially over the parliamentary ratification of the Treaty on European Union signed at Maastricht – illustrate this tendency. In the end, Major was only able to pass this measure on the casting vote of the Speaker, despite the fact that he had a small, but 'working' majority in the Commons. In 2002–4, Blair's Labour government faced even larger rebellions over the war with Iraq and other matters, and only survived the crucial votes because the Labour majority in the Commons was huge and because the Conservatives gave him their support. In a key vote over the war with Iraq in 2002, 139 Labour MPs voted against the government, the largest rebellion since 1846 and the Repeal of the Corn Laws. In 2003, on top-up fees, 72 Labour MPs rebelled, which was the biggest rebellion on the second reading of a bill since 1945. The government, of course, won both votes. But these record-breaking statistics owe more to Labour's huge majority than to the independence of their backbenchers, so the party was able to survive the rebellions. Labour was not defeated once in its first two terms after 1997 on a whipped vote, while every other government since 1966 had been defeated at least once on a whipped vote. But with the re-election of Labour in 2005 with a slimmer majority (of 66), things changed, and on the proposal contained in the Terrorism Bill in November 2005, to intern terrorist suspects without trial for 90 days, Tony Blair's government suffered its first defeat (by 31 votes) since 1997 as the result of a backbench rebellion, in which 49 Labour MPs voted against the government. This was swiftly followed by a further defeat on the same bill, with 51 Labour MPs in revolt. The biggest Labour revolt of the third term was on the second reading of the Education Bill (2006), which was carried only through Conservative support and which saw 52 Labour MPs revolt. There were two more defeats for the government in 2006 on the Religious and Racial Hatred Bill, which limited the right to free speech, but these were due to small revolts (of 26 and 21) and were the result of poor management of the whips, who on one occasion told Tony Blair that his vote would not be needed, so he could go home – and the vote was then lost by a majority of one.

The growing professionalism of backbench MPs

Norton attributes this growing independence of backbenchers to the fundamental and very important issues that modern MPs have faced (such as Europe and war with Iraq), and also to the fact that the people attracted to politics are rather different now from how they were in the past. There are more people coming into the Commons to pursue politics as a career than there were in the past, and as a result they are less willing to see themselves just as 'lobby fodder'. Sometimes, a rather cynical picture is drawn of the backbench 'rebel', as someone who has failed in a ministerial career or is never likely to be able to follow one, or as a 'maverick', a well-known troublemaker with some psychological defects. But from a more positive viewpoint, the 'rebel' is someone who takes his or her responsibilities for scrutiny and representation seriously. There is no question that MPs have to work harder in the twenty-first century than they did in the past. Since the 1970s, there has been a well-documented rise in constituency correspondence, and MPs are now expected to spend a great deal of time answering constituents' letters and emails and dealing with their problems. Interest groups and pressure groups also correspond frequently with MPs. All MPs now hold regular 'surgeries' in their constituencies to listen to the worries of their electorate. There has been some growth in allowances and staffing to help them deal with this increased workload. A long-standing debate surrounds the question of whether MPs should concentrate full time on their work in Parliament or should extend their experience of the 'real world' by continuing to hold down another job as well. The debate is increasingly out of date now as MPs find themselves forced to do more and more constituency work and as Parliament becomes a body which conducts some of its business in the mornings, rather than in the afternoons and evenings as in the past. The gradual increase in the number of women MPs, some of whom may also have family commitments, perhaps increases this concentration on parliamentary work. The scandals of the 1990s, collectively described as incidences of 'sleaze', harmed the reputation of Parliament, but concerned only a tiny minority of MPs, the great majority of whom are hard-working and conscientious people. Nevertheless, stepping back a little, it would not be safe to conclude that growing professionalism among MPs will make any serious dents in the essential nature of our system of government, which without a complete reform (which is not likely to happen) will remain one based on a fusion of powers and a powerful executive supported by a strong party system. These two factors make the modern British Parliament essentially rather weak in comparison with other legislatures around the world.

> **?** *Question:* Discuss the view that the House of Commons is no longer important in British politics.

Activity

1 Using Google, type in the name of a recent Act of Parliament (e.g. The Human Rights Act, 1998; or The Scotland Act, 1998) and have a careful look at it. What does it tell you about the law-making process? Is it longer or shorter than you expected? Is it clear? Is it complicated?

2 Have a class debate on what current issue to write to your local MP about. When you have decided, compose a brief letter in which you set out your main points about the issue. Ask the MP what he intends to do about the issue. Tell the MP that the letter is written as a result of a class debate – keep the letter brief! Get your classmates to sign it and then send it to your MP, at the House of Commons. See if you get a reply. What does this process tell you about the representative nature of the MP's role?

3 Back to Google: search for 'White Paper', and have a look at one on recent issues. How do they differ from Acts of Parliament looked at above? What do they tell you about the consultative work that precedes legislation, and the representative role of Parliament?

4 Now go onto the Parliament website (see below), and look up a select committee. What can you learn about its membership, its chairman, its current work and reports? What does it tell you about the scrutiny function of Parliament? Compare notes with a classmate who has looked up a different committee.

SUMMING UP

The 'mother of Parliaments' has seven main functions: representation, legislation, taxation and finance, scrutiny, debate, legitimation and recruitment of ministers. The leading chamber of Parliament, the House of Commons, performs all these roles, according to its supporters, reasonably well. But in each case there are doubts expressed by critics about how effective Parliament really is. The central problem lies in the 'parliamentary system of government', the key feature of the British political system. Since the executive and legislature are fused, and since in practice the executive dominates the legislature, it is difficult for Parliament to function effectively. Add to this the strength of the party system in the UK and the power of the whips, and we have a recipe for poor scrutiny and, arguably, weaknesses in other areas of parliamentary function as well. But at least Parliament can act decisively when it is needed, and the presence of the Prime Minister and Cabinet actually inside the House of Commons means that they can be directly questioned by MPs, which can produce a very high level of scrutiny. New Labour under Tony Blair made some efforts to modernize the House of Commons, but these did not result in major change – perhaps inevitably, since no government is likely to legislate to reduce government power significantly, and it is in this respect that reform of Parliament would be most useful. However, Gordon Brown's announcements of further parliamentary reform, made as virtually his first action on taking office, may make a substantial difference to Parliament's powers of scrutiny.

Further reading

Philip Cowley, *The Rebels: How Blair Mislaid his Majority* (Politico's, 2005): lively academic study of party loyalty in Parliament.

D. Judge, *The Parliamentary State* (Sage, 1993): fascinating academic defence of Parliament's importance.

David Judge, *Political Institutions in the UK* (Oxford University Press, 2005): goes well beyond Parliament, setting it in its wider context.

P. Norris and J. Lovenduski, *Political Recruitment* (Cambridge University Press, 1994): in-depth analysis of this important issue.

Philip Norton, *Parliament in British Politics* (Palgrave, 2005): the standard work on the topic – tends to be very favourable towards Parliament.

P. Riddell, *Parliament Under Blair* (Politico's, 2001): analysis of recent trends by a high-class journalist.

Websites

www.parliament.uk (official site of Parliament)

The House of Lords

Making connections

The problem with studying the House of Lords at the moment is that it is at present undergoing reform and is in a transitional stage of the process. It is also by no means clear what will happen to it in the future. So it is impossible to write a very conclusive account of the membership of the Lords, or of its powers. It probably exaggerates the importance of the Lords to give them a whole chapter to themselves, but the fact that they are in the middle of these reforms justifies it. In the end, though, the House of Lords is actually a rather unimportant body politically.

11

The House of Lords

KEY TOPICS

- The House of Lords as a part of Parliament
- The House of Lords in historical perspective
- The composition of the House of Lords
- The functions and powers of the House of Lords

SETTING THE SCENE

The previous chapter mainly dealt with the House of Commons, the most important chamber of Parliament. But much of what was said there applies to both Houses, to the Lords as well as the Commons. This chapter focuses on the Lords all by itself. Although definitely inferior to the Commons, the House of Lords is of great interest to political scientists at the moment because it is in the process of being substantially reformed, constituting, arguably, the most significant part of the Labour government's constitutional reforms.

11.1 The House of Lords as a part of Parliament

The House of Lords, or Upper House, is one of the two chambers of Parliament, the other being the House of Commons. Although called the Upper House, the House of Lords is very much inferior to the House of Commons. We therefore have a curiously unbalanced legislature in Britain, although officially it is said that it is bicameral, as opposed to unicameral.

The advantages of **bicameralism** are as follows:

> **Bicameralism:** the system which operates when a representative assembly has two distinct houses or chambers.

- A second house can act as a 'revising' legislative chamber. It provides a second opportunity to look at bills and remove any problems by providing further legislative scrutiny. The government itself can take advantage of this opportunity and pick up problems of drafting which have not emerged in the House of Commons.

- Bicameralism provides a second level of scrutiny of the executive. It is important that this parliamentary function (scrutiny) is carried out thoroughly, and if there are two chambers it is more likely that it will be.
- There is scope for different functions to be performed by the two separate chambers, since each can specialize and find more time to fulfil these functions. In the USA, for example, the Senate and the House of Representatives have certain individual and exclusive powers which they do not share.
- In a bicameral system, different types of representation are possible; it is very common for one of the two houses to represent the regions in a federal state. Bicameralism is therefore particularly suited to a large, federal country like Canada, Australia or the USA. Bicameralism may also be useful where a proportional system of representation is used for one chamber and hence the link between constituents and representatives is rather weak: in the other chamber a stronger constituency link may be arranged by using some other electoral system.
- Bicameralism may also be useful in a country where there are tensions between different ethnic, religious or national groups, and where a unicameral system might place too much power in the hands of the majority group. In a bicameral system, a series of checks and balances will reduce the threats that may come from 'the tyranny of the majority'.

The advantages of **unicameralism** are perhaps less clear than those of bicameralism, and in most liberal democracies there are two chambers. But there are good democratic or liberal objections to bicameralism. The Abbé Sieyès, the French constitutional expert of the French revolutionary period, put forward a strong case (in 1789) for not having a second chamber: if it is doing its job well, it becomes obnoxious to the first chamber; and if it is not doing its job well, it is redundant.

The case for unicameralism may be summarized as follows:

> **Unicameralism:** a system with only one chamber or house in the representative assembly.

- Unicameralism is particularly suited to smaller countries, with a unitary structure, where there is little need for a second chamber – for example, Israel. The new devolved assemblies in Wales and Northern Ireland and the revived Scottish Parliament are all unicameral.
- Under a unicameral system, the government will be less likely to meet with obstructions and hence there will be strong government. Rapid decision-making will be possible.
- There is no danger of clashes between the two chambers if there is only one, and no difficulty about deciding which of the chambers is superior.
- If checks and balances are required (both for the unicameral legislature and for the executive), these may be available from other sources, from a written constitution and a strong judiciary, for example.

Question time in the House of Lords

- The unicameral system may be more democratic, since the will of the voters may be converted more directly into action in such a system. If this action is based on the will of the majority, so be it, for democracy is the rule of the majority.

Is the Westminster Parliament a unicameral or a bicameral legislature?

At first sight this seems to be a stupid question. In theory, Britain obviously has two houses or chambers in its Parliament: the House of Lords and the House of Commons. The problem is that, in practice, this is hardly true, for several reasons.

First, the House of Commons has far more power than the Lords, so legislative and scrutiny functions are not very successfully performed in the Lords. In addition, the Commons can overrule virtually any decision taken by the Lords, so there seems little point in the Lords disagreeing with the Commons. Until the removal of most of the hereditary peers in 2000, the Lords had a built-in Conservative majority, making it less likely that they would provide very effective scrutiny of a Conservative government or, indeed, very unbiased scrutiny of a Labour government. Since 1997, the House of Lords has been under threat of major reform, and has found it difficult at times to perform its functions very effectively. As a result, the House of Lords cannot act as an effective check on the House of Commons.

Second, the present composition of the House of Lords is such that it cannot claim to be representative of anyone except itself. It cannot fulfil the function of representing the regions, and certainly not of protecting the rights of minorities. Lords are generally old, drawn from the upper and middle classes and regarded as out of touch with the rest of the people.

Third, the House of Lords lacked – and still lacks – democratic legitimacy. It therefore finds it difficult to make a mark in a democracy.

For all these reasons, Britain must count as having a quasi-unicameral (virtually unicameral, very like a unicameral) legislature. Alternatively, Britain could be described as a weak bicameral system.

 Question: Discuss the view that the United Kingdom no longer needs a second chamber.

11.2 The House of Lords in historical perspective

The reason for these difficulties with the British bicameral system lie in the history of Parliament and of the House of Lords, and this history needs to be studied in order to understand the political and constitutional position of the House of Lords at the moment.

Medieval birth of Parliament (*c.* 1250)

The development of Parliament involved both the ordinary people (commoners in the House of Commons) and the feudal nobility (in the Lords), working together to act as a check on the power of the King. In the Middle Ages, members of the nobility were the leading figures and were able to dominate the Commons. Hence they developed as the Upper House, superior to the Commons.

The House of Lords in the English Revolution (*c.* 1640–89)

The power of the king was further eroded during what has been called the English Revolution. Parliament, led by the Commons, defeated the Stuart King, Charles I, in the English Civil Wars and then had him beheaded. For a brief period, the House of Lords was also abolished. In 1660, both the King and the House of Lords were restored, but as a result of the Glorious Revolution of 1688–9, the King's powers were now severely limited. In contrast, the House of Lords recovered all its power and during the eighteenth century remained highly significant in British politics.

The rise of democracy (1832–85)

The late eighteenth and nineteenth centuries witnessed a number of revolutions, in America and in many parts of Europe, in which the power of the kings and the nobility was reduced. But Britain, having had a limited revolution in the seventeenth century, avoided a more extreme one a century later. Instead, there was a gradual process of reform, when Parliament itself changed the political system piecemeal, without drawing up a new written constitution. Gradually, more and more men were given the vote, until, by 1885, almost all men could vote (women had to wait until 1918 for partial suffrage and 1928 for full suffrage). This process of spreading democracy obviously strengthened the Commons and weakened the Lords. But the House of Lords prevented any serious threat to its powers from developing, largely by avoiding a clash with the Commons. The nearest they came to a serious dispute was in 1831–2 as the Commons passed the Great Reform Bill, which extended the right to vote to more of the male population. The Lords at first voted against the bill, as a result of which there was extensive rioting by the people in support of reform. In order to get the measure through the Lords, the king threatened to make a large number of new lords who would vote in favour of it. So, in the face of this threat the Lords passed the Reform Bill, and for many years after that the peers kept a lower profile, and hence kept their powers intact. Most people accepted, however, that sooner or later the House of Lords would itself have to be reformed.

The Parliament Act (1911)

In the last years of the nineteenth century the Lords began to forget their need to give way to the Commons. In 1893, they opposed the Commons over Irish devolution, and as a result the measure failed to pass. Then again, in 1910, the Lords defeated the 'People's Budget', a measure devised by the Liberal, David Lloyd George, which threatened to tax aristocratic inheritance. This was a bold and foolish step for them to take, since, even in the Middle Ages, the Lords had accepted that matters of taxation should be decided in the Commons. The result was that the government called a second general election, within only a few months of the previous one, and won popular support for a reform of the Lords. Armed with this electoral mandate, the government again threatened to create new reforming peers in sufficient numbers to force the measure through, with the result that the first reform of the Lords was finally passed. The Parliament Act of 1911 reduced the power of the Lords to one of delaying legislation, and re-emphasized that they should not interfere with financial matters (see below). For the reforming Liberals, this Act was just the first step in a root-

and-branch reform of the Lords which they hoped would follow soon after. In the event it never did.

The Labour Party and reform of the Lords (1949 and 1969)

The Liberals – and before them the Whigs – had been at the forefront of the move to reform the Lords, and in 1911, it was the Liberals H. H. Asquith and Lloyd George who had achieved this. As the Liberal Party declined, the Labour Party emerged as the party that would continue these constitutional reforms. But the Labour Party was divided on this issue. To many on the left of the party, reform of the Lords seemed to be an issue which was irrelevant to the economic and social concerns of the working class. As a result, Labour failed to do very much about the Lords. In 1949, Clement Attlee extended the scope of the Parliament Act of 1911 a little (this will be discussed below). The big chance for Labour came in 1969 when the government of Harold Wilson proposed a major reform of the composition and powers of the House of Lords. In the end, this measure failed because of divisions within the party: left-wingers were afraid that if the House of Lords were reformed, it would become more powerful as a result. What they feared was that the reformed Lords would then obstruct the Commons, which might mean that a Labour Party elected to bring in social and economic reforms for the working class would be prevented from doing so by the reformed House of Lords. When the Labour proposals were put before the House of Commons in 1969, they were defeated by a combination of Labour rebels (led by the aristocratic left-winger Tony Benn) and the Conservative opposition. This jealousy in the House of Commons and fear there of a revival in the power of the House of Lords has been – and still is – the great obstacle in Britain in the path of achieving a genuinely bicameral legislature.

Conservative defence of the House of Lords (1945–97)

The modern Conservative Party of the twentieth century was not committed to fighting to the death to preserve the House of Lords. In fact, it could see that the best way to preserve the Lords might be to reform it. In 1832 and again in 1911, the Tories had given in to the threats of the Commons. The Salisbury family (leading Tory politicians in the Lords for over a century) developed a theory of surrender to the Commons known as the Salisbury Convention, which has become practically a constitutional principle, and will be discussed later. But a seemingly minor step brought in by the Conservative Party in the post-war era strengthened the Lords considerably. In 1958, the Life Peers Act was passed, which enabled the government (through the Crown) to make 'life peers' – people who would hold a non-hereditary peerage for life. This gradually changed the composition of the Upper House, as self-confident ex-ministers and other representatives of the 'great and the good' were promoted to the Lords, injecting a much-needed infusion of new blood and also a new air of authority. The Lords began a modest revival after 1958 and, within 20 years, levels of attendance were up and members were working hard at fulfilling their constitutional functions. In addition, this measure gave the Prime Minister a new area of patronage – something which Prime Ministers like a great deal. A second measure introduced by the Conservatives was less significant, but interesting: in 1963 an Act was passed enabling people to renounce their peerages – that is to say, to give up their entitlement to being a member of the House of Lords. This enabled Lord Home to give up his peerage and become, after being elected MP, the Conservative Prime Minister, albeit briefly. It also allowed Viscount Stansgate to become Tony Benn.

New Labour's protracted reform of the Lords (1997–)

When Labour returned to power in 1997, it planned to reform the Lords, along with much else in the constitutional sphere. The reforms have not been completed, so the discussion of the Lords that follows is inevitably somewhat inconclusive and will need to be presented in historical format. Labour's reforms have largely concerned the composition of the House of Lords; there has been relatively little change to the formal legislative powers of the chamber.

11.3 The composition of the House of Lords

To understand the composition of the House of Lords, it is necessary to look at the position before the reforms of 1999. Next, we need to consider the arrangements for the so-called transitional House, created in 1999. Finally, it is necessary to speculate about what the final Labour settlement will look like.

Original composition

Before 1999, the House of Lords was composed of four main components, all unelected.

Hereditary peers

There were about 750 hereditary peers ('peers' means 'lords'). They are the descendants of people given a title by a monarch which they can pass on to their heirs; in recent years very few new hereditary peers have been made. For more than two centuries, the creation of new peers has largely been a political matter, and most people given titles by the Crown have been recommended for this by the Prime Minister. Further back in history, the Lords were simply the richest people in the country. Noble titles are duke, marquis, earl, viscount and baron, but they are all called lords or peers. Before 1999, all the hereditary peers could sit in the House of Lords, but fewer than a third were regular attenders: in 1996–7, only 184 hereditary peers attended more than half the sittings; some attended none. They were, overwhelmingly, white, elderly, male and Conservative in politics; most were very wealthy. Some could trace their ancestry back hundreds of years and lived in stately homes; some were the descendants of royal bastards; some were descended from rich businessmen who had, in effect, bought their titles.

Life peers

Created gradually over the years since 1958, these now number about 600. They are given a peerage for life: the title cannot be handed down to their descendants. These peers also tend to be old, since the award of a life peerage is generally given to former members of the House of Commons who have either retired or who have failed to be re-elected as an MP. Life peers are more evenly spread among the main political parties and some make a point of being crossbenchers or independent. A few life peers are women. In constitutional terms, the creation of peers is the work of the monarch, done on the 'advice' of the Prime Minister. In other words, the Prime Minister uses his powers of patronage to award peerages. There are rules in place to ensure that a minority of the life peers appointed every year come from the opposition parties.

Bishops and archbishops

There are 24 bishops and 2 archbishops of the Church of England, all of whom are members of the House of Lords. They are all male, almost always white, elderly and conservative in tendency, if not politically. The Church of England had formerly been the dominant religion in the country, which accounts for the presence of the bishops in the House of Lords, but nowadays, even among Christians, members of the Church of England are a minority.

Law lords

These were formed from the 12 most senior judges in the country who meet as appeal judges (called 'Lords of Appeal in Ordinary') in the House of Lords, when it is acting as a court of appeal (this function of the House of Lords is discussed below). In addition, retired Lords of Appeal, the Lord Chancellor and retired Lord Chancellors could sit in the Lords. The Lord Chancellor was head of the legal system, and also presided over the House of Lords in the same way the Speaker chairs the Commons. At present, there are 26 law lords.

Transitional composition

In 1997, the Labour government came to power having pledged in its manifesto to bring in reform of the House of Lords. It set up a commission under Lord Wakeham, a Conservative peer and former Cabinet minister, to consider what form the reforms should take. Meanwhile, Parliament passed a House of Lords Act in 1999 which brought in a new transitional form of membership of the Lords, pending decisions to be made in light of Wakeham's report. According to this transitional format, the House of Lords was composed as follows:

Hereditary peers

In order to pass the House of Lords Act through the House of Lords (always a problem for matters of reform), the Labour government came to an agreement with the Conservative peers that the transitional House would still have some hereditary peers. After a good deal of unseemly haggling, they decided that there should be 92, and the Weatherill Amendment (named after Lord Weatherill, the distinguished former Speaker of the House of Commons who proposed it) was accepted by the government. A small number of these remaining 92 hereditary peers were royal officials (the Lord Great Chamberlain and Earl Marshall, for example), but the majority were so-called 'representative hereditary peers'. Each peer who wished to be considered for this position was to submit a brief statement of views to be considered by the hereditary peerage as a whole, who then voted on who to select as their representatives. The system also allows for 'by-elections' if one of the representative peers dies. It is worth emphasizing that the House of Lords Act did not abolish the titles of the other hereditary peers, but just barred them from sitting in the House of Lords.

Life peers

These positions remain and continue to be created, in quite large numbers recently. In addition, the Labour Party has added a very small number of 'people's peers'. Advertisements have been placed in the press calling for 'ordinary' people to apply to become a member of the House of Lords. The people's peers selected have generally been unusual 'ordinary people'; in fact, they are difficult to distinguish from the sort of people who were normally given a life peerage. The well-meaning gesture that creating these people's peers was greeted with widespread derision by the media. Since 2000, the Prime Minister has been assisted in his choice of life peerages by the advice of a House of Lords Appointments Commission, which nominates non-party-political peers, while the party leaders nominate (as in the past) peers to represent their parties. Between its creation and May 2006, the Commission recommended 36 peers to the Prime Minister.

Box 11.1 Political parties in the House of Lords, March 2008

	Hereditary peers	Life peers	Total
Conservative	48	154	202
Labour	4	212	216
Liberal Democrat	5	73	78
Crossbencher	32	164	196
Bishops (non-partisan)			26
Others (minor parties / Independent)	2	12	14
Total	89	615	732

Note: Excludes 16 peers who are on 'leave of absence'
Source: http://www.parliament.uk (visit this site for an update)

Labour overtook the Conservatives as the largest party in the Lords in May 2005, for the first time in the party's history. This was a result of the removal of the bulk of the hereditary peers (who were mostly Conservatives), and also a policy of creating quite a large number of new life peers after 1997. Labour still does not have a majority in the Lords, however. The crossbenchers are an interesting group, roughly as numerous as the Labour and Conservative peers. They publish their own weekly notice of forthcoming business (a job done in the parties by the Whips), but it would be contrary to their essential nature to vote together as a bloc.

Bishops and archbishops

These remain represented, as before.

Law lords

The law lords are also still in the House of Lords, until the Constitutional Reform Act of 2005, which is discussed below, comes into force in 2009.

Proposals for the future composition of the Lords

The arrangements made in the 1999 House of Lords Act were essentially transitional. The Wakeham Commission reported in 2000, and was very cautious: it recommended removing the hereditary peers, but keeping law lords, bishops and life peers. In addition, Wakeham recommended that some future members (he felt the House ought to consist of about 550 members) should be elected, while the remaining new members should be appointed or nominated. But there was no clear statement on the crucial question of how many should be elected and how many nominated: Wakeham gave a range of alternatives.

The Labour Party manifesto of 2001 echoed the promise made in the manifesto of 1997 that the House of Lords would be made 'more representative and democratic'. One thing that Labour seemed to be agreed on was that the 92 hereditary peers would, in the future, be removed once and for all. But Labour was divided on the issue of how to recruit new members of the Lords:

The government bench in the House of Lords

those on the left of the party favoured an all-elected House, as did the Liberal Democrats, and at times (in a perhaps opportunist mood) the Conservative leadership also supported this. But Tony Blair was opposed to having a very strong elected element, and finally, early in 2003, he announced his support for a fully appointed chamber. During the course of 2002 and 2003, opinion in Parliament was generally swinging away from having an elected component in the reformed Lords. A group called the Campaign for an Effective Chamber was set up by Sir Patrick Cormack and Lord Norton, the latter a political scientist whose academic work has focused on Parliament and who is also a Conservative peer. This pressure group, and the knowledge that the Prime Minister supported appointment rather than election, began to turn opinion around. When a free vote was taken in the Commons on the issue in February 2003, there was no very clear outcome, partly (a cynic might say) because MPs were asked to vote on seven alternative options. However, the fact is that more of them voted in favour of a fully elected House of Lords than voted against it, although slightly more MPs voted for one that would be 80 per cent appointed than for other options.

By the time of the Queen's Speech in November 2003, this vote in the Commons had been forgotten, and the government announced that it had decided in favour of an all-appointed House of Lords. It was proposed that the House of Lords Appointments Commission, which had already been set up in 1999, would be given statutory authority to nominate non-partisan members of the Lords (crossbenchers), although the nomination of party members would presumably still stay in the hands of the party leaders. By the Constitutional Reform Act – proposed first in 2003, then delayed and finally passed in

March 2005, to be implemented fully by 2009 – the office of Lord Chancellor has been reformed and the law lords are to be removed from the House of Lords. This obviously affects the composition of the Lords to some extent. These steps have been taken to ensure the independence of the judiciary, and will be discussed in more detail below and also in the chapter on that subject (chapter 12).

The 2005 Labour manifesto suggested that government thinking (as a result of backbench pressure) was swinging back towards accepting that the Commons should decide on a free vote whether to have an elected element in the new House of Lords, and if so in what proportions to the nominees. One thing which confirmed this move away from an appointed House and which may have kick-started the process of reform again was the protracted police investigation in 2006–7 into the so-called 'cash for peerages' scandal. Allegations were made that senior figures in 10 Downing Street, including the Prime Minister himself, might have been involved in raising loans to finance the 2005 election by offering to grant peerages to substantial donors. This clearly meant that the case for continuing with the system by which the House of Lords was staffed by people essentially nominated by the Prime Minister was difficult to sustain. However, in 2007, the police announced that there was insufficient evidence to bring any prosecutions against Tony Blair or his colleagues in relation to this scandal. But the bad taste of a two-year investigation remained.

Box 11.2 The 2007 White Paper

Early in 2007, the government published a White Paper proposing the following:

- All remaining hereditary peers should leave; remaining life peers could continue to sit or be pensioned off. Bishops would remain, but fewer of them. Retired members of the new Supreme Court will be offered a seat.
- A fully appointed chamber is regarded as outdated, so there would be a mixture of appointed and elected members. This represented a climb-down by Blair.
- The Commons should decide what proportion of elected members and what proportion of appointees there should be. The White Paper speaks frequently of a 50:50 split, but it is up to a free vote in the Commons. The Leader of the House at the time, Jack Straw, suggested that MPs should be able to vote preferentially on a range of options (from 100 per cent elected to 100 per cent appointed) but this was rejected by the Commons, and MPs decided to vote on each option in turn, as they did (unsuccessfully) in 2003.
- The elected members should be chosen at the time of European Parliament elections on yet another electoral system, the 'partially open party List', with a third of the chosen number of elected members being chosen every four years, and sitting for a maximum of 12 years.
- There should be 20 per cent non-party and 80 per cent party members in the new chamber.
- A new statutory Appointments Commission should make the final choice of who is to be chosen for the appointed part of the chamber. Diversity would be one criterion for appointment.
- The total membership would be 540. The name of the 'reformed chamber' would be decided in the future.

In March 2007 the House of Commons had a free vote on the various options open to them. Two of the options carried a clear majority (all-elected and 80 per cent elected) and all the other permutations were rejected. The larger Commons majority (337:224) was, somewhat to everyone's surprise, in favour of a wholly elected chamber; there was a smaller majority (305:267) for an 80 per cent elected membership. Blair himself voted for a 50:50 (appointed/elected) house. Shortly afterwards, the House of Lords itself voted and, not surprisingly, expressed a preference for a fully appointed House. It remains to be seen what will be done as a result of these votes. The new Prime Minister, Gordon Brown, is committed to further Lords reform, but he has other priorities as well.

Since 1997, MPs have faced a real dilemma, essentially over whether to create a new House of Lords which is largely appointed (or nominated), one which is elected or one which is a mixture of these two elements. It is worth examining briefly the arguments for both methods in a little more depth.

Arguments for the appointment of members

Patronage

Even if (as is proposed) an independent Appointments Commission were to make some nominations, the majority of them would still be made by the Prime Minister and by the leaders of the opposition parties. Patronage protects executive dominance of the Lords and hence of Parliament. It is also largely in the interests of the Commons, which is, after all, itself a purely elected element of Parliament, and which can claim superiority over an appointed Lords as a result.

Loyalty

A system of patronage would entail a subservient and largely redundant House of Lords. Those appointed would continue to be, in the main, party loyalists with a Commons career behind them, and they would not seek to upset relations with the Commons. Also, if nominated they would lack the democratic legitimacy which would allow them to challenge the Commons. These may seem like points of criticism, but from the perspective of the House of Commons they are not.

New blood

On a more positive note, the House of Lords could receive a much-needed infusion of new blood through a well-handled system of nomination. Racial minorities, religious groups apart from the Church of England, women and a range of professions and trades could be brought into the legislature. This might be easier to achieve through appointment than election.

Crossbench independence

A sense of crossbench independence could continue to flourish in the Lords if the nomination process were sensibly used. Obviously, the nomination of peers would largely mean the nomination of party loyalists, whose names (as now) would be put forward by each of the political parties, but Wakeham suggested that the Appointments Commission should aim for a 20 per cent crossbench element.

A cautious approach

A largely nominated House is a cautious step, in keeping with much of what Labour has already done in the sphere of constitutional reform. It might pave the way for further changes possibly in the future. It is not unprecedented to have a nominated element in the legislature of a liberal democracy. The Canadian Upper House, for example, is not elected, and is well respected.

Too many elections

There are enough elections as it is, without adding any more. Participation rates may be harmed by too frequent exposure to elections.

Election systems

How would members be elected if they were not appointed? Wakeham wanted a third of his elected element to be voted in every five years from regional party lists; they would sit for 15 years in total. Another suggestion was that party lists should be drawn up at the time of a general election and the elected members of the Lords would be chosen from these lists in the same proportion as the party strength in the Commons shown by the election. Having a nominated chamber would avoid these dilemmas.

Distinction from the Commons

It might be argued that there would be two types of elected MPs if the elected option was decided on: 'real' MPs in the Commons and second-rate elected politicians in the Lords. The really ambitious and able would aim for a career in the Commons. This would obviously not be good for the House of Lords or Parliament as a whole.

Proportionality

There are also significant difficulties surrounding the proportion of elected members to have in the Lords, if it is decided to opt for a mixture of nomination and election.

Arguments for a system of election

It is unclear whether the new House of Lords will be entirely elected, but there is a possibility that a part of its membership will be, and the arguments in favour of election remain the same.

Democratic representation

It seems very odd for a modern legislature in a liberal democracy not to be elected.

The kingdom 'united'

There is an opportunity here to complement the devolution reforms. The reformed Upper House could be used to provide representation for the devolved regions, and also for England, which is at present under-represented at Westminster because of the so-called 'West Lothian Question'. This would help to draw the rather disunited kingdom together. Upper chambers often have this role in federal states.

Improved scrutiny

The Lords could develop a really strong role in terms of scrutiny and legislation if it had the legitimacy of fair elections behind it. As a result of this, the power of the executive might be checked to some degree. It is frequently said that the executive is too powerful in Britain and this would be a way of solving this.

Improved representation

Party list elections, if adopted for the House of Lords, could provide better representation of women and ethnic minorities.

Modernization

An elected Lords would enhance the Labour objective of modernization. It might be easier to have young people brought into the House of Lords through elections. Appointees will tend to be people of experience and a fairly large number will continue to be ex-MPs. This would, it could be argued, leave the Lords looking much as it does today: old-fashioned and elderly.

Enhanced authority

The Lords would have greater authority if elected and could behave with greater sense of confidence in their relations with the Commons and the executive.

 Question: What are the main advantages of a fully elected second chamber?

Have a classroom debate on the motion: 'This house would abolish the House of Lords'. Appoint three speakers on either side of the debate:

(a) one to propose the motion
(b) another to second the proposition
(c) a third to sum up the case for the proposition.

On the other side you should have:

(d) one to oppose the motion
(e) another to second the opposition
(f) a third to sum up.

The speakers give brief speeches in the order (a), (d), (b), (e); the audience can then raise points of their own and, finally, speakers (c) and (f) sum up.
To make it more interesting, you could conduct a 'parliamentary debate', with the speakers sitting facing each other on either side of a long table; interruptions by opposing speakers are allowed on this system, with the interrupter raising a point of information (usually a question designed to expose a weakness in the argument of the other side). The interrupter stands up, and the person speaking then decides whether to take the point of information or not. If the speaker will not allow the interruption, the interrupter has to sit down. At the end, the audience and the debaters can vote. You could take two votes; the first to decide which team argued most clearly and effectively; the second on the political issue involved, irrespective of how well debated it was. You could even hold a vote on the issue at the beginning of the debate, and see whether opinions have been shifted by the end. You will need a chairman to maintain order, and also a time-keeper to ensure that the speakers do not exceed the time-limits you may impose on them.

11.4 The functions and powers of the House of Lords

The functions of the House of Lords are, on the whole, the same as those of the Commons, but it has less power than the lower chamber, as the Commons is sometimes called, to fulfil these functions. The functions are summarized in figure 11.1. Before discussing these functions, look at box 11.3, which describes one role that has just been removed.

Constitutional function

The House of Lords has sometimes been called the 'watch-dog' of the Constitution – that is to say, a body which has a particular role in protecting the

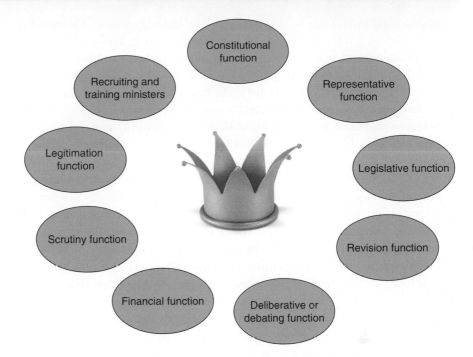

Figure 11.1 The main functions of the House of Lords

Box 11.3 The former judicial function of the House of Lords

As has been said, this function is in the process of being abolished, but needs to be briefly mentioned here. It was a curiosity – a confusing one – that the phrase 'House of Lords' was used to describe the highest court of appeal in England as well as the upper chamber of our legislature. The Lords of Appeal in Ordinary (also known as the Appellate Committee of the House of Lords, and also known as the 'law lords') used the chamber of the House of Lords to hear cases on appeal, usually in the mornings. This judicial function really had almost nothing to do with the present-day House of Lords as a part of Parliament. Indeed, between 1873, when Gladstone removed the Lords of Appeal from the House of Lords to another courtroom, and 1875, when Disraeli put them back, this function did not exist. The only real cross-over between this specialist judicial function and the real legislative work of the House of Lords as a part of Parliament came from the fact that the Lords of Appeal were also members of the House of Lords – that is to say, they had the right to attend the House of Lords as part of Parliament. They held this position for life, so could attend the House of Lords as legislators after their retirement as judges. However, the creation of a new Supreme Court in 2005, which comes fully into force in 2009, removes this function, and takes the entire judicial element away from the Lords. At the same time, the Lord Chancellor has ceased to hold both the position of head of the judiciary and that of chairman (or 'Speaker', to use the House of Commons terminology) of the House of Lords. These changes were designed to secure the complete independence of the judiciary. The loss of the law lords from the Lords may be held to weaken it, because their legal expertise has disappeared, and the House of Lords has lost a group of people who tended to keep a watchful eye on human rights. On 4 July 2006, the House of Lords chose its first Lord Speaker, to replace the Lord Chancellor.

Constitution from misuse by the Commons and by the executive. This may be because it was the Lords who, in the nineteenth century, had a tendency to hold up the reforming measures passed by a more radical Commons. On the whole, however, this function, if it ever existed in reality, is now a dead letter. The only remnant of it is to be found in the Parliament Act of 1911. Under this Act, the House of Lords is permitted to veto completely any bill which the Commons passes to extend the life of Parliament beyond the five years laid down in that Act. In other words, if the Commons decided not to have an election five years after the last one, the House of Lords could force them to do so. It is difficult to see how the Lords would actually do this, however. When the Human Rights Act was debated in 1998, there was discussion about whether the Lords should be given some special role in protecting human rights, but in the end it was decided not to do more than set up a Joint Committee on Human Rights, with members of the Lords and Commons working together on it. The creation of this Committee perhaps reflects a continuing constitutional focus in the Lords. If the decision is taken to give a future reformed House of Lords some role, through its membership, in pulling together the various parts of the devolved United Kingdom, this might also allow it to perform a sort of constitutional role. In 2001, as a result of the constitutional reforms of the Labour government, the Lords set up a Select Committee on the Constitution, which examines all bills to assess their constitutional impact, and undertakes policy enquiries in the field. In March 2005, when the Lords imposed significant amendments on the government's Terrorism Bill,

The Lord Speaker is elected by their lordships, has a five-year term and can be re-elected only once. The salary is £102,000, with £35,000 'expenses', which the newspapers were ungracious enough to criticize as being quite a lot for doing very little. The lucky person elected in July 2006 was Baroness Hayman – shown here

there was talk of the peers acting as defenders of ancient rights like habeas corpus (the right to a trial before imprisonment).

Representative function

Does the House of Lords have a representative role? Of course, in the past it did have a representative role – it represented the aristocracy in the legislature, and in a very direct way, since all of the aristocracy could meet there. It still does represent the aristocracy under the bizarre transitional arrangements of 1999, since the 'representative peers' are elected to the Lords by everyone else with the title of baron and above who cares to vote. Setting this curiosity (which is not likely to endure very long) aside, the presently constituted House of Lords does not conform at all easily to any of the models of representation described above in chapter 10. The peers are not fairly elected, they do not therefore act as delegates or representatives of their electors and they are certainly a very poor cross-section of British society. They are generally elderly, male and upper class. In March 2008, there were 148 women in the Lords and 601 men, which is not much worse a ratio than in the elected House of Commons.

The only case that can be made out for the House of Lords as a representative body is to say that it contains a wide range of experience and wisdom. Many of the life peers, it is argued, have the experience of being doctors, architects, academics, engineers, soldiers, judges, clergymen, etc., and this enables them to bring a fresh approach to their debates. Hence, a breadth of opinion is represented in the House of Lords. These arguments are also used in favour of a nominated chamber for the future. But there is no systematic way in which professional interests are represented there.

A perhaps better argument for the House of Lords as a representative group is to say that party loyalties are less strong there. This is due, first, to a tradition of crossbench independence and, second, to the fact that, by definition, life peers have already soaked up as much prime ministerial patronage as the British honours system will allow and hence have nothing to lose by 'disloyalty'. Third, unelected life members of a legislature (whether hereditary or not) do not need to toe the party line in order to get re-elected. So, members of the House of Lords represent a greater variety of views than members of the Commons do because they are not simply representing party views. All in all, though, it is probably safest to conclude that members of the House of Lords at present represent only themselves and their party, if they belong to one. The way in which they are at present appointed is also called into question by efforts to see the peers as in any way representative. The patronage of the Prime Ministers and, to a lesser extent, of the leaders of the other parties is the really significant factor in appointments at the present. So peers represent the leaders, past and present, of the political parties.

Legislative function

The Parliament Acts

With legislation, we have at last a function which the Lords can be said unambiguously to fulfil. The legislative role of the Lords is clearly defined by the two Parliament Acts, one passed in 1911 and the second in 1949. The first of these Acts reduced to a period of two parliamentary sessions (roughly two years) the time for which the Lords can hold up a piece of legislation which has passed the House of Commons. The second cut the time down to one session, or a maximum of one year and one month. This is sometimes called a suspensive veto, since it can only suspend a measure for a time, but it cannot veto – or overturn – it completely. Under the first Parliament Act, this right was said not to extend to 'money bills', and (as has been said) the Lords were allowed an absolute veto on measures to extend the period between general elections to a period of more than five years. Of course, this power to hold up legislation could be quite considerable, if it were carefully used in the last year before a general election. If the legislation being held up by the Lords failed to pass because an election had been called, and then the opposition came into power and did not choose to reintroduce it, the suspensive veto would have turned into an absolute veto, but only because that was the will of the electors of the House of Commons. On the whole, however, the Lords has, since 1911, tried hard to avoid outright confrontation with the Commons. The fact that the Parliament Acts have only been used seven times since 1911 by the Commons to enforce its will on the Lords shows this.

The Salisbury Convention

One reason for the fact that the Parliament Acts have been so infrequently used is because of this constitutional convention, devised first by the Conservative Prime Minister of the late Victorian period (1895–1902), Lord Salisbury, and also attributed to his descendant, another Lord Salisbury who was prominent in the House of Lords in the Attlee era. This convention simply says that the Lords ought to avoid defeating a legislative proposal on which a governing party has fought an election, or, in modern terms, which is based on the party's election manifesto. Obviously, it is a little difficult at times to apply this rule, since manifesto promises can be rather vague and legislation is very precise, but on the whole the Lords have stuck to this approach. In 2005, however, the Liberal Democrats in the Lords announced that they did not consider themselves any longer bound by this convention, on the grounds that the composition of the Lords was now less unrepresentative of the political views of the country than the Commons. The Liberal Democrat leader in the Lords, Lord McNally, called the Salisbury Convention 'the last refuge of legislative scoundrels'.

Box 11.4 Use of the 1911 and 1949 Parliament Acts

Because of the power over the Lords which, since 1911, the Commons has been able to exert, it is extremely rare for a government bill to be defeated in the Lords, and hence for the Parliament Acts to be invoked. This has happened on seven occasions. The 1914 Government of Ireland Act and the Welsh Church Act of the same year required the use of the 1911 Act. In 1949, the second Parliament Act had to be passed using the first Act. It was not for another 50 years that this second Act had to be used. In 1990 the Lords (on a free vote) defeated the War Crimes Bill and in 1999 it defeated the Sexual Offences (Amendment) Bill. On both occasions, these measures did eventually pass through the agency of the Parliament Act. The Lords felt that both measures were ones on which public opinion was against the government of the day. The first enabled the police to prosecute (mostly) Nazi war criminals and the second reduced the age of consent for homosexuals to 16. Neither vote exactly recommends the Lords to people of an enlightened outlook. More recently, the Act had to be used to pass the 2004 Hunting with Dogs Act, which banned fox-hunting. The use of the Parliament Act to force through the last measure was strongly criticized by the Countryside Alliance, which, in 2004–5, launched an unsuccessful legal challenge in the courts to the 1949 Act, on the grounds that it had been passed against the votes of the House of Lords and therefore could not be used to steamroll through the Act abolishing fox-hunting. The judiciary did not agree with this challenge. It is interesting to note that the Parliament Acts have never been used by a Conservative government, despite the fact that the Conservatives have dominated British politics since 1911. There could not be a better indication of where the sympathies of the members of the House of Lords have generally lain.

Within the framework set out by the Parliament Acts and the Salisbury Convention, the House of Lords is a legislative chamber which works in much the same way as the House of Commons. Bills can be introduced in the Lords first, before the Commons, although the government must be careful, because such measures will not qualify for the protection of the Parliament Act (that is, if they pass the Lords first, and the Commons then amends them and the Lords then votes down that amendment, the Commons cannot insist on getting their way within a year and a month). More normally, legislation comes to the Lords after it has been passed in the Commons. It now passes through the same process of three readings, and possibly a committee and report stage, as in the Commons. If it is amended or defeated in the Lords, the bill then returns to the Commons. Sometimes a protracted process of negotiation develops over amendments made in the Lords in a process known as 'Ping-Pong', which, as its name suggests, involves a bill that has been passed in the Commons being amended in the Lords and then returning to the Commons for them to consider and vote on the amendments. The bill then returns to the Lords for the changes made (or unmade) in the Commons to be reconsidered. This process can carry on again and again if there is no agreement between the two chambers. Ultimately, the Lords will get its way in Ping-Pong in the short term, unless the Commons backs down, but the Commons can then overturn the amended bill using the Parliament Act, if MPs are willing to wait a year. The passage of the Prevention of Terrorism Act in March 2005 involved a protracted period of Ping-Pong, which involved a continuous meeting in both chambers for 30 hours. Obviously, Ping-Pong is where the Lords can be very effective and where it justifies its bicameral existence, and provides useful legislative scrutiny. The Prevention of Terrorism Bill was a bad bill in many ways, harmful to civil liberties, and it was somewhat improved through Ping-Pong because the government had to make concessions to the Lords in order to pass the legislation, which was a matter of urgency because earlier anti-terrorist measures were about to expire. Ping-Pong may be irksome to the government of the day, but in order to produce good legislation, it will clearly be helpful to have an extensive process of scrutiny going on. The weight of experience in the Lords is obviously important here: the law lords will spot deficiencies in drafting, and semi-retired politicians will have retained their nose for potential political problems. But, on the other hand, if an elected government finds that its legislation is being regularly interfered with by a group of people who may be well meaning and highly experienced but who are, in the end, not elected, that government might have some cause to complain, and so might the people who elected it. Another aspect of the legislative work of the Lords is that they can propose Private Members' Bills just as the MPs can in the Commons. This enables controversial social and moral matters to be brought onto the agenda.

Since the reforms of 1999 in the composition of the Lords, it has become a more active body in opposing the government, despite its increasingly pro-Labour composition. During the course of the 2001–5 Parliament, the government was defeated on 245 occasions in the Lords, which was more than four times the rate of defeat compared with the Conservative years 1979–97, and more than twice as often as under the first Blair government. Political scientist Philip Cowley concludes: 'Of the two Houses of Parliament, therefore, it has been the Lords that has been more of a block on the government in recent years.'

Revising function

According to Lord Norton, the leading political scientist to write on Parliament, this is the most significant aspect of the work of the House of Lords. Clearly it is one of the strongest arguments for a bicameral system. The Commons considers legislation as thoroughly as it can, but in the Lords, after a brief pause, this legislation is looked at again and can be revised. Here the legislative scrutiny that is undertaken is not necessarily against the interests of the government; clearly the government needs its legislation to be as good as possible. The main mechanism by which the Lords undertakes this process of legislative revision is by proposing amendments to bills. The energy with which the Lords undertakes this role is shown by the fact that in the 2002–3 session of Parliament, the Lords considered 9,782 amendments to bills, of which 2,996 were passed. There were 207 votes on amendments to bills, 83 of which were lost to the government. The government will be very happy to accept amendments which improve a bill. Of course, one thing that this revising function in the Lords means is that it also gives the government a chance to revise its own legislation by itself proposing amendments in the Lords, and this (rather than wrecking tactics by the opposition) accounts for many of the amendments put up by the Lords.

Deliberative or debating function

The defenders of the House of Lords claim that the Upper House is very good at debating. The reason given for this is that the members of the Lords are highly experienced and drawn from a wide variety of backgrounds, so they can bring this wealth of experience and knowledge to bear on the subject under debate. They are also less prone to political point-scoring in the Lords, it is said, because the members are often crossbenchers or beyond the reach of the threats and promises of the whips. This deliberative function is sometimes alleged to be a reason for having an appointed rather than an elected house, because the ability to draw on this expertise will disappear if members of the Lords become mere professional politicians. However, it is probably best not to see debating as a separate function of the Lords: it would seem very odd to have a constitution which set aside taxpayers' money just for debating, however good the debating was. The fact is that debating is much better seen as a mechanism, as a tool; it is through debating that the functions of scrutiny and legislation are carried out. The only possible opening for those who say that there is a separate deliberative function is to say that not all debates in the Lords are to do with scrutiny or legislation. This is probably true; some of the debates look, to the cynic, like debating for the sake of it. In one month, April 2003, the House of Lords had general debates on (not all at once, but on separate days) the following: Atlantic salmon, terrorism and religion, disabled people, and tourism. In the same month, at various times, they had mini debates on: public interest immunity, the Congo, East Africa, specialized health services, coalmining, and MRSA in hospitals. It is conceivable that all these debates could count as scrutiny, but it may be better to see them as an attempt to influence policy in the long term. Whether anyone takes much notice is unclear. There are probably ways in which the retired great and good can as effectively seek to have an influence on policy; for example, by writing letters to the papers.

The Economic Affairs Committee is one of the permanent investigative committees of the House of Lords

Financial function

Here, the House of Lords has no power at all to thwart the will of the House of Commons, because, as has been said, the 1911 Parliament Act expressly forbids interference with money bills, and indeed even before 1910 it had been accepted by the Lords that it should avoid doing so. What constitutes a 'money bill' is decided by the Speaker of the House of Commons, but it is accepted that the definition cannot be too wide: i.e., a 'money bill' must principally be a financial one. Nevertheless, the Lords exercises its right to debate financial matters, and all bills, including money bills, have to pass the Lords as well as the Commons.

Scrutiny function

Scrutiny is the field in which the House of Lords finds one of its strongest roles. We have already looked at legislative scrutiny. It is true, however, that in technical terms a vote of no confidence in the Lords would have no impact on the government of the day. In addition, ministers of the Crown are mainly accountable to and responsible to the Commons, simply because that is where they sit. Some Conservative governments have had senior ministers in the Lords, and in 1982 Lord Carrington, the Foreign Secretary, resigned following the doctrine of individual ministerial responsibility, so in a way he was held responsible to the Lords. But this is an anomaly. Nevertheless, the Lords can hold the government to account by focusing public and media attention on an issue. Just as with legislation, so with scrutiny of the executive, the procedure in the Lords follows the same pattern as in the Commons. There are debates on matters of public importance just as there are in the Commons. The House of Lords prides itself on the knowledge and wisdom its members bring to these debates. Ministers have to answer questions in the Lords, just as they do in the Commons. Each government department has a minister in the House of Lords, and there is a regular programme of questions for ministers. Questions for a written answer can also be made.

There are select committees in the House of Lords, just as there are in the Commons. They do not follow quite the same pattern, but a number of them have, over recent years, gained a reputation for skilful scrutiny. These include the Lords Select Committee on Science and Technology, set up in 1979, which has no counterpart in the Commons and has a number of peers on it who have academic and industrial experience in the area. Obviously, this committee can have an important role in influencing government policy in this field. The second committee to have acquired a reputation for good scrutiny is the Lords Committee on the European Union, established in 1974, which has its counterpart in the Commons now, but which nevertheless has a significant part to play. It scrutinizes draft European legislation, and works through no fewer than six sub-committees, with a total membership of about 70 peers. Since 2001, there have been two new select committees: on the Constitution (mentioned above) and on Economic Affairs, which can look into broad economic matters, especially those concerned with the monetary policy of the Bank of England, but which would be well advised not to meddle further with the budget after the events of 1910–11. There is also a Delegated Powers Scrutiny Committee, which looks at proposed legislation to see whether what is called the delegated powers contained in the bill are appropriate; these are powers given to ministers to make regulations in the future. Finally, it is necessary to mention a potentially significant Joint Committee on Human Rights, which is attended by members of both the Lords and the Commons, and was created after the Human Rights Act came into force in 2000.

Legitimation function

It is difficult to say whether the House of Lords plays a part in giving the political system as a whole, and especially the process of legislation, any legitimation. It used to be thought that the glamour that attached to hereditary wealth (whether in the royal family or the peerage) gave strength to a political system in an age where the old feudal world was giving way to an age of democracy. This point is made in the work of Walter Bagehot, published first in 1865, where he talks about the need for 'dignified' parts of the Constitution. Somewhat later (1919), the German sociologist Max Weber wrote about the strength of what he called 'traditional' sources of authority. Is any of this still true now? It seems very unlikely. In fact, the authority of the elderly and 'wise' seems in the twenty-first century to be more or less completely at an end. Until the House of Lords is finally reformed, this legitimizing function may be said to be dormant. Whether election or nomination will provide the better chance of giving the House of Lords authority is the most important question facing the reformers of the Upper House.

Recruitment and training of ministers

This is not really a significant function of the Lords either, especially after the reform of the post of Lord Chancellor (previously the only significant minister to sit in the Lords). There are government ministers in the Lords, as there are in the Commons, but they are there because the parliamentary system requires it, and by and large they are junior figures. There are shadow ministers too. The political parties have their structures in the Lords, with a Leader of the House and whips. But the government does not use the House of Lords to any large extent as a reservoir of talent that it can dip into in order to staff the government. The last major government minister to sit in the Lords was Lord Carrington as Foreign Secretary (1979–82), and this was considered rather old-fashioned at the time. The last peer to be prime minister was Lord Salisbury in 1902, and when the Conservative Party in 1963 selected Lord Home to be their leader – and hence Prime Minister – on the retirement of Harold Macmillan, he had to renounce his peerage and become plain Alec Douglas Home, in order to be elected as an MP. This was a form of recruitment and training, but it was very rare, even then. Since 1997, Labour have used the House of Lords as a way of appointing five second-ranking political figures to the government; in all three cases the person appointed was from outside the political world, and the rapid way in which someone can be made a part of Parliament by being given a peerage was the reason for doing this. The three appointments were all rather controversial: Lord Falconer was ennobled in order to become Solicitor General, and was then given other responsibilities – for example for the ill-fated Millennium Dome at Greenwich – and he then became Lord Chancellor; Lord Simon was given a peerage in order to become a minister in the Department of Trade and Industry; and Lord Macdonald was ennobled to become a junior minister in the Scottish Office. When Gordon Brown became Prime Minister in 2007, he ennobled Digby Jones, making him a government spokesman in the Lords on business; and also Mark Malloch Brown, who became a minister in the Foreign Office. But setting these rather exceptional appointments aside, the fact is that the House of Lords tends to be used as a retirement home for redundant MPs and ministers: this is sometimes referred to as being 'kicked upstairs'. Or, to put it in a more positive way, the wisdom and expertise of former ministers is used to strengthen the Lords.

Question: Distinguish between the roles and the powers of the House of Commons and the House of Lords.

SUMMING UP

The years since 1997 and the election of a reforming Labour government have been decisive in the history of the House of Lords, and it has changed more as a result of the 1999 House of Lords Act than at any time in its history, at least since 1911. The 2005 Constitutional Reform Act was also a major reform of the Lords; Labour has promised further reforms to complete this process. Membership is the current area for debate. Essentially, the remaining hereditary element will at some point in the future be banished from the House, and it seems likely that the chamber will be composed of either appointed or elected peers, or (most likely) some mixture of the two. Reform of the functions of the House of Lords have been largely neglected by Labour. Wakeham proposed a very modest change to functions, but the government has shown little enthusiasm even for this. The Human Rights Act has given the Lords no major special role in guarding rights, although the House contributes to the Joint Parliamentary Committee on Human Rights. However, in 2005 the judicial function was abolished, with the Lords of Appeal being hived off and the office of Lord Chancellor reformed. But while this is a highly significant reform from the perspective of the judiciary, it removes a function of the House of Lords which was not central to it as part of Parliament. Suggestions were made by Peter Hain, Leader of the House of Commons in 2004, that a reduction in the delaying powers of the House of Lords is a possibility, reducing them from the current one year to six months. The 2005 Labour manifesto talked of codifying the key conventions governing the work of the Lords, and of reducing to a maximum of 60 days the time the Lords can take to pass most bills. It also spoke of developing forms of scrutiny which would complement those of the Commons. But even without any further legislation directly affecting the functions of the House of Lords, it seems possible that changes in membership may in fact have a gradual, indirect effect on the functions. The House of Lords may be strengthened by the removal of the remaining hereditary peers, so it may play an enhanced role. It is said that the House of Lords was strengthened after 1958 by the creation of life peers and, as a result, it became more confident. If a system of appointment and election increases the representation of women and of minority groups in the Lords, perhaps once again the House will claim a constitutional role as protector of Human Rights. It is possible that the nomination by an independent Appointments Commission of people representing different interests, religions and professions, etc. may strengthen scrutiny. It is likely that the Lords may become more party political in its outlook as a result of these reforms of membership, and this would probably also strengthen its role. But in truth, it would be wrong to expect too much from the second phase of Labour's reforms of the House of Lords. Labour does not wish to create a strong House of Lords, and has not enhanced its powers. The House of Commons has decided against creating a strong rival. Perhaps we should not be too surprised at this.

Further reading

Philip Norton, *Parliament in British Politics* (Palgrave, 2005): written by an academic who is also a member of the House of Lords.

M. Russell, *Reforming the House of Lords* (Oxford University Press, 2000): looks at the recent developments and possible trends for reform.

D. Shell, *The House of Lords* (Harvester Wheatsheaf, 1992): straightforward account of the politics of the Lords, pre-Blair.

The House of Lords: Reform (Cm.7027, HMSO, Feb. 2007): the White Paper on Lords reform, available online from the Stationary Office website.

Websites

www.official-documents.gov.uk (Stationary Office: for White Paper)

www.parliament.uk (Parliament)

CHAPTER
12

The Executive: Prime Minister and Cabinet

Making connections

The main focus here is on the Prime Minister and the Cabinet. It is important when studying the executive in the UK not to fall into the trap of believing that everything stems from the Prime Minister and hence of neglecting the other parts of the core of British politics. So this chapter needs to be considered in relation to the next one concerning ministers and civil servants.

CHAPTER 1

The Executive: Prime Minister and Cabinet

KEY TOPICS

- The role of the executive
- Who runs the executive?
- The Prime Minister
- The Prime Minister's Office
- A British presidency?
- Different styles of prime ministerial leadership
- Limitations on the power of the Prime Minister
- The Cabinet
- What factors influence the Prime Minister's appointments to the Cabinet?
- Do we have Cabinet government?

SETTING THE SCENE

We now reach the heart of the political system: the executive, or government. There will be two chapters dealing with this substantial topic. This first one looks at the Prime Minister and the Cabinet; chapter 13 will look at ministers and the civil service.

The executive: one of the three 'powers' or 'branches' of the system of government. The executive's prime responsibility is to use the power of the state to govern the country by executing the laws passed by the legislature, or by taking actions sanctioned in other ways by the representative assembly, and by supporting the judiciary in enforcing the laws.

12.1 The role of the executive

At the heart of the modern political system in all countries is an **executive**. In some ways, it is the most significant part of the whole political system. It is always in existence (although in the hands of different politicians and parties at different times), while the legislature will generally only meet for set periods. Without the support of the executive, the judiciary would be powerless to act. The other two branches of the system of government revolve around it. The executive in Britain is very often referred to as the government, a term which leads to some confusion, but also emphasizes the importance of the executive as the most powerful of the 'branches of the system of government'. There are two different ways in which the executive can be analysed.

1 *Elected or unelected.* In a liberal democracy, the executive is composed of two distinct parts: elected and unelected. The elected part of the executive in Britain is led by the Prime Minister and consists of the Cabinet and the other ministers who do not attend the Cabinet. The unelected part consists of what are called civil servants, professional experts in administration or government, who work for the elected members of the government.

2 *Local (and devolved) or central.* Most of this chapter will focus on the work of the central executive: the ministers and officials who work largely in that part of London called Whitehall. But local government is carried on throughout the country by officials and councillors who work for the local community at city, county, borough, district and parish levels. In addition, devolution to Scotland, Wales, Northern Ireland, London and the regions of England adds another level of government, as does the development of the European Union.

The functions or role of the executive (especially at central government level) may be defined as follows.

A support for the other branches of government

For the reasons given above, the executive tends to be the leading branch of government in all liberal democracies. According to some commentators, this is particularly true in Britain, which is said to suffer from 'executive dominance'. The executive branch generally has a role in supporting both the other branches. The legislature in Britain is particularly dependent on the executive, which has the power to call the legislature into emergency session and to dissolve it in preparation for an election. Although the judiciary is, in theory, independent, it also depends for support on the executive. The execution of justice in Britain is a cooperative effort in which the executive works closely with the judiciary and legislature.

A democratic, representative function

It is the function of government to exercise the will of the people in executive matters. In a democracy the executive is elected and is therefore in a sense a representative body. It needs therefore to act in the interests of the people if it is to be re-elected at the next election. It will offer a statement of its governmental intentions in its party manifesto at the election, as will the parties which are in opposition but are seeking to become the future government. Thus the executive must rule according to the principles of what is called 'representative government'.

Responsive government

In addition to this, the government needs to respond to the will of the people as expressed in the various groups and institutions which link the people and the executive. Pressure groups, political parties, the media and what is vaguely called public opinion will influence the government in what it does. This is known as responsive government.

To govern responsibly

But although the executive branch has to be responsive and representative in a liberal democracy, it must also run the country and do so in a responsible or sensible way. It may be necessary for the executive to exercise a leadership role and to run ahead of public opinion on unpopular issues like immigration or defence.

An administrative role

Just as a business has to be efficient in its operations, so the government should attempt to run the country, or administer it, as well as possible according to the rules of good government. The link between successful business practices and good government has been particularly highlighted in recent years, and the leader of the executive branch is sometimes called a chief executive by political scientists, which is a phrase also used to describe the managing director of a business.

To cover the great range of government business

The government must specialize and show expertise in a wide range of policy areas. The areas of government responsibility have steadily increased in the last century, and there are few sectors of national life which are not touched at least to some degree by government activity. There is a list of the 2008 Cabinet departments and ministers in table 12.2 (see page 431). A brief summary of the main areas of government responsibility is as follows:

Finance and economic policy	Foreign policy and defence
Home affairs (police, prisons, etc.)	Health
Education	Social policy and welfare
Transport	Trade, industry
Employment	Farming and fisheries
The environment	Sport, culture and tourism

12.2 Who runs the executive?

There is a long-running and important question about where power really lies in Britain's executive. Before going into detail on each of the elements of the executive, it is important to give an overview of this controversy.

Parliamentary government

According to constitutional theory, at the heart of the British system of government is Parliament, which holds the executive to account. This is the constitutional principle of parliamentary sovereignty, which is discussed in chapter 9 on the British Constitution. It is also true that Parliament can dismiss the executive on what is called a vote of no confidence, and so Parliament does look as though it is in control. But for at least the last century, in practice the executive has dominated the legislature and not vice versa (this point is also discussed in chapter 10). So, on the whole, the idea that Parliament dominates the executive in Britain is unacceptable as a way of describing the political realities of the present day. In 2007, one of Gordon Brown's first acts when he became Prime Minister was to announce a future programme of constitutional reform designed to 'limit the powers of the executive', largely by making it more accountable to Parliament. These proposals are listed in chapter 9 on the Constitution. However, although Brown may effect some theoretical, constitutional changes in this respect, he will not change the fact that, whatever the powers of Parliament, the party with the majority in the House of Commons dominates Parliament, and that party also runs the executive. So, it would be naive to conclude that his proposals will fundamentally alter the balance of power between executive and legislature.

Cabinet government

Writing in 1865, the great constitutional authority Walter Bagehot said in his book, *The English Constitution*, that the secret of the British political system was that it wasn't Parliament that dominated the government, but the Cabinet. The Cabinet, he said, was the 'buckle which fastens', the institution that binds the whole political system together, the 'hyphen' which joins the legislature to the executive. The Cabinet consists of the 20-odd ministers who work with the Prime Minister in governing the country. If the Cabinet is in fact in charge of the executive, the Prime Minister is just a member of the Cabinet, with more authority than each of the other members, but less than the body as a whole. He or she is 'primus inter pares' or 'first among equals'. According to the constitutional theory of Cabinet collective responsibility, the Cabinet as a whole resigns in the event of a successful vote of no confidence in the House of Commons, thus emphasizing the view that Cabinet government is the reality. On the whole, however, modern writers have been quick to deny that the Cabinet is in fact still in charge, although the fall in 1990 of Margaret Thatcher reminds us that the role of the Cabinet is not entirely negligible.

Prime ministerial government

When the Labour statesman and academic Richard Crossman edited a new edition of Bagehot's book in 1963, he wrote an influential introduction to it in which he said that Bagehot needed updating on this point. Crossman's view was that Britain no longer had Cabinet government, because twentieth-century Prime Ministers were so effectively dominant over their Cabinets that we had to talk instead about prime ministerial government. In a rather confusing twist, this dominant prime ministerial role is sometimes described as presidential. Michael Foley, while sensitive to the fact that the word 'presidential' introduces almost as many difficulties as it solves, is the academic who has done most to spread the view that we now have a British presidency.

The core executive

Exasperated by this long-running debate over where power really lies in the British executive, political scientists, especially Patrick Dunleavy, Rod Rhodes and Martin Smith, have emphasized that power in Britain is actually rather widely diffused. The Cabinet, Prime Minister and government ministers wield power, but so too do junior ministers, senior civil servants and the chief executives of government agencies. The relationship between these people at the core, or heart, of British government is not best seen as one of rivalry, but of interaction in a complex web of relationships.

Whitehall

Whitehall is the street in London where many government departments have their offices, and it has become a shorthand term for the civil service. According to one rather cynical view of things, which perhaps lends some support to the analysis of the core executive given above, it is the senior civil servants who actually run the country, while the politicians try to claim the credit when something goes right. The best analysis of this view is found in the 1980s television comedy programme, *Yes, Minister*.

Party government

Richard Rose, a most inventive political scientist of recent years, has argued that in Britain the real power lies within the major political parties, and that when a particular political party is in government, this is in fact where the real power lies. According to this view, the Cabinet and the Prime Minister need at all times to be aware of the feelings within their political party. Such a view begs a further question, namely: where does power lie within the political party?

It is, of course, highly likely that there is an element of truth in all these views about where power lies within the British executive.

12.3 The Prime Minister

The obvious answer to the question about where power lies in the British political system is to say that it is with the Prime Minister, and on the whole this is probably the best answer to give. The Prime Minister seems, on balance, to control more resources than his potential rivals in the core executive. The resources (or powers) of the Prime Minister are not clearly defined because of the unwritten nature of the British constitution, but the main points can be summarized as follows.

The first minister, or head of the government

The Prime Minister is the leading figure in the government. Since the days of Robert Walpole (in power 1721–42), there has always been a single person who is, in constitutional theory, appointed by the Crown to lead the government. This person is appointed by the monarch because he or she is the leading figure in a party or group of parties that can command a majority in Parliament. As soon as the result of an election is known, the future Prime Minister visits Buckingham Palace to have his or her position confirmed. The Prime Minister speaks to the monarch at least once a week about the conduct of public affairs. Most importantly, he or she can request what is called a dissolution of Parliament from the monarch – that is to say, can ask the monarch to bring the session of Parliament to a close and call a general election. This means that the Prime Minister has the power to decide when there will be an election. In this process of liaison with the monarch, the Prime Minister is acting as the leader of the government.

The chairman of the Cabinet

The modern idea of a Cabinet is not as old as that of the Prime Minister, but since the late eighteenth century the two have been closely linked. The Prime Minister is head of a Cabinet of ministers and has to call a meeting of the Cabinet roughly once a week; he or she can decide on the precise timing of the meetings and their length and format. The Prime Minister sets the agenda of Cabinet meetings, chairs them and approves the minutes. Associated with the Cabinet is an elaborate system of committees and a civil service department headed by the Cabinet Secretary. This Cabinet system is, in effect, dominated by the Prime Minister, who decides what Cabinet committees there will be and who will be on them.

Gordon Brown on the steps of 10 Downing Street with his wife Sarah after becoming Prime Minister on 27 June 2007

The leader of the government team

The Prime Minister appoints the members of the Cabinet, and all government jobs are approved by him or her. The Prime Minister can 'reshuffle' the Cabinet from time to time, moving ministers from department to department, getting rid of unsuccessful or elderly ministers and bringing in talented new-comers. It is true that the Prime Minister does not have a completely free hand here, but his or her power is still very great. The decision about when a minister should resign after a failure or scandal is in effect the decision of the Prime Minister, who can create new ministerial departments, reorganize and amalgamate them and decide which ministers have a seat on the Cabinet and which do not. Tony Blair reorganized and renamed the Department for Work and Pensions and the Department for Education and Skills; he created new departments in the shape of the Office of Deputy Prime Minister (which he later abolished), the Department of the Environment, Food and Rural Affairs, and the Department of Constitutional Affairs; and in 2007, he supported plans to create a new Department of Justice. In a reshuffle in 2004, Blair attempted to abolish the office of Lord Chancellor, but then discovered (after he had announced that he had done so) that he required, uniquely in this case, an Act of Parliament to do it, so he was forced to make a hurried change to his plans. The appointment of Gordon Brown as Prime Minister in 2007 saw the final creation of the Ministry of Justice and an orgy of renaming and reorganizing. Education and Skills became two ministries: first, Children, Schools and Families; second, Innovation, Universities and Skills. The prosaic Trade and Industry became the baroque Business, Enterprise and Regulatory Reform.

The minister for the civil service

The whole system of government depends on the Prime Minister and not just the elected ministers, but also the non-elected, professional civil service. The Prime Minister supervises promotion at the higher levels of the civil service. The Prime Minister may also reorganize the civil service, reform and restructure it and change its overall complexion and attitude.

The holder of great powers of patronage

The Prime Minister, as has been said, appoints, promotes and dismisses people in the government and to some extent in the senior civil service too. The British Commissioner at the European Union is also nominated by the Prime Minister. In addition, he or she advises the Queen on appointments to the House of Lords and to the senior judiciary. Both these last two pieces of patronage are currently under review and will be limited in the future, and even at the moment the Prime Minister does not have a completely free hand. A large number of other appointments to what can broadly be called the Establishment are at the disposal of the Prime Minister: positions in the Church of England, at certain universities and in the armed forces. Again, the Prime Minister will generally follow expert advice on these appointments. Finally, the honours system is dominated by prime ministerial patronage: peerages, knighthoods and the various other civilian medals and awards which are distributed by the monarch, to a large extent on the Prime Minister's behalf. It is possible to exaggerate this power of patronage, however, because (apart from the appointment of ministers) the PM has to act according to protocol and has to consult various groups.

Coordinator of government policy and ideology

Working with individual ministers, and through the Cabinet, the Prime Minister coordinates government policy. This process begins before an election is won, when the broad outlines of policy are sketched out – and then supervised – by the prospective Prime Minister in his or her party's manifesto. If elected, the Prime Minister will be expected to ensure that this policy statement is implemented; he or she tends to give the development of policy a particular ideological flavour and in some ways tries to lead the government in this area too. Thatcher led her governments as a Thatcherite; Mr Blair has been a 'New Labour' Prime Minister. It remains to be seen what Brown will develop into; he made it clear on his appointment that he would be different from Blair, but perhaps more in terms of style than ideology.

The overseer of the work of Cabinet colleagues

Not only do Prime Ministers coordinate policy, they also get involved, to a greater or lesser extent, in the work of their Cabinet colleagues, depending on their particular interests and abilities. Some Prime Ministers are more inclined to do this than others, but all will be interested in the really important areas of policy, such as foreign affairs, economic policy and home affairs. Some Prime Ministers seem to want to control all policy and treat individual ministers as subordinates whose function it is to carry out their orders. Others are more collegial in their approach.

The leader of the major political party in the House of Commons

The Prime Minister will, by definition, be head of the largest political party in the House of Commons and will have a role in leading that party. This role continues after the Prime Minister has taken up residence in 10 Downing Street. He or she will attend party conferences, and will work closely in running the party with party officials in London. Part of this role will include fundraising for the party, and electioneering.

The chief spokesman for the party and the government in Parliament

Gordon Brown answering Prime Minister's Questions in the Commons

The Prime Minister is in some respects the most important person in Parliament, although the level of prime ministerial attendance in the House of Commons has declined over the past century. Nowadays the Prime Minister tends to leave the day-to-day management of Parliament to the Leader of the House and government whips. But nevertheless he or she will be there to lead major debates – for example on the Queen's Speech at the opening of Parliament. The Prime Minister answers questions in the Commons once a week, and appears before the Liaison Committee, which consists of the chairpersons of select committees, twice a year. The Prime Minister is supposed to make major announcements in Parliament – as has been said, it is essentially the Prime Minister's decision when to call a general election and dissolve Parliament.

The chief government and party spokesman in the country

The Prime Minister has a role as the chief communicator of his or her political party and the chief spokesman for the government. This goes beyond a parliamentary role and involves frequent appearances in the media, on television, writing newspaper articles, and giving interviews or press conferences. Tony Blair started the process of giving a monthly press conference, rather like the President of the USA. This has been criticized on the grounds that the Prime Minister ought to be making announcements in the House of Commons.

Representative of the country abroad and a national figurehead at home

The Prime Minister has increasingly adopted roles which, in the past, have been associated with the head of state or a member of the royal family. Visits to foreign dignitaries, attendance at summit meetings and at the funerals of foreign heads of government and state, the communication of expressions of grief or condolence to countries struck by some disaster: all of these seem increasingly to be part of the work of a Prime Minister. Even at home, the

Table 12.1 Post-war Prime Ministers		
1945–51	Clement Attlee	Labour
1951–5	Winston Churchill	Conservative
1955–7	Anthony Eden	Conservative
1957–63	Harold Macmillan	Conservative
1963–4	Alec Douglas-Home	Conservative
1964–70	Harold Wilson	Labour
1970–4	Edward Heath	Conservative
1974–6	Harold Wilson (again)	Labour
1976–9	James Callaghan	Labour
1979–90	Margaret Thatcher	Conservative
1990–7	John Major	Conservative
1997–2007	Tony Blair	Labour
2007–	Gordon Brown	Labour

Prime Minister is expected to perform similar ceremonial functions, and can generally be expected to appear on television in the event of a serious accident or the death of someone famous.

12.4 The Prime Minister's Office

To support the Prime Minister in his role, there is a Prime Minister's Office, centred on 10 Downing Street, which is both the Prime Minister's home (although Tony Blair and his family actually chose to live in number 11, where the accommodation is larger) and his office. The number of support staff has grown in recent years, but is still relatively small, especially in comparison with the huge staff that works for the President of the USA for example. In 1998, Tony Blair's immediate political staff in 10 Downing Street only numbered 152 but he was still accused of having enhanced the role of his staff by bringing in additional political advisers. Different Prime Ministers organize their Office in different ways, and give their close advisors different titles, and Tony Blair and Gordon Brown have done this too.

Box 12.1 Prime Minister Brown's Office, 2007–

The Prime Minister's Office at the beginning of the Brown premiership was led by the following people, and this list gives some idea of the work in general of the Office under any Prime Minister in recent years:

Tom Scholar is Chief of Staff and Principal Private Secretary, who reports directly to the Prime Minister, has direct responsibility for leading and coordinating operations in Number 10 and runs the Prime Minister's Private Office. This is obviously a very significant role for someone. Scholar is a career civil servant, who previously worked for Brown at the Treasury. Blair created the role of Chief of Staff to work alongside the longer-established Principal Private Secretary; Brown has amalgamated the two roles, which seems to make more sense.

Gavin Kelly is Deputy Chief of Staff, and a Special Adviser – that is, a partisan appointee, from outside the civil service.

Michael Ellam is Director of Communications and the Prime Minister's Spokesman. He is a civil

servant. This was the job held in the early Blair days by Alastair Campbell. Ellam worked for Brown at the Treasury.

Damian McBride, a Special Adviser, advises the Prime Minister on political press issues.

Sue Nye, a Special Adviser, is Director of Government Relations (replacing Blair's Ruth Turner, who in 2006–7 was arrested for her alleged part in the loans for peerages scandal).

Dan Corry, a Special Adviser, is Head of the Policy Unit.

Jeremy Heywood, a civil servant, is Head of Domestic Policy and Strategy.

Jon Cunliffe is a civil servant. His title is Head of International Economic Affairs, Europe and G8 Sherpa. He worked for Brown at the Treasury.

Simon McDonald, a civil servant and former ambassador to Israel, is Head of Foreign and Defence Policy.

- There seems to be a growing expectation that the main media focus is on the Prime Minister. Television tends to concentrate on personalities and characters, and this has the effect of emphasizing the role of the Prime Minister, rather than focusing on institutions like Cabinet and Parliament, which are the real essence of democratic politics. The television cameras need a picture.

- There develops a politics of 'leadership', according to Foley. We judge political parties and their success by whether they are well led. The key to successful leadership is portrayed in the press as being a matter of whether leaders are 'tough'. This becomes a sort of obsession in the media, and policies and issues, at the real heart of politics, are forgotten because of an unhealthy emphasis on 'style' rather than 'substance'.

- Political parties have been in decline in a number of respects (see chapter 7) and this makes it easier for a leader to dominate his or her party. Again, media attention focuses on party unity, and MPs realize that if they are to win support from the voters they need to make the party look united. This is achieved best if the party has a relatively small membership compared with political parties in the past. Party leaders try to distance themselves from their parties and hence gain wider political support: Foley calls this 'spatial leadership'.

- The decline in the prestige of the British monarchy makes the Prime Minister adopt more of the functions of a head of state.

- There is an increase in international meetings as the links between Britain and the wider world increase. These seem to require the attendance of the Prime Minister, as a sort of combined foreign minister and head of state. This again focuses the spotlight on the PM.

Journalist Nick Cohen has gone one better than Foley and has written not of a British presidency under Blair, but of a monarchy under King Tony. Gordon Brown was accused of being a 'control freak' when he was Chancellor of the Exchequer, but since becoming Prime Minister he has worked very hard to exude a feeling of relaxation and collegiality. It remains to be seen whether he really does break out of the presidential mould or not.

 Question: In what ways is the UK political system becoming more presidential?

12.6 Different styles of prime ministerial leadership

The idea that there has been a major shift in the nature of the Prime Minister's role in Britain is open to criticism for two main reasons: first, because

Box 12.2 Margaret Thatcher

In 1979, the Conservatives won a general election under the leadership of their greatest post-war leader, Margaret Thatcher, and there began a period of 18 years of Conservative dominance. Thatcher gradually developed a new ideology and a new set of policies which challenged some, but not all, of the post-war consensus. These policies represented a significant shift to the right in British politics. Thatcher's aim was to 'roll back the frontiers of the state', but at the same time to make sure that what remained of the state should be strong and effective. Thatcher was a successful vote-winner and there were three election victories for her (1979, 1983, 1987). She was loved and loathed in equal measure in Britain: many people found her tough and straightforward; others saw her as  arrogant and out of touch. She had the good fortune to face a divided and demoralized opposition. Her foreign and defence policy did not depart from the post-war consensus of alliance with USA, retreat from Empire and involvement in Europe. But she gave an impression in 1982 when she fought Argentina over the Falkland Islands that she still had some of the old spirit of the British Empire about her. Her gradually harsher approach to relations with Europe also suggested that here she might take a new approach. This toughness earned her the nickname 'The Iron Lady'. Margaret Thatcher fell from power in 1990 when her Cabinet colleagues lost confidence in her ability to lead them. The main issues were the ill-judged poll tax, an unpopular local tax which she decided to introduce. This showed that she was out of touch with public opinion and it worried Conservative MPs who knew they had a general election to face within two years. But it was Thatcher's increasingly anti-European approach which led to the main quarrels with her Cabinet. Most of her closest colleagues were willing to support the creation of a European currency and closer links with Europe, but Thatcher was showing signs by the late 1980s that she wished to depart from the consensus on this matter. In 1990, the Conservative ministers and MPs voted to dismiss her as their leader and hence she lost her job as Prime Minister, to be replaced by John Major.

there is sufficient evidence, and some of it quite recent, that different Prime Ministers follow different styles of leadership; second, because the way in which a Prime Minister behaves is subject to considerable external pressure, which varies from time to time, and which affects the type of leadership that is exercised. There is quite a body of literature on this subject, but one analysis which is particularly useful is that of Philip Norton. He divides Prime Ministers into four groups:

1 *Innovators*. Some Prime Ministers have an individual goal they wish to achieve, with their own party often not fully committed to supporting it. This clearly affects how they work and what type of leadership role they adopt. Examples of this type of leader include Thatcher and Edward Heath. It might be possible to put Blair in this category too.
2 *Reformers*. Some Prime Ministers have the desire to implement the ideological agenda of their own political party. An example here would be Clement Attlee, the Labour Prime Minister in the years 1945–51.

3 *Egoists.* Those in this group are simply power-hungry and wish to remain in power at all costs, without really having a clear idea of what they wish to achieve. Harold Wilson is sometimes seen as falling into this category, as is Tony Blair by some of his critics.

4 *Balancers.* Prime Ministers of this sort face grave difficulties in their political parties, or perhaps in the country as a whole, and their main aim is survival and the maintenance of peace. John Major can be seen as one of these, as can James Callaghan, and maybe Harold Wilson, if we are to be charitable.

Whether we agree with Norton's analysis or not, it is quite clear after a moment's thought that the idea that there has been some progressive growth in the power of the Prime Minister, or that there is a single typical style of

---

Box 12.3 John Major

Major was Prime Minister from 1990 to 1997, taking over from Margaret Thatcher, and won one further election victory for the Conservatives in 1992, rather to his surprise. He was more willing to work with his colleagues than Thatcher had been and he projected a much softer and less combative image than his predecessor. But in many respects he continued her policies: he had, after all, been a senior Cabinet minister during Thatcher's period as Prime Minister, so he might be expected to follow her policies to some extent. On Europe, he was willing to be more friendly to our partners in the EEC and he signed the famous Treaty of Maastricht which  set up the European Union. Major also abandoned the hated poll tax. But the economic policy he followed was thoroughly Thatcherite, involving further privatization and continued efforts to reduce government spending and borrowing. Further moves towards the development of a more business-orientated approach in the civil service and in the public services were also continued, as was the tough stance on law and order. So Major differed from Thatcher on matters of style rather than substance. In 1990, after all, when it was clear even to Thatcher that she would be dismissed by her colleagues, she had thrown her support behind Major as her successor, because she was sure that he would continue her work.

Activity

It is only really possible to judge a Prime Minister after he or she has served a few years in office; so you should keep an eye on Gordon Brown and try to assess where he fits into Norton's scheme. Try to make an early assessment. Giving evidence, make a case for saying that Brown fits into all the categories of Prime Minister given in Norton's analysis.

leadership, is clearly wrong. Thatcher was a strong and overbearing Prime Minister, but in 1990 she fell from power as a result. John Major, one of the longest-serving Conservative Prime Ministers, ran an extremely collegial system, working closely with his colleagues.

Tony Blair, for all his critics, allowed the Chancellor of the Exchequer, Gordon Brown, to run the economic policy of the country virtually by himself, while concentrating his own efforts on other areas of policy. It may be that Brown, in response to criticisms that were made of Blair, may move away from the presidential style. In the end, the saying of a Prime Minister at the beginning of last century, H. H. Asquith, is still true: 'The office of Prime Minister is what its holder chooses and is able to make of it.' It remains to be seen into which category of Prime Minister Brown will fall.

Box 12.4 Blair and Brown

The second most important person in the British executive is often the Chancellor of the Exchequer, who runs the government's economic policy. A strong economy is the key to electoral success for a party in government, and the great ideological divisions of the twentieth century, which until recently defined the outlook of the major political parties, have been over economic policy. Prime Ministers in the past have often been reluctant to allow a Chancellor too much leeway because of the significance of this role. Ted Heath and Harold Wilson tended to dominate economic policy themselves. Thatcher had a love–hate relationship with her two most significant Chancellors, Geoffrey Howe and Nigel Lawson. She fell out quite spectacularly with the latter over currency policy, leading to Lawson's resignation in 1989. Blair had also, by all accounts, a tempestuous relationship with his long-standing Chancellor, Gordon Brown. It is widely believed that Brown had always wanted himself to become Prime Minister, and that in 1994, when Blair was elected as party leader, he made an informal arrangement with Brown at the Granita, an Islington restaurant, agreeing to this succession. In 2005, Blair confirmed that he would resign at some point in his third term, and it was generally assumed that

the Labour Party would then choose Brown to replace him. This of course came to pass in the summer of 2007, although throughout 2006 Blair seemed very reluctant to name the day.

There had also been rumours throughout the Blair premiership that the two men quarrelled from time to time over policy. Brown was sometimes portrayed as a more genuine Labour politician, committed to some vestiges of 'Old' Labour values. This was despite the fact that in many respects Brown had followed a Thatcherite economic policy. Blair had virtually surrendered control of all economic policy to Brown and this control extended beyond the economy, since public spending has an impact on all aspects of social policy. So Brown largely ran Blair's domestic affairs. This may make us reassess the view that the Prime Minister under Blair became a presidential, even a regal, figure. British government under Blair looked in practice more like a partnership of two than a monarchy. It seems possible that the Brown premiership will be more presidential than Blair's, for the very good reason that Blair actually wasn't very presidential.

Tony Blair and Gordon Brown together on a walkabout in Sheffield

? *Question:* Describe what is meant by 'prime ministerial style'.

12.7 Limitations on the power of the Prime Minister

The Prime Minister's power is limited in a number of significant ways. As has been said, different Prime Ministers have different styles and different aims.

Prime ministerial overload

Prime Ministers have a large number of roles to perform. From one angle this gives them great power, but from another, it limits their power, because it will mean that they are constantly besieged by demands on their time. This will essentially tire them and make it necessary to delegate responsibility and hence hand power down to others. A hard-working person like Gordon Brown will be in a better position to cope than most people, but even he will get tired as the pressure mounts.

The Cabinet and ministerial colleagues

This topic will be dealt with more fully later, but clearly it limits the freedom of action of any Prime Minister to a large extent. No Prime Minister can survive for long without the support of the majority of his or her Cabinet colleagues. It is important that they support their Prime Minister whole-heartedly in what she or he plans to do. The fall of Thatcher in 1990 is often said to have been largely the work of her Cabinet. She had been becoming more and more unpopular in the country as a whole as a result of the poll tax (or 'community charge' as she preferred to call the new local tax she introduced), and because of the presidential style of her leadership. In 1990 there was a challenge to her leadership of the Conservative Party, which was perfectly legal according to the party's rules. The system meant that there were potentially three rounds of voting among Conservative MPs, with new candidates entitled to stand in both the first and second round. Only Michael Heseltine stood against Thatcher in the first round and he won fewer votes than she did, but he gained a sufficient number to damage her authority to such an extent that her Cabinet colleagues persuaded her, in a succession of face-to-face interviews, not to stand in the second round, thus leaving the way open for John Major to be elected and hence to become Prime Minister. So, in a bloodless *coup d'état*, Thatcher was removed from office to a large extent by the work of her colleagues. John Major also had difficulties in his second ministry with some of his Cabinet, particularly John Redwood and Michael Portillo, because of their under-hand opposition to his policies, especially on the subject of Europe and also because of their own leadership ambitions. Blair had to work very closely with Brown, his Chancellor of the Exchequer, and according to some commentators there were sometimes periods of friction between the two men. Brown enjoyed the advantage of being able to reshuffle the Cabinet thoroughly when he took over as Prime Minister, hence ensuring the exclusion of his enemies and rivals.

The Prime Minister's own political party

This is an extension of the last point. Beyond the Cabinet there are the MPs and the officials who run the party, and then the wider membership in the country who meet annually at the party conference. A Prime Minister has to retain the support of the party in order to succeed. Blair was fortunate in being able on the whole to change his approach to policy and ideology in step with changes of opinion in his party. But at times, on certain issues he seemed to go further than they wanted. In 2003–4, over Iraq, university costs for students and foundation hospitals, he found himself struggling to win votes in the House of Commons despite having, on paper, a huge majority. In November 2005, he lost a vote in the House of Commons, for the first time in his premiership, when 49 Labour MPs rebelled on the Terrorism Bill. In 2004, there were even rumours that a significant number of Blair's Cabinet colleagues were dissatisfied with his leadership and would have preferred Gordon Brown as leader of the party. By 2005, this pressure had led Blair to take the unprecedented step of announcing that he would cease to be leader of the Labour Party during his third term, and hence virtually hand the position over to Brown. This dented Blair's authority to such an extent that, according to credible reports, when he was undertaking his post-election Cabinet reshuffle in the summer of 2005, he was forced to modify his plans to restructure the Office of Deputy Prime Minister and to move the Secretary of State for Education to another job, because the two people concerned (John Prescott and Ruth Kelly) objected. Gordon Brown as Prime Minister needs to balance the Blairite and the 'Old' Labour wings of his party.

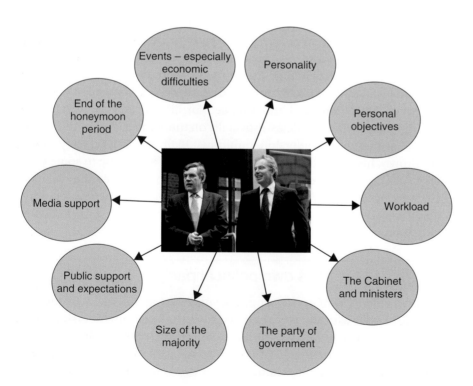

Figure 12.1   Factors limiting prime ministerial power

The size of the Commons majority

Tony Blair was blessed between 1997 and 2005 with two very large majorities, won in successive general elections. This was an important factor in his success, and in his ability – and his government's ability – to get programmes passed in Parliament. However, it is arguable that because his majority was so huge, some dissidents on the backbenches were more willing to cause trouble than they would otherwise have been. In 2003–5, there were a number of Labour backbench revolts which greatly reduced the government's theoretical majority in the Commons. So perhaps it is better to have a large (rather than an enormous) majority. But governments with small majorities, such as that of Wilson and Callaghan in the period 1974–9 and then of John Major in 1992–7, can suffer considerably in the event of a backbench revolt. Over Europe, Major had great problems within his own party and only managed to ratify the Maastricht Treaty with a majority of one vote because of backbench revolts. This sort of difficulty undermines a Prime Minister's authority more generally, in the media and among the voters as a whole. Blair found this out for himself in his third term, with a reduced majority, and his first defeat in 2005 on the Terrorism Bill. Brown has of course inherited this slimmer majority from Blair and in March 2008 he faced back-bench rebellions over his Counter-Terrorism Bill.

Public opinion

MPs and the party faithful will be happy with a Prime Minister who is ahead in the opinion polls, but will tend to show their concerns when public opinion turns against the Prime Minister. This was an important factor in the fall of Thatcher: as the opinion polls turned against her, MPs in her party who sat for marginal constituencies began to fear that if she were allowed to continue in power she would lose them their jobs at the next general election, and they were therefore willing to support a rival as party leader. In 2007, Brown enjoyed a 'Brown bounce' in the opinion polls, but no honeymoon lasts forever.

Media support

If a Prime Minister is to be popular and hence successful, he or she needs the support of a large section of the media. This is, in itself, dependent on the popularity of the Prime Minister. The Murdoch press is often credited, especially by the newspapers themselves, with having more influence than they really have, but when they transferred their support from Major to Blair in the mid-1990s, it was certainly harmful to Major's electoral chances. However, if Major had still been popular in the country, it is very unlikely that the *Sun* and *The Times* would have changed sides in the way they did. Brown initially enjoyed a very favourable press, largely because of the novelty factor.

Honeymoon period

A Prime Minister can generally expect support during the first years of his or her premiership, but gradually this support begins to decline. This was certainly true of Major and Blair. Major's honeymoon period was short-lived (1990–2); Blair's was much longer, but it did eventually run out in about 2002. Thatcher, on the other hand, was at first never personally very popular with her party or the electorate, and her honeymoon really began after the Falklands conflict, three years after her election triumph of 1979. Brown's honeymoon was very short-lived: it lasted no longer than about three months and then came to a rather abrupt end.

Lame ducks

When Tony Blair announced in 2005 that he would stand down in favour of Gordon Brown, he started a process in which his authority gradually ebbed away. It was to be two years before he actually went, and perhaps the main problem was that he took such a long time leaving. Another difficulty was that he did not actually say precisely when he would go, and pressure grew in 2006 for him to step down sooner rather than later. Ministers became less sycophantic, and MPs openly spoke against Blair. What is more, a quarrel began in the Labour Party over whether Brown should take over, or some other Blairite instead. This aura of decline and drift was reminiscent of the last years of Major's government, although the problem there was falling opinion poll ratings. By 2006, Blair was also facing these, in addition to the uncertainties over when exactly he would stand down. But this lame duck experience for Blair was a great advantage for Brown, since it gave him the chance to claim that his appointment meant a change with the past. One Prime Minister's lame duck is the next Prime Minister's honeymoon.

The feel-good factor

If the electorate is happy, it will tend to be satisfied with its Prime Minister. This especially applies to economic prosperity. Low unemployment rates, low levels of inflation and an absence of major financial disasters are all good for the Prime Minister's authority. Major's loss of popularity followed very quickly after the Black Wednesday currency crisis of 1992, which undermined public economic confidence in his government. The popularity of the Conservatives in the early 1990s was also associated with the 'negative equity' problem caused by the crash in the housing market. Foreign policy triumphs like the Falklands War of 1982 are also good for a Prime Minister's reputation, but are not always easy to arrange, as Tony Blair discovered over Iraq.

'Events, dear boy, events'

When the legendary Conservative Prime Minister, Harold Macmillan (1957–63), was asked by a journalist what he most feared, this was what he

---

Box 12.5 The Deputy Prime Minister

For more than 200 years there was no Deputy Prime Minister, and then, in the late twentieth century, the office seemed to have become semi-permanent. It could be argued that this shows the growing importance of the office of Prime Minister. If the Prime Minister is indispensable, he or she must have a deputy. Somebody has to be deputed to have a finger on the nuclear button. The first Deputy Prime Minister was Clement Attlee, who was in coalition with Churchill during the Second World War. After 1945, when Attlee himself became Prime Minister, he appointed Herbert Morrison as his deputy. Anthony Eden was Churchill's deputy, but after 1955 there was no one in the post until the Conservative, R. A. Butler, was appointed Deputy Prime Minister to Harold Macmillan in 1962–3. There followed another long gap until 1979, when first William Whitelaw (1979–88) and then Geoffrey Howe (1989–90) were appointed to the post by Thatcher. After Howe, the office was vacant until Major made Michael Heseltine his deputy in 1995. John Prescott was Deputy Prime Minister from 1997 to 2007 – throughout Blair's premiership. In practice, the appointment seems to be made largely in order to help the Prime Minister in his or her prickly relationship with the political party. There seems to be nothing in the role itself which cannot be done within the Cabinet Office or be deputed to others in the Cabinet. But the growth of Cabinet committees in recent years does mean that an important figure is needed to chair them, and this may be another reason for the rise in the profile of the office. The appointment of a Deputy Prime Minister does not affect the true hierarchy within the Cabinet, which places the Chancellor of the Exchequer, the Foreign Secretary and the Home Secretary as the most important figures after the Prime Minister. Mrs

Thatcher appointed Whitelaw because of his legendary skills with the 'grandees' of the party and the 'Wets', with whom Mrs Thatcher always felt uncomfortable. Blair appointed Prescott in the same spirit in 1997, in order to keep the working-class left wing of the party in order. Both Whitelaw and Prescott were noted in their different ways as very smooth political operators, behind a rather eccentric, thoroughly English veneer of buffoonery. Major appointed Heseltine perhaps as a sort of replacement for Whitelaw, but also to keep a potential rival out of trouble. At first, Prescott combined his post with being Secretary of State for the Environment, Transport and the Regions, but was relieved of some of these duties after some embarrassing problems. The Office of the Deputy Prime Minister was then set up for Prescott and, until May 2006, it retained responsibility for local government, planning, housing, voting and social exclusion, but these functions were presumably transferable, and would not obviously form part of what most people would expect to be the job description of a Deputy Prime Minister. Prescott was aided in this work by no fewer than five government ministers. In 2006, after an embarrassing sex scandal, Prescott was relieved of all these duties, but kept the title (and pay) of Deputy Prime Minister. Then, just as it seemed that the job would become a permanent part of the British Constitution without anyone really noticing, it all came to an end. When Brown became Prime Minister in 2007, he did not appoint a deputy, but instead chose Harriet Harman, who had been elected Deputy Leader of the Labour Party by the party membership, as Leader of the House of Commons, Minister for Women and Labour Party Chair. It looks as if the Deputy Prime Ministership did not survive John Prescott's eventful career.

drawled in reply. He meant that unforeseen events can crop up, especially perhaps abroad, which tend to throw the political system into chaos and are sometimes difficult to handle. Macmillan perhaps had in mind the Suez crisis of 1956, which was caused by Colonel Nasser's seizure of the Suez Canal and which then led to a major diplomatic and military failure for Britain and to the 'retirement on grounds of ill health' of the Conservative Prime Minister, Anthony Eden, but which allowed Macmillan himself to become Prime Minister.

> **Question:** Discuss the view that the limits on the power of the Prime Minister are too few and too ineffective.

12.8 The Cabinet

Members and size

Brown's first and second **Cabinets** consisted of 23 members of the government, with four more junior ministers listed as also attending; the precise number varies from time to time but it is generally about that size, or a little larger. Blair's last Cabinet had also been 23-strong, with one additional attender. Cabinet ministers are all members of the Commons or Lords, mainly the former. Every Cabinet member since 1945 has been a member of the party which has won the previous general election – that is to say, there have been no coalition governments since then. The Prime Minister will always be a member of the Cabinet, and acts as the chairman of the meeting. The other great offices of state are also always in the Cabinet: Chancellor of the Exchequer, Home Secretary and Foreign Secretary. All the other ministries are generally represented in the Cabinet too, but a certain amount of discretion is allowed to the Prime Minister on whether to include the more minor ministers, and whether to include the Chief Whip or the Chairman of the Party.

The Cabinet: the chief ministers who work with the Prime Minister (who is also a member of the Cabinet) in running the country. 'The Cabinet' also describes the regular meetings of these members of the government.

Harriet Harman arriving at Downing Street on her first day as Deputy Leader of the Labour Party

Meetings

The Cabinet meets roughly once a week while Parliament is in session. Meetings are called by the Prime Minister and it is up to him or her when these meetings take place. Some Prime Ministers have used the Cabinet more frequently than others: Blair was not a great exponent of Cabinet government, and some of his Cabinet meetings only lasted for half an hour or so. Others have had two-day meetings, and 'Away Day' meetings at Chequers, the Prime Minister's official country residence, to discuss strategy – for example, in the run-up to a general election – but these are rare events.

Cabinet secrecy

Cabinet secrecy is an important constitutional convention or rule. For 25 years after a meeting, what has been said there is considered secret. The reason for this is to encourage open discussion between colleagues, which would be difficult to achieve if their disagreements were made public. Cabinet secrecy is closely linked to the idea of Cabinet collective responsibility, which will be discussed below. It is also part of a more general culture of confidentiality in British government: the view that discussions between individual ministers, and between ministers and their civil servants, are confidential. Like all good constitutional conventions, this one is frequently broken. Leaks occur, and ex-Cabinet ministers publish their diaries and memoirs. Harold Wilson famously leaked to the press the fact that he had held a Cabinet meeting to tell his colleagues not to leak the details of Cabinet discussions to the press. Former Cabinet ministers are now supposed to show an early draft of their memoirs to the Cabinet Secretary before publication. This followed revelations in the published diaries of Richard Crossman and Barbara Castle. But it did not prevent subsequent revelations by Tony Benn and Alan Clark. There are no sanctions which, in practice, can be used against a former minister who reveals secrets. After she had resigned as a minister in the previous year, Clare Short in 2004 made quite damaging revelations drawn from information she had seen as a Cabinet minister in the run-up to the war with Iraq, including the fact that the Secretary-General of the United Nations and members of the UN Security Council were bugged by British Secret Services. Nothing was done to punish her. In 2008 the Information Commissioner ruled that Cabinet minutes of discussions about Iraq in 2003 should be made public, but the government appealed against this ruling.

Cabinet collective responsibility

The great constitutional convention, or rule, which concerns the Cabinet says that all the members of the Cabinet are together (or collectively) responsible for all the actions of the government. In fact this is now extended to collective ministerial responsibility, which involves all the junior ministers outside the Cabinet too. The Shadow Cabinet adopts a similar approach, in the rather different circumstances of opposition. The doctrine of collective responsibility has three basic points:

1 The discussions in Cabinet can involve disagreement and are kept secret (see above).
2 Once a decision has been made, the Cabinet must stick to it collectively. Ministers must not criticize each other in public. If a minister does

disagree with the agreed line on something, he or she must resign from the government, but can carry on as a backbench MP. Alternatively, they could just maintain a respectful silence on the issue. Resignation is most likely if the issue about which there is disagreement is one closely linked to the minister's own responsibility or particular interests, or if it is a matter of great national importance.

3   If the government is defeated on a vote of no confidence in the House of Commons, the whole government must resign, and there will be a general election. The Prime Minister cannot resign individually in such circumstances and pass the job on to another member of the Cabinet. The only time since the end of the Second World War that a government has been defeated on a vote of no confidence was 1979, when the Labour government of James Callaghan did not have a majority in the Commons, and when, in any case, a general election was imminent.

The most important resignations from Blair's government on the grounds of collective responsibility were in 2003 by three ministers who disagreed with the government's decision to send troops to Iraq. The leading figure here was Robin Cook, as Leader of the House of Commons, a Cabinet minister and also a former Foreign Secretary. There were some famous resignations under Thatcher which came about because ministers disagreed with aspects of policy: Michael Heseltine in 1986, Nigel Lawson in 1989 and Geoffrey Howe in 1990. Heseltine's resignation was interesting because not only did he disagree with the decision taken by his colleagues, he also said when he resigned that Thatcher had not allowed a full discussion of the issue (the Westland helicopter case) in the Cabinet.

But there are also interesting examples of ministers who were allowed, and even encouraged, by the Prime Minister to remain in the Cabinet despite the fact that they were known to disagree with government policy. Most recently, in 2003 Blair persuaded Clare Short to stay on as Overseas Development Secretary even though she was known to oppose the war on Iraq. He did this because he did not want two Cabinet ministers to resign at once, and because he told her she would be involved after the war in channelling overseas aid to Iraq. Short remained in the Cabinet, but a few months later resigned, because of the ridicule that had been heaped on her by the press for her apparent hypocrisy over the matter. It was well known after 1992 that a number of members of Major's Cabinet disagreed with the Cabinet line on Europe, but they were not forced to resign. In the first Thatcher government (1979–83), there were also disagreements over economic policy which did not lead to resignations. It is clearly difficult to maintain complete Cabinet agreement, and unrealistic to expect that it could be maintained. Since collective responsibility is a constitutional convention, the Prime Minister is free to interpret it as he or she thinks best. In 1969, Harold Wilson allowed public Cabinet dis-

Table 12.2 Brown's second Cabinet (2008)	
Prime Minister First Lord of the Treasury Minister of the Civil Service	Gordon Brown
Chancellor of the Exchequer	Alistair Darling
Secretary of State for Foreign and Commonwealth Affairs	David Miliband
Secretary of State for Justice and Lord Chancellor	Jack Straw
Secretary of State for the Home Department	Jacqui Smith
Secretary of State for Defence; Secretary of State for Scotland	Des Browne
Secretary of State for Health	Alan Johnson
Secretary of State for the Environment, Food and Rural Affairs	Hilary Benn
Secretary of State for International Development	Douglas Alexander
Secretary of State for Business, Enterprise and Regulatory Reform	John Hutton
Leader of the House of Commons (and Lord Privy Seal), Minister for Women, Labour Party Chair	Harriet Harman
Secretary of State for Work and Pensions	James Purnell
Secretary of State for Transport	Ruth Kelly
Secretary of State for Communities and Local Government	Hazel Blears
Parliamentary Secretary to the Treasury and Chief Whip	Geoff Hoon
Secretary of State for Children, Schools and Families	Ed Balls
Minister for the Cabinet Office, Chancellor of the Duchy of Lancaster	Ed Miliband
Secretary of State for Culture, Media and Sport	Andy Burnham
Secretary of State for Northern Ireland	Shaun Woodward
Leader of the House of Lords (and Lord President of the Council)	Baroness Ashton of Upholland
Chief Secretary to the Treasury	Yvette Cooper
Secretary of State for Innovation, Universities and Skills	John Denham
Secretary of State for Wales	Paul Murphy

agreements over trade union reform and then again, in 1975, he permitted ministers to campaign on different sides of the debate over the European referendum, saying that he had suspended the constitutional convention.

Cabinet committees

The Cabinet looks rather unimportant until we consider the wider governmental system in which it is located. There are a large number of Cabinet

committees and sub-committees which depend on the Cabinet for their existence. Their number and importance grew after 1945, although until as
recently as 1992 their composition and functions were secret. Some political
scientists argue that since the 1970s, these committees have been somewhat in
decline, but they are still significant. After the 2005 election, the number of
Cabinet committees (and sub-committees) was cut from 61 to 44, but Blair
announced that he wanted them 'to assume a more central role in the operation of the government', perhaps in answer to criticism that he had used them
less in his first two terms. Cabinet committees are appointed by the Prime Minister, and they either deal with a particular area of policy (a standing committee) or a particular crisis or issue that crops up (an ad hoc committee). The
Prime Minister will chair some committees, and appoints the chairs of the
other committees, often using the Deputy Prime Minister, the Chancellor of
the Exchequer or some other senior Cabinet member. The committees make
decisions that have the force of Cabinet decisions, or they prepare papers for
the Cabinet itself. If the members of a committee disagree on a subject (which
is rare), the topic can be taken to the Cabinet for a decision. In 1997, Tony Blair
invited the leader of the Liberal Democrat Party to join a Cabinet committee
that was set up to discuss policy on constitutional reform, and Paddy Ashdown
accepted. This was unusual in constitutional terms, since previously all
members of these committees had been members of the majority governing
party or were neutral civil servants. Blair did this because the Liberal Democrats were closely associated with Labour in constitutional reform. When
Charles Kennedy became leader of the Liberal Democrats, he stopped attending the Committee. Probably the most famous Cabinet committee is the War
Cabinet, much loved by the media, which is brought together when a war
breaks out: in recent years, for example, over Iraq (2003), Afghanistan (2002),
Kosovo (1999), Iraq (1991) and the Falklands (1982). The committee consists
principally of the Prime Minister, the Secretary of State for Defence, the
Foreign Secretary and the leading military chiefs. Another favourite with the
media is 'COBRA' (Cabinet Office Briefing Room A, originally abbreviated BRA,
but changed by some intelligent spin-doctor into COBRA), which is used for
meetings about civil emergencies like floods and terrorist attacks.

Cabinet Secretary and Cabinet Office

There is an important civil service department which works with the Cabinet:
the Cabinet Office. It is headed by the Cabinet Secretary, currently Sir Gus
O'Donnell, who is the senior Home Civil Servant. The Cabinet Secretary
attends Cabinet meetings and takes the minutes. He has a regular, weekly
meeting with the Prime Minister, and there will also be less formal contacts as
required: his office is in Downing Street. He is responsible for managing the
whole Cabinet system and is therefore in charge of helping the Prime Minister

coordinate government policy and supervise government ministers and civil servants. The Cabinet Secretary has a weekly meeting with the senior civil servants from all the government departments, which helps inter-departmental liaison. In effect, the Cabinet Office is part of the Prime Minister's informal 'department', and the Prime Minister will be in very frequent contact with the Cabinet Secretary. The existence of this Office helps to explain why the Prime Minister can survive without a major department of his or her own. It also suggests that the old question about who is in charge, Prime Minister or Cabinet, is really not the right question to ask: the Prime Minister and Cabinet work together, and the Cabinet Office helps them to do this.

 Question: Assess the role of the Cabinet in government decision-making.

12.9 What factors influence the Prime Minister's appointments to the Cabinet?

Although the Prime Minister has great power in the area of appointments to the Cabinet, there are also considerable limitations on that power. This makes us reflect on whether the theory that we have prime ministerial government in the UK is correct.

Constitutional conventions

There are certain constitutional conventions that the Prime Minister must observe when forming a Cabinet. Cabinet members must be in Parliament, and the great majority must be in the House of Commons. It is possible to import into the Cabinet an important person from outside the world of politics, and make him or her a Lord, but the normal route is through the Commons.

It was generally thought that ministers needed to come from the majority party in Parliament, of which the Prime Minister is, by definition, the head, and as far as the Cabinet goes this is true. However, when Brown became Prime Minister he asked Paddy Ashdown, former leader of the Liberal Democrats, to join the Cabinet as Minister for Northern Ireland. Ashdown could see that this would damage his own party and refused. But Brown did appoint Digby Jones, former head of the CBI, as a junior minister (but not in the Cabinet) in the Lords in 2007. It emerged that Jones was not a member of the Labour Party and probably had Tory sympathies, but he was willing to 'take the Labour whip' – that is to vote with the Labour Party in the House of Lords. If there is a coalition, new rules apply to appointments to the Cabinet, but there has not been a coalition government in the UK since 1945.

Another convention that the Prime Minister cannot ignore is that the heads of the chief ministries cannot be left out of the Cabinet – for example, the Chancellor of the Exchequer, the Home Secretary or the Foreign Secretary.

Personal judgement

The Prime Minister will follow his or her own personal judgement when making appointments to the Cabinet. Friends and political allies will obviously be easier to work with than rivals or enemies. Blair was on terms of personal friendship with Peter Mandelson, Lord Irvine and Lord Falconer, for example, all of whom gained important positions in the Cabinet. Gordon Brown promoted his friends Ed Balls and Des Browne.

The 'One of Us' syndrome applies also. The Prime Minister will work best with others from the same strand of the party. Thatcher was fond of asking of people: 'Is he one of us?' She wanted to be associated with right-wing Conservatives (Thatcherites) and she despised the One-Nation Tories – or 'Wets', as she called them. Similarly, Blair was happiest with New Labour, Third Way people rather than Old Labour.

There is also the 'Tent' syndrome, to use the analogy of the US President Lyndon B. Johnson. He claimed that it is better to have people who are potential rivals or threats 'inside the tent' rather than outside it, where they may do more damage.

Abilities

The abilities of the available potential ministers need to be considered. Some people of outstanding ability will be almost impossible to exclude from the Cabinet. The Prime Minister will look for people with particular skills.

- They need parliamentary skills in debating, public speaking and answering questions.
- Ministers require administrative ability, since they will have to run a large government department.
- A Cabinet minister should ideally have had experience as a junior minister, perhaps in a number of departments.
- A politician needs political cunning.
- A requirement of modern Cabinet ministers is that they should be good on TV.
- Ideally, not too much scandal should be associated with them in the fields of sex and money.

Specialisms

MPs tend to have specialisms; they concentrate on particular areas of government from the beginning of their careers, speak on debates on these subjects and get onto the select and standing committees which deal with them. Hence, these specialists will be best suited for the ministerial jobs in their particular field. For example, Douglas Hurd was a Foreign Office civil servant before becoming a politician, so he was well suited to becoming Foreign Secretary under Thatcher and Major. Frank Field had been Chair of the Social Security Select Committee, so seemed ideal for the job as Pensions Minister in 1997.

External factors

There are many external factors that might limit the range of choice available to the Prime Minister. The media have their favourites and their hate figures, and the Prime Minister will inevitably be affected by this. For example, Peter Mandelson was never popular in the press, and this may have influenced Blair in his decision to sack him from the Cabinet (twice). This same sentence could have been written with the name David Blunkett substituted for that of Mandelson.

The party is a significant factor. Certain ministers are very popular with the party, making it difficult to get rid of them, or creating pressure to appoint them. Clare Short allegedly held onto her post in the Cabinet in 2003 despite her opposition to the war with Iraq because of her support in the Labour Party, although after a while she decided to resign herself. This becomes a crucial factor if the Prime Minister is weak, with a small majority, under media pressure or facing external crises.

All parties are coalitions of different factions and tendencies, and the Prime Minister generally has to balance these when forming the Cabinet. Thus Blair held onto Prescott to please Old Labour. Thatcher always had Whitelaw in the Cabinet as a tame representative of the Tory landed gentry.

'A ministry of all the talents'

This phrase was used 200 years ago to describe what we would now call a coalition government. Gordon Brown resurrected it in 2007: he claimed he would draw on government experts regardless of their political views. In fact, at the centre in the Cabinet, this made little difference because, as has been said, Ashdown refused to join. But a number of junior ministers and government advisers came from outside the Labour Party. In other respects, Brown's new Cabinet did try to balance New Labour (e.g. the Miliband brothers) and Old Labour (e.g. left-winger Alan Johnson) as well as one convert from the Conservatives (Shaun Woodward).

The inherited Cabinet

A newly appointed Prime Minister (or leader of the opposition) will often find a Cabinet (or Shadow Cabinet) already in place. Since these people will generally have played a major part in electing the leader, and will have worked as a team for some years already, it will be very difficult to change them for new people immediately. In this way, Major had to live with his Thatcherite inheritance, and Thatcher took six years from her appointment as leader of the Conservative Party to get rid of all of the 'Wets', as she called the Conservative ministers who disagreed with her hard-line policies. All but seven of Brown's Cabinet in 2007 had served in previous Blair Cabinets, and the newcomers were all in relatively minor jobs. In addition, in the Labour Party, the Shadow Cabinet members are all elected by the party, and the only influence the leader of the party has over this is to assign the particular roles to each of the elected members. This situation severely limits what a Labour leader in opposition can do. This rule ceases to apply, however, once Labour is in government, although it is clearly difficult for the Prime Minister to sack his colleagues immediately.

Diversity

Blair had eight women in his last Cabinet and Brown had five in his first and six in his second: this is a higher proportion of women to men than in the House of Commons, but obviously less than in the population as a whole. Jacqui Smith was made Home Secretary in 2007, the first woman to hold one of the three top Cabinet jobs; women generally tend to get the more lowly Cabinet jobs. In terms of race, there have been, and still are, several very effective Cabinet ministers of Jewish origin, but currently no member of the Cabinet is black or Asian, although Baroness Scotland (of Afro-Caribbean origin), appointed Attorney General by Brown, has the right to attend Cabinet meetings when required by a discussion of legal matters. All in all, diversity has not been a subject for discussion to any large extent in the UK when it comes to a Prime Minister choosing his or her team, unlike in the USA.

Activity

Look at the current membership of the Cabinet and assess the reasons for each appointment – you may need to use Google to find out a bit about the biography of the members. Why were they appointed? Which of the criterion given in the section above about appointments to the Cabinet apply in each case? Were they appointed for their experience, for their role within the party, to balance factions, because of loyalty to the Prime Minister, because they were inherited or because of their experience?

Question: What factors affect the appointment of ministers?

12.10 Do we have Cabinet government?

In summary, it is useful to look briefly at the case for and against saying that the Cabinet is the dominant force in the executive.

Yes: the Cabinet is the dominant force

The Cabinet has a dominant role in British government; it has considerable 'resources' at its disposal. As has been said earlier on in this chapter, Walter Bagehot believed that the British system of government was indeed dominated by the Cabinet. It had a central coordinating role, since it was the 'buckle' that linked government to Parliament. The central constitutional doctrine of Cabinet collective responsibility seems to support such a view. It is the entire Cabinet that resigns in the event of a vote of no confidence in the Commons, not just the Prime Minister. When this happens, there has to be a general election. Cabinet solidarity and Cabinet secrecy support this essential principle, which emphasizes the central role of the Cabinet. A positive analysis of the modern role of the Cabinet certainly includes an important list of functions which clearly demonstrate the Cabinet's continued importance:

- Major governmental decisions need the formal approval of the Cabinet.
- If there is a dispute between ministers, or a genuine split in the government over policy, the 'final court of appeal' is said to be the Cabinet. Once it has spoken, everyone in the government has to agree, or pretend to agree or resign.
- The Cabinet acts as a brake on over-hasty action: the Prime Minister or individual ministers may be encouraged to think twice if the Cabinet urges caution.
- The Cabinet is a secret forum of debate, with everyone of importance on hand to offer views. That way a really high-level discussion on a difficult issue will take place.
- The Cabinet legitimizes government decisions. If a decision is known to have been made in the Cabinet, it acquires the authority of Cabinet support, in the eyes of the party, Parliament and the people. It is not just the decision of one person, the Prime Minister.
- The Cabinet is the symbol of the collective executive. It tells us that we are governed not by one person, but by a group. If it did not meet regularly, we would not have that reassurance.

- In times of war, the importance of a collective approach to government is emphasized when the War Cabinet comes into existence, although this is a scaled-down version of the real thing, and is technically a Cabinet committee.
- Prime Ministers who ignore the Cabinet face criticism from academics and, to a lesser extent, their colleagues. This is because there is quite a strong feeling in British politics that the Cabinet should not be ignored. Blair was criticized for this, especially towards the end of his period in office. As a result, when Brown took over in 2007, he tried to give the impression that his approach would be more collegial and that he would treat the Cabinet with more respect.

No: the Cabinet is not actually so powerful

Many modern commentators have suggested that the UK has prime ministerial, not Cabinet, government. By meeting in so-called 'bilaterals' – one-to-one meetings with individual ministers – the Prime Minister undermines the Cabinet. The growing 'presidentialism' of the Prime Minister has been stressed by Richard Crossman (in 1965) and Michael Foley (in 2000). The argument is that as Cabinet government has declined, so prime ministerial government has risen. The failure of the Cabinet to subject the case for war with Iraq to close scrutiny led Peter Hennessy to accuse it of being 'the most supine [spineless] Cabinet since 1945'. This was seen in particular in the fact that the Attorney General's advice on whether the war with Iraq would be legal according to international law was only given to the Cabinet in the form of a brief summary and that no member of the Cabinet asked to see the full version.

There is plenty of evidence to suggest that the Cabinet is not, in practice, very powerful:

- It meets infrequently, generally only once a week while Parliament is in session, and less often while Parliament is in recess.
- Its meetings are quite short – under Blair, sometimes only half an hour.
- Since the 1960s, the Cabinet seems to have declined in importance, meeting less frequently and in shorter session than in the past. More broadly, there have been accusations from former ministers for some time (for example, Richard Crossman under Harold Wilson, Michael Heseltine under Margaret Thatcher and Clare Short under Tony Blair) that the Cabinet is being sidelined.
- It is undermined by the existence of so many committees; these are where the real work of government goes on. All that the Cabinet does is to apply a rubber stamp of formal approval to what has been decided elsewhere. This point raises the question, however, of what we mean when we talk about 'Cabinet': do we mean the formal weekly meetings (which seem to

be less important nowadays) or do we mean the complex system of Cabinet committees? Cabinet committees are actually less numerous and probably less important now than they were 30 years ago, but they still play a significant role in the system of government.

- The power of the Prime Minister over the Cabinet is considerable. The Prime Minister calls the Cabinet into session, decides how long the meetings will be and how often they will be held, decides the agenda and the number and composition of the committees, and edits the minutes. Ultimately membership of the Cabinet is also decided by the Prime Minister, since he or she appoints and dismisses ministers. From time to time, Prime Ministers 'reshuffle' the Cabinet, promoting some ministers and demoting others all at the same time. The PM can create whole new ministries and amalgamate others, and decide if a ministerial job is worthy of a seat on the Cabinet. The Prime Minister is responsible for drawing up a code of conduct for ministers and for deciding whether ministers should resign if they break any part of the code.

SUMMING UP

Different Prime Ministers have different styles. Tony Blair was noted for three main features in his approach to government. The first two of these distinctive characteristics are ones that he shares with some other Prime Ministers, but the third is unique. First, Blair tended to work with a strong team in Downing Street, who enjoyed his trust and with whom he conducted business in an extremely informal way. Some critics have argued that his personal advisers have enjoyed more power than Cabinet ministers – Anthony Adonis in the Downing Street Policy Unit, for example, being the real power behind government educational policy. But this informality and tendency to work with an 'inner ring' of trusted friends is not new. Most post-war Prime Ministers have worked in this way, although Blair may have taken it further than others did. Second, Blair certainly ran the Cabinet down in status, at least in terms of the formal meetings. Although this continues a trend first observed in the 1960s by Richard Crossman, Blair took it to a new level. The way in which the Attorney General's advice on the legality of the war with Iraq was not even discussed in the Cabinet, and not even given to Cabinet members in its full form, symbolizes this very well. Third, Blair shared his power with another extremely powerful minister, the Chancellor of the Exchequer, who was, broadly speaking, given control over most aspects of domestic policy, and even latterly made some forays into the foreign arena, visiting Africa in 2006. This duopoly at the heart of British government is virtually unique in modern politics. It suggests, perhaps, that Brown's premiership will not, in terms of the style of government, be markedly different from Blair's. As Chancellor of the Exchequer, Brown enjoyed a close relationship with his political advisers, such as Ed Balls, and he was notably dictatorial, gaining a reputation as the 'Iron Chancellor' in his relations with Cabinet colleagues. The main difference between a Brown and Blair premiership may simply be that Brown will continue to run the treasury while also attempting to take over Blair's national leadership role. It will be fascinating to see how this shapes up.

> **?** *Question:* Discuss the view that 'the Cabinet no longer makes the key decisions'.

Further reading

M. Burch and I. Holliday, *The British Cabinet System* (Harvester, 1996): academic study of the Cabinet and wider executive core.

M. Foley, *The British Presidency* (Manchester University Press, 2000): lively and famous study of the modern Prime Minister's role.

P. Hennessy, *The Prime Minister* (Allen Lane, 2000): classic study by a master of anecdote and analysis – eminently readable.

P. Hennessy, *Cabinet* (Blackwell, 1986): still relevant and lively.

N. McNaughton, *The Prime Minister and Cabinet* (Hodder, 1999): straightforward analysis, ideal for the AS beginner.

J. Major, *Autobiography* (HarperCollins, 1999): straight from the horse's mouth – what it was like from the inside.

James Naughtie, *Rivals* (First Estate, 2002): radio presenter tells the story of the Brown–Blair relationship.

Robert Preston, *Brown's Britain* (Short Books, 2006): a study of the 'Iron Chancellor'.

A. Rawnsley, *Servants of the People* (Penguin, 2001): amusing analysis of a high-class journalist.

R. A. W. Rhodes and P. Dunleavy, *Prime Minister, Cabinet and Core Executive* (Macmillan, 1995): lively academic launch of the idea of a core executive.

Peter Riddell, *The Unfulfilled PM* (Politico's, 2005): lively biography of Blair.

M. Smith, *The Core Executive in Britain* (Macmillan, 1999): updates and develops the core executive theme.

M. Thatcher, *The Downing Street Years* (HarperCollins, 1993): the tragic story of Thatcher's rise and fall, as told by the lady herself.

Websites

www.cabinet-office.gov.uk (Cabinet Office site)

www.number-10.gov.uk (Prime Minister's site)

www.ukonline.gov.uk (for links to government departments)

www.direct.gov.uk (guide to UK government)

Ministers and Civil Servants

Making connections

As has been said, this topic links into the last one: after all, senior ministers are members of the Cabinet. The important question of where power really lies in the UK is also carried on here. The relationship between the elected and the unelected parts of government is briefly dealt with, and might provide an area for further study through case studies. Case studies might involve the study of a government department, or of a quango: these bodies have websites and it could be interesting to test the value of the Freedom of Information Act by seeing what they can tell you about themselves. If quangos and civil service departments don't excite you, then a study of a scandal associated with the resignation of a minister might be more interesting: look in the newspaper archives.

CHAPTER 13

Ministers and Civil Servants

KEY TOPICS

- Ministers and accountability
- Ministerial resignations
- The civil service: traditional features
- Changes to the civil service since 1979
- Open government and freedom of information
- The relationship between civil servants and ministers

SETTING THE SCENE

The last chapter dealt with the Prime Minister and his senior ministers in the Cabinet. But there are other elected members of government: the junior ministers. This chapter looks at the role and work of all ministers, both within the Cabinet and outside it. It then turns to the work of the civil service, the permanent, non-elected officials who work with the ministers in the executive.

13.1 Ministers and accountability

The Cabinet is composed of ministers, and outside the Cabinet there are junior ministers who support their Cabinet colleagues in running the departments of state. The number of ministers in each department depends on its importance and size. Junior ministers divide into three groups. First, Ministers of State, who are often quite significant political figures who will deputize for the Secretary of State and be expected to speak in the Commons on a particular area of departmental specialization. Second, Parliamentary Under-Secretaries of State, whose role is less important than the Ministers of State, working perhaps in a smaller department. Finally, the lowest order of minister are the Parliamentary Private Secretaries (PPS), who are MPs, often at the beginning of their careers, and who are assigned to individual ministers to give support. They are sometimes nicknamed 'bag carriers' because they often seem to be travelling around the country or abroad with their minister, hovering in the background with a sheaf of papers or an important file. Altogether, the government generally has about 90 members of the House of Commons on its payroll as Cabinet ministers, junior ministers, PPSs and whips.

Accountability or responsibility

The key concept connected with ministers is **accountability**, or responsibility as it was in the past known. The accountability of ministers in a democracy is to the people, and it may be direct, with the people hearing of the work of ministers through the media. More normally, however, it is said that ministers are accountable to the people through Parliament. This accountability or responsibility involves explaining policies and the work of government clearly and honestly. It also involves taking the blame if a mistake is made or a serious foreseeable problem is not avoided. This blame-taking may involve resignation.

There are two main forms of accountability in the British political system. First, the elected element of the executive (the Prime Minister, ministers at Cabinet level and the junior ministers) are collectively responsible to Parliament and hence to the people – this is collective responsibility. As has been said in chapter 12, on a vote of no confidence the entire government resigns and asks the electorate for its opinion of them. Even without a vote of no confidence, which is a rare measure, the government is held to account at each general election when the electorate votes on the government's past record as well as their future plans.

The second form of accountability which needs to be discussed here is individual ministerial responsibility. This can be divided into two. First, departmental responsibility. Every minister, but especially a minister of Cabinet rank, is responsible to the people through Parliament for his or her work. If a major error or problem arises in a government department, the minister must be prepared to explain it to Parliament, and if it is serious enough, the minister must resign. One aspect of this accountability is that a minister is expected to tell the truth to Parliament. Again, it is a resigning matter if the minister is found to have lied or concealed the truth. A further aspect is that the minister is expected to be responsible to some degree for the work of the civil servants in his or her department, who are not personally answerable to the people or Parliament for what they do. Second, there is also a form of accountability which is labelled 'personal responsibility'. Ministers are responsible for their own personal behaviour and if they do not maintain high standards of moral conduct they are expected to resign. This usually is a matter of sexual scandal, but can also involve financial irregularities.

> **Accountability**: the way in which a person is held responsible by someone else for his or her work, and must explain truthfully what has been done, and must apologize or resign in the event of some failure.

Question: Define 'individual ministerial responsibility'.

13.2 Ministerial resignations

There are five reasons why a minister may resign:

1 *Non-political reasons.* A minister may simply wish to return to the back-benches or, in the famous words used first by Norman Fowler when he resigned from Thatcher's Cabinet, 'spend more time with the family'. A more recent example of this is the resignation of Alan Milburn as Secretary of State for Health in 2003. There are always suspicions expressed in the press when this happens that a minister is actually resigning because of the third reason given below. So it was assumed that Fowler was out of sympathy with Thatcher's style. But unless a minister says that this is the case, we cannot really quarrel with the reason he or she gives for resigning.

2 *After a vote of no confidence in the House of Commons.* As we have already seen, every member of the government resigns when this happens.

3 *On the doctrine of collective Cabinet responsibility.* If a minister disagrees with what the Cabinet decides to do, he or she must either pretend to agree or resign. This is also discussed in chapter 12.

Peter Mandelson, Secretary of State for Northern Ireland, announcing his resignation to the media

4 *Individual personal accountability.* If a minister is discovered to have done something which is considered morally wrong, it is generally felt that he or she should resign. Recent examples of this include David Mellor in 1992, for having an affair with someone who promptly told the lurid details to the newspapers; Ron Davies in 1998, for allegations of being 'picked up' by a homosexual on Clapham Common; Peter Mandelson in 1998, for failing to declare a large loan given him by another Labour politician, Geoffrey Robinson, when he applied for a mortgage; Peter Mandelson, for a second time, in 2001 after Blair had reappointed him, for applying personal pressure to get a British passport for an Indian businessman S. P. Hinduja, who was under investigation in his own country. The two resignations of David Blunkett (in 2004 and 2005) were also on grounds of personal misconduct. In 2008, Peter Hain resigned because he was being investigated by the police for alleged fund-raising irregularities.

5 *Individual departmental responsibility.* If a minister is responsible for a failure within his or her department he or she should resign. The famous example of this is Sir Thomas Dugdale, who resigned in 1954 after a failure in his department over the compulsory purchase of Crichel Down. The interest of this historical case is that the mistake was quite trivial and had been made by a civil servant who cannot by any stretch of the imagination be said to have been supervised directly by Dugdale. Although, apparently, Dugdale was keen to resign anyway for other reasons, it remains true that this type of responsibility for all actions within a department is by modern standards considered unusual. In 1982, the Foreign Secretary, Lord Carrington, and two other members of his department resigned for failing to prevent the Argentinean invasion of the Falklands Islands. This is a classic example of a minister taking responsibility for a major problem, probably largely to protect the Prime Minister's position. More recent examples include the resignation of Stephen Byers in 2002 as Secretary of State for Transport: this followed a series of problems in his department including difficulties over the failure of Railtrack, the privatized railway company, an email sent out from his political adviser, Jo Moore, encouraging colleagues to 'bury bad news' on 9/11, and an obscure quarrel with another public relations expert, Martin Sixsmith. In 2002, Estelle Morris resigned alleging she was not as 'effective' at her job of Education Secretary as she would like. She did not apologize for anything specific, but there had been a number of education problems, including those surrounding the introduction of the AS exams and their marking. In 2004, the minister responsible for immigration, Beverley Hughes, resigned after damaging whistle-blowing within her department which revealed that the immigration service had not been doing what she said it was doing, the final straw coming when the minister was exposed as having misled the public in a television interview. In 2006, Charles Clarke resigned after a series of problems in the Home Office, which

culminated in the damaging revelation that hundreds of foreigners who had been convicted of crimes in the UK with the recommendation from the judge that after their sentence had been served, they should be deported, had in fact been released from prison without this happening.

What factors decide when a minister resigns on the grounds of individual ministerial responsibility?

Constitutional convention

The British Constitution is unwritten, and ministerial resignations are governed by convention. It is true that this is now written out and made public in the document entitled *Questions of Procedure and Code of Conduct for Ministers*, but this document cannot specify what should be done in each instance. This was shown when David Blunkett resigned for the second time, in 2005; at first, the Prime Minister argued that although Blunkett had broken the code by taking employment after his previous resignation (rather than waiting for two years) and by not consulting the Committee of Standards on this employment, he should not be disciplined about it. So there is much room for flexibility and manoeuvre, and whether a minister resigns or not is really decided by political circumstances more than anything else.

The severity of the case

It is unlikely that any minister these days would resign on a relatively trivial matter like Crichel Down.

The speed with which a minister accepts responsibility

There is always a temptation to deny that a mistake has been made, but the case of Beverley Hughes in 2004 shows that an immediate apology and explanation is probably the best course of action, because she did not do this and, as a result, the problem festered and the press swarmed around the open wound. Trying to cover something up will only work if it is successful. Lying to Parliament or the media is a certain route to resignation if it is found out.

The confidence of the Prime Minister

Does a minister resign or is he or she actually asked to resign by the Prime Minister? Even if a minister resigns, the Prime Minister may refuse to accept the resignation. The support of the Prime Minister is obviously crucial. Blair supported Stephen Byers more than once before his final fall. He also made quite sure that he did not lose Geoff Hoon after the invasion of Iraq in 2003, which had thrown up some information about failures in the Ministry of Defence. In 1992, John Major was very keen to prevent his Chancellor of the Exchequer, Norman Lamont, from resigning after the Black Wednesday currency crisis, which was the most serious economic problem since the IMF loan of 1977. Lamont offered to resign, but Major persuaded him to stay on in order to calm the money markets. Lamont resigned, however, a year later, in part as a result of pressure in the media.

The strength of parliamentary criticism

Some ministers are popular among the government's backbenches which makes it difficult for them to be sacked, and helps them cling on to power. The governing party may see calls for resignation from the opposition as motivated by partisan spite and may rally around the minister. The opposition itself may have its own reasons for wishing the minister to remain. For example, Geoff Hoon had sympathy from MPs on the Conservative benches in 2003 because they had supported the war with Iraq. And in 2002, the Conservatives probably wanted Byers to stay on in power because he was so unpopular in the press.

Press and media attacks

The press has a legitimate role to play in politics in holding government ministers to account, since they communicate political information to the people. But journalists also have a tendency to pursue campaigns against some politicians merely out of a desire to show their power or because there is a tendency for newspapers to imitate one another and hence to gang up and bully a minister in trouble. This certainly has its impact. Mandelson's second resignation in 2001 owed much to media attacks, as did those of Estelle Morris, Stephen Byers and David Blunkett. On the other hand, the Prime Minister may wish to take on the press and try to face down the attacks. In the case of Hoon, this seems to have worked. Similarly, although the Deputy Prime Minister, John Prescott, became the butt of media attacks in 2006, as the scandal of his affair with his secretary was revealed, Blair refused to ask for his resignation. In a very curious move, in the reshuffle which followed the revelation of the scandal, Blair took away most of the responsibilities associated with the Office of the Deputy Prime Minister, but left Prescott with his job title and pay.

Decline in doctrine of responsibility?

If ministers were to resign whenever there was a problem in their department, the continuity of government would be lost because resignations would be so frequent. In addition, it does seem to be contrary to modern, more relaxed attitudes to morality for ministers to resign for having an affair. Nevertheless, there are probably just as many resignations now as there were in the past. Still, the idea of responsibility is being eroded, partly by changes to the civil service, which are discussed later in this chapter, and this may be a more serious matter. In 2007, after the latest failure in his department involving its failure to process the information sent from abroad concerning the conviction of British criminals, the Home Secretary, John Reid, refused to admit any personal responsibility and announced that a civil servant was to be sacked.

Box 13.1 Mysterious resignations

Although political scientists analyse the reasons for ministerial resignations according to constitutional principles, in the real world politicians are keen not to make the reasons for their resignation crystal clear. It is sometimes in the government's interests to make it look as though a minister has resigned because he or she has been hounded from office by a cruel set of journalists. When Estelle Morris resigned as Secretary of State for Education in 2002, she seemed almost too frank, saying that she was simply not tough enough for the job. In fact, she had presided over a number of departmental blunders and presumably was therefore resigning because she took responsibility for these mistakes. She was responsible in constitutional terms to the people (through Parliament) for running her department well. But by saying she was not good enough for the job, she made the Prime Minister look more managerialist, wisely moving his personnel around the business like the successful Chief Executive Officer of a multinational company.

David Blunkett's first resignation, in December 2004, was even more mysterious. According to the Prime Minister he resigned with his integrity intact. But the press revealed that he had had an affair with a married woman, and he was claiming to have fathered at least one of her children. In the past this would have been sufficient for a ministerial resignation on the grounds of individual 'moral' responsibility – a minister being expected to uphold high standards of decency. Most people would agree nowadays that Blair was right not to demand his resignation on these grounds. As he said at the time, even ministers are entitled to a private life. But Blunkett also admitted that he had used a House of Commons railway pass for his girlfriend (which is illegal) and his girlfriend (by then less friendly towards him) claimed that he had used his influence as Home Secretary to secure a very quick grant of a visa for her Filipino nanny. The official inquiry into the visa affair concluded that either Blunkett had wrongly supported the application (hence he was still resigning on the grounds of individual 'moral' responsibility; and also because he had lied about it), or that his officials had wrongly fast-tracked the application without him having specifically asked for it (hence he had presided over a departmental cock-up and was taking responsibility for that). By the time the inquiry reported, Blunkett had resigned. He made no resignation speech in the House of Commons: perhaps just as well, since, had he done so, he would presumably have had to explain why he was resigning.

Both Morris and Blunkett were widely praised among their colleagues when they resigned. But it did not help Blunkett much in 2005, when he resigned for a second time; all the public and media could remember was that in 2004 he had resigned over something disreputable, and that Blair had brought him back to the Cabinet in less than six months. But it was interesting to note that even in 2005, Blair continued to say that there was no stain on Blunkett's reputation, although he resigned, in effect, for breaking the *Code of Conduct for Ministers*. Blunkett continued to claim that he had done nothing wrong.

Question: Discuss the view that the convention of individual ministerial responsibility is no longer important in British politics.

Activity

Using the news websites (BBC, *Guardian*, etc.) and Google, research the case of Des Browne, Minister of Defence, whose resignation was demanded by the opposition parties and the press in April 2007 following the Iran hostages crisis. A number of British sailors and marines were audaciously kidnapped by the Iranian Revolutionary Guards while they were searching shipping in the Persian Gulf. After being held captive in Iran for nearly a fortnight, and being paraded on Iranian television, these British service personnel were released. Browne was responsible for the defence forces which had been humiliated by this incident. In addition, he then allowed the service personnel to sell their stories to the media for large sums of money, despite the fact that this was contrary to the Official Secrets Act and the fact that government servants owe a legal duty of confidentiality to their employer. When this decision was criticized in the media and by the opposition, Browne reversed his decision and forbade any more selling of stories to the press. But by then, two such stories had appeared in the papers and on TV. What are the rights and wrongs of the case? On what grounds was the resignation of the minister demanded? What was his defence against these demands? What happened in the end to the minister? Why?

13.3 The civil service: traditional features

The executive in all liberal democracies consists of two elements: an elected political element and an unelected body of professional administrators or bureaucrats. In the UK, the Prime Minister, the Cabinet and the ministers make up the elected, political group. The day-to-day work of administration is carried on by what is called the civil service. The name civil service is a reminder of how British government is built on ancient foundations. Civil servants are servants of the monarch, or, in modern terms, of the state. They are civilians, to distinguish them from the armed services, the military servants of the state. Many of the major government departments have their offices in the area of London called Whitehall and, as a result, the civil service is often referred to as 'Whitehall'. There are at present about half a million of these civil servants, working for the central government. In addition, local and devolved government in the country as a whole has a large number of local government officers in its employ. Political scientists are most interested in the top civil servants, who number about 4,000, and what follows

Box 13.2 Bureaucracy

In everyday usage, the word 'bureaucracy' has a negative sense: it means an overuse of paperwork, a love of petty regulation and the extension of power into regions which are best left outside the sphere of government. Right-wing politicians tend to use the word in this negative sense quite a lot, and it is not difficult to see many examples in everyday life (not just in government) of how there is a creeping tendency of managers and administrators to extend their work. But there is a perfectly neutral use of the word in political science. A bureaucracy is simply a civil service, or the administrative branch of a political system. As such, it does the really important work of running the country, of taxing and spending, largely (it is hoped in a democracy) in the interests of the people. There can be very few people who do not benefit in the end from the work of civil servants. This bureaucracy – in the neutral political science sense – can therefore be 'bureaucratic' (in the negative sense) or not, depending on how efficiently it is organized.

tends to concentrate on them. The civil service in Britain has changed greatly since 1979, and it is important to look at its traditional features before examining how they have changed in recent years. Finally, we need to consider how the two parts of the executive – the political and the professional elements – interact.

Traditional features of the civil service

The British civil service was thoroughly reformed in the mid-nineteenth century as a result of the movement for change which developed from the Northcote–Trevelyan Report of 1854. These changes resulted in the creation of a bureaucracy the main features of which are still with us even after the more recent developments which started with the election of Margaret Thatcher in 1979. The traditional characteristics of the Northcote–Trevelyan civil service are permanence, neutrality, anonymity and confidentiality. To these, we might add a fifth, which is that the senior civil service was expected to be a meritocracy of generalists.

Permanence

Civil servants form, according to the traditional model, the permanent part of the government, unlike ministers, who are elected politicians and who change with elections and resignations. These bureaucrats regard the civil service as their career and they expect to be in their posts for their working lives. This contrasts with senior civil servants in the USA, who mostly change with each change of President. Permanence is supposed to encourage a sense of duty (a 'public service ethos'), expertise and experience. It gives to British government a degree of continuity, which would be lost if the top civil servants were replaced with every change of government. This might be said to be particularly important in foreign policy, for example, where foreign

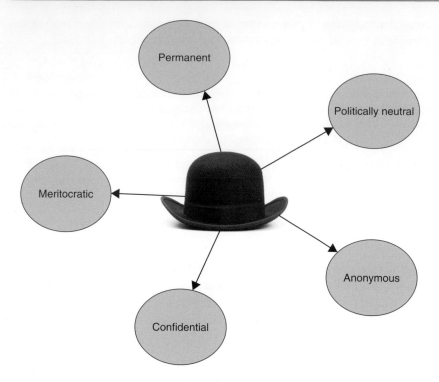

Figure 13.1   Traditional features of the civil service

countries have a right to expect Britain to maintain a consistent approach in its relations with them. The Foreign Office in the UK is often said, for example, to be more pro-Arab than its equivalent (the State Department) in the USA, and this would be a 'Foreign Office view', which belongs as much to the permanent officials as to their elected bosses.

Political neutrality

Civil servants are meant to be politically neutral or non-partisan. The advice they give should be expert and neutral, and not biased. They should be prepared to criticize a minister, rather than agree with him or her all the time. A group of 'yes men' would not give the best advice, so it is good for civil servants to debate freely with their ministers. Once a policy has been decided on, however, civil servants should implement it obediently, even if they disagree with it. The first part of this equation contrasts with the position in the USA, where the top civil servants are largely party appointments who are not expected to hide their allegiance.

Anonymity

Civil servants, on the traditional model, are supposed to be anonymous, and not subject to direct public scrutiny, or media attention. If they were known publicly, this would lead to questions about their neutrality. The doctrine of ministerial accountability or responsibility means that it is ministers (not civil servants) who report to Parliament on what their departments have done, and who are responsible to Parliament for any failures.

Confidentiality

Civil servants' advice to ministers is confidential, to use the polite British euphemism for secret. This enables ministers and civil servants to cover up mistakes, and, on a more positive note, helps civil servants to give frank advice. There may be security issues at stake too, which require secrecy in defence, foreign policy and market-sensitive economic matters.

Senior civil servants: a meritocracy of generalists

Prior to the Northcote–Trevelyan Report, senior members had been recruited on the basis of patronage. People who knew government ministers and royal courtiers were able to get well-paid and not particularly difficult jobs for their friends and relations: this was known at the time as jobbery. The civil service envisaged by Northcote and Trevelyan would recruit people for their permanent jobs by competitive examination, and at the senior level also on the basis of their university degrees. The point of this was to obtain the best recruits, to create an elite of government officials: a 'meritocracy'. As a result, the British civil service was supposed to be as successful and powerful as the civil service of Imperial China had been, and, to reflect this, senior civil servants took to calling themselves 'mandarins', the Chinese word for government official. British mandarins were not expected to have studied political science or public administration at university, as their counterparts in Germany and France were, but were 'generalists', people with a broad liberal education (generally in the classics), but with no particular expertise for being an official in, for example, the Ministry of Agriculture – apart from being able to read Virgil in the original.

 Question: What is meant by civil service neutrality?

13.4 Changes to the civil service since 1979

The British civil service was much admired for its professionalism in the years after Northcote–Trevelyan. But in the period after 1945 it came under scrutiny by reformers. The two traditional features which were most criticized were neutrality and meritocracy. The other features were not commented on very much, and the assumption was that they were reasonable and well suited to the British political system. Critics both on the left and right of the political spectrum argued that the advice of senior civil servants was not actually very neutral, because civil servants all shared the outlook and prejudices of a single class: the English upper-middle class. They were not in fact a meritocracy as the Victorian reformers had hoped, but were recruited on the basis of a modern form of jobbery, mostly from the universities of Oxford and Cambridge and the major public schools. The Labour Prime Minister Harold Wilson appointed a commission under Lord Fulton which, in its Report of 1968, recommended changes to the civil service to make it genuinely meritocratic and to allow civil servants from the lower grades of the profession to be promoted within the service. But since the civil service was left to implement these reforms itself, very little actually changed.

Thatcher's election in 1979, however, began a gradual process of reform to the civil service, which has changed the system radically. It is nevertheless true that, despite this, the civil service still operates to some degree according to the same principles as in the past. These principles have all been challenged, but an analysis of the British civil service at present will accept that it is still built on a modified version of the traditional principles of permanence, neutrality, anonymity, confidentiality and even meritocracy and generalism.

Reductions in numbers of civil servants

The main Thatcherite attack on the civil service had actually little to do with its traditional features, but was based on the view that it was expensive and over-manned. The New Right view, in fact, was that almost all state activity was illegitimate and that the 'frontiers of the state' should be 'rolled back'. It is also the case that all administrative and clerical work (in banks and insurance offices, for example) in the last 20 years has become increasingly automated. The civil service has been reduced in numbers since Thatcher started the process. In 1979 there were 732,000 civil servants; by 1999 there were 460,000. But by 2005 the number had grown again to 530,000, and at the beginning of 2007, there were 550,000 civil servants (which was down by 4,000 over the previous three months). In 2004, Blair's government announced ambitious plans to reduce the size of the service, on the basis of an efficiency review carried out by Sir Peter Gershon. This announcement was partly made in response to Conservative plans to do the same, and also to the way in which the figures were rising again. The plan was to reduce numbers to about the levels of 1999, but it remains to be seen whether this will actually be achieved. It may be worth noting that new technology is not cheap and that a reduction in the number of civil servants has not always resulted in a reduction in administrative costs. The installation of the latest IT equipment has often involved a scandalous waste of public money too. Generalist mandarins and reforming politicians have not proved particularly effective at managing change of this sort.

Attack on pay and privileges

Thatcher demanded more work from and gave less pay to a group of workers who in the past had been reasonably well cared for. This process has continued, although it is more evident at the lower end than at the top of the pay scales. Senior civil servants have continued to be awarded medals and honours when they retire.

Cost-cutting pursuit of efficiency

Starting with the work of the Efficiency Unit at 10 Downing Street, each government department was encouraged by Thatcher to reduce its costs. From 1982, the Financial Management Initiative was launched, also to save money. In 2004, both the Labour government and the Conservative opposition announced plans to reduce costs further, largely by sacking civil servants. The fact that these announcements were made more than 20 years after Thatcher had launched the process suggests that the pursuit of efficiency and lower costs has been a rather slow process.

Next Steps and executive agencies

The biggest change to the civil service began in 1988 with the so-called Next Steps programme. The idea was to hive parts of government departments off into semi-independence, setting up executive agencies, run (allegedly) on strict lines of efficiency; for example, the Benefits Agency, the Child Support Agency and the Teachers' Pensions Agency. By 1996, these agencies – which numbered 102 – accounted for 71 per cent of the civil service. This still left a core of Whitehall departments, headed by their mandarins, or senior civil servants, who continued to be directly employed by the state. The executive agencies are headed by chief executives, often not from a civil service generalist background, but drawn from the less rarefied and refined atmosphere of business and commerce. They tend to be run on business lines, which may or may not involve saving taxpayers' money. The growth of these agencies has tended to threaten traditional views of civil service accountability and anonymity. The chief executives have not been able to hide in the background and have been forced to give a public account of the activities of their organizations. Rather conveniently at times, this has meant that ministers have been able to blame the chief executives if something goes wrong, rather than taking responsibility for failures themselves, as was the theory in the past. Thus, in a speech in November 2005, the Prime Minister attacked the Child Support Agency for inefficiency, although he was presumably responsible for it, since it is a government body.

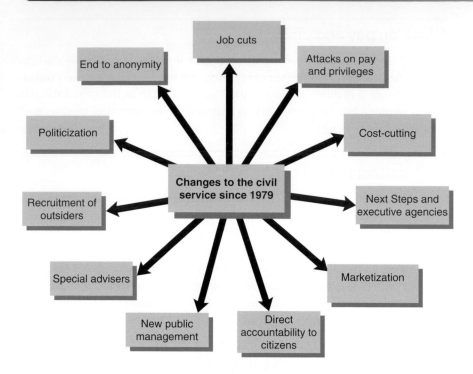

Figure 13.2   Changes to the civil service since 1979

Market testing, marketization and the Private Finance Initiative

From 1992, the civil service was encouraged to look to private enterprise to perform ancillary functions, and put cleaning, typing, etc. out to tender. Market testing, the first initiative in this area, involved each government department 'testing' the market to see whether any of its operations could be performed more cheaply by employing outside contractors rather than in-house employees. Marketization means the introduction of free-market methods into the working of government departments, by encouraging competition between different sections of the department in an effort to save money. One way that was used to involve business in government was to develop the Private Finance Initiative, which involves using private capital to develop building projects. Like the introduction of executive agencies these initiatives have the tendency to change the relationship between the civil service and ministers and to expose the former to more direct financial scrutiny. Labour has continued to follow this policy enthusiastically, especially where the development of large capital projects is involved. These are now largely funded by private capital in order to make the government's public sector borrowing requirement (an economic measure of legendary importance) look better than it is.

Direct accountability to citizens

From 1992, Major's government developed the idea of having a Citizen's Charter. The Charter was simply a statement of the rights of citizens in relation to public services. Although ridiculed at the time, this initiative brought in a change to practices across the whole of the public services. It brought in targets, performance figures, standards and a much more consumer-orientated approach. Again, this tends to mean that civil servants now relate directly to citizens rather than through the medium of the minister.

New public management

Since the 1980s, new management methods have been introduced in all areas of public service: state education, the National Health Service and the civil service. This system developed under Thatcher and Major; it was connected to the Citizen's Charter and continued to be enthusiastically pursued under New Labour. Its main features include an emphasis on hierarchy and differences in pay between the lower and higher grades, an aggressive approach to personnel management, the proliferation of paperwork – according to its critics – and an emphasis on target-setting and quality assurance.

Special advisers

Prime Ministers and ministers have always used outside advisers, but the widespread use of such advisers in the civil service developed most strongly under Thatcher, and continued to do so under Labour. In every government department at the senior level, there are now a small number of political advisers. These people undermine almost every feature of the traditional civil service: they are temporary appointments, they are generally well known – if not to the public, at least to journalists – and they are not expected to be neutral. They have a useful role to play in ensuring that government business is carried out and, above all, they help the career civil servants by acting as a channel of communication between the bureaucrats and the ministers. There seem, therefore, to be two civil services emerging in the twenty-first century at the top level: a traditional career civil service and a body of temporary political appointments who, in theory, are there to advise the minister, but who look a little as if they are actually also there to supervise the old-fashioned mandarins. It is worth keeping this in perspective though: in 1997 there were 38 special advisers in the civil service and another 8 in the Prime Minister's Office; in 2003, after six years of New Labour, the figures had risen dramatically to 81 and 27 respectively. But this needs to be set against the fact that in 2002 there were 4,020 senior civil servants in total. When he became Prime Minister, Gordon Brown announced his opposition to the Prime Minister's use of the royal prerogative and issued an Order in Council (a prerogative action) that took away from special advisers at Number 10 the right to give orders to civil servants. Brown announced that he would define the powers of special advisers in a civil service bill. There has also been an increased use by ministers of advice from think-tanks like Demos, Charter 88 and the Adam Smith Institute, which also may seem to undermine the mandarins.

Outsiders

There has been a growth in recruitment to the senior levels of the civil service of people from outside the government bureaucracy, with wider experience in the 'real world' and with professional expertise (as economists, lawyers, accountants, etc.). By 2007, it was estimated that one in five of the senior service came from this background. This undermines notions of permanence and the traditional model of recruitment. Nevertheless, it is worth remarking that after three decades of change, only a relatively small number of mandarins no longer fit the old Victorian stereotype.

Politicization

There were accusations that, under Thatcher, there was a tendency towards politicization of the civil service. This means that the supposedly neutral civil service becomes biased politically towards the party currently in power. In periods of one-party dominance (which we have enjoyed in Britain since 1979), this is obviously a possibility. The Prime Minister, after all, appoints the top civil servants, and promotions within departments are subject to the approval of the minister responsible for the department and, at the highest level, of the Prime Minister. It would not be beyond the realms of possibility that a meritocrat would see the value of dropping his or her neutrality in order to gain promotion. In the end, these accusations are almost impossible to substantiate: although civil servants are expected to be neutral, they are also expected to be loyal and discrete. Such accusations of politicization were also levelled against Blair. Thus, the Cabinet Secretary in 2001, Sir Richard Wilson, was accused of doing political business for Blair, for example when Peter Mandelson resigned in 2001. It may be worth pointing out, though, that the debate over the politicization of the civil service is a little out of date by now, since the growing use of political advisers in government departments means that a form of open politicization is now officially recognized. In addition, the institutionalized role of political advisers means, in effect, that the old-style traditional mandarins can be left to be as neutral as they were in the past, because the politics has already been taken care of by the advisers.

An end to anonymity

In recent years, this too has been under attack, as some of the evidence given above also shows. In addition, it is worth pointing out that civil servants are sometimes called before Commons select committees. This happened to David Kelly in 2003, when he was so publicly berated by the Commons

---

Box 13.3 The Nolan Report

The Nolan Report into Standards in Public Life (1995) was critical of the civil service in some respects, and led to the creation of a Civil Service Code. This code has encouraged 'whistle-blowing' by civil servants. This means that civil servants are encouraged to reveal any maladministration in their departments which it may not be possible to remove through the normal channels. Whistle-blowing may involve a civil servant in breaking the rules of anonymity and also implies a change in the confidential relationship between ministers and civil servants. The code also laid down guidelines to stop the revolving door syndrome, by which senior civil servants would, on retirement, be taken on by private firms in areas related to their previous department. If this practice is stopped, it will help prevent politicization of the civil service and may also reduce the costs of government.

Foreign Affairs Committee that it may, according to critics, have contributed to the depression which then led him to take his own life. Judicial and other inquiries into failures of government policy have also involved the naming of specific individual civil servants: for example, in the report in 2002 on the arms to Sierra Leone scandal, and in the Scott Report on arms to Iraq in 1996.

A civil service bill

There have been suggestions made for at least a decade that an Act of Parliament should be passed to define more clearly the position of the civil service, especially in terms of its relationship to ministers. Essentially, the Act would give parliamentary approval to the traditional model of the role of civil servants, but establish it on a modern basis in terms of the impact of recent changes that have been made to the civil service like the growth of political advisers. This would be part of a growing trend towards the piecemeal codification of the British Constitution which has been evident since 1997. In October 2004, the government published a draft bill for consultation, but the measure has not been enacted. If passed, this Act would define the role of political advisers, clarifying what they can and cannot do, give a clear statement of the core principle of civil service neutrality and govern the recruitment and management of civil servants. The Green Paper, *The Governance of Britain*, published by Gordon Brown as almost his first action when he became Prime Minister in 2007, promised to introduce the civil service bill in the next parliamentary session and to include in it a definition of the powers of special advisers, denying them the power to give orders to civil servants.

'Not fit for purpose'

On being appointed Home Secretary in 2006, John Reid boosted the morale of his civil servants by declaring publicly that the Home Office was 'not fit for purpose'. As more and more administrative problems emerged, Reid continued to blame his workforce, until, early in 2007, he announced plans to break up the Home Office and hive off a separate Department of Justice at some unspecified time in the future. It is difficult to find a better image of the new role of the Civil Service, as the butt of ministerial attacks. What makes Reid's comments unfair is that his own government had been running the Home Office for the past nine years, during which time it would have been possible to initiate the reforms required to make the department less unfit.

 Question: Discuss the role of the higher civil service in policy-making.

Box 13.4 Quangos

Quasi-autonomous non-government organizations (Quangos) are bodies that are funded and appointed by the government, but are partly independent of it, and are not part of a specific government department. The precise definition of what is and what is not a quango is not very clear. The classic analysis made in the Pliatzky Report of 1980 distinguished between advisory, executive and judicial quangos, or tribunals. The BBC (according to some definitions) is a quango. The Higher Education Funding Council, the body that finances universities, is also a quango. Locally, quangos help run hospitals as hospital trusts, and fund economic projects, as regional development agencies. Bodies like Ofsted, Ofwat and Oftel, which claim to regulate the public services or privatized industries, are also quangos. These quangos have been widely criticized in the past, both by Margaret Thatcher and by New Labour. They seem to lack democratic accountability: the people who run them are appointed and not elected, and they cost a great deal of government money. All efforts to reform them have failed, and their numbers have grown inexorably. The process by which state activity has been privatized, or partly privatized, has required regulation and new bodies to distribute government money. The reorganization of the civil service into agencies also justifies the existence of bodies which are to some degree free-standing and flexible – although technically agencies do not count as quangos. It seems impossible to carry on effective government in the modern world without using bodies like quangos. What is more, voter apathy, especially at local level, means that a system of appointing the members of these bodies rather than electing them is about the only practical way in which it can be done. In 2004, the Conservative opposition launched an attack on the growth of quangos, and in 2005, Gordon Brown responded by abolishing or amalgamating some of the ones that came within the Treasury's area.

13.5 Open government and freedom of information

A further area in which the role of the civil service has been modified in recent years has been in the development of a more open approach to government information, with the growth of open government.

Open government is the free access of citizens to government information. In some countries like Sweden and Norway, citizens have a right to access almost all government documents. The USA has a very strong Freedom of Information Act which means that it has been possible for British journalists to find out quite a lot about the UK's secret services by looking at CIA files. In contrast, there has been in the past quite a closed or secretive system of government in UK. The main features of this traditional British secrecy are:

- Civil service confidentiality. The traditional model of the civil service insisted that advice given by a civil servant to a minister was confidential or secret.
- Cabinet secrecy, under the doctrine of Cabinet collective responsibility.
- A general culture of secrecy in government: secrecy is particularly important in relation to security and defence issues, which have played a

significant part in British politics in the past century as a result of Britain's part in two world wars, the Cold War, the Northern Irish problem and the so-called war on terror.

- The Official Secrets Acts (1911 and 1989), which were passed to enforce secrecy on matters of defence and security, but also in other areas of policy too. These Acts make it a criminal offence for a government employee to release information without official permission.
- The control of government information by the Press Secretary at 10 Downing Street.
- The 'lobby' system, by which certain favoured journalists are given un-attributable briefings by the Press Secretary.

However, this tradition of secrecy in government is gradually being balanced by developments which mean that Britain is slowly being brought into line with other liberal democracies in this area. Furthermore, there has been a long tradition of a free press and of free speech in Britain, which has meant that the secrecy of the British state has, in practice, always been rather leaky. As a result, yet another of the traditional features of British government is being challenged, and there have been a number of developments in the movement towards more open government. These include the following:

- Hansard reporting of Parliament. At least Parliament itself has been open to reporting for more than 200 years. Hansard is the official record of everything said in Parliament and of all documents tabled as part of the work of Parliament.
- Parliament has been televised since the late 1980s.
- Justice must be seen to be done, and the judicial branch in the UK has always been open to reporting, except in exceptional circumstances (involving children, for example, or matters of national security). But the courts have as yet avoided the intrusion of television cameras.
- In answer to criticisms of the Thatcher regime, in 1992 John Major launched the Open Government Initiative. Civil Service departments were encouraged to open government up as much as possible to public inquiries. Major was keen that citizens should have full information about public services (school league tables, etc.) as part of the Citizen's Charter measure.
- The Nolan Report (1995) and Scott Report (1996), which followed inquiries into government scandals, both emphasized the need for more openness in government.
- The Data Protection Act (1998) came fully into force in 2001 and allows people access to information about themselves which is stored both electronically and on paper. The Human Rights Act (1998) also offers protection here too.
- The Freedom of Information Act (2000).

The Freedom of Information Act

The Labour government elected in 1997 pledged to bring in a Freedom of Information Act. The hopes of the Campaign for Freedom of Information, an important pressure group led by Maurice Frankel, were that government information would be made freely and cheaply available to citizens. Campaigners were to be disappointed by the legislation when it was finally passed, because it severely restricts what information can be made available. If a minister feels that the information might cause harm, he or she can refuse to allow it to be revealed; information held by the government about individuals or businesses can be kept confidential and not revealed to other individuals or businesses; security matters are still restricted; Cabinet secrecy is maintained; civil service advice remains confidential; and the cost for an individual to obtain information may be high.

But although modest in comparison with the corresponding measure in the USA, when the Freedom of Information Act came fully into force in 2005, it did make quite a difference to government in Britain. A post of Information Commissioner has been set up to ensure that both the Freedom of Information Act and the Data Protection Act are administered correctly, and people can appeal to this official if they are in dispute with a government department over information.

It is perhaps significant that in the days before the Act came into operation it was reported that some departments had started a major programme of document-shredding. In addition, late in 2004 the government announced that any information given to investigative journalists would at the same time be published on the internet. This has been interpreted as an attempt to deter reporters from looking for a scoop among government records, because anything they discovered would immediately be available to their rivals. Early in 2005, papers relating to the Black Wednesday currency crisis of 1992 were revealed to a journalist who had used the Act to request them. This caused controversy, since the Conservatives claimed that the government was happy to reveal economic papers which might damage the reputation of a previous Conservative government, while being unwilling to release information that might lead to criticisms of its own economic policies. On a more positive note, in 2005 the Attorney General's advice made in 2003 to the Cabinet on the legality of the war with Iraq was made public, although it had taken a great deal of pressure to achieve. Even more surprising, early in 2007, the advice given by his civil servants to the Chancellor of the Exchequer, suggesting the dangers of his windfall tax on pension funds ten years before, was made public. Early in 2008, the Information Commissioner called for Cabinet minutes on the war with Iraq to be released.

Late in 2006, the government announced that it was considering making access to information a little more difficult, on the grounds of expense. The

Act limited access on the grounds of cost: up to a maximum of £600 for a government department and £450 for any other body which came under the scope of the Act. What was proposed was that these costs should be fully economic ones – that is, they should include the time taken to research the request by civil servants. It was feared that this would limit access in complex cases. In addition, the government said it was considering limiting access to people or organizations who were using the system too often; it suggested a limit of four requests per year. It remains to be seen what will happen as a result of these suggestions, which were received with howls of protest from the media and pressure groups.

To make matters worse, in 2007, a Private Member's Bill introduced by Conservative MP David Maclean passed the House of Commons which would have exempted much of the work of MPs from the Freedom of Information Act. The argument in favour of this was that the confidentiality of correspondence between constituents and MPs needed to be preserved. Cynics argued that the real reason for the bill was that it would have stopped the press from having access to information about MPs' expenses. The bill seemed to some to have underhand government support and the public outcry against it led, in the end, to it failing to pass Parliament, when no member of the House of Lords was found who was prepared to sponsor it.

Evaluation of freedom of information

Before leaving the subject of open government, it is worth asking whether it is always good to have open government, or whether it should be limited in some ways. Table 13.1 gives arguments for and against having freedom of information.

 Question: What is meant by open government?

13.6 The relationship between civil servants and ministers

One final view of the British executive that needs to be considered is whether in fact the whole system is actually run by the civil service. This is the main theme in the 1980s television series *Yes, Minister*. It is worth bearing in mind that this series was scripted by two former civil servants. The important question lying behind this debate is: what is the best way to describe the relationship between ministers and civil servants? There has been much debate

Table 13.1 Arguments for and against freedom of information

FOR	AGAINST
It is necessary to have free access to information if the executive is to be held to account by the people.	There are problems of security and defence which require official secrecy.
It is impossible to have a really free press without freedom of information.	There are issues of privacy which might be raised. The government holds information about its citizens which is confidential, and which most people would not wish to be made available to other people, even if they want to access to their own files themselves.
Freedom of information helps guarantee academic freedom, and allows academic researchers and think-tanks to help inform the policy-making process.	The government has information about businesses which should not be made available to their rivals.
Effective parliamentary scrutiny is impossible in a climate of secrecy.	Some information is sensitive, and if it were revealed, it might harm the economy or successful administration in other areas.
The work of pressure groups is enhanced.	Cabinet secrecy is an important constitutional principle and essential to ideas of collective Cabinet responsibility.
An effective opposition is only possible if opposition politicians have access to government information.	Civil Service neutrality is preserved by the confidentiality of civil service discussions.
In a democracy people have a right to know about how their government conducts itself.	Efficient government is best carried on in an atmosphere of relative secrecy. The cost on civil service time would be great if a very comprehensive system of free information were to be introduced. Most of this cost would be used in practice only to satisfy the curiosity of a few obsessive people, or to sell more newspapers.

among political scientists and politicians over the years about this, and four main 'models' have emerged. We will briefly describe them in what follows.

Traditional model

According to the traditional model, as has been said, ministers decide on policy and it is voted on by the people. Civil servants advise the minister, but once the minister has decided what course to follow, the civil servants then implement that decision. The minister is accountable to the people through

Parliament for what his or her department does. According to a phrase often used, civil servants are 'on tap, but never on top'. They are anonymous because only the minister is directly accountable. Their advice to ministers is confidential because they work in a trusting, cooperative relationship with them. They give neutral advice because such advice is best; it means that they will point out the problems in anything ministers suggest and will not agree with ministers just to flatter them. It might be pointed out that there are some problems with this traditional view of the relationship between ministers and civil servants. Is a civil servant's loyalty owed to the government of the day, or is it to the state itself? The only constitutionally valid answer seems to be that the civil servant is loyal to the Crown and hence to the state. This may lead to a conflict between loyalty to the minister (as demanded by the traditional model) and loyalty to the state. In 1985, for example, a senior civil servant, Clive Ponting, was put on trial under the Official Secrets Act because he revealed confidential information to an opposition MP about the controversial sinking of the Argentinean warship, the *Belgrano*. Ponting's defence was that he was acting in the interests of the state even if he was disobeying a minister. Although the judge advised the jury to convict Ponting, arguing that the interests of the state coincided with those of the government, the jury disagreed and the he was found innocent, although he had clearly not behaved like a good civil servant according to the traditional model.

New Right or bureaucratic over-supply model

This view influenced Margaret Thatcher and encouraged her to reform the civil service, and it certainly challenges the traditional model, suggesting that it is the civil servants not the ministers who are 'on top'. According to New Right analysis, civil servants ruthlessly seek to build up their own power simply in order to increase their numbers, pay and privileges. Whenever a policy was proposed by a minister, civil servants would just work out what was in it for them. Since reforms of the 1980s and 1990s, and the substantial reduction in the size of the civil service, it now seems unlikely that this is still true, although further cuts in manpower in 2004 suggest that there may have been something in it.

Left-wing or Marxist model

This is another analysis which criticizes the traditional model and is based on the view that the civil service has more power than might be thought. According to this model, put forward, for example, by Tony Benn, the civil service is dominated by an upper-class elite whose ideas are formed by their education and background. They will inevitably oppose socialist measures, and use their power to obstruct a radical reformer as a minister. But if this is true, how was it possible for Thatcher to reform them?

Liberal democratic model

This is a saner model than the previous two, but it does not accept the traditional picture entirely. Like the previous two models, it stresses the strength of the civil servants and the weakness of the ministers. The main points are these:

- Ministers are outnumbered by their civil servants and so they obviously find it difficult to win a debate with them.
- Ministers are temporary, civil servants are permanent. Ministers change their jobs on average about every two years, although under Major and Blair there was a tendency towards longer terms for ministers in their departments. Again this enables the 'departmental view' developed by the permanent civil servants to prevail, and this will limit a minister's freedom of action. In ten years of Labour government, John Reid was, successively: Minister of Transport, Leader of the House of Commons, Secretary of State for Scotland, Secretary of State for Northern Ireland, Secretary of State for Health, Secretary of State for Defence and Home Secretary.
- Ministers are amateurs, civil servants are experts. This is especially the case when a minister comes into office after a long period in opposition. None of Blair's ministers in 1997 had ever been in Cabinet before.
- Civil servants have the detailed information, ministers do not. Ministers have to rely on civil servants to provide them with evidence.
- Civil servants can work together, and undermine a minister by coordinating their opposition to a policy they dislike collectively. This view of the civil service is called the 'Whitehall Village model'.
- Ministerial overload. Ministers have other roles to play: in Parliament, in their party, before the media, as a constituency MP. So they are not really on top of their jobs. Civil servants have more time.
- Even if a minister gets a policy proposal past the civil servants, it is they who are responsible for implementing it, and they can subtly change it in the process if they like.

When we consider the points made above, it is hardly surprising that ministers have been keen to appoint political advisers to support them within the department they are trying to run. Put crudely, at times the minister needs spies in the department and needs to have some politically reliable supporters there.

SUMMING UP

We can return finally to the idea that British government is not actually a battle for supremacy between rival players: the Prime Minister and ministers; the Prime Minister, ministers and the party; government and Parliament; ministers and civil servants. The core executive model of British government stresses that all the players mentioned above have a part: each group has its strengths (its 'resources') and each has its limitations. There is always tension between the groups, but not conflict; it is a creative tension, which helps keep things balanced. Taking this core executive view and applying it to the relations between ministers and civil servants, we have to acknowledge that the 'traditional model' on this subject is not really acceptable. The fact is that senior civil servants will play an important part in making policy. And, in constitutional terms, some people might argue, it is not entirely wrong that they should play this role, at least not until the civil service is so thoroughly politicized that it becomes a servant of the government and not of the state.

? *Question:* Explain the relationship between civil servants and ministers.

Further reading

Christopher Foster, *British Government in Crisis* (Hart, 2005): wide-ranging analysis of recent changes and challenges.

J. Greenwood, R. Pyper and D. Wilson, *New Public Administration in Britain* (Routledge, 2002): academic dissection of the core executive.

P. Hennessy, *Whitehall*, 2nd edn (Pimlico, 2001): a classic work by the master of lively engaging writing on politics.

N. McNaughton, *The Civil Service* (Hodder, 2000): very reliable introductory topic book.

R. A. W. Rhodes, *Transforming British* Government, 2 vols (Macmillan, 2000): lively and stimulating academic study.

Derek Scott, *Off Whitehall* (I. B. Tauris, 2004): an insider's view of government at the centre.

Websites

www.ukonline.gov.uk (for links to government departments)
www.civil-service.gov.uk (Civil Service)
www.homeoffice.gov.uk (Home Office)
www.mod.gov.uk (Ministry of Defence)
www.fco.gov.uk (Foreign and Commonwealth Office)
http://www.direct.gov.uk (guide to government)

The Judiciary

Making connections

The judiciary is often not the favourite topic of students of politics because it doesn't seem to be a very 'political' one. It worth trying to find recent contemporary cases in the newspapers, especially in the field of judicial review and human rights, to illustrate this area: they are more numerou than might be thought and they provide a useful illustration of the political importance of the judiciary. There have been number of disputes between the government and the judiciary, and it is worth keeping an eye on the media for further examples, which in the present climate are probably likely to occur. The position of the highest court in the land (and the focus of most attention from political scientists) is the process of reform and this also adds to the interest of th subject. This chapter, especially the section on rights, links chapter 9 (on the Constitution) and the initial look at citizenship in chapter 1. The section on constitutional refor in chapter 9 links to the reform of the law lords discussed in this chapter.

CHAPTER 14

The Judiciary

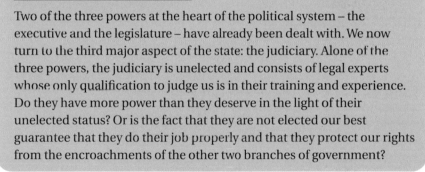

KEY TOPICS

- What is the judiciary?
- Judicial independence
- Judicial neutrality
- Rights and the redress of grievances

SETTING THE SCENE

Two of the three powers at the heart of the political system – the executive and the legislature – have already been dealt with. We now turn to the third major aspect of the state: the judiciary. Alone of the three powers, the judiciary is unelected and consists of legal experts whose only qualification to judge us is in their training and experience. Do they have more power than they deserve in the light of their unelected status? Or is the fact that they are not elected our best guarantee that they do their job properly and that they protect our rights from the encroachments of the other two branches of government?

14.1 What is the judiciary?

The judiciary: the third branch of government, which deals with judging, the law and the law courts. The word 'judiciary' is sometimes also used simply to mean 'the judges'.

In Britain, it is sometimes tempting to ignore the **judiciary** in a discussion of politics. The law seems more like a profession, like engineering or architecture, and it would be unusual to find a chapter on engineering or architecture in a textbook on politics. But it is wrong to take such a view, for several reasons.

First, the law and how it is interpreted in the courts is central to all politics. The job of the executive in large part is to propose changes to the law, and the function of Parliament is then to legislate, to make these changes into legal enactments. Parties contest elections on a manifesto promising changes to the law, and when elected they are supposed to carry out these promises of legislation. Pressure groups often also support specific changes in the law. So the democratic process is bound up with making law, and hence the question of how law is then enforced in the courts is of considerable significance.

Second, the common law tradition in Britain means that judges themselves make law, as well as judge by it. Common law, the law of our land, is older than Parliament and it works by judges setting precedents in the judgements they make on each case (this is sometimes called 'case law'). Quite rightly, in a parliamentary democracy, Parliament can then make a new law which will overrule a judge's precedent for future cases. But in the detail of the law, the judges have a valuable legislative role to play. Parliament cannot legislate for every single case: that is the role of the judiciary.

Third, the executive and the participants in the political process as a whole are subject to the rule of law. If a politician is suspected of corrupt electoral practices, the law courts will be used to judge that politician, just as an ordinary citizen will be judged on suspicion of having committed a crime. Thus, Tony Blair was questioned by the police in 2006 and 2007 over the alleged breach of the law in the cash for peerages scandal. In the same way, maladministration in the executive is subject to legal scrutiny through what is called judicial review. From time to time, judicial inquiries are set up to look into matters concerning the government. The most important example in recent times was the inquiry led by Lord Hutton into the death of the government scientist Dr Kelly, which reported in January 2004. The judiciary is to some extent the watchdog of the whole political process. Without a written constitution, however, the role of the judiciary in the UK is in this area somewhat limited, at least in comparison with some countries, especially the USA.

Fourth, British citizens look as individuals to the judiciary to redress grievances and protect their rights. They may need to do this in the face of a government which is exceeding its powers or is acting unreasonably. The passage into British law of the European Convention on Human Rights in 1998 gives added force to this point.

A brief overview of the British judicial system

There are hundreds of judges and courts in this country. The system is made more complicated by the fact that there is a separate legal structure in Scotland, with its own courts and judges. Essentially, the legal system deals with two types of case: criminal and civil. There are separate courts for each.

Criminal courts

The arrest and prosecution of a criminal is the business of the executive, acting through the police and the Crown Prosecution Service. A crime is an action which is directed against the whole community, even if there is only one individual victim. So the state takes upon itself the prosecution and the punishment of the criminal, and the judiciary does the judging. Minor cases

The statue of Justice stands above the Central Criminal Court, fondly known as the Old Bailey, which until 1902 was Newgate prison and is a famous court for criminal cases in England

are heard in magistrates' courts. Magistrates, or Justices of the Peace, are generally part-time judges, often with no professional knowledge of the law. Their experience and training, and the support they receive from lawyers employed by the court to help them, enables them to hear cases involving, for example, minor motoring offences, theft, assault or drugs. More serious cases are sent to the Crown Courts: the Old Bailey is a well-known example of such a court. The system is different in Scotland, with most cases heard before the Sheriff or District Courts, and very serious ones going to a High Court.

Civil courts

If an individual (or group) is damaged, perhaps financially or in some other way by another individual or group, and if this is not a matter of criminal activity, the individual harmed can bring a civil case against the wrongdoer. So, for example, if an employee is wrongfully dismissed, or if a householder is in dispute with his or her builder over failure to complete a job, this may lead to a civil case. In such cases, the judiciary provides judgements according to the law of the land. At first, these may be in small-claims courts, or employment tribunals, where the case will be heard by people often even less professionally qualified than Justices of the Peace. Serious cases are heard in county courts, and the really difficult problems will be dealt with by the High Court. In Scotland the sheriff courts and the Court of Session are the equivalent of the county courts and High Court under English law.

The Court of Appeal

After judgement in the lower courts, in both civil and criminal cases, if people feel they have been unfairly treated in the trial, there may be a chance for an appeal. In an appeal, another court looks at the case again and decides whether it was properly conducted by the lower court. This is heard in England in the Court of Appeal.

The Supreme Court

Really important or difficult appeals may be heard in the highest court in the land, by the judicial committee of the House of Lords – i.e., by the 'law lords'. From 2009 this court will be called the Supreme Court, as a result of the Constitutional Reform Act of 2005. The judges who hear cases in this highest court of appeal are all highly respected and very experienced. The law lords (or Lords of Appeal in Ordinary, to give them their full title) generally meet in groups of five, drawn from a total team at present of twelve. In addition to their function as judges, the law lords also work as members of the political institution, the House of Lords, and they remain in the Lords as life peers even after they have retired as judges. By the Constitutional Reform Act of 2005, the judges of the Supreme Court will cease to be part of the House of Lords. In other respects, they will continue to work much as before, but with a new name and in a new building. This important reform is further discussed later on in this chapter and also in chapter 11 on the House of Lords.

Europe

There is an important European aspect to the judiciary, too. The European Court of Justice (ECJ) is the final court of appeal in matters of European Union law, and it therefore has jurisdiction in Britain over certain types of (largely economic) matters. It sits in Luxemburg, and the judges are drawn from all the member states of the European Union, including Britain. The European Court of Human Rights (ECHR) sits in Strasbourg, and is easy to confuse with the ECJ. It hears appeals under the European Convention of Human Rights, to which Britain is a signatory. Since Britain incorporated the convention into its law as the Human Rights Act in 1998, it is unlikely that there will be as many appeals to Strasbourg as in the past, but the option is still there.

 Question: What is the role of the judiciary?

Box 14.1 Law and justice

The law is easy enough to define: it is the rules made for citizens by the legislature as interpreted by the judiciary, and enforced by the executive, who control the police and prison service. In a democracy, all these three branches of government are responsible to the people they serve. Justice is more difficult. John Rawls, an American liberal political philosopher, says simply that it is 'fairness'. Justice is the ideal of a good system of law, and more widely of a well-run political system. It looks obvious, therefore, that our legal system should be based on justice. On top of the Old Bailey, London's old criminal court, is a statue of 'Justice', a beautiful woman dressed in a classical robe, blindfolded (because judges should be unbiased) and holding the scales of justice (because the judge needs to weigh the evidence carefully). Lawyers and their clients often appeal to the justice of their case, and one of the grounds for judicial review (discussed later in this chapter) is that the rules of 'natural justice' have been broken. But it doesn't take long to see that there can be problems in saying that law should be based on justice. There will be disagreements over what justice means. To some it is unjust to experiment on animals; to others it is not. But law should be clear: if a majority of the population wants to stop animal experimentation, it will be stopped by a law passed in Parliament. Consider another case: most people would say that it is wrong to cheat on a girl or boyfriend, but would you want to have this unjust action made illegal? Should people be put in prison for marital infidelity? Another problem is that in some cases the law is not seen as being based on justice. While the 30 mph speed limit is part of our law, it would not really be seen as being based on unchanging principles of justice, and many people do exceed the limit where they think they can get away with it. On the other hand, they would be conscience-stricken if they were to kill or injure a child while speeding. Should we obey a law which is unjust? At Nuremburg, where the Nazi war criminals were put on trial, the claim that the defendants were 'only obeying orders' was not allowed. This should be especially the case in a liberal democracy, where the penalties for breaking the rules are less severe than in Hitler's Germany. On the other hand, we should be able to campaign for a change in the law in a democracy, and some people argue we should wait until this change in the law, rather than break it as a matter of principle.

14.2 Judicial independence

Judicial independence: the freedom of the judiciary from interference in its activities by the other two branches of government, the executive or legislature, and also from pressure exerted by the media or public opinion.

It is best to begin by looking at the theory – why **judicial independence** should exist – and then at the practice – whether or not it does exist. There is some overlap between these two points, since if in Britain we feel that judicial independence ought to prevail, then it is likely that to some extent it will do so. There is also some overlap between judicial independence and judicial neutrality, and indeed some confusion between the two. Judicial neutrality will be dealt with later on in this chapter. Judicial independence also involves the judiciary being unelected, and hence independent of the pressure that may be exerted on them by public opinion. In the USA some judges are elected and as a result candidates up for election or re-election for these posts have to try to convince the voters of their fitness for office by being harsh in the punishments they hand down or claim they will impose if given the job. If the judiciary is independent of the government, of Parliament and of the influence of the electorate, it is more likely to be strong enough not to bow to the pressure of the media.

The theory of judicial independence

Liberal democracy

It is difficult to conceive of a liberal democracy which did not insist on the rule of law and on an independent judiciary. Judiciaries which are not independent, but which can easily be interfered with by the government, tend to be associated with totalitarian regimes like Stalin's Russia, where the judiciary willingly supported Stalin in his paranoid 'show trials' by which he killed the people he thought were plotting against him.

Separation of powers

This idea goes back to the eighteenth century (at least), when it was developed by the great French political philosopher, Baron de Montesquieu, in *De l'esprit des lois*, which was first published in 1748. Montesquieu believed there were three essential elements to a system of government: the legislature (which makes laws); the executive (which administers the laws) and the judiciary (which judges according to the laws). As far as Montesquieu was concerned, a well-organized political system was one where these three branches of government were kept separate. This idea was taken up by the framers of the American Constitution (1787) and it is still strongly supported in the USA. It is often said that in Britain the separation of powers does not exist, and that instead there is a practical 'fusion of powers', which is the precise opposite. This fusion is based on the constitutional idea that Parliament is sovereign, and on the political fact that in practice in a parliamentary system of government, the executive is able to control Parliament. However, the judiciary is left out of this account, and there is no reason to suppose that the judiciary should to any large extent be involved in this relationship of fusion. Even in Britain, then, in theory we adhere to the idea of a separation of the judiciary from the other branches of government.

The tradition of the common law

From quite early in English history, the judicial system was seen as a defence of the rights of the people against the encroachments of the King and his government. Even medieval kings were careful to respect the law, and Magna Carta (1215) is still revered as a document in which legal rights were defined very early in English history. In the Stuart era, when Parliament fought King Charles I, part of the strength of Parliament's case came from the support given to it by famous judges, like Edward Coke. Again, in the eighteenth century, the rights of the individual were defended against the power of a corrupt Parliament by the careful use of legal precedent. At each stage in this struggle, the fact that the judicial system was free from the control of king and Parliament meant that royal and parliamentary arrogance could be controlled by an outside agency.

The rule of law

In the late nineteenth century the great constitutional expert, A. V. Dicey, included the 'rule of law' as one of the principles underpinning the British Constitution. He said there were three aspects to the rule of law. First, 'that no man is punishable or can be lawfully made to suffer . . . except for a distinct breach of the law established in the ordinary legal manner before the ordinary courts of the land.' Second, that no one (not even the Prime Minister, or a government minister) is above the law, so anyone can be brought to trial if they do wrong. Third, Dicey said, the Constitution itself is composed to some extent of judicial decisions that have been made in the past and which guarantee the right to free speech and the right to hold public meetings, for example. The idea of the rule of law is clearly based on notions that there should be an independent judiciary to defend this rule of law.

The European context

By signing the European Convention of Human Rights (ECHR) and then incorporating it into British law as the Human Rights Act (HRA) in 1998, the

The European Court of Human Rights building in Strasbourg

UK accepted judicial independence and impartiality: 'everyone is entitled to a fair and public hearing within a reasonable time by an independent and impartial tribunal' (Article 6). The ECHR and HRA are discussed more fully at the end of this chapter. In 2000, in the case of McGonnell, the ECHR raised questions about the independence of the judicial system of Guernsey, where the Bailiff exercised powers very similar to those of the UK's Lord Chancellor. It was this case, above all others, which precipitated the reforms (in the 2005 Constitutional Reform Act) to be discussed later on.

Individual rights and judicial review

If individual rights are to be protected, it is essential that there should be an independent judiciary, otherwise the government could use the machinery of the state and the judiciary together to remove these rights. Judicial review is the process (to be discussed later on) by which the courts can question (or review) the legality of government actions. Again, without an independent judiciary, it is difficult to see how an effective process of judicial review can be carried out.

Judicial neutrality

This is a separate issue to be discussed later, but it is clear that it is to some degree connected to judicial independence. Judges cannot be neutral if they are not independent, and vice versa. The first type of bias a judge must avoid (in order to be neutral) is bias in favour of the government.

While the independence of the judiciary seems in essence to be a very good thing, it might be worth pondering whether certain checks and balances are missing from the British Constitution when it comes to the judiciary. The judges in Britain are not elected (as they are in many instances in the USA) and yet they play an increasingly important role in public life. The pursuit of further independence for the judiciary seems like a very good thing, but it ought to be accompanied by some scrutiny and accountability.

How independent is the judiciary?

In 2005, after a long and difficult passage through Parliament, the Labour government passed a Constitutional Reform Act. This measure was designed to answer accusations that the British judiciary was not actually fully independent, or perhaps that judges were not seen to be independent. We will begin by looking at the evidence which may have prompted this reform, and then look at the measures which have been taken to remove the fears of those who said the judiciary was not fully independent.

Complete judicial independence cannot be claimed

Constitutional theory: parliamentary sovereignty

If Parliament is sovereign, it is difficult to maintain that the judiciary is independent, since it must be subordinate to Parliament. Subordinates cannot be independent. Dicey had an answer to this: the best defence of the rule of law, he said, was the sovereignty of Parliament. By this, he seems to have meant that Parliament would fight to protect such an obviously good thing as the rule of law (and hence an independent judiciary). But what parliamentary sovereignty in practice means is that every aspect of the legal system is subject to parliamentary reform; Parliament can abolish courts, change the law and decide on what penalties and punishments can be applied in the courts. In 2005 Parliament, under the control of a powerful executive, pushed through its Terrorism Act, which established the Home Secretary's right to imprison or detain terrorist suspects without what would normally be considered a fair trial. This measure was somewhat watered down after protests in the House of Lords, but even after these modifications, Parliament had effectively removed an important judicial power, not to mention a significant civil right.

Political practice: the fusion of powers

In the UK, there is such a close fusion of powers in practice between the executive and the legislature that it is difficult to believe that this does not rub off on the judiciary, especially in its relations with the executive.

The law lords

The most senior judges (the law lords) were, until the reforms of 2005 (to be discussed next), members of the House of Lords, and continued to have this role even after they had retired as senior judges. This meant that members of the judiciary were part of the legislature, which looked like a breach of judicial independence. The law lords were, by convention, expected not to play a part in the obviously political debates in the Lords, but it seemed clearly sensible that they should be consulted on laws which very closely affect the system of justice. In some cases, law lords were quite active legislators. The 2005 Constitutional Reform Act invalidates this example of a fusion of powers.

The Lord Chancellor

The head of the legal system in Britain, and himself a judge (at least in theory – in practice he acted as a judge very rarely), was until 2005 the Lord Chancellor. It is well known, however, that the Lord Chancellor was a 'political appointment', made by the Prime Minister. The Lord Chancellor was a member of the government, and sat in the Cabinet. In addition, the Lord

Chancellor was in effect the leading government figure in the House of Lords, in the second chamber of the legislature, and chaired meetings there as the Speaker does in the House of Commons. This seemed to indicate that the judiciary was not independent. Even if this is dismissed as just a relic of our medieval past, we have to consider the wider picture, the context in which the Lord Chancellor operated. The legal system was run by the Lord Chancellor's Department, in conjunction with the Home Office – both government departments. However, this supposed breach of judicial independence was removed by the government's legislation of 2005, when the office of Lord Chancellor was reformed and a Department of Constitutional Affairs (DCA) was created under a Secretary of State, who in future will not also be a judge. In addition, in 2007 the government created the Ministry of Justice, which took over the work of the DCA and also some of the work of the Home Office which had to do with the judicial system. This Department of Justice will closely resemble similar bodies in other liberal democracies abroad and will limit itself to running the administrative side of the judicial system

The appointment of the judiciary?

Appointments to the judiciary are made by the Crown, which has meant, in effect, that, until the reforms of 2005, they were part of government patronage. The Prime Minister appointed to the Court of Appeal and to the Judicial Committee of the House of Lords (the 'law lords'), having sought advice on his appointments from the Lord Chancellor. The Lord Chancellor appointed judges below this level. To quote political scientist Gillian Peele, writing in 2002: 'It is difficult to believe that a prime minister with Blair's legal connections would not take a strong interest in legal appointments.' The appointment of judges had gradually become somewhat less secretive and informal a process than it had been in the past. In 1994, the Lord Chancellor at that time (Lord Mackay) allowed a process of open competition to be used to appoint circuit judges, and from 1997 the next Conservative Lord Chancellor (Lord Irvine) extended this approach to High Court judges. In Scotland, the devolved Parliament is involved in a process of vetting the appointment of senior judges in something like the way in which the Senate in USA is involved in such appointments. The pressure group Justice called for a similar reform to be introduced in England and Wales, and also for the setting up of an independent Judicial Appointments Commission to make the initial nominations for Parliament to confirm. So, the process of judicial appointments before 2005 might have led us to question whether such appointments were free from partisan bias, and hence whether the judiciary was independent of the executive. It was both initial appointments and subsequent promotions within the judiciary which were a matter of political patronage, and perhaps the biggest question-marks were over the process by which judges were promoted to the highest positions. However, Labour's reforms in 2005 passed all judicial appointments over to an independent Judicial Appointments Commission, again removing this threat to judicial independence.

The dismissal and payment of the judiciary

In constitutional theory, by the Act of Settlement of 1701, senior judges hold their posts 'during good behaviour' and can be dismissed on a vote in both houses of Parliament. This obviously breaches judicial independence. But such a step has been taken only once, when a judge was dismissed in 1830 on such a vote for smuggling whiskey. The fact that this was so long ago might reassure us that, in practice, the judiciary is independent at least of Parliament. The payment of judges is now also kept out of the political arena: since 1971 there has no longer been an annual debate in Parliament about it – the salaries are fixed by an independent body (the Top Salaries Review Body). Criticisms of judges in Parliament are possible, but infrequent.

The role of the Home Secretary

The police service, prisons and policies relating to crime and law and order are dealt with by the Home Office, a government department headed by the Home Secretary. There is nothing very sinister about this; it is common throughout the world for government ministers to play this role. But from time to time it does lead to problems, partly because the Home Secretary runs a government department which can pass legislation on matters connected with crime and disorder through Parliament with comparative ease. This can compromise the independence of the judiciary if the legislation interferes with the right of judges to decide how to judge for themselves. One such issue surrounds the imposition of mandatory sentences. These are sentences which Parliament makes it compulsory for judges to impose in

Gordon Brown appointed Jacqui Smith as Home Secretary when he formed his first Cabinet

certain cases, and they now exist for murder, and also for repeat offences of a serious nature. In 2003, they were also introduced for possession of guns. Obviously, Parliament is sovereign and can therefore decide this matter, but it does look as though judges are being sidelined by this sort of law. However, one area of Home Office interference in sentencing was changed when, in 2002, the law lords themselves, using the Human Rights Act, decided that the Home Secretary could not over-rule decisions made by the Parole Board on the release of prisoners. But in January 2004 the decision in the case of Maxine Carr, when the Home Secretary changed the rules on the early release of prisoners precisely in order to prevent Carr being let out, suggests that the Home Office can still interfere in this area. David Blunkett, Labour's Home Secretary until late 2004, came into conflict on several other occasions with the judiciary, and made a number of populist speeches denouncing the un-elected 'liberal' judiciary's interference with the Home Office's allegedly more robust approach to crime and to terrorism. Clearly, this sort of approach looks a little like one branch of government trying to put pressure on another, and makes one question whether the principle of judicial independence is fully respected in the UK. Blunkett's successors, Charles Clarke and John Reid, were also critical of a number of judicial decisions.

The judiciary is independent

Some of what has just been said actually establishes a case for saying that the judiciary is in fact independent. Broadly speaking, this is the best answer to give, especially after the passage of the 2005 Constitutional Reform Act.

The 2005 Constitutional Reform Act

This Act should remove, when it comes fully into force in 2009, many of the concerns mentioned above about the independence of the judiciary. As has been said, it establishes a Supreme Court to replace the law lords. This means that the link between the legislature and the judiciary, created by the fact that the law lords sat in the House of Lords as legislators, disappears. The Act also reforms the office of Lord Chancellor, making the Lord Chief Justice (currently Lord Phillips of Worth Matravers, appointed in 2005) – a judge with no links to the legislature or executive – the head of the judiciary in place of the Lord Chancellor, with the additional title of President of the Courts of England and Wales. He will be responsible for the training, guidance and deployment of judges. He will also have the job of representing the views of the judiciary to Parliament and ministers and could in that capacity raise any concerns the judiciary might have over its independence. For the first time, the Act enshrines in law a duty on government ministers to uphold the independence of the judiciary. Ministers will be specifically barred from trying to influence judicial decisions through any special access to judges. Finally, the

Constitutional Reform Act will create an independent Judicial Appointments Commission to appoint judges, removing the role of the Lord Chancellor and the Prime Minister in this area. Technically, appointments will still be made by the Secretary of State for Constitutional Affairs (the government minister who has inherited the executive functions of the Lord Chancellor, renamed in 2007 as Secretary of State for Justice), so it is possible that quibbles over judicial independence may continue. There is also a minor issue over the fact that appointments to the 'independent' Commission will be made by the government itself. Late in 2007, Brown's new government announced that it was considering further legislation to remove entirely the involvement of the Lord Chancellor in judicial appointments.

Judicial review

Judicial review is the process by which the action of a government department or other public body can be 'reviewed' by a judge if a citizen feels that the department has acted wrongly. Through judicial review, the rule of law is applied to the workings of government. This process has grown in importance in the past 40 years, and many of the decisions made by judges clearly demonstrate the independence of the judiciary. It will be dealt with at greater length later in the chapter when we come to discuss rights. Recent cases of judicial review have seen frequent reprimands issued by the courts, especially against the Home Office, and especially on the application of immigration regulations. In 2007, there was a judicial review of the government's refusal to implement the recommendations of the Ombudsman on providing compensation to people who had lost money through the collapse of a number of private pension plans, which they claimed they had contributed to on the advice of the government. The judge came down firmly on the side of the disappointed pensioners, and against the government. This demonstrates, in this case at least, that the judge was not swayed by a desire to support the government.

Judges defend the rights of citizens

This will also be discussed later on, and is a disputed area, but on the whole the evidence suggests that judges are quite willing to oppose a government and defend individual rights. The 1998 Human Rights Act obviously enhances the role of judges here.

The *sub judice* rule

This is widely observed by Parliament and the government. When a matter is said to be *sub judice*, it means that it is being dealt with by the courts, and the rule is that no public discussion of the matter should go on in Parliament, or in the press, because this discussion might prejudice the case, by influencing the judge or jury. The application of this rule clearly shows that there is an acceptance of the need for judicial independence. Ministers are generally very careful not to comment on individual cases in this way, although sometimes they cannot resist the temptation to do so. In 2004, the Prime Minister expressed in Parliament his revulsion at the crimes committed by some British soldiers in Iraq while they were being tried by a court martial.

European influences

If there is to be an appeal to the European Court of Human Rights, which meets outside Britain, then this immediately establishes an independent court of appeal on matters of rights, since, if the court is outside the country, it must be independent of interference by the British government. The same argument also applies to the European Court of Justice, to which the British can also appeal on matters of European law.

Political culture

All political parties accept the need for judicial independence and opposition parties would seize on evidence of pressure being exerted by the government

---

Box 14.2 The judges and major public inquiries

Major public inquiries are held from time to time to look into matters of controversy, and these are often headed by a senior judge. Recent examples include:

- the inquiry into standards in public life (Lord Nolan: 1995)
- the inquiry into the sale of arms to Iraq (Sir Richard Scott: 1996)
- the inquiry into the police handling of the murder of Stephen Lawrence (Sir William Macpherson: 1999)
- the inquiry into the death of government scientist Dr Kelly (Lord Hutton: 2003)

It is clear that these inquiries need a person of standing and integrity to lead them, and also clear that the process is a sort of judicial one. But the reason that senior judges are chosen is largely to do with the perceived neutrality and independence of the judiciary. This supports the view that the judges are both neutral and independent. However, it also brings judges right into the political arena, calling into question their cherished independence (and neutrality). The Scott Report, for example, was presented, when it was finally published, in such a way as, in effect, to prevent any really successful political challenge from being mounted against the government of the day. This was not really the fault of Scott himself, but was perhaps the result of giving a judge, whose experience is essentially non-political, the responsibility of looking into an intensely political matter. So judges cannot escape from politics, and yet they wish to be independent of the democratic process and they reject interference from an elected Parliament and an elected executive. There would certainly seem to be a paradox here, but one that we cannot really blame the judges for. It is the politicians who use the judiciary to head these inquiries, the purpose of which is almost always to win time – time during which the issue is expected to cool, and time during which the ministers or other politicians responsible for the problems can find new jobs to avoid the need to resign if criticized by the inquiry's report. In the USA, inquiries of this sort tend to be the responsibility of committees within the legislature, composed of elected representatives, who seem to do the job quite well, despite not being judges.

on the courts if there were any. It is well known in the legal profession that the courts should be independent, and lawyers are careful to guard this judicial freedom; they have ample opportunity in court to express concerns if they feel there has been any breach of the independence of the judiciary. The Bar Association and Law Society (the two professional associations for lawyers) would be quick to condemn any attacks on judicial independence. It would certainly be grounds for appeal if it were discovered that a judge had responded to political pressure during the course of a trial. As with much else in British politics, perhaps the best defence of important principles is the freedom of the press. There are significant pressure groups involved in this area too, especially Liberty, Charter 88 and Justice.

 Question: How independent are judges from Parliament and the executive?

14.3 Judicial neutrality

Judicial neutrality: the absence of bias in the judiciary – religious, social, gender, sexual, political or racial bias, for example.

It is clearly crucial to the question of whether the judiciary protects the rights of citizens to know that members of the judiciary are unbiased, or neutral, in their judgements. It is easy to confuse **judicial neutrality** with judicial independence, and the two are connected. If the judiciary is dependent on the executive to some degree, this might bias its decisions in the direction desired by the party of government. It is on the matter of political bias that there is likely to be most confusion between judicial neutrality and judicial independence. If judges are biased towards a particular political party, it looks as though this might be because they are not independent of the executive. But in a democracy where there is not continual one-party dominance, it is likely that bias towards one particular party is due more to factors other than judicial dependence on the executive. However, since there have been long periods of one-party dominance in Britain's recent history (1979–97, Conservative dominance, for example), there may be something in the view that political bias is a result of judicial dependence.

We will now look at some of the evidence in favour of the view that the judiciary is not neutral.

J. A. G. Griffiths, *The Politics of the Judiciary*

This book was published first in 1977, and has been through several editions since then. It is still relevant to some degree today. The essential point made by Griffiths was that the judiciary was drawn largely from middle-aged, male members of the white, upper-middle class, and that it adopted the outlook of such people. This meant that judges were biased in their judgements in favour of middle-aged, white, upper-middle-class males. Essentially, the judges were prejudiced in favour of conservative values, Griffiths thought. This might not be overtly partisan bias, but more a tendency to support a small-c conservative outlook on social matters. This bias was demonstrated, Griffiths thought, in the way in which the judiciary applied the law against people from outside this group, especially in politically sensitive trials.

Recruitment

Griffiths's point about recruitment to the judiciary is still relevant today. To be a judge, you need to have been a barrister or solicitor. In fact, most judges have been barristers rather than solicitors. The legal profession requires long, expensive training, and lawyers are well-paid people; this is especially true of barristers. In fact, the number of judges who have been to public school as well as the number who have been to Oxford or Cambridge has increased in recent years. In 1999, Labour Research found that 80 per cent of senior judges had been to public school and 86 per cent had been to Oxford or Cambridge. In 2007, there were no ethnic minority law lords, Heads of Division or Appeal Court judges, and there was only one (described as being of 'mixed' ethnic origin) high court judge; only 9 out of 639 circuit judges came from ethnic minorities. There had never been a woman law lord until 2003, when Brenda Hale was appointed; there is currently no female Head of Division, and there are only 3 woman among the 37 appeal court judges, 10 among the 108 high court judges, and 73 female circuit judges. It may be that gradually, as more females and more people from ethnic minorities go into the legal profession, more of these will be promoted to become judges. But this process is bound to take time, since judges are not appointed until they are quite old and highly experienced. As for the tendency for judges to be drawn from the rich and well educated, this may be more difficult to deal with. Obviously, we do not want under-educated judges.

Judicial discretion

Judicial neutrality, or its absence, is only really an issue if judges have the freedom to exercise discretion in their judgements. Clearly there would be no point in having a judge at all if judgements were simply automatic. There must be some discretion exercised by judges. Judging involves the application of a broad general statement of what is right or wrong in a particular area, in other words a law, to a specific case. Because these cases vary so much, the judge needs discretion to apply the law, or to guide the jury in how they should apply the law. Sentencing may also require the use of discretion, with the judge able to vary the severity of the sentence from case to case.

Griffiths's argument depended on taking the view that a considerable degree of discretion is allowed to judges under English law. There certainly is some truth in this view, and English law has always prided itself on the fact that judges can themselves change the law by establishing precedents which involve new interpretations of what the law means.

Biased judgements

Against racial minorities

The racial bias of the judicial system as a whole (which should therefore include the police and the prison service as well as the judiciary) is something which, over the years, has been a cause for concern. The Macpherson Inquiry into the death of Stephen Lawrence which reported in 1999 revealed 'institutional racism' in the police. Recent examples suggest that this may extend to the judiciary. For example, in 2001 there were riots in Bradford, which seemed to have a racial aspect to them. The disturbances in the Asian area of Manningham were (according to the Asian population there) followed by sentences which were far stiffer than those which were imposed after rather similar disturbances a day later in the predominantly white area in the same city. The Commission for Racial Equality has pointed to continuing concerns about how, even today, there seems to be a bias against racial minorities in the whole system of justice.

Against women

The principal complaint from women's groups has in the past surrounded rape cases, when male judges have proved unsympathetic to female victims of these crimes. Helena Kennedy, in *Eve Was Framed* (1992), was able to give good evidence for anti-female bias among the judiciary. It is arguable that such evidence is now a little out of date, and that the judiciary has moved with the times and is more careful to avoid bias in this area than in the past.

Against the Labour movement

Much of Griffiths's evidence was used to show that the judiciary supported governments (especially Conservative governments) and employers in their quarrels with trade unions. In the 1970s and 1980s especially, there were a number of politically sensitive trials of this sort, where judges seemed to be very ready to make judgements against workers.

Against welfare policies

One famous case from the 1970s seemed to support Griffiths: the Fare's Fair case. The Labour group on the Greater London Council campaigned in local elections on a promise to cut local bus fares by increasing local taxation. It won the election and then implemented this policy. A judgement in the High Court prevented it from implementing this policy on the grounds that the local authority had exceeded its powers (it was *ultra vires*, to use the jargon). This seemed to support Griffiths's view that the courts opposed welfare policies, and the case did also seem to involve a good deal of judicial discretion.

Judgements in favour of national security

The miscarriages of justice surrounding the attempts in the 1970s and 1980s to round up various groups of IRA bombers (the cases of the Guildford Four, Birmingham Six and Maguire Seven especially) did involve the judiciary, but the main blame in these cases attached to the police. Whether these cases involved, as is sometimes said, anti-Irish bias on the part of the police and judiciary is questionable, since if the real IRA culprits had been picked up, they would presumably also have been Irish in the same way as the unfortunate people so tragically mistreated by the system. There is always something of a suspicion in high-profile national security cases that somewhere lurking behind them there is collusion between the secret service (part of the executive) and the judiciary, and hence that they involve a breach of judicial independence. But this may be merely the paranoia which the existence of a secret service tends to engender. The case of Clive Ponting in 1985 was certainly a worrying one, since the judge supported the view in his judgement that the government of the day could define what the interests of the state are, and that a civil servant should not reveal information to Parliament if it showed that a minister had lied to Parliament. Fortunately for the judicial system, and despite the judge's direction, the jury was less keen than the judge to give up its rights to the government, and Ponting was found not guilty. Again, the judge seems to have been guided by some sort of desire to protect national security and official secrecy.

The arrogance of the judiciary

Judges are often seen as being out of touch, and they come from a profession which is not noted for its concerns over how it is regarded by the public. One problem is that in order to preserve the independence of the judiciary, it is virtually impossible to remove them – they cannot easily be sacked. Unlike most public servants, they seem to be subject to very little 'quality control' or appraisal. Hence judges who are biased are very difficult to replace or re-educate.

Next, we look at some evidence in favour of the view that the judiciary is neutral.

Griffiths is out of date

Griffiths's book is still valuable, but even when it was first published it too was accused of not being entirely unbiased. Three decades later, it does appear to be somewhat out of date. Perhaps the book in itself had some influence in helping develop a more unbiased judiciary.

Recruitment

There is still a real problem over recruitment to the judiciary, especially in terms of its social composition. This does not inevitably result in a lack of neutrality, but it is simply wrong, whether it does or not. The judiciary needs to be a more representative cross section of the community than it currently is, if only because all powerful elite groups should be representative. But more women and more people from ethnic minorities have come into the legal profession in recent years and gradually, as they get older, they will be promoted into the higher ranks of the judiciary. In 2003, the first woman was appointed as a law lord. It is very surprising such an appointment had not been made any earlier, but these things do take time. Changes in the appointments procedure which have been brought in over recent years do make the system look more democratic, and the creation of an independent Judicial Appointments Commission will certainly make a difference in the future. The change brought in under Thatcher, by which the judiciary ceased to be a monopoly for barristers and was opened up to solicitors, should also help democratize the judiciary to a small extent: solicitors generally come from a slightly different part of the middle class than barristers. Judicial discretion is probably a little more prevalent now than it was in Griffiths's day, but it is not necessarily in itself a cause of bias.

A more liberal senior judiciary

During the 1990s many of the judges seemed to become more liberal in their attitudes. Thatcher had succeeded in annoying the legal profession, and tried to reduce the power of barristers (by opening up their work to solicitors). A number of high-profile cases in the 1990s, especially judicial reviews of decisions by the Home Office, put the judges at odds with the government, for example on immigration issues. The macho crime policies of the early 1990s were also criticized by prominent members of the judiciary: Lord Scarman called for a Bill of Rights, and other legal figures demanded constitutional reform. The advent of New Labour led to the promotion of more liberal figures, e.g. Lord Woolf as Lord Chief Justice (who followed another liberal, Lord Taylor, who had been appointed under the Conservatives).

A danger of liberal bias? The Hoffmann case

The best evidence that Griffiths is out of date is provided by the fact that in recent years suggestions have been made (by the then Labour Home Secretary David Blunkett, for example) that the judiciary is becoming too liberal. Obviously it would be wrong if the judiciary were to go from one biased extreme to another. The best evidence for this is provided by the actions of Lord Hoffmann in the case of the extradition of General Pinochet of Chile, which came to a conclusion in 2000. The former dictator of Chile had come to England for medical treatment and was promptly faced by demands for his extradition to Spain to stand trial there for torture. The case came before the law lords on a number of occasions, and it emerged that one of the judges involved, Lord Hoffmann, was a leading member of Amnesty International, a liberal pressure group which was involved in the case and which strongly supported Pinochet's extradition. It might be worth saying that when this emerged, Hoffman withdrew from the case, and that eventually Pinochet was not extradited and was allowed by the law lords to go back to Chile (largely on grounds of ill health, which miraculously disappeared when he got home).

A liberal consensus on race and gender

It is difficult to be precise about this, but there is evidence that attitudes in the judiciary (and in society as a whole) have changed considerably since Griffiths wrote his book. New Labour has worked hard to develop a culture in which racial and gender bias are no longer acceptable. It is argued that this extends to the judiciary.

Trade union legislation

As a result of the legislation passed by the Conservative governments between 1979 and 1997, there is much less scope for judges to interpret the law in such a way as to disadvantage trade unions for the simple reason the law is now clearly and unambiguously framed in such a way as to disadvantage trade unions even before the judiciary is involved. Trade unions themselves have changed in the light of this legislation, and they are now much less militant than in the past. These changes have largely taken trade unionism out of the debate about judicial neutrality.

Changing attitudes to national security

The end of the Cold War and the advent of peace in Northern Ireland have both meant that there is less pressure on the judiciary to support the national interest and official secrecy in their judgements, although more recent developments with the emergence of the 'war on terror' seem likely to bring a new security challenge to judicial neutrality. It may be that the approach will be different. It is interesting, for example, to see that the former Lord Chief Justice, Lord Woolf, spoke out against certain anti-terrorism legislation on the grounds that it might reduce civil liberties, showing the more liberal nature of the modern judiciary. In late 2004 the law lords unanimously used the Human Rights Act to oppose the detention without trial of suspected foreign terrorists in British prisons, thus condemning a Home Office policy and government anti-terrorist legislation. This judgement led in 2005 to changes in the law in the Terrorism Act, although these changes were also condemned by a number of law lords as they passed through Parliament on the grounds that they were in themselves harmful to civil rights.

Box 14.3 Are judges too powerful?

Are judges now so powerful that they ought to be subject to greater democratic scrutiny? If judges were independent of the government and of Parliament, would democracy be enhanced or would it be constrained? On the face of it, it would seem to be good that judges are both independent and neutral; in a democracy, on the other hand, there would seem to be problems with this. Recent developments have enhanced the political role of judiciary, considering 'political' in its broadest sense:

- the rise of European law in the light of the Factortame Case (1990) and its supposed threat to parliamentary sovereignty (see chapter 15 for more details of this case);
- the increasing use of judicial review;
- the development of a human rights role for the judiciary after the Human Rights Act of 1998;
- the political involvement of judges in high-level public inquiries;
- the development, according to some legal academics, of 'judicial activism' among the judiciary – that is to say, an increasing tendency to interpret the law in new ways without waiting for Parliament to legislate;
- the potential involvement of the law lords in reviewing the relationship between the Westminster Parliament and the devolved assemblies set up under recent legislation (although they have never yet heard a case on this subject).

All this points to a growth of judicial power at a time when judicial independence from the elected elements of the constitution is being increased. There may be room in the future for complaint here. In the USA, the senior federal judges (including those of the Supreme Court) are all nominated for appointment by a directly elected official – the President – and are only confirmed in their appointments after intense scrutiny, of a highly political sort, by the elected representatives of the US people in the Senate. In the 2004 US election, the question of who would be appointed to the Supreme Court by the future President became in itself an election issue. A vote for Bush was seen as a vote in the future for a conservative Justice. It is interesting to note that since the creation of the Scottish parliament, senior Scottish judges are also appointed after a process of parliamentary approval. It is not necessary for judicial independence that judges should be immune from democratic scrutiny, although getting the balance right is a difficult job.

The right of appeal makes judicial bias difficult

Since there is almost always a possibility of appeal (and now appeal outside the UK to the European Court of Human Rights), this has always made judicial bias difficult. Furthermore, there are pluralist checks and balances in place: the press, pressure groups, MPs, academics like Griffiths, as well as the legal professional bodies all make the use of judicial bias difficult.

 Question: To what extent are judges politically neutral?

14.4 Rights and the redress of grievances

Civil rights apply to a particular country; human rights are said to be those rights which everyone across the world ought to have. But the way in which these terms are used is rather flexible. For example, what should be called 'civil rights' according to the definition above are called 'human rights' in the 1998 Human Rights Act. The phrase 'civil liberties', in general usage, means much the same as civil rights, but some authorities distinguished them from civil rights. According to this view, civil rights are those rights set out positively in a formal list or statement of rights which has constitutional force, like the UK's 1998 Human Rights Act. In contrast, civil liberties are said to be the negative freedoms which the English common law allows to citizens: the gaps in the law where people are free to do what they like because there is no law against doing it. On this definition, therefore, the British had no rights before 1998, but only liberties. It needs repeating, though, that the way in which these three terms (civil rights, human rights, civil liberties) are used is often rather imprecise. In what follows, the term 'civil rights' is generally used in preference to the other two.

> **Civil rights**: special freedoms which citizens of a country enjoy and which are protected by the law.

A list of civil rights or liberties would probably include the ones shown in figure 14.1 (this is not an exhaustive list). In addition to these legal or political rights, there are also social rights – that is, rights which the citizen can claim to certain welfare or social benefits. These are the most debated rights, and they vary considerably from country to country. The different political parties also differ in their attitudes to these rights: those on the left of the political spectrum tend to be rather generous in what they would include in a list of social rights. On the other hand, conservatives often take the view that the individual citizen should as far as possible provide for him or herself, and not rely on the state for social rights. See figure 14.2 for a list of social rights.

For reasons of space – not because they are not important – the discussion of rights that follows will be concerned largely with the legal or civil rights and liberties, and will ignore the issue of social rights.

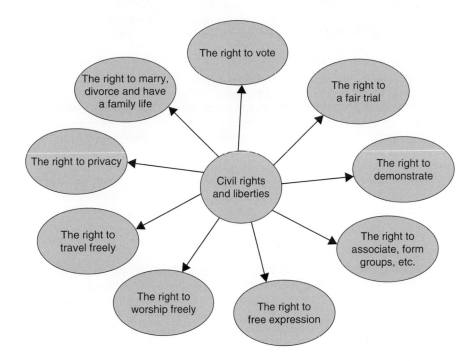

Figure 14.1   Civil rights and liberties

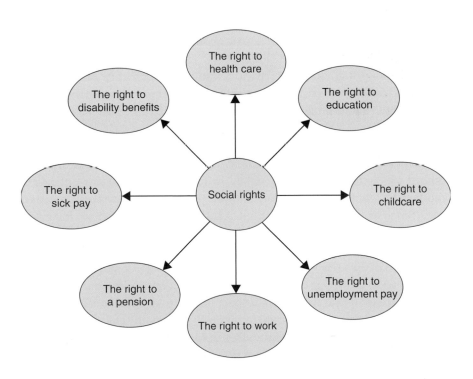

Figure 14.2   Social rights

Box 14.4 Natural and positive rights

Are rights natural? The claim that they are belongs to a tradition in political philosophy which goes back to the Ancient Greeks, but which was particularly strong in the sixteenth and seventeenth centuries. According to this view, justice is a God-given quality, which nature implants in the hearts of all sane people. Justice leads to rights and these rights also have a God-given status. Just as we have physical attributes given us by nature, so we have rights given us by nature. This notion of natural rights is important because it links to the modern idea of human rights and it emphasizes how important rights are. But the modern scientific tradition finds it difficult to accept an idea of natural rights, and Jeremy Bentham, writing 200 years ago, dismissed natural rights as 'nonsense on stilts'. The problem is that the concept of natural rights is a nice idea (it expresses a hope that people's rights ought to be protected), but it defies the realities of the situation: many people do not have their rights respected, so they do not seem to be very 'natural'. The alternative is to see rights as the result of legislation, as being 'positive', to use the philosophical jargon. So, the concept of positive rights emphasizes the need for some legal system actually to state these rights in a declaration or act of some sort, and then to enforce these rights through the courts. Still, there is no reason to dismiss natural rights entirely, even if we accept that positive rights express the truth better. As Plato showed in the *Gorgias* two and a half millennia ago, what is natural for man is to live together with others in society: so it is natural for man to base his positive laws on some conception of justice, but only when rights become positive do they assume a real (or natural) form!

How well are rights protected? How well are grievances redressed?

There has been for a long time a debate about how well rights are protected in this country, and how well individual grievances are redressed. The decision to pass a Human Rights Act in 1998 to some degree grew out of this debate, although some critics of the Act argue that rights were well protected already. There follows a brief analysis of the main points which are raised in this debate.

The rule of law

Before 1998, constitutional theory in Britain said that we did not need a modern Bill of Rights, or a declaration of rights such as existed in other countries. Since we did not have a written constitution, we also did not have a Bill of Rights. In almost every other country, there were written constitutions, following the American and the French examples of the late eighteenth century, and as part of these constitutions there were such lists or statements of rights. But in the UK there was not. A. V. Dicey, the great authority on the Constitution, maintained that the British respect for the rule of law meant that there was no need for such a statement of rights. In Britain, the citizen was allowed to do anything that was not expressly forbidden by the law and the law was drawn up by Parliament in such a way as to preserve this freedom. To a very large extent, it could be said that this was true, although there were exceptions where, in individual cases, rights were invaded. Protection of rights did not depend on there being a constitutional statement of rights. What was more important was the political culture that lay behind it. However, in recent years this approach to rights has become increasingly less popular and, finally, in 1998 Labour passed a Human Rights Act. So in a sense, the British citizen is now protected in both ways: by the new Act and also by the traditional rule of law route.

Parliament

MPs should take up individual cases where the rights of their constituents have been invaded, and of course they do. Some MPs also campaign to defend rights, especially of particular groups. As a whole, Parliament is also keen to defend rights more generally, by seeing that they are not infringed by its legislation. But when matters of national security arise (as over terrorism) it is difficult to do so, and MPs have tended to support government calls for emergency legislation. But the executive cannot rely on this, as was shown in November 2005 when the proposal to detain terrorist suspects for 90 days without trial was voted down in the Commons, and replaced with a limit of 28 days.

Judicial independence and judicial neutrality

The section above on judicial independence is also relevant to the discussion of how well rights are protected. If the judiciary is independent, presumably rights are protected better. A neutral judiciary will defend rights better. One that is biased against women or racial minorities, for example, will not.

Pluralist checks and balances

The press, public opinion, professional associations and pressure groups (Amnesty, Liberty, Charter 88, Justice) all help to guard our rights. MPs will also act in this way too, responding to the concerns of constituents or minority groups and acting on behalf of particular causes. The Labour MP Chris Mullin was a significant figure in helping secure the release of the Birmingham Six and other victims of miscarriages of justice connected to the problems in Northern Ireland.

Specific mechanisms by which grievances of citizens are redressed

There are a number of ways in which citizens can seek redress if they consider their rights have been invaded, and these will now be discussed in turn.

Judicial review

This is an important way in which citizens can protect their rights in the face of government interference or mismanagement. In the past three or four decades, it has grown to a considerable extent: in 1974 there were 160 applications for judicial review; in 1996, there were 3,800; in 2005, there were 5,381 (of which 744 were granted a right to a hearing). The passing of the Human Rights Act in 1998 added greatly to its scope. If a citizen feels that a government department (or any organization) has failed to take into account his or her rights or liberties, the citizen can apply for a judicial review of what has happened. This means that a court will examine the events or incident and will then decide if an injustice has indeed been done. Before 1998, however, the power of judicial review was limited, because the court could not pronounce on whether the government's action had been right or wrong. All the court could do was decide whether the government department had gone through the proper legal process in arriving at the decision. Hence, judicial review provided a rather limited defence of rights. In the USA, judicial review means that the Supreme Court can declare a piece of legislation to be unconstitutional; in the UK the doctrine of parliamentary sovereignty prevents this. In 1996, about a quarter of the applications for judicial review were not granted by the courts, because they did not fit into the rather limited range of cases where judicial review can apply. In addition, it may cost the citizen money to attempt to find a remedy this way, and it will certainly take time. The grounds for a judicial review are illegality, procedural impropriety, a denial of natural justice, irrationality and disproportionality, and finally a denial of human rights. Each will be briefly explained.

Illegality

A public body must abide by the law and cannot act without legal authority to do so. If it does, it is said to be acting *ultra vires* (beyond its powers). So in 1977, in the case *Laker Airways v. Department of Trade*, the court decided that the Secretary of State for Trade had exceeded his powers in stopping Laker from competing with British Airways on the transatlantic route. In 1995, the Court of Appeal decided that the Foreign Secretary had acted illegally in funding the Pergau Dam in Malaysia. In 1997, the Secretary of State for Social Security was judged to have acted illegally in denying asylum-seekers benefits.

Procedural impropriety

A public body must follow the procedures laid down by law in coming to its decisions; it cannot cut corners. In 1995, a government move to close the London–Fort William railway sleeper service was judged unlawful because there had been insufficient consultation.

A denial of natural justice

Government departments must follow procedures which do not offend against the rules of natural justice: they must not show bias and partiality. So the dismissal of the Chief Constable of Brighton in 1964 by the Brighton Watch Committee was found to be illegal because he had not been given a hearing to defend himself.

Irrationality and disproportionality

In rather the same way, decisions must be reasonable and also proportional. So in 1993, for example, the Court of Appeal decided that the opening and reading by prison officers of all prisoners' letters was disproportionate.

The Human Rights Act

As has been said, since 1998, there has been this important addition to the lawyer's arsenal in bringing cases up for judicial review. This is discussed separately below.

Tribunals and inquiries

The use of these was restructured by the Tribunals and Inquiries Act of 1971. There are tribunals to hear the case if citizens feel they have not received justice in such matters as national insurance, pensions, housing, education, the National Health Service and immigration. These tribunals are cheap, quick and accessible. On the whole, they provide an easy route by which a citizen can get a remedy in these important, if slightly mundane, matters. Inquiries are held into planning matters, and can be an extremely lengthy business: for example, inquiries into the building of nuclear power stations, airport extensions and new roads.

The Ombudsman

In 1967 the office of Parliamentary Commissioner for Administration, or Ombudsman, was created, on the model of a Scandinavian official of the same name. The Ombudsman receives complaints from people who believe that a government department has mistreated them. All appeals have to go through an MP, so that the citizen first complains to his or her constituency MP and the MP then contacts the Ombudsman. This obviously tends to restrict access somewhat. In addition, the Ombudsman has no power to force a government department to comply if he or she feels that an injustice has been done, although on the whole government departments do comply. There has been a steady growth in cases investigated by the Ombudsman, but most are quite trivial, and the expectations raised when the office was first created have probably not been realized. There have also been a specialist Ombudsman set up in a number of specific areas, e.g. for Northern Ireland, the NHS and for local government.

The rights of minority and disadvantaged groups

Three main groups in British society which were in the past discriminated against and placed at a disadvantage in comparison with the rest of society have been given certain rights to protect their position. The three groups are ethnic minorities, women and the disabled. It is only possible to comment briefly here on this important area.

Ethnic and religious minorities

In the 1950s and 1960s, ethnic minority groups were discriminated against in Britain, and three Race Relations Acts were passed, in 1965, 1968 and 1976, outlawing discrimination in employment, education, housing and in the provision of services. The last of these Acts set up the Commission for Racial Equality (CRE), a government body which has worked to reduce discrimination. In 2000 a Race Relations Amendment Act was passed to try to remove 'institutional racism' from public bodies.

Women

Discrimination against women led to the Equal Pay Act of 1970, which makes it illegal for an employer to pay women less than men. In 1975 a more extensive measure, the Sex Discrimination Act, was passed, setting up the Equal Opportunities Commission (EOC).

Disabled

The disabled had to wait until 1995 for a Disability Discrimination Act to be passed, which also set up a Disability Rights Commission (DRC).

Although these three groups have been given particular consideration by this legislation, there has not been any real attempt in the UK to bring in a policy of affirmative action or positive discrimination. This might perhaps be criticized, especially if we compare the situation in Britain with that in USA where racial minorities do enjoy some additional protection under a variety of affirmative action programmes. There has also been some opposition in Britain to singling out these groups for special treatment and setting up commissions to deal with the problems of each. The passing of the Human Rights Act (to be discussed next) led to moves to roll all three Commissions (CRE, EOC, DRC) into a single Commission for Equality and Human Rights, with a wider and more general remit.

The European Convention on Human Rights (ECHR) and the Human Rights Act

In 1998, the protection of British rights became a live political topic with the passing of the Human Rights Act. It is necessary to spend some time looking at this measure.

Background: Britain signs the ECHR

In 1950 a body called the European Council (which at the time consisted of 15 members, and it is important to remember is not part of the European Union) drew up the ECHR. Britain was a member of the European Council and signed the Convention. Indeed, British legal experts played an important part in drawing up the Convention, which was a list of rights and was quite similar to the UN Universal Declaration of Human Rights which had been drawn up in 1945. The view prevalent in Britain at the time was that British citizens had their rights protected by the British respect for the rule of law, and, in effect, Britain more or less ignored the ECHR. A European Court of Human Rights was set up in Strasbourg, to hear appeals under the Convention, but at first no one in Britain could use it.

British appeals allowed to the European Court (1965–97)

In 1965, Harold Wilson's Labour government allowed British citizens to take cases to Strasbourg where they felt their human rights had been invaded. It did seem odd that Britain had signed the ECHR but that her citizens had no access to the courts to use it, and Wilson put this right. Between 1965 and 1997, a total of 98 cases against the British government were brought before the court by UK citizens. In 50 of these cases, the court upheld the complaint. The British government then made some reparation and changed its procedures to make sure that no one in the future would have their rights invaded in the same way. The government did this under the international treaty it had signed and not because it was bound by British law to do so. An example of this would be the way in which the caning of children in British schools was stopped in the 1980s as a result of a case brought under the ECHR.

Labour adopts the policy of 'incorporation'

So British citizens could use the ECHR to protect their rights, but only by going through the expensive process of taking the case to Strasbourg. Lord Scarman, a famous liberal law lord, first suggested in 1974 that the Convention should be made part of British law, should be 'incorporated'. If this were done, citizens in the UK could simply bring a case before the British courts, and needed only to go to Strasbourg on appeal. This idea was taken up again in the 1990s by various pressure groups like Charter 88 and by

> **Box 14.5 Rights protected under the European Convention on Human Rights, and Human Rights Act**
>
> - Article 2: Right to life
> - Article 3: Prohibition of torture
> - Article 4: Prohibition of slavery and forced labour
> - Article 5: Right to liberty and security
> - Article 6: Right to a fair trial
> - Article 7: No punishment without legal conviction
> - Article 8: Right to respect for private and family life
>
> - Article 9: Freedom of thought, conscience and religion
> - Article 10: Freedom of expression
> - Article 11: Freedom of assembly and association
> - Article 12: Right to marry
> - Article 14: Prohibition of discrimination
> - Protocol 1, Article 1: Protection of property
> - Protocol 1, Article 2: Right to education
> - Protocol 1, Article 3: Right to free elections

supporters of liberal law reform like Lord Lester. It then started to form part of New Labour's constitutional reform plans, and featured in the manifesto of 1997.

The 1998 Human Rights Act

In 1998 Parliament passed the Human Rights Act, which came into force in 2000. This Act made ECHR part of British law. It is a rather limited measure in constitutional terms. It was written in such a way as to protect the great constitutional doctrine of parliamentary sovereignty. It does not give the judiciary the power to 'strike down' Acts of Parliament because Parliament is sovereign. In the USA the Supreme Court can declare unconstitutional an Act of Congress, a presidential action or a measure taken by an individual state, in which case it will cease to have any force. In the UK this cannot happen. If a judge decides that a citizen's rights have been harmed by something which is done according to an Act of Parliament, all the judge can do is to send a 'declaration of incompatibility' to Parliament saying that the law is incompatible with the Human Rights Act. As a result, Parliament is expected (but not compelled) to take some action, just as it used to take action after a judgement from Strasbourg in the past. The judge can go a step further if he or she feels there is an urgent need for new legislation, but again Parliament is under no obligation to issue a remedial order to sort things out. A remedial order is a parliamentary measure by which an existing Act of Parliament can rapidly be amended in light of a judgement of incompatibility with the Human Rights Act being made by a judge. This has only happened once, when the 1983 Mental Health Act was amended in this way.

Alternatively, Parliament can respond to an adverse judgement under the Human Rights Act by bringing in new primary legislation. There is also no mechanism in the UK by which a constitutional court, as it can in France, is able to declare a bill before Parliament to be unconstitutional. But the Human Rights Act does say that on introducing a bill, the government minister responsible for it has to issue a 'certificate of compatibility' with the Human Rights Act (although this does not mean a judge in the future must be bound by this opinion). In 2001, a joint parliamentary committee (of Lords and Commons) on human rights was set up, which also looks at new legislation with an eye to its compatibility. In 2004, for example, this committee issued a report critical of the 2001 Anti-Terrorism, Crime and Security Act by which foreign terrorist suspects had been detained without trial in Britain. The law lords agreed late in 2004 and used the Human Rights Act to declare the detention illegal. The government, however, did not immediately accept that it was under any obligation to release the prisoners or to change the legislation. But by March 2005 these prisoners had been released, although they were still severely restricted by orders limiting their freedom while they lived out of prison. At the same time, a new Terrorism Act was passed, by which future terrorist suspects, both British and foreign, would be placed under various forms of restrictions (curfews, tagging, house arrest, etc.) The government had therefore responded to the law lords' judgement, although in the process it had developed another threat to the rights of British citizens. This clearly indicates the weakness of the Act.

The impact of the Human Rights Act

Constitutional impact

As has been said, the Act was carefully written to preserve the constitutional theory of parliamentary sovereignty. What is more, the Act itself allows Parliament to 'derogate' from it, or suspend it in some particulars if it feels it necessary to do so: the 2001 anti-terrorism law, for example, derogated from Article 6 (the right to a fair trial) on the grounds of national security. But in practice, the Act as a whole does look rather as if it is an entrenched measure, and one that will not be removed very easily. If this is the case, parliamentary sovereignty seems to be threatened, in practice if not in theory. On the other hand, in 2004, the Conservatives were seriously suggesting that they would repeal the Act if they came to power, so this indicates that it may be very far from entrenched. The Act is particularly important in this constitutional respect because, although it is just one among many constitutional reforms introduced since 1997 by Labour, in most countries a written constitution includes a statement of rights. So the Human Rights Act is very much a constitutional document.

Impact on the judiciary

In constitutional theory, judges are no more powerful after the passage of the Human Rights Act than they were before. In practice, however, they do seem to have developed a rather stronger role, which should be seen as part of an overall increase in judicial power. In 2001 – and again in 2003 – there were a number of high-profile clashes between the judges and (predictably) the Home Office, especially over the application of rules on immigration and asylum. In the 1990s, lawyers defending immigrants and asylum-seekers found a sympathetic hearing in the courts on judicial review, where they argued that the government was not applying its own rules fairly. Since then, their power to cause havoc for the Home Office has been increased by the ability they have to complain on the much broader point that the rules, even if fairly applied, in themselves may involve a breach of human rights. But all this can be exaggerated. In the first year of its application, the Human Rights Act led to judges issuing only three 'declarations of incompatibility'.

Impact on the protection of rights

There was an immediate increase in the use of human rights as a remedy in the courts following the introduction of the Human Rights Act. The scope of 'judicial review' has been greatly enhanced by the passage of the Act. There were 600 cases brought in the first year of its application, of which 15 per cent were successful. Most commentators take the view that this rise in cases will be sustained and will increase. Britain is becoming a country where individual rights are being defended more and more strongly. But the Human Rights Act may not really have plugged a gap in the system: it may not be the case that before 2000 our rights were not protected. What seems to be happening is that the British are simply getting an appetite for bringing cases to court to protect their rights, whereas in the past they would have spent their money in some other way.

Statutory interpretation

Not only do citizens now have a right to a more extensive judicial review under the Human Rights Act, but, in addition, judges can interpret all legislation in the light of the Human Rights Act. This means that in judgements made by the courts, the rights of citizens will be taken into account in addition to other legal considerations. Existing law will be applied by the courts in the light of the Human Rights Act insofar as this is possible.

Equality and Human Rights Commission

The role of this body, which started up in 2007, is to work with the government, Parliament and the courts to promote human rights in Britain and end discrimination and harassment of people because of their religion, disability, race, age, gender or sexual orientation. It consists of a merger of three separate equality commissions: the Disability Rights Commission, the Commission for Racial Equality and the Equal Opportunities Commission.

Criticisms of the Human Rights Act

There were concerns expressed from the very beginning in some quarters about the introduction of a Human Rights Act in Britain. As the bill was passing through Parliament, the strongest complaints were from defenders of the rights of a free press, who were concerned that the Act might be used to restrict their freedoms. The Act has indeed been used to protect a right to privacy (for example, in the case of Naomi Campbell, who in 2004 won her case against the *Daily Mirror* on the grounds that it had breached her right to privacy by publishing a photograph of her leaving a rehab clinic), which was previously impossible under English law, but whether this is such a bad thing is open to debate. David Blunkett, when Home Secretary, was very critical of the way in which the judiciary used its power to limit his freedom of action, and was also in general terms quite critical of what he typified as the 'liberal' defenders of civil liberties who had been unwilling to acknowledge the threat of terrorism and of serious crime. This seemed strange in some ways coming from a member of the government that was itself responsible for passing the Human Rights Act. The Conservative opposition have continued from time to time to express their concerns about the Act. In August 2004 the then Shadow Home Secretary, David Davis, developed a sustained attack on the 'compensation culture', which he said was developing in the UK in part as a result of the Human Rights Act. This was leading to a great growth in claims for compensation from schools and hospitals, Davis said, although he admitted that most of these were not brought under the Act. Some were, however, and he claimed that a convicted murderer had been able to force prison authorities into allowing him to access pornography in his cell by threatening to use the Human Rights Act. In 2005 in preparation for the election, the Conservatives announced that if they were elected they would begin a 'review' of the Act, with a view to repeal or at least reform parts of it. Their intention is to develop a 'modern British Bill of Rights', stressing duties as well as rights, defining core liberties, avoiding some of the problems associated with the Human Rights Act and protecting jury trial and equality under the law. In 2007, Gordon Brown announced that his government would proceed in enacting a Bill of Rights and Duties, which would supplement the Human Rights Act, rather in the ways already suggested by the Conservatives.

Box 14.6 Anti-terrorism legislation, 2001–5

The Terrorism Act (2000)

Even before 11 September 2001, this Act defined terrorism. It gave the government powers to ban organizations which fell under this terrorist definition and to seize terrorist property and finances; it gave powers to the police to stop and search on the grounds of terrorism; and it created offences of raising money for terrorism and training terrorists.

The Anti-Terrorism Crime and Security Act (2001)

Following 9/11, the government rushed through this Act, which allowed it to detain foreign terrorist suspects without trial or charge, and without seeing the evidence against them. This was partly, ironically, to protect the human rights of such detainees, who might suffer death if they were deported to their home countries. However, in passing this law, the government 'derogated' from, or opted out of, the Human Rights Act (as it was entitled to do), on the grounds of national security. The Act set up a court called the Special Immigration Appeals Commission, which met in secret without a jury and allowed only specially vetted lawyers to appear before it. This body was to hear appeals from those detained.

This led to the detention of 11 men in Belmarsh high security prison, 9 of whom appealed to the House of Lords, which found in their favour in December 2004. The law lords said that it was wrong to discriminate against foreigners by allowing their detention without trial, and that there were not sufficient grounds to derogate from the Human Rights Act, and hence that the Anti-Terrorism Act was unjustified. In the words of Lord Hoffmann: 'The real threat to the life of the nation comes not from terrorism but from laws such as these.'

The Prevention of Terrorism Act (2005)

This was the government's response to the ruling on the 'Belmarsh nine'. It allowed the government to use 'control orders' against terrorist suspects, whether foreign or British; these involved house arrest, banning the use of computers and phones, and surveillance. The foreign suspects were then let out of prison, and put under these orders. Many of them have since absconded.

The Terrorism Act (2005)

Following the terrorist attacks in London in July 2005, the government proposed to give the police the power to detain terrorist suspects without charge or trial for up to 90 days. It was this which raised the strongest civil liberties objections in Parliament, and in the end the government reduced the period to 28 days. This Act also banned 'glorifying, exalting or celebrating' terrorism, and the promotion of terrorism or incitement to terrorism. The government was given powers to deport foreigners involved in the promotion of terrorism.

Tony Blair invented a new freedom to explain all this: 'Here in this country and in other nations round the world, laws will be changed, not to deny basic liberties but to prevent their abuse and protect the most basic liberty of all: freedom from terror.'

The Counter-Terrorism Bill (2008)

Parliament began debating a new measure under Brown, designed to extend the detention period to 42 days and taking further anti-terrorism measures.

Threats to civil liberties

What has been written above may seem unduly positive about how well rights are being protected in the UK. At each stage of the argument, however, there are opportunities to question whether rights really are well guarded. If

After the London bombings of 7 July 2005, legislation was introduced which enhanced police and government powers in order to protect the public from acts of terrorism

the independence and impartiality of the judiciary are questioned, then it is likely that rights will not be protected. There are certainly reasons to doubt that minority groups or those who have been discriminated against in the past do have their rights protected, even now. The Human Rights Act has its deficiencies. Perhaps two additional drawbacks need to be emphasized. First, a feature common to most judicial systems is that they are not run on welfare lines: in other words, citizens generally have to pay to protect their rights and, as everyone knows, going to law is expensive. There is a system of legal aid, by which the poorer sections of the community can receive financial assistance in protecting their rights, but the system is by no means generous and excludes people on middle incomes. The second threat to rights comes from the desire for security in a world where crime and terrorism are politically sensitive issues. Thus, in 1994 the Conservative Home Secretary, Michael Howard, passed the Criminal Justice and Public Order Act, which gave the police power to stop people gathering to listen to music 'with a repetitive beat' (at 'raves'), set up a national DNA database, introduced a crime of trespass and abolished the 'right to silence' (which in the USA is part of the Constitution, and which went back in British law to the Middle Ages).

In 2000, 2001 and 2005 the Labour Home Secretaries, David Blunkett and Charles Clarke, brought in anti-terrorism measures which essentially removed the right of habeas corpus (an ancient right to have a trial before being imprisoned which is also part of the US Constitution), as well as the rights to free speech and association (see box 14.6). In 2008, Gordon Brown introduced further anti-terrorism legislation. In 2005, the government passed the Serious Organized Crime and Police Act, which, among other things, banned demonstrations of one or more persons without police approval within one kilometre of the Houses of Parliament. Using this Act, they arrested a colourful eccentric called Brian Haw, who, since 2001, had been conducting a (peaceful) one-man peace protest across the road from Parliament. Shortly afterwards, two peace protesters were arrested for reading out the names of British servicemen killed in Iraq in front of the war memorial (or Cenotaph) in Whitehall. A journalist reported in 2006 that she was questioned by police for having a picnic with her children on the grass outside Parliament, because she had baked a cake with the word 'Peace' iced on the top of it. In 2007, Brown announced that he was prepared to consult over re-establishing the right to demonstrate in the vicinity of Parliament, and hence to repeal this clause in the 2005 Act.

Another anti-libertarian case to hit the headlines in 2005 occurred with the arrest and questioning by police of Walter Wolfgang on suspicion of terrorism, because he (an 81-year-old Labour Party member) had shouted 'Rubbish' during a speech by Jack Straw during the 2005 Labour Party Conference. There are plans to introduce compulsory ID cards, which could be seen as an invasion of privacy and a denial of the presumption of innocence. Individual privacy has also been invaded by the placing of more and more CCTV cameras in many public places. All these measures seem, when looked at one at a time, to some degree justified, but taken together they do seem to represent a huge invasion of individual liberty – all in the name of collective security, but arguably just to make a political point or to save the political bacon of politicians in the event of a rise in the crime figures or a terrorist attack. These illiberal laws are passed with relative ease because of parliamentary sovereignty, which (according to its greatest advocate, A. V. Dicey) is supposed to be such a great defence of the rule of law. To its credit, however, in November 2005, the House of Commons refused to endorse the move to allow detention without trial of terrorist suspects for 90 days. But this exception tends to emphasize the previous occasions when Parliament had tamely accepted a reduction of rights in the name of national security.

Question: Critically examine the attempts to extend citizens' rights since 1990.

Activity

Look up the European Convention on Human Rights and make notes on the contents of the Convention. What problems do you see with the Convention? Are there any rights you would exclude? What are its strengths? Discuss with classmates the following issues:

1 Should the right to privacy be more important than the right to free speech? Should 'celebrities' and politicians have a right to privacy?
2 In 2007, the government told the Catholic Church that it would have to allow gay couples to use its adoption agencies in the same way as straight couples. This was contrary to the religious views of the Church. Was the government right to do this?
3 Recent cases involving Muslim girls wearing veils at school have resulted in the expulsion of children who have refused not to wear them. Have these children had their rights respected or not?
4 Should prisoners be allowed the right to vote?
5 The government justifies its anti-terrorism legislation on the grounds that it is defending the most basic human right of citizens, the right to life. How justifiable is this claim?

SUMMING UP

The political role of the judiciary has changed considerably since Labour was elected in 1997. On the positive side, reforms have been introduced which establish the independence of the judiciary, by changing the relationship between it and the other two branches of the system of government. The 2005 Constitutional Reform Act (CRA), when fully implemented, will radically alter the position of the judiciary in the British constitution. As far as judicial neutrality is concerned, the anxieties expressed by J. A. G. Griffiths in the 1970s seem now rather outdated, and modern judges at times appear more liberal than a Labour government. But the composition of the senior judiciary is only slowly changing, although the new Appointments Commission set up by the CRA will begin to make a change as more women and people from beyond the white, Anglo-Saxon establishment are appointed. The landmark Human Rights Act of 1998 has also radically altered the attitudes of the British to their civil liberties, or, as we should now think of them, their human rights. But this reform is not without its critics, and not merely those on the right of politics who might have an instinctive dislike of a culture of rights. Is the judiciary developing too much power in the light of these changes, and also in the light of the development of European law, with its potential to overturn the essentially democratic doctrine of parliamentary sovereignty? Are we developing a new aristocracy of unelected judges willing to stand up to an executive which, for all its faults, is at least representative of the people?

Further reading

K. D. Ewing and C. A. Gearty, *Freedom under Thatcher* (Clarendon, 1990): illustrates well the starting point for Labour's reforms of the judiciary.

J. A. G. Griffith, *The Politics of the Judiciary* (Fontana, 1997): still worth looking at – the classic left-wing critique of the judiciary.

H. Kennedy, *Eve was Framed* (Chatto and Windus, 1992): a further attack on the judicial system from a modern feminist perspective.

S. Lee, *Judging Judges* (Faber and Faber, 1988): a reply to Griffiths.

Websites

www.humanrights.gov.uk (Government's Human Rights Unit)
www.lcd.gov.uk (Lord Chancellor's Department)

The European Union

Making connections

The intricate details of how the European Union works are a little difficult to absorb, partly because the system is so different from what we are used to in the UK. It is important to see the EU not only as a system with a history, but also as a lively issue in British politics, a topic on which people disagree. When seen as an issue of this sort it perhaps becomes more engaging as a topic. It is an area on which people often take up prejudiced or rapidly formed views; it is better to approach it with an open mind and to consider all sides of the issue before coming to a conclusion on it.

15

The European Union

KEY TOPICS

- The history of the European Union
- The institutions of the European Union
- Is there a 'democratic deficit' in Europe?
- The single currency
- British political parties and the European Union
- The impact of the European Union on British politics
- Arguments for and against the European Union

SETTING THE SCENE

The politics of the United Kingdom has been changed radically since the 1970s by developments in two important areas: Europe and devolution. The final two chapters deal with these huge issues. First, Europe. Since 1973 we have been part of the organization of European states which forms what was originally called the European Economic Community (EEC, or Common Market), and is now the European Union (EU). Membership of this Union has caused political turmoil in Britain at various times, and has also had a profound impact on our political and constitutional arrangements. It is still the biggest single political issue facing the country, but one which politicians sometimes try to ignore and which the citizens often find perplexing.

The European Union (EU): the group of (currently) 27 European countries which have joined together to promote their economic well-being and to foster good relations between themselves.

15.1 The history of the European Union

The **European Union** grew out of the desire among European countries to prevent another conflict from developing after the end of the Second World War (1939–45). Starting with 6 countries in 1957, it is at present composed of 27. The history of Europe in the post-war period is dominated by the history of the EU. For the United Kingdom, the development of the EU has been, in its quiet way, one of the most important political issues of the period. It continues to be an area of great interest. It is difficult to say exactly what the EU is at present, because it has changed and developed in the past, and there seem to be indications that it will continue to develop in the future. Before looking at the politics of British membership, it is important to examine the history of the development of the EU.

1951: The Treaty of Paris

This was signed by six countries (France, West Germany, Italy, the Netherlands, Belgium and Luxemburg) and set up the European Coal and Steel Community. This body was created to ensure that there was no over-production or harmful competition in the production of coal and steel between the states that signed the treaty. The Treaty of Paris was part of a general movement in Europe which took place in the years after the Second World War and was intended to develop better relations between the former combatants of the war. The European Council had agreed to the European Convention on Human Rights in 1950, and the Western European Union had been formed in 1954 to coordinate foreign and defence policy. The European Coal and Steel Community was run by institutions rather like those that developed later into the European Union and is therefore counted as one of its chief forerunners.

1957: The Treaty of Rome

This was signed by the six founding members and set up the European Economic Community (EEC). The ear 1957 is taken as marking the real foundation of what later became the European Union. The aim was to remove restrictions on trade between the member states and to develop a Common Agricultural Policy, so that food supply and agricultural employment could be secured using the methods already employed to deal with coal and steel. At the same time, the European Atomic Energy Community was created, to develop nuclear power stations. The Treaty of Rome envisaged further integration between the states, and spoke of the need for an 'ever closer union' in Europe.

1973: Britain joined the EEC

The question of whether Britain should join the EEC had been discussed, both in Europe and in Britain, ever since it had been first set up. There had been unsuccessful attempts to join in the 1960s, which had been blocked largely by the President of France, Charles de Gaulle. Finally, in 1973, under the Conservative Prime Minister Edward Heath, Britain joined. When the Labour Prime Minister, Harold Wilson, came to power, he decided to hold a referendum on European membership (in 1975) in which the British people voted two to one in favour of staying in the EEC.

1986: The Single European Act (SEA)

This was an agreement among the members of the EEC to develop economic integration further in order to achieve a completely free market between the states. By the SEA, members agreed to uphold 'four freedoms': the free movement of goods, services, labour and capital. In order to get fair competition between member states, it was also necessary to develop common environ-

---

Box 15.1 The enlargement of the European Union

The EU has grown since its beginnings. The growth has been an uneven, complicated process.

1957: The original six were France, West Germany, Italy, Belgium, the Netherlands and Luxemburg. At first the EEC, as it was then, seemed resistant to accepting new members. At various times in the 1960s Britain showed a willingness to join, but was refused entry.

1973: The first major enlargement occurred, involving the United Kingdom and two other closely associated countries: Denmark and Ireland.

1981: Greece joined.

1985: Spain and Portugal joined. At the same time, Greenland left. Greenland had been part of Denmark and had joined along with that country. After becoming independent of Denmark, Greenland also left the EU.

1989: The Berlin Wall came down, leading to the reunification of Germany, which brought East Germany into the EU automatically. By now the process of enlargement was quite well established, and by the Treaty of Maastricht (1992) a series of criteria were laid down to decide whether a country qualified for membership or not.

1995: Austria, Sweden and Finland joined.

2004: The largest phase of enlargement, when former communist countries were the most significant of ten new members: Malta, Cyprus, Estonia, Latvia, Lithuania, Poland, the Czech Republic, Slovakia, Slovenia and Hungary. Cyprus is divided between a Turkish Cyprus and a Greek Cyprus: only the latter joined, although it had been hoped that membership would lead to the reunification of the two parts. This enlargement added 20 per cent to the population of the EU, 23 per cent to its area and 4 per cent to its economy.

2007: Two further countries joined: Rumania and Bulgaria.

The future: Some European countries do not wish to join because they prize their independence and neutrality too highly: Switzerland, Norway and Iceland. The qualifications to join are geographical (part of Europe, interpreted quite loosely though), economic (reasonably rich) and political (democratic and liberal). Some countries will probably join later, but do not yet qualify on economic or political grounds: Serbia, Croatia, Bosnia, Albania, Montenegro and Macedonia. Turkey may join eventually, although great controversy surrounds this application. There have been occasional suggestions that the North African states, Algeria, Morocco and Tripoli, might join, but this seems unlikely, partly on geographic grounds. Would Russia ever wish to join? The country qualifies as much as some other countries, but is probably too proud. Many people in the Ukraine would like to do so eventually, and the issue became an important one there in the disputed presidential election of 2004.

mental and social policies, and hence the SEA involved developments in these areas too. In addition, the institutions of the EU needed to be strengthened after 1986 in order to prevent one or more states from opposing the achievement of economic integration by vetoing measures against their national interest.

1992: The Maastricht Treaty

This treaty, also know as the First Treaty on European Union (TEU), created the EU on the basis of the earlier agreements already described. It was signed by the member states at a meeting held at Maastricht, a town in the Netherlands. The treaty repeated the aim of achieving an 'ever closer union', but, at Britain's insistence, it avoided using the word 'federal' with regard to Europe.

John Major, the Conservative Prime Minister, negotiated the treaty on Britain's behalf and faced huge political problems, largely among his own party at home, in doing so. In the end, he did not accept the whole treaty, but secured agreement that Britain should have two major opt-outs from its full provisions. The first concerned the really significant issue decided at Maastricht, which was a timetable for the introduction of the European Single Currency. Major refused to commit Britain to joining the new currency, but reserved the right to join at a later date than the other member states. Second, Major refused to agree to the Social Chapter, part of the treaty which bound its signatories to strengthening the rights of workers. But Britain agreed to the rest of the treaty, which extended the powers of the institutions of the Union, and made tentative moves towards a common outlook in four areas of policy: justice, home affairs, foreign policy and security. In these areas, Maastricht was largely sketching future possibilities rather than deciding anything very concrete. One significant step forward was the creation of the idea of European citizenship, the most tangible aspect of which has been the adoption in Britain of a new EU passport. The political repercussions in Britain over the treaty were immense. Although Major was able to win the election of 1992, he faced massive political problems immediately afterwards, as he attempted to get the treaty ratified in Parliament (he had decided against calling a referendum because he was afraid he would lose). For at least two years, the issue dominated British politics and caused major divisions in the Conservative Party.

1997: The Treaty of Amsterdam

Also known as the Second Treaty on European Union, this was negotiated by the outgoing Major government and signed by Tony Blair as soon as he came to power. The signing of the treaty was delayed so that it would not become an election issue in 1997. This treaty developed European cooperation further in a number of areas, and strengthened the institutions a little more. It built on agreements made earlier at Schengen in Luxembourg, abolishing border controls between member states and making provisions for a common European immigration policy. Britain did not sign up to the Schengen Agreement and has also opted out of the border and immigration arrangements made at Amsterdam. The Amsterdam Treaty also made some important decisions about the entry of new members to the Union.

2000: The Nice Treaty

This was another attempt at strengthening the institutions of the EU in their relations with the member states. This treaty was necessary because the expansion of the EU (planned for 2004) required a change in the representation of the member states on the various bodies which run the Union. Stronger cooperation on defence and foreign policy was promised, including the creation of an EU military 'rapid reaction force'. It was also agreed that there would be moves towards open frontiers between member states, and cooperation on immigration policy.

2002: The single currency, or euro

For many years, the idea of a single European currency had been discussed. In the late 1980s these plans were pushed ahead by Jacques Delors, President of the European Commission (see below). Margaret Thatcher at first opposed these plans, but in 1989, against her better judgement, she signed up to the Exchange Rate Mechanism (ERM), the early attempt to coordinate currency policy as a prelude to adopting the single currency. However, in 1992 Britain fell out of the ERM after a catastrophic collapse in the value of the pound on what became known as 'Black Wednesday' (16 September). At Maastricht, Major had reached agreement with the other European member states on condition that Britain could opt out of joining the single currency. Denmark and Sweden also got opt-outs. The other members worked towards adopting a single currency, which was launched first in 1999, and which became a reality in 2002, when its coins and notes began to circulate. Twelve of the fifteen members joined the euro zone (Greece after a delay, having not initially met the economic requirements). Britain, Denmark and Sweden refused to join, at least for the moment. In 2008, Cyprus and Malta joined the euro zone.

2003–4: The EU Constitution

There was no written constitution for the EU, only a series of treaty agreements (as mentioned above). There was pressure, therefore, to draw up a constitution, and a 'convention', or commission, was set up under Valéry

Giscard d'Estaing, former President of France, to do so. In 2003, a draft constitution was debated by the European Council, and these discussions continued into 2004. The debate was largely about what the document should say, rather than whether or not it was right to have a constitution. In April 2004, to everyone's surprise, Tony Blair announced that he would hold a referendum on the issue, to allow the British people to have their say. He said the referendum would be held after the next general election, planned for 2005. Finally, in June 2004, the Constitution was agreed by the leading politicians of the member states, including Britain. The political parties in the UK lined up in a predictable way: Labour and the Liberal Democrats were in favour, Conservatives against. But before any decisions could be taken in the UK, in May 2005 referendums were held in France and the Netherlands, and in both cases the people voted 'No'. It looked as if the EU Constitution had failed and that it would be forgotten.

2007: Reform Treaty of Lisbon

However, in 2007, a new Reform Treaty, containing many of the elements of the 2004 Constitution, but without actually being a constitution, was agreed at a European Council meeting in Brussels and finally signed in Lisbon. Signing the treaty was virtually Blair's last action as Prime Minister. The government quickly announced that there was no need for a referendum on this treaty, although many Euro-sceptics said that there should be one, since more than 90 per cent of it resembled the earlier document. The Reform Treaty was required, its supporters argued, to enable the new EU members to be successfully amalgamated in the machinery of the Union.

Question: Discuss the view that the Maastricht Treaty has been the most important development in the European Union since the Single European Act.

15.2 The institutions of the European Union

Two themes intertwine in the government of the EU and find themselves expressed in the institutions of government of the Union: intergovernmentalism and supranationalism.

Intergovernmentalism describes how the EEC tended to run its affairs in the early days, especially after the so-called Luxemburg Compromise of 1968, when General de Gaulle, the President of France, insisted that nation-states should retain a veto over important affairs. De Gaulle wanted a 'Europe des patries' – a Europe of nation-states. On the whole, most British governments have tended to agree with de Gaulle that this is the best way to run the Union.

Intergovernmentalism: the theory that the European Union should be run by the governments of the member states cooperating as if they were members of an alliance or loose club of states.

Map of the European Union

Supranationalism would turn Europe into a sort of federation, with no right of national veto by the member states. Europe would become a 'United States of Europe' rather like the United States of America, where each individual state (Texas, California, etc.) has some sovereignty and some recognized powers, but there is a unifying federal authority in Washington, DC which binds all the states together. This is the vision of how Europe should develop held by Jean Monnet, who was the most significant of the founding fathers of the EEC, and by many of the subsequent Presidents of the Commission.

In practice the way in which the EU is run is a mixture of both intergovernmentalism and supranationalism. The chief institutions of the EU are the European Council, the Council of Ministers, the European Commission, the European Court of Justice and the European Parliament. It is also important to mention intergovernmental conferences, which have made very significant decisions for the Union.

> **Supranationalism**: the theory that the European Union should develop institutions which have power and sovereignty transferred to them by the member states, so that they can take decisions of their own accord.

Intergovernmental conferences

IGCs are meetings of the heads of government of the member states of the EU. They have been held to discuss all the major new treaties that have been signed: the Treaty of Paris, the Treaty of Rome itself, the Single European Act, the two Treaties on the Union and the Treaty of Nice. They are intergovernmental in name and also in practice, since at Maastricht the UK negotiated some changes to the treaty and also opt-outs, as did Denmark and then Sweden in rather the same way.

The European Council

This is a more regular and formal meeting of the heads of government of the member states than the IGCs and the other various summits that have been held. Every six months, the heads of government meet in an atmosphere of informality and discuss broad strategy for the Union. These meetings sometimes prepare the way for IGCs, and are obviously rather similar and clearly intergovernmental. Every six months, one of the member states takes over the presidency of the European Council and is expected to host the meetings and set their agendas. The proposed EU Constitution of 2004 suggested that the Council should meet four times a year and that an individual should be elected by qualified majority vote (see below on this) to the presidency of the European Council for a term of two and a half years. The President would claim to represent the EU on foreign and security matters, would negotiate between member states and 'drive forward' the work of the European Council. This has now been accepted by the Treaty of Lisbon (2007).

The Council of Ministers

This is a similar sort of body to the European Council. In fact, it comprises a number of meetings of the various ministers of the member states, discussing policy separately, but called, rather confusingly, the (singular) Council of Ministers. Thus the transport ministers of all the states will meet regularly to discuss transport, and the agriculture ministers will meet separately to discuss their area of policy. There are 23 of these groupings in total, arranged according to departmental area. The Council of Ministers is the decisive law-making body of the Union, although it works closely with the Commission and Parliament. Policy is discussed in more detail by the Council of Ministers than it has been discussed in the IGCs or European Council. It looks very intergovernmental, because the discussions are between representatives of each individual member state. In the early days of Europe, decisions were taken by unanimous agreement of the members of the Council of Ministers. But the Council is now perhaps not as intergovernmental as it seems, since the ability to use a veto has become less and less available to the representatives of the member states as the EU has developed.

Gradually, unanimous decision-making has been replaced in many areas by the growth of what is called 'qualified majority voting' (QMV). Under QMV, each member is given a number of votes on the Council of Ministers according to its size. At present, Britain has 29 votes. To get a measure passed on the Council currently requires 232 out of the total of 321 votes: more than a simple majority, but obviously less than unanimity. This system of voting has been, as can be imagined, a great source of disagreement and controversy over the years. When decisions had to be unanimous, it emphasized the intergovernmentalism of the Union, but now that changes can be made according to QMV, Europe begins to look as though it is run on a supranational basis. The Council of Ministers has a permanent staff known as the Committee of Permanent Representatives (COREPER, from its French acronym), made up of civil servants from each country, which looks after its business when it is not meeting. It is in the Council of Ministers that the future shape of EU policy is laid down, and that the law of the EU (its regulations and directives) is largely developed. In this, it works with the Commission and the European Parliament, but it is the really significant institution in making these decisions.

The Commission

This body comprises both the executive (with the Council of Ministers) and the civil service of the Union. It is a permanent body housed in Brussels and is in some ways the most powerful institution in the EU. It is headed by commissioners, chosen for four-year terms from each of the member states. Before 2004, the larger states each had two commissioners; since enlargement in 2004, there has been one commissioner from each member state. Each commissioner has a departmental responsibility for some area of policy within the EU (fisheries, environment, farming, etc.) – these departments are called Directorate-Generals (DGs). Since 2004, the more significant DGs have

The European Parliament Building in Strasbourg

been the responsibility of the larger states. So, Peter Mandelson, for example, when he became Britain's commissioner in 2004, was given control over the DG that dealt with international trade, clearly one of the most important jobs in the Commission.

There is a President of the Commission – who could be described as the President of the European Union – who is at present chosen from among the commissioners and approved by the European Parliament. The Commission makes laws, with the support of the Council of Ministers, and then enforces its legislation. In practice, the Commission also drives forward the process of integration and provides the continuing pressure to achieve an 'ever closer Union'. In 2004, for example, it was the Commission that used the European Court of Justice to insist that the Council of Ministers force Germany and France to abide by the Union's economic rules, which had been agreed on by member states as necessary to run the euro successfully. The Council of Ministers, the intergovernmental body, had been prepared to ignore the breach of the rules by these two major nations, but the supranational Commission – headed by nationally chosen commissioners – used the law to stop it. Of course, its independence is also limited by the need to work within the wider intergovernmental framework.

The European Parliament

The EP is the representative body of the European Union, and, since 1979, has been directly elected every five years by the people of Europe. It meets in Strasbourg, but has a chamber in Brussels too, to be near the Commission; it also occasionally meets in Luxemburg. There are currently 785 Members of the European Parliament (MEPs), of whom 78 come from the UK. The EP's powers have steadily increased with each treaty. It does not initiate legislation, which is odd for a representative assembly, but it does scrutinize it. It is probably best described as a 'revising chamber' when it comes to legislation, a bit like the UK's House of Lords. Although weak in legislative terms, it is stronger when it comes to scrutiny, especially scrutiny of the Commission. It has the power to veto the EU's annual budget and also to dismiss the Commission. It did take the drastic step of sacking the Commission in 2002 following a financial scandal, although in practice many of the old commissioners were reappointed very quickly afterwards. The EP also has the power to reject the new Commission when it is appointed every four years, having made enquiries about the people nominated by the member states. In 2004 it used this power to prevent the Italian nominee from taking up his job when it was revealed that he held rather illiberal views, but it had to do this by threatening to refuse to ratify the appointment of the whole Commission, because it has no formal power to reject individual commissioners. The EP cannot be described as intergovernmental because it represents people rather than governments, although MEPs are elected through the party system and hence have links with the national governments. It is also difficult to see it as supranational, since its powers are limited, but as it develops confidence, it has the potential to become stronger.

The European Court of Justice

The ECJ is the body which judges whether member states and organizations within them have followed the law of the European Union. EU law takes the form of regulations (binding orders) and directives (enforceable instructions to a member state to take steps itself to abide by an EU decision) and it is these measures that are enforced by the ECJ, which also is the final court of appeal in these matters. The Commission uses the ECJ to discipline member states that do not abide by the rules: the court is therefore supranational. One judge is drawn from each of the 27 member states, but obviously they judge impartially.

 Question: 'The European parliament lacks power.' Discuss.

15.3 Is there a 'democratic deficit' in Europe?

Since the 1980s, there have been concerns expressed about the fact that the EU has developed without a great deal of democracy to accompany it. This lack of democracy has been called the 'democratic deficit'. The main concerns may be said to be as follows.

Weakness of the European Parliament

The introduction of direct elections in 1979 was clearly a step in the right direction, but the low levels of participation in these elections, notably in the UK, is worrying. The real problem, however, is the weakness of the European Parliament. The role of the EP is discussed above, and although it has increased its powers, these remain small. Both the intergovernmental (Council) and the supranational (Commission) institutions of the EU have been reluctant to make the EP more powerful or more democratic. The supranationalists have not supported a body which may be a thorn in the side of the Commission; the intergovernmentalists on the Council do not wish to see their own freedom removed. As the only directly elected democratic body in the EU at the moment, the Parliament would probably acquire more legitimacy if its members sought to be genuinely representative of their constituencies. In a federal (or quasi-federal) state, the role of representatives must inevitably be in large part the representation of local or regional interests. The EP makes little effort to do this, and hence fails in the primary function of an elected body – representation. There have been steps taken to make the Parliament more powerful, but there is another problem here: a more powerful EP does not necessarily improve democracy. Each MEP represents about seven times the number of people represented by a domestic MP. Would democracy be improved if the MEP were to take over some of the functions of the MP? Simple arithmetic suggests not, especially bearing in mind that turnout for EP elections is about half what it is for national general elections.

Elite politics

No popular movement existed to support application for membership of what became the European Union, or indeed to oppose the Euro-scepticism which emerged on the Right in the UK in the 1990s. There has been no substantial pressure group in favour of European integration in this country, no grassroots movement with petitions and demonstrations. On the contrary, opposition to the EU has produced some quite popular single-issue political parties – for example, the Referendum Party and the UK Independence Party. A referendum was held in 1975 over membership of the EU (after the UK had joined) and elite support for a 'yes' vote in the referendum was almost overwhelming. No further referendum has been held in the UK on the growth of the powers of the EU, although referendums have been held in other member states. Referendums were, however, promised on European Monetary Union and the new EU Constitution. Where the subject of the EU enters domestic politics in the UK, it does so as a subsidiary theme, which parties seek to exploit to gain support. No general election was ever fought mainly on this issue. British people are mostly ignorant of European affairs and receive a highly biased account of them from the often strongly anti-European popular press. Turnout in European elections in the UK is – even by British standards – low. Opinion polls indicate that the British are generally apathetic or hostile towards European integration, and the single currency. Opinion polls also show a division in attitudes: while the upper and middle classes and the business community in Britain are generally in favour of the EU, the working class is hostile. Much of the work of the EU is shrouded in mystery. The Commission is a closed body and meetings of the Council of Ministers were, until recently, conducted entirely in secret, although there has lately been some attempt at greater transparency.

Scrutiny in the UK

The intergovernmental structures of the EU have not been very strongly subjected to democratic scrutiny in the UK. The mechanisms for parliamentary scrutiny in the UK were very weak until quite recently: the main forum for scrutiny was a committee of the unelected House of Lords, which itself suggests a sort of institutionalized democratic deficit. There is now more time allowed for Commons scrutiny of EU legislation and there is a Minister of State for Europe in the Foreign and Commonwealth Office (not exactly a major post, although at times the minister has attended the Cabinet without actually being a 'member'). Before 1997, attendance at meetings of the Council of Ministers was occasionally left to senior civil servants, but ministers must now themselves make the effort to attend. All this suggests that some attempts have been made to reduce the democratic deficit. It needs also to be emphasized that large areas of policy are now settled in Europe, and it is therefore important to have structures by which they may be scrutinized in the UK. What seemed in the past to be lacking, though, was very much input from domestic, democratically elected representatives at the early stages of policy-making. Scrutiny in Parliament was a process undertaken largely when it was already too late to change very much. The Treaty of Amsterdam sought to improve matters in this area, by ruling that there should be a six-week interval between the tabling of a legislative proposal and its insertion on the Council agenda, specifically to allow national legislatures more time to discuss the issue, and presumably give their advice to the minister who would legislate at Brussels.

Judges

The power of unelected judges has been enhanced by the EU. Judges can use EU law to strike down the legislation passed by an elected UK Parliament. This is significant, given the worries voiced in recent years about the political bias of the judiciary, and adds weight to concerns about the way in which Europe seems to strengthen elites in the UK.

Presidentialism

The growing tendency observed by some commentators for the UK Prime Minister to assume a more elevated role as a sort of 'presidential' figure is enhanced by the rise of EU. This suggests a movement away from democratic politics. The focus is now centred on the Prime Minister as he or she attends intergovernmental conferences, and meetings of the European Council. The very extensive patronage of the Prime Minister is also enhanced by access to nominations to the Commission and other EU institutions.

Subsidiarity

There is no doubt that European statesmen are aware of the democratic deficit and are concerned about the problem. There has been a gradual process of democratizing the European institutions, but since democratization tends to go hand in hand with the growth of supranationalism, there are problems. Article 3b of the Maastricht Treaty, which was included with the support of the British, made reference to the principle of **subsidiarity** in an attempt to make a new approach to the question. Using the principle of subsidiarity, the Maastricht Treaty says that decisions should be taken by the EU, 'only if and insofar as the objectives of the proposed action cannot be sufficiently achieved by the Member States and can therefore, by reason of the scale or effects of the proposed action, be better achieved by the Community'. As has been pointed out, subsidiarity might imply that some decisions are best taken at subnational level, in the regions or localities.

> **Subsidiarity**: the theory that it is best to take all political decisions as close to the people concerned as possible, i.e. at the most subsidiary level (e.g. a decision affecting one town would be taken in that town).

 Question: Discuss the view that there is a 'democratic deficit' in the European Union.

15.4 The single currency

The biggest single European issue for Britain in the last two decades has been whether to adopt the euro in place of the pound sterling. After briefly examining the history of this issue, it is important to look at Labour and Conservative Party views on the matter.

The history of the single currency

1989

After much internal division between the senior figures of the Conservative Party, Margaret Thatcher was persuaded, against her better judgement, to join the Exchange Rate Mechanism (ERM), which was a preliminary stage in the EEC preparations for adopting a single currency. The move towards a single European currency had been going on since before Britain first joined in 1973. The great struggles over this within the Conservative Party contributed to Thatcher's fall from power in 1990.

1991–2

When John Major negotiated the Maastricht Treaty, he arranged for a British opt-out on the single currency. In other words, Britain reserved the right not to join the single currency when the time came for a final decision. John Major did this to avoid too much internal division within his own party, especially in the run-up to the general election of 1992.

1992: Black Wednesday

The pound suffered from massive, speculative currency dealing which reduced its value initially by about 15 per cent in relation to other currencies, and which led Britain to withdraw from the Exchange Rate Mechanism. The cost to the government of supporting the pound as the crisis unfolded was put at £3.3 billion. The British press blamed the German Central Bank for failing to support the pound, but the fact is that Thatcher had overvalued it and hence it was vulnerable to speculation. This made it politically impossible for Major to rejoin the ERM, which meant that Britain could not adopt the euro when it was launched in 2002. Black Wednesday immeasurably strengthened the hand of the Conservative Euro-sceptics, and although it helped Blair achieve power in 1997, it also made it impossible for him to adopt the euro.

Box 15.2 Labour and the euro

Labour has said that it is broadly in agreement with the idea of adopting the euro, but will only do so when the time is right and with the agreement of the people. In 1997, as one of his first measures, the then Chancellor of the Exchequer, Gordon Brown, created what is virtually an independent British central bank when he gave the Bank of England the ability to set interest rates. This measure was seen as a first step towards working with the European Central Bank, which was set up by the Maastricht Treaty to manage the monetary policy of the euro zone. Brown also unveiled his five economic tests for deciding when the time would be right for Britain to adopt the euro:

1 There must be sustainable convergence between the British economy and the economies of the euro zone.
2 There must be sufficient flexibility in the euro zone to deal with economic change once Britain had joined.
3 Investment in the UK should not suffer.
4 The financial services industry (the 'City' of London) should not be harmed as a result of joining.
5 Britain should only join if doing so were good for employment.

These tests were first applied by the Treasury in 2003, when Brown announced that he could not at that point support an application for membership. The government undertook to test the situation annually thereafter to see if joining could be recommended. Many commentators took the view that Brown's economic tests were not sufficiently objective for them to be taken seriously, and that they were a political smokescreen for delaying making a decision until the political situation was right. If the Treasury decided the tests had been passed, the next step would be to put the question to the people in a referendum, with the government recommending that they should vote in favour of the new currency. But the British people have remained stubbornly opposed to supporting the adoption of the euro, and the British press, especially the Murdoch papers, has also on the whole been opposed. So, the economic tests are a good political measure, since they enable the government to put off a decision. There was speculation that Brown was personally less enthusiastic about the euro than Blair, and in any case there are reasons for being a little cautious about joining. When it was first launched, the euro was quite weak and lost value against the dollar, and the British economy has grown faster since 1997 than the economies of most countries which adopted the euro. So there were some economic reasons for not joining the euro zone immediately. But officially there was no real disagreement between Brown and Blair on this matter: both supported joining the euro when the time was right. This time has not yet arrived and it is likely that Brown's promotion to Prime Minister makes it even less likely that the UK will adopt the euro in the near future.

1997: general election

The election was affected by the issue of the single currency. The Referendum Party campaigned on the single issue of holding a referendum on the euro. This put great pressure on the Conservative Party and made it more strongly Euro-sceptic than ever. All three major parties followed the Referendum Party in promising that, if elected, they would hold a referendum on the issue. The difference was that the Referendum Party was promising to hold an immediate referendum, but the other parties did not say

Box 15.3 Conservatives and the euro

Conservative policy on the euro after 1997 looks very different from that of Labour, but in practice was not so very different. Between 1997 and 2003, the Conservative leaders – William Hague and especially Iain Duncan Smith – were quite strongly Euro-sceptic. Hague's policy, which Duncan Smith followed, was that the Conservatives would not rule out eventual adoption of the euro, but that it should be delayed for some time. In 2001 Hague proposed that if the Conservatives won the election of that year, adopting the euro would be put off for at least the duration of two more Parliaments, or about ten years. The reason for this approach was to give voters the chance to express their opposition to the euro by voting Conservative, but also to avoid antagonizing the pro-European section of the party too much by declaring total opposition. It looked like a rather contradictory policy, but was not very different from that of Labour. Michael Howard, after his election as Conservative leader in 2003, gradually emerged with an even more uncompromising opposition to the euro than his predecessors. The Conservatives were now more clearly opposed to joining the euro zone than in the past, and this was made clear in their manifesto of 2005. They said then they supported a referendum on the issue but would advise people to vote no. The Conservative position has changed little since the election of David Cameron as leader, but there has been a marked softening of tone on the subject of the European Union.

when they would hold one. Since 1997, the attitude of the Labour government and the Conservative opposition has not significantly altered on the issue.

15.5 British political parties and the European Union

The European Union has been one of the major issues facing Britain since the 1950s. Not surprisingly, it has caused great difficulty for the main political parties. They have disagreed between themselves over the issue, and there have been quite frequent disagreements actually within the parties.

Division between the British political parties

The EU has been an issue which cuts across the main divisions between the two major British parties, and as a result it has forced the parties into adopting new positions in relation to one another. This can be shown by examining briefly the history of how the issue has affected the main parties. Ever since the EU became a subject for discussion in British politics (in about 1960), there have been more periods of agreement or consensus between the two major parties on Europe than there have been of disagreement. The main periods of adversary politics or conflict over the topic have been 1960 and

Box 15.4 Possible positions on the European Union

It is probably best to think of a spectrum of opinion among political parties and the population in general on the European Union. But to simplify, this spectrum can be divided in a number of ways. Obviously there is a straightforward division between those who are in favour of Britain being a member of the European Union and those who are not: pro-Europeans and anti-Europeans. The anti-Europeans can then be split into two groups depending on their other political views. First, there are socialist anti-Europeans, who see the EU as a 'rich man's club' designed to fleece the working class. This is a dying breed, it is fair to say, since the advent of New Labour, but it was once a very prominent group in the party. Second, there are nationalist anti-Europeans, who sometimes overlap with the socialist anti-Europeans, but are generally to be found on the right of British politics and who see the EU as a threat to national independence.
Pro-Europeans could be analysed in the same way as the anti-Europeans: social democrat pro-Europeans, who welcome the way in which regional aid, workers' rights, environmental and human-rights issues are strengthened by the EU, and liberal economic (or capitalist) pro-Europeans, who welcome the opportunities for economic growth and business enterprise which stem from the EU. Another way to analyse the two factions is according to the strength of their feelings on the issue. Anti-Europeans cannot really be separated in this way: they are united in opposition, and it is not possible to be moderate or extreme about leaving the EU – they just want to leave. But pro-Europeans are divided into two groups. First, there are the Euro-sceptics. These people wish to remain members of the EU, but are sceptical about the value of further integration and a strengthening of the institutions of the EU. The second group consist of europhiles or enthusiastic pro-Europeans, who welcome the creation of the EU and are pleased at the prospect of a strong, active Union, with Britain at the heart of it. At present – and indeed for the past 40 years – the majority of the British political elite has been found in one or other of these last two major camps. The British people have been less keen, but a majority of them has probably also been pro-European.

1962 and between 1980 and 1987, because at these times the Labour Party was officially committed to opposition to the EU while the Conservative Party was in favour.

1960–2

The Conservative Party under Harold Macmillan announced its desire to join the EEC, in a spirit of capitalist pro-Europeanism. Hugh Gaitskell, the leader of the Labour opposition, much to everyone's surprise, announced his opposition to joining the EEC at the 1962 party conference. In doing so, he used the language of what we have called nationalist anti-Europeanism (see box 15.4), saying that to join would mean 'the end of a thousand years of history'. His real motive may have been to appeal to the left wing of his party, which distrusted him as a man of the centre. The left of the Labour Party had socialist objections to the EEC.

1962–80

During this period, Harold Wilson and James Callaghan both tried to steer the Labour Party back to a pro-European position, but did so against a background of great divisions within the party. The impression given, though, was that the Labour Party was more suspicious than the Conservative Party was of Europe.

1980–7

The Labour Party emerged in this period as being in favour of withdrawal from the EEC, while the Conservatives were in favour of continued membership.

1987–2005

Labour became again a pro-European party and gradually began to adopt the position of being more in favour of Europe than the Conservatives, who were becoming more sceptical on the issue.

2005–present

Cameron has tentatively moved the Conservative Party a little back into the centre-ground, even on the contentious issue of Europe. Under Brown, the Labour Party will probably be a little less enthusiastic about Europe than it was under Blair.

Hence, on the issue of Europe, the two main British political parties moved into different positions, and underwent a process of realignment. At the beginning of the period, the Labour Party was less pro-European and the Conservative Party more pro-European. By the 1990s their positions had been reversed, and a realignment had taken place: the Conservatives had become more sceptical and the Labour Party more enthusiastic. At first, this continued to be the case in Labour's third term. In 2005, the pro-European Conservative, Ken Clarke, was rejected in the leadership elections, confirming the party's Euro-scepticism. Labour, on the other hand, continued to support eventual membership of the euro zone and would have endorsed support for the European Constitution. The sharpness of the divisions between the two parties on Europe may perhaps be a little blunted by the election of the centrist David Cameron as Conservative leader, who wishes to modernize the party, and also by the choice of Gordon Brown as leader of Labour, since he is known to be more cautious on Europe than Blair.

Division within the main British political parties

Political parties ought to be united; otherwise, they cannot fight one another for power. The media and the public apparently prefer their parties to be 'led' by people who can unite the party. But on Europe, both parties have always been to some degree divided, and at times very seriously and bitterly divided. Again, the parties have taken it in turns to be more divided on the subject.

1960–81

Labour was certainly more divided than the Conservatives on the issue. By the time of the crucial debates of 1970–2, when Britain joined the EEC under a Conservative government, the division was virtually 50:50 in the Labour Party. On the whole, the left of the party was more opposed to Europe than the right. This division ran right through the party to the Cabinet, and on the referendum of 1975 Wilson 'suspended' the constitutional convention of Cabinet collective responsibility because it was impossible for his colleagues to agree on Europe. Things went from bad to worse after that, and in 1981 the right wing of the Labour Party split away to form the Social Democratic Party (one of the forerunners of the Liberal Democrats), mainly on the basis of this issue. The Conservative Party did have a small and noisy group which opposed the EEC during these years, but the bulk of the party supported membership. Ironically, it was those on the right of the Conservative Party who opposed membership, for patriotic reasons.

1980–present

For a few years under Thatcher in the 1980s, both parties seemed on the surface largely united – Labour in opposition to the EEC and the Conservatives in favour. But after 1986, when Thatcher enthusiastically supported the Single European Act, divisions began to emerge in the Conservative Party on the issue. Thatcher began to develop Euro-sceptic views, which were adopted by the nationalist right wing of the party. Under Major (1990–7), the Conservatives were seriously divided over whether to support the single currency and also over the Maastricht Treaty. Major faced a small but very effective group of opponents on these issues. After 1997, this group of Euro-sceptics took control of the party under Hague and Duncan Smith: their aim was to prevent further growth of the powers of the Union, but they did not support withdrawal. The Euro-enthusiasts in the party, led by Ken Clarke, tended to find themselves increasingly marginalized by the growing strength of the Euro-sceptics. Supporters of Europe among Conservative MPs tend to come from an older generation; with each election after 1987, the number of Conservative Euro-sceptics to have been elected grew. Michael Howard won election in 2003 as leader of a party of which most MPs were Euro-sceptics of one sort or another. At first, Howard seemed to be trying to unite the party around a slightly more moderate approach to the questions. But in 2004 and 2005, perhaps under some pressure from the UK Independence Party, and also out of a desire to differentiate the Conservatives clearly from Labour, Howard reverted to the Euro-scepticism of his two immediate predecessors as leaders. The Conservative Euro-enthusiasts are a rather small group now. David Cameron, appointed as leader in late 2005, wanted to modernize his party and part of this may involve moving away from Euro-scepticism and adopting a more constructive approach to the EU. Cameron must be careful, however, not to alienate the right wing of his party, and force some of his voters into the arms of UKIP, which has been picking up quite a few disaffected Conservative votes. Meanwhile, the Labour Party became increasingly united over Europe in the 1990s and rather surprisingly united around a pro-European approach. The main reason for this may have been that Labour became united on more or less every issue during this period in a desperate effort to achieve power. Under the surface, there were certainly different emphases in the Labour Party over the question of the EU, but on the whole they did not lead to serious intra-party quarrels. The new generation of Labour MPs, especially those swept to power in the New Labour landslide of 1997, has been increasingly enthusiastic about Europe. The succession of Gordon Brown, however, probably shifted the party a few degrees away from his predecessor's Euro-enthusiasm.

Box 15.5 The European Union and three great events in British party politics

The European Union has had a dramatic impact on the party politics of the last three decades, as is shown by the part the issue played in three great events involving both parties in these years.

Labour nearly falls apart (1970–5)

For 20 years (at least) before 1970, the Labour Party had been a difficult coalition of socialists and social democrats, of the left and right; but it had held together. Over joining the EEC, Labour nearly split between the pro-Europeans (largely on the right) and the anti-Europeans (largely on the left). Harold Wilson was able, just about, to keep the party together, by holding a referendum in 1975 and by allowing the Cabinet to disagree in public on the matter. But Labour in the 1970s was gradually sinking in the polls and in 1979 Margaret Thatcher came to power, in part due to the very public divisions in the Labour Party on Europe.

Labour does fall apart (1981)

Finally, in 1981 the right wing of the Labour Party did split away, and formed the Social Democratic Party (SDP), which in 1988 joined the Liberal Party to form the Liberal Democrats. It was partly over Europe that this split took place, although the classic divisions between left and right were also important. The leading figures in the new SDP were Euro-enthusiasts: the most prominent, Roy Jenkins, had been a European Commissioner. Without its right-wingers after 1981, the Labour Party declared its desire to withdraw from Europe completely.

The Conservatives sack their leader (1990)

In 1990, against a background of declining public support for their party, Conservative MPs decided to get rid of their most successful post-war Prime Minister, Margaret Thatcher. A leadership challenge in the party led to John Major being chosen in her place. There were other issues involved – for example, the poll tax. But it was over Europe and Britain's membership of the Exchange Rate Mechanism, the forerunner of the single currency, that the real disagreements between Thatcher and the other leading figures in her party became clear. Thatcher had become increasingly sceptic, while her chief opponents in the leadership election (Heseltine, Major and Hurd) were essentially pro-European. Hence, she was voted out of Downing Street by her own MPs.

Question: Explain the term 'Euro-sceptic'.

15.6 The impact of the European Union on British politics

Membership of the European Union has been one of the great political and constitutional issues of the post-war period and has affected almost every aspect of the British political system. The impact of the EU on the two major British political parties has already been discussed. What follows is a discussion of how the topic of Europe has affected other political areas.

The impact of the EU on national sovereignty

National sovereignty, or the sovereignty of the British state and its citizens, is the ability of the UK to decide matters for itself. Quite clearly, membership of EU has involved a considerable loss of national self-government, or sovereignty. There is now a range of EU institutions which run alongside the UK political institutions and which in a number of areas have some impact on the independent decision-making of these UK bodies. In addition, British citizenship has been profoundly affected by our membership of the EU. British citizens are now also EU citizens, and can go and live anywhere they like in the Union. In the same way, nationals of other EU countries can come and live in Britain, although their entitlement to UK state benefits is to some degree restricted. There is no escaping from the conclusion that British sovereignty has been eroded. All that can be said against this view is to make a series of qualifications.

First, it is possible to say that this sovereignty has been 'pooled', or is now 'shared'. In federal states like the USA, sovereignty is said to be divided between the central federal authority and the individual states – e.g., Texas, California, etc. This might also be said of European supranational institutions. Second, insofar as the EU is largely still an intergovernmental organization, UK sovereignty is preserved at the level of policy-making and legislation by British representation on the Council of Ministers and European Parliament. Finally, if the purpose of the sovereignty of the democratic state is to mobilize the sovereignty of the people, and if the EU can become truly democratic and overcome its so-called 'democratic deficit', then the sovereignty of the people will be preserved.

The impact of the EU on parliamentary sovereignty

This is a difficult constitutional topic, which is dealt with more fully in chapter 9. Parliament is sovereign in the UK because it is the place where the sovereignty of the state and the people is said to be located. But sovereignty is clearly affected by the fact that the EU can, in some matters, make laws for the UK – as is the independence of the UK legislature, Parliament. Part of the difficulty is that parliamentary sovereignty is the key theoretical principle underpinning the whole of the British Constitution, and it seems shocking for it to be breached in this way. There is, however, an answer to this: Parliament itself willingly gave up its power by ratifying the accession of the UK to the EEC, passing in 1972 the European Communities Act, by which it was explicitly stated that in certain circumstances EU law would take precedence over home-grown parliamentary law. So Parliament agreed to limit itself, thus preserving the doctrine of parliamentary sovereignty. In addition, any future Parliament could invoke the principle of parliamentary sovereignty and reclaim the independence of our state. The main difficulty with accepting that we still have parliamentary sovereignty lies in the fact that the 1972 European Communities Act seems to be able to bind future Parliaments after its passage. A key aspect of the doctrine of parliamentary sovereignty has been the idea that no Parliament can 'bind its successor', or make a law which no future Parliament can repeal. But the European Communities Act does seem to have this effect. However, the Act has this effect because no Parliament has sought to overturn it explicitly, and a Parliament might do so in the future. The idea of sovereignty is essentially a paradoxical one when it relies on the doctrine that no sovereign Parliament can bind its sovereign successor. The best practical demonstration of this alleged loss of parliamentary sovereignty came with the famous Factortame Case (see box 15.6).

The effect of the EU on the decisions of the UK government

Decisions made by the British government can be overruled by the EU if it deems that its own laws have been contravened. The body in the Union which does this is the European Commission and it uses the European Court of Justice (ECJ) to enforce its decisions. This happens throughout the EU, and the UK government is actually extremely good at abiding by EU law in comparison with many other EU states. Thus in 1989, the ECJ ruled against the UK government just once, while other member-states had a total of 79 rulings against them. Between 1982 and 1989 there were 20 referrals of the British government to ECJ for breach of EU law, which was the second lowest number of any state. Examples of how British governments have had to modify their policy include the following.

Box 15.6 The Factortame Case (1991)

It had been clear since the Treaty of Rome in 1957 that European law could overrule national laws. There has been no secret about this, and the 1972 European Communities Act clearly accepts (and 'legalizes') this. The case which made this crystal clear as far as the UK was concerned was the Factortame Case. The Spanish fishing company of this name appealed through the UK courts against decisions of the British government restricting their actions. The government had acted using the Merchant Shipping Act passed by Parliament in 1988. Factortame argued that the law of the EEC allowed them to act as they did, and that the British government could not use the 1988 Act to prevent them. In 1991, the House of Lords heard this case on appeal, and consulted the European Court of Justice (as they were bound to do under EU law) on the case. As a result, the judges in the House of Lords decided in favour of Factortame and 'struck down' the 1988 Merchant Shipping Act. This seems to be a clear denial of either (1) the aspect of parliamentary sovereignty by which the law courts have to apply the law enacted by Parliament – that is, the 1988 Merchant Shipping Act; or (2) the aspect of parliamentary sovereignty which says that no Parliament can bind its successor, since quite clearly the Merchant Shipping Act was passed by a Parliament 16 years after the 1972 European Communities Act. Either way, it does not look good for parliamentary sovereignty. In practical political terms, the real problem may simply be one of poor parliamentary draughtsmanship. The legal experts who drew up the Merchant Shipping Act should have made sure it did not conflict with European law. There is no formal mechanism in the British political system to ensure that new legislation does not conflict with EU law (as there is now for the Human Rights Act), so it rested with the courts to judge the 'constitutionality' of parliamentary action.

In 1987, an EU directive on acid pollution was enforced on the UK, so that steps had to be taken to reduce sulphur dioxide and nitrogen oxide emissions from power stations. This seems to show the EU in a good light: environmental protection of this sort must be a matter of international law, and it is right for the EU to protect Germany and the Scandinavian countries which are downwind of our acid-rain pollution. Clearly it would be unpopular for a domestic government to take a measure like this, which would be very expensive, without EU pressure.

In 1986, the EU forced the UK government to set up the National Rivers Authority at the time of the privatization of the water companies in England and Wales. The Thatcher government had proposed to privatize the control of rivers to these commercial suppliers of water. Here, EU action is more contentious, unless one argues that the state of the UK's rivers affects foreign countries. Without this argument, this looks like EU interference in internal UK activity, which seems not to concern anyone apart from the UK electorate, who can control a government's actions through the normal agency of the ballot box. It was, however, a step taken by the Commission on the basis of European law which the UK had played a part in enacting.

Government ministers are clearly very closely involved in the work of the EU, attending meetings of the Council of Ministers, especially if their

"EU regulations – you have to plant this instead"

department is strongly involved in the work of the EU. The Foreign and Commonwealth Office takes a lead in European affairs, although the Prime Minister also maintains a close interest. The Cabinet Office coordinates the European policy of different government departments, through a European Secretariat. The Treasury, the Department of Trade and Industry and the Department for Environment, Food and Rural Affairs are also most deeply involved in the affairs of Europe. Civil service links with Brussels are, of necessity, very strong, with senior mandarins attending meetings of the Council of Ministers and working closely with the UK representatives on the Committee of Permanent Representatives (COREPER). These COREPER officials are Whitehall civil servants, a third from the Foreign and Commonwealth Office, and the remainder seconded for two-year stretches by their UK departments.

Some areas of public policy are decided in Europe

The EU decides public policy for its members in a growing number of areas. To look on this in a favourable light, the UK plays a part in these decisions, and of course in some sense thereby exercises power over other member states. But from a more negative perspective, policy for the UK is decided abroad. Some areas are completely exempt from EU interest but they are not many.

The three areas most likely to be largely unaffected by the EU in the future are welfare, foreign and defence policy, and justice and home affairs.

Welfare

It is extremely unlikely that in the near future the EU will directly involve itself in the social security arrangements of member states, which vary considerably from country to country, and which are an extremely expensive drain on the resources of a state. Similarly, policies on education, health and personal social services are costly, and subject to much variety across Europe. However, the EU has already had an impact on the age of retirement in this country, after equality judgements by the ECJ ruled that both men and women should retire at the same age. There are also several EU educational programmes, like Erasmus, and language-teaching initiatives.

Foreign and defence policy

Under the two treaties on European union, there are ambitious aspirations for policy harmonization in this area, in the expectation of creating a common foreign and security policy. But intergovernmentalism will probably also persist. NATO still exists and will be Europe's main defensive alliance in the future. The divisions in Europe over the Balkans in the 1990s and over Iraq in 2002–4 show how unlikely it is that policy will be decided by the EU and not in each member state.

Justice and home affairs

The Maastricht Treaty envisaged a gradual process by which policy in these areas would be increasingly harmonized, but beyond cooperation on immigration, borders and the creation of Europol (a scheme for linking police forces across Europe), it is unlikely that great progress will be made. It is significant that in recent years there has been growing cooperation between the police forces of the eastern counties of England with their counterparts across the Channel. It is now a requirement in the Kent Constabulary that candidates for senior posts be competent in at least one European language. Overall, however, there are such huge differences in the legal systems and in the approach to law and order across Europe that it will be impossible to create a single European system in this area of policy for many years to come.

But, beyond these areas, the policy impact of the EU is quite significant.

Agriculture and fisheries

Policy in this area is almost all made by the EU. There is a Common Agricultural Policy and also a Common Fisheries Policy, which in recent years has produced a number of demonstrations by British fisherman, who are bitter about the way in which their freedom to fish is restricted, and also by the way in which fishermen from other member states are given access to 'British' fisheries.

Trade and economic policy

This is a huge area, and the impact of the EU on government policy here is clearly considerable. At its simplest, it is not possible for the UK to impose restrictions on either exports or imports, or indeed to raise or lower tariffs, without European approval. In 1990, the ECJ ruled that the UK government should receive £44.4 million from British Aerospace, which the government had overpaid to the company when it sold British Leyland to them. Such a payment was a form of government subsidy, which was forbidden by European law. It is reckoned that 80 per cent of all regulations affecting the production, distribution and exchange of goods in the EU are now European rules, not home-grown national ones.

Taxation and the UK budget

Value Added Tax (VAT) was introduced in Britain when it joined the EU and it is the source of most EU funds. It is now harmonized, more or less, all over the EU. The convergence criteria for joining the euro zone dictate to prospective members the level of their deficit, debt, inflation rates and interest rates. A reminder that this was the case was delivered in 2004 when the European Court of Justice imposed large fines on Germany and France for failing to keep to these rules. Under the 1986 Single European Act the harmonization of tax levels was a key factor, so that member states can compete fairly with one another. In December 1998, at the Vienna European Council, the question of Britain's tax rates was raised: tax is low in Britain compared with other European countries and this may give the country a trading advantage over the others. European integration in the future seems likely to involve greater tax harmonization.

Currency policy

If the UK adopts the euro, it will lose control over its own currency, and the value of the currency will be decided in the European Central Bank in Frankfurt. But even without joining the euro zone, British currency policy has, since the 1980s, been greatly affected by Europe. In the mid-1980s, the Chancellor of the Exchequer, Nigel Lawson, began to 'shadow the German mark' – that is, to tie the value of the pound to the strongest European currency. Even after the crash of the pound on Black Wednesday in 1992, this policy continued. Since 1997, Labour has been officially committed to eventual membership of the euro zone, and hence its currency policy could be said to be governed to some extent by that goal.

Environmental policy

As the examples given above of EU action over acid-rain and river-management show, this is an area of policy where the EU plays a very active part. More than 200 EU directives and regulations have been issued on environmental matters. In 1993, a European Environment Agency was established to act as an information centre on the subject.

Transport policy

The EU has taken an interest in fostering trans-European road links. Ironically, the environmental concerns of the EU which made the Commission respond to complaints about British road schemes at Twyford Down and Newbury in the 1990s need to be set against the background that these road schemes were actually built in response to EU strategic road network plans.

The impact of the EU on the Westminster Parliament

The constitutional point about the supposed loss of parliamentary sovereignty involved in joining the EEC has already been discussed. There is also an important political issue here. Insofar as large policy areas are now discussed and decided outside the UK, parliamentary power has been seriously undermined. As veteran Labour politician Tony Benn claims, the power of ministers has been enhanced at the expense of Parliament, in that they now decide these matters without needing to pass legislation in Parliament. However, ministers cannot entirely bypass Parliament in European affairs, and there are now parliamentary committees which scrutinize EU policy. There is a well-regarded House of Lords Select Committee on European Affairs, although the very fact that it belongs to the inferior second chamber lessens its impact. In the Commons there is a Select Committee on European Legislation, which examines draft proposals for additions to EU law from the Commission, although it has limited powers to do very much about this legislation after it has scrutinized it. At various times, the work of Parliament has been greatly influenced by debates on European affairs. This has had a significant impact on Parliament. The debates under Edward Heath in 1971–2, and then in 1974–5 under Wilson, took up a great deal of parliamentary time. One of best examples of the impact of Europe on Parliament was seen in 1992–3, when Major tried to secure the ratification of the Maastricht Treaty. There were a number of extremely close votes in the Commons on the Maastricht debates, caused largely by divisions within the Conservative Party. The Maastricht Bill took 200 hours to debate and there were 600 amendments proposed to it. Despite what Tony Benn says, this suggests that parliamentary power was in some senses enhanced as a result of the intensity of disagreement on this issue.

The impact of the EU on political parties

The effect of the controversies over Britain's membership of the European Union on the two major parties has already been discussed, but it is important to recognize that other parties have also been affected.

In the 1990s, the UK saw the development of two anti-European political parties. The UK Independence Party (UKIP) was formed to oppose British membership of the EU. It contested a number of seats in the 1992 and 1997 elections, to no great success, but in 1999 gained three seats on the European Parliament. In the European elections in June 2004, to most people's surprise, it won 12 seats and was in third place behind the two major parties, and ahead of the Liberal Democrats. In the 2005 general election, the party, led by a former Conservative MP, Nigel Farage, collected 2.8 per cent of the national vote (up from 2.1 per cent in 2001), but because of the first-past-the-post electoral system got, of course, no MPs.

The Referendum Party contested the 1997 general election and was the brainchild, ironically, of the MEP for Paris, the late Sir James Goldsmith, a very rich British businessman. The Referendum Party won an extraordinary 811,827 votes in 1997, making it easily the most successful fourth party in English politics for as long as there have been elections. It ran on the platform of calling a referendum on EU membership, and gained support largely from disaffected Conservative voters in the South of England. Since Sir James's death, the party has been disbanded but it continued as the Referendum Movement, an anti-European pressure group.

The Green Party received a considerable boost in 1989 when it got an extraordinary 14.9 per cent of the vote in the European Parliament elections of that year. At that time, the elections for the EP were conducted under the FPTP system, so the Green Party gained no seats. The Grünnen in Germany, and other environmental parties in Europe, were strong at that time, and this doubtless encouraged voters to support the British Green Party. The development of an EU interest in environmental issues following the Single European Act contributed too. In subsequent European Parliament elections, conducted under a more proportional electoral system, the Greens have gained representation: two seats in both 1999 and 2004.

The Liberal Democrat Party (and its various predecessors) has been a committed supporter of the European cause since the issue entered British politics, although there have been occasional Liberal Euro-sceptics. The Liberal Party underwent a substantial revival in the early 1970s, but by 1979 was again in decline. It was rescued from further decline by the issue of Europe, which was to a large degree instrumental in creating a new party, the Social Democratic Party, which in 1981 split away from Labour. In an alliance with the Liberals in the 1983 election, the SDP came close to becoming the second British political party. After 1987, this alliance became the Liberal Democrat Party, which, it can therefore be claimed, owes its existence to the issue of Europe. The party's last three leaders, Paddy Ashdown, Charles Kennedy and Menzies Campbell, have tended to be a little muted in their support for Europe while in the election spotlight, but the fact remains that the Liberal Democrats are the party of Europe in British politics, and will continue as such under Nick Clegg.

The impact of the EU on the judiciary

One aspect of politics in the UK in the past 25–30 years has been the increasing role of the judiciary, in protecting the rights of citizens and in limiting the free action of the executive branch of the political system. This has been coupled with concerns expressed about the independence, impartiality and representative nature of the judiciary. The rise of the judiciary has been encouraged by the power given it under the European Communities Act to give 'direct effect' to European law, and to 'strike down' parliamentary law if it conflicts with it. This was dramatically shown in the Factortame Case (discussed above in box 15.6). The separate matter (because it is not technically anything to do with the EU) of the incorporation of the European Convention on Human Rights into British law by the 1998 Human Rights Act is having a similar effect, bringing judges into the political arena. The judiciary cannot use the Human Rights Act to strike down an Act of Parliament in the same way that it can use European law, but it can write to Parliament declaring that an Act is incompatible with the Human Rights Act, and Parliament should then take its own actions to change the law.

The impact of the EU on pressure groups

Some of the cause pressure groups have been created just because of Europe. For example, there is a European Movement which fosters support for integration; in 1999, the Britain in Europe group was set up, headed by Colin Marshall, former Chairman of British Airways; and opposition to the euro has also produced pressure groups: Business for Sterling and the Save the Pound campaign. Environmental cause groups have also been given an impetus from the opportunities for lobbying presented by the EU interest in environmentalism. Cause pressure groups like Friends of the Earth and Greenpeace are supranational political groups, reflecting the globalization of which the EU is also in a sense a symptom.

But it is the sectional or interest groups that have been most aided by the existence of the EU. After 1979, such groups found it increasingly difficult to get a hearing in British politics. This was particularly true of the trade unions, but also of the representatives of employers and of industry. They were compensated to some degree with a growing role in Brussels. The EU is in some senses a 'corporatist' organization; that is, it subscribes to the view that governments should work in their economic policies in close cooperation with the 'social partners', with representatives of organized labour and of business. Corporatism was the standard post-war view in Britain of how interest groups should be treated, a view supported by both Labour and Conservative governments until 1979, when Thatcherism ended it. The European commitment to this corporatism is shown by the existence in Brussels of the

Economic and Social Committee, which puts the views of the representatives of national interest groups to the Commission and Council. The network of advisory committees of the Council and Commission (the 'comitologie', as it is known) also welcomes an input from pressure groups. Individual trade unions, and their peak organization, the Trades Union Congress (TUC), maintain offices in Brussels, as do business associations and also their peak organization, the Confederation of British Industry. Large UK companies have Brussels representatives too, or work through professional lobbyists there. The National Farmers' Union has been enthusiastically engaged in Europe, and Sir Henry Plumb – one of its past Presidents – became a successful MEP, rising to be the first British President of the European Parliament. In 1988, Jacques Delors, the President of the Commission at that time, gave a speech to the Trades Union Congress, prompting its General Secretary to claim that 'Delors is our shepherd'. British lobbying firms have been particularly successful in Brussels, representing businesses from all over the Union, not just from the UK. There is apparently a saying in EU circles that 'the Brits run Brussels', meaning that lobbyists from the UK play a significant role there. There are supranational links between such interest groups. Thus, the European agricultural interest has a European-wide peak group which lobbies the EU institutions on behalf of European farmers.

There are other European peak organizations which also lobby at Brussels, representing several industries and trade unions. Among the more important of these 'Euro-groups' are:

- The Committee of Professional Agricultural Organizations of the European Community
- The Union of Industries of the European Community
- European Bureau of Consumer Unions
- European Trade Union Confederation
- European Environmental Bureau
- Banking Federation of the European Community

The impact of the EU on subnational politics

The nationalist parties in the UK (the Scottish National Party and Plaid Cymru) were at first opposed to the EEC. They argued that there was little point in breaking away from the UK, only to be admitted to a larger and even more remote state. The same was true of the Ulster Unionists, for rather different reasons. Their fierce British patriotism resented any abridgement of sovereignty. They had given a parliamentary constituency to the most virulent right-wing opponent of Europe during the 1970s, Enoch Powell, when he was ejected from the Conservative Party for his opposition to the official party line on Europe. But during the 1980s, as European integration developed and as

European policy involved greater regional economic aid, the nationalists began to soften towards Europe, and became enthusiastically in favour of it. They feel that the EU will give Scotland and Wales the security and support they need to survive as independent states outside the UK. So it might be argued that the growth of Scottish and Welsh nationalism, and hence also of the devolution these countries have been granted by Westminster to weaken this nationalism, is caused to some degree by the development of the EU. The settlement of Northern Ireland at the time of the Good Friday Agreement (1998), which involves complex changes to citizenship in that province, may also owe something to developments in Europe on this issue. If British and Irish citizens are now, as a result of membership of the EU, European citizens, the old struggles over Northern Irish identity begin to seem less relevant.

A number of British regions, especially Merseyside, the Highlands and Islands of Scotland, and Cornwall have benefited substantially from EU regional aid. Following the Maastricht Treaty, a Committee of the Regions was set up in Brussels to provide the Commission and Council with advice on matters of concern to the regions of Europe. All UK regions are represented on this Committee of the Regions, and most of the larger local authorities maintain some sort of permanent representation in Brussels. In 1995, also in response to Maastricht, the UK was divided into eight regions, which have a regional office, or Regional Development Agency. The Labour Party while in opposition proposed to give these regional offices a democratic basis and to give to the regions of the UK a real institutional structure. Once in power, the Labour government was rather slow to turn these proposals into firm commitments, but in November 2004 the north-eastern region held a referendum over whether to create a regional assembly there, and decisively rejected the proposal. In 2007, the new Brown government quietly dropped further discussion of English regional assemblies. But English Regional Development Agencies remain, and owe their existence, to some extent, to the influence of Europe.

Activity

A counterfactual exercise is one in which you consider what would have happened if history had turned out differently. It is useful because it helps us evaluate what actually did happen and its impact more clearly. With a classmate consider two cases:

1 If we had withdrawn from the European Economic Community as a result of the referendum of 1975, what would have been the probable consequences? Organize your answer in terms of beneficial and harmful consequences.
2 In the 1990s, some on the right of British politics argued seriously that Britain should join the North American Free Trade Area, with the USA, Canada and Mexico. What would have been the good or bad impact of doing this?

Question: Discuss the constitutional impact that membership of the European Union has had on the United Kingdom.

15.7 Arguments for and against the European Union

There is a whole range of opinion concerning the European Union, as has been said, which can be found represented in all the main parties. For the purposes of analysis and evaluation, we can polarize arguments into two groups: for and against the EU. The arguments in favour of the EU are generally to be found expressed by Labour and the Liberal Democrats and the arguments against by the Conservatives. Here, a dozen arguments are presented: the first six will start off with the positive points in favour of the Union; the second six will start with criticisms. The list is not meant to be exhaustive and the reader should be able to add additional points on both sides of the argument.

Peace and security

For the EU

Supporters of the EU argue that peace in Europe since 1945 – the end of the Second World War – has been maintained by the cooperation between former enemies which the Union has fostered. In addition, the inclusion after 2004 of the former Warsaw Pact countries cemented good relations with them which had started only as recently as 1989, when communism in Eastern Europe began to crumble. The efforts to include Turkey in the future will also, it is argued, lead to an improvement in relations with Middle Eastern, Islamic countries, which have been a matter of concern in recent years. It is therefore reasonable, Euro-enthusiasts argue, to develop a common European foreign and defence policy. This does not threaten the links between Europe and the USA, since American foreign policy has always supported the development of the EU.

Against the EU

In response, opponents of the EU argue that Europe would have been at peace after 1945 in any case, and the inclusion of the Eastern European countries came after 1989 not before, so peace between East and West in Europe was not a result of anything done by the European Union. The problems in the former Yugoslavia in the 1990s were a sign that post-war Europe was not immune to conflict and also that the EU had no answer to these issues. It remained for NATO to try to sort out Kosovo, after the scandal of non-intervention in Bosnia. What is more, the prospects for further European cooperation seem rather small, in view of the failure of Europe to agree on a common policy over the Iraq crisis in 2002–4, and also the reluctance of European members of NATO (apart from the UK) in 2006–8 to get seriously involved in the dangerous parts of Afghanistan.

Prosperity and economic growth

For the EU

The main argument in favour of the EU is that membership has helped the British economy to grow. The Single European Act of 1986 led to completely free movement of goods, services, capital and labour, and this is very helpful to the British economy, which has always been strongly geared towards overseas trade. The enlargement of the Union extends the economic opportunities of the member states by opening up potentially valuable areas for trade and investment. The adoption of the euro will also enhance these economic benefits.

Against the EU

On the other hand, it can be argued that there would have been economic growth in Europe in the second half of the twentieth century even without the EU. In fact European growth rates have actually been rather modest since 1957, much less than those in the Far East and the USA, for example. In addition, European countries which have remained outside the EU, like Switzerland, have enjoyed economic prosperity nevertheless. Indeed, Norway and other European countries outside the EU have been able to negotiate free trade agreements with the EU, which have given these countries all the economic advantages of membership without any of the political disadvantages.

Globalization

For the EU

The world is becoming a smaller place with the growth of electronic communications, world trade and commerce. These developments suggest that the days of the nation-state are numbered and that larger political blocs are needed in the modern world. It is important that European countries band together in order to negotiate better trade relations with USA and the growing Asian economies. Together, the European countries will have more impact than they would if they attempted to negotiate individually.

Against the EU

This argument does not add up. If globalization is an inevitable economic process driven by changes in technology, then there is really no point in attempting to further it – or, indeed, to protect oneself against it – by joining the EU. In addition, Britain's real economic and cultural partners are in the 'English-speaking' world: the USA and the British Commonwealth. The way in which joining the EU has drawn Britain away from these global partners has been a move away from a world-view into a narrow regional approach to politics.

Civilization

For the EU

One argument in favour of the EU is that there is a common European culture, which it is important to nurture and develop. Membership of the EU avoids narrow nationalism and develops a sense of civilization by connecting us to the world of, for example, Michelangelo, Voltaire, Beethoven, etc. At a more practical level, membership of the EU might bring tangible benefits for students through the Erasmus and Socrates programmes which have developed to enable them to study in foreign universities.

Against the EU

It is quite possible to be part of European culture without being a member of the EU. It may in practice be more important for the British to respect their own culture and traditions. In any case, many British people are from African, Asian and American cultural traditions and feel excluded when notions of European culture are stressed.

Environment

For the EU

It is important to develop regional policies to deal with problems of environmental pollution, since the winds and tides mean that such problems cannot be restricted to one country. The EU has already had an impact in reducing pollution, taking action over acid rain and setting standards of food safety, for example. The institutions of the EU are ideally framed to enable further environmental problems to be dealt with in this way. It is for this reason that the Green Party has enjoyed some success in the European Parliament elections. The British Green Party can cooperate with other European environmental movements as a result.

Against the EU

If the EU were really interested in the environment, fundamentalist environmentalists argue, it would not be so keen to encourage economic growth, the real engine of pollution in the modern world. In any case, there are other international bodies which can encourage environmental cooperation between countries, above all the United Nations, which has in recent years tried to negotiate reductions in carbon dioxide emissions in the Kyoto Treaty (1998), for example.

Law and order

For the EU

It is important to develop links with our regional neighbours to fight international crime, people smuggling, vice and terrorism. The creation of Europol (a European police force) brings benefits in terms of shared intelligence and a cooperative effort. There are already advantages for Britain which derive from having a common European policy on extradition. This will lead in the end to some further harmonization of legal systems.

Against the EU

It is quite possible to develop policing and intelligence links without being part of a supranational body like the EU. Most shared intelligence on terrorism comes from outside the EU, and it is important in a globalized world to have international, not regional, links. Harmonization of legal systems is unnecessary and undesirable.

The budget

Against the EU

One of the strongest arguments against continued British membership of the EU is that it costs the British taxpayer money. A portion of VAT receipts go direct to the EU. In 2005, Britain contributed in gross terms 13.1 per cent of the EU budget; the total budget in 2007 totalled 126.5 billion euros. Britain is the second biggest net (i.e. considering the total paid and deducting what is received in return) contributor to the EU budget, paying about twice what France does. Only Germany, which is a richer country, makes a larger net contribution than the UK, paying about a third more. The EU budget pays for the institutions and employees of the Union, but also provides money to member states according to certain rules. The largest item of expenditure is on the Common Agricultural Policy (CAP), which is bad for Britain because it does not have a very large agricultural sector (see more on this below).

Increasing parts of the EU budget go to helping the poorer regions of the EU. Again, this does not benefit the UK very much, because it is generally very rich in comparison with other parts of the Union. In 2006, Tony Blair negotiated away Britain's budget rebate, which had been won by Thatcher in recognition of the fact that Britain gets so little back from the budget, and by the time this has come fully into force (it is being phased in gradually), Britain's unequal share in the budget will be even greater.

For the EU

Other countries, notably Germany, suffer more from the same problem. Germany contributes more than the UK and gets little in return directly. This is part of the responsibility of the richer countries in the EU. In fact, the budget in the long run benefits everyone, especially the more advanced economies like the UK. If money is redistributed to the poorer regions, they become richer and spend their money on goods and services from more advanced regions like the UK.

The Common Agricultural Policy (CAP)

Against the EU

Ever since the UK joined the EU, there have been complaints about the CAP, which consumes about half the EU budget and provides subsidies to farmers: in 2007, this was computed to be 55.1 billion euros. It tends to slow down the modernization of farming in areas where small farms are the norm – as in France, for example, where the government is generally strongly opposed to reform of the CAP. It has sometimes created stupid and wasteful outcomes: 'wine lakes' and 'butter mountains' – huge stockpiles of produce which the EU buys at a high price from farmers and then stores, again at a high cost. This is done because once the CAP has guaranteed an intervention price, it has to pay the farmers, however much they produce. To avoid this, in the 1990s the CAP developed a policy of 'set-aside', which involved paying farmers *not* to cultivate part of their land. So, the argument goes, the CAP is wasteful, expensive, harms agriculture and cannot be changed. In addition, it harms the developing world, because farmers there cannot compete with EU farmers, who are guaranteed a high price by the CAP.

For the EU

The CAP made sense in the post-war era, in order to feed the growing population of Europe. Furthermore, British farmers have benefited from the CAP. It is slowly being reformed, as French resistance is worn down, and payments are increasingly made to farmers to encourage environmentally friendly policies. As Europe expands, it is inevitable that the CAP will decline in importance, and payments will be made to rural areas on other grounds than agricultural subsidy.

Threat to national sovereignty

Against the EU

Perhaps the strongest argument against the EU is based on the fear that the independence of Britain and its very existence as a nation-state is threatened by membership. This point has been discussed already to some extent. Critics argue that it is unlikely that, as the EU develops, Britain will ever be able to extricate itself. The abandonment of the currency and adoption of the euro will make this even more difficult. The fact that parliamentary sovereignty is a key principle of the British Constitution supports this argument, since this seems also to be threatened by membership.

For the EU

The argument against this view could be based on two different premises. First, we could say that it is actually good to give up national sovereignty, because it tends to lead to conflict and trouble with other nations. Alternatively, we could argue that there is not actually a huge onslaught on our sovereignty involved in membership of the EU. Britain has joined a 'club' of other nations, and could always withdraw.

Democratic deficit

Against the EU

This issue is debated above. There certainly does seem to be a democratic case to be made against the EU, which has developed without much in the way of popular involvement. A further point to be made here is that the majority of the British people are suspicious of the EU, and do not want to extend European integration any further. Opinion polls show the majority of the British to be opposed to the adoption of the euro, which is the main reason why British governments have not yet signed up to it. There is a vicious circle here: the EU is undemocratic, people are not involved and as a result the EU is unpopular with people.

For the EU

On the other hand, it could be argued that there are steps being taken to remove the democratic deficit and as a result the EU will become both more democratic and more popular. The unpopularity of the EU may owe more to the propaganda of the British newspapers. The only national newspapers to support the EU are: the *Guardian*, the *Financial Times*, the *Observer* and the

Mirror. It will be noticed that three of the above are not 'popular' tabloids, and that none of them belongs to Rupert Murdoch. When the British people have the EU properly explained to them, they tend to support it, as was shown by the 2:1 vote in favour of continued membership in the 1975 referendum.

Immigration and xenophobia

Against the EU

There has been a long-running right-wing problem in post-war Britain with issues of immigration, which in more recent years has tended to revolve around the question of asylum-seekers and refugees. Especially with the enlargement of 2004, this led to right-wing arguments against the EU, as increasing numbers of immigrants from the rather poorer new member states have come to Britain. This feeling is whipped up by some newspapers, and is worryingly associated with the rise of extreme parties like the British National Party and, to a lesser extent, the UK Independence Party. The inclusion of Bulgaria and Rumania in 2007 also raised these concerns, with the result that the British government restricted access to the British job market to people from these countries, as did many other EU nations.

For the EU

This argument can be overstated: Britain is increasingly multicultural, and race relations are in some ways better than in France or Germany. The value to the expanding British economy of a flexible migrant workforce is obvious, especially since many 'native' Britons are reluctant to do certain types of job. There is also a flip side to immigration: many Britons now move abroad, especially to retire in Spain or France.

Dull uniformity and patriotism

Against the EU

Politics is often a matter as much of the heart as of the head. As Napoleon said, 'Men are ruled by their dreams.' Probably the strongest objection to European integration derives from a sort of romantic patriotism: a mixture of nostalgia and tradition. People simply wish to remain different and separate, without necessarily disliking the French or Germans. They want to retain their quirky British way of doing things and to keep this important aspect of their sense of who they are, of their identity.

For the EU

Two arguments could be developed against this. First, it could be said that the past should be left behind and the future welcomed. Opposition to the EU does seem to be an outlook which is strongest among the older generation, and weakest among the young. On the other hand, we could simply deny that adopting a European identity as well as a British identity is a threat: there is no need to destroy what is good about the past in order to support what is good about the future.

> **Question:** What are the advantages of European integration?

SUMMING UP

In 1973, Britain joined what we now call the European Union (EU). This was probably the most significant event in post-war British history. Since then, the EU has developed into a major force in world politics, and the powers of the EU have expanded considerably. The impact of this institution on all aspects of British politics has been immense. Above all, British sovereignty has been weakened, and the power of our 'sovereign' Parliament has, in theory, been reduced, as shown by the Factortame case. Every aspect of British politics has been changed as a result of our membership of the EU. Pressure groups now operate in Brussels, in an attempt to influence policy there. Political parties have had to work with the parties of other countries in order to function within the European Parliament. For example, in 2006, David Cameron announced that the Conservatives MEPs would cease to work at some point in the future with the 'European People's Party' and would set up a new grouping of its own. Government, Parliament, the Civil Service, the devolved assemblies and executives, and local government have all been forced to adapt to Britain's membership of EU. At the same time, great political crises have erupted since the 1960s over the issue of Britain's role in Europe. In recent times, the subject of whether we should join the euro zone and also whether we should support the adoption of a new Constitution for Europe have been suggested as worthy subjects for national referendums. It seems unlikely that in the future this seminal issue will not continue to have a huge impact on the UK.

Further reading

A. Davies, *British Politics and the EU* (Hodder, 1998): a straightforward analysis of the topic.

S. George, *An Awkward Partner* (Oxford, 1998): historical analysis of Britain's difficult relationship with the EU.

J. McCormick, *Understanding the EU* (Macmillan, 1999): useful study of the EU and its politics.

N. Nugent, *The Government and Politics of the European Union* (Palgrave, 2002): standard study of how the EU works.

Websites

www.europa.eu.int (European Union)
www.fco.gov.uk (Foreign Office)
www.fedtrust.co.uk (Federal Trust)
www.ukip.org (United Kingdom Independence Party)

Devolution

Making connections

The most important aspect of this topic to sort out concerns the similarities and differences between the devolved systems used in the various areas, which vary to some extent. There are important links to be made with chapter 9 on the Constitution and chapter 15 on Europe. It is in this area that constitutional reform under Labour governments since 1997 has achieved what will probably be its most lasting legacy. The discussion of the state in chapter 1 also provides useful links to this topic.

Devolution

SETTING THE SCENE

This final chapter deals with a major topic which, although by no means new, has developed very strongly since the 1970s in Britain: devolution. This topic, like that of Europe discussed in chapter 15, calls into question the nature of our state and raises important issues about British nationality and citizenship. As Scotland, Wales and Northern Ireland adapt to their new position within the United Kingdom, how does this affect England?

16.1 The nation

Before dealing with devolution, it is important to look first at the concept of the nation and nationalism, which provide an important background to the subject. Chapter 1 contains a discussion of 'the state', and this analysis of the nation follows to some degree from that.

Nation is a difficult concept to define. One problem is that people use the word interchangeably with 'country' and 'state'. For example, the United Nations is the association which brings together almost all the states of the world, but is not called the 'United States', for understandable reasons. We can ignore this use of the word 'nation'. But there are other complications. Sometimes there is complete overlap between the state and the nation. The French are a nation and most of them live in France. The term 'nation-state' has been used to describe a country like France where state and nation overlap. But even with France there are problems. For example, there are the Basques, a people who live in south-west France and also over the border in north-east Spain, and who claim – with as much justice as anyone else – to be a nation with a language completely different from either French or Spanish. Arguably, the Basques should therefore be called a nation, but they do not have their own state.

In the Basque country, some of the Basque people are nationalists and wish to set up their own independent Basque state. **Nationalism** has been an extremely important ideology in the last 200 years, arguably the most important political force in the history of those years. It remains very powerful. James G. Kellas, a political scientist writing in 1991, distinguished between three sorts of nationalism:

> **Nation**: a group of people who feel bound together by common racial, cultural or geographical ties.

> **Nationalism**: the ideology or set of political beliefs held by nationalists, who are people who wish to emphasize the importance of their national identity, often in order to create an independent country for their nation to live in.

1 *Ethnic nationalism* is based on exclusive racial or ethnic definitions of who qualifies as part of the nation. This is the harmful nationalism of the Germans under Hitler, and modern nationalists tend to be careful to avoid such a racist view of the nation. It also suffers from intellectual difficulties because it is very difficult to define what a 'race' really is.

2 *Social nationalism* is less exclusive than ethnic nationalism and sees the nation as more broadly bound together by social, cultural, geographical or perhaps linguistic ties. This would be the best way to describe most modern nationalist movements. A Scottish nationalist, for example, would not reject support from anyone who lived in Scotland, regardless of whether they were 'racially' Scottish or not.

3 *Official or state nationalism* is a feeling of patriotism which the state attempts to foster in order to develop unity and solidarity among its citizens. Historically, 'state building' has often been encouraged by this sort of nationalism, which relies heavily on education and ceremony to do its work. Official nationalism can build on social nationalism as described above, but it might need to create a new, artificial nation to do so. The Canadians comprise a nation, for example, with a strong sense of national pride, but most of them come originally from either France or the British Isles, and obviously also from a wide range of other, different social or ethnic nationalities. The Canadian state can build a nation by emphasizing the common interests of Canadians rather than the separate identities of French-Canadians, or Canadians from Britain, etc.

What nations are there in the United Kingdom?

The state nation

The official answer to the question, 'What nation exists in the United Kingdom?' is that the people of the United Kingdom are British. 'British' is a generic term for people who live in the four historic nations of the British Isles: England, Scotland, Wales and (Northern) Ireland. There is clearly a problem with Ireland, since three-quarters of the island of Ireland is now independent and the people there cannot therefore be called British. Many of the people of Northern Ireland, although officially British, also reject this British identity and since 1998 they have been able to have dual British and Irish nationality.

The cultural nations

In addition to being British, most people in the United Kingdom also identify themselves as being from the four nationalities – English, Scottish, Welsh and Irish – associated with the ancient historic nations which went to form the United Kingdom. This is less true of the English, the great majority of the population, who have somewhat arrogantly tended to confuse 'British' with 'English', although recent surveys show that there is a growing sense of Englishness. The United Kingdom is therefore rather odd as a country since it consists of people most of whom think of themselves as having a sort of unofficial dual identity as English-and-British, Scottish-and-British, etc.

Box 16.1 What is the United Kingdom?

A thousand years ago there were four separate countries which made up the British Isles, each under its own separate ruler or rulers: England, Scotland, Wales and Ireland. Gradually, these countries came together, partly as a result of wars, partly by agreement.

Wales was largely conquered by the English, and King Edward I of England made his son Prince of Wales in 1301. This is the reason why Wales is called a 'Principality' and the title (just an honorary one nowadays) 'Prince of Wales' is still given to the eldest son of the King or Queen of England. In 1536 and 1543, two Acts of Parliament, sometimes called 'Acts of Union', were passed, which brought Wales more closely into the same political system as England, giving the Welsh representation in Parliament.

Scotland kept its independence from England despite repeated invasions, but in 1603, by an accident of birth, King James VI of Scotland became James I of England, and the two Crowns were united. This was the beginning of the United Kingdom. In 1707, by mutual agreement, the Scots abandoned their parliament and began to send their MPs to join the English in Westminster. This was agreed by the Act of Union.

Box 16.1 *(continued)*

Ireland was repeatedly attacked by the English and finally conquered by Oliver Cromwell in the seventeenth century. A century before, Henry VIII had claimed to be King of Ireland. An Act of Union was made between Ireland and Great Britain (i.e. Scotland, Wales and England) in 1801, when the parliament in Dublin was abolished, and Irish MPs came to Westminster. The tragic history of Ireland in the 100 years that followed involved a great struggle by the Catholics in the south of the country to recover from the British their right to rule themselves, opposed by the Protestants from the north who wished to remain part of the Union. This was solved (at least temporarily) by the Government of Ireland Act (1920), which set the south on the road to independence – as what eventually became the Republic of Ireland – but kept Northern Ireland as part of the United Kingdom.

Hence it can be concluded that our country, the United Kingdom of Great Britain and Northern Ireland, is technically about a century old.

16.2 Constitutional background

States can be classified in different ways, according to their constitutions, and what the constitutions lay down about how they are to be governed. One of the ways of classifying states is to decide whether they are federal or unitary. This subject is also discussed in chapter 10 on the Constitution.

A unitary state

Sovereignty is the ultimate or supreme political power. Obviously some of this power will be handed down to local government, so the details of, say, roads, footpaths, street-lights, etc. can be dealt with in a way which is sensitive to local needs. But the point about a **unitary state** is that this dispersal (or 'decentralization') of power is made by the centre and can be modified or withdrawn by the centre. In the past, the United Kingdom has generally been described as a unitary state: Parliament at the 'centre' of the country, in Westminster, is described as sovereign, and from time to time it can modify the rules under which local government can operate. As will be seen later, there are some doubts about whether Britain is a very good example of a unitary state, but on the whole this description still seems the best one.

> **Unitary state**: one in which sovereignty is located in one place, concentrated at the 'centre' of the state.

A federal state

In a **federal state** the central authority cannot withdraw the power which is granted to the region if the constitution does not allow it. An example of a federal state is the United States of America, where each of the 50 'states' (Texas, California, etc.) is guaranteed by the Constitution the right to decide

> **Federal state**: one in which the constitution lays down that sovereignty is shared between the central authority and local and regional authorities.

Box 16.2 Centre and periphery

States would ideally have their political centre, the capital, at the geographic centre of the country. They very rarely do, however, because states are generally the product of historical developments stretching back over centuries. Capitals tend to be situated in the most important economic centres and are often located on or near the coast, rather than in the most convenient administrative position, which would presumably be somewhere in the middle. London is very far from the geographic centre of the UK or even of England. The same is true, in their respective states, of Paris, Moscow, Berlin, Washington, Beijing, etc. It is not so true of Rome, but Rome was deliberately chosen as the capital of Italy in the 1860s because it was at the geographic centre. The result of this asymmetry in the location of capitals is that it makes a strong case for decentralization, even for federalism. According to Stein Rokkan and Galen Irwin – in *Economy, Territory, Identity: Politics of West European Peripheries* (Sage, 1983) – people in the 'peripheries' – that is, the outlying areas of the state – develop feelings of resentment because they are distant from the capital and feel powerless to affect decisions taken there. This is made worse by the fact that the capital is (by definition) situated in the economically rich part of the country. It is made even worse still because being the capital adds to the wealth of the area, by providing employment for civil servants, who in London have to be paid more money than their colleagues in other parts of the country because it is so expensive to live in London! One way around this was adopted by the founding fathers of the USA, who deliberately deprived their capital, Washington, DC, of democratic representation so that it could not benefit too much from being the capital. It remains unrepresented in the Senate and some of the worst areas of inner-city deprivation and poverty are to be found there.

---

on a whole range of matters, like the death penalty, for example, which in a unitary state would be decided at the centre. A federal state usually retains at the centre, through its constitution, powers over defence, foreign policy, the currency and other major economic matters. The powers that are granted to the regions tend to be matters of social and domestic policy, like education, health care and transport, for example. In such a system, the powers of the regions and of the centre are protected by the Constitution: they are entrenched. Federal powers can therefore only be changed by constitutional amendment, which is usually a lengthy and difficult process. A constitutional court usually exists to judge whether there has been any breach of the constitutional laws if there is a dispute between the region and the central authority.

Is the United Kingdom really a unitary state?

Constitutional authorities support the view that the United Kingdom is a unitary state. One of the key principles of the British Constitution is parliamentary sovereignty, which implies a unitary state. According to this principle, Parliament is the democratically elected representative of the sovereign

Table 16.1 Federal versus unitary states

Arguments for a FEDERAL state	Arguments for a UNITARY state
Large states prefer federalism: Canada, the USA, Australia and South Africa. The regional diversity that is a product of this geographic fact is more easily recognized through a federal system. Communication used to be an issue for large states, although this is less relevant today.	Smaller countries often prefer a unitary state, since they may wish to emphasize their strength, and may feel that too much division within the state will weaken it. The problems with regional diversity and communications obviously disappear here.
Countries with linguistic or culturally diverse populations may favour federalism. There are more likely to be tensions between the centre and the periphery if there is a language difference. In Quebec, a province of Canada, most of the population speaks French and came originally from France; the other provinces are English-speaking. In a federal system, this difference must be recognized.	Cultural similarities may be strengthened in a unitary state: they may help to bind together a state which otherwise could be divided. In addition, a relatively homogeneous state may prefer a unitary system. Why emphasize differences when unity may bring harmony and strength?
Federalism is more democratic: it attempts to solve one of the problems associated with representative democracy. The purest form of democracy is when people literally rule themselves as the Ancient Athenians (in theory) did. The larger the unit of representation – the more people a member of a representative body represents – the further away from this ideal of democracy we get. Federalism has more chance to give power straight to the people. The concept of subsidiarity is discussed in chapter 15.	There is no reason why a unitary state should not have a system of local government and hence allow for local representation. Some unitary states are quite decentralized: in some ways, Britain allows quite a lot of diversity in local educational provision, for example, and yet Britain is a unitary state.
Representation is improved in a federal system. Those who are represented have better access to their representative; lobbying is facilitated when the representative lives alongside to the people represented and can gauge the mood of the people more easily.	Participation is encouraged when people feel they have a say in genuine national issues. Asking people to vote frequently for minor local officials is no way to improve participation.
Participation is improved if people feel that local issues are important to politicians and if they feel local politicians have the power to deal with them.	Federalism leads to complications in the political process. There will be quarrels over jurisdiction: representatives at the centre and the periphery will try to claim powers beyond what the Constitution grants them, and this will cause dissension. The real power will be granted to unelected judges, in the constitutional court, which will then settle such matters. The experience of the USA confirms this.

Table 16.1 (*continued*)	
Arguments for a FEDERAL state	**Arguments for a UNITARY state**
The tensions that can develop between the capital city at the centre of the political system and the regions are likely to be reduced if people feel that they have contact with local politicians who can represent their views forcibly at the centre. There is less likelihood that a region will seek to break away from the centre under a federal system.	Unitary states encourage fairness in the provision of public services and the distribution of national resources. There will be uniform access to a National Health Service, for example, in a unitary system. Federalism will mean diversity and hence unfairness. There will also be competition between regions for the distribution of benefits from the centre, which will encourage division.
Local issues are understood by local populations and by locally accountable politicians: it is simply inefficient to refer these small matters repeatedly to the capital city for an answer.	Unitary states will be more administratively efficient, and will cut out a useless level of bureaucracy.

British people, and it can make or repeal any law it wants. So, the British state must be sovereign, because in federal states the powers of the regions are entrenched, or protected from repeal or amendment, unless there is a formal process of constitutional amendment. There is generally also in a federal state a constitutional court, like the Supreme Court in the USA, which can adjudicate in matters of dispute between the centre and the regions, as on all matters of a constitutional sort. But, there is only one location of sovereignty in Britain – the Parliament at Westminster – and there is no constitutional court. There is not even, according to an extreme interpretation, a constitution, since what might be described as such is actually unwritten, or uncodified. Any powers which the Westminster Parliament grants to a city – for example, Liverpool – or a county – for example, Essex – can be revoked by a later Parliament. The history of local government in Britain is littered with examples of Westminster changing the powers and boundaries of local authorities at all levels. So, Britain is not a federal state. If Britain is not a federal state, the argument goes, it must be unitary.

But are there more than the two alternatives: federal or unitary? Two further interesting suggestions have been made: that Britain is either a union state or a quasi-federal state.

Is Britain a 'union state'?

This is the description given by Rokkan and Irwin. They make comparisons between Britain and other countries like France, Spain and the Netherlands, which grew up as a result of historical changes that linked a number of previously separate countries together. As has been said, the United Kingdom of Great Britain and Northern Ireland was established by Acts of Union: the Act of Union with Scotland of 1707, and the Act of Union with Ireland of 1801 (amended in 1920 by the Government of Ireland Act, which gave Eire its freedom). In addition, the constitutional historian Sir Geoffrey Elton referred to the Acts of 1536 and 1543 as the Union with Wales. So, the British state has been built up by three agreements between England and its neighbours. The relationship between England and these neighbours involved important concessions from the centre, which created or pre-served in each of the three regions certain rights and privileges. So, even if the United Kingdom is not technically a federal state, it is an extremely odd unitary state.

Even before devolution, there were in some respects more significant diff-erences between how things were managed politically in Scotland and England than there were between how things were done in Texas and Cali-fornia, for example. The Act of Union with Scotland preserved the Scottish legal system, with its three criminal verdicts ('Guilty', 'Not Guilty' and 'Not Proven'). Scotland had its own banknotes, educational qualifications (Highers instead of A-levels), established religion (Presbyterian and not Epis-copalian) and since 1939 the Scottish Office (created in 1886 first in London), composed of the civil servants who administered Scottish government, has been located in Edinburgh.

Wales was less different politically from England, but after 1964 the Welsh Office was housed in Cardiff. Northern Ireland was also in a uniquely diff-erent relationship with Westminster. To take one example, elections in Northern Ireland have for some time been held under a different electoral system from those on the 'mainland' and there is also a separate party system in the 'Province'. To add one final quirky example, even after the Act of 1920, which created the Irish Free State with Dublin as its capital, Irish citizens were able to go and freely settle in Britain and vote in general elections.

If we consider the position of the Channel Islands and the Isle of Man, where British people pay less tax than the rest of their fellow citizens, more complexity emerges. But while all these examples emphasize the differences within the United Kingdom, it is worth repeating that in constitutional terms none of them was entrenched, and all could be overturned by the sovereign Parliament in Westminster.

Is Britain quasi-federal?

Since 1997, the relationship between the centre and the regions of Britain has been altered by the process known as devolution, which will be discussed next. This has also had a profound effect on whether we can seriously regard the United Kingdom as unitary. The political scientist Vernon Bogdanor has used the phrase 'quasi-federal' to describe the new situation. 'Quasi' is Latin for 'as if' or 'in some ways', so Bogdanor means that Britain has become a federal state of some limited sort as a result of devolution. This question will be further discussed later in the chapter.

Multi-level governance

'New modes of governance' or 'multi-level governance' are terms which have entered the language of political science. 'Governance' means the exercise of political power. So 'multi-level governance' describes how, since the last decade of the twentieth century, the way in which political power is wielded has been to some degree made more complicated and less centralized. The supposedly sovereign British state is now situated in a rather complex web. In some senses superior to the British state is the European Union and a number of other regional and global networks to which Britain belongs. The levels of governance have also become more elaborate below the United Kingdom, as power has been devolved to the historical nations, Scotland, Wales and Northern Ireland, and even to the English regions. These developments challenge the traditional views of how power is exercised in the modern state and challenge even whether this modern state can still be held to exist.

Devolution: the process by which a superior political authority at the centre grants power and rights to an inferior authority in a region of the country.

16.3 Devolution

The word '**devolution**' was first used in this context by the eighteenth-century Whig political philosopher Edmund Burke, when he proposed granting some rights of self-government to what were then the American colonies. Since the 1960s in the United Kingdom there has been a strong movement to give further power to Scotland, Wales and, in a different context, Northern Ireland, and after 1997 this movement resulted in action which has devolved much power to these three regions. Devolution does not necessarily lead to the creation of a federal state, since federalism means that powers granted to an inferior level of government are permanent and entrenched. But, as Bogdanor says, it does move the state towards federalism, to a sort of quasi-federalism, and certainly emphasizes the oddity of the British union state. The process of devolution seems at first sight to be a peculiarly British movement, but at roughly the same time in France and Spain there has been a process of handing power to the regions. France officially remains a unitary state, but has lost much of the centralization for which it was once famous. As for Spain, it is very similar to Britain in its developments in this area, and it is unclear whether it should, as a result, be described as a unitary or a federal state. Nor is this recent movement towards devolution confined to Europe: developments in the federal United States of America in the 1980s and 1990s reversed the trend towards centralization and were described by one enthusiast as a 'devolution revolution'.

Administrative devolution is the process by which the civil servants (the bureaucracy) who administer a region return to that region, rather than doing their work from the capital. Thus, as has been said, the Scottish Office was moved to Edinburgh in 1939: although it was linked to a Cabinet minister who spent much time in Westminster, the actual work of Scottish government was run from Edinburgh itself, from an office staffed almost entirely by Scots. The same was true of Wales, but not until 1964, when the Labour government of Harold Wilson took the first modern steps in the direction of devolution. It could be argued that Wales has essentially stuck at this stage of administrative devolution, even after the New Labour changes that followed 1997, as will be shown. As for Northern Ireland, it had administrative devolution from 1920, but was the first region also to be granted legislative devolution.

Legislative devolution is the process by which a regional representative assembly is granted the power by the central authority to make certain laws in the region. This is clearly a more serious and substantial measure of devolution. It is the type of devolution that has been granted to Scotland and Northern Ireland, but not fully to Wales. This sort of devolution clearly nudges the process in the direction of federalism; it is difficult to imagine a region within a federal system which did not have law-making powers. Nevertheless, it is worth pointing out that local councils (borough, city, metropolitan, county, district and even parish councils) have the power to make what are called 'by-laws': closing roads, imposing fines for public drinking of alcohol, repositioning lamp-posts, etc. So, there was a good deal of legislative power exercised at local level even before devolution in Britain. What matters is the importance of the issues over which the devolved assembly can legislate.

16.4 Scotland and Wales

What political factors were responsible for devolution coming onto the political agenda in recent years? Why did the Labour government bring in devolution? It is necessary to look first at devolution to Scotland and Wales, whose processes were rather similar, before turning to Northern Ireland and finally within England itself, where things have been very different.

The reasons in favour of (and against) devolution are not unlike those in favour of federalism, which have already been listed above. Devolution is claimed by its supporters to improve democracy, representation, participation, accountability and the efficiency of government. It does this without the formal creation of a federal system, which would be very difficult to achieve in the UK without drawing up a written constitution or attacking the idea of parliamentary sovereignty.

Cultural separateness

Wales and Scotland had a tradition of separateness which went back to the days when they had been independent countries of their own. Wales has a sense of independent cultural identity associated with the Welsh language, which is spoken by about one-fifth of the population. It is true, however, that the Welsh language divides the Welsh people into a Welsh-speaking group in the more rural north of the country, and an English-speaking group in the south, and that the language issue has strengthened the opposition to devolution among the English-speaking majority in Wales. In Scotland there is only a tiny group of Gaelic speakers (about 1.5 per cent), but a strong sense of separateness derived from the Scottish legal tradition, educational system and differences from England in terms of religion and local government.

Tension between the centre and the periphery

As Rokkan and Irwin have shown, there are often feelings of resentment against the centre, against the capital, expressed by people who live at some distance from it. The capital city tends to attract more wealth and to acquire a sense of glamour, while the outlying regions can stagnate economically and feel a mixture of neglect and exploitation. This leads to the demand for devolution, or, at its most extreme, for independence.

Administrative devolution

Even before the advent of a movement for legislative devolution, a reasonably full degree of administrative devolution had already been granted to both Wales and Scotland. In a way, the completion of this process after 1997 was a logical next step. Even in the legislative sphere there were, before 1997, well-developed mechanisms in the Westminster Parliament for the separate scrutiny, especially of Scottish, but also of Welsh legislation, with a number of committees of the House of Commons working with the secretaries of state.

The rise of nationalism

In both Wales and Scotland, nationalist parties grew quite strong in the 1960s, demanding complete independence for their countries. The Scottish Nationalist Party (SNP) gained 30 per cent of the Scottish vote in October 1974, and 11 MPs; this has been its greatest electoral success to date. Plaid Cymru (in English, 'the Party of Wales') also gained its highest level of support at that election: 10.7 per cent of the Welsh vote, and 3 MPs. This sudden increase in support for the nationalists is a little difficult to account for, but has something to do with a general dissatisfaction at the time with the two major political parties, which also helped to revive the fortunes of the Liberal Party. There was a general movement also in the 1960s and 1970s for people to become interested in new political issues, and the rise in support for nationalism has been linked to the growth of other 'new social movements', as they are called, such as feminism, environmentalism and the peace movement. The discovery of North Sea oil off the coast of Scotland fuelled resentment in Scotland, with nationalists arguing that the profits from the oil would end up south of the border.

Response to the rise of nationalism

Both the Labour Party and the Liberals had sympathy with ideas behind devolution, and were forced into taking some action by the rise of nationalism, which looked as though it might deprive them of some of their votes in areas where both parties (especially Labour) have traditionally had considerable support. Hence, in the 1970s the policy of devolution was developed as a way of diluting the demands of the nationalists. The idea was to detach the moderate Scots and Welsh who were in favour of a greater degree of self-government from the more extreme nationalists. The result was that the Labour government of James Callaghan legislated to hold referendums in 1979 in Wales and Scotland on the subject of devolution: both referendums failed (referendums are discussed in more detail in chapter 2). There was simply insufficient support in Wales for devolution: those opposed to devolution outnumbered those in favour four to one. But in Scotland a clear majority of the Scottish voters were in favour. However, an amendment to the bill which had introduced these referendums, made by a Labour backbencher who was hostile to devolution, laid down that it was necessary for over 40 per cent of those entitled to vote, not just those who turned out to vote, to support the measure for it to pass. Only 32.5 per cent of the Scottish electorate supported devolution in 1979, so it failed.

The impact of Conservative rule on the demand for devolution, 1979–97

The Conservative Party under Edward Heath had been quite sympathetic to calls for devolution, but when Margaret Thatcher took over from him as leader in 1975 she returned to the unionist roots of the party and opposed all calls for devolution. John Major followed Thatcher in this, and in the closely contested election of 1992 he is credited with winning crucial votes in England because of the way he highlighted Labour plans to 'break up the United Kingdom'. The tensions between the London centre and the Welsh and Scottish peripheries were made worse by the economic and social problems of the early Thatcher years, with the run-down of the steel and coal industries. Thatcher was always unpopular in Scotland and made matters worse by introducing the community charge – or poll tax – which was a regressive form of local taxation that fell heavily on the poor, to Scotland in 1988, two years before it was adopted in the rest of the country. This caused demonstrations and a Scottish National Party (SNP) campaign of civil disobedience. The demand for devolution, even independence, was strengthened by the 18 years of Conservative rule because no matter how unpopular the government was in Scotland and Wales, it continued to win elections because of English votes. By 1997, the Conservatives were so unpopular outside England that they did not win a single parliamentary seat in either Wales or Scotland.

New Labour

The revival of the SNP in the face of the poll tax stimulated Labour enthusiasm for devolution, especially in Scotland. In 1989, Labour and the Liberal Democrats met with all pro-devolution elements of Scottish life in a constitutional convention, and this was the beginning of the plans that were implemented in 1997. It is worth reflecting on the fact that after the resignation in 1983 of Michael Foot (who, like his predecessor as leader of the party, James Callaghan, sat for a Welsh constituency), all Labour leaders have been either Welsh or Scottish. The New Labour Party was looking for radical policies in new areas to replace the social and economic policies of Old Labour which had been abandoned, and these were found in constitutional reform, especially devolution. The new Clause IV of 1995 clearly announced this conversion to constitutional change.

 Question: State the case in favour of devolution in the UK.

16.5 How devolution functions in Scotland and Wales

The devolution referendums (1997)

As soon as Labour was elected to government in 1997 it set in train the process of devolution. The first step was to hold two referendums – again! These have been discussed in chapter 2. The 1997 Welsh referendum – as in 1979 – just asked the Welsh whether or not they wanted a devolved assembly. But the 1997 Scottish referendum asked two questions: the first about devolution and the second about whether the Scots wanted to give their new devolved parliament the power to vary the level of income tax by up to three pence in the pound. This immediately shows that devolution for Scotland was to be a more serious affair than devolution for Wales. The 1997 referendums of were decided on a simple majority of the voters, unlike in 1979. However, the result in Wales gave some backing to the arrangements of 1979, because on a low turnout (50.1 per cent) only a tiny majority voted 'yes' (50.3 per cent). So the legitimacy of the decision to devolve power to Wales was questionable. Nevertheless, the result in 1997 was 'yes' in Wales, as it was also in Scotland, where there was a 'yes' vote on both questions. Following these referendums, the legislation was passed through Parliament in 1998, and devolution was granted to both countries.

The new electoral systems

Elections were held in May 1999 to elect the representative bodies set up by the legislation and further elections were held in 2003 and 2007. The electoral system used in both countries was the same. There were to be fixed-term elections every four years. The voting method adopted was the additional member system (AMS), which is discussed in chapter 3. This is a hybrid proportional electoral system, which allows political parties considerable control over the selection of candidates, but still retains a constituency link. This was particularly the case since the closed system was adopted, where the voter cannot alter the order in which the party list is presented. The reason that a proportional system was adopted was apparently because Labour was worried that under a first-past-the-post system the SNP might gain control of the Scottish Parliament – Labour thought that this would be all but impossible under AMS. The 2007 election proved them wrong, however: it resulted in the formation of a minority SNP executive.

For the sake of consistency, the system had also to be given to Wales and the Greater London Assembly.

The devolved institutions

The new electoral system led to the election of a Scottish Parliament of 129 Members of the Scottish Parliament (MSPs) in Edinburgh, and a Welsh Assembly (in Welsh, 'Senned') of 60 Members of the Welsh Assembly (MWAs) in Cardiff. The greater importance of the Scottish body is shown by both its size and its title. The government of Wales is known as the Welsh Executive, and is headed by a First Secretary for Wales. The Scottish Executive is headed by a First Minister. Again, the different terminology used the two leaders is interesting. These executives work with the permanently staffed bureaucracies

The new Scottish Parliament buildings in Edinburgh

which had existed in Edinburgh and Cardiff since the days of administrative devolution and which are now named the Scottish Civil Service and the Welsh Office.

Financial powers

There is a considerable difference in the power granted to the two authorities: Scotland has more power than Wales does to run its affairs. The Scottish Parliament can vary the rate of income tax in Scotland by three pence in the pound, although in practice it has never actually used this power. In both Scotland and Wales, the main way in which the new devolved executives can make a difference is by allocating funds differently between departments. They are given block grants by the British Treasury and can then divide this money up as they choose, spending more on education, for example, if they wish (as indeed they have).

The Chamber is where meetings of the Scottish Parliament are held

Legislative powers

Here there is also a difference between Scotland and Wales. The Scottish Parliament can pass primary legislation. Scottish bills, which in the past had gone through the Westminster Parliament, changing the law in Scotland, now pass through the Parliament in Edinburgh instead. The Welsh Assembly has no such power, but can pass secondary legislation (as, of course, can the Scottish Parliament). Secondary legislation consists of detailed orders made by a government minister, using powers given by a piece of primary legislation passed, in the case of Wales, by the Westminster Parliament. This is a considerable power and enables the Welsh Executive to respond to Welsh needs more effectively, and to be scrutinized more carefully by the Welsh Assembly.

Areas with which these devolved institutions can deal

The new devolved institutions are given control over the usual social and economic concerns that regional government generally deals with. Apart from the very significant fact that the Scots have the power of primary legislation, the list of areas which have been devolved are very similar: local government, education, health and social care, culture, leisure and the arts (including the important Welsh language question, of course), agriculture, fisheries and food, housing, environment and planning, heritage and sport, industry, economic development, training and transport. In addition, the Scottish Parliament can legislate on the Scottish legal system and on Scottish law. The 1998 Scotland Act, which created the devolved system there, has 20 pages of 'reserved matters', areas which the government of Britain at the centre reserves for itself. These are generally predictable: matters of foreign policy, defence, immigration, constitutional affairs, most budgetary matters, the currency and major economic policy, and social security benefits. But also reserved are abortion, broadcasting and holding referendums – potentially very contentious issues.

Relations with Westminster and Whitehall

Devolution at first made no difference to the representation of Scotland and Wales in the UK Parliament, although in 2005 the number of Scottish constituencies in Westminster was reduced by 14, as will be discussed in the next section on the West Lothian Question. There is still a Welsh Secretary and a Scottish Secretary in the Cabinet, although their role has obviously changed, and the holders of these jobs now may combine them with other responsibilities. They are now intermediaries between the new assemblies and executives and the central government and Parliament in London. The various departments within the Scottish and Welsh Executives make agreements, or concordats, with the corresponding departments at the centre, in Whitehall, in which they work out the details of how they will work together. The possibility of a clash over 'competence' is obviously much greater in Scotland; that is, a clash between the Scottish Parliament and the Westminster Parliament over whether a piece of Scottish legislation goes beyond the powers granted to the Scottish Parliament, whether it is **ultra vires** (Latin for 'beyond its powers'). There is an elaborate series of safety nets to prevent this:

> **Ultra vires**: Latin for 'beyond its powers'. When a local or devolved government goes beyond its legal powers, it is said to act *ultra vires*.

- The Scottish Executive has to certify that a bill is within the areas of competence of the Scottish Parliament when it is introduced there.
- The Presiding Officer of the Scottish Parliament (the equivalent of the Westminster 'Speaker') can step in to stop debate if a matter is *ultra vires*, but can be overruled by a vote of the MSPs.
- The Secretary of State for Scotland has limited powers of veto over legislation which goes beyond the bounds of what is allowed.
- The Judicial Committee of the Privy Council (in effect, the law lords, to be replaced by the new Supreme Court) will act as a sort of constitutional court if there is serious disagreement between Westminster and Edinburgh.

Developments in Welsh devolution

A case was made from the very start by some for extending the rather limited powers granted to the Welsh Assembly. This led to the setting up of the Richards Commission, which reported in 2004, recommending that the Welsh Assembly should have primary legislative powers, be enlarged to 80 members, and be elected by STV. The Richards Report also said that tax-varying powers were desirable for Wales but not essential. The UK government did not accept the recommendations, and the White Paper published in 2005 entitled *Better Governance for Wales* merely recommended that the Welsh Assembly should be given greater power to scrutinize the work of the Welsh Executive. The Welsh Executive should be separated from the Assembly (rather than acting as a committee of the Assembly as in the past), and hence more subject to its oversight, as was the case with the Scottish Executive, and of course the UK government. The Welsh Executive would be able to request the Secretary of State for Wales (in London), by using an 'Order in

Council', to modify and add provisions to legislation which affects Wales. In the future, the White Paper recommended that a referendum on granting primary legislative powers to the Assembly could be held if supported by two-thirds of the Assembly and also supported in Westminster. In addition, candidates for the Welsh Assembly would be banned from standing both for the additional member list and as constituency representatives. These modest changes were put into law by the 2006 Government of Wales Act.

> **?** **Question:** How does devolution in Scotland differ from devolution in Wales?

16.6 The impact of Scottish and Welsh devolution

Constitutional impact: asymmetric devolution

One impact of devolution has been to raise interesting constitutional questions, especially concerning the nature of the union state or quasi-federal constitution. The first point is that devolution has been unequal or asymmetrical. It is different in Wales from how it is in Scotland. If one adds in the fact that it is also different in Northern Ireland, and then again in London and the English regions, the system looks ramshackle. No one in the USA would dream of giving fewer powers to the state of New Hampshire than to the state

'Since Scottish devolution he just does what he wants'

of Texas just because Texas is bigger, for example. Yet this seems to be what has happened in the UK. One answer to this criticism is that the whole point of devolution is to respond to local needs sensitively, and Wales simply did not want to have as much power given it as Scotland. But, as the current First Secretary for Wales, Rhodri Morgan, has pointed out, it is not surprising if Welsh devolution is not popular in Wales if it does not give Wales much independence. The real losers from this asymmetry, however, are the English, as the West Lothian Question shows.

The West Lothian, or English, Question

When the question of devolution first came seriously onto the political agenda in 1978, the Labour MP for West Lothian, Tam Dalyell, coined this phrase. The West Lothian Question applies to devolution in Scotland and Northern Ireland, but not in the same way in Wales, because the Welsh Assembly has no primary legislative power. The question is simply this: why should a Scottish member of the Westminster Parliament be able to debate and vote on matters which concern England, while an English MP cannot legislate on the same matters in Scotland after they have been devolved to Scotland? Recently, it has been called the English Question because it is so important for English representation. There is a further twist to this, since a Scottish member of the Westminster Parliament has more control over English education (for example) than over Scottish education, since the latter is a matter dealt with by the devolved Parliament in Edinburgh. Thus, in 2004, the government won the crucial debates over 'top-up fees' for university students because, although many English Labour MPs voted against the measure, there were enough votes from Scottish Labour MPs to carry it through. This is despite the fact that the top-up fees will not be paid by Scottish students, because the Parliament in Edinburgh, which was controlled by Labour and the Liberal Democrats, voted against the policy for Scotland.

The West Lothian, or English, Question is a problem that goes to the heart of the debate over devolution and over the nature of the British Constitution. In a proper system of federalism, with a written constitution, such a problem would not exist. Various proposals have been made to resolve the question, but the Labour government is very unlikely to do anything which might harm its control over English affairs. Labour's main answer to the issue has been to propose the introduction of regional devolution within England. But this does very little to get to the root of the problem, and, in any case, efforts to create elected assemblies in the English regions look unlikely to succeed, as will be shown below. One problem, connected in some ways to the West Lothian Question, which has been settled, derives from the fact that before devolution, Scotland had more MPs at Westminster per head of the population than England did. The reason for this was to compensate Scottish MPs for the difficulties involved in representing distant, and often very large (in terms of area), constituencies. A boundary revision which came into force in 2005 reduced the number of Scottish MPs at Westminster by 14 (from 73 to 59) and has, therefore, to some extent removed one aspect of the West Lothian Question, although Scotland is actually still over-represented in Westminster by about four MPs. The Conservative Party is committed, however, to legislating to resolve the issue if ever it is elected to power at Westminster and to devise a system of 'English votes for English laws' – probably by banning Scottish MPs from voting on a bill which the Speaker declares to be an 'English' one. When Gordon Brown became Prime Minister in 2007, he made it clear that he would not adopt this policy. However, he did make some concessions by giving nine of his new ministers a responsibility for each of the regions of England, including London. This corresponds to the Cabinet posts for ministers responsible for Wales, Scotland and Northern Ireland. Quite what these ministers are supposed to do is unclear, but Brown also proposes that they should be scrutinized by nine regional Commons select committees.

Parliamentary sovereignty and the unitary state

Has devolution threatened the central constitutional doctrine of parliamentary sovereignty? The 1998 Scotland Act, which devolved power to Scotland, insisted that it 'does not affect the power of the Parliament of the United Kingdom to make laws for Scotland'. So the important constitutional idea that the Westminster Parliament is sovereign, and hence that the state is unitary, is preserved. Parliament at the centre could always withdraw the powers that have been devolved to Scotland and Wales, and indeed it has had to do that with respect to Northern Ireland within a very short time of power being devolved there because of the continued tensions within the province. However, the distinction between legal sovereignty and political sovereignty is useful here. Legally, and in terms of constitutional theory, Parliament certainly could re-establish direct rule over Scotland and Wales, but politically, in terms of the practicalities of the matter, it seems very unlikely that this could happen in the foreseeable future. Although the Conservative Party opposed devolution as it passed through Parliament, it has not pledged to overturn the measures if it were to win a general election in the UK, for the very practical reason that it would be politically extremely difficult, and would almost certainly strengthen nationalist tendencies in both Scotland and Wales.

The impact of devolution on the political parties

The three major political parties always had, to a greater or lesser extent, some separate Scottish and Welsh organizations, but since devolution these have had to be strengthened. Devolution has extended to the party system, in which there are now structures in place to run the parties on a separate basis in Scotland and Wales. One area which obviously needs regional control is the selection of candidates for election, a particularly difficult issue with the additional member system, which requires party lists in addition to straightforward constituency representation. The question of the selection of a party leader in Wales, and indeed of the whole conduct of politics there, led to some difficulties within the Labour Party. The problem arose largely because the party leadership in London wanted to control decision-making in this area and chose to put pressure on the Welsh party to get its way.

The first person selected to be First Secretary in Wales, Ron Brown, was acceptable both to Labour headquarters in London and to the Welsh Labour Party. But in late 1998, Brown had to resign over a sex scandal, and Labour Party 'control freaks' then essentially imposed Tony Blair's preferred candidate, Alun Michael, on the party as the future First Secretary, in preference to Rhodri Morgan, who was more popular in Wales, but who was considered too Old Labour by Blair. The selection process for Welsh leader involves an 'electoral college', which works in the same way as the process by which the leader of the UK Labour Party has been elected since 1981. This allowed the Labour leadership to put pressure on the trade unions in Wales, an important part of the 'electoral college', in order to select Michael. (A very similar process of pressure was used to impose Frank Dobson on the London Labour Party as candidate for mayor in preference to Ken Livingstone, with similarly bad results.) However, in the 1999 elections for the Welsh Assembly, the Labour Party then failed to secure an absolute majority, in part because of the fuss over the leadership appointment and the bad taste this had left. Alun Michael wanted to form a coalition with the Liberal Democrats, but he could not talk his party into agreeing to this, and he tried to carry on as a minority leader. But he had a great deal of trouble controlling both his party and the Welsh Assembly as a whole, and in February 2000 the Assembly passed a vote of no confidence and so he resigned. At this point, Rhodri Morgan finally became leader of the party in Wales; he promptly entered a coalition with the Liberal Democrats and remains, at the time or writing, an effective and popular First Secretary, who has not turned out to be particularly Old Labour.

The impact of the new electoral systems

This has already been dealt with in chapter 3, but it is worth repeating that party politics has been affected to a large extent by the introduction of more proportional systems in Wales and Scotland.

- Small political parties have been given a chance of representation: the Green Party and the Scottish Socialist Party are the best examples.

- The winner-takes-all effect has been reduced. This forced Labour into coalition in Scotland with the Liberal Democrats, which lasted from 1999 to 2007, and a similar coalition briefly in Wales, with periods of Labour minority government in between in Wales.
- The Liberal Democrats have benefited from a more proportional electoral system, and also because Labour was prepared to go into coalition with them.
- The party list system has enabled the parties to recruit more women candidates: since 2003, half the Welsh members have been women. Female representation has also markedly increased in Scotland.

The development of coalition and minority government

Labour in Scotland was in coalition with the Liberal Democrats from 1999 to 2007. This did not really lead to weak government, as some critics of coalitions have suggested it would. It gave the Liberal Democrats a say in Scottish affairs which might be argued to have been disproportional to their real electoral weight, since in both 1999 and 2003 they were the fourth party in the elections. But they had worked with Labour for devolution since the 1970s and Labour was unlikely to go into coalition with either the Scottish National Party or the Conservatives. One criticism of proportional systems is that voters do not know in advance what will result from their decision to vote in a particular way, because it is not until after the election that politicians will gather together in the proverbial 'smoke-filled rooms' and decide the shape of the coalition in the light of the election results. This argument does not hold with regard to the elections for the Scottish Parliament because – at least in 2003 – the electorate was only too well aware that a Labour/Liberal

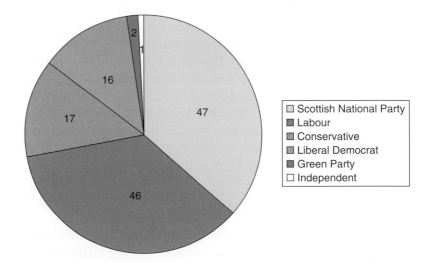

Figure 16.1 Results of the 2007 Scottish general election

Democrat coalition was likely, so the argument that voter choice is reduced by the 'smoke-filled rooms' effect of proportional representation is not borne out. After 2007, the rather surprising result of the election in Scotland was the emergence (after a long delay) of a minority government led by the Scottish National Party.

The same sorts of comment apply, to a lesser extent, in Wales, where a similar coalition was set up 2000–3. Labour survived (just about) in a minority in 1999–2000, and then again with exactly half of the Assembly seats after 2003. After 2007, Labour decided to form a coalition with Plaid Cymru; and the decision to do this does bear out the 'smoke-filled rooms' argument, since it was certainly unexpected before the election.

Policy initiatives in the devolved regions

As might be expected, devolution meant that in domestic affairs Wales and Scotland developed distinctive approaches, especially to education, an area for which the Welsh and Scots have traditionally shown more respect than the English. In Wales, the SATs introduced by Thatcher and maintained by Blair have been abolished, and the sixth-form curriculum has been reformed with the introduction of a Welsh baccalaureate. In Scotland, school teachers have seen their salaries enhanced after decades of neglect under successive Conservative and Labour administrations, and the ill-conceived student university fees introduced into the rest of Britain by Labour have been rejected. In Wales, the ban on the sale of beef on the bone, in response to the BSE scare, was lifted well before it was removed in England. Fox-hunting with hounds was abolished in Scotland before the Westminster Parliament passed legislation on the matter, and the state resumed responsibility in Scotland for the cost of old peoples' homes (as was the case in Wales), which had been withdrawn by the British government under John Major. A number of these changes were due to Liberal Democrat pressure on their Labour coalition colleagues in Scotland and Wales. This caused some tensions within the Labour Party. On the whole, however, because between 1999 and 2007 we have had a Labour government at the centre and Labour-dominated executives in Cardiff and Edinburgh, there have not yet been any real rifts between the devolved governments and the UK government. It remains to be seen whether the election of an SNP executive in 2007 will lead to any show-downs with the Labour government at Westminster.

Has devolution been a success?

It is probably too early to say, and in any case judgement is likely to depend on one's political standpoint. On the positive side, the system which was devised appears to have worked quite smoothly, although there have been some problems in Wales. However, devolution does not seem to have been hugely popular with the people of Wales and Scotland, as the disappointing turnout figures in the Scottish and Welsh elections have shown. There have been complaints in both Cardiff and Edinburgh about the costs involved, especially in building new offices for the assemblies. If the whole point of devolution was to remove the demand for independence, then at first this appeared to have been successful: in the 2003 elections, both SNP and Plaid Cymru lost votes and seats. But 2007 saw the growth of support for the SNP and, to a lesser extent, for Plaid Cymru, so it could be argued that devolution has had the opposite effect, as some Conservatives had predicted back in 1997.

Question: Why have some Scottish and Welsh nationalists criticized Labour's programme of devolution?

16.7 Northern Ireland

The reasons for devolution in Northern Ireland are to some extent the same as those for Scotland and Wales. The fact that Northern Ireland is separated from the rest of Britain by the sea obviously adds a further case for devolution. But there is another and unique dimension which has to be considered briefly here, since devolution for Northern Ireland has been seen

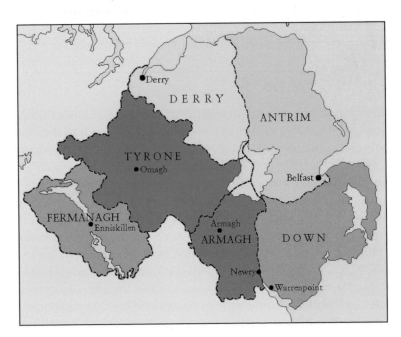

Northern Ireland

as a solution to the problem of inter-communal strife and terrorist violence in the province.

Devolution as a result of partition (1920)

The tragic history of the United Kingdom's relations with Ireland reached a sort of stopping-point in 1920 when the forerunner of the modern Republic of Ireland was given its independence from Britain. However, Ireland was partitioned and Northern Ireland remained part of the UK because the majority of its population consisted of Protestants who mainly wished to remain British – they are described as Unionists, or supporters of the Union with the mainland. A sizeable minority of the population of Northern Ireland, however, were Catholics and largely nationalist, wishing to be given their independence from Britain and to join up with the rest of Ireland as a free state. Although the word was not widely used at the time ('Home Rule' was the preferred term), in 1920 Northern Ireland became the UK's first experiment in devolution. A Parliament was set up in Stormont Castle, on the outskirts of Belfast, to rule the province. The Stormont Parliament ran Ulster until 1972 and it showed that devolution can sometimes have its problems. The British government allowed the majority group, the Protestants, to rule Northern Ireland in a high-handed and discriminatory way. The Unionists changed the voting system so that it favoured the majority, redrew the boundaries of local government in their own interests and ensured that more was spent on educating, housing and employing Protestants than Catholics. Majoritarian devolution in Ulster, government by the majority and for the majority, resulted in a sort of apartheid system, under which the minority Catholic population were exploited and discriminated against.

Suspension of devolution (1972)

In the 1960s a movement grew up among the nationalist, Catholic community, inspired by the similar protests of Dr Martin Luther King Jr in the USA, to oppose the discriminatory rule of the Stormont Parliament. Riots and violence between the Catholic and Protestant communities developed. The nationalism of the Catholics (their desire to be part of the Republic of Ireland) clashed with the fervent unionism or loyalism of the Protestant majority, who wished to remain part of the UK. The British sent in an army in 1969 to restore order, but this only made the situation worse. In 1972, the Stormont Parliament was abolished and Britain imposed 'direct rule' on Northern Ireland, ending the sorry history of 50 years of devolution. Terrorism developed on both sides and the province descended into economic decline, government by virtual martial law, and sporadic acts of mindless violence. The nationalist terrorists, led by the Irish Republican Army (IRA), attacked British and unionist targets, while the loyalist or unionist terrorists, the Ulster Defence Association (UDA) and the Ulster Volunteer Force (UVF) replied in kind.

Attempts to reach a power-sharing agreement

British military occupation of Northern Ireland was inevitable, but generally made things worse not better. The aim of the British government after 1972 was more or less the same whichever party was in power in Westminster – namely, to restore devolved government in Northern Ireland, but to establish it on a basis of 'power-sharing', not majority rule. The idea was to create a permanent coalition government in Northern Ireland, which would unite Catholics (nationalists) and Protestants (unionists) in running the country according to principles of democratic fairness. The model to be followed was the systems used in the Netherlands and Belgium, where different religious and linguistic groups have managed to live together. Such a system has been described as 'consociational democracy' by political scientist Arendt Lijphart, and depends on establishing a 'grand coalition' government in which both sides can be represented. The first attempt to reach such an agreement was negotiated at Sunningdale in 1973, but failed the following year, due both to poor handling by Harold Wilson's British government and also to the inflexibility of the Ulster politicians. Another 20 years of violence and direct rule followed, which cannot be described fully here because of lack of space.

The Sinn Fein delegation at the Northern Ireland peace talks in 1998

The Good Friday Agreement (1998)

The 'troubles' in Northern Ireland came to an end in 1998 as a result of three factors:

1 Patient diplomacy by Thatcher, Major and Blair, and support for this policy from the Republic of Ireland.
2 A decision was taken by the leaders of the main Catholic/nationalist terrorist group, the Provisional IRA, especially Jerry Adams, to pursue their aims by peaceful means.
3 A similar decision was made by the Protestant/loyalist paramilitary groups.

At last, on Good Friday 1998, an agreement was signed in Belfast which established the peace process. Britain declared that it had no 'selfish' interest in keeping Northern Ireland as part of the UK and that the desire of the majority of Ulster people to remain British would be respected. The IRA and loyalist paramilitaries agreed to give up their armed struggle. Devolution would be established on the basis of power-sharing. There would be limited cross-border links with the Republic of Ireland, which would hold a referendum on whether or not to renounce its constitutional claim to the north. There would also be a referendum in the north over whether to accept the agreement. This referendum was duly held in 1998 and produced a result in favour of the agreement and a return to devolution. Details of the referendum are described more fully in chapter 2.

On the whole, the referendum was a success in that turnout was high and the result was a strong 'yes' vote. The main problem was that a larger proportion of the minority Catholic population voted in favour of the agreement than did people from the majority Protestant population, who clearly had more to lose from power-sharing. This reveals one significant difficulty with referendums, namely that they generally only give the voters two alternatives. The Protestants were not allowed to vote on a return to devolution of a majoritarian sort, which most of them probably supported, nor were the Catholics offered the opportunity to vote for a reunification of Ireland. On the other hand, if voters had been given this genuine choice, it is unlikely that peace would have been established in Northern Ireland.

16.8 How devolution functions in Northern Ireland

A Northern Ireland Assembly of 108 members is elected, and an Executive, with a First Minister, is drawn from and responsible to the Assembly.

Elections

Elections are held according to the single transferable vote (STV) system, different from elections to the devolved assembles on the mainland, but a system that is favoured in Northern Ireland. Obviously, it is important there to reassure the two communities that they will be represented on a strictly proportional basis, and STV should give that reassurance. It is also hoped that moderates in each community may transfer their vote to other moderate candidates in the opposing community rather than to the more extreme candidates within their own sectarian group. The elections were (in theory) to be held every four years, on a fixed-term basis. In practice, the British government delayed the 2002 elections (the second set of elections) because they hoped this would produce a result which they preferred. In fact, it did not have this effect when the elections were finally held in 2003.

The Northern Ireland Assembly

Like the Scottish Parliament, the Assembly has primary legislative powers. The areas of competence which can be handled in Belfast, and the areas which are 'excepted' and are dealt with in Westminster, are very similar to those given under the terms of devolution to Scotland. For Northern Ireland, there is a third group of policy areas, called 'reserved'. At present, these are kept by West-minster, but they could in the future be transferred to Belfast. They include (predictably) security, some legal matters and trade. Unlike the Scottish Parliament, the Northern Ireland Assembly has no tax-varying powers.

Jurisdiction

Matters of dispute between Westminster and Belfast over jurisdiction are to be referred to the Judicial Committee of the Privy Council (to be replaced by the Supreme Court in 2009), as with the other devolved assemblies.

Power-sharing

The power-sharing mechanisms used in Northern Ireland are unique in the UK. Members of the Assembly, when elected, must register their 'identity' ('Unionist', 'Nationalist' or 'Other'). As a result, the representatives of each community are clearly identified in the Assembly. This has been criticized as encouraging sectarianism, but it is essential in order to make power-sharing work. It allows mechanisms to operate which ensure that contentious legislation must pass with the 'parallel consent' of a majority of those of both major political identities. In other words, laws are not made by a simple majority in Northern Ireland but by a majority from each of the two communities. Put crudely, if a majority of the Nationalists disagree with a law, it will not pass, even if a majority of the overall Assembly want it to pass.

The Executive

The Executive must have a First Minister and Deputy First Minister from the different communities, and all other government ministers and the chairs of the Assembly's committees are shared out among the various political parties of both communities according to strict rules of proportionality.

Citizenship

Citizens of Northern Ireland may choose to hold Irish as well as UK citizenship. There is a commitment that the British government will not surrender the sovereignty of Northern Ireland without the consent of a majority of the population. This statement is made to reassure the Protestant majority that there will be no 'sell-out' by the British government handing Northern Ireland over to the Republic of Ireland.

Links with the Republic of Ireland

There are three links established with the Republic of Ireland: the North–South Ministerial Council, the British–Irish Intergovernmental Conference and the British–Irish Council (or 'Council of the Isles'), which also has Welsh and Scottish representatives.

16.9 Has devolution for Northern Ireland been successful?

It is worth emphasizing that it is very difficult to judge devolution in itself apart from the other recent events in Northern Ireland. The only judgement we are likely to come to is in terms of whether peace has been maintained in Northern Ireland, and this is a far larger and more complex question.

Terrorist attacks

There were continued terrorist outrages after the Good Friday Agreement, especially by breakaway factions of the IRA, which did not accept the ceasefire. The most horrific example was the Omagh bombing in 1998, which was the work of the Real IRA and which killed 29 people in the worst atrocity of the whole 'troubles'. But since then, terrorist violence has gradually declined to very low levels.

There was also in the early days a continued high level of inter-communal tension and violence, best shown by the problems surrounding parades, or traditional marches, especially by Unionists.

Elections

For nine years after the Good Friday Agreement there was no successful, permanent establishment of the devolved institutions. Two elections were held in this period (1998 and 2003), but the second election had been delayed by a year because the British government was afraid that it would produce a result which would strengthen extremism. The more extreme parties in both communities did indeed strengthen their positions following 1998, which was the reason why the 2002 election was delayed. The more moderate Ulster Unionist Party (UUP) was pushed into second place among Unionists by the Democratic Unionist Party (DUP); the Social Democratic and Labour Party (SDLP) was overtaken by Sinn Fein (SF). It is fair to add that the latter is less extreme now than it was in the past and that the DUP has also mellowed.

Cooperation between parties

The Unionist parties had initially shown a reluctance to cooperate with the Nationalists. Until 2007, the DUP (after 2003 the largest party in the Assembly) refused to sit in an Executive with Sinn Fein, the Nationalist party associated with the IRA. The other Unionist party, the UUP, was divided over whether to join Sinn Fein in the Executive. Its leader at the time, David Trimble, who was made First Minister when the Executive was briefly formed in 1999, had been prepared to do so, but he was under pressure from more hard-line party members not to do so.

Decommissioning of weapons

Sinn Fein at first did not succeed in delivering on its promise to decommission weapons, at least to the satisfaction of the Unionists. It was this issue which delayed the initial meeting of the Assembly and which caused it to break down subsequently. However, a declaration by Sinn Fein in April 2005, in the run-up to the UK general election, suggested that it was possible that a decisive act of decommissioning might at last be a possibility. This declaration was partly the result of intense lobbying of Sinn Fein to make such a statement, especially in America, following the murder of Robert McCartney early in 2005, and the popular campaign in Northern Ireland led by the murdered man's sisters and partner against the alleged IRA involvement in his murder.

Northern Ireland Assembly

The Assembly first met in 1999 after a delay of a year because all the members could not initially agree to work together. An executive was briefly formed, with representatives from both communities, but devolution has had to be suspended in total on four occasions by the British government and direct rule reimposed. Between 2002 and 2007, no executive was formed; instead, there was direct rule from the UK. Negotiations between Sinn Fein and the Democratic Unionist Party late in 2004 seemed to come close to an agreement to form an executive. These were brought to an abrupt end, however, after the announcement by the police that the IRA had been involved in a major bank robbery in Belfast, and Sinn Fein was suspected by the Unionists of having had knowledge of this crime. As a result, efforts to form a power-sharing executive – and hence to resume the devolved institutions – came to an end again.

However, things looked more hopeful in 2006. In October the St Andrews Agreement was made between the Northern Ireland parties and the British and Irish governments. This Agreement envisaged a re-creation of the power-sharing executive, the holding of elections in 2007 and a restoration of devolved government to the province. The crux of the matter was that Sinn Fein agreed to recognize the Police Service of Northern Ireland. For many years, Sinn Fein had been suspicious of the police as a symbol of Unionist oppression, but reforms to the service made since 1998 had reassured them. As a result, the UK government agreed to restore justice and policing by 2008 to Northern Ireland as areas which would not be reserved to the government in Westminster. Nevertheless, Ian Paisley of the DUP refused to endorse the immediate re-creation of the executive, but nor did he reject the plans entirely. In January 2007, Sinn Fein announced that it was willing to give its official support to the Police Service of Northern Ireland. This announcement made the British government hopeful that the DUP would, as a result, be willing to join a power-sharing executive with Sinn Fein. So the decision was taken to hold elections in March 2007. These elections confirmed the DUP and Sinn Fein as the two dominant parties. Following the elections, a much more positive feeling began to emanate from Northern Ireland, with Ian Paisley meeting leaders of Sinn Fein, and in May 2007 it was finally announced that he would set up a power-sharing executive with them.

It is worth concluding, therefore, on a positive note: three elections have been held, and the Executive and Assembly did briefly function. In 2007, they met again, and devolved government has been restored. Since the horrors of Omagh, the level of violence has decreased markedly. Inter-communal violence has also declined and there is increased economic prosperity in Northern Ireland. The peace process is working, but the political will to make power-sharing devolution function successfully has only just been shown. It would be wrong to draw too many conclusions about the success of devolution, however, since Northern Ireland is such a special case.

> **Activity**
>
> 1 Empathetic exercise: Empathy involves trying to put yourself in the position of someone else. It is valuable in helping us evaluate different political stand-points. With three classmates develop a role-playing discussion between (a) a member of the SNP/Plaid Cymru, (b) a right-wing Conservative, (c) a Labour supporter in Scotland/Wales, (d) a Liberal Democrat supporter. Act out a dialogue between these people in front of the class.
> 2 Conduct the same exercise from a Northern Ireland perspective with an imagined debate between (a) a Sinn Fein supporter, (b) a supporter of the SDLP, (c) a supporter of the DUP, (d) a supporter of the UUP, (e) a supporter of the Alliance Party, (f) the Secretary of State for Northern Ireland.

16.10 Regional devolution in England

In addition to the major developments in Scotland, Wales and Northern Ireland, the Labour governments since 1997 have also pursued a more limited aim of encouraging regional and local government in England by devolving a limited degree of power there too. The only really successful area where this policy has been applied is in Greater London.

Greater London

There were several reasons put forward for a policy of devolution for Greater London.

An unusual form of 'devolution'

Some of the arguments used in favour of devolution for Scotland, Wales and Northern Ireland seem to run counter to the reasons for devolution in London. Obviously, the idea that London is a peripheral region, disengaged from the centre, is hardly tenable. Still, as in most capital cities there are areas of poverty in London as well as areas of wealth and privilege. It is even doubtful whether 'devolution' is quite the right word to use, since what has been done for London simply looks like a piece of local government reorganization.

A desire to undo the work of previous Conservative governments

In 1986, by an act of what looked a little like political spite, Margaret Thatcher abolished the Greater London Council, a body which had taken over from the London County Council which itself dated back to 1888. She did this, according to her critics, because she was annoyed by what she saw as the political extremism of the Labour council which ran London under Ken Livingstone, who was demonized at the time in the right-wing press as 'Red Ken'. Thatcher felt that the individual London boroughs were strong enough to run their areas for themselves and that there was no need for an additional tier of local government. She did, however, leave intact the Inner London Education Authority to run the capital's schools.

A desire to give the capital a single local government

Labour was committed in 1997 to giving London back a single, unifying tier of government to coordinate the work of the London boroughs. Labour argued that no other great capital city in the world lacked such an overarching system of local government. This reform would be particularly important, it was claimed, in order to improve transport in the city.

A general desire to revive local government

There was also a desire to try to revive local government, not just in London, but throughout the country. Local government was thought generally to be in decline and commanded very little attention in the media or from the public. Participation levels in local government were very low, especially in terms of

London Mayor, Ken Livingstone

turnout at local elections. One way to improve this was to have directly elected mayors in the major cities, and London was to be the first one. If the mayor were a figure who commanded the attention of the media, this would lift the whole profile of local government. The way in which mayors in the USA captured the public imagination there was cited in favour of this view.

The implementation of reform in London

Referendum

The implementation of reform in London followed the same pattern as in Scotland, Wales and Northern Ireland. A referendum was held in 1999 on whether to bring in the proposed changes. Details of the referendum and the subsequent elections are given in more detail in chapter 2. The result was a resounding 'yes', but the turnout was very low.

A mayor for Greater London

The most important aspect of the proposal was to have a directly elected mayor for Greater London. This was a deviation from the parliamentary system which had been used in Wales, Scotland and Northern Ireland, where the First Secretary and First Ministers were not directly elected but chosen by the assemblies to which they were responsible. The mayor of London was expected to be a presidential post, separate from the Greater London Assembly and not responsible directly to it, but to the people of London. The thinking here was presumably, as has been said, to give the position of mayor greater prominence. The elections to the position of mayor were to be made by yet another new system, in this case the supplementary vote system. Elections were to be on a fixed term every four years, as elsewhere in the world of devolution.

Assembly

A Greater London Assembly was to be elected at the same time on the additional member system, as was used in Scotland and Wales. The Greater London Assembly consists of 25 members, from whom the mayor draws a Cabinet to help him in his work.

Powers

The powers of the mayor and Assembly are limited. There are two principal areas. The first is policing: the Metropolitan Police Commissioner works with the mayor; it is worth adding that the Home Office keeps a very close eye on the activity of the police and it is unlikely that the mayor or Assembly will affect this much. Second, London transport is under the mayor's control. Again, the freedom of action of the mayor here is limited. The mayor is also a figurehead for London, and clearly could use the role to develop, over time, more powers.

The impact of the reforms in London

A high-profile mayor

This aim was clearly successful. Ken Livingstone, the first mayor to be elected, has seldom been out of the spotlight of publicity. His personal popularity is shown by the fact that he was elected first as an Independent, and then re-adopted as the Labour candidate for mayor. His most successful action was the implementation in 2002 of the 'congestion charge' in central London, which was so successful that it was decided in 2004 that it should be extended beyond the centre of the capital to the Western inner suburbs – which duly happened in 2007. This measure was a considerable gamble when it was introduced, but seems to have worked successfully, and will probably be copied in other parts of Britain. The government even began a national debate in 2007 over whether a system of 'road pricing' should be adopted nationwide: needless to say, it did not meet with unreserved support.

The powers of the mayor were at first quite modest. Even in the field of transport, the mayor is weak, largely because he lacks financial power. The Labour government was determined to rebuild the London Underground using a Private-Public Partnership scheme. Livingstone conducted a strong campaign to have the project paid for entirely out of taxation: he lost.

Party power

The selection of a Labour candidate for mayor caused difficulties in 2000 rather like those connected to the selection of a Welsh First Secretary. In the end, pressure from the 'control freaks' at the top of the party persuaded the London Labour Party's electoral college to choose Frank Dobson as their candidate, largely because Blair distrusted Ken Livingstone. Having been refused the party's nomination, Livingstone therefore stood as an Independent and, amid great media hype, won. Four years later, in 2004, Labour decided to readmit him to the party and to adopt him as the Labour candidate – he won again. Over the central question of who selects candidates, the Labour Party leadership had been thwarted.

A low-profile Assembly

As might have been expected, the Assembly has been an anonymous body, with little impact. However, small parties have gained some representation in the elections, which are conducted under principles of proportional representation, leading to successes for the Green Party and the UK Independence Party, in line with similar gains for minor parties in Scotland and Wales.

Further powers for the mayor

In response to the criticism that London's mayor had been given limited powers, the government decided in 2007 that the he or she would be given further powers by Parliament. The new areas in which the mayor can be involved include: planning, waste, culture and sport, health, climate change and appointments to other governmental bodies in London. In addition, it is interesting to see that Livingstone managed gradually to extend his reach of his own accord, establishing links with other cities all around the world, for example, and being involved in the preparation for the London Olympic Games.

Regional government in England outside London

Labour also came to power in 1997 intending to devolve some power to the English regions, or at least to bring in some changes to local government there. As a result there have been fitful and, it has to be said, rather unsuccessful attempts to do this. The thrust has been in two directions: directly elected mayors (to be discussed in the next section) and regional assemblies.

Regional assemblies

In 1995, under John Major's Conservative government, in response to encouragement from the European Union, the country was divided into regions, which correspond to the European Parliament constituencies established when the regional closed party list electoral system was introduced in 1999. There are eight English regions, and each was initially given a skeletal regional administration, under a Regional Development Agency. These bodies were more active in areas where EU funds were made available, and consisted of civil servants drawn from local and central government, responsible to representatives of the relevant local councils.

When Labour came to power in 1997, it announced plans for changes to make these agencies more democratic by attaching them to elected regional assemblies, which would be like the other devolved assemblies in the UK. The reasons for this were:

- to make the Regional Development Agencies more democratic and accountable;
- to regenerate local government;
- to create a more symmetrical system, so there was at least some devolution all round;
- to answer in some measure the West Lothian Question (discussed above);
- to answer a genuine desire in certain outlying areas of England for some structures sensitive to local needs;
- to respond to a sort of regionalism, a local patriotism in certain areas.

The English regions

The idea was not initially very popular with anyone, and faced (almost alone of Labour's constitutional reform proposals) a concerted campaign of opposition from the Conservative Party. Even within the Labour Party doubts were expressed about the plans, although they were enthusiastically supported by the Deputy Prime Minister, John Prescott. There were therefore delays. However, in 2004 it was announced that referendums would be held in November that year in three regions (the north-east, north-west and Yorkshire-and-Humberside) to decide whether to go ahead with the plan. In July 2004 it was abruptly announced that the balloting would only take place in the north-east. The reason given was that it had been planned to conduct the referendum by postal ballot and that there had been complaints about the use of such an electoral process in the June 2004 local and European elections in the other two regions. So it was decided not to proceed with the referendum there. Cynics argued, however, that the government had been concerned that the result would have been negative in these two regions and had cancelled the referendums for that reason. When the vote was taken in the north-east in November 2004, the result was a decisive 'no' vote. On a turnout of 47.8 per cent (boosted by the postal ballot), 78 per cent of the voters opposed the creation of a regional assembly. The people of the region simply did not see the point of setting up a new tier of local government with the limited powers that were being offered. The referendum result in the north-east has forced Labour to reconsider its policy on English regional devolution. It seems likely that there will not be English regional assemblies now. This was confirmed in 2007, when Gordon Brown announced that English regional assemblies (but not development agencies) were to be scrapped.

16.11 Local government and directly elected mayors

Local democracy

There is an important and complex system of local government in the United Kingdom, as in all liberal democracies, which needs to be briefly discussed here. It is fair to say that it is a rather neglected area of the politics of the country, and that, arguably, it is somewhat in decline at the moment. The development of devolution as part of Labour's recent constitutional reforms has been intended in part to give a fresh impetus to the system of local government. The key concept here is democracy. If the people are to rule themselves (as they must in a democracy), they ought to be deeply involved in local decision-making. This is important in order to develop fully ideas of representation and participation, the key aspects to democracy. Local decisions concern people closely and are ones where their input is most useful, since they know how things should be done at the level of the community. Direct democracy (arguably the purest form of democracy) ought to be more of a realistic possibility at a local level, where the number of people involved is small. Representatives should be closest to those they represent at this level of government and should find it easiest to take the opinions of the local population on matters of interest to them. However, in practice, local government in Britain is subject to very strict control from central government, so local democracy is to some extent undermined. The boundaries, powers, spending and the very existence of local councils are strictly controlled by central government, using the sovereignty of Parliament to legislate if local government is thought to be in need of reform.

The structure of local government in the UK

Local government in Britain dates back many centuries, and has always been based on a number of tiers or levels, and on making a distinction between the local government of towns (known as boroughs and metropolitan areas) and of rural areas (known as counties). Over the centuries the geographic divisions and boundaries of local government have been redrawn many times, and this restructuring has continued into recent times. The most recent reorganization dates from the Major government and the work of the Local Government Commission of 1993–8. This Commission made a compromise settlement which differs slightly for the different regions.

Scotland and Wales

In Scotland and Wales there are, respectively, 32 and 22 unitary authorities. These authorities divide up these two countries between them and have the same responsibilities. They are 'unitary' because there is no other level of government involved. They replace in many cases a system where there were two levels of local government, one on top of the other, which shared responsibilities among them. This use of unitary authorities has proved useful in the light of the devolution for Scotland and Wales which Labour introduced, which would have looked very unwieldy if there had been two layers of local government underneath it.

England

In England there are three different systems employed:

1   There are now 46 new unitary councils, in areas where a single layer of local government has been thought to be useful. For example, Peterborough is now run as a unitary council, where formerly it had been part of Cambridgeshire. Many people hoped that these unitary councils might be used everywhere in England but such a radical step was avoided by the Local Government Commission which opted instead for retaining the counties discussed next.

2   There are 34 county councils. The counties were the ancient divisions of the country which date back to Saxon times, and have been retained

because of the strong sense of local identification that there is with them. Each county is divided into a number of district councils (there are 238 in total). So the County of Cambridgeshire, for example, is divided into South Cambridgeshire, the City of Cambridge and so on. The county has responsibility for some services and the district for others. In rural areas there are also parish councils which deal with the concerns of villages.

3   There are 36 metropolitan districts or boroughs. These are also unitary authorities, running largely urban areas. London has also 33 boroughs of its own, which have since 1999 been grouped under a Greater London Authority with a mayor and Assembly (this is discussed above).

Councillors and officers

Local councils are run by elected councillors, who face elections every four years, in a complicated system by which a proportion are re-elected every year. The major political parties contest these local elections rather in the same way as they fight over the general elections. The permanent staff of local councils, the civil servants, are known as local government officers, and they work under the scrutiny and direction of the elected councillors. There is a complicated relationship between local councils and central government, with officers responding to directions from Whitehall and working within the guidelines set by Parliament and the government at the centre.

The responsibilities of local government

There is a complex division of responsibilities between the various layers of local government. The main responsibility of local government is the delivery of local services, among which the most significant are as shown in figure 16.2.

The financing of local government

Until 1988, the rates (a tax on houses and land) provided some part of local government finance to pay for the services listed above, and the central government provided the rest. Between 1988 and 1993 Margaret Thatcher's community charge or poll tax (an unpopular local tax, which took little account of variations in income) was used to replace the rates, and in 1993 this was replaced by a council tax, which is a modified form of the rates. Local councils have a limited degree of freedom in charging what rate of council tax they feel they need to fund their spending. But local councils now get the bulk of their money from central government (about 75 per cent), in addition to any charges they may directly make (for car parks, etc.). Some part of this money given by central government is derived from the 'business rate', a tax on local business properties. Since central government pays so much, it controls the

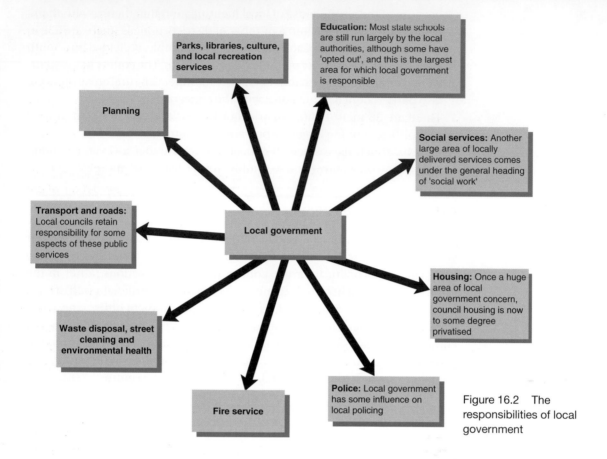

Figure 16.2   The responsibilities of local government

spending of local councils very strictly, using the Audit Commission, a central government watchdog, to do so. The central government can in the end decide how much a local council will charge through the council tax, and can limit its spending.

Local government in crisis?

Commentators sometimes look back with nostalgia to the great days of local government of a century ago when community effort and pride transformed the great cities and counties of Britain. Since then, they argue, there has been a great decline in local government, and, increasingly, central government has stepped in to run things. The main problems seem to be as follows.

Local participation has declined

The turnout in the 2006 local elections (when turnout was not boosted by being held at the same time as other more important elections) was only 36 per cent. People take a decreasing interest in local democracy and turnout at local elections has fallen away sharply. At the same time, political parties have found it difficult to recruit people willing to play a part as local councillors, who tend, increasingly, to be retired people drawn from a rather narrow social class. A census of local councillors in 2001 found that 97.5 per cent were white, 37.5 per cent of them were retired, 64.5 per cent were from a background described as managerial or professional and their average age was 57.

Funding crisis

The poll tax introduced by Thatcher was a notorious failure, and its replacement, the council tax, is also open to criticism. Above all, more and more of the costs of local government have increasingly been met in recent years by central government, which undermines local democracy, since the level of services and taxes cannot be set locally, and are not subject to local accountability.

Less local control of local services

The National Health Service is now almost entirely outside the system of local government. Further and higher education are run almost entirely from the centre and more and more schools are also outside direct local control. Much local provision in other areas has been privatized as a result of the reforms of the 1980s and 1990s. This is especially true of council housing. So, local government seems increasingly irrelevant.

Geographical divisions

The structure and geographical divisions of local government have been frequently changed in the past half century and no entirely satisfactory system has been adopted.

Relationship between central and local government

This has changed since 1979 and the election of Thatcher. Whereas in the past local and central government sought to work in partnership, in more recent years local government has been seen increasingly as a client of central government, carrying out instructions from the centre. This has undermined local independence, confidence and a sense of local accountability. Voters in local government elections can no longer be at all clear that their vote will make any difference to how local services are delivered, since so much is decided centrally.

Labour and local government since 1997

As might be expected, Labour has responded to the challenges of local government since 1997 with a mixture of new and old techniques. On the one hand, the Thatcherite tendency to encourage privatization (now known as

Best Value) and to squeeze local government expenditure has continued. On the other hand, as part of its movement towards devolution, Labour has encouraged developments in local government which have sought to develop local democracy, participation and a sense of regional and local self-reliance.

The Local Government Act (2000)

This has been the major piece of local government reform undertaken by Labour. It was the culmination of years of discussion of how local councils should organize themselves. Under the Act, large local authorities (with a population of more than 85,000 – mainly the unitary authorities, counties and metropolitan councils) were given three possible options on how to run their affairs:

1 They could opt for a directly elected mayor who would work with a Cabinet drawn from the local council. This would be rather similar to the system introduced for Greater London. If a council opts for this model it has to hold a referendum. In addition, if more than 5 per cent of the electorate petition for such a system, a referendum has to be held.
2 A slight variant of the first system is that a directly elected mayor may work with a council manager (whom the mayor appoints) rather than a Cabinet.
3 A Council leader elected by the council should work with a Cabinet of not more than 10 councillors. This model replaces a system by which the council was divided into a number of committees, each responsible to the council for running a specific area of policy (housing, planning, etc.).

The local government White Paper (2006)

A further local government reform was announced by the publication of a White Paper in 2006 – *Strong and Prosperous Communities* – which was then adopted by Gordon Brown in 2007. The main thrust of the reforms proposed is to empower local communities so that they can take a greater control over their own affairs, to some extent by bringing pressure to bear on their local councils. There will be more consultation through Citizen Juries, and the creation of a Community Call for Action, by which people can 'demand action' on specific issues from their councils. Thus, power will be 'devolved' from councils to people, and 'active citizenship' will be encouraged. It is likely therefore that Brown will continue to reform local government, and an early indication of this was the announcement in 2007 that a number of new single-tier, unitary local authorities would be created in areas where previously there had been a two-tier system.

Directly elected mayors

The reasons for introducing these into England are much the same as the reasons for setting up a London mayor: to regenerate local government, to draw publicity to it by focusing on personalities and, hence, to improve participation. Following the reasonably successful launch of the London mayor, the process was floated more generally, as a result of the 2000 Local Government Act. The take-up of directly elected mayors has been patchy, and no major city outside London has adopted the system. Labour had hoped that Liverpool or Newcastle (for example) might do so, but this has not been the case. As has been said, if there is demand for a directly elected mayor, then a local referendum is held, and if the population vote 'yes', elections for a mayor are held.

Between 2001 and 2006 (mainly in the early years), there were 34 referendums and they have resulted in 12 towns and cities adopting a mayor. The impact of this measure has been patchy. In Middlesbrough, a controversial ex-policeman, Ray Mullin, was elected. He has brought public attention to a number of problems in his town, and in a sense can be judged a success. There is always a limit to what can be achieved in local government, in any case. The election as mayor in Hartlepool of Stuart Drummond, who was disguised as the local football mascot and dressed in a monkey costume, obviously seems to bring the office into disrepute. It shows how an Independent can be elected when turnout is low. The campaign to elect Drummond was backed by a local radio station in order to highlight the absence of local provision for young people in terms of entertainment, and, it could be argued, if it did achieve this, then it can be held to have been legitimate. Drummond turned out to be a reasonably successful mayor and was re-elected in 2005. All except one of these new mayors has decided to work with a Cabinet rather than a council manager. All in all, this aspect of Labour policy on devolution and local government reform has been rather undramatic, although probably less a failure than the effort to create a system of elected regional assemblies. Local government in England still remains something of a problem for believers in democracy, representation and political participation.

 Question: Discuss the view that elected local government and devolved government are important elements of democracy in Britain.

SUMMING UP

We live in exciting times for students of politics. The development of devolution has been one of the great steps taken by the reforming Labour government elected in 1997. It reignites the great issue of Home Rule, which dominated Victorian and Edwardian politics. Scotland, Wales and Northern Ireland have since 1997 been profoundly changed in their relations with the United Kingdom. Britain has moved from being a unitary state to being in the limbo of 'quasi-federalism'. Scotland has acquired a Parliament, with limited taxation powers and the ability to pass primary legislation in a number of domestic areas. What is more, Scotland was ruled by coalition government from 1998 to 2007, and then by the Scottish Nationalist Party thereafter. The changes in Wales have been less dramatic, although in 2006 the powers of the Assembly were to some degree extended, and after the 2007 election, Plaid Cymru joined Labour in a coalition. After 30 years of bitter struggle, it looks possible that Northern Ireland may at last be in the process of being settled, and accepting a power-sharing executive. If this is achieved, it will stand as one of the great achievements of Tony Blair's premiership. The process seems to be set to continue and develop too. A revival of nationalism in Scotland and Wales calls into question the devolution settlement of 1997–8, and the SNP is already preparing for a referendum on the status of Scotland within the Union, which as far as the party is concerned ought to lead to a vote for independence.

Further reading

V. Bogdanor, *Devolution in the United Kingdom* (Opus, 2001): dissection of the problem by the great expert in the field.

V. Bogdanor, *Joined-Up Government* (British Academy, 2006): wide-ranging academic study which goes beyond local and regional government.

J. Kellas, *The Scottish Political System* (Cambridge, 1975): fascinating insight into the ancient regime in Scotland.

C. Pilkington, *Devolution in Britain Today* (MUP, 2002): sane introduction for the sixth-form student.

G. Stoker (ed.), *The New Politics of Local Government* (Basingstoke, 2000): academic analysis by a leading expert in the field.

Websites

www.snp.org.uk (Scottish National Party)
www.plaidcymru.org.uk (Plaid Cymru)
www.nio.gov.uk (Northern Ireland Office)
www.local-regions.odpm.gov.uk (Local & Regional section of the Office of the Deputy Prime Minister)
www.scotland.go.uk (Scottish Executive)
www.scottish.parliament.uk (Scottish Parliament)
www.wales.gov.uk (Welsh Executive)
www.ni-assembly.gov.uk (Northern Ireland Assembly)

Glossary

Abstention: deliberately not voting, as a positive act, having carefully considered the alternatives (as opposed to not voting through apathy). A genuine act of abstention is a piece of political participation.

Access point: a point of contact between the people with power politically and those protest movements or pressure groups which seek to influence them: e.g. Parliament, government departments, law courts, local and devolved government, the EU.

Accountability: the way in which a person is held responsible by someone else for his/her work, and must explain truthfully what has been done, and must apologize or resign in the event of some failure.

Adversary politics: the way in which political parties conduct themselves in constant disagreement and debate.

Authority: the quality possessed by a political leader or a government which has legitimacy or a right to rule.

Bandwagon effect: the way in which the opinion polls may encourage people to jump on the bandwagon, and vote for the party which is ahead in the polls.

Bicameralism: the system which operates when a representative assembly has two distinct houses or chambers.

Boomerang effect: the way in which opinion polls may encourage people to vote for the losing party identified in an opinion poll if they are horrified at the prospect of the other party winning.

Cabinet: the chief ministers who work with the Prime Minister (who is also a member of the Cabinet) in running the country. 'The Cabinet' also describes the regular meetings of these members of the government.

Cause pressure groups: associations which have as their main aim the achievement of influence over a particular area of policy. In other words, they focus above all on a single aim, or a cause. Because they try to promote their cause, these pressure groups are also called promotional groups.

Citizen: the individual member of a state.

Civil rights: special freedoms which citizens of a country enjoy and which are protected by the law.

Class dealignment: the tendency since about 1970 for the decline of the simple link between the working class and voting Labour and the middle class and voting Conservative.

Confederation: an association of states which retain their independence but which join together for their mutual economic or diplomatic benefit.

Consensus: agreement, so when parties agree this can be seen as consensus politics.

Constitution: a set of rules, or constitutional laws, setting out how a political system in a particular state should operate, how the citizen is related to the state and what rights the citizen can claim.

Democracy: the system of government where the people rule themselves.

Devolution: the process by which a superior political authority at the centre grants power and rights to an inferior authority in a region of the country.

Digital democracy or e-democracy: a form of direct democracy where the people make political decisions, or are consulted by the government, using the internet.

Direct democracy: government of the people by the people, immediately and with no intervention from elected politicians.

Electoral mandate: the authority to implement a programme or policy given to a government as a result of winning an election.

European Union (EU): the group of, at present, 27 European countries which have joined together to promote their economic well-being and to foster good relations between themselves.

Executive: one of the three 'powers' or 'branches' of the system of government. The executive's prime responsibility is to use the power of the state to govern the country by executing the laws passed by the legislature, or by taking actions sanctioned in other ways by the representative assembly, and by supporting the judiciary in enforcing the laws.

Factionalism: the way in which political parties often divide into sub-groups, divided over policy, ideology or strategy; if they become very serious, these divisions can even lead to a party splitting up.

Federal state: one in which the constitution lays down that sovereignty is shared between the central authority and local and regional authorities.

First-past-the-post (FPTP): an electoral system which involves two or more candidates standing for election, the electors being given one vote each, and the candidate who wins most votes being declared the winner. In recent years it has also been called the Single Member Plurality System (SMPS).

Floating voters (or swing voters): voters who are not naturally or reliably attached to a particular party and who vote for different parties at different times.

Functional representation: the representation of different interests (professions, or social or economic groups, for example) through the existence of associations (generally sectional pressure groups) dedicated to representing their views, and keeping government informed of their needs and grievances.

Hybrid electoral system, also known as a mixed system: one which combines features of FPTP and PR, or even combines features of majoritarian and PR systems.

Insider pressure group: one which has strong links with those people who have political power, and is therefore in a good position to influence policy.

Intergovernmentalism: the theory that the European Union should be run by the governments of the member states cooperating as if they were members of an alliance or loose club of states.

Judicial independence: the freedom of the judiciary from interference in its activities by the other two branches of government, the executive or legislature, and also from pressure exerted by the media or public opinion.

Judicial neutrality: the absence of bias in the judiciary – religious, social, gender, sexual, political or racial bias, for example.

Judiciary: the third branch of government, the branch which deals with judging, the law and the law courts. Hence, the word 'judiciary' is sometimes also used simply to mean 'the judges'.

Landslide election: an election which gives the winner a large majority and which is also a turning point, bringing in a new party to government.

Legislation: law-making; laws, especially those passed by Parliament.

Legitimation: the conferring of legitimacy, the process by which political 'power' is transformed into 'authority', by which force is made legitimate or morally acceptable.

Liberal democracy: a state where the people rule themselves but in addition the rights of the citizen are protected by law.

Majoritarian electoral system: generally used to describe one which ensures that the winning candidate is elected with an absolute majority (more than 50 per cent) of the vote; sometimes used to describe first-past-the-post systems.

Nation: a group of people who feel bound together by common racial, cultural or geographical ties.

Nationalism: the ideology or set of political beliefs held by nationalists, who are people who wish to emphasize the importance of their national identity, often in order to create an independent country for their nation to live in.

One-nation Toryism: the idea, derived from Disraeli, that the Conservative Party should aim to reunite the country by working to reduce the gap between rich and poor and by developing a strong sense of patriotism.

Outsider pressure group: one which is not blessed with the degree of contact enjoyed by an insider group, and which cannot therefore have such influence.

Parliamentary sovereignty: the ultimate political power in the United Kingdom, exercised on behalf of the people by their elected representative body.

Party identification (or partisan alignment): the way in which particular people consistently support the same political party, adopting its ideology and voting for it on a regular basis.

Party system: the way in which parties operate together within the wider political system, specifically, the number of parties in the country, and the relative strengths of the parties.

Political participation: the way in which citizens get involved in the political process. A participatory democracy is one where citizens are encouraged to take an active part in political life.

Political power: the ability to get things done, to change something in the country or to decide to keep it the same.

Political recruitment: the way in which people are drawn into politics itself at an active level, generally by becoming politicians.

Post-legislative referendum: one which gives the electorate the say on whether to adopt a piece of legislation which has already passed Parliament; if the people agree, the government is mandated, or commanded by them, to act.

Pre-legislative referendum: one held before legislation has passed Parliament on the issue in question: in pure constitutional terms, Parliament could ignore the result; it is only a piece of advice given to Parliament by the people.

Pressure group: an association of people who try to influence those who have political power.

Primary pressure groups: those that have political pressure as their main concern.

Proportional representation (PR): under an electoral system run according to the principle of proportional representation the number of votes cast for each party is matched more or less exactly by the proportion of seats in the assembly allocated to each party.

Referendum: a vote on a specific issue (or specific issues) by the electorate as a whole.

Representative or indirect democracy: the system where the people elect politicians to govern on their behalf.

Salient issue: one which the voters consider to be important.

Scrutiny: the act of overseeing or examining the work of one of the branches of government by another. It generally applies to the oversight of the executive by the representative assembly. The purpose of scrutiny is to expose the errors of government, thus ensuring accountability and good government.

Secondary pressure groups: those which have other primary concerns, and which use political pressure occasionally and incidentally to their chief interests, which may be commercial, charitable or social in nature.

Sectional pressure groups: associations which have as their main aim the defence of the interests of a particular section of the community. For this reason they are sometimes called interest groups.

Social contract: an agreement between the citizen and the state, by which the citizen receives benefits, while the state claims duties, or obligations.

Social democracy: the ideology which seeks to gain gradual and moderate social improvements for the people through democratic processes, and is based on a belief in the value of social cooperation, but not necessarily state ownership.

Socialism: the view, founded on a strong belief in human equality, that private property should be replaced by 'social ownership'.

Sovereignty: supremacy or ultimate political power.

State: a country which is independent of all others; the permanent political authority within an independent country.

Subsidiarity: the theory that it is best to take all political decisions as close to the people concerned as possible, i.e. at the most subsidiary level (e.g. a decision affecting one town would be taken in that town).

Supranationalism: the theory that the European Union should develop institutions which have power and sovereignty transferred to them by the member states, so that they can take decisions of their own accord.

Swing voters (or 'floating' voters): those who can swing in either political direction, and are willing to vote for any party that convinces them it is right for them to do so.

Tactical voting: using your vote in the most effective way, especially to express a negative preference. It is negative voting: voting against a particular party rather than voting in favour of a particular party.

The Third Way: 'New Labour's' ideology, which is an attempt to steer a centre path between old-fashioned socialism and Thatcherite conservatism, but one based on Labour principles of community and social justice.

Traditional conservatism: values are based on a love of the past, a respect for tradition and a desire for stability.

Turnout: the measure of how many people vote (or 'turn out' to vote) in elections. In the UK it is usually expressed as the ratio of voters (those who actually do vote) to electors (those entitled to vote because they are on the electoral register), expressed as a percentage.

Ultra vires: Latin for 'beyond its powers'. When a local or devolved government goes beyond its legal powers, it is said to act *ultra vires*.

Unicameralism: a system with only one chamber or house in the representative assembly.

Unitary state: one in which sovereignty is located in one place, concentrated at the 'centre' of the state.

Voter volatility: the changeable nature of modern voters, who are willing to switch their votes from one party to another.

Westminster Parliament: the United Kingdom's supreme legislative and representative assembly.

Index